THE
GODHEAD

―――――――――― ⧉ ――――――――――

NEW SCRIPTURAL INSIGHTS ON THE
FATHER, THE SON, AND THE HOLY GHOST

Other books by Duane S. Crowther

THE
GODHEAD

NEW SCRIPTURAL INSIGHTS ON THE
FATHER, THE SON, AND THE HOLY GHOST

DUANE S. CROWTHER

HORIZON PUBLISHERS
SPRINGVILLE, UTAH

This is not an official publication of The Church of Jesus Christ of Latter-day Saints. The opinions and views expressed herein belong solely to the author and do not necessarily represent the opinions or views of Cedar Fort, Inc. Permission for the use of sources, graphics, and photos is also solely the responsibility of the author.

ISBN 13: 978-0-88290-828-1

Published by Horizon Publishers, an imprint of Cedar Fort, Inc., 2373 W. 700 S., Springville, UT, 84663
Distributed by Cedar Fort, Inc. www.cedarfort.com

Cover design by Nicole Williams
Cover design © 2007 by Lyle Mortimer

Printed in the United States of America

10 9 8 7 6 5 4 3 2 1

Printed on acid-free paper

IF YOU COULD HIE TO KOLOB

If you could hie to Kolob In the twinkling of an eye,
And then continue onward With that same speed to fly,
Do you think that you could ever, Through all eternity,
Find out the generation Where Gods began to be?

Or see the grand beginning, Where space did not extend?
Or view the last creation, Where Gods and matter end?
Methinks the Spirit whispers, "No man has found 'pure space,'
Nor seen the outside curtains, Where nothing has a place."

The works of God continue, And worlds and lives abound,
Improvement and progression Have one eternal round.
There is no end to matter; There is no end to space;
There is no end to spirit, There is no end to race.

There is no end to virtue; There is no end to might;
There is no end to wisdom; There is no end to light.
There is no end to union; There is no end to youth;
There is no end to priesthood; There is no end to truth.

There is no end to glory; There is no end to love;
There is no end to being; There is no death above.
There is no end to glory; There is no end to love;
There is no end to being; There is no death above.

—William W. Phelps
1792–1872

Cassette Talk Tapes by the Author

Anarchy in America: Prophecies of Events Preceding the Establishment of the New Jerusalem
Are You Saved? A Mormon's View of Faith, Works, Grace, and Salvation
Armageddon
Biblical Proofs of the Book of Mormon
Biblical Proofs of the Restored Church
Doctrinal Evidences that Mormons Are Christians: A Refutation of Misleading Statements Circulated by Anti-Mormon Critics
Exaltation and the Kingdoms of Glory
Forty Keys to Family Emergency Readiness
From First Draft to First Edition: A Step-by-Step Guide to Self-Publishing
God Speaks Through Prophets Today
God's Eternal Plan of Salvation
The Great and Abominable Church in Prophecy
He Comes in Glory: The Second Coming of Jesus Christ and Events Prophesied to Precede It
How to Recognize Spiritual Promptings
How to Seek the Gifts of the Spirit
Interpreting the Book of Revelation
Israel: Past, Present and Future
Joseph Smith: A True Prophet of God
The Last Days in Prophecy (6-tape set)
A Latter-day Saint View of Christ and the Trinity
Life After Death, the Spirit World, and the Kingdoms of Glory (6-tape set)
Missionary and Temple Work for the Dead
Nephi's Panoramic Preview: 2,500 Years in Prophecy
The New Jerusalem and Council at Adam-ondi-Ahman
Paradise: The Spirit-world Home of the Righteous
Recognizing Techniques of Deception in Anti-Mormon Literature
The Resurrection: Doctrine, History and Prophecy
Through Death Unto Life Everlasting
Understanding Isaiah in the Book of Mormon
Why Join the Mormons?
World War III: God's Judgments Upon the Nations
Ye Must Be Born Again

TABLE OF CONTENTS

PREFACE

The Prophet Joseph Smith said:

I want your prayers and faith that I may have the instruction of Almighty God and the gift of the Holy Ghost, so that I may set forth things that are true and which can be easily comprehended by you, and that the testimony may carry conviction to your hearts and minds of the truth of what I shall say. . . .

I wish to go back to the beginning to the morn of creation. There is the starting point for us to look to, in order to understand and be fully acquainted with the mind, purposes and decrees of the Great Eloheim, who sits in yonder heavens as he did at the creation of the world. It is necessary for us to have an understanding of God himself in the beginning. If we start right, it is easy to go right all the time; but if we start wrong we may go wrong, and it will be a hard matter to get right.

There are but a very few beings in the world who understand rightly the character of God. The great majority of mankind do not comprehend anything, either that which is past, or that which is to come, as it respects their relationship to God. They do not know, neither do they understand the nature of that relationship. . . . *If men do not comprehend the character of God, they do not comprehend themselves.* I want to go back to the beginning, and so lift your minds into more lofty spheres and a more exalted understanding than what the human mind generally aspires to. . . .

My first object is to find out the character of the only wise and true God, and what kind of a being He is; and if I am so fortunate as to be the man to comprehend God, and explain or convey the principles to your hearts, so that the Spirit seals them upon you, then let every man and woman henceforth sit in silence, put their hands on their mouths, and never lift their hands or voices, or say anything against the man of God or the servants of God again. (Joseph Smith, Jr., *History of the Church*, 6:302–4)

What Motivated the Writing of This Book?

As will be clearly shown in chapter 1, *man must have a correct knowledge of God to be able to attain eternal life!* This realization, and the quest for increased understanding of this all-important subject, has been a powerful motivator for me. That quest has also been a unique challenge. The subject is vast in scope, profound in depth, lofty in its aim, and eternal in its dimensions. It's also burning in its desire, thought-provoking in its pondering, and demanding in its call. But it is tantalizing in the avenues for new thought which it has provided and humbling in its weight of responsibility.

My objective has been, from its inception, to glean from the scriptures a clear understanding of the character and nature of God, indeed, of all three members of the Godhead. Of necessity, it has required the confronting of differing points of view and wrestling with deep thoughts and philosophies, doctrines and dogmas.

Examining the many varied beliefs about God leads one to encounter both great truths and noxious errors. It also requires one to sift through thousands of pages of often-conflicting but deeply held opinions. It has required weighing opposing doctrines and striving to penetrate to their sources and origins. It has called for questioning what is based on the rock of sound, scripture-based doctrine, as opposed to expository writings that tickle the eye and ear but have only a sandy foundation.

Computer Tools Made an Important Difference

What is different in this book, as opposed to the thousands of books penned on the subject in past epochs, is the lightning speed of scripture searches. It is only in the past two decades that copies of all four of the Latter-day Saint standard works have been available on computer software, with effective search-engine programs to drive them, so word-searches could be used to scout out elusive passages and insights.

Still, with this remarkable tool available, an almost overwhelming new challenge quickly emerged: the large quantity of time and energy required to sift through many hundreds of scripture passages to discern which are pertinent to the subject at hand. With this challenge, one soon is reminded of the need for true patience!

What does one find when computerized word searches are run? Here, for example, are word counts for just a few significant terms: (1) Lord: 10,522 "hits"; (2) God, 7,526; (3) Lord God, 2,724; (4) Father, 2,716; (5) Jesus, 1,285; (6) holy, 1,180; (7) Christ, 1,108; (8) Spirit, 1,091; (9) Jesus Christ, 447; (10) Ghost, 272; (11) Holy Ghost, 262; (12) Only Begotten Son, 35; (13) Jehovah, 14; etc. Searching these and hundreds of other terms requires one to quickly but carefully scan every passage, recognize and determine the meaning of each passage in its context, and then evaluate and decide where and how each selected passage should be used. That process has required many months of work!

There's no doubt that all that computer searching made it possible to tie numerous scriptural passages together that haven't previously been linked by other scholars, either in the world of general Christian scholarship or among Latter-day Saint researchers and expositors.

This book doesn't set forth new doctrines, but it assembles multitudes of rather "unknown" scriptural phrases and passages into solid patterns that in many instances have rarely or never been addressed in Mormondom. That's been one of the writing objectives: to find and emphasize previously overlooked fragments which, when combined together, set forth new patterns of comprehension and richer, deeper understandings.

Written with a Latter-day Saint Perspective

It's obvious that this is a book written by a Latter-day Saint author with a lifetime background in Latter-day Saint theology. Its author is one who firmly believes that within the four canonized Latter-day standard works is where the truest and broadest understandings of the nature of God reside. The Bible provides a broad doctrinal base, but it is the Book of Mormon, Doctrine and Covenants, and the Pearl of Great Price that add clarification, provide essential explanations, and furnish further insights that bring the whole picture into sharper focus.

It should be clearly understood that I am not an official spokesman for The Church of Jesus Christ of Latter-day Saints. Church leaders didn't ask me to write this book, nor did anyone from the Church supervise, direct, or edit my writing. This isn't a "Latter-day Saint book," it is "a book written by a Latter-day Saint." That nuance of difference is a major factor in the minds of many individuals, both Latter-day Saints and non-Latter-day Saints. I make no claim to infallibility, but I readily acknowledge that spiritual promptings and confirmations to include various items were sometimes felt and were a sweet blessing.

The most daunting task of all has been to write to both Latter-day Saint and non-Latter-day Saint readers, concerning hundreds of deep concepts, in such a way that significant new insights are communicated, yet on a level where most everyone can understand what is being written. Then too, there's the challenge of writing in a style where the written words won't induce unavoidable slumber for all those who peruse these pages.

And should it be written in a meek style where no one will feel challenged by opposing viewpoints, or should dogmas that have evolved out of the great Apostasy be specifically identified and challenged? This author chose the latter course.

Differences with "Trinitarian" Doctrines Will Be Identified

This book isn't written with an "axe to grind." It isn't intended as a book which attacks other churches nor harangues against their beliefs. But circumstances place me in an awkward predicament: the book's objective is to gather together and present, in as concise and coherent a fashion as possible, what the four Latter-day Saint standard works teach about the three members of the Godhead: God the Father; God the Son, who is Jehovah/Jesus Christ; and God the Holy Ghost. That can't be done without very distinct differences becoming evident between scriptural doctrines and the radically different views of numerous Christians who believe in what they call "the trinity." I call them "trinitarians." Their belief in a "three-in-one" God keeps clashing with hundreds of the scriptures that will be cited herein.

That "trinitarian" belief system originated as early as the fourth century AD, beginning to be stated in creedal form in the Council of Nicæa in AD 325. That "three-in-one" belief in the nature of God passed down through what became the Roman Catholic and Greek Orthodox churches. Powerful "anathemas" required absolute obedience and allegiance to the various doctrines set forth in the different creeds. These resulted in religious excommunications, purges, expulsions, shunnings, and martyrdoms—practices which were frequently abused as the churches grew in power and wealth.

During the dark ages when religious warfare was the order of the day, many, many thousands were annihilated, maimed, or tortured by church inquisitions if the individuals refused to subscribe to the doctrines which the various creedal statements mandated.

The "three-in-one" doctrines continued to be embraced by the churches that came into being with the Protestant Reformation. They linger today as basic doctrines of many of the "mainline Christian churches," still based on ancient creeds formulated, revised, and perpetuated in a series of "ecumenical councils" over many centuries.

And then, an entirely different understanding of the true nature of the Godhead burst upon the scene! It happened in the spring of 1820, when God the Father and God the Son Jesus Christ stood side by side as they conversed with a young lad named Joseph Smith, Jr. In an instant, Joseph learned that the Father and the Son are two separate, distinct individuals, not two different manifestations of a single Divine Being. And Joseph saw that they had physical shapes, like human bodies, rather than being shapeless, immaterial, everywhere-at-once beings who were only incorrectly defined as incorporeal "spirits."

When one of the two Divine Beings said to Joseph, "This is My Beloved Son. Hear Him!" Joseph learned that he was to be tutored by none other than Jesus Christ. One of the glorious insights which Jesus conveyed to Joseph that day concerning the churches whose roots were based in those "trinitarian" creeds was that "all their creeds were an abomination in his sight" (JS—H 1:17–19).

With the rapid growth of The Church of Jesus Christ of Latter-day Saints in the past century, hundreds of thousands of new converts have joined the ranks of Mormondom in a multitude of the nations of today's world. Many of these good people came with "trinitarian" backgrounds and ideas. Perhaps some of those ideas still linger in their latent belief systems. It is hoped that this book will help them recognize that "three-in-one" teachings conflict with the scriptures cited herein. Those differences will be pointed out and clarified.

Methodologies Used in Writing This Book

In modern times, the Prophet Joseph Smith put the nature of God in a new perspective. He also laid out a path whereby those who truly desire to do so can move toward eternal life and the qualities of Godhood. In a great 1844 conference address to twenty thousand of the Saints in Nauvoo, Illinois, he said: *"When we understand the character of God, and know how to come to Him, he begins to unfold the heavens to us, and to tell us all about it. When we are ready to come to him, he is ready to come to us"* (Joseph Smith, *History of the Church*, 6:308).

Truly an amazing amount of knowledge has been revealed in the four standard works about the three exalted, perfected members of the Godhead. However, that knowledge hasn't been provided "on a platter." Rather, it has been revealed in the scriptures "line upon line, precept upon precept; here a little, and there a little" (D&C 128:21). Very few have assembled these bits and pieces into coherent categories and groupings where they together provide profound new insights. Unfortunately, there are many such insights which have laid "just beyond the grasp" of many Latter-day Saints during past decades.

In this book, scriptural patterns have been sought which define essential doctrines without the need for outside interpretation. With that objective, guiding statements from Latter-day Saint prophets and leaders have occasionally been included to add additional insights, but such statements are cited herein rather sparsely; *the objective has been to build this book on a sound scriptural basis*. That's not to say or imply, by any means, that high value is not placed on the teachings and guidance of Latter-day Saint prophets and General Authorities. It most certainly is, but gathering and analyzing their teachings on the nature and character of the members of the Godhead is a challenge so vast and time consuming that the task has been left for others to perform.

Like most books, this volume has its own set of identifying "quirks." Some of them are briefly listed here:

The use of ellipses: Many of the passages on the nature of God cited in this book tended to include more than a single idea. To pursue all of those concepts, passage after passage, would provide such a tangle of tangents as to make comprehension extremely difficult, and it would make this already-long book three or four times as long. Therefore, the decision was made to delete the tangents and cite only the words pertinent to the subject being discussed. It's like pruning and thinning peach trees: one needs to lop off the branches which encumber the central growth of the tree and reduce the number of buds on the branches so the remaining peaches will grow large and sweet. When you see ellipses [. . .], know that tangential (but often-fascinating) phrases and verses have been removed to focus the flow of on the particular message being considered in that section.

The use of italics, bold type, and underlinings: Those who teach writing sometimes say that good writing doesn't need words placed in italics, bold, or all-capitals to make a point. But in a book of this kind, it is felt that the reader is best served when key thoughts and words that might easily be otherwise overlooked are highlighted as a service to the reader. Throughout the book, the italics included are placed there by the author, unless the phrase "italics in the original" is included in the citation.

This book contains numerous lists, often presented in paragraph form. Occasional items of particular importance are placed in bold type, sometimes as in-list subheadings, sometimes to emphasize concepts or items of particular importance which might otherwise be overlooked. On rare occasions, key words have been bolded and italicized in situations where the applicable portion of the item already is in italic or bold type. Again, the goal is to be "reader friendly" by bringing key concepts to the reader's attention without creating distractions.

The use of bullets: Bullets [•] have been used in many chapters herein when numerous scriptural passages are being cited to simplify identifying where these passages begin and end. It would have been preferable to have all those passages presented in list form, rather than placed one after another in paragraph form. However, knowing that putting them all in list form would have added at least another hundred pages to the book and raised the purchase price considerably, I elected to use paragraph styling, with the cited passages separated by bullets.

The use of square brackets: Some of the authors whose statements are cited herein have inserted their personal viewpoints and commentaries in parenthetical expressions ( ). When I insert comments or clarifications within scriptural passages, or in quotations from other authors, it has been done using square brackets [ ].

Source citation methodology: The notation style typically used in the social sciences, of identifying a quoted source by placing the author's name in parentheses at the end, followed by the page number, has been utilized (i.e., Jones, 206). However, because this style can be frustrating to the reader, I have often included the book title or identifying words from the title so readers won't have to turn to the bibliography to satisfy their curiosity concerning what the title is of the book being cited. Again, being "reader friendly" is the goal. The footnoting of most citations has been avoided because of the time-consuming and space-occupying challenges which they pose for typesetters and page-layout personnel.

Presenting meaningful scripture groupings: A major objective has been to present scriptures in such a way that they interpret themselves and don't call for outside interpretation. If my work in this book is properly done, readers won't say

"Brother Crowther says . . ." Rather, they'll say, "Brother Crowther has tied together broad scriptural patterns that show that . . . , and that's great, because I never understood it that way before."

Since many of the scriptural patterns laid out in this book are not compiled or listed in other LDS works, an effort has been made to assemble enough of them to clarify the pattern and establish its place for use in further studies. Sometimes this listing of passages slows the flow of the book. Feel free to jump ahead to the next section if you wish; the lists will still be there when you want to come back and study them in more depth.

Presenting occasional new thoughts and theories: If this book is well written, some readers, hopefully, will discover a host of ideas which are new to them. However, the strong patterns of supporting scriptures will make them aware that the concepts which they've just discovered have been there for centuries; it is they, individually and collectively, who are learning about them, not the world at large.

Occasionally, when key insights yearn to be considered, but where they go beyond the evidence of scripture, a theory will be suggested or presented for future consideration, but it will be clearly labeled as theory, not as doctrine. (Remember the Lord's instruction, that Church members are to *"Teach ye diligently . . . , that you may be instructed more perfectly in . . . theory"*? A workable theory is a hypothesis—a pattern of thought which is not yet fully substantiated but which merits appropriate consideration as further evidence is sought for and gathered and molded into a cohesive whole. But I recognize that gospel theories still need to be based "in principle, in doctrine, in the law of the gospel, in all things that pertain unto the kingdom of God, that are expedient for you to understand: Of things both in heaven and in the earth, and under the earth; things which have been, things which are, things which must shortly come to pass; . . ." [D&C 88:78–79].)

If theories are advanced herein, they'll be clearly labeled as such. Watch for "we don't really know, as yet," "the scriptures don't clarify that," words or phrases such as "perhaps," "it's possible that," "it may be that," "we might discover that," "consider the alternate meaning that," and so forth.

"You Have Got to Learn How to Be Gods Yourselves"

Back to Joseph Smith's 1844 conference address, in order to add a little additional insight before this preface is concluded. Brother Joseph said, *"Here, then, is eternal life to know the only wise and true God; and you have got to learn how to be Gods yourselves, . . . And I want you to know that God, in the last days, while certain individuals are proclaiming his name, is not trifling with you or me"* (Joseph Smith, *History of the Church*, 6:306).

I regard that statement as a profound truth. To help myself and others to move forward in the quest for greater understanding concerning the many aspects of the nature of God the Father, God the Son Jehovah/Jesus Christ, and God the Holy Ghost, this book delves into numerous areas that I, at least, have never seen compiled in depth in Latter-day Saint writings. I hope that this collection of scriptural insights on numerous aspects concerning those who govern this earth from on high will prove useful to many. I hope too that these insights will constitute true patterns that will help shape mankind's personal quests to become "exalted beings."

This book, then, is the result of some deep digging on subjects of profound importance. I truly hope that it will increase scriptural and doctrinal understanding for many Latter-day Saints and others who may read it. May it be an instrument for good in the lives of many people!

The manuscript has been crafted and written prayerfully. I hope that those who read it will do so in like manner, prayerfully looking for understanding and enlightenment through the Holy Spirit and truly seeking for guidance and confirmation of the scriptural truths it presents as they read.

If they, and you, will do so, then may God truly bless you!

—Duane S. Crowther

PART ONE

THE BROAD ARRAY OF CHRISTIAN BELIEFS ABOUT GOD

CHAPTER 1

THE IMPORTANCE OF KNOWING GOD

It Is Life Eternal to Know the Godhead and Associate with Them Eternally

Our Lord and Savior, Jesus Christ, twice gave very succinct definitions of the eternal goal for which His righteous followers should strive. In the last week of His mortal life, while pouring out His innermost feelings to His beloved Heavenly Father in prayer, He said,

> Father, the hour is come; glorify thy Son, that thy Son also may glorify thee:
> As thou hast given him power over all flesh, that he should give *eternal life* to as many as thou hast given him.
> *And this is life eternal, that they might know thee the only true God, and Jesus Christ, whom thou hast sent.* (John 17:1–3)

Again, in these last days, the great Creator and Redeemer of mankind repeated this same definition, but in expanded form, saying that "*This is eternal lives—to know the only wise and true God, and Jesus Christ, whom he hath sent*" (D&C 132:24).

In another revelation He stressed that "*eternal life . . . is the greatest of all the gifts of God*" (D&C 14:7).

Eternal Life: The Greatest of All the Gifts of God

The Prophet Lehi saw in vision this "greatest gift" of eternal life, symbolized as a tree:

> *I beheld a tree, whose fruit was desirable to make one happy.*
> And it came to pass that I did go forth and partake of the fruit thereof; and I beheld that *it was most sweet, above all that I ever before tasted.* Yea, and I beheld that the fruit thereof was white, to exceed all the whiteness that I had ever seen.
> *And as I partook of the fruit thereof it filled my soul with exceedingly great joy;* wherefore, I began to be desirous that my family should partake of it also; for I knew that it was desirable above all other fruit. (1 Ne. 8:10–12)

Later, when the Spirit of the Lord desired to show Lehi's son, Nephi, the interpretation of his father's vision, the Spirit asked Nephi, "Knowest thou the meaning of the tree which thy father saw?" Nephi replied: "*Yea, it is the love of God, which sheddeth itself abroad in the hearts of the children of men; wherefore, it is the most desirable above all things.*" And then the Spirit amplified that understanding, observing: "*Yea, and the most joyous to the soul*" (1 Ne. 11:21–23).

An intriguing promise made by the Christ is recorded in the book of Revelation, which closely relates to the visions of the Tree of Life seen by Lehi and his son Nephi. He promised that "*To him that overcometh will I give to eat of the tree of life,* which is in the midst of the paradise of God" (Rev. 2:7).

Jesus often spoke of the great joy embodied in the goal of eternal life during his mortal ministry. For instance, while standing in a boat in the Sea of Galilee, He told parable after parable to the crowd of interested listeners gathered on the nearby shore. He said:

> The kingdom of heaven is like unto *treasure* hid in a field; the which when a man hath found, he hideth, and *for joy* thereof goeth and selleth all that he hath, and buyeth that field.
> Again, the kingdom of heaven is like unto a merchant man, seeking goodly pearls:
> Who, when he had found one *pearl of great price,* went and sold all that he had, and bought it. (Matt. 13:44–46)

While preparing Joseph Smith, Oliver Cowdery, and David Whitmer to restore his church and gospel to the earth, the Master gave them this revelation concerning the glorious joy of eternal life with God:

> *Remember the worth of souls is great in the sight of God;* . . .
> And *how great is his joy* in the soul that repenteth!
> Wherefore, you are called to cry repentance unto this people.
> And if it so be that you should labor all your days in crying repentance unto this people, and bring, save it be one soul unto me, *how great shall be your joy with him in the kingdom of my Father!*
> And now, *if your joy will be great with one soul that you have brought unto me into the kingdom of my Father, how great will be your joy if you should bring many souls unto me!* (D&C 18:10, 13–16)

Other scriptural incidents bear witness of man's longing for eternal life, like the New Testament account of the man who ran to Jesus "and kneeled to him, and asked him, Good Master, *what shall I do that I may inherit eternal life?*" (Mark 10:17, see also Luke 10:25; Luke 18:18).

And like the Lamanite king who queried Aaron, the missionary who was teaching him, saying: "*What shall I do that I may have this eternal life of which thou hast spoken?* Yea, what shall I do that I may be born of God, having this wicked spirit rooted out of my breast, and receive his Spirit, *that I may be filled with joy, that I may not be cast off at the last day?* Behold, . . . I will give up all that I possess, yea, I will forsake my kingdom, that I may receive this great joy" (Alma 22:15).

Be Ye Perfect, like the Father and the Son!

When the resurrected Christ appeared to his followers in the new-world land of Bountiful, He said to them: "*I would that ye should be perfect even as I, or your Father who is in heaven is perfect*" (3 Ne. 12:48). Since He had by then attained His resurrection, He apparently was willing to amplify His very similar statement previously made in His great Sermon on the Mount. He had previously said, *"Be ye therefore perfect, even as your Father which is in heaven is perfect"* (Matt. 5:48). It is significant that in his Inspired Version of the Bible, the Prophet Joseph Smith was prompted to change this passage to read: *"Ye are therefore commanded to be perfect . . ."* (JS—M 5:50).

So, who, and what, is God, and what is perfection? And on a broader scale, what are the natures of the three members of the Godhead: God the Father; his firstborn son, Jesus Christ; and God the Holy Spirit, the Holy Ghost? **And is it truly a central doctrine of Christianity that man, indeed—mankind—is to strive to become Christlike in character, to the point that he can actually gain the attributes and status of Godhood?**

Jesus said unto the children of men: "Follow thou me. . . . *and do the things which ye have seen me do"* (2 Ne. 31:10, 13). Jesus told his disciples, "I have given you an example, *that ye should do as I have done to you"* (John 13:15). When He was among the Nephites He said to them: *"What manner of men ought ye to be?* Verily I say unto you, *even as I am"* (3 Ne. 27:27).

And, to where is that supposed to lead? That all-important phrase in Christ's Sermon on the Mount seems to loom large in this context: "seek ye first the kingdom of God, and his righteousness; *and all these things shall be added unto you"* (Matt. 6:33).

Latter-day Saints Believe in "the Godhead," Not "the Trinity"

Most of the "first-person" words spoken by a member of the Godhead, as recorded in the four standard works of The Church of Jesus Christ of Latter-day Saints, are the statements of a single individual, who is primarily known by two different names, though He has many dozens of other titles. His premortal name was and is *Jehovah.* His mortal and postmortal name is *Jesus, the Christ.*

He, in turn, provides hundreds of other details about His Father, in numerous places throughout the scriptures. His Father typically is known in the scriptures as *God the Father.* Jesus also conveys, in numerous other passages, many other insights about the third member of the Godhead: *the Holy Ghost.*

Most of the scriptural statements made by God in the *Old Testament* are statements made by Jehovah, though they are identified in the King James and many other Bible versions as having been made by the LORD (written in small-capital letters). This name change will be explained in detail later.

When the forthcoming mortal birth of the Son of God was first announced by the angel Gabriel, the angel told Mary that "thou shalt conceive in thy womb, and bring forth a son, and shalt call his name JESUS" (Luke 1:31). The *New Testament,* and most portions of the other three Latter-day Saint volumes of scripture (the *Book of Mormon,* the *Doctrine and Covenants,* and the *Pearl of Great Price*), usually refer to him as Jesus Christ when speaking of his mortal ministry and of his ongoing postmortal ministry.

These three divine personages: God the Father, God the Son Jehovah/Jesus Christ, and God the Holy Ghost, are sometimes linked together under the word *Godhead.* However, the term *Godhead* only appears three times in the scriptures: all in the New Testament: Acts 17:19, Romans 1:20, and Colossians 2:9, and all three of these passages are allusions rather than fully descriptive terms.

Several centuries after the mortal sojourn of Jesus Christ in the meridian of time, as the great "falling away" from many of the true doctrines of Christ was well under way, religious philosophers coined the term "trinity" as an inclusive term for God the Father, God the Son, and God the Holy Ghost. The term "trinity" is not a scriptural term—it never appears in the Old or New Testaments. Unfortunately, that word became so infused with non-scriptural perceptions of the true natures of the three members of the Godhead that Latter-day Saints, along with those of a number of other faiths, do not regard it as an appropriate descriptive term for their concept of God. Those differences will become more apparent in the various chapters of this book.

Throughout this book, various comparisons will be made between Latter-day Saint beliefs and the doctrinal creeds and beliefs by those who adhere to "trinitarian" dogmas. The doctrinal bases for both belief systems: (1) the Latter-day Saint concept that the Father, Son, and Holy Ghost are a Godhead composed of three separate and distinct beings and (2) the Catholic-Protestant "trinitarian" belief that there is only one God, one substance, but it is comprised of three distinct persons. The scriptures upon which each of the two beliefs are based will be presented and analyzed. The results will definitely prove interesting and thought-provoking!

God Expects and Intends to Be Known and Acknowledged throughout the Earth

It is abundantly apparent, from many dozens of passages in the scriptures, that Jehovah, who is Jesus Christ, expects to be known, respected, honored, worshiped, reverenced, and properly regarded as a king and a God. He, by divine assignment, was commissioned by His Father to rule over all the events of this earth. As previously cited at the beginning of this chapter, God the Father "*hast given him power over all flesh, that he should give eternal life to as many as [God the Father] hast given him*" (John 17:2). Therefore, in obedience to this divine calling, Christ created this earth, came to it in the meridian of time to teach His doctrines and to give His mortal life as an atoning sacrifice for the sins of all mankind, and will return in His "Second Coming" in glory to cleanse the earth of sin and to rule and reign here for a thousand-year millennial era as the King of all mankind. He most certainly is entitled to the appropriate honor and glory for these positions and accomplishments. Indeed, when He returns to the earth, "every knee shall bow," and "every tongue shall swear" to acknowledge his coming and His right to rule and reign here upon the earth as its king and its God (Isa. 45:23).

The Lord Wants Man to Both Know and Understand Him

Two key passages on this principle have already been cited in this chapter: (1) "*And this is life eternal, that they might **know** thee the only true God, and Jesus Christ, whom thou hast sent*" (John 17:3), and (2) "*This is eternal lives—to **know** the only wise and true God, and Jesus Christ, whom he hath sent*" (D&C 132:24).

A passage from the Old Testament book of Jeremiah stresses the importance of both *knowing* and *understanding* God: "Let not the wise man glory in his wisdom, neither let the mighty man glory in his might, let not the rich man glory in his riches: *But let him that glorieth glory in this, that he **understandeth** and **knoweth** me, that I am the* LORD *which exercise lovingkindness, judgment, and righteousness, in the earth: for in these things I delight, saith the* LORD" (Jer. 9:23–24).

Other passages speak more specifically about knowledge and understanding concerning the nature of God. For instance, the Book of Mormon Prophet Jacob commented on attaining a perfect knowledge of Christ: He said, "Seek not to counsel the Lord, but to *take counsel from his hand. . . . be reconciled unto him through the atonement of Christ*, his Only Begotten Son, . . . and *be presented as the first-fruits of Christ unto God*, having faith, and obtained a good hope of glory in him . . . marvel not that

I tell you these things; for *why not speak of the atonement of Christ, and **attain to a perfect knowledge of him?***" (Jacob 4:10–12).

The Prophet Mormon wrote that *"the Spirit of Christ is given to every man, that he may know good from evil;* wherefore, I show unto you the way to judge; for every thing which inviteth to do good, and to persuade to believe in Christ, is sent forth by the power and gift of Christ; *wherefore ye **may know with a perfect knowledge** it is of God"* (Moro. 7:16).

The scriptures are filled with passages about both (1) the importance of knowing-God and (2) the importance of understanding God. What follows in the next section are lists of key passages on each of those two topics.

Key Passages on Knowing and Understanding God

Without pursuing these topics in depth, here are two sets of twenty-five brief examples of historical events and divine manifestations. All assert **the importance of knowing God**. Together, they demonstrate the far-reaching significance and impact of God's name, power, and supremacy, as well as his mercy, protection, and love for his people, being known among the people throughout the earth, and in all eras of time. Most certainly, the concept that there is a God, and that He guides and directs the affairs of men, has been a major missionary theme in all gospel dispensations. God knows how to best accomplish his eternal purposes. Remember, *"the Lord knoweth all things from the beginning; wherefore, he prepareth a way to accomplish all his works among the children of men; for behold, he hath all power unto the fulfilling of all his words"* (1 Ne. 9:6).

All of the following examples are drawn from the Old Testament, and all of them emphasize that man is to **know** God. Ten will be cited here; references will be provided for an additional 15 selected passages:

1. **Moses to Pharoah:** "Thus saith the LORD, *In this thou shalt **know** that I am the LORD:* behold, I will smite . . . upon the waters which are in the river, and they shall be turned to blood" (Ex. 7:17–18).

2. **God to Moses, when Pharoah's charioteers were pursuing the Israelites fleeing toward the Red Sea:** *"the Egyptians shall **know** that I am the LORD, when I have gotten me honour upon Pharaoh, upon his chariots, and upon his horsemen"* (Ex. 14:18).

3. **Moses and Aaron, telling the Israelites about manna from heaven:** *"then shall ye **know** that the LORD hath brought you out* from the land of Egypt" (Ex. 16:6).

4. **God, through Moses, to the Israelites:** "I have led you forty years in the wilderness: your clothes are not waxen old upon you, and thy shoe is not waxen old upon thy foot. . . . *that ye might **know** that I am the LORD your God* (Deut. 29:5–6).

5. **King Solomon, at the dedication of the Jerusalem temple:** "The LORD our God be with us, as he was with our fathers: let him not leave us, nor forsake us: That he may incline our hearts unto him, to walk in all his ways, and to keep his commandments, and his statutes, and his judgments, which he commanded our fathers. . . . *That all the people of the earth may **know** that the LORD is God"* (1 Kgs. 8:57–58, 60).

6. **A writer of psalms:** *"**Know** ye that the LORD he is God: it is he that hath made us, and not we ourselves; we are his people, and the sheep of his pasture"* (Ps. 100:3).

7. **Elijah, calling down fire from heaven in his contest with the 450 priests of Baal:** "LORD God of Abraham, Isaac, and of Israel, *let it be **known** this day that thou art God in Israel, and that I am thy servant,* and that I have done all these

things at thy word. Hear me, O LORD, hear me, *that this people may* **know** *that thou art the LORD God*" (1 Kgs. 18:36–37).

8. ***God's prophecy of the gathering of Israel, spoken through Isaiah:*** "kings shall be thy nursing fathers, and their queens thy nursing mothers: they shall bow down to thee with their face toward the earth, and lick up the dust of thy feet; and *thou shalt* **know** *that I am the LORD . . . and all flesh shall know that I the LORD am thy Saviour and thy Redeemer, the mighty One of Jacob* (Isa. 49:23, 26).

9. ***God's prophecy of the return of scattered Israel, through Jeremiah:*** "I will set mine eyes upon them for good, and I will bring them again to this land: . . . *And I will give them an heart to* **know** *me, that I am the LORD:* and they shall be my people, and I will be their God: for they shall return unto me with their whole heart" (Jer. 24:6–7).

10. ***God's purpose for His Sabbath days, through Ezekiel:*** "Moreover also I gave them my sabbaths, to be a sign between me and them, *that they might* **know** *that I am the LORD that sanctify them*" (Ezek. 20:12).

See also: [11] Ex. 16:12; [12] Ex. 31:13; [13] Deut. 4:39; [14] Deut. 7:9; [15] Deut. 13:3; [16] Deut. 31:12–13; [17] Josh. 4:23–24; [18] Judg. 17:13; [19] 1 Chr. 28:9; [20] 1 Kgs. 20:13; [21] 2 Kgs. 19:19; [22] Isa. 60:14, 16; [23] Jer. 31:33–34; [24] Ezek. 34:27, 31; [25] Ezek. 38:21–23.

Of equal significance and import are the dozens of passages that stress **the importance of understanding God.** Again, without pursuing these topics in depth, here are 25 brief examples of scriptural statements that present many of the aspects concerning the necessity of man being able to truly understand God, his creations, his commandments, and explanations of principles leading to godliness. Again, ten will be cited here; then references will be provided for an additional 15 selected passages:

1. ***A Proverb of Solomon:*** "*incline thine ear unto wisdom, and apply thine heart to* **understanding**; . . . *Then shalt thou* **understand** *the fear of the LORD, and find the knowledge of God. For the LORD giveth wisdom: out of his mouth cometh knowledge and* **understanding** (Prov. 2:2, 5–6).

2. ***An angel to Daniel:*** "Fear not, Daniel: for *from the first day that thou didst set thine heart to* **understand***, and to chasten thyself before thy God,* thy words were heard, and I am come for thy words" (Dan. 10:12).

3. ***John: Christ gave them understanding and discernment:*** "we know that the Son of God is come, and *hath given us an* **understanding***, that we may know him that is true,* and we are in him that is true, even in his Son Jesus Christ. This is the true God, and eternal life (1 Jn. 5:20).

4. ***Nephi: the Lord enlightens man's understanding:*** "my soul delighteth in plainness; for after this manner doth the Lord God work among the children of men. *For the Lord God giveth light unto the* **understanding***;* for he speaketh unto men according to their language, *unto their understanding*" (2 Ne. 31:3).

5. ***Jacob: God takes away the understanding of the wicked:*** "because of their blindness, which blindness came by looking beyond the mark, they must needs fall; for *God hath taken away his plainness from them, and delivered unto them many things which they cannot* **understand**, because they desired it. And because they desired it God hath done it, that they may stumble" (Jacob 4:14).

6. ***Mormon writes on the plates according to understanding God gave him:*** "now I, Mormon, proceed to finish out my record, which I take from the plates of

Nephi; and I make it *according to the knowledge and the* **understanding** *which God has given me"* (W of M 1:9).

7. **King Benjamin: open your hearts and minds:** "I have not commanded you to come up hither to trifle with the words which I shall speak, but that you should hearken unto me, and open your *ears* that ye may hear, and *your hearts that ye may* **understand**, and *your minds that the mysteries of God may be unfolded* to your view" (Mosiah 2:9).

8. **God: commandments given to provide understanding:** "Behold, I am God and have spoken it; these commandments are of me, and were given unto my servants in their weakness, after the manner of their language, *that they might come to* **understanding**" (D&C 1:24).

9. **God: man is given understanding when he asks:** "Speaking unto you that you may naturally understand; but unto myself my works have no end, neither beginning; *but it is given unto you that ye may* **understand**, *because ye have asked it of me and are agreed"* (D&C 29:33).

10. **God: understand how and what to worship:** *"I give unto you these sayings that you may* **understand** *and know how to worship, and know what you worship, that you may come unto the Father in my name, and in due time receive of his fulness"* (D&C 93:19).

See also: [11] 1 Kgs. 3:11–12; [12] Ps. 53:1–2; [13] Rom. 3:10–12; [14] Eph. 4:17–18; [15] Alma 26:35; [16] D&C 10:63; [17] D&C 32:4–5; [18] D&C 50:21–22; [19] D&C 76:8–10; [20] D&C 76:12–13; [21] D&C 78:10; [22] D&C 88:11, 13; [23] D&C 88:78; [24] D&C 97:14; [25] D&C 138:11.

The Higher Priesthood Holds the Key of the Knowledge of God

An individual, on his own, can do much to know and understand the nature of God; indeed, the natures of each of the three members of the Godhead. However, the scriptures make it plain that to attain to the higher levels of understanding on this important subject, priesthood power and authority are essential aspects, and access to the essential priesthood ordinances, especially those of the temple, is required. The Doctrine and Covenants indicates that "this greater priesthood [the Melchizedek Priesthood] administereth the gospel and *holdeth the key of the mysteries of the kingdom, even the key of the knowledge of God.* Therefore, in the ordinances thereof, *the power of godliness is manifest"* (D&C 84:19–20).

A later passage indicates that **"The power and authority of the higher, or Melchizedek Priesthood**, is to hold the keys of all the spiritual blessings of the church—To have the privilege of *receiving the mysteries of the kingdom of heaven*, to have the heavens opened unto them, to commune with the general assembly and church of the Firstborn, and **to enjoy the communion and presence of God the Father, and Jesus the mediator of the new covenant**" (D&C 107:18–19).

The profound epistle written by Joseph Smith in 1842 concerning baptism for the dead, which was canonized as D&C section 128, adds further insights on "the powers of the Holy Priesthood" as the doorway to "glory and honor, and immortality and eternal life." The final sentence of verse 14, cited below, adds further insight of great significance: *"This, therefore, is the sealing and binding power, and, in one sense of the word, the keys of the kingdom, which consist in the key of knowledge."* This is a key section of Joseph Smith's important letter:

Now the great and grand secret of the whole matter, and the *summum bonum* of the whole subject that is lying before us, *consists in obtaining the powers of the Holy Priesthood*. For him to whom these keys are given there is no difficulty in obtaining a knowledge of facts in relation to the salvation of the children of men, both as well for the dead as for the living.

Herein is glory and honor, and immortality and eternal life—The ordinance of baptism by water, to be immersed therein in order to answer to the likeness of the dead, that one principle might accord with the other; to be immersed in the water and come forth out of the water is in the likeness of the resurrection of the dead in coming forth out of their graves; hence, this ordinance was instituted to form a relationship with the ordinance of baptism for the dead, being in likeness of the dead.

Consequently, the baptismal font was instituted as a similitude of the grave, and was commanded to be in a place underneath where the living are wont to assemble, to show forth the living and the dead, and that all things may have their likeness, and that they may accord one with another—that which is earthly conforming to that which is heavenly, as Paul hath declared, 1 Corinthians 15:46, 47, and 48:

Howbeit that was not first which is spiritual, but that which is natural; and afterward that which is spiritual. The first man is of the earth, earthy; the second man is the Lord from heaven. As is the earthy, such are they also that are earthy; and as is the heavenly, such are they also that are heavenly. And as are the records on the earth in relation to your dead, which are truly made out, so also are the records in heaven. *This, therefore, is the sealing and binding power, and, in one sense of the word, the keys of the kingdom, which consist in the key of knowledge*. (D&C 128:11–14)

Personal Unrighteousness Robs Man of His Knowledge and Understanding of God

Several passages from the Bible are presented here that warn of the process that occurs when individuals fail to serve God with all their heart, might, mind, and strength. Those cited represent many others which warn of the same outcomes.

The Apostle Paul, for instance, wrote concerning the downward spiral which results from unrighteousness. He tells how previously gained knowledge of God leaves men on the road to personal wickedness and apostasy without excuse:

I am not ashamed of the gospel of Christ: for it is the power of God unto salvation to every one that believeth; to the Jew first, and also to the Greek.

For therein is the righteousness of God revealed from faith to faith: as it is written, The just shall live by faith.

For the wrath of God is revealed from heaven against all ungodliness and unrighteousness of men, who hold the truth in unrighteousness;

Because *that which may be known of God is manifest in them; for God hath shewed it unto them.*

For the invisible things of him from the creation of the world are clearly seen, being understood by the things that are made, even his eternal power and Godhead; *so that they are without excuse:*

Because that, *when they knew God, they glorified him not as God, neither were thankful; but became vain in their imaginations, and their foolish heart was darkened.*

Professing themselves to be wise, they became fools, . . .

Wherefore God also gave them up to uncleanness through the lusts of their own hearts, to dishonour their own bodies between themselves:

Who changed the truth of God into a lie, . . .

And even as they did not like to retain God in their knowledge, God gave

them over to a reprobate mind, to do those things which are not convenient;

Being filled with all unrighteousness, fornication, wickedness, covetousness, maliciousness; full of envy, murder, debate, deceit, malignity; whisperers,

Backbiters, haters of God, despiteful, proud, boasters, inventors of evil things, disobedient to parents,

Without understanding, covenantbreakers, without natural affection, implacable, unmerciful:

Who knowing the judgment of God, that they which commit such things are worthy of death, not only do the same, but have pleasure in them that do them. (Rom. 1:16–22, 24–25, 28–32)

In his epistle to the Galatians, Paul writes of converts who were wicked prior to their conversion, and again after being converted and having known God, they have slipped back into their previous wickedness once again: "Howbeit then, when ye knew not God, ye did service unto them which by nature are no gods. *But now, after that ye have known God, or rather are known of God, how turn ye again to the weak and beggarly elements, whereunto ye desire again to be in bondage?* (Gal. 4:8–9).

In his epistle to Titus, Paul wrote of the personal downfall and loss of personal righteousness of "many unruly and vain talkers and deceivers," and warning that nothing is regarded as pure by those who are "defiled and unbelieving":

Whose mouths must be stopped, who subvert whole houses, teaching things which they ought not, for filthy lucre's sake.

One of themselves, even a prophet of their own, said, The Cretians are alway liars, evil beasts, slow bellies.

This witness is true. Wherefore rebuke them sharply, that they may be sound in the faith;

Not giving heed to Jewish fables, and commandments of men, that turn from the truth.

Unto the pure all things are pure: but unto them that are defiled and unbelieving is nothing pure; but even their mind and conscience is defiled.

They profess that they know God; but in works they deny him, being abominable, and disobedient, and unto every good work reprobate. (Titus 1:11–16)

The Apostle John contrasted those who had "the spirit of truth" with those who had yielded to the "spirit of error," and stressed that **love and a firm knowledge of God is what characterizes the righteous:**

Ye are of God, little children, and have overcome them: because greater is he that is in you, than he that is in the world.

They are of the world: therefore speak they of the world, and the world heareth them.

We are of God: he that knoweth God heareth us; he that is not of God heareth not us. Hereby know we the spirit of truth, and the spirit of error.

Beloved, let us love one another: for love is of God; and every one that loveth is born of God, and knoweth God.

He that loveth not knoweth not God; for God is love.

In this was manifested the love of God toward us, because that God sent his only begotten Son into the world, that we might live through him.

Herein is love, not that we loved God, but that he loved us, and sent his Son to be the propitiation for our sins.

Beloved, if God so loved us, we ought also to love one another. (1 Jn. 4:4–11)

Summary

1. A major blessing and qualifier, for those who are to gain eternal life and be eligible to dwell in God's glorious kingdom, is that they have come to know God the Father and the other members of the Godhead.

2. Eternal life is the greatest of all the gifts that God offers to His children. It is symbolized as the tree of life, as a treasure, and as a pearl of great price in the scriptures.

3. Man is commanded to seek perfection, preparing himself for the higher blessings he will receive when various aspects of eternal perfection will be conferred upon him.

4. Latter-day Saints believe that the Father, Son, and Holy Ghost constitute a divine combination which the Bible refers to as the "Godhead."

5. To the contrary, they do not embrace the "three-in-one" concept of the nature of God, so they typically refrain from referring to the combined members of the Godhead as the "trinity" because of the numerous unscriptural connotations which are implied in the term by those of other faiths.

6. God expects to be known and acknowledged throughout the earth.

7. The Lord wants man to both know and understand Him. Twenty-five key passages on knowing God were presented, and twenty-five passages on the importance of understanding were also listed.

8. The Melchizedek Priesthood holds the keys of the knowledge of God, but personal unrighteousness can cause man to lose the intimate knowledge of God which he had attained in the days of his righteousness.

9. Again, it is life eternal to know the Godhead and associate with them eternally!

CHAPTER 2

WHAT TODAY'S CHURCHES TEACH ABOUT GOD

A Comparison of Major Denominations' Beliefs Concerning the Nature of God

One of the most informative ways to understand the "trinitarian" doctrines found among the "mainline Christian" churches, and to determine what sects reject those three-in-one doctrines, is to read what they report as being their doctrines in books on comparative religions.

In seeking to present capsulized statements from a broad selection of religious denominations and beliefs, I have intentionally sought the insights of non-Latter-day Saint authors so as not to be regarded as having a pro-Latter-day Saint slant in the statements cited. He has selected Simon & Schuster's popular guide *Religions of America* as an appropriate source for the brief statements cited in this chapter. It is a concise work, and its latest edition is considered to be among the most accurate and informative of the recent sources available.

Edited by Leo Rosten, *Religions of America* is one of the best-known of this genre of religious reporting. First published under the title *A Guide to the Religions of America* in 1955, the publishers adopted the current title in 1963. Those purchasing the book in 2005 probably purchased the 33rd edition, which shows *Ferment and Faith in an Age of Crisis* and *A New Guide and Almanac* as subtitles. That printing also asserts that it is *The completely revised, updated, and expanded edition of the classic book* and states that *Over 300,000 copies of the previous editions have been sold.*

The first half of the book consists of answers to questions submitted by noted and respected authorities, leaders, or scholars. These individuals were deemed qualified to speak authoritatively for their respective ecclesiastical groups.

In his Editor's Preface, Rosten's reason for utilizing a question-and-answer format is eloquently stated:

> PART ONE is in question-and-answer form. I asked the questions; the authors wrote the answers.
>
> What I insisted upon was direct, simple, candid answers. What I rejected was theological jargon or sonorous cant. *The question-and-answer form is the surest road I*

know to clarity, and the best way of avoiding those lofty ambiguities and irritating hair-splittings which, alas, characterize so much of the literature on religion. (Rosten, 17)

In this chapter, brief excerpts which characterize each faith's beliefs concerning the nature of God are cited so that their widely varying views can be compared.

Greek Orthodox

In answer to the question "What Are the Main Doctrines of the Eastern Orthodox Church?" and "What Is the Basic Creed of the Orthodox Church?" the following was supplied:

> *Orthodoxy believes that God is one in substance and a Trinity in person. Orthodoxy worships one God in the Trinity and the Trinity in unity, neither confusing the persons nor dividing the substance.*
>
> Orthodoxy hold the creation to be the work of the blessed Trinity and believes the world is neither self-created nor has it existed from eternity; it is the product of the wisdom, the power, and the will of one God in Trinity. *God the Father is the prime cause of the creation, God the Son perfected the creation, and God the Holy Ghost gives it life.*
>
> The Orthodox believe that our Lord Jesus Christ, while truly God, *begotten of the same substance as the Father and consubstantial with Him,* is also truly a man in every respect except sin. The denial of His humanity would constitute a denial of His incarnation and of our salvation.
>
> The official creed accepted by Orthodoxy, formulated and adopted by the First Ecumenical Council of Nicæa (AD 325) and the Second Ecumenical Council of Constantinople (AD 381), is generally known as the Nicæan Creed. It reads as follows:
>
> "I believe in one God, the Father Almighty, maker of heaven and earth and of all things visible and invisible; and in one Lord Jesus Christ, *the only begotten Son of God, begotten of His Father before all ages*: light of light, very God of very God, *begotten, not made, consubstantial with the Father,* by Whom all things were made, Who for all men and for our salvation came down from heaven, and *was incarnate by the Holy Ghost* of the Virgin Mary, and was made man; and was crucified also for us under Pontius Pilate. He suffered and was buried; and the third day *He arose again* according to the Scriptures, and ascended into heaven, and *sitteth on the right hand of the Father.* And He shall come again with glory to judge both the quick and the dead, whose kingdom shall have no end.
>
> "And I believe in the Holy Ghost, the Lord and giver of life, who proceedeth from the Father, who with the Father and Son together is worshiped and glorified, and who spoke by the prophets.
>
> "I believe in one, holy, catholic and apostolic church; I acknowledge one baptism for the remission of sins. I look for the resurrection of the dead, and for the life of ages to come." (Rosten, 117)

Roman Catholicism

In answer to the questions "Are Roman Catholicism and Eastern Orthodoxy More Alike Than Different in Their Beliefs?" and "What, Then, Are the Main Differences Today Between the Eastern Orthodox Church and the Roman Catholic Church?" the following insights were supplied:

> Yes. Actually, *the basic tenets of both bear the sanction of the same seven ecumenical councils, the last of which took place in AD 787, when the Eastern and Western branches*

of Christianity were still united. . . . In doctrine, the Eastern Orthodox Church differs from Roman Catholicism in the following:

1. *The Roman Catholic Church holds that the holy spirit proceeds "and from the Son" (a doctrine known as the "filioque" clause) as well as from the Father. Eastern Orthodoxy believes that the holy spirit proceeds only "from the Father."* (Rosten, 115)

Episcopalian

In answer to the query "What Are the Basic Beliefs of Episcopalians?":

They are affirmed in the Apostles' Creed and the Nicene Creed. The Apostles' Creed is the ancient baptismal statement of faith. As used in Episcopalian services, it runs:
I believe in God the Father Almighty, Maker of heaven and earth:

And in Jesus Christ his *only* Son our Lord: *Who was conceived by the Holy Ghost,* Born of the Virgin Mary: Suffered under Pontius Pilate, Was crucified, dead, and buried: He descended into hell; The third day He rose again from the dead: He ascended into heaven, And sitteth on the right hand of God the Father Almighty: From thence He shall come to judge the quick and the dead.

I Believe in the Holy Ghost: the holy Catholic Church; The Communion of Saints:

The Foregiveness of Sin: The Resurrection of the body; And the Life everlasting. Amen.

The Nicene Creed, used at the service of Holy Communion, is an expanded statement of the Christian faith, essentially the same as the Apostles' Creed.

Both creeds state the main points of Christian belief in a pictorial and dramatic form. *Some of the phrases are clearly "symbolic" (as, "sitteth on the right hand of God the Father," which of course **could not be literally true**)*; some parts are historical in intention (as "born," "crucified," "dead," "buried," "rose again"); and some parts are theological such as "of one substance," in the Nicene Creed, although *more often the theological affirmations are phrased in the pictorial language that the early Church took over from its Jewish background.* (Rosten, 99)

In response to the question "What Is the Episcopal Position About the Trinity?" the following was supplied:

The trinity is the Christian teaching about God. In the light of man's experience of God's working in the world, Christians have been driven to assert that God *is* as He *reveals* Himself. *He is Creative Reality (God the Father); He is Expressive Act (God the Son); He is Responsive Power (God the Holy Spirit).* Yet He is *one* God. This is "theology."

What matters most, in the Book of Common Prayer, about the Trinity is that we worship God and experience Him in a "trinitarian" fashion. (Rosten, 101)

Lutheran

"What Are the Basic Tenets of the Lutheran Creed?" brought the following response:

Lutherans don't claim any doctrines different from the common Christian faith described in the New Testament and *first summarized in the Apostles' Creed.* We are created by God, but we employ the freedom given us by God to disobey our Creator. The result is continual tragedy in human life. But God does not abandon us in our tragedy. He shares it with us.

In Christ, He reveals Himself as the Savior God, suffering punishment and death so we may share with Him in the resurrection from death. Through faith in Christ, a new life begins in us. It is nourished by God's gifts through His Word and sacraments. The Word is recorded in the Bible, but *the Word itself is a living, active thing* through which the Holy Spirit stirs us to growth in understanding and obedience to God's will. (Rosten, 158–59)

In response to the query "Do Lutherans Believe in the Holy Trinity?" this response is presented:

> *They do,* along with orthodox Christians of all ages. *God the Father is our Creator. God the Son is our Redeemer. God the Holy Ghost is the Sanctifier and Nourisher of our souls. Yet there is one God in three personalities.*
>
> It is not possible to make any essential Christian teaching—such as how God could be a man, how the dead can live eternally, how one God can be three personalities—conform to mathematical formulas or submit to scientific proof. *Such things are beyond the range of human reasoning* and are matters of faith. (Rosten, 162)

Presbyterian

Their response to the question "Do Presbyterians Believe in the Trinity?" was:

> *Yes.* The Trinity is frequently invoked in worship, at every baptism, and in the benediction at the close of each service. *When God is spoken of as three persons— Father, Son, and Holy Spirit—Presbyterians do not think of Him as three individuals. That is tritheism. One God reveals Himself in three manifestations.*
>
> The word "Persons" used of the Godhead is employed in the same sense as "persona." *It signifies a character or a representation.* Various analogies have been employed by theologians to explain this doctrine but most Presbyterians accept it by faith. (Rosten, 203–4)

Methodist

"What Is the United Methodist Attitude Toward the Trinity?"

> To United Methodists *the doctrine of the Trinity is one of the most important ways of thinking about God.* It describes God as creator, savior, and divine presence and power in history. Within United Methodist liturgies, there are many references to trinitarian theology. (Rosten 173–74)

"What Distinguishes Methodists from Other Protestant Denominations?"

> *The Methodist Church retains, in general, the theology of the Anglican Church, from which it sprang.* Some Methodist parishes preserve much of the Protestant Episcopal liturgy. On the other hand, in some Methodist churches, the services of worship are very informal. Within the 40,000 American Methodist churches, there is probably as wide variation in types of thought and worship as there is between Methodists, Presbyterians, Congregationalists, and others. (Rosten, 178)

"How Do United Methodists 'Theologize'?"

> The 1972 general conference of this church adopted a significant, newly worded statement on Doctrine and Doctrinal Standards. The conference agreed that *Articles of Religion and Confession of Faith "are not to be regarded as positive, juridical norms for doctrine, demanding unqualified assent on pain of excommunication."* They are, rather, landmarks in the church's theological journey. (Rosten, 182)

The Church of Jesus Christ of Latter-day Saints

Latter-day Saints will recognize the name of Richard L. Evans, who wrote the information concerning The Church of Jesus Christ of Latter-day Saints while serving as a member of the Quorum of the Twelve Apostles prior to his death in 1971. An author's note to readers concerning the latest edition of *Religions of America* states that "Dr. Evans' article was submitted to The Church of Jesus Christ of Latter-day Saints, for such changes or corrections as might be thought appropriate. A few changes, approved by the First Presidency of the Church, have been included in this version. Where the text is not that of Dr. Evans, the initials [TFP] (The First Presidency) identify it." (Rosten, *Religions of America*, 186)

In answer to the question Do Mormons Believe in the Holy Trinity? Elder Richard L. Evans responded:

> Yes. *The Latter-day Saint accepts the Godhead as three literal, distinct personalities: God the Father; His Son, Jesus the Christ (who is one with the Father in purpose and in thought, but separate from Him in physical fact); and the Holy Ghost, a Personage of spirit* (Acts 7:55, etc.). Here, *the Mormon points to literal scriptural language.* He believes in a loving, understanding *Father who made his children "in his own image"* (Genesis 1:27), and Jesus His Son is said to be in *"the express image of his person"* (Hebrews 1:3). (Rosten, 189)

His response to the query What Do the Mormons Believe About Jesus Christ? was:

> They believe Him to be the Son of God, *"the only begotten of the Father" in the flesh.* They believe in His atoning sacrifice and literal resurrection. They accept Him as the Savior and Redeemer of mankind. They look to Him as the "one mediator between God and men" (I Timothy 2:5), and pray to the Father in His name. They believe that He will come again and reign on earth (Acts 1:9–11). (Rosten, 189)

Elder Evan's answer to the question "Do Mormons Believe in the Virgin Birth?" was "Yes. The Latter-day Saint accepts the miraculous conception of Jesus the Christ." (Rosten, 189)

Baptist

The following is their response to the question "Do Baptists Accept the Doctrine of the Trinity?":

> Most Baptists do.
> This is a basic doctrine of Christianity. The trinitarian formula, "in the name of the Father, and of the Son, and of the Holy Ghost," is used at every baptism.
> *The sublime mystery of the Trinity, of the eternal and infinite essence of God manifested in three persons—these, the Baptist leaves to theologians to interpret.* He accepts them. (Rosten, 30)

Seventh-day Adventist

In answer to the question "Do Seventh-day Adventists Believe in the Trinity?" the following is recorded:

> They do. Reverently they worship Father, Son, and Holy Spirit, *"three Persons in one God."* And they do so because they believe this to be the teaching of the Bible

concerning God in His relation to this world and the human race. (Rosten 247)

However, their response to the query "How Do Seventh-day Adventists Differ from Other Protestants?" seems to reflect on how they view "trinitarian" doctrines:

> Seventh-day Adventists claim that *they are not inventors of new doctrines but recoverers of old truths—truths long eclipsed by the infiltration of pagan traditions and superstitions into the Christian Church.* (Rosten, 245)

United Church of Christ

The question "What Is the United Church of Christ Creed?" is answered in these words:

> Traditionally the Congregational Christian churches were *non-creedal*, although many individual churches adopted their own statements of faith. The Evangelical and Reformed Church had a statement of faith for the whole denomination. An important aspect of the negotiations toward union was agreement upon *a Statement of Faith to be regarded "as a testimony, not a test of faith."* In the Preamble to the Constitution accepted by the uniting churches there is this affirmation: "[The United Church of Christ] *claims as its own the faith of the historic Church expressed in the ancient creeds and reclaimed in the basic insights of the Protestant Reformers.* It affirms the responsibility of the Church in each generation to make this faith its own in reality of worship, in honesty of thought and expression, and in purity of heart before God." (Rosten, 277)

Their answer to the question "Do You Believe in the Holy Trinity?" is:

> Yes. The Statement of Faith begins: "We believe in God, the Eternal Spirit, Father of our Lord Jesus Christ . . ." The Holy Spirit is referred to separately as "creating and renewing the Church of Jesus Christ, binding in covenant faithful people of all ages, tongues and races." (Rosten, 278)

Christian Scientist

Their response to the question "What Is the Attitude of Christian Scientists Toward the Trinity?" is:

> By the Trinity, Christian Scientists mean the unity of Father, Son, and Holy Spirit—*not as three persons in one but as Life, Truth, and Love, or three offices of one divine Principle.* (Rosten, 72)

Quaker

The question "What Is the Attitude of Friends Toward Jesus?" is answered in this manner:

> Quakers have a common belief in the revelation of God in Christ. There is a variety of points of view among Friends, but there is a universal witness (a common faith) that *God expressed His love historically in Jesus of Nazareth and eternally through the Spirit of Christ.* To many Friends, these are two experiences of the same reality—the historical Jesus and the risen Christ within. . . .
> Christianity has to do with accepting Jesus as leader and example, and with doing what he commands. *It does not have to do with speculations as to his metaphysical nature.*

Friends, in their private opinions, run the gamut from Christian orthodoxy to extreme unorthodoxy. Yet even those Friends who refuse to label themselves Christians *are likely to cite their disillusionment with forms of Christianity that seem preoccupied with making up doctrines about Jesus* instead of following his message and example. (Rosten, 226)

Their response to the query "How Do Friends Feel About the Trinity?" is:

Again, there is wide freedom for personal opinion. It must be remembered that Quakerism is based on a religious way of life rather than accepted dogmas. The Quaker faith is a religion of experience. Whatever is known experimentally about God, the Holy Spirit, the Christ Within, becomes the true guide. *Friends tend to believe in the immanence of God rather than His transcendence.*

"Trinity" is a term not found in Scripture and is an example of unnecessary speculation—of turning Christianity into a religion about Jesus instead of the religion of following Jesus. (Rosten, 227)

Disciple of Christ

When asked "What Are the Basic Beliefs of Your Creed?" the representative for this faith wrote, in part:

The church professes no doctrine or dogma beyond belief in Jesus Christ; all other matters are therefore open to individual interpretation, even the characteristics mentioned here as being distinctively Disciple.

The Disciples *reject the use of creeds* when applied as tests to determine "rightness of belief."

Disciples, from the very beginning of the movement, *have objected to matters that tend to divide Christianity. They have therefore rejected creeds and dogma with vehemence.* They have opted strongly for the right of every Christian to read the scriptures for himself or herself and to decide on matters of opinion.

There is no church authority that fixes a position on doctrine. (Rosten, 85)

In response to the question "Do the Disciples Believe in the Holy Trinity?" the following was supplied:

The Disciples have had little trouble in discarding most of the dogmas that sprang up between the first century and the nineteenth. Hence, *speculation about the Holy Trinity and the nature of a triune God* has bothered them little or not at all. They baptize in the name of the Father, Son, and Holy Spirit, as Christ commanded. *The name of the Father, Son, and Holy Spirit is the Comforter promised in the New Testament,* but they do not worry over its constitution or the nature of its operations. They accept its guidance as constantly enlarging the horizons of Christian thought. They are not concerned about such matters as original sin or predestination. (Rosten, 88)

Jehovah's Witness

The beginning of their reply to the question "What Are the Teachings of Jehovah's Witnesses?" is as follows:

That *Jehovah is the only true God.* His sovereignty has been challenged by Satan, who caused the rebellion in Eden and who puts the integrity of all men to the test. God's primary purpose is the vindication of this sovereignty. In carrying out this purpose, God sent Jesus to earth to provide the ransom sacrifice and to lay the foundation for God's new system of things.

In response to the question "Do Witnesses Believe in the Holy Trinity?" the following is presented:

> *Jehovah's Witnesses believe that Jehovah God and Christ Jesus are two distinct persons and are not combined with a so-called "Holy Ghost" in one godhead called a Trinity.* The "Holy Spirit" is not a person. It is God's active force. (Rosten, 133)

Unitarian Universalist

The question "What Do the Names "Unitarian" and "Universalist" Mean?" was answered, in part, in these words:

> *"Unitarian" was a theological term, applied in the sixteenth century, to those who denied the doctrine of the trinity.* Unitarians thought that the idea of equating Christ with God was unscriptural, illogical, and unnecessary.
>
> "Universalist" stood for the teaching that salvation was not for a limited few—the elect—but was a gift of God for all. The joys of a final reconciliation with God were ultimately available to all men, regardless of their errors or doubts. No God of love, the Universalists declared, could eternally damn any one.
>
> Both Unitarians and Universalists, although focusing on different doctrines, were thus affirming the importance of human beings as not separated from God, and their natural ability to know and do what is right. (Rosten, 264)

Their answer to the question "Do Unitarian Universalists Believe in God?" is:

> Unitarian Universalists believe that all persons must decide about God for themselves.
>
> In their churches are agnostics, humanists, even atheists—as well as nature worshipers, pantheists, and those who affirm a personal God. All recognize, however, that *the word "God" is a stumbling block to religious communication for many people because it has so many meanings.* All know also that there is no special virtue in being able to declare, "I believe in God." (Rosten, 265)

The question "Do Unitarian Universalists Think That Jesus Christ Was Divine?" brought this response:

> In a sense they think that every person is divine—that is, that there is goodness and worth in everyone. Some call it a "divine spark," others simply "human dignity."
>
> However, *Unitarian Universalists see no need for the concept of a special divinity in Christ, and they clearly reject any notion of God's requiring the sacrifice of "His Son" to atone for human "sin."*
>
> Nor do they see the need for a Messiah of the Jewish hope or the Savior of Christian belief. But they are inspired by the life and teachings of Jesus as an extraordinary fellow human being. (Rosten, 267)

Varying Levels of Acceptance or Rejection of the "Trinitarian" Formula

It is obvious that there are numerous levels of acceptance or rejection of the "trinitarian" "one God in three persons" formula. Even a cursory scanning of the above statements of belief voiced by designated representatives of the various churches shows the tremendous wide variance in the level of acceptance accorded to the "trinitarian" formula. Note, for instance, these brief portions of the statements quoted above:

1. The **Episcopalians**, for instance, stated that they subscribed to the Nicene Creed and the Apostles' Creed but denied the literal nature of certain aspects of those creeds, saying that *"Both creeds state the main points of Christian belief in a pictorial and dramatic form. Some the phrases are clearly 'symbolic'* (as, 'sitteth on the right hand of God the Father,' which of course could not be *literally* true)."

2. The **Methodists** reported that they adopted a significant statement in 1972 that their Articles of Religion and Confession of Faith *"are not to be regarded as positive, juridical norms for doctrine,* demanding unqualified assent on pain of excommunication."

3. The **Baptists** only hold that "most Baptists do" accept the "doctrine" of the Trinity, and they express the reservation that "The sublime mystery of the Trinity, of the eternal and infinite essence of God manifested in three persons—*these, the Baptist leaves to theologians to interpret,"* in effect asserting that the "trinitarian" dogma is beyond the comprehension of their typical members.

4. The **Seventh-day Adventists** acknowledge that pagan ideologies are involved with "trinitarian" dogma: "Seventh-day Adventists claim that they are not inventors of new doctrines but *recoverers of old truths—truths long eclipsed by the infiltration of pagan traditions and superstitions into the Christian Church."*

5. When various congregational churches united to form **The United Church of Christ**, they felt it necessary to formulate a statement of faith for the whole denomination. An important aspect of their negotiations toward union was the agreement that their Statement of Faith, which dealt in part with the traditional Christian beliefs, was to be regarded *"as a testimony, not a test of faith."* They didn't want their individual church memberships to hinge on belief in the "trinitarian" dogmas.

6. **Christian Scientists** have completely redefined the term trinity and separated themselves from the ancient creedal statements: "By the Trinity, Christian Scientists mean the unity of Father, Son, and Holy Spirit—*not as three persons in one but as Life, Truth, and Love, or three offices of one divine Principle."*

7. **Quakers** have never accepted the ancient Christian creeds. "Quakerism is based on a religious way of life rather than accepted dogmas. . . . *'Trinity' is a term not found in scripture and is an example of unnecessary speculation*—of turning Christianity into a religion about Jesus instead of the religion of following Jesus."

8. **Disciples of Christ**, "from the very beginning of the movement, have objected to matters that tend to divide Christianity. *They have therefore rejected creeds and dogma with vehemence. . . . The Disciples have had little trouble in discarding most of the dogmas that sprang up between the first century and the nineteenth.* Hence, speculation about the Holy Trinity and the nature of a triune God has bothered them little or not at all."

9. **Jehovah's Witnesses** "believe that Jehovah God and Christ Jesus are two distinct persons" and are not combined with a so-called "Holy Ghost" in one godhead called a Trinity."

10. **Unitarian** "was a theological term, applied in the sixteenth century, *to those who denied the doctrine of the trinity.* Unitarians thought that the idea of equating Christ with God was unscriptural, illogical, and unnecessary."

A Comparison of Beliefs Concerning Deity of Non-Christian Faiths

Agnostic

Also included in Rosten's collection of religious groups was a section on Agnostics. This was the response a noted agnostic furnished to the query "How Does an Agnostic Regard Jesus, the Virgin Birth, and the Holy Trinity?"

> *Since an agnostic does not believe in God, he cannot think that Jesus was God.* Most agnostics admire the life and moral teachings of Jesus as told in the Gospels, but not necessarily more than those of certain other men. Some would place him on a level with Buddha, some with Socrates, and some with Abraham Lincoln.
>
> Nor do they think that what he said is not open to question, since they do not accept any authority as absolute.
>
> *They regard the Virgin Birth as a doctrine taken over from pagan mythology, where such births were not uncommon.* (Zoroaster was said to have been born of a virgin; Istar, the Babylonian goddess, is called the Holy Virgin.) *They cannot give credence to it or to the doctrine of the Trinity,* since neither is possible without belief in God. (Rosten, 288)

Jew

In response to the query "Do Christianity and Judaism Agree on Anything? On What Points Do They Differ?" the following was given concerning the nature of God:

> *Jews do not accept the divinity of Jesus as the "only begotten Son" of God.* Jews recognize Jesus as a child of God in the sense that we are all God's children. The ancient rabbis taught us that *God's greatest gift is the knowledge that we are made in His image.* Jews also cannot accept the principle of incarnation—God becoming flesh. It is a cardinal tenet of our faith that *God is purely spiritual; He admits of no human attributes.*
>
> *Nor can Judaism accept the principle of vicarious atonement—the idea of salvation through Christ.* It is our belief that every man is responsible for his own salvation. We believe that no one can serve as an intermediary between man and God, even in a symbolic sense. We approach God—each man after his own fashion— without a mediator. (Rosten, 144–45)

The following statements are also of interest concerning their beliefs about man's relationships with God:

> Christians and Jews share the same rich heritage of the Old Testament, with its timeless truths and its unchanging values. They share their belief in the fatherhood of one God—all-knowing, all-powerful, ever-merciful, the God of Abraham, Isaac, and Jacob. They share their faith in the sanctity of the Ten Commandments, the wisdom of the prophets, and the brotherhood of man. . . . Judaism holds that man can most genuinely worship God by imitating those qualities that are godly: As God is merciful, so must we be compassionate; as God is just, so must we deal justly with our neighbor; as God is slow to anger, so must we be tolerant. . . . He who is beloved of his fellow man is beloved of God. . . . From their earliest childhood, Jews are taught that He [God] is to be worshiped out of love, not out of fear. (Rosten, 143–44)

"Unchurched" Americans

In his survey, Leo Rosten also included a large group which he designated as "Unchurched" Americans. In response to the question "Who Are the Unchurched?" the furnished response was:

The "unchurched" are those millions of Americans who choose not to identify themselves with any of the organized religions.

We should distinguish between those people who are merely indifferent or inactive and *those who decline to join a church out of conviction.* It is this latter group—those who do not join a church out of principle—whom we shall consider here. (Rosten, 255)

The response to the query "Are the Unchurched Purely Negative in Their Beliefs?" was:

For the unchurched, religion is a personal and nonsectarian matter rather than a question of church affiliation or formal ritual. *Still others completely reject the concept of religion, viewing it as a relic of ancient superstition and authoritarian tradition.* Some will admit that they experience familiar "religious" feelings, such as awe and wonder, but experience difficulty even with the word "religion"—*because it has so many associations with sectarian strife, bigotry, and repression. . . .* Jewish and Christian religious beliefs, which have so profoundly shaped Western ideas, have assumed that man's moral and spiritual life is derived from God and is dependent upon God. But if we look to other spiritual traditions—the teachings of early Buddhism, for example—we find a deeply religious attitude that does not draw from a claim of divine attitude. (Rosten, 256–57)

This group includes philosophical attitudes such as those held by Humanists, by Deists, and also by Pantheists:

The overwhelming percentage of avowed humanists belong to no organization to promote their distinctive religious or ethical beliefs. Some humanists, on the other hand, cherish religion for its cultural and moral value and see nothing inconsistent in joining religious bodies that interpret religion in liberal, humanistic terms.

Liberal churches, Reform and Reconstructionist Jewish congregations, and Quaker meetings—all are fellowships that have attracted many who hold humanistic interpretations of religion. So, strictly speaking, not all people of humanistic belief are unchurched." . . .

Deists are people who believe in a Supreme Being or Creator but reject the idea of divine revelation, sacred scriptures, or miracles. They believe in a Deity who established an orderly universe but does not interfere in the working of nature's laws.

Many of the unchurched, of course, hold such beliefs. They may respect Jesus and other religious sages as wise teachers, but they deny that such figures were supernaturally inspired. . . .

Pantheism is the belief that there is no God except nature or the universe itself. Nature is an impersonal creative unity or whole, the pantheist believes.

Although the word "pantheist" has come to sound old-fashioned and is seldom used any more, many of the unchurched have a deep sense of awe and reverence for nature or the cosmos, which they accept as self-existing. (Rosten, 257–60)

Numerous other churches and religious faiths acknowledge the existence of Jesus Christ but do not regard Him as a divine being with the qualities of Godhood. These include:

1. The **Unification Church**, founded by Sun Myung Moon in 1954 in South Korea.
2. The **Unity School of Christianity**, founded by Charles (1854–1948) and Myrtle (1845–1931) Fillmore in 1889 in Kansas City.
3. **Spiritualism (Spiritism)**, an ancient belief popularized by Kate and Margaret Fox (sisters) in 1848 in Hydesville, New York.

4. **Scientology**, a group founded in 1954 in California by L. Ron Hubbard (1911–1986).
5. **New Age**, a movement popularized in part by Shirley McLaine in the 1980s–1990s, is based on Eastern mystics, Hinduism, and paganism.
6. **Hinduism** began between 1800 and 1000 BC in India and has many sects.
7. **Hare Krishna** was founded in 1965 in New York by A.C. Bhaktivedanta Swami Prabhupada (1896–1977). This religion is based on Hindu teachings from the AD 1500s.
8. **Transcendental Meditation** was founded in 1959 by Maharishi Mahesh Yogi in California, based on Hinduism and yoga.
9. **Buddhism**, an offshoot of Hinduism, was founded about 525 BC in India by Buddha (Siddhartha Gautama).
10. **Islam** was founded by Muhammad (570–632) about AD 610, in Mecca and Medina.
11. The **Baháí World Faith** was founded in 1844 in Iran by Mizra Ali Muhammed (the Bab) and Mizra Husayn Ali (Baháúllah).

Beware of the Implications of the Term "Trinity"

In this day of political wrangling, when numerous judges for the Supreme Court and other high judicial offices are being nominated by one political party and challenged by the other party, the use of the term "litmus test" has emerged. *The typical dictionary definition of the term is "a test in which a single factor (as an attitude, event, or fact) is decisive." The use of the term "Trinity" has become a litmus test.*

When the staff of Leo Rosten asked the question "Do _____ believe in the Holy Trinity," it posed a dilemma for various faiths. These denominations have strong beliefs concerning God the Father, God the Son Jesus Christ, and God the Holy Spirit, but yet they don't believe in the "one God in three persons" formula which was formalized in the Nicean Creed. To the contrary, they believe in one Godhead composed of three separate persons: the Father, Son, and Holy Ghost.

But because of the "litmus test" implications of the question, "Do you believe in the Trinity," the question has come to mean "Do you believe in a true God or a false god," and "Are you a Christian." The question is typically posed by members of denominations which accept the creeds formulated in the earthly Catholic councils as the foundation of their belief in God. If the respondent's reply to the question is "no," rather than "yes," the respondent is categorically branded as a believer in a false god and hence is not considered to be a Christian. Little opportunity is afforded for the respondent to clarify his beliefs.

Rather than be subjected to this categorical rejection and denunciation, respondents feel compelled to answer the "do you believe in the trinity" question in the affirmative. *They answer yes to the question, then state and clarify their belief system as they give further explanations.* This is what Elder Richard L. Evans, of the Latter-day Saint Council of the Twelve did when he responded to the Rosten-group's query, "Do Mormons Believe in the Holy Trinity?" He answered in the affirmative, *but then immediately clarified that the Church's belief most definitely did not follow the "one God in three persons" concept of the ancient creeds.* He wrote:

> Yes. The Latter-day Saint accepts the Godhead as three literal, distinct personalities:
> God the Father; His Son, Jesus the Christ (who is one with the Father in purpose and

in thought, but separate from Him in physical fact); and the Holy Ghost, a Personage of spirit (Acts 7:55, etc.). Here, *the Mormon points to literal scriptural language.* He believes in a loving, understanding *Father who made his children "in his own image"* (Genesis 1:27), and Jesus His Son is said to be in *"the express image of his person"* (Hebrews 1:3). (Rosten, 189)

So, should the word trinity be used by Latter-day Saints in reference to their belief in the Godhead of God the Father, God the Son Jesus Christ, and God the Holy Spirit? They should be aware that people of other faiths who use the term "trinity" most definitely are not using it in that more general, "godhead" fashion. *To them, the term most certainly has reference to what they call a mystery because they can't explain it: the one God in three persons formula.*

The eleventh edition of the *Merriam-Webster's Collegiate Dictionary* defines the word "trinity" in this manner: "[state of being threefold, fr. L *trinus* threefold] *the unity of Father, Son, and Holy Spirit as three persons in one Godhead according to Christian dogma.*"

In my opinion, *the dictionary definition using the words "according to Christian dogma" loads and biases the term, making it unusable as a legitimate part of Latter-day Saint terminology.* It is recognized, however, that some Latter-day Saints have used the term in their discussions of the nature of God and the roles of the Father, Son and Holy Ghost in the Godhead, perhaps confusing rather than clarifying their explanations through the term's usage, especially if their words are to be heard or read by others who are not from a Latter-day Saint background and understanding.

Two examples cited from dictionaries of theology should suffice to make it clear that the term "trinity" definitely is not just a generalized term referring to the Father, Son and Holy Spirit. For instance, the *Westminster Dictionary of Christian Theology*, in its eight-page article titled "Trinity, Doctrine of the" begins with these two paragraphs:

> *The doctrine of the Trinity is primarily a christological doctrine and its most widely accepted form is a product mainly of the fourth century AD.* It was the christological concerns of the early Christian centuries which persistently motivated and which finally fashioned most of classical "trinitarian" doctrine, and in modern times the declared purpose of that doctrine still is to point to the presence and action of God in this world in Jesus the Christ (economic Trinity). Although "trinitarian" doctrine as we know it was prefigured in some authors before the fourth century and underwent some minor developments since then, *its basic form owes more to the controversial needs of that century and to the religious imagery accepted by Christians and non-Christians alike at that time than to any other influence either before or since.*
>
> *Scriptural authority for the development of trinitarian doctrine has become a much-debated topic,* but in view of the supreme normative role which all Christian traditions in one way or another accord to scripture, *it is a topic that is likely to be debated for some time to come.* Views on this topic range from the conviction that trinitarian doctrine is little more than a summary of explicit data otherwise scattered across O. T. and N. T., *to the assertion that it is an important aid in worship but without any real foundation in the Bible* (Richardson). In between these extremes Emil Brunner, for instance, argues that a trinitarian doctrine which respects the strict "economic" order of salvation and revelation, the order in which Father, Son and Spirit come "after one another," is biblical, whereas *"essential" Trinities which place the "persons alongside one another" in a transcendent relationship represent no more than an aberration of theological thought*

which, however, has dominated church preaching from the fifth century onward. (Richardson & Bowden, *Westminster Dictionary of Christian Theology*, 581)

Other theological dictionaries also universally make it clear that the term "Trinity" is not just a general term referring collectively to the Father, the Son, and the Holy Spirit. Rather, *it is a term which pre-supposes the "one God in three persons" concept of the Nicene Creed.* The second example to be cited is found in Muller's *Dictionary of Latin and Greek Theological Terms.* The lengthy discussion of the term "Trinity" begins as follows:

> **Trinitas:** *Trinity*; viz., *the existence of God as one in essence* (*essentia*, q.v.) *and three in person* (*persona*, q.v.). *The doctrine of the Trinity arises out of the church's reflection on the biblical declaration that God is one, but is known as Father, Son, and Spirit.* The correlation of the way in which God is known through his self-revelation and the way in which God truly is in himself constitutes the necessary presupposition of true doctrine, i.e., of the truth of the revelation itself; therefore, *the revelation that God is one and the revelation that God is three cannot be reduced to an eternal oneness and a temporal or economical threeness. Equally, the oneness cannot be defined in such a way that it ultimately abolishes the threeness, or the threeness in such a way that it ultimately abolishes the oneness.* **Trinity, therefore, is an attempt to avoid both a monadic oneness and tritheistic view of God through the affirmation that God is one in essence and three in person.** The terms used to elucidate this doctrine come from both the patristic and the medieval church. (Muller, *Dictionary of Latin and Greek Theological Terms*, 306–7).

Hence, I suggest that Latter-day Saints not confuse the term "trinity" with the more general term "godhead," which does not carry such a "three-in-one connotation, when trying to explain Latter-day Saint doctrines pertaining to the nature of God.

Summary

1. Authorized representatives of various religions responded to requests that they state the beliefs of their respective faiths. Brief citations from these statements are found in this chapter.
2. The compiler of these statements chose a question-and-answer format because he felt it would be "the best way of avoiding those lofty ambiguities and irritating hairsplittings which, alas, characterize so much of the literature on religion."
3. The Eastern Orthodox, Roman Catholic, Episcopalian, Lutheran, Presbyterian, Methodist, Baptist, Seventh-day Adventist, and United Church of Christ indicate that their doctrines concerning the nature of God are based on ancient Catholic creeds such as the Nicene Creed and the Apostles' Creed.
4. Several of these churches, in their authorized statements cited above, include limiting statements which indicate varying degrees of contrary or differing beliefs in their ranks concerning whether the ancient creeds are fully accepted as being true beliefs concerning God's nature.
5. Several other denominations, including The Church of Jesus Christ of Latter-day Saints, indicated very strong beliefs in the power and divinity of God the Father, God the Son, and God the Holy Ghost, but they do not accept the "one God in three persons" formula set forth in the ancient creeds.

6. Many other faiths have very different concepts of who and what God is:

A **Christian Scientists** envision the unity of Father, Son, and Holy Spirit "not as three persons in one but as Life, Truth, and Love, or three offices of one divine Principle."

B **Quakers** state that "Christianity has to do with accepting Jesus as leader and example, and with doing what he commands. It does not have to do with speculations as to his metaphysical nature."

C The **Disciple of Christ** faith "professes no doctrine or dogma beyond belief in Jesus Christ," and they "reject the use of creeds when applied as tests to determine 'rightness of belief,' " apparently regarding them as "matters that tend to divide Christianity."

D **Jehovah's Witnesses** "believe that Jehovah God and Christ Jesus are two distinct persons and are not combined with a so-called "Holy Ghost" in one godhead called a Trinity."

E **Unitarians** "denied the doctrine of the trinity" and "thought that the idea of equating Christ with God was unscriptural, illogical, and unnecessary."

F **Unitarian Universalists** stated that they "see no need for the concept of a special divinity in Christ," and they "reject any notion of God's requiring the sacrifice of 'His Son' to atone for human sin."

G Sun Myung Moon's **Unification Church** does not believe in the trinity but believes that "God created the universe out of himself; the universe is God's 'Body.' "

H The **Unity School of Christianity** does not believe in the trinity, nor that God is an actual being, but only an "invisible impersonal power" that is "in everything."

I **Spiritualists** believe that "God is infinite intelligence," an "impersonal power controlling the universe."

J Followers of **Scientology** do not accept the biblical concept of God but instead believe that everyone is "a 'theton,' an immortal spirit with unlimited powers over its own universe."

K Followers of the **New Age Movement** have their individual concepts of God, but many believe that "Everything and everyone is God. God is an impersonal force or principle, not a person."

L Adherents of **Hinduism** believe that "God is 'The Absolute,' a universal spirit," and that "Everyone is part of God (Brahman) like drops in the sea."

M Followers of **Hare Krishna** believe that "God is Lord Krishna," who is "a personal creator," and that "the souls of all living things are part of him."

N Those who practice **Transcendental Meditation** believe that "each part of creation makes up 'God' (Brahman)." Their "Supreme Being is not personal." They hold that "All creation is divine; [and] 'all is one.' "

O **Buddhism** is mostly atheistic. Many Buddhists "do not believe in a God or Supreme Being of any kind."

P Followers of **Islam** believe that "God (Allah) is one"; a God who "is a severe judge" though sometimes merciful and is not depicted as loving. They believe that "Jesus is one of up to 124,000 prophets sent by God to various cultures. . . . Jesus was born of a virgin, but is not the Son of God. He was sinless, but not divine or God Himself."

Q   Members of the **Bahái World Faith** believe that "God is an unknowable divine being" who has revealed himself through nine "manifestations," or religious leaders, including Moses, Buddha, Confucius, Jesus, Muhammad, and Baháúllah.

R   **Jews** do not "accept the principle of incarnation—God becoming flesh. It is a cardinal tenet of [their] faith that God is purely spiritual" with "no human attributes." They also do not believe in the divinity of Jesus.

7. It is obvious that vastly different concepts of the nature of God exist, even among churches and religious organizations that recognize the existence and mortal ministry of Jesus Christ.

8. The author cautions Latter-day Saints not to use the term "trinity" as a synonym for the term "godhead" because it causes confusion for those of other faiths as well as for Latter-day Saint members. To non-Latter-day Saints, the term "trinity" conveys the meaning of "the existence of God as one in essence and three in person," and they often use belief or non-belief in their concept of the trinity as a "litmus test" to determine whether others are "Christians."

PART TWO

ATTRIBUTES AND PHYSICAL NATURES OF GODHEAD MEMBERS

CHAPTER 3

ATTRIBUTES OF MEMBERS
OF THE GODHEAD

The Approaches Used in This Chapter

Over the centuries, many authors have attempted to define and explain numerous attributes of God. Some characteristics have been presented well; others have become entangled in philosophical reasoning which are in direct conflict with scriptural principles. Some reasons why they're in conflict? (1) They attempt to describe "God," while making no distinction between the various characteristics of the different members of the Godhead. (2) They are, at times, locked into creedal statements from ancient times which are in direct conflict with the scriptures. (3) They are immersed in ancient philosophical hypotheses, often reaching back to Plato and other Greek philosophers, which became embedded in the thinking and writing of early Christian Fathers and Apologists. (4) They sometimes get carried away in their own imaginations, reasoning and analyzing scriptural passages, waxing so eloquent that they interpret the passages far beyond the limits of their stated meanings.

This chapter is an effort to view God through both Latter-day Saint and non-Latter-day Saint eyes. Several Bible and theological dictionaries, all based in "trinitarian" beliefs, have been identified and used as "typical" reference guides. It should be recognized that these non-Latter-day Saint theological sources are attempting to identify "God" as a single individual, while this chapter is addressing the characteristics of three different beings: God the Father, God the Son, and the Holy Spirit.

In some instances, statements will be cited from these theological sources that are in conflict with biblical teachings or scriptural passages from other Latter-day Saint scriptures. These conflicting statements will be identified as such, but space will not be devoted to refuting them in this chapter. Readers should find ample refutation for them in other chapters of this work.

One major assumption is made in this chapter. Since all three members of the Godhead have achieved perfection, it is assumed that the three of them share the same attributes, eternal perspectives, life-concepts, and emotional characteristics. Little effort has been made to differentiate concerning which of the three members of the Godhead are being spoken of in the hundreds of scriptural passages cited here. In most cases, that will be obvious; in some passages which merely speak of "God," it may prove beneficial to examine their contexts for a more in-depth understanding and subject identification.

Defining God from the Scriptures: "Trinitarian" Approaches

To set the stage, two brief excerpts are cited. The first is from Erickson's *Christian Theology:*

> When we speak of the attributes of God, we are referring to *those qualities of God which constitute what he is.* They are the very characteristics of his nature. We are not referring here to the acts which he performs, such as creating, guiding, and preserving, nor to the corresponding roles he plays—Creator, Guide, Preserver.
>
> *The attributes are qualities of the entire Godhead.* They should not be confused with *properties*, which, technically speaking, are the distinctive characteristics of the various persons of the Trinity. Properties are functions (general), activities (more specific), or acts (most specific) of the individual members of the Godhead.
>
> *The attributes are permanent qualities. They cannot be gained or lost. They are intrinsic.* Thus, holiness is not an attribute (a permanent, inseparable characteristic) of Adam, but it is of God. *God's attributes are essential and inherent dimensions of his very nature.* (Erickson, *Christian Theology*, 265)

The second citation is from the *Evangelical Dictionary of Theology:*

> In the Scriptures the divine attributes are not above God, beside God, or beneath God; *they are predicated of God.* God is holy; God is love. These characteristics do not simply describe what God does, they define what God is. . . . The Scriptures . . . make God known. The attributes are inseparable from the being of God. . . . In knowing the attributes, then, we know God as he has revealed himself. . . .
>
> *Much of our knowledge of God's attributes is analogical or figurative, where Scripture uses figures of speech.* Even then, however, the point illustrated can be stated in nonfigurative language. *So all our understanding of God is not exclusively analogical.* The revealed, nonfigurative knowledge has at least one point of meaning the same for God's thought and revelationally informed human thought. . . . We may be far from fully comprehending divine holiness and divine love, but insofar as our assertions about God coherently convey relevant conceptually revealed meanings, they are true of God and conform in part to God's understanding. (Elwell, et al., *Evangelical Dictionary of Theology*, 452–53)

Some Concerns on the "Most Basic of Definitions" Cited Above

The two above citations, from typical theological treatises, raise intrinsic conceptual differences of major proportions between the definitions and approaches coined and utilized by the deep thinkers of ancient Christianity (which were founded in the thought-processes of Plato and his contemporaries) and Latter-day Saint precepts based not only on the Bible but the Latter-day Saint scriptures which clarify and amplify them, as well as other insights revealed through Latter-day Saint prophets.

What red flags do these two citations raise? Two issues leap to the forefront:

Red flag number 1. From *Christian Theology*: "*The attributes are permanent qualities. They cannot be gained or lost. They are intrinsic.* Thus, holiness is not an attribute (a permanent, inseparable characteristic) of Adam, but it is of God."

What's the red flag? The phrases "The attributes are permanent qualities. They cannot be gained or lost. They are intrinsic," followed by "holiness" as an example. Some of the un-acquirable and can't-be-lost qualities they regard as being intrinsic only to God are believed by Latter-day Saints to be acquirable and to be can-be-lost qualities to man and to God: holiness (sanctification) being one of them (see D&C 20:31–34).

"Trinitarians" believe that God "always was God"; they also fought major theological battles concerning whether Christ "always was God." Latter-day Saints regard Godhood as an exalted priesthood office and believe that man, assisted by the grace of God, can attain Godhood, as did Jesus Christ. They also believe that when the scriptures provide glimpses of God the Father in the premortal life, they are glimpsing one generation of deity in an eternal ongoing line of generations, rather than being shown back to the very, absolute beginning of "beginningless eternity."

Part of this line of Latter-day Saint thought comes from a general conference discourse given by the Prophet Joseph Smith on April 7, 1844. Since it was given, in part, as a funeral sermon commemorating the recent death of a faithful member, King Follett, the discourse has come to be known as the "King Follett Discourse." It is lengthy and profound, and worthy of in-depth study. Only a small portion of it is cited in this context, to set the stage for this chapter:

> *God himself was once as we are now, and is an exalted man, and sits enthroned in yonder heavens!* . . . It is the first principle of the gospel to know for a certainty the character of God, . . . that he was once a man like us; yea, that *God himself, the Father of us all, dwelt on an earth, the same as Jesus Christ himself did*; . . . and *you have got to learn how to be Gods yourselves, and to be kings and priests to God, the same as all Gods have done before you,* namely by going from one small degree to another, and from a small capacity to a great one: from grace to grace, from exaltation to exaltation. . . .
>
> How consoling to the mourners when they are called to part with a husband, wife, father, mother, child, or dear relative, to know that, although the earthly tabernacle is laid down and dissolved, they shall rise again to dwell in everlasting burnings in immortal glory, not to sorrow, suffer, or die any more, *but they shall be heirs of God and joint heirs with Jesus Christ. What is it? To inherit the same power, the same glory and the same exaltation, until you arrive at the station of a god, and ascend the throne of eternal power, the same as those who have gone before. What did Jesus do? Why, I do the things I saw my Father do when the worlds came rolling into existence. My Father worked out his kingdom with fear and trembling, and I must do the same*; and *when I get my kingdom, I shall present it to My Father, so that He may obtain kingdom upon kingdom, and it will exalt Him in glory.* He will then take a higher exaltation, and *I will take his place, and thereby become exalted myself.* So that *Jesus treads in the tracks of His Father, and inherits what God did before*; and *God is thus glorified and exalted in the salvation and exaltation of all His children.* It is plain beyond disputation, and you thus learn some of the first principles of the gospel, about which so much hath been said.
>
> When you climb up a ladder, you must begin at the bottom, and ascend step by step, until you arrive at the top; and so it is with the principles of the gospel—you must begin with the first, and go on until you learn all the principles of exaltation. *But it will be a great while after you have passed through the veil before you will have learned them. It is not all to be comprehended in this world; it will be a great work to learn our salvation and exaltation even beyond the grave.* (Joseph Smith, *History of the Church*, 6:305–7)

It should be understood, of course, that Latter-day Saints believe that God the Father, God His Son Jesus Christ, and God the Holy Ghost are the *only* Gods who have, or ever will have, governing power pertaining to *this* earth during its mortal probation.

Red flag number 2. The "trinitarians," based on Plato's logic, think they are defining what they sometimes refer to as "the great first cause" or the "one and only God," and believe they are delving back to "the very beginning" of beginningless eternity. In contrast, Latter-day Saints believe that the scriptures as they are presently available to mankind don't go all the way back, forever and ever, but only portray events in "recent" premortal generations—those generations which encompass the preparations for the creation of this present earth and those key players who made those preparations and enacted this earth's spiritual and physical creation.

But back to red flag number 2: how do those "trinitarian" scholars of past and present apply Plato's logic and early Greek methodologies? *Their typical approach in delving into the scriptures to learn the nature of God is to draw philosophical analogies—in other words, to not take the scriptures at face value, but to reason beyond the scriptures to attempt to fit God into their preconceived notions,* perhaps based on some of Plato's "forms." *This is called "allegorical interpretation."*

This red flag is found in Elwell's *Evangelical Dictionary of Theology* citation above: "*Much of our knowledge of God's attributes is **analogical or figurative**, where scripture uses figures of speech.* Even then, however, the point illustrated can be stated in non-figurative language. *So all our understanding of God is not exclusively **analogical**.*" As will be seen in several chapters in this book, *they take much of the most forth-right biblical evidence that conveys the true nature of God and side-step it, calling the passages "anthropomorphisms," etc.*

In contrast, the Latter-day Saint approach to scripture regards many of those discarded passages as literal statements. What was *Joseph Smith's approach to scriptural interpretation*? These were his comments, for instance, in reference to the Savior's parable of the prodigal son:

> *What is the rule of interpretation? Just no interpretation at all. Understand it precisely as it reads.* I have a key by which I understand the scriptures. I enquire, what was the question which drew out the answer, or caused Jesus to utter the parable? It is not national; it does not refer to Abraham, Israel, or the Gentiles, in a national capacity, as some suppose. *To ascertain its meaning, we must dig up the root and ascertain what it was* that drew that saying out of Jesus. (*History of the Church,* 5:261)

Before beginning brief considerations of the various "attributes" which are typically cited when theological treatises, bible dictionaries, and similar works, several foundational principles understood primarily (and perhaps *only*) by Latter-day Saints are first presented:

Some Latter-day Saint Foundations

I. Members of the Godhead Are Three *Separate* Beings

Several verses from the Doctrine and Covenants are appropriate in this context. This section, D&C 130, contains important items of instruction given by Joseph Smith the Prophet, at Ramus, Illinois, April 2, 1843:

> When the Savior shall appear we shall see him as he is. *We shall see that he is a man like ourselves.*
> And that same sociality which exists among us here will exist among us there, only it will be coupled with eternal glory, which glory we do not now enjoy.
> *John 14:23—The appearing of the Father and the Son, in that verse, is a personal*

appearance; and the idea that the Father and the Son dwell in a man's heart is an old sectarian notion, and is false.

In answer to the question—Is not the reckoning of God's time, angel's time, prophet's time, and man's time, *according to the planet on which they reside?*

I answer, Yes. But there are no angels who minister to this earth but those who do belong or have belonged to it.

The angels do not reside on a planet like this earth;

But they reside in the presence of God, on a globe like a sea of glass and fire, where all things for their glory are manifest, past, present, and future, and are continually before the Lord.

The place where God resides is a great Urim and Thummim.

This earth, in its sanctified and immortal state, will be made like unto crystal and will be a Urim and Thummim to the inhabitants who dwell thereon, whereby *all things pertaining to an inferior kingdom, or all kingdoms of a lower order, will be manifest to those who dwell on it;* and *this earth will be Christ's. . . .*

The Father has a body of flesh and bones as tangible as man's; the Son also; but the Holy Ghost has not a body of flesh and bones, but is a personage of Spirit. Were it not so, the Holy Ghost could not dwell in us.

A man may receive the Holy Ghost, and it may descend upon him and not tarry with him. (D&C 130:1–9, 22–23)

Concerning the Holy Ghost, the Pearl of Great Price contains this unique statement which enumerates many of His powers and responsibilities: • "by the Spirit ye are *justified, . . .* Therefore it is given to abide in you; the *record of heaven*; the *Comforter*; the *peaceable things* of immortal glory; the *truth* of all things; that which *quickeneth* all things, which *maketh alive* all things; that which *knoweth* all things, and hath *all power* according to *wisdom, mercy, truth, justice,* and *judgment*" (Moses 6:60–61).

2. The Three Members of the Godhead Are All Spirit Beings

The scriptural passage "*God is a Spirit: and they that worship him in spirit and in truth*" (John 4:24) is a correct statement. The fact that God the Father and God the Son have resurrected, glorified, tangible bodies does not negate the fact that they still are spirit beings.

Likewise, all God the Father's *not-yet-mortal children*, as His spirit-children off-springs, are spirits.

Likewise, all God the Father's children who are *mortal beings* are spirit beings with physical bodies superimposed over their spirit bodies. Thus, mortal beings can "worship him [God] *in spirit* and in truth" (John 4:24).

Likewise, God the Father's children whose *mortal bodies are in the grave*, while they have progressed to their next phase of life in the spirit world, are still spirit beings.

Likewise, God the Father's children who *have been resurrected* are still spirits, though they now have glorious, immortal, physical, tangible bodies superimposed over their spirit bodies—glorified bodies that will remain coupled with their spirit bodies for all eternity.

Unfortunately, those without Latter-day Saint scripture don't know what a spirit really is. They are unaware that "There is no such thing as immaterial matter. *All spirit is matter, but it is more fine or pure, and can only be discerned by purer eyes; We cannot see it; but when our bodies are purified we shall see that it is all matter*" (D&C 131:7–8).

Nor do they understand that physical bodies have the form, shape, appearance, and organs of the spiritual bodies over which they are superimposed. See Ether

3:15–16, in which the premortal Christ told the brother of Jared: • "Seest thou that ye are created after mine own image? Yea, even all men were created in the beginning after mine own image. Behold, *this body, which ye now behold, is the body of my spirit; and man have I created after the body of my spirit;* and even as I appear unto thee to be in the spirit will I appear unto my people in the flesh."

In contrast to these understandings, "trinitarian" books and articles paint an entirely different perspective of God's spirit nature. For instance, the *New Bible Dictionary*, in its descriptive article on God, states: "In this respect we must distinguish between God and His creatures that are spiritual. *When we say that God is pure spirit, it is to emphasize that he is not part spirit and part body as man is. He is simple spirit without form or parts, and for that reason he has no physical presence.* When the Bible speaks of God as having eyes, ears, hands and feet, it is an attempt to convey to us the senses that these physical parts convey, for if we do not speak of God in physical terms we could not speak of him at all. This, of course, does not imply any imperfection in God. *Spirit is not a limited or restricted form of existence, it is the perfect unit of being*" (Douglas, et al., "God," *New Bible Dictionary*, 427).

It would be difficult to find a paragraph with less scriptural substantiation and more direct conflict with the scriptures than this one!

3. Members of the Godhead Are Personal, Living, Active Beings

The members of the Godhead are separate, living, active beings. They interact with one another. They actively create, oversee, and control earth events, sustain their followers, make covenants, preserve Israel, build the church, and judge all justly. God the Father sent His Son to this earth to perform His atoning sacrifice, and then He raised Him from the dead.

The Godhead members actively seek the growth and eternal progress of all mankind, especially those who will acknowledge and obey them. In their separate roles they give commandments, call and inspire prophets, communicate inspiration and revelation, and hear and answer prayers.

The Father, Son, and Holy Ghost each have personal capabilities of intelligence, emotion, and volition. They know who they are and what their purposes are. They have a keen sense of identity, meaning, and purpose, as will be demonstrated in hundreds of instances throughout this book.

Dozens of passages make reference to the "living God," using the title in reference to both God the Son and God the Father. For instance, concerning God the Son, Jehovah: • "Joshua said, Hereby ye shall know that *the living God* is among you" (Josh. 3:10). • "who is this uncircumcised Philistine, that he should defy the armies of *the living God?*" (1 Sam. 17:26). • "My soul thirsteth for God, for *the living God*" (Ps. 42:2). • "the LORD is the true God, he is *the living God*" (Jer. 10:10). • "fear before the God of Daniel: for he is *the living God*" (Dan. 6:26). • "they be called the children of *the living God*" (Rom. 9:26). • "we trust in *the living God,* who is the Saviour of all men" (1 Tim. 4:10). • "ye are come unto mount Sion, and unto the city of *the living God,* the heavenly Jerusalem" (Heb. 12:22). • "they . . . reviled against Moses and against *the true and living God*" (1 Ne. 17:30).

Other "living God" passages make direct reference to **God the Father** (usually while identifying the Christ as His Son): • "thou art that Christ, *the Son of the living God*" (John 6:69). • "a man shall endure to the end, in following the example of *the Son of the living God*" (2 Ne. 31:16). • "hear the words of Jesus Christ, *the Son of the* *living God*" (3 Ne. 30:1). • "I am Jesus Christ, *the Son of the living God*" (D&C 14:9). • "baptism in the name of Jesus Christ, *the Son of the living God*" (D&C 55:2).

Thus it is evident that the scriptural term the "living God," like dozens of other scriptural titles, is used in reference to both the Father and the Son, but it definitely does not imply that they are the same being. It is a descriptive term, not an actual name.

4. Members of the Godhead Are Eternal Beings

Members of the Godhead are eternal beings, as are all mankind. This statement does not mean, however, that God nor Man have always existed in their present forms. Latter-day Saints know that prior to being born as spirit children, they previously existed as **intelligences**, which are eternal: • "they existed before, they shall have no end, they shall exist after, for they are gnolaum, or eternal" (Abr. 3:18; see 3:18–24). • "Man was also in the beginning with God. Intelligence, or the light of truth, was not created or made, neither indeed can be. All truth is independent in that sphere in which God has placed it, to act for itself, as all intelligence also; otherwise there is no existence" (D&C 93:29–30).

Concerning the **eternal future**, Latter-day Saints believe that the members of the Godhead, as well as all mankind, will exist eternally. They agree with numerous passages such as: • "Blessed be the Lord God of Israel for ever and ever" (1 Chr. 16:36). • "David said, Blessed be thou, Lord God of Israel our father, for ever and ever" (1 Chr. 29:10). • "Stand up and bless the Lord your God for ever and ever" (Neh. 9:5). • "the Lord sitteth King for ever" (Ps. 29:10). • "this God is our God for ever and ever" (Ps. 48:14).

The scriptures repeatedly assert that **mankind also will live forever:** • "*that thou mayest prolong thy days upon the earth, which the Lord thy God giveth thee, for ever*" (Deut. 4:40). • "The secret things belong unto the Lord our God: but *those things which are revealed belong unto us and to our children for ever*" (Deut. 29:29). • "*For thou hast confirmed to thyself thy people Israel to be a people unto thee for ever*: and thou, Lord, art become their God" (2 Sam. 7:24). • "*For thy people Israel didst thou make thine own people for ever*; and thou, Lord, becamest their God" (1 Chr. 17:22).

5. Members of the Godhead Are Unchanging in Their Natures, Desires, and Purposes

The members of the Godhead are eternally consistent in their purposes, attributes, standards, and impartial expectations for all mankind. Their acts are never arbitrary or capricious. All mankind can rely on their integrity, have confidence in their counsels and commandments, and chart their life's courses based upon their hope of eternal rewards which the Godhead members extend to everyone. Also, mankind knows that they are created in the image of God, with divine potential and infinite worth.

Concerning the **unchangeable natures** of the members of the Godhead, the scriptures say: • "Every good gift and every perfect gift is from above, and cometh down from *the Father of lights, with whom is no variableness, neither shadow of turning*" (James 1:17). • "Wherein God, willing more abundantly to shew unto the heirs of promise *the immutability of his counsel*, confirmed it by an oath: That by two immutable things, in which *it was impossible for God to lie*, we might have a strong consolation, who have fled for refuge *to lay hold upon the hope set before us: Which hope we have as an anchor of the soul*, both sure and stedfast" (Heb. 6:17–19). • "I say unto you he [God] *changeth not; if so he would cease to be God*; and he ceaseth not to be God, and *is a God of miracles*" (Morm. 9:19). • "I know that God is *not a partial God, neither a changeable being*; but he is unchangeable from all eternity to all eternity" (Moro. 8:18). • "we know that there is a God in heaven, who is infinite and eternal, *from everlasting to everlasting the same unchangeable God*, the framer of heaven and earth, and all things which are in them; And that he created man, male and female, *after his own image and in his own likeness, created he them*" (D&C 20:17–18).

There are passages that speak of God being the same yesterday, today and forever (see Heb. 13:8; 1 Ne. 10:18; 2 Ne. 2:4; 2 Ne. 29:9; Morm. 9:9; 10:19; and D&C 20:12; 35:1). These are true statements. (However, *problems arise when individuals incorrectly define how they think God was or is, and then assert that he can't change from that incorrect definition. They fail to recognize that divine beings have walked, and continue to walk, the pathway of eternal accomplishment of eternal beings—the path upon which mortal man has also embarked*.)

However, these passages concerning being "the same yesterday, today and forever" do not mean that God is so rigid that he will not alter His course of action if conditions among men change and require a different action or approach than what God first projected. Many of His instructions are based on prior actions of man, and **God is willing to change His instructions** if and when He sees wayward man's repentance and efforts to move toward righteous outcomes. See, for instance, Jonah 3:1–4:11, where the Lord spared the city that was to be destroyed when the people of Nineveh repented and believed in God.

And **God can be negotiated with.** See Gen. 18:23–33, where Abraham sought that Sodom be spared; and Alma 10:21–23, where the prayers of the righteous temporarily spared the wicked city of Ammonihah from destruction.

How does God grow? Through new creations, new progeny, and the acquiring of additional glory—generated through the actions of those who function in His behalf as well as through His own ongoing achievements. As Christ taught concerning His Father in the Lord's Prayer: • "*For thine is the kingdom, and the power, and the glory, for ever*" (Matt. 6:13). He grows, in part, by molding His children into priests and kings: • "*Jesus Christ* . . . hath made us kings and priests **unto God** and **his Father**; to him be glory and dominion for ever and ever" (Rev. 1:5–6). [Notice the three generations mentioned in this remarkable verse! See also Col. 2:2: • "to the acknowledgement of the mystery of *God*, and of the *Father*, and of *Christ*" and Col. 3:17: • "do all in the name of the Lord *Jesus*, giving thanks to *God* and the *Father* by him."]

6. Members of the Godhead Are Perfect Beings

Numerous scriptural passages assert the perfection of members of the Godhead. Again, as in many of the descriptions of members of the Godhead cited in this chapter, some of the passages refer to the perfection of God the Father while others are clearly speaking of the perfection of Jehovah/Jesus Christ.

Those making reference to **the perfection of God the Father** include: • "Be ye therefore perfect, even as *your Father which is in heaven is perfect*" (Matt. 5:48). • "be ye transformed by the renewing of your mind, that ye may prove what *is that good, and acceptable, and perfect, will of God*" (Rom. 12:2). • "Old things are done away, and all things have become new. Therefore I would that ye should be perfect even as I, or *your Father who is in heaven is perfect*" (3 Ne. 12:47–48).

Passages specifically referring to **the perfection of Jehovah**, who is Jesus Christ, include: • "He is the Rock, *his work is perfect*: for all his ways are judgment: a God of truth and without iniquity, just and right is he" (Deut. 32:4). • "As for God, *his way is perfect*; the word of the LORD is tried" (2 Sam. 22:31; Ps. 18:30). • "The *law of the LORD is perfect*, converting the soul" (Ps. 19:7). • "Though he were a Son, yet learned he obedience by the things which he suffered; And *being made perfect*, he became the author of eternal salvation unto all them that obey him" (Heb. 5:8–9). • "therefore God himself atoneth for the sins of the world, to bring about the plan of mercy, to appease the demands of justice, that *God might be a perfect, just God*, and a merciful God also" (Alma 42:15). • "These are they who are *just men made perfect through Jesus* the mediator of the new covenant, who wrought out this *perfect atonement* through the shedding of his own blood" (D&C 76:69). Notice Heb. 5:8–9, which speaks of Christ "being made perfect," which seems to indicate that perfection is an "attained" quality, not an "intrinsic" one.

It is interesting to note that there are considerably more **biblical passages admonishing man to strive to attain perfection** than there are passages asserting the perfection of members of the Godhead. Since Latter-day Saints believe that man's ultimate objective is to attain personal perfection, and hence Godhood, while "trinitarians" do not believe in such a doctrine, it seems appropriate to cite some of those passages about man attaining perfection in this context, as follows: • "*Noah was a just man and perfect* in his generations, and *Noah walked with God*" (Gen. 6:9; see Moses 8:27: "*Noah was a just man, and perfect* in his generation; and he walked with God, *as did also his three sons, Shem, Ham, and Japheth*"). • "the LORD appeared to Abram, and said unto him, I am the Almighty God; *walk before me, and be thou perfect*" (Gen. 17:1). • "*Thou shalt be perfect with the LORD thy God*" (Deut. 18:13). • "God is my strength and power: and *he maketh my way perfect*" (2 Sam. 22:33). • "*Let your heart therefore be perfect* with the LORD our God, to walk in his statutes, and to keep his commandments" (1 Kgs. 8:61). • "*Asa's heart was perfect* with the LORD all his days" (1 Kgs. 15:14; 2 Chr. 15:17). • "O LORD, remember now how *I have walked before thee in truth and with a perfect heart*, and have done that which is good in thy sight" (2 Kgs. 20:3). • "Solomon my son, know thou the God of thy father, and *serve him with a perfect heart and with a willing mind*: for the LORD searcheth all hearts, and understandeth all the imaginations of the thoughts" (1 Chr. 28:9). • "the people rejoiced, for that they offered willingly, because *with perfect heart they offered willingly* to the LORD" (1 Chr. 29:9). • "all the work of Solomon was prepared unto the day of the foundation of the house of the LORD, and until it was finished. *So the house of the LORD was perfected*" (2 Chr. 8:16). • "Thus shall ye do in the fear of the LORD, faithfully, and *with a perfect heart*" (2 Chr. 19:9). • "the LORD said unto Satan, Hast thou considered my servant Job, that there is none like him in the earth, *a perfect and an upright man*, one that feareth God, and escheweth evil?" (Job 2:3). • "It is God that girdeth me with strength, and *maketh my way perfect*" (Ps. 18:32). • "*I will behave myself wisely in a perfect way. O when wilt thou come unto me? I will walk within my house with a perfect heart*" (Ps. 101:2). • "brethren, farewell. *Be perfect*" (2 Cor. 13:11). • "that we may *present every man perfect* in Christ Jesus" (Col. 1:28). • "All scripture is given by inspiration of God . . . *That the man of God may be perfect*" (2 Tim. 3:16–17). • "these all, having obtained a good report through faith, received not the promise: God having provided some better thing for us, that *they without us should not be made perfect*" (Heb. 11:39–40; see D&C 128:15: "as Paul says concerning the fathers—that they without us cannot be made perfect—*neither can we without our dead be made perfect*). • "God of all grace, who hath called us unto his eternal glory by Christ Jesus, . . . *make you perfect*" (1 Pet. 5:10). • "Ye are not able to abide the presence of God now, neither the ministering of angels; wherefore, continue in patience *until ye are perfected*" (D&C 67:13). • "that which is governed by law is also preserved by law and *perfected and sanctified by the same*" (D&C 88:34).

Obviously, some of these passages concerning man's being perfect are not focused on ultimate perfection; though just as obviously, some of the others definitely seem to have that focus.

7. Members of the Godhead Are Exalted Above Their Mortal Creations

The non-Latter-day Saint world has labeled this quality of Deity "transcendence." *The concept of the transcendence of God is that a God is a being who is higher than the things he creates.*

Having attained Godhood and exaltation, God the Father, God the Son, and God the Holy Ghost are infinitely exalted above their creations.

However, this concept is frequently carried to extremes in "trinitarian" theological treatises which sometimes delight in emphasizing the "nothingness" of man in contrast to the "incomprehensible greatness" of God. In contrast, Latter-day Saints, knowing the glorious promises God the Father has made to His spirit children, understand that God seeks man's ultimate outcome to be "like Father, like son"!

Latter-day Saints know that they lived with God the Father, God the Son, and God the Holy Ghost prior to the creation of this earth, and that they had a one-on-one relationship with them in premortality. They knew and understood the nature of exaltation, for they saw those who had attained Godhood functioning in those roles and responsibilities. They knew that as they came to earth to undergo their mortal probation, their memories of those premortal relationships would be blocked. However, to aid them here in mortality, the scriptures present descriptions of the members of the Godhead as they reveal themselves, or each other, to man.

Passages which emphasize the **greatness of the members of the Godhead** include: • "The LORD reigneth; let the people tremble: he sitteth between the cherubims; let the earth be moved. Let them praise thy great and terrible name; for it is holy" (Ps. 99:1–3). • "LORD, thou hast been our dwelling place in all generations. *Before the mountains were brought forth, or ever thou hadst formed the earth and the world, even from everlasting to everlasting, thou art God*" (Ps. 90:1–2). • Solomon's prayer dedicating the newly built temple in Jerusalem: "LORD God of Israel, there is no God like thee, in heaven above, or on earth beneath, who keepest covenant and mercy with thy servants that walk before thee with all their heart: . . . But will God indeed dwell on the earth? behold, *the heaven and heaven of heavens cannot contain thee;* how much less this house that I have builded?" (1 Kgs. 8:23, 27).

Latter-day Saints do not agree with commentaries which assert that "the creature could never hope to become equal to his Creator or understand all the workings of his mind (Rom. 11:33–36)" (*Insight on the Scriptures*, 1:969), or "to seek to be as God in a biblical perspective is not deeper spirituality but rebellious idolatry or blasphemy." (Elwell, et al., "God," *Evangelical Dictionary of Theology*, 458).

Passages that emphasize **the significance of man and his eternal potential to attain perfection** as creations of God include: • "*Be ye therefore perfect,* even as your Father which is in heaven is perfect" (Matt. 5:48). • "His lord said unto him, Well done, thou good and faithful servant: thou hast been faithful over a few things, *I*

will make thee ruler over many things: enter thou into the joy of thy lord" (Matt. 25:21).
• "The disciple is not above his master: but *every one that is perfect shall be as his master"*
(Luke 6:40). • *"the glory which thou gavest me I have given them*; that they may be one,
even as we are one: I in them, and thou in me, *that they may be made perfect in one"*
(John 17:22–23). • "he gave some, apostles; and some, prophets . . . *For the perfecting
of the saints,* for the work of the ministry, for the edifying of the body of Christ *Till
we all come . . . unto a perfect man,* unto the measure of the stature of the fulness of
Christ" (Eph. 4:11–13). • "But ye are come unto . . . the heavenly Jerusalem, and to an
innumerable company of angels, To the general assembly and church of the firstborn,
which are written in heaven, and to God the Judge of all, *and to the spirits of just men
made perfect"* (Heb. 12:22–23). • "God, . . . According as his divine power *hath given
unto us all things that pertain unto life and godliness,* through the knowledge of him that
hath called us to glory and virtue: Whereby are given unto us exceeding great and precious promises: that by these *ye might be partakers of the divine nature,* having escaped
the corruption that is in the world through lust. And beside this, giving all diligence,
add to your faith virtue; and to virtue knowledge; And to knowledge temperance; and
to temperance patience; and to patience *godliness*; And to *godliness* brotherly kindness;
and to brotherly kindness charity" (2 Pet. 1:2–7). • "The Spirit itself beareth witness
with our spirit, that *we are the children of God: And if children, then heirs; heirs of God,
and joint-heirs with Christ*; if so be that we suffer with *him*, that we may be also glorified together" (Rom. 8:16–17). • *"come unto Christ, and be perfected in him,* and deny
yourselves of all ungodliness; and if ye shall deny yourselves of all ungodliness, and love
God with all your might, mind and strength, then is his grace sufficient for you, that *by
his grace ye may be perfect in Christ*; and if by the grace of God ye are perfect in Christ, ye
can in nowise deny the power of God. And again, if ye by the grace of God are perfect
in Christ, and deny not his power, then are ye sanctified in Christ by the grace of God,
through the shedding of the blood of Christ, which is in the covenant of the Father
unto the remission of your sins, *that ye become holy, without spot"* (Moro. 10:32–33).

8. Members of the Godhead Are "in" Man

Doctrine and Covenants section 88 provides unique insights concerning *the Light
of Christ*: • *"This is the light of Christ.* As also he is in the sun, and the light of the sun,
and the power thereof by which it was made. As also he is in the moon, and is the light of
the moon, and the power thereof by which it was made; As also the light of the stars, and
the power thereof by which they were made; And the earth also, and the power thereof,
even the earth upon which you stand. *And the light which shineth, which giveth you light,
is through him who enlighteneth your eyes, which is the same light that quickeneth your
understandings; Which light proceedeth forth from the presence of God to fill the immensity
of space—The light which is in all things, which giveth life to all things, which is the law by
which all things are governed, even the power of God* who sitteth upon his throne, who is
in the bosom of eternity, who is in the midst of all things" (D&C 88:7–13).

Other faiths, though they don't know about and understand the light of Christ,
speak of this manner in which God is in and throughout everything as "*immanence*."
A typical non-Latter-day Saint description of immanence is:

> *By this we mean his all-pervading presence and power within his creation.* He does
> not stand apart from the world, a mere spectator of the work of his hands. He per-
> vades everything, organic and inorganic, acting from within outwards, from the

centre of every atom, and from the innermost springs of thought and life and feeling, a continuous sequence of cause and effect. . . . Paul, in addressing the men of Athens, . . . affirms his immanence as the one who "is not far from each one of us, for 'In him we live and move and have our being' (Acts 17:24, 28)." (Douglas, et al., "God," *New Bible Dictionary*, 427)

Through the power of the light of Christ, God is able to dwell on high and at the same time be with man here on earth: • "thus saith the high and lofty One that inhabiteth eternity, whose name is Holy; *I dwell in the high and holy place, with him also that is of a contrite and humble spirit*, to revive the spirit of the humble, and to revive the heart of the contrite ones" (Isa. 57:15).

The *power and influence of the Holy Ghost* can also descend from on high and dwell within individuals. As cited above, • "*the Holy Ghost has not a body of flesh and bones, but is a personage of Spirit. Were it not so, the Holy Ghost could not dwell in us. A* man may receive the Holy Ghost, and *it may descend upon him and not tarry with him*" (D&C 130:2–3). • Paul's second epistle to Timothy instructs him: "That good thing which was committed unto thee keep by *the Holy Ghost which dwelleth in us*" (2 Tim. 1:14). • An early D&C revelation contains the words, "behold, I will tell you in your mind and in your heart, by *the Holy Ghost, which shall come upon you and which shall dwell in your heart*. Now, behold, this is the spirit of revelation" (D&C 8:2–3).

Though members of the Godhead dwell on high, they are also immediately aware of, and in communication with, their children on this and other earths, as necessary, through the light of Christ, through the Holy Ghost, through angelic beings, and through the sanctified-earth communication system described in D&C 130:7–9: "where all things . . . are continually before the Lord."

Elwell, in the *Evangelical Dictionary of Theology*, describes various other aspects and levels of God's ability to be "in" man as follows:

> *Just as persons may be present to one another in varying degrees, God may be present to the unjust in one sense and to the just in a richer way.* A person may simply be present as another rider on a bus, or much more significantly as a godly mother who has prayed daily for you all your life. God is graciously present in forgiving love with the converted, who by faith have been propitiated, reconciled, and redeemed by Christ's precious blood. They become his people, he becomes their God. God dwells in them as his holy place or temple. *The relational oneness of thoughts, desires, and purposes grows through the years.* That unity is shared by other members of Christ's body who are gifted to build each other up to become progressively more like the God they worship, not metaphysically, but intellectually, ethically, emotionally, and existentially. (Elwell, 458–59)

However, many Latter-day Saints do not accept the usage of the trinitarian-popularized term "*omnipresent*" in connection with the members of the Godhead. The dictionary definition for this term is "*present in all places at all times*" (*Merriam-Webster's Collegiate Dictionary*, 11th edition, 865).

While the light of Christ is everywhere present within His creations (D&C 88:12–13), and while Christ and other heavenly beings can move faster than lightning from one place to another, both God the Son and God the Father have tangible, physical bodies that of necessity are in only one place at a time. God the Holy Ghost, a being only of spirit, is believed to have a spirit body which is in the shape of a human's mortal body; that form is also believed to only be in one place at one time, though his influence can be within many human minds and hearts at the same time.

This understanding differs radically from the typical trinitarian concept that God is completely without bodily shape. Thus their literature makes such statements as "Although God is not limited by space or time, or the succession of events in time, he created the world with space and time" (Elwell, et al., *Evangelical Dictionary of Theology*, 453).

What scriptural passages are typically cited by "trinitarians" in support of their "omnipresent" God-is-everywhere hypothesis? Eight passages are presented: • (1) "Can any hide himself in secret places that I shall not see him? saith the LORD. Do not I fill heaven and earth? saith the LORD" (Jer. 23:24). • (2) "But will God indeed dwell on the earth? behold, the heaven and heaven of heavens cannot contain thee; how much less this house that I have builded?" (1 Kgs. 8:27). • (3) "who is able to build him an house, seeing the heaven and heaven of heavens cannot contain him?" (2 Chr. 2:6). • (4) "Whither shall I go from thy spirit? or whither shall I flee from thy presence? If I ascend up into heaven, thou art there: if I make my bed in hell, behold, thou art there. If I take the wings of the morning, and dwell in the uttermost parts of the sea; Even there shall thy hand lead me, and thy right hand shall hold me" (Ps. 139:7–10). • (5) "The eyes of the LORD are in every place, beholding the evil and the good" (Prov. 15:3). • (6) "For where two or three are gathered together in my name, there am I in the midst of them" (Matt. 18:20). • (7) "God that made the world and all things therein, seeing that he is Lord of heaven and earth, dwelleth not in temples made with hands; . . . That they should seek the Lord, if haply they might feel after him, and find him, though he be not far from every one of us: For in him we live, and move, and have our being; as certain also of your own poets have said, For we are also his offspring" (Acts 17:24, 27–28). • (8) "One God and Father of all, who is above all, and through all, and in you all" (Eph. 4:6).

These passages, for the most part, present the image that God's communication systems and knowledge systems are far-reaching and absolute in their penetration, rather than that God's physical being (which they deny exists) is actually present. These passages pose significant interpretational dilemmas for "trinitarians" if they seek to interpret them literally in terms of where God actually is at any one moment. If that is the way they should be perceived, then the rest of the references to God's physical being should also receive literal interpretation: they speak of God's eyes, His right hand holding someone, His literally being in the midst of groups of believers, and that God literally is the Father of all mankind, and that mankind actually are His offspring. That literal interpretation sounds far closer to Mormonism than "trinitarianism"!

9. Members of the Godhead Have All Power

(Mark 14:36; Luke 1:37). *The three members of the Godhead are omnipotent,* which means that *each of them have all and unlimited power, and with that power, all things can be accomplished.* The scriptures teach that: • "Jesus beheld *them,* and said unto them, With men this is impossible; but *with God all things are possible*" (Matt. 19:26; Mark 10:27; Luke 18:27). • "Christ said, "Abba, *Father, all things are possible unto thee*" (Mark 14:36). • *"For with God nothing shall be impossible"* (Luke 1:37). • "Alleluia: for *the Lord God omnipotent* reigneth" (Rev. 19:6). • *"with power, the Lord Omnipotent* who reigneth, who was, and is from all eternity to all eternity, shall come down from heaven among the children of men" (Mosiah 3:5, 17–18, 21). • "we know of their surety and truth, because of *the Spirit of the Lord Omnipotent*" (Mosiah 5:2). • "that Christ, the *Lord God Omnipotent,* may seal you his" (Mosiah 5:15).

With their unlimited powers, the members of the Godhead are able to do whatever they will, in the way that they will it. They do not do anything contrary to their nature of righteousness, wisdom, and holy love. They usually do not do everything by their own immediate agency; rather, they often utilize angelic and human agents, and, when necessary, they delegate their tremendous powers to their priesthood agents. Christ told His followers: • "If ye have faith as a grain of mustard seed, ye shall say unto this mountain, Remove hence to yonder place; and it shall remove; and *nothing shall be impossible unto you*" (Matt. 17:20).

The ancient scriptures are replete with **examples of God extending His great powers to men:** • The Pearl of Great Price records that the Lord told Enoch that "*all flesh is in my hands*, and I will do as seemeth me good" (Moses 6:32), and then gave to Enoch such power that when he spake the word of the Lord, "the *earth trembled*, and the *mountains fled*, even according to his command; and the *rivers of water were turned* out of their course; and the roar of the lions was heard out of the wilderness" (Moses 7:13). • The Old Testament reports that God gave Elijah the Tishbite power to *stave off famine* (1 Kgs. 17:13–16), to *raise a boy from the dead* (1 Kgs. 17:17–24), and to *call down fire from heaven* (1 Kgs. 18:19–39). • The Book of Mormon reports that God granted unlimited powers to Nephi: to "*smite the earth with famine, and with pestilence, and destruction*"; to rend and *move mountains*, and to *seal and loose* on earth and in heaven (see Hel. 10:4–11).

Members of the Godhead determine the outcome of events—either unconditionally or conditionally. They may determine some events to come to pass unconditionally (see, for instance, Isa. 14:24–27, where the LORD vows to break the Assyrian forces). However, many events in history have been planned conditionally, depending either upon *the obedience of people*, or upon their *permitted disobedience to God's divine precepts*. See, for instance, • "If my people, which are called by my name, shall humble themselves, and pray, and seek my face, and turn from their wicked ways; *then will I hear from heaven, and will forgive their sin, and will heal their land*" (2 Chr. 7:14). • "But the Pharisees and lawyers *rejected the counsel of God against themselves*, being not baptized of him" (Luke 7:30). • "Wherefore *God also gave them up to uncleanness through the lusts of their own hearts*, to dishonour their own bodies between themselves" (Rom. 1:24).

However, the eternal purposes of the Godhead are not frustrated but fulfilled in the way they choose to accomplish them. See, for instance, • "[Christ,] in whom also we have obtained an inheritance, being predestinated according to *the purpose of him who worketh all things after the counsel of his own will*" (Eph. 1:11).

Members of the Godhead have and exercise control over nature, over the weather and other elements of earth's physical makeup, though they apparently do not routinely control weather events. For instance, • "thus saith the LORD God of Israel, The barrel of meal shall not waste, neither shall the cruse of oil fail, *until the day that the LORD sendeth rain* upon the earth" (1 Kgs. 17:14). • "*Thou, O God, didst send a plentiful rain*, whereby thou didst confirm thine inheritance, when it was weary" (Ps. 68:9). • "see the works of the LORD, and his wonders in the deep. For *he commandeth, and raiseth the stormy wind*, which lifteth up the waves thereof" (Ps. 107:24–25). • "Let us now fear the LORD our God, *that giveth rain, both the former and the latter*, in his season: he reserveth unto us the appointed weeks of the harvest" (Jer. 5:24). • "thus saith the Lord GOD; *I will even rend it with a stormy wind* in my fury; and there shall be *an overflowing shower* in mine anger, and *great hailstones* in my fury to consume it" (Ezek. 13:13). • "rejoice in the LORD your God: for *he hath given you the former rain moderately*, and he will cause to come down for you the rain, the former rain, and the latter rain in the first month" (Joel 2:23). • "your Father which is in heaven: for *he maketh his sun to rise* on the evil and on the good, and *sendeth rain* on the just and on the unjust" (Matt. 5:45). • "there arose a great storm of wind, and the waves beat into the ship, so that it was now full. . . . And he [Jesus] arose, and rebuked the wind, and *said unto the sea, Peace, be still*. And the wind ceased, and there was a great calm" (Mark 4:37, 39).

Members of the Godhead use and control priesthood power. They not only have the personal power to bring to pass their purposes in the way they purpose them, they also direct the priesthood authority throughout all the realms they control, in order to accomplish what they will: • "Thy name shall be called no more Jacob, but Israel: *for as a prince hast thou power with God* and with men" (Gen. 32:28). • "*God is my strength and power*: and he maketh my way perfect" (2 Sam. 22:33). • "God exalteth by his power" (Job 36:22). • "God, How terrible art thou in thy works! *through the greatness of thy power* shall thine enemies submit themselves unto thee" (Ps. 66:3). • "when he had called unto him his twelve disciples, *he gave them power against unclean spirits, to cast them out, and to heal all manner of sickness and all manner of disease*" (Matt. 10:1). • "the seventy returned again with joy, saying, Lord, even the devils are subject unto us through thy name" (Luke 10:17). • "And this greater priesthood administereth the gospel and holdeth the key of the mysteries of the kingdom, even the key of the knowledge of God. Therefore, *in the ordinances thereof, the power of godliness is manifest*. And without the ordinances thereof, and the authority of the priesthood, the power of godliness is not manifest unto men in the flesh" (D&C 84:19–21). • "The Melchizedek Priesthood holds the right of presidency, and *has power and authority over all the offices in the church in all ages of the world, to administer in spiritual things*" (D&C 107:8). • "the rights of the priesthood are *inseparably connected with the powers of heaven*, and that the powers of heaven cannot be controlled nor handled only upon the principles of righteousness" (D&C 121:36). • "*a power which records or binds on earth and binds in heaven*. Nevertheless, in all ages of the world, whenever the Lord has given a dispensation of the priesthood to any man by actual revelation, or any set of men, *this power has always been given*" (D&C 128:9). • "the long-promised day has come when every faithful, worthy man in the Church may receive the holy priesthood, *with power to exercise its divine authority*, and enjoy with his loved ones every blessing that flows therefrom" (OD 2).

10. Members of the Godhead Have All Knowledge

Members of the Godhead are omniscient, a term which means that *they have all knowledge*. Their intellectual capabilities are unlimited, and they use them fully and perfectly. • Christ's disciples testified to Him that "Now are we sure that *thou knowest all things*" (John 16:30), and • Peter told Him "Lord, *thou knowest all things*; thou knowest that I love thee" (John 21:17). • "God is greater than our heart, and *knoweth all things*" (1 Jn. 3:20). • "Neither is there any creature that is not manifest in his sight: but *all things are naked and opened unto the eyes of him with whom we have to do*" (Heb. 4:13).

Members of the Godhead know all inward thoughts and outward acts of humanity: • "For *the ways of man are before the eyes of the LORD,* and he pondereth all his goings" (Prov. 5:21). • The LORD said, "*they did evil before mine eyes,* and chose that in which I delighted not" (Isa. 66:4). • Jeremiah poured out his heart to God, saying, "we are left but a few of many, *as thine eyes do behold us*" (Jer. 42:2). • The Book of Mormon account of the people of Alma who were being persecuted by the Lamanites records that they "did pour out their hearts to him; and *he did know the thoughts of their hearts*" (Mosiah 24:12), and the Lord answered them saying, "Lift up your heads and be of good comfort, for *I know of the covenant which ye have made unto me*; and I will covenant with my people and deliver them out of bondage" (Mosiah 24:13), and then "*the burdens which were laid upon Alma and his brethren were made light*; yea, the Lord did strengthen them that they could bear up their burdens with ease, and they did submit cheerfully and with patience to all the will of the Lord" (Mosiah 24:15). • In the Doctrine and Covenants, Jesus Christ revealed that he is "The same which *knoweth all things*, for *all things are present before mine eyes*" (D&C 38:2).

The judgments of members of the Godhead are formed in the awareness of all the relevant data. They know everything that bears upon the truth concerning any person or event. • Thus, the Prophet Jacob testified that "by the help of the all-powerful Creator of heaven and earth *I can tell you concerning your thoughts*, how that ye are beginning to labor in sin" (Jacob 2:5). • King Benjamin told his people "I can tell you, that if ye do not watch yourselves, and *your thoughts, and your words, and your deeds*, . . . even unto the end of your lives, ye must perish" (Mosiah 4:30). • And the Prophet Alma testified that "if we have hardened our hearts against the word, . . . we shall be condemned. For *our words* will condemn us, yea, all *our works* will condemn us; we shall not be found spotless; and *our thoughts* will also condemn us; and in this awful state we shall not dare to look up to our God" (Alma 12:13–14).

Their *foreknowledge of forthcoming events* is included in the knowledge of the members of the Godhead. Thus, the scriptures record the divine statement that • "My name is Jehovah, and *I know the end from the beginning*" (Abr. 2:8). • Peter wrote his first epistle to those whom he called the "Elect according to *the foreknowledge of God the Father*, through sanctification of the Spirit, unto obedience and sprinkling of the blood of Jesus Christ" (1 Pet. 1:2). • Alma taught that valiant men were called to be priesthood holders in the premortal life "*according to the foreknowledge of God*, on account of their exceeding faith and good works" (Alma 13:3), and he continued, saying that God's priesthood was "prepared from eternity to all eternity, *according to his foreknowledge of all things*" (Alma 13:7).

Members of the Godhead, speaking through their prophets, have used *prophecies of coming events to prove that the* LORD *is God*. • Thus Jehovah revealed, through Isaiah, that "I *am* God, . . . *Declaring the end from the beginning*, and from ancient times *the things* that are not yet done, saying, My counsel shall stand, and I will do all my pleasure: . . . yea, *I have spoken it, I will also bring it to pass*; I have purposed it, I will also do it" (Isa. 46:9–11). • "*I have declared the former things from the beginning*; and they went forth out of my mouth, and I shewed them; I did them suddenly, and they came to pass" (Isa. 48:3). • "For as the rain cometh down, and the snow from heaven, and returneth not thither, but watereth the earth, and maketh it bring forth and bud, that it may give seed to the sower, and bread to the eater: *So shall my word be that goeth forth out of my mouth: it shall not return unto me void, but it shall accomplish that which I please*, and it shall prosper in the thing whereto I sent it" (Isa. 55:10–11). • "Write the vision, and make it plain upon tables, that he may run that readeth it. For *the vision is yet for an appointed time, but at the end it shall speak, and not lie*: though it tarry, wait for it; because it will surely come, it will not tarry" (Hab. 2:2–3).

11. Members of the Godhead Are Wise

God is perfectly wise. In addition to knowing all the relevant data on any subject, God selects ends with discernment and acts in harmony with His purposes of holy love. Man may not always be able to see that events in their lives work together for a wise purpose, but they can know that God chooses from among all the possible alternatives the best ends and means for achieving them. God not only chooses the right ends, but also chooses them for the right reasons: the good of His creatures and thus His glory.

Members of the Godhead not only have *unlimited wisdom,* they also have the ability to grant it to man here on earth: • *"I have filled him with the spirit of God, in wisdom, and in understanding, and in knowledge,* and in all manner of workmanship" (Ex. 31:3). • "they feared the king: for they saw that *the wisdom of God was in him,* to do judgment" (1 Kgs. 3:28). • *"God gave Solomon wisdom and understanding* exceeding much, and largeness of heart" (1 Kgs. 4:29). • "the LORD give thee *wisdom* and understanding" (1 Chr. 22:12). • "God is mighty, and despiseth not any: he is mighty in strength and *wisdom"* (Job 36:5). • "God giveth to a man that is good in his sight *wisdom, and knowledge, and joy"* (Eccl. 2:26). • "Blessed be the name of God for ever and ever: for *wisdom and might are his"* (Dan. 2:20). • "O the depth of the riches both of *the wisdom and knowledge* of God!" (Rom. 11:33). • "Christ the power of God, and *the wisdom of God"* (1 Cor. 1:24). • "O the *wisdom* of God, his mercy and grace!" (2 Ne. 9:8). • "come to a knowledge of the goodness of God, and his matchless power, and his *wisdom,* and his patience" (Mosiah 4:6). • "Believe in God; believe that he is, and that he created all things, both in heaven and in earth; believe that *he has all wisdom, and all power,* both in heaven and in earth" (Mosiah 4:9). • "my God; for *he has all power, all wisdom, and all understanding; he comprehendeth all things,* and he is a merciful Being" (Alma 26:35).

12. Members of the Godhead Are Holy

Godhead members are morally spotless in character and action. They are upright, pure, and untainted with evil desires, motives, thought, words, or acts. They are holy, and as such they are the source and standard of what is right. They are free from all evil, and love all truth and goodness. They value purity and detest impurity.

They cannot approve of any evil, and they have no pleasure in evil: • "thou art not a God that hath pleasure in wickedness: *neither shall evil dwell with thee"* (Ps. 5:4), and cannot tolerate evil: • *"Thou art of purer eyes than to behold evil,* and canst not look on iniquity" (Hab. 1:13). They abhor evil and cannot encourage sin in any way: • *"God cannot be tempted with evil, neither tempteth he any man"* (James 1:13–14).

Holiness is not solely the product of their wills, but a characteristic of their eternal natures. They will the good because they are good. And because members of the Godhead are holy, they consistently hate sin and are repulsed by all evil without respect of persons.

The Holy Ghost is called holy not only because He is a member of the Godhead and thus shares the holiness of their divine natures, but because one of His essential functions is to produce holy love in the hearts of those who have been redeemed.

Scriptural passages concerning the Gods' holiness include: • "Who is like unto thee, O LORD, among the gods? who is like thee, *glorious in holiness,* fearful in praises, doing wonders?" (Ex. 15:11). • "I am the LORD your God: ye shall therefore sanctify yourselves, and ye shall be holy; *for I am holy*" (Lev. 11:44). • "Ye shall be holy: for *I the LORD your God am holy*" (Lev. 19:2). • "God sitteth upon *the throne of his holiness*" (Ps. 47:8). • "Exalt ye the LORD our God, and worship at his footstool; for *he is holy*" (Ps. 99:5). • "Exalt the LORD our God, and *worship at his holy hill; for the LORD our God is holy*" (Ps. 99:9). • "God hath spoken in *his holiness*" (Ps. 108:7). • "thus saith the Lord GOD, *the Holy One of Israel*" (Isa. 30:15). • "I am the LORD thy God, *the Holy One of Israel*, thy Saviour" (Isa. 43:3). • "Thus saith the LORD, thy Redeemer, *the Holy One of Israel*; I am the LORD thy God" (Isa. 48:17). • "I am the LORD your God dwelling in Zion, *my holy mountain*" (Joel 3:17). • "Art thou not from everlasting, O LORD my God, *mine Holy One?*" (Hab. 1:12). • "a spirit of an unclean devil, . . . Saying, Let us alone; what have we to do with thee, thou Jesus of Nazareth? art thou come to destroy us? I know thee who thou art; *the Holy One of God*" (Luke 4:33–34). • "declared to be the Son of God with power, according to *the spirit of holiness*" (Rom. 1:4). • "*Holy, holy, holy, Lord God Almighty*, which was, and is, and is to come" (Rev. 4:8). • "thus saith the Lord, thy Redeemer, *the Holy One of Israel*" (1 Ne. 20:17). • "all men come unto God; wherefore, they stand in the presence of him, to be judged of him *according to the truth and holiness which is in him*" (2 Ne. 2:10). • "they shall know that the Lord is God, *the Holy One of Israel*" (2 Ne. 6:15). • "*O how great the holiness of our God!* For he knoweth all things, and there is not anything save he knows it" (2 Ne. 9:20). • "*Holy, holy are thy judgments*, O Lord God Almighty" (2 Ne. 9:46). • "the Lord of Hosts shall be exalted in judgment, and *God that is holy* shall be sanctified in righteousness" (2 Ne. 15:16). • "The heavens is a place where God dwells and *all his holy angels*" (Alma 18:30). • "thy maker, thy husband, the Lord of Hosts is his name; and thy Redeemer, *the Holy One of Israel*—the God of the whole earth shall he be called" (3 Ne. 22:5). • "when ye shall be brought to see your nakedness before God, and also the glory of God, and *the holiness of Jesus Christ*, it will kindle a flame of unquenchable fire upon you" (Morm. 9:5). • "the Lord God has spoken it; and honor, power and glory be rendered to *his holy name*" (D&C 20:36). • "Which glory is that of the church of the Firstborn, even *of God, the holiest of all*, through Jesus Christ his Son" (D&C 88:5). • "all men, everywhere, must repent, or they can in nowise inherit the kingdom of God, for *no unclean thing can dwell there, or dwell in his presence*; for, in the language of Adam, *Man of Holiness is his name*, and the name of his Only Begotten is the Son of Man, even Jesus Christ" (Moses 6:57). • "Behold, I am God; *Man of Holiness is my name*; Man of Counsel is my name; and Endless and Eternal is my name, also" (Moses 7:35).

13. Members of the Godhead Are Gods of Truth and Integrity

Since the Father, Son, and Holy Ghost all are Gods of integrity, eternally committed to truth and righteousness, *they do not and cannot lie*. They determine what, and how much, to reveal to mankind in the various stages of man's progress; but what they reveal is truth, and man should regard their revelations as truth—straightforward, unadulterated truth.

That statement takes on special meaning in the context of this study, in which many hundreds of passages concerning the nature of God found in the scriptures are cited. However, it is recognized that much of the Christian world sidesteps or ignores the vast majority of them because of erroneous interpretational methods adopted close to two millennia ago in order to mold doctrines into the warped philosophical "forms" of Platonic thought.

The scriptures clearly assert that • "The LORD God, merciful and gracious, long-suffering, and abundant in *goodness and truth*" (Ex. 34:6). • "I will publish the name of the LORD: ascribe ye greatness unto our God. He is the Rock, his work is perfect: for all his ways are judgment: *a God of truth and without iniquity, just and right is he*" (Deut. 32:3–4). • "the Strength of Israel *will not lie* nor repent" (1 Sam. 15:29). • "thou hast redeemed me, *O LORD God of truth*" (Ps. 31:5). • "O LORD, thou art my God; I will exalt thee, I will praise thy name; for thou hast done wonderful things; *thy counsels of old are faithfulness and truth*" (Isa. 25:1). • "they shall be my people, and I will be their God, *in truth and in righteousness*" (Zech. 8:8). • "it was *impossible for God to lie*" (Heb. 6:18). • "they bear record according to *the truth which is in the Lamb of God*" (1 Ne. 13:24). • "all men come unto God; wherefore, *they stand in the presence of him, to be judged of him according to the truth and holiness which is in him*" (2 Ne. 2:10). • "The *Spirit of truth* is of God" (D&C 93:26). • "O Lord God Almighty . . . thou sittest enthroned, with glory, honor, power, majesty, might, dominion, *truth, justice, judgment*, mercy, and an infinity of fulness, from everlasting to everlasting" (D&C 109:77).

Numerous other passages characterize members of the Godhead as *being faithful and true*. These words are assertions of both *their integrity and their reliability*. And these assertions are made not only of them personally but of their words and commandments also.

The scriptures give assurance that there is no lack of fidelity in the persons, thoughts, or promises of any of the three members of the Godhead. They say: • "The LORD be *a true and faithful witness* between us" (Jer. 42:5). • "Let us hold fast the profession of our faith without wavering; (for *he is faithful* that promised)" (Heb. 10:23). • "If we confess our sins, *he is faithful and just to forgive us our sins*" (1 Jn. 1:9). • "God is faithful, who will *not suffer you to be tempted above that ye are able*" (1 Cor. 10:13). • "If we believe not, yet *he abideth faithful: he cannot deny himself*" (2 Tim. 2:13). • "These things saith the Amen, *the faithful and true witness*, the beginning of the creation of God" (Rev. 3:14). • "I saw heaven opened, and behold a white horse; and he that sat upon him was called *Faithful and True*" (Rev. 19:11). • "I heard a voice from the Father, saying: Yea, *the words of my Beloved are true and faithful*" (2 Ne. 31:15). • "Search *these commandments*, for they are true and faithful" (D&C 1:37). • "These sayings are true and faithful; wherefore, *transgress them not, neither take therefrom*" (D&C 68:34).

14. Members of the Godhead Function in a Patriarchal, Family-oriented Environment

Throughout scriptural history, members of the Godhead have been recorded as functioning in a family environment and *performing acts which foster familial relationships*. For instance, the scriptures say: • "I will bless them that bless thee [Abram], and curse him that curseth thee: and *in thee shall all families of the earth be blessed*" (Gen. 12:3). • "behold, my covenant is with thee [Abraham], and *thou shalt be a father* of many nations. Neither shall thy name any more be called Abram, but thy name shall be Abraham; for *a father of many nations have I made thee*. And I will make thee *exceeding fruitful*, and I will make nations of thee, and kings shall come out of thee. And *I will establish my covenant between me and thee and thy seed after thee in their generations* for an everlasting covenant, to be a God unto thee, *and to thy seed after thee*" (Gen. 17:4–7). • "*thy seed shall be as the dust of the earth*, and thou [Jacob] shalt spread abroad to the west, and to the east, and to the north, and to the south: and *in thee and in thy* seed shall all the families of the earth be blessed" (Gen. 28:14). • "At the same time, saith the LORD, will *I be the God of all the families of Israel*, and they shall be my people" (Jer. 31:1), and • "Joseph nourished his father, and his brethren, and all his father's household, with bread, *according to their families*" (Gen. 47:12).

The basic societal unit, organized under the direction of the members of the Godhead both on earth and in heaven, is the family. The scriptures clearly indicate that • "*God setteth the solitary in families*" (Ps. 68:6). As God began to reveal his will through his prophets, the emphasis was on families from the beginning. Thus • "Adam blessed God and was filled, and began to *prophesy concerning all the families of the earth*" (Moses 5:10).

Throughout the standard works of the Church, emphasis has continually been on maintaining the integrity and sanctity of the marriage unit. Thus Jesus taught, • "Have ye not read, that he which made them at the beginning *made them male and female*, And said, For this cause shall a man leave father and mother, and shall cleave to his wife: and they twain shall be one flesh? Wherefore they are no more twain, but one flesh. What therefore God hath joined together, let not man put asunder" (Matt. 19:4–6; Mark 10:6–9). The Apostle Paul wrote that • "I bow my knees unto *the Father* of our Lord Jesus Christ, Of whom the whole family in heaven and earth is named" (Eph. 3:14–15). In modern times, the Lord has instructed, • "*whoso forbiddeth to marry is not ordained of God*, for *marriage is ordained of God unto man*. Wherefore, it is lawful that he should have one wife, and *they twain shall be one flesh*, and all this that the earth might answer the end of its creation; And that it might be filled with the measure of man, *according to his creation before the world was made*" (D&C 49:15–17). Provisions have been made for the *sealing of eternal family relationships* (D&C 132), and entry into the "*new and everlasting covenant of marriage*" through temple priesthood ordinances is a requisite for a man or woman to attain exaltation in the celestial kingdom; without it, "*That is the end of his kingdom; he cannot have an increase*" (D&C 131:1–4).

From the beginning of mortal time, genealogies have been kept and honored. When the law of Moses was given, strict laws concerning all manner of family relationships were given. Chastity and fidelity were required, and those restrictions and instructions have been maintained down through time.

It is clear that this pattern of marriage and family life which constitutes the basic organizational unit here on earth is fashioned after life in the eternal, celestial realms. As Jesus taught, • "*Thy will be done on earth as it is in heaven*" (3 Ne. 13:10; Matt. 6:10). Just as parenthood is ordained here on earth, it must certainly exist in heaven. Numerous scriptures make it clear that God the Father is the Father of His firstborn son, Jesus, a son whom He repeatedly identifies as "*my beloved son*." Parents, apparently come in pairs; one cannot become a father without a mother also existing, so it is assumed that Jesus, and all mankind, are the offspring of heavenly progenitors.

It is also assumed that God's eternal family and extended families are organized in the *patriarchal order*, as is the structure of mortal families which are patterned here on earth after their heavenly counterparts. This structural organization is integral, then, to all God's revelations to mankind, including hundreds of passages in the Bible, many more in the other standard works, and in God's numerous revelations to modern prophets (for instance, *The Family: A Proclamation to the World*). Therefore, the assertion that God exists and functions in a structured family relationship is set forth here as a basic attribute of Godhood.

15. Members of the Godhead Are Filled with Love

Through their grace, and because of their great love, members of the Godhead extend benefits, deserved or undeserved, to those who are in need of their loving care. They give of themselves for the well-being of those loved. Their love is the love of parents for their children, for God the Father truly is the father of all His spirit children. The love of Jesus Christ is as the love of the adopted Father for those who accept His gospel and become His adopted sons and daughters: • *"he hath chosen us in him before the foundation of the world,* that we should be holy and without blame before him in love: Having predestinated us unto *the adoption of children by Jesus Christ* to himself" (Eph. 1:4–5). • *"God so loved the world, that he gave his only begotten Son,* that whosoever believeth in him should not perish, but have everlasting life. For God sent not his Son into the world to condemn the world; but that the world through him might be saved" (John 3:16–17).

Through the love of the members of the Godhead, mortals are prompted to care for the sick, the needy, the aged, the poor, and others in need. Love is a settled purpose of will involving the whole person in seeking the well-being of others.

God has commanded His faithful followers, instructing them that *"thou shalt love the* LORD *thy God* with all thine heart, and with all thy soul, and with all thy might" (Deut. 6:5).

But **what do the scriptures say about the love of members of the Godhead for mortals** here on earth? • "the LORD thy God turned the curse into a blessing unto thee, because *the* LORD *thy God loved thee"* (Deut. 23:5). • "the LORD *loved Israel* for ever" (1 Kgs. 10:9; 2 Chr. 9:8). • *"For God so loved the world, that he gave his only begotten Son,* that whosoever believeth in him should not perish, but have everlasting life" (John 3:16). • "*the Father himself loveth you,* because ye have loved me" (John 16:27). • *"God loveth* a cheerful giver" (2 Cor. 9:7). • "Be perfect, be of good comfort, be of one mind, live in peace; and *the God of love and peace shall be with you"* (2 Cor. 13:11). • "But God, who is rich in mercy, for *his great love wherewith he loved us,* . . . hath quickened us together with Christ" (Eph. 2:4–5). • "the *love of Christ,* which passeth knowledge" (Eph. 3:19). • "walk in love, as *Christ also hath loved us"* (Eph. 5:2). • "ye yourselves are taught of God to love one another" (1 Thess. 4:9). • "God hath not given us the spirit of fear; but of power, and *of love,* and of a sound mind" (2 Tim. 1:7). • "whoso keepeth his word, in him verily is *the love of God* perfected" (1 Jn. 2:5). • "what manner of *love* the Father hath bestowed upon us, that we should be called the sons of God" (1 Jn. 3:1). • "Hereby perceive we *the love of God,* because he laid down his life for us" (1 Jn. 3:16). • "He that loveth not knoweth not God; for *God is love.* In this was manifested *the love of God toward us,* because that God sent his only begotten Son into the world, that we might live through him" (1 Jn. 4:8–9). • "we have known and believed the love that God hath to us. *God is love*; and he that dwelleth in love dwelleth in God, and God in him" (1 Jn. 4:16). • "the Lord God hath given a commandment that all men should have charity, which *charity is love"* (2 Ne. 26:30). • "God has had mercy on us, . . . *he loveth our souls as well as he loveth our children"* (Alma 24:14). • *"I will encircle thee in the arms of my love.* Behold, I am Jesus Christ, the Son of God" (D&C 6:20–21). • "the Holy Spirit, *which God bestows on those who love him,* and purify themselves before him" (D&C 76:116).

The love of God is a unique phenomenon, because **many who have had near-death or life-after-death experiences have commented on the nature of God's love** that they experienced there. A few brief extracts from *Life Everlasting* (2nd revised edition, 2005) will illustrate the glorious love some of them have described: • "There was no worry, no sorrow, no pain; all that was gone. It was like being in perfect understanding, perfect knowledge, *perfect love*, perfect acceptance" (p. 57). • "I will never forget the feeling of being totally enveloped in warmth, . . . it was *a feeling of warmth, of love, of compassion*—it was a tangible feeling, almost physical in nature. This wonderful feeling enveloped me" (57). • "The peace I felt was wonderful, a perfect tranquility and warmth, for *I was surrounded by an unconditional love*. The love was everything that I had hungered for but seemed unable to find in life. All the anger, hate, pain, and fear that I had previously felt were removed. *Pure love and peace* were all around me" (57). • "I never felt *so accepted, so loved, and so calm*. . . .It was like all the beautiful things in my life intensified a trillion times. It was nothing I have ever seen or felt before. *Love doesn't even begin to describe what I felt, but it's the only word I know to explain the sensation*" (58). • "I had never felt such an overwhelming sense of *peace, and acceptance, and total love*, . . . there was not judgment. Just mercy and acceptance" (58). • "When I left my body I was encompassed with a higher power. It felt like *complete wholeness, tranquility, peacefulness*, . . . *Definitely love*, definitely. There are no words in the English language to describe it. It's more than love; *the word love is just the tip of the iceberg*, so to speak. . . . It was everything" (58). • "When we got close to the Savior, I felt *a tremendous love emanating from him*. It's hard to describe, but *you could feel it all around him*. And I felt a similar enormous love for him" (62). • "He gathered me in his arms and began to . . . comfort me. He gave me *such a warm feeling of love*, and . . . I've never felt anything like it. *It was warm, it was love, it was joy*—I didn't want it to end. It was the most thrilling feeling I had ever experienced before or since" (63). • "I was filled with peace, I felt calm, and there was an assurance that the peace would stay with me. *There was an overpowering love coming from Him to me—I could feel it*. . . . There were the love and comfort that he gave" (66).

16. Members of the Godhead Grant Their Grace to Repentant Mankind

The dictionary waxes eloquent when it comes to the word *grace*, supplying an extended list of meanings and synonyms. Some of those are: "1a. ***unmerited divine assistance given humans for their regeneration or sanctification***; b. a virtue coming from God; c. a state of sanctification enjoyed through divine grace. 2a. Approval, Favor; b. Mercy, Pardon; c. a special favor: Privilege; d. disposition to an act or instance of kindness, courtesy, or clemency; e. a temporary exemption: Reprieve. Syn.: see Mercy" (*MerriamWebster's Collegiate Dictionary*, 11th Edition, 542).

Perhaps the first definition, "unmerited divine assistance given humans for their regeneration or sanctification" is the most appropriate definition for the scriptures cited here. Notice, especially, the other blessings repeatedly associated with the term grace: • "*the* LORD *will give grace and glory*: no good thing will he withhold from them that walk uprightly" (Ps. 84:11). • "we believe that *through the grace of the Lord Jesus Christ we shall be saved*" (Acts 15:11). • "*Grace to you and peace* from God our Father, and the Lord Jesus Christ" (Rom. 1:7, 1 Cor. 1:3; 2 Cor. 1:2). • "The *grace of the Lord Jesus Christ*, and the *love of God*, and the *communion of the Holy Ghost*, be with you all" (2 Cor. 13:14). • "*For by grace are ye saved through faith*; and that not of yourselves: *it is the gift of God*" (Eph. 2:8). • "*Grace, mercy, and peace*, from God our Father and Jesus Christ our Lord" (1 Tim. 1:2). • "God . . . hath saved us, and called us with an holy calling, not according to our works, but *according to his own purpose and grace, which was given us in Christ Jesus before the world began*" (2 Tim. 1:9). • "*Grace be with you, mercy, and peace,* from God the Father, and from the Lord Jesus Christ, the Son of the Father, *in truth and love*" (2 Jn. 1:3). • there is no flesh that can dwell in the presence of God, save it be *through the merits, and mercy, and grace of the Holy Messiah*" (2 Ne. 2:8). • "remember, after ye are reconciled unto God, that *it is only in and through the grace of God that ye are saved*" (2 Ne. 10:24). • "we know that it is *by grace that we are saved,* after all we can do" (2 Ne. 25:23). • "the Lord God showeth us our weakness that we may know that *it is by his grace, and his great condescensions* unto the children of men, that we have power to do these things" (Jacob 4:7). • "we know that *justification through the grace of our Lord* and Savior Jesus Christ is just and true; And we know also, that *sanctification through the grace of our Lord* and Savior Jesus Christ is just and true, to all those who love and serve God with all their mights, minds, and strength" (D&C 20:30–31).

Thus it is the grace of God which bridges the gap between the result of man's best efforts and the much higher demands of justice; without His grace no man can be saved.

17. Members of the Godhead Treat All Mankind Impartially

Members of the Godhead deal impartially with all mankind and ***do not capriciously play favorites.*** Everyone can expect a "fair deal" from them. The scriptures say: • "there is *no iniquity with the LORD our God, nor respect of persons*" (2 Chr. 19:7). • "Of a truth I perceive that *God is no respecter of persons*: But in every nation he that feareth him, and worketh righteousness, is accepted with him" (Acts 10:34–35). • "there is *no respect of persons* with God" (Rom. 2:11). • "*he that doeth wrong shall receive for the wrong which he hath done*: and there is *no respect of persons*" (Col. 3:25). • "I the Lord am willing to make these things known unto all flesh; For *I am no respecter of persons*" (D&C 1:34–35). • "*all flesh is mine, and I am no respecter of persons*" (D&C 38:16).

However, God's impartiality does "play favorites" to the extent that members of the Godhead are ***committed to bless the righteous and to ultimately chastize the unrighteous.*** This policy has been revealed throughout the scriptures since the beginning of time. See, for instance, Deuteronomy 28, where for the entire chapter the LORD promise to bless the Israelites temporally and spiritually if they are righteous (Deut. 28:1–14); but to curse, smite and destroy them if they turn to wickedness (Deut. 28:15–68). See also Deut. 30:1–20.

But ***it is the conduct of man which determines whether they will reap blessings or cursings,*** not any capriciousness on the part of Godhead members: • "*men are free according to the flesh; and all things are given them which are expedient unto man.* And they are free *to choose liberty and eternal life,* through the great Mediator of all men, or *to choose captivity and death,* according to the captivity and power of the devil; for he seeketh that all men might be miserable like unto himself. And now, my sons, I would that ye should look to the great Mediator, and hearken unto his great commandments; and be faithful unto his words, and *choose eternal life,* according to the will of his Holy Spirit; And *not choose eternal death,* according to the will of the flesh and the evil which is therein" (2 Ne. 2:27–29).

Also, the scriptures repeatedly have indicated that ***God will chasten those He loves,*** in an effort to teach and correct them. This, perhaps, is in the same mode as parents today who will reprimand their young children to keep them from wandering into the street or to teach them to be unselfish as they interact with their playmates. • "Behold, *happy is the man whom God correcteth*: therefore despise not thou the chastening of the Almighty" (Job. 5:17). • "My son, despise not the chastening of the LORD; neither be weary of his correction: For *whom the LORD loveth he correcteth*; even as a father the son in whom he delighteth" (Prov. 3:11–12). • *"For whom the Lord loveth he chasteneth* . . .If ye endure chastening, God dealeth with you as with sons" (Heb. 12:6–7). • *As many as I love, I rebuke and chasten*: be zealous therefore, and repent" (Rev. 3:19). • "the Lord seeth fit to chasten his people; yea, *he trieth their patience and their faith"* (Mosiah 23:21). • "in the days of their iniquities hath *he chastened them because he loveth them"* (Hel. 15:3). • "I, the Lord, will contend with Zion, and plead with her strong ones, and *chasten her until she overcomes and is clean before me"* (D&C 90:36). • *"all those who will not endure chastening, but deny me, cannot be sanctified"* (D&C 101:5). • *"my people must needs be chastened until they learn obedience*, if it must needs be, by the things which they suffer" (D&C 105:6).

Numerous **warnings of the fairness of God, at the time of judgment**, have been recorded to help men understand the implications of their present actions as they relate to their personal Judgment Day. Three of the most poignant are: • (1) "I beseech of you that ye *do not procrastinate the day of your repentance until the end*; for after *this day of life, which is given us to prepare for eternity*, behold, if we do not improve our time while in this life, then cometh the night of darkness wherein there can be no labor performed. *Ye cannot say, when ye are brought to that awful crisis, that I will repent, that I will return to my God.* Nay, ye cannot say this; for that same spirit which doth possess your bodies at the time that ye go out of this life, that same spirit will have power to possess your body in that eternal world" (Alma 34:33–34). • (2) "Yea, and there shall be many which shall say: Eat, drink, and be merry, for tomorrow we die; and it shall be well with us. And there shall also be many which shall say: Eat, drink, and be merry; nevertheless, *fear God—he will justify in committing a little sin; yea, lie a little, take the advantage of one because of his words, dig a pit for thy neighbor; there is no harm in this; and do all these things, for tomorrow we die; and if it so be that we are guilty, God will beat us with a few stripes, and at last we shall be saved in the kingdom of God.* Yea, and there shall be many which shall teach after this manner, *false and vain and foolish doctrines*, and shall be puffed up in their hearts, and shall seek deep to hide their counsels from the Lord; and their works shall be in the dark" (2 Ne. 28:7–9). • (3) "if our hearts have been hardened, yea, if we have hardened our hearts against the word, insomuch that it has not been found in us, *then will our state be awful, for then we shall be condemned. For our words will condemn us, yea, all our works will condemn us; we shall not be found spotless; and our thoughts will also condemn us; and in this awful state we shall not dare to look up to our God*; and we would fain be glad if we could command the rocks and the mountains to fall upon us to hide us from his presence. But this cannot be; *we must come forth and stand before him in his glory, and in his power, and in his might, majesty, and dominion, and acknowledge to our everlasting shame that all his judgments are just; that he is just in all his works*, and that he is merciful unto the children of men, and that he has all power to save every man that believeth on his name and bringeth forth fruit meet for repentance. And now behold, I say unto you *then cometh a death, even a second death*, which is a spiritual death; then is a time that whosoever dieth in his sins, as to a temporal death, shall also die a spiritual death; yea, *he shall die as to things pertaining unto righteousness"* (Alma 12:13–16).

18. Members of the Godhead Follow a Premortal Plan of Redemption for Mankind

This plan is called by various names in the Book of Mormon, where it is reported in far more detail than the other Latter-day Saint scriptures. Those names include (in alphabetical order): (1) the great and eternal plan of deliverance from death; (2) the great plan of mercy; (3) the great plan of the Eternal God; (4) the great plan of redemption; (5) the merciful plan of the Great Creator; (6) the plan of happiness; (7) the plan of mercy; (8) the plan of our God; (9) the plan of redemption; (10) the plan of restoration; and (11) the plan of salvation.

General references to the plan include: • "This is the **plan of salvation** unto all men, through the blood of mine Only Begotten, who shall come in the meridian of time" (Moses 6:62). • "my soul delighteth in the covenants of the Lord which he hath made to our fathers; yea, my soul delighteth in his grace, and in his justice, and power, and mercy in the **great and eternal plan of deliverance from death**" (2 Ne. 11:15). • "will ye reject all the words which have been spoken concerning Christ, . . . and make a mock of the **great plan of redemption**, which hath been laid for you?" (Jacob 6:8). • "what could I write more than my fathers have written? For have not they revealed the **plan of salvation?**" (Jar. 1:2). • "now, my son, go thy way, declare the word with truth and soberness, that thou mayest bring souls unto repentance, that the **great plan of mercy** may have claim upon them" (Alma 42:31).

It is significant to note that this plan *"was laid from the foundation of the world"* (Alma 12:25, 30) "through Christ" (Alma 22:13). Entire books have been written on the many facets of this God-devised plan. It is sufficient, in this context, to cite some of its key principles from the book of Alma, where it is explained in greatest detail. Obviously, some of the pivotal events of the history of this earth are built around the various elements of this plan:

• (1) "For as *death hath passed upon all men*, to fulfil the **merciful plan of the great Creator**, *there must needs be a power of resurrection*, and *the resurrection must needs come unto man by reason of the fall*; and the *fall came by reason of transgression*; and because man became fallen *they were cut off from the presence of the Lord*" (2 Ne. 9:6).

• (2) "O how great the **plan of our God!** For on the other hand, *the paradise of God must deliver up the spirits of the righteous*, and *the grave deliver up the body of the righteous*; and *the spirit and the body is restored to itself again*, and *all men become incorruptible, and immortal*, and *they are living souls*, having a perfect knowledge like unto us in the flesh, save it be that *our knowledge shall be perfect*" (2 Ne. 9:13).

• (3) "Now, *if it had not been for the* **plan of redemption**, which was *laid from the foundation of the world*, there could have been *no resurrection of the dead*; but there was a plan of redemption laid, which *shall bring to pass the resurrection of the dead*, of which has been spoken" (Alma 12:25).

• (4) "therefore *God conversed with men*, and *made known unto them the* **plan of redemption**, which *had been prepared from the foundation of the world*; and this he made known unto them according to their faith and repentance and their holy works" (Alma 12:30).

• (5) "Therefore *God gave unto them commandments*, after having made known unto them the **plan of redemption**, that *they should not do evil*, the *penalty thereof being a second death*, which was an everlasting death as to things pertaining unto righteousness; for *on such the plan of redemption could have no power*, for *the works of justice could not be destroyed*, according to the supreme goodness of God" (Alma 12:32).

• (6) "But God did call on men, in the name of his Son, (this being the **plan of redemption** which was laid) saying: *If ye will repent and harden not your hearts, then will I have mercy upon you, through mine Only Begotten Son*; Therefore, *whosoever repenteth, and hardeneth not his heart, he shall have claim on mercy through mine Only Begotten Son,* unto *a remission of his sins*; and these *shall enter into my rest*" (Alma 12:33–34).

• (7) "Aaron did expound unto him the scriptures from the creation of Adam, laying *the fall of man before him, and their carnal state* and also the **plan of redemption**, which was *prepared from the foundation of the world, through Christ*, for all whosoever would believe on his name. And *since man had fallen he could not merit anything of himself*; but *the sufferings and death of Christ atone for their sins*, through *faith and repentance*, and so forth; and that *he breaketh the bands of death*, that the grave shall have no victory, and that the sting of death should be swallowed up in the hopes of glory" (Alma 22:13–14).

• (8) "For *it is expedient that an atonement should be made;* for according to the **great plan of the Eternal God** there *must be an atonement made, or else all mankind must unavoidably perish*; yea, all are hardened; yea, all are fallen and are lost, and *must perish except it be through the atonement which it is expedient should be made*" (Alma 34:9).

• (9) "I say unto thee, my son, that the **plan of restoration** is *requisite with the justice of God*; for it is *requisite that all things should be restored to their proper order.* Behold, it is requisite and just, according to the power and resurrection of Christ, that *the soul of man should be restored to its body,* and that *every part of the body should be restored to itself*" (Alma 41:2).

• (10) "*if Adam had put forth his hand immediately, and partaken of the tree of life, he would have lived forever,* according to the word of God, *having no space for repentance*; yea, and also the *word of God would have been void*, and the **great plan of salvation** would have been frustrated. But behold, *it was appointed unto man to die . . .* and man became lost forever, yea, *they became fallen man*" (Alma 42:5–6).

• (11) "Therefore, *according to justice*, the **plan of redemption** could not be brought about, *only on conditions of repentance of men in this probationary state*, yea, this *preparatory state*; for except it were for these conditions, *mercy could not take effect except it should destroy the work of justice.* Now the *work of justice could not be destroyed; if so, God would cease to be God*" (Alma 42:13).

• (12) "And thus we see that *all mankind were fallen, and they were in the grasp of justice*; yea, the *justice of God, which consigned them forever to be cut off from his presence.* And now, the **plan of mercy** could not be brought about *except an atonement should be made*; therefore *God himself atoneth for the sins of the world*, to bring about the **plan of mercy**, *to appease the demands of justice, that God might be a perfect, just God, and a merciful God also*" (Alma 42:14–15).

• (13) "Now, *repentance could not come unto men except there were a punishment*, which also was eternal as the life of the soul should be, *affixed opposite to the plan of happiness*, which was as *eternal also as the life of the soul.* Now, *how could a man repent except he should sin?* How could he sin if there was no law? How could there be a law save there was a punishment?" (Alma 42:16–17).

19. Members of the Godhead Govern Man with Justice, Mercy, and Probation

As asserted in the premortal plan of redemption, the requirements of both justice and mercy must be met, and the two principles maintained in effect through the operation of man's repentance and obedience to God's commandments.

Their justice is based upon the rule of law; those laws having been revealed to mankind from on high. Blessings are derived from obedience to God's laws: • *"There is a law, irrevocably decreed in heaven before the foundations of this world, upon which all blessings are predicated—And when we obtain any blessing from God, it is by obedience to that law upon which it is predicated.* (D&C 130:20–21).

Man may turn away from his former righteousness, and justice requires punishment for that wickedness: • "although a man may have many revelations, and have power to do many mighty works, yet if he boasts in his own strength, and sets at naught the counsels of God, and follows after the dictates of his own will and carnal desires, *he must fall and incur the vengeance of a just God upon him"* (D&C 3:4).

In like manner, *if a wicked person repents and turns to righteousness, his former sins can be forgiven*. Significant passages in the book of Ezekiel explain this aspect of God's justice:

> ye say, The way of the Lord is not equal. Hear now, O house of Israel; Is not my way equal? . . .
>
> When a righteous man turneth away from his righteousness, and committeth iniquity, and dieth in them; for his iniquity that he hath done shall he die.
>
> Again, *when the wicked man turneth away from his wickedness that he hath committed, and doeth that which is lawful and right*, he shall save his soul alive.
>
> Because he considereth, and turneth away from all his transgressions that he hath committed, he shall surely live, he shall not die. (Ezek. 18:25–28 {18:19–32; see also 33:7–20})

Many scriptures make reference to the need for members of the Godhead to adhere to *the principle of justice*: • "Just balances, just weights, a just ephah, and a just hin, shall ye have: I am the LORD your God" (Lev. 19:36). • "He is the Rock, his work is perfect: for *all his ways are judgment: a God of truth and without iniquity, just and right is he"* (Deut. 32:4). • "what doth the LORD require of thee, but to *do justly, and to love mercy, and to walk humbly* with thy God?" (Mic. 6:8). • "Great and marvellous are thy works, Lord God Almighty; *just and true* are thy ways, thou King of saints" (Rev. 15:3). • "I must cry unto my God: *Thy ways are just"* (2 Ne. 26:7). • "I am about to go down to my grave, that I might go down in peace, and my immortal spirit may join the choirs above in singing the praises of *a just God"* (Mosiah 2:28). • "if that man repenteth not, and remaineth and dieth an enemy to God, *the demands of divine justice* do awaken his immortal soul to a lively sense of his own guilt, which doth cause him to shrink from the presence of the Lord, and doth fill his breast with guilt, and pain, and anguish" (Mosiah 2:38). • "I would that ye should be steadfast and immovable, always abounding in good works, that Christ, the Lord God Omnipotent, may seal you his, that you may be brought to heaven, that ye may have everlasting salvation and eternal life, through the wisdom, and power, *and justice, and mercy of him who created all things, in heaven and in earth, who is God above all"* (Mosiah 5:15). • "Therefore ought ye not to tremble? For salvation cometh to none such; for the Lord hath redeemed none such; yea, neither can the Lord redeem such; for he cannot deny himself; for *he cannot deny justice when it has its claim"* (Mosiah 15:27). • "when every nation, kindred, tongue, and people shall see eye to eye and shall *confess before God that his judgments are just"* (Mosiah 16:1). • "it is better that a man should be judged of God than of man, for *the judgments of God are always just*, but the judgments of man are not always just" (Mosiah 29:12). • "O Lord God Almighty, hear us in these our petitions, and answer us from heaven, thy holy habitation, where thou sittest enthroned, with glory, honor, power, majesty, might, dominion, *truth, justice, judgment, mercy*, and an infinity of fulness, from everlasting to everlasting" (D&C 109:77).

At the opposite end of the scale is ***the principle of mercy***. Numerous scriptures speak of the willingness of Godhead members to show mercy to mortal mankind; to enable God to be both "a perfect, just God, and a merciful God also." In their mercy, the members of the Godhead modify or withhold their judgments in accordance with their knowledge of the needs, desires and acts of man.

Note that several of the passages cited predicate God's mercy on man's prior repentance: • "The LORD God, *merciful and gracious*, longsuffering, and abundant in goodness and truth" (Ex. 34:6). • "(For *the LORD thy God is a merciful God;*) he will not forsake thee, neither destroy thee, nor forget the covenant of thy fathers which he sware unto them" (Deut. 4:31). • "*the LORD your God is gracious and merciful*, and will not turn away his face from you, if ye return unto him" (2 Chr. 30:9). • "thou art *a God ready to pardon, gracious and merciful*, slow to anger, and of great kindness" (Neh. 9:17). • "*for thy great mercies' sake* thou didst not utterly consume them, nor forsake them; for *thou art a gracious and merciful God*" (Neh. 9:31). • "Gracious is the LORD, and righteous; yea, *our God is merciful*" (Ps. 116:5). • "turn unto the LORD your God: for *he is gracious and merciful*, slow to anger, and of great kindness" (Joel 2:13). • "Great and marvelous are thy works, O Lord God Almighty! Thy throne is high in the heavens, and thy power, and goodness, and *mercy* are over all the inhabitants of the earth; and, because *thou art merciful*, thou wilt not suffer those who come unto thee that they shall perish!" (1 Ne. 1:14). • "*I will be merciful unto them*, saith the Lord God, if they will repent and come unto me; for mine arm is lengthened out all the day long, saith the Lord God of Hosts" (2 Ne. 28:32). • "seek not to counsel the Lord, but to take counsel from his hand. For behold, ye yourselves know that *he counseleth in wisdom, and in justice, and in great mercy*, over all his works" (Jacob 4:10). • "my joy is carried away, even unto boasting in my God; for he has all power, all wisdom, and all understanding; he comprehendeth all things, and *he is a merciful Being*, even unto salvation, to those who will repent and believe on his name" (Alma 26:35). • "*God himself atoneth* for the sins of the world, *to bring about the plan of mercy*, to appease *the demands of justice*, that *God might be a perfect, just God, and a merciful God* also" (Alma 42:15).

A scriptural summation of justice versus mercy is found in the forty-second chapter of the book of Alma:

> But there is a law given, and a punishment affixed, and a repentance granted; *which repentance, mercy claimeth; otherwise, justice claimeth the creature and executeth the law*, and the law inflicteth the punishment; *if not so, the works of justice would be destroyed, and God would cease to be God.*
>
> But God ceaseth not to be God, and *mercy claimeth the penitent*, and mercy cometh because of the atonement; and the atonement bringeth to pass the resurrection of the dead; and *the resurrection of the dead bringeth back men into the presence of God; and thus they are restored into his presence, to be judged according to their works, according to the law and justice.*
>
> For behold, *justice exerciseth all his demands*, and also *mercy claimeth all which is her own*; and thus, none but the truly penitent are saved.
>
> What, *do ye suppose that mercy can rob justice?* I say unto you, Nay; not one whit. If so, God would cease to be God.

And thus God bringeth about his great and eternal purposes, which were prepared from the foundation of the world. And *thus cometh about the salvation and the redemption of men, and also their destruction and misery.* (Alma 42:22–26)

20. Members of the Godhead Take Pleasure in Righteousness, Feel Anger Toward Wickedness

Members of the Godhead find pleasure and experience joy over obedient followers here on earth. A broad variety of scriptural passages indicate their satisfaction and pleasure.

A number of passages, for instance, express **the pleasure of God the Father over the actions of His son, Jesus Christ:** • "This is my beloved Son, in whom I am well pleased" (Matt. 3:17). • "he that sent me is with me: the Father hath not left me alone; for *I do always those things that please him*" (John 8:29). • "*For it pleased the Father that in him* [Christ] *should all fulness dwell*" (Col. 1:19). • "Behold my Beloved Son, in whom I am well pleased, in whom I have glorified my name—hear ye him" (3 Ne. 11:7). • "Listen to him who is the advocate with the Father, who is pleading your cause before him—Saying: Father, behold the sufferings and death of him who did no sin, *in whom thou wast well pleased*" (D&C 45:3–4).

Other passages express **the Lord's pleasure with specific actions taken by individual church members:** • "*The* LORD *is well pleased for his righteousness' sake*; he will magnify the law, and make it honourable" (Isa. 42:21). • "it shall be given thee, also, to make a selection of sacred hymns, as it shall be given thee, *which is pleasing unto me,* to be had in my church" (D&C 25:11). • "do the work of printing, and of selecting and writing books for schools in this church, that little children also may receive instruction before me *as is pleasing unto me*" (D&C 55:4).

Some passages are the expressions of **righteous individuals who are commenting on the rewards of their efforts to please God:** • "whatsoever we ask, we receive of him, because we keep his commandments, and *do those things that are pleasing in his sight*" (1 Jn. 3:22). • "by the fear of the LORD men depart from evil. *When a man's ways please the* LORD, he maketh even his enemies to be at peace with him" (Prov. 16:6–7).

Other passages express **God's pleasure with the church as a whole, or with groups of saints** within the church: • "the only true and living church upon the face of the whole earth, *with which I, the Lord, am well pleased,* speaking unto the church *collectively* and not individually" (D&C 1:30). • "your wives and your children, many of whose feelings are exceedingly tender and chaste and delicate before God, *which thing is pleasing unto God*" (Jacob 2:7). • "Thus saith the Lord unto you who have assembled yourselves together to receive his will concerning you: Behold, *this is pleasing unto your Lord, and the angels rejoice over you*; the alms of your prayers have come up into the ears of the Lord of Sabaoth, and are recorded in the book of the names of the sanctified, even them of the celestial world" (D&C 88:1–2).

There are passages which express **God's pleasure over specific actions, projects, and beneficial activities** which members may pursue: • "I will praise the name of God with a song, and will magnify him with thanksgiving. *This also shall please the* LORD better than an ox or bullock" (Ps. 69:30–31). • "Children, obey your parents in all things: for *this is well pleasing unto the Lord*" (Col. 3:20). • "let us offer the sacrifice of praise to God continually, that is, the fruit of our lips giving thanks to his name. But to do good and to communicate forget not: for *with such sacrifices God is well* *pleased"* (Heb. 13:15–16). • *"I, the Lord, am well pleased* that there should be a school in Zion" (D&C 97:3).

A few passages express **God's pleasure derived from His own actions**: • "it hath *pleased the* LORD to make you his people" (1 Sam. 12:22). • "now hath God set the members every one of them in the body [his church], *as it hath pleased him"* (1 Cor. 12:18). • *"it pleaseth God* that he hath given all these things [various foodstuffs] unto man; for unto this end were they made to be used, with judgment, not to excess, neither by extortion" (D&C 59:20).

In a different vein, as beings who delight in justice, righteousness, and holiness, the members of the Godhead are truly repulsed by corruption, injustice, and any kind of unrighteousness that destroys bodies, minds, spirits, families, communities, and nations. *The scriptures often speak of God's righteous indignation at evil. Though members of the Godhead are slow to anger, they will in no way leave the wicked unpunished.*

Thus, the scriptures express various **behaviors or attitudes which are displeasing** to Godhead members: • *"the carnal mind is enmity against God:* for it is not subject to the law of God, neither indeed can be. So then they that are in the flesh cannot please God" (Rom. 8:7–8). • "But *without faith it is impossible to please him:* for he that cometh to God must believe that he is, and that he is a rewarder of them that diligently seek him" (Heb. 11:6). • "with some I am not well pleased, for they will not open their mouths, but *they hide the talent which I have given unto them,* because of the fear of man" (D&C 60:2). • *"without faith no man pleaseth God;* and with whom God is angry he is not well pleased; wherefore, unto such he showeth no signs, only in wrath unto their condemnation" (D&C 63:11). • "I, the Lord, am *not pleased with those among you who have sought after signs and wonders* for faith, and not for the good of men unto my glory" (D&C 63:12). • "I, the Lord, am not well pleased with the inhabitants of Zion, for *there are idlers among them; and their children are also growing up in wickedness; they also seek not earnestly the riches of eternity,* but *their eyes are full of greediness.* These things ought not to be, and must be done away from among them" (D&C 68:31–32) • "I, the Lord, am not well pleased with many who are in the church at Kirtland; For *they do not forsake their sins,* and their wicked ways, *the pride of their hearts,* and *their covetousness,* and *all their detestable things,* and observe the words of wisdom and eternal life which I have given unto them" (D&C 98:19–20).

Other passages are the Lord's **expressions of displeasure over the improper actions of individual wayward saints**: • "he hath need to repent, for I, the Lord, am not well pleased with him, for *he seeketh to excel, and he is not sufficiently meek before me"* (D&C 58:41). • "I, the Lord, am not pleased with my servant . . . *he exalted himself in his heart, and received not counsel, but grieved the Spirit"* (D&C 63:55). • "there are many things with which I am not pleased; behold, *he aspireth to establish his counsel instead of the counsel which I have ordained,* even that of the Presidency of my Church; and *he setteth up a golden calf* for the worship of my people" (D&C 124:84).

But the scriptures forthrightly show that members of the Godhead feel and express more than mere displeasure. There are situations where **God's anger and wrath** are vented against the wicked. However, the scriptures report that • "thou art a God ready to pardon, gracious and merciful, *slow to anger,* and of great kindness," (Neh. 9:17). • "The LORD is *slow to anger,* and great in power" (Nah. 1:3). Also, • "rend your heart, and not your garments, and turn unto the LORD your God: for he is gracious and merciful, *slow to anger,* and of great kindness, and repenteth him of the evil" (Joel 2:13).

In contrast, though, they say that • "God judgeth the righteous, and *God is angry with the wicked every day*" (Ps. 7:11). But they also say that God will abate his anger if the wicked are repentant: • "But if ye will repent and return unto the Lord your God *I will turn away mine anger*, saith the Lord; yea, thus saith the Lord, blessed are they who will repent and turn unto me, but wo unto him that repenteth not" (Hel. 13:11). And there is balance between blessing the righteous and punishing the wicked: • "*The hand of our God is upon all them for good that seek him; but his power and his wrath is against all them that forsake him*" (Ezek. 8:22).

It is interesting to note that in almost all instances where the LORD speaks of His anger, the situation involves either (1) idolatry and the serving of pagan gods, (2) rebellion against Him and His prophets, or (3) other instances of gross obedience to His commandments. Concerning rebellion, one prophet said, • "Wherefore, we would to God that we could persuade all men *not to rebel against God, to provoke him to anger*" (Jacob 1:8).

General statements on what will cause God's anger and wrath: "He that believeth on the Son hath everlasting life: and *he that believeth not the Son shall not see life*; but *the wrath of God abideth on him*" (John 3:36). • "For the wrath of God is revealed from heaven *against all ungodliness and unrighteousness of men, who hold the truth in unrighteousness*" (Rom. 1:18). • "For this ye know, that no *whoremonger*, nor *unclean person*, nor *covetous man*, who is an *idolater*, hath any inheritance in the kingdom of Christ and of God. Let no man deceive you with vain words: for *because of these things cometh the wrath of God upon the children of disobedience*. Be not ye therefore partakers with them" (Eph. 5:5–7). • "Mortify therefore your members which are upon the earth; fornication, uncleanness, inordinate affection, evil concupiscence, and covetousness, which is idolatry: *For which things' sake the wrath of God cometh on the children of disobedience*" (Col. 3:5–6). • "in nothing doth man offend God, or *against none is his wrath kindled*, save those who *confess not his hand in all things*, and *obey not his commandments*" (D&C 59:21). • "signs come by faith, unto mighty works, for without faith no man pleaseth God; and *with whom God is angry he is not well pleased*; wherefore, unto such he showeth no signs, only *in wrath unto their condemnation*" (D&C 63:11).

21. Members of the Godhead Control Length of Life and Time of Death of All Mankind

Members of the Godhead determine when and where man comes to earth, fix the allotted length of his stay in mortality, and choose the time of man's departure from mortality into the next phase of his existence: the spirit world. However, there is substantial evidence that every individual, in his premortal existence, made choices which affected these God-level decisions and which determined many of the situations and challenges he would encounter on earth as part of probation here. (See *Life Everlasting* [2nd revised edition, 2005], 81–155.)

Scriptures which speak of members of the Godhead determining aspects of man's mortal birth and death include: • "Remember . . . When the most High divided to the nations their inheritance, when he separated the sons of Adam, *he set the bounds of the people according to the number of the children of Israel*" (Deut. 32:7–8). • "*The LORD killeth, and maketh alive: he bringeth down to the grave, and bringeth up*" (1 Sam. 2:6). • "Man that is born of a woman is of few days, . . . *his days are determined, the number of his months are with thee, thou hast appointed his bounds that he cannot pass*"

(Job 14:1, 5). • *"A time to be born, and a time to die"* (Eccles. 3:2). • The Savior went unharmed in several situations where he suffered bodily attack because *"his hour was not yet come"* (John 7:30; 8:20). • "God that made the world and all things therein, . . . hath made of one blood all nations of men for to dwell on all the face of the earth, and *hath determined the times before appointed, and the bounds of their habitation"* (Acts 17:24, 26). • *"thus did I, the Lord God, appoint unto man the days of his probation*—that by his natural death he might be raised in immortality unto eternal life, even as many as would believe; And they that believe not unto eternal damnation; for they cannot be redeemed from their spiritual fall, because they repent not" (D&C 29:43–44). • *"For there is a time appointed for every man*, according as his works shall be" (D&C 121:25). • *"Thy days are known*, and thy years shall not be numbered less" (D&C 122:9).

22. Members of the Godhead Regard Man's Mortal Life as a Probationary State

The premortal concepts of justice versus mercy are overlaid over the concept that this *mortal life is a probationary state*. This understanding is initially based on a pivotal passage found in the third chapter of the book of Abraham:

> And there stood one among them that was like unto God, and he said unto those who were with him: *We will go down, for there is space there, and we will take of these materials, and we will make an earth whereon these may dwell;*
>
> And *we will prove them herewith*, to see if they will do all things whatsoever the Lord their God shall command them;
>
> And they who keep *their first estate* [their premortal training] shall be added upon; and they who keep not their first estate shall not have glory in the same kingdom with those who keep their first estate; and they who keep *their second estate* [their mortal probation] *shall have glory added upon their heads for ever and ever.* (Abr. 3:24–26).

This mortal life, then, is *a period of testing*, following what is believed to be a very intensive premortal training period. To put this mortal probationary situation into perspective, compare the premortal state to attending the university. Then, if Peter's comment "that one day is with the Lord as a thousand years, and a thousand years as one day" (2 Pet. 3:8) is taken somewhat literally, then man's stay on earth is equal to about a 2- to 3-hour "final exam." Just as textbooks are inaccessible for most university exams, man's memory of premortal events has been blocked as he took up his mortal body. He's on his own as God "proves him." And just like the final exam is a significant part of one's university-class grade, so the individual needs to really strive to do his best; that "do-your-best" attitude should characterize his life activities during mortality if he is wise.

The scriptures, particularly the Book of Mormon, put great emphasis on mortal life as being one's period of probation: • "Wherefore, if ye have sought to do wickedly *in the days of your probation*, then ye are found unclean before the judgment-seat of God; and no unclean thing can dwell with God; wherefore, ye must be cast off forever" (1 Ne. 10:21). • "the day should come that they must be judged of their works, yea, *even the works which were done by the temporal body in their days of probation"* (1 Ne. 15:32). • "And the days of the children of men were prolonged, according to the will of God, that they might repent while in the flesh; wherefore, *their state became a state of probation*, and their time was lengthened, according to the commandments which the Lord God gave unto the children of men" (2 Ne. 2:21). • "wo unto him that has the law given, yea, that has all the commandments of God, like unto us, and that transgresseth them, and *that wasteth the days of his probation*, for awful is his state!" (2 Ne. 9:27). • "for none of these can I hope except they shall be reconciled unto Christ, and enter into the narrow gate, and walk in the strait path which leads to life, and *continue in the path until the end of the day of probation*" (2 Ne. 33:9). • "there was a space granted unto man in which he might repent; therefore *this life became a probationary state; a time to prepare to meet God*; a time to prepare for that endless state which has been spoken of by us, which is after the resurrection of the dead" (Alma 12:24). • "And thus we see, that *there was a time granted unto man to repent, yea, a probationary time*, a time to repent and serve God" (Alma 42:4). • "Therefore, as they had become carnal, sensual, and devilish, by nature, *this probationary state became a state for them to prepare*; it became a preparatory state" (Alma 42:10). • "Therefore, according to justice, the plan of redemption could not be brought about, *only on conditions of repentance of men in this probationary state*, yea, this preparatory state; for except it were for these conditions, mercy could not take effect except it should destroy the work of justice. Now the work of justice could not be destroyed; if so, God would cease to be God" (Alma 42:13) • "behold, *your days of probation are past; ye have procrastinated the day of your salvation until it is everlastingly too late*, and your destruction is made sure; yea, for ye have sought all the days of your lives for that which ye could not obtain; and ye have sought for happiness in doing iniquity, which thing is contrary to the nature of that righteousness which is in our great and Eternal Head" (Hel. 13:38). • *"Be wise in the days of your probation*; strip yourselves of all uncleanness; ask not, that ye may consume it on your lusts, but ask with a firmness unshaken, that ye will yield to no temptation, but that ye will serve the true and living God" (Morm. 9:28). • "And *thus did I, the Lord God, appoint unto man the days of his probation*—that by his natural death he might be raised in immortality unto eternal life, even as many as would believe" (D&C 29:43).

The scriptures also indicate that **God intentionally proves man** during his time of mortal probation. • "Behold, I will rain bread from heaven for you; and the people shall go out and gather a certain rate every day, *that I may prove them, whether they will walk in my law, or no*" (Ex. 16:4). • "Moses said unto the people, Fear not: for *God is come to prove you*, and that his fear may be before your faces, that ye sin not" (Ex. 20:20). • "And thou shalt remember all the way which the LORD thy God led thee these forty years in the wilderness, to humble thee, *and to prove thee, to know what was in thine heart*, whether thou wouldest keep his commandments, or no" (Deut. 8:2). • "Who fed thee in the wilderness with manna, which thy fathers knew not, that he might humble thee, and *that he might prove thee*, to do thee good at thy latter end" (Deut. 8:16). • "establish the just: for *the righteous God trieth the hearts and reins*" (Ps. 7:9). • *"For thou, O God, hast proved us: thou hast tried us"* (Ps. 66:10). • *"I will try you and prove you herewith*. And whoso layeth down his life in my cause, for my name's sake, shall find it again, even life eternal" (D&C 98:12–13).

The members of the Godhead's **attitudes concerning mortal death** deserve comment before concluding this chapter on their attributes and defining motives. It is apparent that they view death only as a doorway to the next phase of life. Just as mortal birth serves as a doorway to man's probation here on earth, death marks the conclusion of this period of probation and testing and allows one to move on to the next phase of eternal growth. Death, obviously, is not the end of one's existence, it is "birth" to the more advanced and glorious opportunities which the spirit world holds for all mankind.

By the same token, *death for an unrepentant person does not mean that the individual is automatically condemned to hell (contrary to "trinitarian" belief). If the individual has never been taught the gospel of Jesus Christ, he will have the opportunity to learn of it in the spirit world:* • "For for this cause was *the gospel preached also to them that are dead,* that they might be judged according to men in the flesh, but *live according to God in the spirit*" (1 Pet. 4:6; see also 3:18–20). After hearing the gospel there, the individual still has the opportunity to repent and then "live according to God in the spirit" to change his eternal life's course.

Jehovah/Jesus Christ, apparently, is willing to terminate life on earth for untaught individuals who are obstructing His master plans for blessing His chosen people Israel, knowing that their transition to the spirit world will create greater opportunities for growth and salvation for those who are not doing well in their earthly probation. • "*The LORD killeth, and maketh alive: he bringeth down to the grave, and bringeth up*" (1 Sam. 2:6).

Knowledge of this important principle helps one to understand the true results of situations in the scriptures where the Lord has called for the slaying of unrighteous individuals. Because of this knowledge, Latter-day Saints recognize the actions of a merciful God in situations where others may regard God's same actions as being harsh, unnecessarily cruel and vindictive.

Before Israel journeyed westward across the Jordan River and began conquering the Land of Canaan, the LORD commanded them: • "Ye shall utterly destroy all the places, wherein the nations which ye shall possess served their gods, upon the high mountains, and upon the hills, and under every green tree: And ye shall overthrow their altars, and break their pillars, and burn their groves with fire; and ye shall hew down the graven images of their gods, and destroy the names of them out of that place" (Deut. 12:2–3). Then the LORD commanded them that they were to completely • "*cut off the nations from before thee,*" and warned them to "*Take heed to thyself that thou be not snared by following them, after that they be destroyed from before thee; and that thou enquire not after their gods,* saying, How did these nations serve their gods? even so will I do likewise. Thou shalt not do so unto the LORD thy God: *for every abomination to the LORD, which he hateth, have they done unto their gods; for even their sons and their daughters they have burnt in the fire to their gods.* What thing soever I command you, observe to do it: thou shalt not add thereto, nor diminish from it" (Deut. 12:30–32).

And then the LORD warned them that their conduct in this matter would serve as a test, of how fully they would follow him: • "*the LORD your God proveth you, to know whether ye love the LORD your God with all your heart and with all your soul*" (Deut. 13:3). At the same time, he warned them of the great danger which lay ahead of them to be tempted to succumb to the worship of false gods (Deut. 13:1–18). So Jehovah instructed Israel to completely destroy the inhabitants of the cities they would be conquering so that idolatry and false-god worship would not make its way among them.

Cases in point are events which are recorded early in the book of Joshua: • When Jericho was conquered by the advancing Israelites, the LORD instructed them to slay every person and animal in the city (with the exception of Rahab, who had previously saved the life of two Israelite spies; Josh. 6:17–21). • All twelve thousand of the inhabitants of the city of Ai were slain by the Israelites (Josh. 8:21–26). • When they fought against the Amorites and the five kings allied with them, the Lord slew more of the enemy with great hailstones than the Israelite warriors slew "with a very great slaughter" (Josh. 10:10–30), leaving no one alive. • Likewise, all the inhabitants of Makkedah, Libnah, Lachish, Eglon, Hebron, Debir, and all who resided in the the countryside from Kadesh-barnea to Gaza, and the land of Goshen were slain (Josh. 10:28–42), and Joshua, obedient to the LORD, • "left none remaining, but utterly destroyed all that breathed, as the LORD God of Israel commanded" (Josh. 10:40). • Joshua chapters 11 and 12 record other great slaughters.

So in all of this, the LORD, apparently, was accomplishing two objectives: (1) He was seeking to safeguard His chosen people, Israel, from the powerful temptations which were awaiting them in all those cities, and (2) He was removing tens of thousands who had never heard of Jehovah or the great plan of redemption, bringing them into the spirit world where they, with their premortal memories restored, could be more easily taught the gospel, and where they would be more receptive to receiving and living it.

One just can't grasp what was happening in many Old Testament situations until the unity of these two purposes is understood. While He was being a stern, militant God, Jehovah also was being an merciful and benevolent Being. Thus, understanding the concept of mortal life being a probationary state, and understanding that God is blessing people when He removes them from the earth and brings them into the more advanced, higher level of the spirit world. Yes, man mourns for the death of his beloved kin, but he should also rejoice in the great blessings that are coming to them as they "graduate" from this probationary world and move on to far better opportunities for eternal growth!

Summary

1. Criticisms of "trinitarian" explanations of the attributes of God include:
   A They attempt to describe God without making distinctions between different members of the Godhead.
   B They are locked into ancient creedal statements which, at times, are in direct conflict with numerous scriptural passages.
   C They are tied into ancient philosophical hypotheses, reaching back to Plato and other Greek philosophers, which influenced the writings of many of the early Christian "fathers."
   D They wax so eloquent that their descriptions go far beyond the limits of the scriptures they are interpreting.
   E Red flag number 1: They regard as "intrinsic" certain qualities which Latter-day Saints believe are not necessarily permanent, "can't be lost" qualities.
   F Red flag number 2: The "trinitarians," based on Greek philosophies, think they are describing "the great first cause," while Latter-day Saints believe that the same passages are describing a particular "generation" of an eternal ancestry of divine beings, but which is not the very first God.
   G "Trinitarians" think they are describing a self-existent God who for all eternity has possessed His God-like attributes, while Latter-day Saints believe that Godhood is a priesthood position that can be conferred upon individuals when they reach the pinnacle of their eternal progression process.
2. A quotation from Joseph Smith's *King Follett Discourse* introduces the concept

that God is an exalted man who worked out His own salvation and exaltation on another earth, just as others need to learn to do and achieve.

3. Some Latter-day Saint foundations are that God the Father and the Son have tangible bodies; the Holy Ghost is a spirit being. The three are completely separate beings, not different manifestations of the same divine being.

4. Members of the Godhead are personal, living beings. They are eternal beings, who are unchanging in their personal attributes, desires and purposes.

5. Members of the Godhead are all perfect beings. They are exalted above their mortal creations (transcendence), and through the light of Christ, they are "in" all things (immanence), though they have form and shape and they themselves are only in one place at any given time.

6. Members of the Godhead have all power (omnipotence), all knowledge (omniscience) and all wisdom.

7. Members of the Godhead all are holy. They are Gods of truth and integrity, and treat all their subjects with impartially: rewarding the righteous, and punishing wickedness.

8. Members of the Godhead function in a patriarchal, family-oriented environment.

9. Members of the Godhead are filled with and characterized by love, grace, and mercy. They take pleasure in righteousness and feel anger toward wickedness.

10. Members of the Godhead follow a set plan of redemption and salvation, devised before the creation of this earth, which guides their actions and decisions concerning mankind.

11. Members of the Godhead govern man with balanced justice and mercy, recognizing that mortal beings are on this earth undergoing a period of probation which is very brief when contemplated in eternal "time."

12. Members of the Godhead control the timing of all mankind's births and deaths, plus events and locales in their mortal lives. They sometimes remove individuals from earth because they are failing their mortal probations so they can receive remedial help and training in the spirit world. They also can remove those who are obstructing the progress of the righteous.

CHAPTER 4

IS GOD ONLY AN "INCORPOREAL," "INVISIBLE" SPIRIT?

God As Spirit

When one reads the works of Catholic and Protestant theologians trying to explain the nature of God, their works very early allude to two New Testament passages, with a typical misinterpretation of both of them. Following their reasoning is instructive.

Dr. R.A. Torrey was a highly respected Bible scholar who lived more than a century ago. His book, *What the Bible Teaches*, carries a notice stating "Copyright 1898–1933 by Fleming H. Revell Company, with a preface to the seventeenth edition," which indicates that his writings have been widely disseminated. He begins with the first chapter titled "**God as Spirit.**" His chapters are organized into "facts" and "propositions." He begins:

> As the aim of this book is to ascertain and state in systematic form what the Bible teaches, the method pursued will be to first give the Scripture statements, and then sum up their contents in a proposition, following the proposition by such comments as may appear necessary.
>
> **I. The fact that God is Spirit.**
>
> Jno. 4:24—"God is (a) Spirit: and they that worship him must worship him in spirit and truth."
>
> FIRST PROPOSITION: God is Spirit.
>
> *QUESTION:* What is spirit?
>
> *ANSWER:* Luke 24:39—"Behold my hands and my feet, that it is I myself: handle me and see; for a spirit hath not flesh and bones, as ye see me have." A spirit is incorporeal, invisible reality. To say God is spirit is to say God is incorporeal and invisible (Compare Deut., 4:15–18). (Torrey, 13)

Interpreting John 4:24: "God is a spirit"

Dr. Torrey takes some quantum leaps in his interpretations here when he assumes that a spirit is incorporeal (*Webster's Dictionary:* "not corporeal: having no material body or form"). His "incorporeal" assumption is not what John 4:24 says! In fact, it is directly opposite to what the John 4:24 passage states. *The context*: Jesus is journeying from Jerusalem to Galilee, passing through Samaria. He stops for water at Jacob's well (near Sychar, Samaria) and engages in conversation with a lady there. She perceives that "thou art a prophet" and comments that her forefathers have long worshiped in that mountain. Jesus replies:

> Ye worship ye know not what: we know what we worship: for salvation is of the Jews.
>
> But the hour cometh, and now is, when the *true worshippers shall worship the Father in spirit* and in truth: for the Father seeketh such to worship him.
>
> *God is a Spirit*: and they *that worship him must worship him in spirit* and in truth. (John 4:22–24)

Thus the Savior twice emphasizes that true worshipers must worship the Father "in spirit and in truth." He says that "the hour cometh, and now is" when true worshipers are worshiping the Father in that manner. The question: how do mortal worshipers worship the Father in spirit?

He's not talking about worshiping through the Holy Ghost—the woman he just met has no concept of such a being.

He likewise is not talking about worshiping God the Father in a "spirited," lively manner. There's no inkling of that meaning put forth in the passage nor in its context.

The only understandable alternative, in order to interpret the passage correctly, is to recognize that living human beings are spirit beings temporarily clothed in mortal bodies. And just as they are to worship the Father in spirit, while still clothed in their mortal bodies, the passage in no way indicates that God the Father does not have a physical body, even though He is a "spirit." *If worshippers can have a physical body clothing their spirit bodies, and thus "worship him in spirit," so also can God have a physical body which clothes His spirit body, as hundreds of other scriptural passages indicate.*

Interpreting Luke 24:39: "Flesh and bones, *as ye see me have*"

Just like Dr. Torrey makes an erroneous interpretation by taking only the first half and not the second half of John 4:24, he makes the same error when dealing with Luke 24:39. This passage also should be seen in context to be better understood.

Luke 24 deals with events which occurred on the first day after Christ rose from the tomb as a resurrected being. Verses 13–35 deal with the experience of the two disciples with whom Christ conversed as they walked toward Emmaus. At the end of that passage, those two disciples have just reported to the Apostles, gathered together in Jerusalem, that "The Lord is risen indeed" (Luke 24:34). Then, while the Apostles were still gathered together,

> And as they thus spake, Jesus himself stood in the midst of them, and saith unto them, Peace be unto you.
>
> But they were terrified and affrighted, and *supposed that they had seen a spirit*.
>
> And he said unto them, Why are ye troubled? and why do thoughts arise in your hearts?
>
> Behold my hands and my feet, that it is I myself: handle me, and see; *for a spirit hath not flesh and bones, **as ye see me have***.
>
> And when he had thus spoken, he shewed them his hands and his feet.
>
> And while they yet believed not for joy, and wondered, he said unto them, Have ye here any meat?

And *they gave him a piece of a broiled fish, and of an honeycomb. And he took it, and did eat before them.* (Luke 24:36–43)

It is the inadequate interpretation of verse 39, which Dr. Torrey and countless other "trinitarians" have made, that is being called in question here. The verse reads: "Behold my hands and my feet, that it is I myself: handle me, and see; for a spirit hath not flesh and bones, as ye see me have." The error arises when they take only the words "a spirit hath not flesh and bones" and understand it as meaning that "A spirit is incorporeal, invisible reality" (Torrey, 13). That is not what the passage says, at all. It says, "a spirit hath not flesh and bones, *as ye see me have*" (Luke 24:39).

Christ was not saying a spirit body does not have flesh and bones, but rather that *the flesh and bones of a spirit body are not of the same composition and density as his resurrected body's flesh and bones.* The Apostles could see the Lord's appearance, and, therefore, they recognized him, but without physical contact they could not discern whether He was still a spirit being or had by then acquired His physical body once again. The Savior's task was to teach them that His spirit body was now clothed with resurrected flesh and bones—elements of a different consistency than the flesh and bones of His spirit body. If He were still only a spirit, as He was after His body "gave up the ghost," their mortal hands wouldn't have been able to feel His body. But He opted to teach them the nature of a resurrected body so He had them all touch Him and discern Him using their sense of touch, and then He sat down and ate the fish and honeycomb while in their presence so they could see His body could now process tangible foodstuffs.

Note also the message conveyed in Luke 24:37: "But they were terrified and affrighted, and *supposed that they had seen a spirit.*" The Apostles obviously knew that a spirit being has the same form and appearance as a mortal being, with head, torso, arms and hands, legs and feet, and all the external and internal parts of a mortal being. A mortal body is merely a tangible covering which is superimposed over a spirit body at birth, and which is removed and placed in the grave when death occurs.

Remember the Creation account in the first two chapters of Genesis. In chapter one "God created man in his own image, in the image of God created he him" (Gen. 1:27). Obviously, that image was in the physical shape and form of a man. But it becomes obvious, when one begins reading chapter two, that the creation of man and of all the earth, recorded in chapter 1, is only a spiritual creation, for as the seventh day begins, there was not yet "a man to till the ground" (Gen. 2:5). It was not until God watered the face of the earth, and breathed into Adam's nostrils the breath of mortal life, that "man became a living soul" (Gen. 2:6–7). These principles are further clarified below, in the section titled: *Latter-day Saint Scriptures Teach about "Spirit" and "Spirit Beings."*

Biblical Passages Teach the Nature of Man's Spirit

Numerous Old Testament biblical passages speak of man's spirit: • When Moses had his great confrontation with the followers of Korah, there came a time when the people cried unto God in prayer, saying: "O God, *the God of the spirits of all flesh*" (Num. 16:22). • Later, Moses prayed unto the LORD, saying: "Let the LORD, *the God of the spirits of all flesh,* set a man over the congregation" (Num. 27:16). • The book of Job states that *"there is a spirit in man"* (Job 32:8). • And the book of Ecclesiastes speaks of death, saying that "Then shall the dust return to the earth as it was: and *the spirit shall return unto God who gave it*" (Eccles. 12:7).

New Testament passages indicate that the early saints understood that spirit beings have form and shape. • "When Jesus came, walking on the tempestuous waves of the Sea of Galilee during the night after he had fed the 5,000, his disciples exclaimed, *"It is a spirit"* when they first saw him (Matt. 14:26). When Peter was miraculously freed from prison and knocked on the gate of Mary's home where many of the saints were gathered, they, thinking him dead, were astonished and said, • *"It is his angel"* (Acts 12:15). • In Hebrews one learns that God is father of spirit beings who become physical beings when they are born into mortality: "We have had fathers of our flesh which corrected us, and we gave them reverence: shall we not much rather *be in subjection unto the Father of spirits*, and live?" (Heb. 12:9). • James, while speaking of the principle of faith, observed that *"For as the body without the spirit is dead*, so faith without works is dead also" (James 2:26). If James' definition that "the body without the spirit is dead" indicates that a "living" being needs both a body and its spirit combined, what does that indicate about the physical status of the "Living God"? Obviously, that the "Living God" has a body! • Peter exclaimed to Jesus that "Thou art the Christ, *the Son of the living God*" (Matt. 16:16). • He later repeated the statement, telling Jesus "we believe and are sure that thou art that Christ, *the Son of the living God*" (John 6:69). (See also Acts 14:15; Rom. 9:26; 2 Cor. 3:3, 6:16; 1 Tim. 3:15, 4:10, 6:17; Heb. 3:12, 9:14, 10:31, 12:22; Rev. 7:2.)

Latter-day Saint Scriptures Teach about "Spirit" and "Spirit Beings"

The nature of spirit beings is one of those many gospel principles for which Latter-day Saints have quite extensive scriptural knowledge which the rest of the world is lacking. They know, for instance:

1. *Man is spirit*: "For *man is spirit*" (D&C 93:33).

2. *Spirit is matter*: "There is no such thing as immaterial matter. *All spirit is matter*, but it is more fine or pure, and can only be discerned by purer eyes; We cannot see it; but when our bodies are purified we shall see that it is all matter" (D&C 131:7–8).

3. *Spirit beings existed premortally and exist eternally*: "If there be two spirits, and one shall be more intelligent than the other, yet these two spirits, notwithstanding one is more intelligent than the other, *have no beginning; they existed before, they shall have no end, they shall exist after, for they are gnolaum, or eternal*" (Abr. 3:18).

4. *Mortal bodies look like their spirit bodies*: "*that which is spiritual being in the likeness of that which is temporal*; and that which is temporal in the likeness of that which is spiritual; *the spirit of man in the likeness of his person*, as also the spirit of the beast, and every other creature which God has created" (D&C 77:2).

5. *The spirit and the body constitute the soul of man*: "*the spirit and the body are the soul of man*" (D&C 88:15; however, not all scriptural passages use the term soul in this manner).

6. *Spirits without their bodies cannot receive a fulness of joy* (until their spirits and bodies are reunited): "The elements are eternal, and *spirit and element, inseparably connected, receive a fulness of joy*; And when separated, man cannot receive a fulness of joy" (D&C 93:33–34).

7. *Man can behold, with the eyes of his spirit, things he cannot see with his mortal eyes*: "But now *mine own eyes have beheld God; but not my natural, but my spiritual eyes*, for my natural eyes could not have beheld; for I should have

withered and died in his presence; but *his glory was upon me; and I beheld his face, for I was transfigured before him*" (Moses 1:11).

8. ***All things and people on this earth were created in spirit form in heaven, prior to the physical creation of this earth***: "Now, behold, I say unto you, that these are the generations of the heaven and of the earth, when they were created, in the day that I, the Lord God, made the heaven and the earth, And every plant of the field before it was in the earth, and every herb of the field before it grew. *For I, the Lord God, created all things, of which I have spoken, spiritually, before they were naturally upon the face of the earth.* For I, the Lord God, had not caused it to rain upon the face of the earth. And *I, the Lord God, had created all the children of men*; and not yet a man to till the ground; for in heaven created I them; and there was not yet flesh upon the earth, neither in the water, neither in the air" (Moses 3:4–5).

9. ***Man's body was formed from the dust of the ground; then God placed man's premortal spirit into the body and the spirit and body, together, became a living soul***: "The Gods formed man from the dust of the ground, and took his spirit (that is, the man's spirit), and put it into him; and breathed into his nostrils the breath of life, and *man became a living soul* (Abr. 5:7).

10. ***God the Father and God the Son Jesus Christ (with others) combined their efforts to create this earth and all who dwell upon it***: "I, God, said unto mine *Only Begotten, which was with me from the beginning: Let us make man in our image, after our likeness*; and it was so. . . . And I, God, created man in mine own image, in the image of mine Only Begotten created I him; male and female created I them" (Moses 2:26–27; see Gen. 1:26–27).

11. ***Man is created in the image of the spirit body of Jesus Christ***: Latter-day Saints have this knowledge because of a manifestation granted to the brother of Jared when he pled with the Lord to touch stones so they could have light in their barges as they crossed the seas:

> I know, O Lord, that thou hast all power, and can do whatsoever thou wilt for the benefit of man; therefore *touch these stones, O Lord, with thy finger*, and prepare them that they may shine forth in darkness; and they shall shine forth unto us in the vessels which we have prepared, that we may have light while we shall cross the sea.
>
> Behold, O Lord, thou canst do this. We know that thou art able to show forth great power, which looks small unto the understanding of men.
>
> And it came to pass that when the brother of Jared had said these words, behold, *the Lord stretched forth his hand and touched the stones one by one with his finger. And the veil was taken from off the eyes of the brother of Jared, and he saw the finger of the Lord; and it was as the finger of a man, like unto flesh and blood*; and the brother of Jared fell down before the Lord, for he was struck with fear.
>
> And the Lord saw that the brother of Jared had fallen to the earth; and the Lord said unto him: Arise, why hast thou fallen?
>
> And he saith unto the Lord: *I saw the finger of the Lord*, and I feared lest he should smite me; for I knew not that the Lord had flesh and blood.
>
> And the Lord said unto him: Because of thy faith thou hast seen that *I shall take upon me flesh and blood*; and never has man come before me with such exceeding faith as thou hast; for were it not so ye could not have seen my finger. Sawest thou more than this?
>
> And he answered: Nay; Lord, show thyself unto me.
>
> And the Lord said unto him: Believest thou the words which I shall speak?

And he answered: Yea, Lord, I know that thou speakest the truth, for thou art a God of truth, and canst not lie.

And when he had said these words, *behold, the Lord showed himself unto him,* and said: *Because thou knowest these things ye are redeemed from the fall; therefore ye are brought back into my presence; therefore I show myself unto you.*

Behold, *I am he who was prepared from the foundation of the world to redeem my people. Behold, I am Jesus Christ.* I am the Father and the Son. In me shall all mankind have life, and that eternally, even they who shall believe on my name; and they shall become my sons and my daughters.

And never have I showed myself unto man whom I have created, for never has man believed in me as thou hast. *Seest thou that ye are created after mine own image? Yea, even all men were created in the beginning after mine own image.*

Behold, this body, which ye now behold, is the body of my spirit; and man have I created after the body of my spirit; and even as I appear unto thee to be in the spirit will I appear unto my people in the flesh. (Ether 3:4–16)

Concerning the Lord's statement "I am the Father and the Son," see chapter titled *Jesus Christ as the Father.*

12. *The resurrection is the reuniting of man's spirit and his body:* "This death of which I have spoken, which is the *spiritual death,* shall deliver up its dead; which spiritual death is hell; wherefore, death and hell must deliver up their dead, and hell must deliver up its captive spirits, and the grave must deliver up its captive bodies, and *the bodies and the spirits of men will be restored one to the other;* and it is by the power of the resurrection of the Holy One of Israel. O how great the plan of our God! For on the other hand, *the paradise of God must deliver up the spirits of the righteous, and the grave deliver up the body of the righteous; and the spirit and the body is restored to itself again, and all men become incorruptible, and immortal, and they are living souls,* having a perfect knowledge like unto us in the flesh, save it be that our knowledge shall be perfect" (2 Ne. 9:12–13).

13. *The Father and the Son have glorified physical bodies; the Holy Ghost has only a spirit body at this time:* "*The Father has a body of flesh and bones as tangible as man's; the Son also; but the Holy Ghost has not a body of flesh and bones, but is a personage of Spirit. Were it not so, the Holy Ghost could not dwell in us*" (D&C 130:22; see also D&C 76:19–24; 110:1–10; Acts 7:55–56).

14. *Deceased spirit beings have form and shape:* Jesus visited them in the spirit prison (1 Pet.4:6, 3:18–20). *Joseph F. Smith, in his Vision of the Redemption of the Dead, saw multitudes of these spirit beings:* "The eyes of my understanding were opened, and the Spirit of the Lord rested upon me, and *I saw the hosts of the dead, both small and great.* And there were gathered together in one place an innumerable company of the spirits of the just, who had been faithful in the testimony of Jesus while they lived in mortality; And who had offered sacrifice in the similitude of the great sacrifice of the Son of God, and had suffered tribulation in their Redeemer's name. All these had departed the mortal life, firm in the hope of a glorious resurrection, through the grace of God the Father and His Only Begotten Son, Jesus Christ. I beheld that they were filled with joy and gladness, and were rejoicing together because the day of their deliverance was at hand. *They were assembled awaiting the advent of the Son of God into the spirit world, to declare their redemption from the bands of death.* Their sleeping dust was to be restored unto its perfect frame, bone to his bone, and the sinews and the flesh upon them, *the spirit*

and the body to be united never again to be divided, that they might receive a fulness of joy" (D&C 138:11–17; see the entire section).

Challenging Torrey's Interpretation of "Image" in Genesis 1:27

Now, back to the writings of Dr. R.A. Torrey in his chapter "God as Spirit." His "creative interpretations" need to be addressed. In particular, his assertion that "*a spirit is incorporeal, invisible reality. To say God is spirit is to say God is incorporeal and invisible*" (Torrey, 13) is based on assumptions which do not hold true with the scriptural message of the Bible. As demonstrated above, they most certainly collide with the revealed knowledge concerning the nature of God and the nature of spirit beings which has been granted to Latter-day Saints. As far as I am concerned, Torrey is 180 degrees off the mark on this subject.

The next part of his exposition shows his intentional avoiding of essential passages while artfully attempting to dodge basic Bible teachings. To quote him:

> *QUESTION*: What does it mean, then, when it says in Gen. 1:27: "God created man *in his own image?*"
>
> The answer to this question is plainly given in the following passages:
>
> Col. 3:10—"And have put on the new man, which is renewed *in knowledge after the image of him that created him.*"
>
> Eph. 4:23, 24—"And be renewed in the spirit of your mind; and that ye put on the new man, which, *after God*, is created *in righteousness and true holiness.*"
>
> Col. 1:15—"Who is *the image of the invisible God*, the first-born of every creature." (Compare I Tim. 1:17.)
>
> The words "image" and "likeness" evidently do not refer to visible or bodily likeness, but to intellectual and moral likeness—likeness "in knowledge," "righteousness" and "holiness of truth." (Torrey, 13; italics his.)

While dealing with Torrey's convenient assumption that "image" only refers to "intellectual and moral likeness," not physical form, shape, and appearance, it must be recognized that his interpretation constitutes a wide leap from the literal message of the Bible.

It is appropriate to go back and quote Genesis 1:24–28 and then *follow the term "image" through the scriptures*:

> And God said, Let the earth bring forth the living creature *after his kind*, cattle, and creeping thing, and beast of the earth *after his kind*: and it was so.
>
> And God made the beast of the earth *after his kind*, and cattle *after their kind*, and every thing that creepeth upon the earth *after his kind*: and God saw that it was good.
>
> And God said, *Let us make man in our image, after our likeness*: and let them have dominion over the fish of the sea, and over the fowl of the air, and over the cattle, and over all the earth, and over every creeping thing that creepeth upon the earth.
>
> So *God created man in his own **image**, in the **image of God** created he him*; male and female created he them.
>
> And God blessed them, and God said unto them, Be fruitful, and multiply, and replenish the earth, and subdue it: and have dominion over the fish of the sea, and over the fowl of the air, and over every living thing that moveth upon the earth. (Gen. 1:24–28)

Rarely is a Bible passage made more clear than this one. There is no talk of "knowledge" or "righteousness" or "holiness" or "truth" here; the passage is clearly speaking of physical nature and appearance. Cattle, creeping things, and beasts were created *after their kind*. Then God created man "*in his image*," and "*after [his] likeness*." Man was born with arms, hands, a torso, legs, feet, a neck, a face, a brain, internal organs. And, as seen above, the physical was a copy of the spiritual.

Genesis 2:4–5 indicates that the creation described in Genesis 1, apparently, is the spiritual creation. The creation described in Gen. 2:6–25 appears to be the physical implementation of that previous creation.

Genesis 5:1–3 shows how the terms "likeness" and "image" continued to be used by the author of Genesis:

> This is the book of the generations of Adam. *In the day that God created man, in the likeness of God made he him*;
> Male and female created he them; and blessed them, and called their name Adam, in the day when they were created.
> And Adam lived an hundred and thirty years, and *begat a son in his own likeness, after his image*; and called his name Seth. (Gen. 5:1–3)

Again, there is no talk of "knowledge" or "righteousness" or "holiness" or "truth" here; the passage is clearly speaking of physical appearance.

The use of the term "image" is also used in a clearly physical sense in Gen. 9:6, when God warned the family of Noah about the sin of murder, saying that • "Whoso sheddeth man's blood, by man shall his blood be shed: for *in the image of God made he man*." Once again, there is no talk of "knowledge" or "righteousness" or "holiness" or "truth" here; the passage is clearly speaking of the physical appearance and the sanctity of the mortal body.

The concept of man being in God's image and likeness reaches beyond physical appearances to the concept of sonship, with mankind literally being regarded as sons and daughters of God the Father. Thus, in the genealogical listing provided in Luke chapter three, the lineage is supposedly traced back from Jesus through Joseph, all the way back to the final step: "[Cainan] Which was the son of Enos, which was the son of Seth, which was the son of *Adam, which was the son of God*" (Luke 3:38). This wasn't a line following "knowledge" or "righteousness" or "holiness" or "truth" in this passage; this was a tracing of paternity and hence, physical likeness.

Jesus, in His day, used the term "image" to portray a physical likeness when He told His disciples: "Shew me the tribute money. And they brought unto him a penny. And he saith unto them, Whose *is this image* and superscription? They say unto him, Cæsar's. Then saith he unto them, Render therefore unto Cæsar the things which are Cæsar's; and unto God the things that are God's" (Matt. 22:19–21).

Paul, writing to the Corinthians, instructed them that "a man indeed ought not to cover his head, forasmuch as *he is the image and glory of God*" (1 Cor. 11:7). Again, image means physical appearance in this passage, not "knowledge" or "righteousness" or "holiness" or "truth."

In 2 Corinthians, Paul writes of man acquiring the glory of God in his face, saying: "But we all, *with open face* beholding as in a glass the glory of the Lord, are changed into the *same image* from glory to glory, even as by the Spirit of the Lord" (2 Cor. 3:18). Again, the "image" subject is physical appearance. So, it's not difficult to interpret the passage four verses later, which says that "the light of the glorious gospel of *Christ, who is the image of God*, should *shine* unto them" (2 Cor. 4:4). What's being said? Christ looks like his Father, and just as Christ's glory shines physically, so does the Father shine physically.

The same understanding applies to Colossians 1:15, which speaks of Christ being in the image of His Father. The passage refers to Christ, the Father's "dear Son":

> [Dear Son:] In whom we have redemption through his blood, even the forgiveness of sins: *Who is the **image** of the invisible God, the firstborn of every creature*: For by him were all things created, that are in heaven, and that are in earth, visible and invisible, whether they be thrones, or dominions, or principalities, or powers: *all things were created by him, and for him: And he is before all things, and by him all things consist.* And he is the head of the body, the church: who is the beginning, the firstborn from the dead; that in all things he might have the preeminence. For it pleased the Father that in him should all fulness dwell. (Col. 1:13–19)

In summary, Dr. Torrey did a disservice to his followers while interpreting Genesis 1:27 when he failed to follow the biblically indicated usage of the terms "image" and "likeness" as meaning physical shape and appearance. Trying to disguise the physical nature and shape of God's bodily form by alluding only to distantly related passages, and crudely interpreting them by stating that "The words 'image' and 'likeness' evidently do not refer to visible or bodily likeness, but to intellectual and moral likeness," just doesn't ring true!

Is God the Father "Invisible"?

Torrey, in the passage being analyzed above, cited the Colossians 1:15 passage about Christ, • "Who is the **image** of *the invisible God*, the firstborn of every creature." The passage clearly seems to be asserting that Jesus Christ has the same appearance as God the Father, since He is "the image" of God the Father, of whom he is the firstborn son.

Unfortunately, Torrey and many other "trinitarian" theologians immerse the passage in metaphysical implications. They "spiritualize" Christ being in the Father's physical image, and instead dwell on the word "invisible."

That word "invisible" only appears in the Bible five times: once in Romans (1:20), twice in Colossians (1:15, 16), once in 1 Timothy (1:17), and once in Hebrews (11:27). A brief examination of the five passages is informative.

1. *The Romans passage* is a rebuke of the "unrighteousness of men." Why? Because they "hold the truth in unrighteousness"—"that which may be known of God is manifest in them, for God hath shewed it unto them," making *"the invisible things of him [God]* from the creation of the world" *"clearly seen*," particularly "his eternal power and Godhead." But "they glorified him not as God," and "professing themselves to be wise, they became fools" (Rom. 1:18–22). Here "the invisible things" are "clearly seen," so they're not invisible at all, are they? Isn't "professing themselves to be wise" but making themselves "fools" what the "trinitarians" are doing when they assert that God is **only** a spirit, and assert that *"a spirit is incorporeal, invisible reality. . . . God is incorporeal and invisible*," as Torrey did above?

In spite of literally hundreds of biblical passages in which God asserts His physical nature, shape, and attributes (see chapter titled: *The Physical Attributes of Godhead Members*), they interpret those passages which refer to God's being in a specific place as only "symbolic" or "figurative." For instance, Leo Rosten's report of the Episcopalian statement of their beliefs, as expressed in the Nicene and Apostles' Creeds, says that *"Some of the phrases are clearly 'symbolic' (as, 'sitteth on the right hand of God the*

Father,' which of course **could not be literally true***)"* (Rosten, 99). To "trinitarians," with their definition of the nature of God which denies his physical attributes, using this passage is like "walking on eggshells" because it reveals their "spiritualized" treatment of the hundreds of literal passages concerning the true nature of God so clearly.

2. *The two* **Colossians** *uses* of the word "invisible" come in consecutive verses. When they are cited in context (rather than making Colossians 1:15 stand by itself), they are extremely problematic for "trinitarians" because they (A) allude to premortal origins (v. 15–16); (B) explain that Christ, not God the Father, was the actual creator who created all things in heaven and in earth (v. 16); (C) explain that all things on earth were created *for* Christ (v. 16); (D) assert that Christ has been given preeminence over the Father (v. 18); and (E) says that "it pleased the Father that in him [Christ] should all fullness dwell" (v. 19):

> In whom we have redemption through his blood, even the forgiveness of sins:
> *Who is the image of the invisible God, the firstborn of every creature:*
> For *by him were all things created, that are in heaven, and that are in earth, visible and invisible*, whether they be thrones, or dominions, or principalities, or powers: *all things were created by him, and for him*:
> And *he is before all things, and by him all things consist.*
> And he is the head of the body, the church: who is the beginning, the firstborn from the dead; that *in all things he might have the preeminence.*
> For *it pleased the Father that in him should all fulness dwell.* (Col. 1:15–19)

It is obvious that the early Catholic creedal statements **definitely are not in harmony** with the profound messages of these verses.

3. *First Timothy 1:17* also presents numerous problems for "trinitarian" theologians. It is obvious that the entire chapter is about Jesus Christ ("God our Saviour" [v. 1], "the glorious gospel of the blessed God" [v. 11], "I thank Christ Jesus our Lord" [v. 12], "the grace of our Lord was exceeding abundant with faith and love which is in Christ Jesus" [v. 14], "Christ Jesus came into the world to save sinners" [v. 15], "Jesus Christ might shew forth all longsuffering, for a pattern" [v. 16], and "the King eternal" [v. 17]). So it is clear that Jesus Christ is the subject of verse 17: "Now unto *the King eternal, immortal, invisible, the only wise God*, be honour and glory for ever and ever" (1 Tim. 1:17).

But Jesus Christ certainly wasn't invisible to His Apostles and other disciples, who saw Him throughout His mortal ministry and then saw Him repeatedly following His death and resurrection (see Luke 24:13–31; Mark 16:12; Luke 24:36–48; Jn. 20:19–23; Mark 16:14; John 20:26–31; John 21:1–25; 1 Cor. 15:6–7; Matt. 28:16–20; Mark 16:15–18; Luke 24:50–51; Acts 1:1–11). Paul taught that "*Christ being raised from the dead dieth no more*; death hath no more dominion over him" (Rom. 6:9; see also Luke 20:36). And Paul wrote to the Philippians that "Our conversation is in heaven, from whence also we look for our Saviour, the Lord Jesus Christ: *Who shall change our vile body, that it may be fashioned like unto his glorious body*" (Phil. 3:20–21).

So the Bible clearly teaches that Jesus Christ now has a resurrected, tangible, spirit-plus-flesh-and-bones body, and that it is eternal—His spirit will never be separated from His body again. Yet 1 Timothy 1:17 calls it "invisible." Does that mean that it does not exist, or does it mean that in most instances the immortal, resurrected Christ does not reveal Himself, meaning make His physical body visible, since the time of His ascension into heaven? If man, after death and resurrection, will be able to "look for our Saviour," and see Him, that means that He still has a physical (but more refined and glorified) body. It is tangible and real. And that is the same situation with God the Father: He has a tangible body, but He doesn't choose to make it visible to man, except in very rare situations. It too can be called "invisible," but that term by no means indicates that it doesn't exist.

A simple comparison: I live high in the Rocky Mountains of Utah. I cannot look East and see New York City, nor can I gaze to the West and see San Francisco. Those faraway cities are "invisible" to me. But I have the knowledge, and the faith, that I can someday visit those cities, literally see them, and physically interact with their inhabitants. So it is with the "invisible" but tangible bodies of God the Son Jesus Christ, and God the Father: I have the scriptural promises and faith that I, and multitudes of others, will someday be able to see and associate with God the Father and His Son, Jesus Christ. Depending on the grace of God the Father and Christ Jesus, and their assessment of our hearts and our worthiness, we will someday see them, if they choose to allow us that privilege.

4. The fifth and final biblical passage which employs the word "invisible" is **Hebrews 11:27**. It constitutes part of the famous "roll call of faith," and in this verse is speaking of Moses:

> By faith Moses, when he was come to years, refused to be called the son of Pharoah's daughter;
> Choosing rather to suffer affliction with the people of God, than to enjoy the pleasures of sin for a season;
> Esteeming the reproach of Christ greater riches than the treasures in Egypt: for he had respect unto the recompence of the reward.
> By faith he forsook Egypt, not fearing the wrath of the king: for *he endured, as seeing him who is **invisible**.* (Heb. 11:24–27)

So in this passage, it is the yet-unborn Jesus Christ whom the author of Hebrews is calling "invisible" to Moses. Yet **Moses was allowed to see Yahweh face to face, on several occasions**: Ex. 3:2–6; 24:9–11, 16–17; 31:18; 33:9–11, 19–23; 34:28–33; Num. 12:6–8; Deut. 5:24. Obviously, the word "invisible" is being used here, as in the other passages cited in this section, in the sense of being *"generally unseen by mortals."* Clearly, the use of the word "invisible," in these five instances where it appears in the Bible, *carries no connotation of "incorporeal" or of "never ever seen because there is no existing form or shape."*

What of John 1:18: "No man hath seen God"?

In this passage the Apostle John, author of the fourth gospel, is giving a "bare-bones" synopsis of the missionary-oriented testimony of John the Baptist. John is quoted as saying, in John 1:18: *"No man hath seen God at any time; the only begotten Son, which is in the bosom of the Father, he hath declared him."*

One can tell if individuals who cite this passage as a proof-text are real seekers after truth by whether they put it in proper interpretational context by citing the other biblical passages which are related to it. If they don't, it's a sure sign that they are trying to obscure, rather than illuminate, the doctrine.

Jesus, in his "Bread of Life" sermon given in Capernaum, said these words:

> No man can come to me, except the Father which hath sent me draw him: and I will raise him up at the last day.
> It is written in the prophets, And they shall be all taught of God. Every man

therefore that hath heard, and hath learned of the Father, cometh unto me.
Not that any man hath seen the Father, *save he which is of God, he hath seen the Father.* (John 6:44–46; see Gen. 32:30; Acts 7:55–56)

Another key passage should also be linked to John 1:18. That key passage is Matthew 11:27: "All things are delivered unto me of my Father: and no man knoweth the Son, but the Father; *neither knoweth any man the Father, save the Son, and **he to whomsoever the Son will reveal him**"* (Matt. 11:27). Joseph Smith's inspired translation of this verse adds interesting amplification. It reads: *"and they to whom the Son will reveal himself; they shall see the Father also"* (JST Matt. 11:28).

These two clarifying passages, then, present an entirely different doctrine, and they both clarify the John 1:18 proof-text cited above. In John 6:46, the Lord clearly states that *"he which is of God, he hath seen the Father."* In Matthew 11:27, the Lord again clearly states that *He will reveal the Father to some individuals,* so they will have seen the Father. Obviously, the Bible tells of many worthy individuals, people who were and are "of God," who saw God, and that is what the Savior is acknowledging in this passage. (See later in this chapter for a listing of many scripture passages which tell of people who saw members of the Godhead.)

Also, it should be recalled from earlier in this chapter that God the Father is the father of spirits, meaning all mortals are His spirit children, so all of us have seen God the Father; we just can't remember it during our mortal probation. When death allows man to lay down his mortal remains, those memories of seeing and being with Heavenly Father will be vivid in their minds.

So, *I suggest that everyone, both Latter-day Saints and non-Latter-day Saints, would do well to link at least these three verses together in a scripture chain: John 1:18, John 6:46, and Matthew 11:27.* I believe that one should never cite just the one without the others. And I firmly believe that when someone cites *only* John 1:18, while knowing the messages of John 6:46 and Matt. 11:27, that person is clearly suspect in his motives and methods and definitely does not deserve to be trusted!

The passage recorded in Doctrine and Covenants section 67 lends significant understanding to this matter of who can see God. It says: *"no man has seen God at any time in the flesh, except quickened by the Spirit of God. Neither can any natural man abide the presence of God, neither after the carnal mind"* (D&C 67:11–12).

There is another related passage which is sometimes proof-texted: 1 John 4:12. That is unique, because John 1:18 and 1 Jn. 4:12 are the only two passages in the entire Bible which in any way purport to convey that God the Father cannot be seen, the erroneous message these proof-texters are seeking to convey. Like the other passages cited above, 1 John 4:12 should be read in context so as to be properly understood:

> Every spirit that confesseth not that Jesus Christ is come in the flesh is not of God: and this is that spirit of antichrist, whereof ye have heard that it should come; and even now already is it in the world.
>
> Ye are of God, little children, and have overcome them: because greater is he that is in you, than he that is in the world.
>
> They are of the world: therefore speak they of the world, and the world heareth them.
>
> We are of God: *he that knoweth God heareth us; he that is not of God heareth not us. Hereby know we the spirit of truth, and the spirit of error.*
>
> Beloved, let us love one another: for love is of God; and every one that loveth is

born of God, and knoweth God.

He that loveth not knoweth not God; for God is love.

In this was manifested the love of God toward us, because that God sent his only begotten Son into the world, that we might live through him.

Herein is love, not that we loved God, but that he loved us, and sent his Son to be the propitiation for our sins.

Beloved, if God so loved us, we ought also to love one another.

No man hath seen God at any time. If we love one another, God dwelleth in us, and his love is perfected in us.

Hereby know we that we dwell in him, and he in us, because he hath given us of his Spirit.

And we have seen and do testify that the Father sent the Son to be the Saviour of the world.

Whosoever shall confess that Jesus is the Son of God, God dwelleth in him, and he in God. (1 Jn. 4:3–15)

Obviously, John's subject in this portion of his epistle is the love of God, and his message is focused in his assertion that • "*love is of God; and every one that loveth is born of God, and knoweth God*" (1 Jn. 4:7). In this passage he gives a good partial explanation of Christ's benediction following the Last Supper, when He prayed for His disciples, and for the people they would in turn convert, petitioning • "*That they all may be one; as thou, Father, art in me, and I in thee, that they also may be one in us*" (John 17:21). Here, John's message is that • "If we love one another, God dwelleth in us, and his love is perfected in us. Hereby know we that we dwell in him, and he in us, because he hath given us of his Spirit" (1 Jn. 4:13). This is a key passage which explains how the Godhead are united as "one," and how the followers of Christ are also united with them: in purpose and in love, but not in the same mysterious "substance."

The phrase "no man hath seen God at any time" seems foreign to the passage. Who knows if it is an unauthorized insertion by some unnamed scribe as 1 John 5:7, sixteen verses later, is known and universally acknowledged to be. We don't know if John, by this time, had ever actually seen God the Father. We do know that He was present on the Mount of Transfiguration, along with Peter and James, when they and Jesus were visited by Moses and Elias (Matt. 17:1–5), and while they were there "a bright cloud overshadowed them: and *behold a voice out of the cloud, which said, This is my beloved Son, in whom I am well pleased; hear ye him.* And when the disciples heard it, they fell on their face, and were sore afraid" (Matt. 17:5–6). Whether John actually saw God the Father, or only heard His voice testifying of the divine Sonship of Jesus, that experience obviously was a powerful witness that God the Father lives, and speaks to man, and that He is a separate being from Jesus rather than the two of them being two different manifestations of the same physical (or metaphysical) "substance."

Other passages are relevant, and should be linked to John 1:18. For instance, Matthew 11:27. Here it is, in context:

At that time Jesus answered and said, I thank thee, O Father, Lord of heaven and earth, because thou hast hid these things from the wise and prudent, and hast revealed them unto babes.

Even so, Father: for so it seemed good in thy sight.

All things are delivered unto me of my Father: and no man knoweth the Son, but the Father; neither knoweth any man the Father, save the Son, and *he to whomsoever the Son will reveal him.* (Matt. 11:25–27)

Here, the Christ clearly teaches that those who "know" the Father are (1) Himself, the Son of God and (2) "he to whomsoever the Son will reveal him" (Matt. 11:27). That verse should most definitely be cross-referenced to John 1:18 and John 6:46. *Likewise, Acts 7:55–56*, in which Stephen sees God the Father and Jesus standing side by side, deserves to be connected to those other key passages. *Latter-day Saints obviously will opt to cross-reference Joseph Smith–History 1:17–20 and Doctrine and Covenants 76:19–23*—two other instances, in addition to Acts 7:55–56, when God the Father and Jesus Christ were seen standing together, side by side.

Can Man See God? Numerous Biblical Passages Say Yes!

• In His "Beatitudes," a central portion of His Sermon on the Mount, the Lord Jesus taught His disciples, • "Blessed are the pure in heart, for *they shall see God*" (Matt. 5:8). This, of course, is eternally impossible if God is an "unchangeable God" and is "incorporeal and invisible." So, is the promise of Jesus that the pure in heart "shall see God" a falsehood? a prophecy which will never be fulfilled? something to be "spiritualized," considered to be only "symbolic," and something that will never literally take place? Or does the problem lie in the unsubstantiateable teaching that God is "incorporeal and invisible"?

• When Jacob, in the Old Testament, proclaimed that • "*I have seen God face to face, and my life is preserved*" (Gen. 32:30), was he bearing false witness, or did he literally see God "face to face"? How would that be possible if the "unchangeable" God is "incorporeal and invisible"? Was Jacob's testimony false, or does the falsehood lie in the "incorporeal and invisible"interpretation?

• When Moses saw the burning bush and heard the voice of God saying, • "I am the God of thy father, the God of Abraham, the God of Isaac, and the God of Jacob," the scriptural account states that • "*Moses hid his face; for he was afraid to look upon God*" (Ex. 3:5–6). Why would he be afraid to look upon God if God is incorporeal and literally has no body or physical shape or form?

• Was God lying when He told Moses to • "Go unto the people, and sanctify them to day and to morrow, and let them wash their clothes, And be ready against the third day: for *the third day the* LORD *will come down in the sight of all the people upon mount Sinai*" (Ex. 19:10–11)?

• If God is incorporeal and invisible, and thus cannot be seen, what did God mean when He told Moses to • "Go down, charge the people, lest they *break through unto the* LORD *to gaze*, and many of them perish" (Ex. 19:21)?

• When the book of Exodus records that Moses and more than seventy elders of Israel ascended the mountain and there • "*they saw God*" (Ex. 24:11), is that a falsehood, or does the falsehood lie in the interpretation that the "unchangeable" God is "incorporeal and invisible"?

• Is it a falsehood when the Bible records that • "as Moses entered into the tabernacle, the cloudy pillar descended, and stood at the door of the tabernacle, and *the Lord* talked with Moses. . . . And *the* LORD *spake unto Moses face to face, as a man speaketh unto his friend*" (Ex. 33:9, 11), or is the dogma false that says God in "incorporeal" and has no bodily form or shape?

• When God rebuked Aaron and Miriam, telling them that with some prophets He would only communicate in visions, but said of Moses that • "*With him will I speak mouth to mouth, even apparently*, and not in dark speeches; and *the similitude of the*

LORD *shall he behold*" (Num. 12:8), wasn't God again saying that He would commune directly with Moses, face to face?

• Was the Old Testament chronicler lying when he wrote that • "there arose not a prophet since in Israel like unto Moses, *whom the LORD knew face to face*" (Deut. 34:10)?

• When the barren parents of Samson received from a heavenly visitor the promise • "thou shalt conceive, and bear a son," they suddenly became terrified, and Manoah said unto his wife, • "We shall surely die, *because we have seen God*" (Jud. 13:22), were they lying in their assertion that they had actually seen God, or does the falsehood lie in the doctrine that the "unchangeable" God is "incorporeal and invisible"?

• Should the biblical testimony concerning Solomon, that • "*the LORD God of Israel, which had appeared unto him twice*" be discarded because of the unscriptural doctrine that God is a formless, incorporeal "everywhere blob," or does the fault lie in the incorrect doctrine itself?

• Is the often-quoted testimony of Job that • "though after my skin worms destroy this body, yet *in my flesh shall I see God*" (Job 19:26) a false testimony, or does the falsehood lie in the doctrine that the "unchangeable" God is "incorporeal and invisible"?

• When the Prophet Isaiah recorded his vivid description of the LORD sitting upon His throne, and his testimony that • "*mine eyes have seen the King, the LORD of hosts*" (Isa. 6:5) is recorded in canonized scripture, should that scripture be disregarded because it is in direct opposition to the God is incorporeal dogma?

• If God has no form or shape, what possible meaning can be drawn from Jesus' rebuke to His Jewish critics that • "Ye have neither heard his voice at any time, *nor seen his shape*" (John 5:37)? His question has no discernable meaning unless God has a shape!

• If Jesus is of the same invisible and intangible "substance" as God the Father, then how is Jesus able to promise His followers that • "he that loveth me shall be loved of my Father, and I will love him, and *will manifest myself to him*" (John 14:21)?

• "When Stephen, who was being challenged and questioned by the unbelieving Jewish Sanhedrin, testified, • "Behold, *I see the heavens opened, and the Son of man standing on the right hand of God*" (Acts 7:55–56), was he lying? Or, if he actually saw the Father and the Son standing side by side, how could that be possible if the "unchangeable" God is "incorporeal and invisible" and if Jesus Christ and God the Father are of the same, undivided "substance," and the "unchangeable" God is "incorporeal and invisible"? Can they be in two places at the same time if they are a single, undivided "substance"? Does the falsehood lie in Stephen's testimony, or in the interpretation that the "unchangeable" God is "incorporeal and invisible"?

• If the mortal Jesus was actually God the Father manifested in mortal form, as asserted in "trinitarian" doctrine and now is a resurrected being which cannot be separated from His resurrected body any more, does that mean that God the Father now has a resurrected body? Or is the Father supposedly still "incorporeal"?

• How should this passage in Hebrews be interpreted? • "Follow peace with all men, and holiness, *without which no man shall see the Lord*" (Heb. 12:14).

• And if God is "incorporeal," and doesn't have a resurrected body, then how can this passage from First John be interpreted? • "Beloved, now are we the sons of God, and it doth not yet appear what we shall be: but we know that, when he shall appear, *we shall be like him; for we shall see him as he is*" (1 Jn. 3:2).

• And finally, if God is a shapeless, incorporeal "everywhere blob," how can the reference in Revelation 22 be interpreted? • "but the throne of God and of the Lamb shall be in it; and his servants shall serve him: And *they shall see his face*; and his name shall be in their foreheads" (Rev. 22:3–4).

Most definitely, numerous Bible passages state, unequivocally, that **God can be seen by man**, under the proper conditions!

Are the Manifestations of God *Not* God Himself?

As Torrey's propositions about the nature of God in his "God As Spirit" chapter continue, the hole he dug for himself with his interpretational statement "*To say God is spirit is to say God is incorporeal and invisible*" (Torrey, 13), continues to grow deeper. His outline using statements of "what the Bible teaches," followed by his "propositions" with their explanations is continued here. However, since almost all of the scriptures he cites are already cited in this chapter, they will be quoted by reference only.

> **II. The manifestation of Spirit in visible form.**
> [He quotes John 1:32 and Heb. 1:7.]
> *SECOND PROPOSITION: That which is spirit may manifest itself in visible form.*
> **III. God manifested in visible form.**
> [He quotes Ex. 24:9, 10.]
> *THIRD PROPOSITION: God has in times past manifested Himself in visible form.*
> **V. What was seen in these manifestations of God.** [One wonders if V, instead of IV, is a typographical error, or whether IV has been edited out of the book in its later editions.]
> [He quotes John 1:18; he then quotes Ex. 33:18–23.]
> *FOURTH PROPOSITION: That which was seen in these manifestations of God was not God Himself—God in his essence—but a manifestation of God.*
> QUESTION: Is there any contradiction between Ex. 24:9, 10 ("Then went up Moses, and Aaron, Nadab and Abihu, and seventy of the elders of Israel; and *they saw the God of Israel*"), Isa. 6:1 ("In the year that king Uzziah died *I saw also the Lord* sitting upon a throne, high and lifted up, and his train filled the temple"), and Jno. 1:18 ('No man hath seen God at any time; the only begotten Son, which is in the bosom of the Father, he hath declared Him")?
> ANSWER: None whatever. To illustrate: A man may see the reflection of his face in a glass. It would be true for the man to say "I saw my face," and also true to say "I never saw my face." *So men have seen a manifestation of God, and it is perfectly true to say those men saw God. No man ever saw God as He is in His invisible essence, and so it is perfectly true to say: "No man hath seen God at any time."* (Torrey, 14–15)

There, in this outline and set of propositions, Dr. Torrey sets forth the illogical, unbiblical, and unwarranted assumption that is characteristic of "trinitarian" theologizing: that (1) God the Father, and also the premortal Jesus Christ, had no bodily shape nor image ("*God in His invisible essence*"), and (2) that which was seen in the numerous appearances of God recorded in the Old Testament was not really God Himself, but only a "manifestation" of God (Torrey wrote: "*That which was seen in these manifestations of God was not God Himself . . . but a manifestation of God*"). In other words, God supposedly "turned on" some type of physical appearance in these numerous appearances recorded in the sacred scriptures, but that wasn't really God Himself; it was only a false representation of His presence.

Only *manifestations* of God? What a broad, sweeping, all-encompassing rationalization and assumption! What a tremendous house of straw has been erected over the misinterpretation of two one-line scriptural phrases: "God is a spirit . . ." (John 4:24) and "No man hath seen God at any time . . ." (John 1:18)

Is there any scriptural evidence, at all, that God "turns His physical appearance on and off" (my terminology) in situations where He wants to be visible? Not one iota! No scripture at all is ever even offered to support this scriptural dodge.

There are literally hundreds of scriptural passages where God, speaking about Himself (speaking in the first person) speaks of His possessing body parts. There are literally hundreds of other scriptural passages where authorized, knowledgeable prophets and Apostles, who most certainly knew about the nature of God and who most certainly had communed directly with Him, speak of God's body parts. Yet the literal nature of all those passages describing appearances of God are rejected, or intentionally ignored by "trinitarian" theologians, or are interpreted by them as only being "metaphors" or "spiritual" or "figures of speech."

Man, Not God, Is Changed When "Eyes Are Opened"

What happens when God or angels appear to man, or when God communicates his will to man? Does God's physical appearance change so He can be seen, or is man somehow changed so he can be receptive to the communication and be preserved as he sees the glory of God? The scriptures, both ancient and modern, make a clear case that *it is man who is changed, not God changing His appearance from an incorporeal being to becoming a manifestation or illusion.* The scriptural term used, when man is being changed to accommodate his communication with deity, typically refers to his eyes being opened. Here are examples:

• When Adam and Eve were being tempted in the Garden of Eden, they were told: "God doth know that in the day ye eat thereof, then *your eyes shall be opened*, and ye shall be as gods, knowing good and evil" (Gen. 3:5, 7). • Hagar, at the well: "*God opened her eyes*, and she saw a well of water; and she went, and filled the bottle with water, and gave the lad drink" (Gen. 21:19).

• Balaam, when an angel blocked his donkey's way: "*the* LORD *opened the eyes of Balaam*, and he saw the angel of the LORD standing in the way, and his sword drawn in his hand" (Num. 22:31; 24:3, 4, 15–16). • Elisha, showing his servant the angelic hosts protecting them from the Syrians: "Elisha prayed, and said, LORD, I pray thee, open his eyes, that he may see. And *the* LORD *opened the eyes of the young man; and he saw*: and, behold, the mountain was full of horses and chariots of fire round about Elisha" (2 Kgs. 6:17, 20). • The Psalmist: "*Open thou mine eyes*, that I may behold wondrous things out of thy law" (Ps. 119:18). • The disciples who were visited by the risen Lord on the road to Emmaus: "And *their eyes were opened, and they knew him*; and he vanished out of their sight" (Luke 24:31). • The Pharisees, questioning the blind man to whom Jesus had restored his eyesight: "What sayest thou of him, that *he hath opened thine eyes*? He said, He is a prophet" (John 9:17, 21, 26, 30, 32). • Paul, telling of his vision of Jesus, calling him to preach to "the Gentiles, unto whom now I send thee, *To open their eyes*, and to turn them from darkness to light, and from the power of Satan unto God" (Acts 26:17–18).

Likewise, the concept of eyes being opened is frequently encountered concerning **God's eyes being opened** to receive the prayers of His petitioners. • Thus Solomon prayed, as his temple was being dedicated, asking God "*That thine eyes may be open toward this house night and day*" (1 Kgs. 8:29). • He prayed "*That thine eyes may be open unto the supplication of thy servant*, and unto the supplication of thy people Israel"

(1 Kgs. 8:52. See also 2 Chr. 6:40–42). • And shortly afterward, "the LORD appeared to Solomon by night, and said unto him, I have heard thy prayer, and have chosen this place to myself . . . *Now mine eyes shall be open, and mine ears attent unto the prayer that is made in this place*" (2 Chr. 7:12–15). • Nehemiah prayed, "O LORD God of heaven . . . *Let thine ear now be attentive, and thine eyes open*, that thou mayest hear the prayer of thy servant" (Neh. 1:5–6). And on, and on.

Now, is there anything different (1) between petitioners asking the LORD to open the eyes of other individuals so they will see visions and angels, (2) petitioners asking the LORD to open His eyes and be attentive to their prayers, and (3) the LORD telling Solomon that His [the LORD's] "eyes shall be open"? Is there any scriptural passage that says that the mortals' eyes were literal but the LORD's eyes were only figurative? There is no basis, whatsoever, for that "figurative" assumption. When the LORD says His eyes will be open, and His ears will be attentive, it seems impossible that anyone in good conscience could attempt to deny the literalness of that passage, and the hundreds of others in which God speaks, in first person, about His body parts and His physical image.

It should be noted that **latter-day scripture also contains very significant passages about eyes being opened as glorious visions are received**: • "By the power of the Spirit *our eyes were opened and our understandings were enlightened*, so as to see and understand the things of God—" (D&C 76:12). • "And while we meditated upon these things, *the Lord touched the eyes of our understandings and they were opened*, and the glory of the Lord shone round about. And we beheld the glory of the Son, on the right hand of the Father, and received of his fulness; And saw the holy angels" (D&C 76:19–21). • "*The veil was taken from our minds, and the eyes of our understanding were opened.* We saw the Lord standing upon the breastwork of the pulpit, before us; and under his feet was a paved work of pure gold, in color like amber. His eyes were as a flame of fire; the hair of his head was white like the pure snow; his countenance shone above the brightness of the sun; and his voice was as the sound of the rushing of great waters, even the voice of Jehovah, . . ." (D&C 110:1–3). • "And as I wondered, *my eyes were opened, and my understanding quickened*, and I perceived that the Lord went not in person among the wicked and the disobedient who had rejected the truth, to teach them; But behold, from among the righteous, He organized his forces and appointed messengers, clothed with power and authority, and commissioned them to go forth and carry the light of the gospel to them that were in darkness" (D&C 138:29–30). • Again, the process of man's being changed in order that he can see God, is best described in scripture by the ancient prophet Moses: "*But now mine own eyes have beheld God; but not my natural, but my spiritual eyes, for my natural eyes could not have beheld*; for I should have withered and died in his presence; but *his glory was upon me; and I beheld his face, for I was transfigured before him*" (Moses 1:11).

But it is all the passages like those listed above that help one to understand John 6:46, the passage which explains the "trinitarian's" favorite proof-text: John 1:18— "*Not that any man hath seen the Father, save he which is of God, **he hath seen the Father**" (John 6:46).

These latter-day visions, in which prophets of God saw either the resurrected bodies of the Father and the Son or the spirit body of Jesus, bear solemn witness that the "trinitarians' " unscriptural interpretation that God is incorporeal, and their unjustified assumption that when members of the Godhead are seen they, in reality, are not being seen but only "manifestations" of them are being viewed, are erroneous and without scriptural support.

Conflicting "Nature of God" Statements Found in Theological Treatises

There was a brief section which was derived from non-Latter-day Saint materials in the preceding chapter that I opted to transplant to this chapter because it, perhaps, would be a better "fit" in this chapter's context. This is what was transferred to this position:

Descriptions of the attributes of God found in "trinitarian" theological treatises often include statements or phrases that are not in accord with scriptural principles. In particular, they lack the additional insights found in the Latter-day Saint scriptures, and they lack essential information which would alter their views if they were more fully informed (and, obviously, if they would accept those volumes as divinely revealed scriptures).

Without belaboring their statements or attempting to refute them in this chapter, several of these conflicting statements concerning the nature of God are pointed out in this brief addendum. Most of them are addressed in other chapters of this book.

A volume selected as a thorough, representative work of "trinitarian" exposition is Elwell's *Evangelical Dictionary of Theology,* which is filled with valuable insights on many subjects. However, under the heading of "*God, Attributes of,*" and the subheading of "*God Is an Invisible, Personal, Living, and Active Spirit,*" the following statements are found. They are listed here followed by their *Evangelical Dictionary of Theology* page numbers:

1. "As a spirit, God is invisible" (451).
2. "No one has ever seen God or ever will (1 Tim. 6:16)" (451).
3. "A spirit does not have flesh and bones (Luke 24:39)" (451).
4. "In transcending the physical aspects of human personhood God thus transcends the physical aspects of both maleness and femaleness. However, since both male and female are created in God's image, we may think of both as like God in their distinctly nonphysical, personal male and female qualities. In this context the Bible's use of masculine personal pronouns for God conveys primarily the connotation of God's vital personal qualities and secondarily any distinctive functional responsibilities males may have" (451–52).
5. "In fact, God is superpersonal, tripersonal. The classical doctrine of the Trinity coherently synthesizes the Bible's teaching about God" (452).
6. "The unity of the one divine essence and being emphasized in the NT concept of a personal spirit implies simplicity or indivisibility. Neither the 'trinitarian' personal distinctions nor the multiple attributes divide the essential unity of the divine being. And that essential, ontological oneness is not torn apart by the incarnation or even the death of Jesus" (452).

Within the next subsection of Elwell's *Evangelical Dictionary of Theology,* titled "*Metaphysically, God is Self-existent, Eternal and Unchanging,*" are other statements which are misleading, or not in harmony with the scriptures, as understood by Latter-day Saints. They are:

7. "God is self-existent. All other spirits are created and so have a beginning. They owe their existence to another" (453).
8. "God's life is from within himself, not anything that had a beginning in the space-time world. God has no beginning, period of growth" (453).
9. "God fills space and time with his presence" (453).

10. "God is not limited by space or time, or the succession of events in time" (453).
11. "God who is present at all times and in all places" (453).
12. "Mankind is not (like Christ) begotten of God or an emanation from God of the same divine nature" (458).
13. "To seek to be as God in a biblical perspective is not deeper spirituality but rebellious idolatry or blasphemy" (458).

Presumably, an adequate rebuttal of some of these statements has been found in this chapter. The next three chapters will address most of the rest of the ideas represented above, though they will not speak directly to these particular statements.

Summary

1. A chapter from the writings of Dr. R.A. Torrey, a well-respected theologian from days past, was selected as a representative basic-level presentation of the "God is a spirit" concept from both Catholic and Protestant theologies, and it was examined and critiqued point by point.

2. In-depth explanations of the most common proof-texts cited on this subject by "trinitarians" were presented. They included John 4:24 (God is a spirit), Luke 24:39 (flesh and bones, as ye see me have), Gen. 1:27 (image), the five biblical passages which refer to God as "invisible" (Rom. 1:20; Col. 1:15, 16; 1 Tim. 1:17, and Heb. 11:27), and John 1:18 (no man hath seen God).

3. Bible passages were cited which teach the nature of man's spirit, followed by a detailed listing of Latter-day Saint teachings about "spirit" and "spirit beings."

4. In answer to the question, "Is God the Father invisible?" the point was made that God has a tangible body which can be seen by man's "spiritual eyes," but that he rarely chooses to show himself to most mortal beings.

5. The author suggests that everyone should cross-reference John 1:18 with John 6:46 and Matt. 11:27.

6. Numerous Bible passages were cited which indicate that man has seen God on many occasions.

7. The erroneous teaching that Bible appearances of God to man were not God Himself but only "manifestations" of God was critiqued and shown to be unscriptural.

8. When God is seen by man, it is not God that is changed so as to be seen. Rather, it is man's spiritual eyes which are opened, no matter whether it is an actual in-person visitation or a vision which is being seen.

9. Numerous statements which conflict with Latter-day Saint understanding of the scriptures were listed from typical "nature of God" theological descriptions so as to demonstrate what many typical "trinitarian" understandings are on those subjects.

CHAPTER 5

THE "THREENESS" AND THE "ONENESS" OF THE FATHER, SON, AND HOLY SPIRIT

How Many Gods Do Christians Worship?

Inherent in the belief system of almost every Christian faith is the core concept that they worship (1) God the Father, (2) God the Father's Son, Jesus Christ, who came and dwelt on this earth in the meridian of time, and (3) the Holy Ghost. That these beings are worshiped is clear indication that they all are regarded as Gods—supreme beings!

Each of these divine personages is identified in the Bible and other scriptures with numerous names, many of which are indicators of some trait or location which identifies them in the minds of those who apply the hundreds of names which they, in the aggregate, hold, and to which they are believed to respond.

Several passages in the New Testament refer to them in cumulative form as the "Godhead" (cf. Acts 17:29; Rom. 1:20; Col. 2:9). The next-to-the-last verse in the Gospel of Matthew very likely is the most-often-quoted of all biblical verses about the members of the Godhead because it mentions each of them individually: "Go ye therefore, and teach all nations, baptizing them in the name of the Father, and of the Son, and of the Holy Ghost" (Matt. 28:19).

So, do the math! How many personages are (1) the Father, (2) the Son, and (3) the Holy Ghost? If your answer is three, you are to be congratulated; you most likely are eligible for promotion from first to second grade if you presently attend grammar school! If your answer is other than three, you may be held over for another year or two.

Unfortunately, some Christian faiths have a math problem and believe that one plus one plus one only equals one! They, apparently, hark back to *The Anathemas of the Second Council of Constantinople, which devised this wording in AD 553*. [Dictionary definition: **Anathema: (a)** a ban or curse solemnly pronounced by ecclesiastical authority and accompanied by excommunication; **(b)** the denunciation of something as accursed; **(c)** a vigorous denunciation (*Merriam Webster's Collegiate Dictionary*, 11th Edition, 45)]. Participants in that Council wrote the creedal statement that:

> If anyone does not confess that the Father and the Son and the Holy Spirit are *one nature or essence* [reality], one power or authority, worshiped as *a trinity of the same*

essence [reality], *one deity in three hypostases or persons,* **let him be anathema.** For there is one God and Father, of whom are all things, and one Lord Jesus Christ, through whom are all things, and one Holy Spirit, in whom are all things" (Leith, "The Second Council of Constantinople," 553). (*Creeds of the Churches,* Anathema I, 46).

This chapter is written to address that mathematical conundrum. How many is one? How many is three? Is there any scripturally justifiable interpretation that exists for the concept that there is only *one* God? ***Does a church council's ancient anathema against anyone believing that there are three distinct beings in the Godhead change the math?*** Does a proclamation that one plus one plus one only equals *one* make that a sacred truth?

In this chapter the implications of this man-created mathematical enigma and the gross hermeneutical errors which may have played a part in its formulation, and later attempts at doctrinal justification for it, will be examined.

Deuteronomists' Efforts to Assert Monotheism by Restructuring Old Testament Scriptures

Does the Bible really teach what ancient theologians termed "monotheism"? Clearly, the Old and New Testament jointly speak of more than one God: God the Father, God the Son Jesus Christ, and God the Holy Ghost. Many hundreds of biblical passages refer to them, both singly and collectively. They often refer to two or more Godhead members being present at the same time, or of one of them speaking to another. Yet ancient interpreters sought to change and mold the Israelite concept of God into belief in only one God.

During the past two decades, interesting new research and biblical historical analysis has shed new light and understanding on what went on in ancient attempts to reshape Israel's concept of deity—a process which apparently was a precursor to the interpretational thinking which shaped early Christian beliefs and creeds.

An English scholar, Margaret Barker, has caused serious reassessment of long-held assumptions. In the introduction to her book *The Great Angel: A Study of Israel's God,* after citing Phil. 2:6–11 and Rom. 1:3–4, she states her thesis:

> All the titles are there: **Son of God, Lord** and **Messiah.** It has been the practice to treat the titles separately, as if each designated a different aspect of belief, and the separate strands were only brought together by the creative theologizing of the first Christians. I should like to explore a different possibility, namely that *these three titles, and several others, belonged together in the expectations and traditions of first-century Palestine, and that the first Christians fitted Jesus into an existing pattern of belief. The rapid development of early Christian teaching was due to the fact that so much of the scheme already existed; the life and death of Jesus was the means of reinterpreting the older hopes.* This is not a new idea; from the beginning Christians have claimed that Jesus was the fulfilment of the hopes expressed in the Old Testament. Our problem is to know exactly what those hopes were, and how they were expressed in first-century Palestine. What did the key words mean? *The discovery of the Dead Sea Scrolls has forced us to redraw the picture of Judaism in the time of Jesus; many of the old certainties have been destroyed by this new knowledge.* Many of the 'sources' for New Testament background studies (writings of the rabbis, the gnostic texts) have now been shown to belong to a period two or three centuries later than the time of Jesus. . . . *the evidence points consistently in one direction and indicates that pre-Christian Judaism was not*

monotheistic in the sense that we use that word. The roots of Christian trinitarian theology lie in pre-Christian Palestinian beliefs about the angels. There were many in first-century Palestine who still retained a world-view derived from the more ancient religion of Israel in which there was a High God and several Sons of God, one of whom was Yahweh, the Holy One of Israel. Yahweh, the Lord, could be manifested on earth in human form, as an angel or in the Davidic king. It was as a manifestation of Yahweh, the Son of God, that Jesus was acknowledged as Son of God, Messiah and Lord. (Barker, *The Great Angel*, 2–3)

Margaret Barker begins her explanation by focusing on what she calls "a crucial distinction":

> This comprehensive treatment does not, however, **distinguish between the two different words for God and therefore ignores a crucial distinction**. There are those called sons of El Elyon, sons of El or Elohim, all clearly heavenly beings, and there are **those called sons of Yahweh or the Holy One who are human**. This distinction is important for at least two reasons: **Yahweh was one of the sons of El Elyon, God Most High. In other words he was described as a heavenly being**. Thus the annunciation narrative has the term 'Son of the Most High' (Luke 1:32) and the demoniac recognized his exorcist as 'Son of the Most High God' (Mark 5:7). *Jesus is not called the son of Yahweh nor the son of the Lord, but he is called Lord. We also know that whoever wrote the New Testament translated the name Yahweh by Kyrios, Lord.* (See, for example, the quotation from Deuteronomy 6:5: 'You shall love Yahweh your God . . .' which is rendered in Luke 10:27 'You shall love the Lord [Kyrios] your God.') *This suggests that the Gospel writers, in using the terms 'Lord' and 'Son of God Most High,' saw Jesus as an angel figure, and gave him their version of the sacred name Yahweh.* (Barker, *The Great Angel*, 4–5)

Throughout the chapter she cites numerous passages showing differences between "sons of El Elyon, sons of El or Elohim, all clearly heavenly beings" and "sons of Yahweh or the Holy One who are human." Then, in chapter 2, she begins the explanation of the Deuteronomic reform, and draws a clear distinction between "the Deuteronomist" and "the Chronicler":

> The great destruction wrought by the Babylonians at the beginning of the sixth century followed hard upon the so-called Deuteronomic reform. What was destroyed was therefore in a state of flux, since *we are by no means certain that the Deuteronomic reform was the wholesale success claimed for it. The two accounts of what happened in the reign of Josiah differ in detail and emphasis: the Chronicler (2 Chr. 34–5)* described finding the lawbook, renewing the covenant and keeping a great Passover; *the Deuteronomist (2 Kings 22–3)* described in detail all the abominations that were swept away and wrote but briefly of the great Passover. We do not know, therefore, what happened at that time. *All we know is that the Deuteronomists wrote themselves into history at this point, since, in 2 Kings, they clearly identified the programme of reform with their own ideals. If this is accurate, then we have evidence for a sweeping away of everything that did not accord with one particular point of view;* if it is not accurate, i.e. *if it is only a retrospective improvement on fact, then we have evidence for a rewriting of history on a massive scale, to the point where it becomes extremely difficult for us to call it history in any modern sense of the word. We should call it propaganda.* It is a common enough phenomenon in this century to see a radical change of government or ruling philosophy accompanied by a rewriting of the past. *If the keynote of the Deuteronomists was an emphasis*

of the exclusion of all other gods, then it is easy to see that any traces of earlier religious practices in Jerusalem, had they been concerned with things other than sacred history, the Exodus and the cult of Yahweh alone, would have had little chance of surviving. It is a fact that the writings of First Isaiah, our best source of information on the pre-Deuteronomic religion of Jerusalem, have no concern for just these things which the reformers made so central. *Here then is the first question: What did they reform, either in fact, or by creative history writing? Was there more, far more, in the religion of pre-exilic Jerusalem, than the later writers wished to perpetuate?* (Barker, *The Great Angel,* 12–13)

It is beyond the scope of this book to pursue this topic in depth. Ms. Barker has done a thorough job, drawing a book-full of evidence (from, as her chapter titles indicate, the Exile, the Old Testament, Wisdom, Angels, the Name, Philo, Jewish Writers, the Gnostics, the first Christians, and the New Testament), *all making the case that God the Father and Jesus Christ are two separate beings, and that Jesus is Jehovah.* What is important, in this context, is that there is strong evidence that Deuteronomist reformers tried to alter the Old Testament so it would appear to be monotheistic in its message. This statement summarizes part of what her book conveys:

> *The restructuring of Israel's traditions and writings during the exile and the years which followed must always be borne in mind when reading the Old Testament. So too must the fact that many traces of the older ways survived, as can be seen in Dan. 7, and were still being removed at the beginning of the Christian era,* as can be seen from the significant differences between the Qumran versions of certain Hebrew texts and those we now use. *Such traces of the older ways as escaped the ancient scribes are often removed by modern readers as they read, since we have all been steeped in one particular view of the Old Testament and its monotheism.* The first Christians did not read it as we do; *they still knew that Yahweh was the son of Elyon.* To read the Old Testament without our customary presuppositions is an illuminating experience. (Barker, *The Great Angel,* 26–27)

Even more enlightening concerning the message of *The Great Angel* is the brief review of that book which she included in her preface to her later work: *The Great High Priest.* She wrote,

> It is no longer wise to consider one form of Judaism as "orthodoxy" and all others as sectarian, it being recognized that *there was a huge difference between Rabbinic Judaism and the varieties of the faith in the second temple period. The Sages had not been preserving the older ways but creating a substantially new system after the destruction of the temple in 70 CE.* Part of the method was defining the canon, but *the books excluded from that Hebrew canon were preserved by Christian scribes. We now know that even the text of the hebrew Scriptures was different before the advent of Christianity. It is becoming increasingly clear that the Old Testament which should accompany the New Testament is not the one usually included in the Bible. An exploration of the "surface" of the Old Testament is no longer enough, nor can "canonical" texts continue to enjoy a privileged position. . . .*
> *The Trinitarian faith of the Church had grown from the older Hebrew belief in a pluriform deity,* and so the earliest Christian exegetes had not been innovators when *they understood the* Lord *of the Hebrew Scriptures as the Second God, the Son of El Elyon.* The One whom they recognized in Jesus had been the Lord, and so they declared "Jesus is the Lord." This was the subject of my book *The Great Angel: A Study of Israel's Second God* (1992). *Monotheism, in the way that it is usually understood by*

biblical scholars, had been a consequence of changes made in the seventh century BCE, and was not part of the older faith. (Barker, *The Great High Priest*, xi–xii)

For further information concerning the many changes to Jewish scriptures and doctrines during the eras discussed above, see chapter 6 in the "Lessons Learned from the History of Hermeneutics" section.

Understanding "Only One God" Passages

This section may be dealing with passages influenced by the Deuteronomists.

Those who assert that there is only one God typically turn to a few Old Testament verses as proof-texts and cite them out of context. Several of these passages appear in the Pentateuch (the first five books of the Jewish and Christian scriptures: Genesis through Deuteronomy in the Old Testament). Most of the others cluster in Isaiah, chapters 43–46.

Before reviewing them, the reader would do well to be aware of certain key scriptural teachings which need to be understood in able to properly understand the meanings of these proof-texts:

1. All the "only one God" passages in the Old Testament have reference to Jehovah, who is frequently addressed or referred to as the LORD (in all capital letters).

2. It is Jehovah who is frequently identified as the God who is the creator of this earth, as the God who covenanted with Abraham, Isaac, and Jacob; and as the God who revealed the Ten Commandments to Moses and said, "I am the LORD thy God, . . . thou shalt have no other gods before me."

3. An overwhelmingly large majority of the hundreds of scriptural passages which identify the physical and emotional character of God are passages which are referring to Jehovah.

The need to apply basic hermeneutical principles of interpretation. One of the basic principles of scriptural interpretation is that the character of the "circumstances peculiar to the writings" must be taken into account. In his well-known textbook *Principles of Biblical Interpretation*, Louis Berkhof summarizes these circumstances under three headings: (1) "the original readers and hearers," (2) "the purpose of the author," and (3) "the time of life, the special circumstances, and the frame of mind" (see Berkhof, 124–28). *In the case of every one of these "only one God" passages typically used as proof-texts, (1) God is speaking to theologically unschooled peoples, and (2) the central point God is stressing is that the Israelites must not worship the false gods of surrounding nations.*

Moses was speaking to a great mass of illiterate slaves who had lived all their lives under the shadows of Egypt's pagan gods. At their first opportunity, when they thought their Prophet Moses was dead, they reverted to idol worship and pagan worship practices, compelling Aaron to make them a golden calf (Ex. 32). In the case of Moses' Egyptian slaves, Jehovah wasn't giving them all the facts about their eternal status and relationships. *He only gave them as much knowledge as they could handle when He said He was the only God they should serve. Today this is called conveying information "only on the need to know" basis.* He'd even taken the higher priesthood, which held "the key to the knowledge of God" out of their midst because of their weaknesses (D&C 84:17–25).

Isaiah, in his day, was dealing with idolatrous Israel and backsliding Judah, both of which were surrounded by nations worshipping dozens of pagan gods who won easy sway by tempting the Abrahamic peoples to "worship" via the tantalizingly attractive sexual rites practiced in their groves and high places. Though the inhabitants of the surrounding lands typically worshiped an entire pantheon of mythical beings whom they regarded as divine beings, the word of the LORD through Isaiah was that backsliding Israel was to worship Jehovah, and Him alone.

Again, in communicating with them, Jehovah was not making deep theological statements on the nature of God, He was telling them to stay away from the fertility rites and idolatries that were all around them. He was making it plain that He, Jehovah, was the divine being who had created this earth and fashioned the process for their spirits to possess mortal bodies upon it. And more important, He was making the point that He, and He alone, would be their Savior and their Redeemer.

While dealing with these peoples on a "need to know" basis, Jehovah did not tell them about God the Father, nor about God the Holy Spirit. They weren't ready for a fuller understanding of the Godhead at that point. They weren't ready to delve into the glorious premortal events which were later revealed and confided to the children of men. It should again be recalled, in this context, that God had previously told Moses, "*only an account of this earth, and the inhabitants thereof, give I unto you*" (Moses 1:35). At that point in their progression, they were only told of the God who was working directly with them on a day-to-day basis: Jehovah, the firstborn Son of God the Father.

When Jehovah spoke through Isaiah and said that "beside me there is no Savior," He was telling backsliding Israel the truth, but certainly not the whole truth. He didn't explain about God the Father or God the Holy Ghost who were backing him up in His responsibilities; He just told them that He was their God, and they should follow Him and no one else. And, for sure, they were to stay away from all the pagan gods whose false priests were everywhere available to tempt them. He didn't explain about the Atonement He would work in their behalf many centuries later, when He would be born into mortality—that event which was to be the focal point of all human history. Though He told them repeatedly that He was their Savior and their Redeemer, few, if any of them, had the slightest inkling of the real meaning of those terms.

In short, **those of the "trinitarian" persuasion who try to assert that these "only one god" passages are profound statements on the nature of God and of the Godhead, rather than specific warnings about the dangers of idolatry, are twisting the scriptures just as hard as they can.** So that they can't separate these proof-text passages from their real contexts, those contexts are included, below, wrapped around the proof-texts they typically recite.

With these background and interpretive principles as their over-arching context, the following passages now are cited. The portion typically cited as "only one God" evidence is in bold italics; the context showing that the passage is given in a context of warning backsliding Israel not to become involved with the false gods of the lands are highlighted in italic type:

• [1] "*I am the LORD thy God*, which have brought thee out of the land of Egypt, out of the house of bondage. *Thou shalt have no other gods before me. Thou shalt not make unto thee any graven image, or any likeness of any thing that is in heaven above, or that is in the earth beneath, or that is in the water under the earth: Thou shalt not bow down thyself to them, nor serve them*" (Ex. 20:2–5; Deut. 5:6–9).

• [2] "in all things that I have said unto you be circumspect: *and make no mention of the name of other gods, neither let it be heard out of thy mouth*. . . . mine Angel shall go before thee, and bring thee in unto the Amorites, and the Hittites, and the Perizzites, and the Canaanites, and the Hivites, and the Jebusites: and I will cut them off. *Thou shalt not bow down to their gods, nor serve them, nor do after their works: but thou shalt utterly overthrow them, and quite break down their images.* And **ye shall serve the LORD your God**" (Ex. 23:13, 23–25).

• [3] "*ye shall destroy their altars, break their images, and cut down their groves*: For **thou shalt worship no other god**: for the LORD, whose name is Jealous, is a jealous God: *Lest thou make a covenant with the inhabitants of the land, and they go a whoring after their gods, and do sacrifice unto their gods, and one call thee, and thou eat of his sacrifice*" (Ex. 34:13–15).

• [4] "Take heed unto yourselves, lest ye forget the covenant of the LORD your God, which he made with you, and *make you a graven image, or the likeness of any thing, which the LORD thy God hath forbidden thee.* For the LORD thy God is a consuming fire, even a jealous God. . . . Unto thee it was shewed, that thou mightest know that **the LORD he is God; there is none else beside him**" (Deut. 4:23–24, 35).

• [5] "**Hear, O Israel: The LORD our God is one LORD** . . . *beware lest thou forget the LORD*, which brought thee forth out of the land of Egypt, from the house of bondage. Thou shalt fear the LORD thy God, and serve him, and shalt swear by his name. *Ye shall not go after other gods, of the gods of the people which are round about you;* (For the LORD thy God is a jealous God among you) lest the anger of the LORD thy God be kindled against thee, and destroy thee from off the face of the earth" (Deut. 6:4, 12–15).

[Adam Clarke, in his commentary on Deut. 6:4, presented a varied list of translations for this famous verse. He wrote: "Hear, O Israel. Shema Yisrael, Yehovah Eloheinu, Yehovah achad. These words may be variously rendered into English; but almost all possible verbal varieties in the translation amount to the same sense: 'Israel, hear! Jehovah, our God, is one Jehovah'; or, 'Jehovah is our God, Jehovah is one'; or, 'Jehovah is our God, Jehovah alone'; or, 'Jehovah is our God, who is one'; or, 'Jehovah, who is our God, is the one Being' " (*The Bethany Parallel Commentary of the Old Testament*, 342–43).]

• [6] "For the LORD's portion is his people; Jacob is the lot of his inheritance. He found him in a desert land, and in the waste howling wilderness; he led him about, he instructed him, he kept him as the apple of his eye. . . . the LORD alone did lead him, and *there was no strange god with him.* . . . But Jeshurun waxed fat, . . . he forsook God which made him, and lightly esteemed the Rock of his salvation. *They provoked him to jealousy with strange gods, with abominations provoked they him to anger. They sacrificed unto devils, not to God; to gods whom they knew not, to new gods that came newly up, whom your fathers feared not.* Of the Rock that begat thee thou art unmindful, and hast forgotten God that formed thee. . . . **I, even I, am he, and there is no god with me**" (Deut. 32:9–10, 12, 13–18, 39).

• [7] "*Have ye not cast out the priests of the LORD, the sons of Aaron, and the Levites, and have made you priests after the manner of the nations of other lands? so that whoso*ever cometh to consecrate himself with a young bullock and seven rams, *the same may be a priest of them that are no gods.* But as for us, **the LORD is our God**, and we have not forsaken him; and the priests, which minister unto the LORD, are the sons of Aaron, and the Levites wait upon their business" (2 Chr. 13:9–10).

• [8] "Ye are my witnesses, saith the LORD, and my servant whom I have chosen:

that ye may know and believe me, and understand that I am he: *before me there was no God formed, neither shall there be after me. I, even I, am the* LORD; *and beside me there is no saviour.* I have declared, and have saved, and *I have shewed, when there was no strange god among you*: therefore ye are my witnesses, saith the LORD, that I am God" (Isa. 43:10–12).

• [9] "Thus saith the LORD the King of Israel, and his redeemer the LORD of hosts; *I am the first, and I am the last; and beside me there is no God.* . . . ye are even my witnesses. *Is there a God beside me? yea, there is no God; I know not any. They that make a graven image are all of them vanity; and their delectable things shall not profit; and they are their own witnesses; they see not, nor know; that they may be ashamed. Who hath formed a god, or molten a graven image that is profitable for nothing?* Behold, all his fellows shall be ashamed: and the workmen, they are of men: let them all be gathered together, let them stand up; yet they shall fear, and they shall be ashamed together. The smith with the tongs both worketh in the coals, and fashioneth it with hammers, and worketh it with the strength of his arms: yea, he is hungry, and his strength faileth: he drinketh no water, and is faint. The carpenter stretcheth out his rule; he marketh it out with a line; he fitteth it with planes, and he marketh it out with the compass, and *maketh it after the figure of a man, according to the beauty of a man; that it may remain in the house.* He heweth him down cedars, and taketh the cypress and the oak, which he strengtheneth for himself among the trees of the forest: he planteth an ash, and the rain doth nourish it. *Then shall it be for a man to burn: for he will take thereof, and warm himself; yea, he kindleth it, and baketh bread; yea, he maketh a god, and worshippeth it; he maketh it a graven image, and falleth down thereto. He burneth part thereof in the fire; with part thereof he eateth flesh; he roasteth roast, and is satisfied: yea, he warmeth himself, and saith, Aha, I am warm, I have seen the fire: And the residue thereof he maketh a god, even his graven image: he falleth down unto it, and worshippeth it, and prayeth unto it, and saith, Deliver me; for thou art my god"* (Isa. 44:6, 8–17).

• [10] "Thus saith the LORD to his anointed, to Cyrus, . . . *I am the* LORD, *and there is none else, there is no God beside me*: I girded thee, though thou hast not known me: That they may know from the rising of the sun, and from the west, that *there is none beside me. I am the* LORD, *and there is none else.* . . . The labour of Egypt, and merchandise of Ethiopia and of the Sabeans, men of stature, shall come over unto thee, and they shall be thine: they shall come after thee; in chains they shall come over, and *they shall fall down unto thee, they shall make supplication unto thee, saying, Surely God is in thee; and there is none else, there is no God. Verily thou art a God that hidest thyself, O God of Israel, the Saviour. They shall be ashamed, and also confounded, all of them: they shall go to confusion together that are makers of idols"* (Isa. 45:1, 5–6, 14–16).

• [11] "*I am the* LORD; *and there is none else.* I have not spoken in secret, in a dark place of the earth: I said not unto the seed of Jacob, Seek ye me in vain: I the LORD speak righteousness, I declare things that are right. Assemble yourselves and come; draw near together, ye that are escaped of the nations: *they have no knowledge that set up the wood of their graven image, and pray unto a god that cannot save.* Tell ye, and bring them near; yea, let them take counsel together: who hath declared this from ancient time? who hath told it from that time? have not I the LORD? and *there is no God else beside me; a just God and a Saviour; there is none beside me.* Look unto me, and be ye saved, all the ends of the earth: for *I am God,* and there is none else" (Isa. 45:18–22).

• [12] *"BEL boweth down, Nebo stoopeth, their idols were upon the beasts, and upon the cattle: your carriages were heavy loaden; they are a burden to the weary beast. They stoop, they bow down together, they could not deliver the burden, but themselves are gone into captivity.* . . . To whom will ye liken me, and make me equal, and compare me, that we may be like? *They lavish gold out of the bag, and weigh silver in the balance, and hire a goldsmith; and he maketh it a god: they fall down, yea, they worship. They bear him upon the shoulder, they carry him, and set him in his place, and he standeth; from his place shall he not remove: yea, one shall cry unto him, yet can he not answer, nor save him out of his trouble.* Remember this, and shew yourselves men: bring it again to mind, O ye transgressors. Remember the former things of old: for *I am God, and there is none else; I am God, and there is none like me"* (Isa. 46:1–2, 5–9).

The point is obvious. The context of every one of these "I am God, and there is none like me" passages shows that they all are connected with the LORD's admonitions to turn away from the false pagan gods who were tempting Israel. Instead, they were to worship *only* Jehovah. It was *He* who created them, guided and protected them, and who would someday atone for their sins and be their Savior. *None* of these passages were explanations of the existence of the other members of the Godhead. Israel was still functioning on a "need to know" basis. Teaching about the existence of God the Father and God the Holy Ghost was to be withheld until the New Testament era when the LORD would come among men in the flesh!

So much for "only one God" proof-texts! It's time to move on to more profound matters.

The Savior's Statements of His Unity and "Oneness" with God the Father

There are two statements made by Jesus Christ that form much of the supposed basis for the three-in-one "trinity" doctrine adopted by the early church as it drifted into apostasy. Both statements were made by the Savior in the final weeks of His mortal ministry.

The *first statement* was made at the very end of His late-Judean ministry, about three months before His crucifixion. He had attended the Feast of Dedication in Jerusalem. While walking in the temple on Solomon's porch, He was confronted by Jews who surrounded Him and challenged Him with this request: "If thou be the Christ, tell us plainly" (John 10:24). Jesus replied to them:

> I told you, and ye believed not: the works that I do in my Father's name, they bear witness of me.
> But ye believed not, because *ye are not of my sheep*, as I said unto you.
> *My sheep hear my voice, and I know them, and they follow me:*
> And *I give unto them eternal life*; and they shall never perish, neither shall any man pluck them out of my hand.
> *My Father, which gave them me, is greater than all*; and no man is able to pluck them out of *my Father's hand.* (John 10:25–29)

And then He made the oft-quoted and almost always misinterpreted statement, "*I and my Father are one*" (John 10:30). This statement angered His challengers to the point that they took up rocks to stone Him. But before they could do so, Jesus challenged them:

Many good works have I shewed you from my Father; for which of those works do ye stone me?

The Jews answered him, saying, For a good work we stone thee not; but for blasphemy; and because that *thou, being a man, makest thyself God.*

Jesus answered them, Is it not written in your law, I said, *Ye are gods?*

If he called them gods, unto whom the word of God came, and the scripture cannot be broken;

Say ye of him, whom the Father hath sanctified, and sent into the world, Thou blasphemest; because I said, I am the Son of God?

If I do not the works of my Father, believe me not.

But if I do, though ye believe not me, believe the works: that ye may know, and believe, that *the Father is in me, and I in him.* (John 10:32–38)

With this rebuttal, His critics again sought to take him. He escaped out of their hands, however, and went into seclusion beyond the Jordan river.

The **second statement** that Jesus made concerning His "oneness" with God the Father was made in an upper room in Jerusalem the night before His martyrdom. Jesus was with His Apostles. In this extended meeting, in which they had eaten the Passover meal, Jesus talked with them in great detail concerning His love for them, the coming and mission of the Holy Ghost, their responsibility to be faithful in the ministry, and the approaching persecution in which some of them would lose their lives. He alluded to His impending arrest and death, and then He lifted up His eyes to heaven and spoke the glorious words recorded in chapter 17 of the gospel of John as the closing prayer—His benediction on the last supper.

In this prayer, He made several references to His unity and "oneness" with the Father, and also His unity with His Apostles. These phrases, again oft-quoted, but with their context almost universally ignored by believers in the "trinity" doctrine, are significant, for **they define the nature of the "oneness" of both the Father and the Son, and also of the true followers of Christ.**

First, He prayed for His followers: "Holy Father, *keep through thine own name those whom thou hast given me,* **that they may be one, as we are**" (John 17:11).

Then, as He continued His prayer, He explained that the same "oneness" which He has with the Father was to be extended to all His followers:

Neither pray I for these alone, but for them also which shall believe on me through their word;

That they all may be one; as thou, Father, art in me, and I in thee, that they also may be one in us: that the world may believe that thou hast sent me.

And the glory which thou gavest me I have given them; **that they may be one, even as we are one:**

I in them, and thou in me, that they may be made perfect in one; and that the world may know that thou hast sent me, and hast loved them, as thou hast loved me. (John 17:20–23)

So these two passages are the most explicit passages in all the Bible explaining the "oneness" of the Father and the Son. "Trinitarians" avoid John chapter 17 like the plague as they write their theologies. Why? because these verses clearly state:

1. *that the oneness of the disciples of Christ is the same oneness as that which unites the Father and the Son* ("that they all may be one; as thou, Father, art in me, and I in thee");

2. *that the disciples are to be one in the Father and the Son* ("that they also may be one in us");

3. *that the oneness of the disciples of Christ with the Father and the Son* ("I in them, and thou in me") *is to serve three purposes:* (a) *to perfect the Saints* ("that they may be made perfect in one"), (b) *to show the world that the Father has sent the Son* ("that the world may know that thou hast sent me"), and (c) *that the world may know the Father loves the disciples of Christ with the same love which He feels for His Son, Jesus Christ* ("and hast loved them, as thou hast loved me").

The Pivotal Doctrinal Choice: One in "Substance" or One in "Unity of Purpose"?

So, in *these pivotal passages (John 10:30 and 17:20–23),* the Christian world is faced with a major doctrinal choice. Does the statement of Jesus Christ that "I and my Father are one" mean that,

1. **God the Father and God the Son and God the Holy Ghost, are together, only** *"one God," of the very same "substance" or "essence,"* as defined in the creeds of early Christendom?

2. Or, does it mean that **the "oneness" of God the Father and God the Son and God the Holy Ghost is an affirmation that they are fully united in purpose, fully agreed in their eternal objectives, fully integrated in their methodology, fully united in mutual love, fully united in their powers and how they use them, and working harmoniously in all their interactions with man here on this earth and with all their creations,** though they are three separate persons, and hence three distinctly separate Gods?

Ponder that question and choose carefully, for it is the most pivotal issue within all of Christianity. It is the central issue that separates the Apostasy from the Restoration. It's the litmus test Evangelicals use when they try to label some Christian faiths as "cults." It's the issue that squares off the "traditional authority" of early Christian councils against the "revealed authority" of the restored gospel, as embodied in The Church of Jesus Christ of Latter-day Saints.

"Three-in-One" Definitions Found in Ancient Creedal Statements

What do the creeds say about the "substance" and the "oneness" of the Godhead? According to this creedal definition, as expounded in the fourth- to eighth-century *Creed of Athanasius:*

1. Whosoever will be saved, before all things it is necessary that he hold the Catholic [true Christian] faith. 2. Which Faith except every one do keep whole and undefiled, without doubt he shall perish everlastingly. 3. And the Catholic [true Christian] faith is this: that *we worship one God in Trinity, and Trinity in Unity;* **4. Neither confounding the Persons; nor dividing the Substance.** 5. For there is one Person of the Father, another of the Son, and another of the Holy Ghost. 6. *But the Godhead of the Father, of the Son, and of the Holy Ghost, is all one:* the Glory Equal, the Majesty Coeternal. 7. Such as the Father is, such is the Son: and such is the Holy Ghost. 8. The Father *uncreate,* the Son *uncreate:* and the holy Ghost *uncreate.* 9. The Father *incomprehensible,* the Son *incomprehensible* and the Holy Ghost *incomprehensible.* 10. The Father eternal, the Son eternal: and the Holy Ghost eternal. 11. And yet they are not three Eternals: but *one Eternal.* 12. As there are not three uncreated, nor three incomprehensibles: but *one uncreated* and *one incomprehensible.* 13. So likewise the Father is Almighty, the Son Almighty: and the Holy Ghost Almighty.

14. And yet they are not three Almighties: but *one Almighty*. 15: So the Father is God, the Son is God: and the Holy Ghost is God. 16. **And yet they are not three Gods: but one God.** 17. So likewise the Father is Lord, the Son Lord: and the Holy Ghost Lord. 18. And yet *not three Lords: but one Lord.* 19. *For like as we are compelled by the Christian verity: to acknowledge every Person by himself to be God and Lord; So are we forbidden by the Catholic [Christian] Religion: to say, There be three Gods, or three Lords.* 20. The Father is made of none: *neither created nor begotten.* 21. *The Son is of the Father alone: not made, nor created, but begotten.* 22. The Holy Ghost is of the Father, and of the Son; *neither made, nor created, nor begotten, but proceeding.* 23. So there is one Father, not three Fathers; one Son, not three Sons; one Holy Ghost, not three Holy Ghosts. 24. And *in this Trinity none is before, or after other*: none is greater, or less than another; 25. But the whole three Persons are coeternal together, and coequal: So that in all things, as is aforesaid: *the Unity in Trinity, and the Trinity in Unity is to be worshipped.* 26. **He therefore that will be saved must thus think of the Trinity.** 27. Furthermore, it is necessary to Everlasting Salvation; that he also believe rightly the Incarnation of our Lord Jesus Christ. 28. For the right Faith is, that we believe and confess: that *our Lord Jesus Christ, the Son of God, is God and Man;* 29. *God, of the Substance of the Father begotten before the worlds*: and Man of the Substance of his mother, born in the world; 30. Perfect God, and perfect Man: of a reasonable soul and human flesh subsisting. 31. Equal to the Father, as touching his *Godhead*: and inferior to the Father, as touching his Manhood. 32. Who although he be God and Man: yet he is not two, but one Christ; 33. One; not by conversion of the Godhead into flesh: but by taking the Manhood into God; 34. One altogether; *not by confusion of Substance: but by Unity of Person.* 35. For as the reasonable soul and flesh is one man: so God and Man is one Christ; 36. Who suffered for our salvation: descended into hell, rose again the third day from the dead. 37. *He ascended into heaven; he sitteth on the right hand of the Father, God Almighty*: from whence he shall come to judge the quick and the dead. 38. At whose coming all men shall rise again with their bodies: and shall give account for their own works. 39. And they that have done good shall go into life everlasting: and they that have done evil into everlasting fire. 40. This is the Catholic [true Christian] faith: which except a man believe faithfully, he cannot be saved. ("The Creed of Athanasius {Symbolum Quicunque}," Melton, *American Religious Creeds*, 1:2–3.) ["The creed has lost popularity in the contemporary era, although it is still accepted and used in the Roman Catholic Church. The Lutherans included the creed in their doctrinal material as part of their broader case for catholic orthodoxy. The text reproduced here is taken from the Lutheran *Book of Concord*. . . . The words in brackets have been inserted into the text by the Lutheran translators to explain their understanding of the word "catholic," which differs considerably from the common meaning of Roman Catholic." (*Ibid.*)]

And, if the interpretation of these passages is that they mean that God the Father and God the Son are the same being, the same "essence," the same "substance" (though the "trinitarian" world remains completely at a loss, even after 2000 years, to define what that "substance" is), **how do they explain Christ's intent that all of His disciples are to be "one" with the Father and the Son, and "in" them, as expressed in John 17:20–23 and numerous other passages** that will be cited?

The answer: **they don't explain it. They side-step it.** It draws no comment in typical expositions of the Catholic/Protestant doctrine of the trinity. Yet it can't be ignored—it holds the key to the correct understanding of the nature of the Godhead!

As will be seen a bit further on in this chapter, it is readily apparent that "substance" is not the right interpretation of the pivotal word "one" when it applies to the

Godhead. Rather, *"unity of purpose"* is the interpretation which is meaningful and valid when speaking of God the Father, God the Son Jesus Christ, and God the Holy Ghost, *especially when the word "one" also includes the millions of other individuals who are true believers in Christ.*

The Doctrine of the "Oneness of God and the Saints" in Other Latter-day Saint Scriptures

The Book of Mormon and other Latter-day Saint scriptures also speak of the Father, the Son, and the Holy Ghost as being "one God." These passages are generally understood to be used in the sense of "one Godhead," meaning the three are united in purpose and intent, as in the context of a priesthood quorum. Thus, Nephi taught:

> • [1] Wherefore, ye must press forward with a steadfastness in Christ, having a perfect brightness of hope, and a love of God and of all men. Wherefore, if ye shall press forward, feasting upon the word of Christ, and endure to the end, behold, thus saith the Father: Ye shall have eternal life.
>
> And now, behold, my beloved brethren, this is the way; and there is none other way nor name given under heaven whereby man can be saved in the kingdom of God. And now, *behold, this is the doctrine of Christ, and the only and true doctrine of the Father, and of the Son, and of the Holy Ghost, which is one God, without end.* Amen. (2 Ne. 31:20–21)

The Prophet Alma, in his words of rebuttal to the lawyer Zeezrom, spoke of the three members of the Godhead in terms of their being one Godhead, as they unite in judging mankind. He said, • [2] "[resurrected beings] shall be brought and *be arraigned before the bar of Christ the Son, and God the Father, and the Holy Spirit, which is one Eternal God*, to be judged according to their works, whether they be good or whether they be evil" (Alma 11:44).

The resurrected Christ himself taught the people in the land of Bountiful concerning the nature of the Godhead as He explained the ordinance of baptism to them, saying: • [3] "after this manner shall ye baptize in my name; for behold, verily I say unto you, that *the Father, and the Son, and the Holy Ghost are one; and I am in the Father, and the Father in me, and the Father and I are one"* (3 Ne. 11:27).

The Savior reiterated His teaching of the unity of purpose of the three members of the Godhead a few verses later, as He explained the nature of His doctrine to the believing Nephites, saying: • [4] "this is my doctrine, and I bear record of it from the Father; and whoso believeth in me believeth in the Father also; and unto him will the Father bear record of me, for He will visit him with fire and with the Holy Ghost. And thus will the Father bear record of me, and the Holy Ghost will bear record unto him of the Father and me; for *the Father, and I, and the Holy Ghost are one"* (3 Ne. 11:35–36).

Just as His profound prayer to His Father in Heaven at the end of the last supper (John 17:1–26, above) holds "landmark status" because of its doctrinal profundity and its clarification of the way in which the three members of the Godhead are united as one, a glorious prayer offered by Jesus here in the Americas stands as a similarly profound "landmark." In this prayer, given at the beginning of His second day of visitation among the Nephites, the Savior sought from God the Father the purification of His newly called twelve disciples in the Land Bountiful so that He could "be in them" in the same way as the Father is in Him, so that all of them could be united with the Father and the Son in "one." The account also describes that cleansing process as it occurred, and closes with Christ's prayer that His newly cleansed twelve disciples might be purified in him as He is glorified in them:

> • [5] now Father, I pray unto thee for them, and also for all those who shall believe on their words, that they may believe in me, *that I may be in them as thou, Father, art in me, that we may be one.*
>
> And it came to pass that when Jesus had thus prayed unto the Father, he came unto his disciples, and behold, they did still continue, without ceasing, to pray unto him; and they did not multiply many words, for *it was given unto them what they should pray,* and they were filled with desire.
>
> And it came to pass that Jesus blessed them as they did pray unto him; and his countenance did smile upon them, and *the light of his countenance did shine upon them, and behold they were as white as the countenance and also the garments of Jesus; and behold the whiteness thereof did exceed all the whiteness, yea, even there could be nothing upon earth so white as the whiteness thereof.*
>
> And Jesus said unto them: Pray on; nevertheless they did not cease to pray.
>
> And he turned from them again, and went a little way off and bowed himself to the earth; and he prayed again unto the Father, saying:
>
> Father, *I thank thee that thou hast purified those whom I have chosen,* because of their faith, and *I pray for them, and also for them who shall believe on their words, that they may be purified in me, through faith on their words, even as they are purified in me.*
>
> Father, I pray not for the world, but *for those whom thou hast given me* out of the world, because of their faith, *that they may be purified in me, that I may be in them as thou, Father, art in me, that we may be one,* that I may *be glorified in them.* (3 Ne. 19:23–29)

Later that same day, as Jesus taught His disciples about future last-days events, He again emphasized His unity of purpose with His Heavenly Father. He taught that • [6] "The Father hath made bare his holy arm in the eyes of all the nations; and all the ends of the earth shall see the salvation of the Father; and *the Father and I are one*" (3 Ne. 20:35).

In yet another appearance among the Nephite Saints, the Savior granted to three of His twelve disciples the privilege of remaining on the earth to preach the gospel and bring souls unto Christ "while the world shall stand" (see 3 Ne. 28:1–23). He then spoke of their ultimate reward when they "shall sit down in the kingdom of my Father," promising them that they will eventually be glorified as the Savior himself will be, involved in that eternal oneness promised to all the faithful who will join with the Father and the Son in the eternities. He told them: • [7] "ye shall sit down in the kingdom of my Father; yea, your joy shall be full, even as the Father hath given me fulness of joy; and *ye shall be even as I am, and I am even as the Father; and the Father and I are one; And the Holy Ghost beareth record of the Father and me*; and the Father giveth the Holy Ghost unto the children of men, because of me" (3 Ne. 28:10–11).

The unity of purpose and joy of the Godhead was anticipated by the Prophet Mormon shortly before his death, as he wrote of the future Judgment Day and the happiness which will be the reward of the righteous following that great day: • [8] "he that is found guiltless before him at the Judgment Day hath it given unto him to dwell in the presence of God in his kingdom, to sing ceaseless praises with the choirs above, *unto the Father, and unto the Son, and unto the Holy Ghost, which are one God,* in a state of happiness which hath no end" (Morm. 7:7).

The doctrine of the absolute and eternal unity of purpose of the Godhead is also emphasized in the Doctrine and Covenants. It first appears there in the revelation granted for the official restoration of Christ's church on April 6, 1830. The revelation speaks of • [9] "those who should come after, who should believe in the gifts and callings of God by the Holy Ghost, which beareth record of the Father and of the Son; *Which Father, Son, and Holy Ghost are one God, infinite and eternal, without end. Amen*" (D&C 20:27–28).

Becoming one with the Savior is part of the glorious reward of those righteous beings who will be resurrected in the first resurrection in connection with the Lord's Second Coming in great glory, • [10] "For a trump shall sound both long and loud, even as upon Mount Sinai, and all the earth shall quake, and they shall come forth— yea, even the dead which died in me, to receive a crown of righteousness, and to be clothed upon, even as I am, *to be with me, that we may be one*" (D&C 29:13).

The theme of "oneness in Christ's church" runs throughout the Doctrine and Covenants, as exemplified in section 31, where the Lord promises Thomas B. Marsh that • [11] "I will bless you and your family, yea, your little ones; and the day cometh that *they will believe and know the truth and be one with you in my church*" (D&C 31:2).

The unity of the Church, in which the righteous believers eventually will become the "sons of God" and one in Christ, in the same way as the Father and Son are one in each other, is again emphasized in section 35: • [12] "Listen to the voice of the Lord your God, even Alpha and Omega, the beginning and the end, whose course is one eternal round, the same today as yesterday, and forever. I am Jesus Christ, the Son of God, who was crucified for the sins of the world, even as many as will believe on my name, *that they may become the sons of God, even one in me as I am one in the Father, as the Father is one in me, that we may be one*" (D&C 35:1–2).

The parable Christ set forth in section 38, as He taught that "every man" should "esteem his brother as himself," again emphasized the required "oneness" of the Church: • [13] "Behold, *this I have given unto you as a parable, and it is even as I am. I say unto you, be one; and if ye are not one ye are not mine*" (D&C 38:27).

Section 50 again explained the nature of the "oneness" of the Godhead, asserting that those who receive Christ will be "in" him, and He would be "in" them. In some mysterious undefined "substance," as the ancient creeds stipulated? No, rather, in unity of fellowship, purpose, and holiness: • [14] "*the Father and I are one. I am in the Father and the Father in me; and inasmuch as ye have received me, ye are in me and I in you*" (D&C 50:43).

Examples of Biblical Passages Where "One" Means "Unity," Not "Substance"

Alexander Cruden, in his *Complete Concordance,* defines the word "one" in three ways and furnishes scriptural examples for his definitions: "[1] *One only, there being no other of that kind,* 1 Tim. 2:5; Heb. 10:14. [2] *The very same,* Gen. 11:1; 40:5; 1 Sam. 6:4. [3] *Some body, any one,* 2 Sam. 23:15" (Cruden, 470). The interpreter's challenge, when dealing with the word "one" in reference to the members of the Godhead, is to properly ascertain which of these senses is being conveyed by the passages being studied and explained.

His three definitions are somewhat difficult to apply to the matter at hand. But in generalities, "trinitarians" attempt to find their definition of the nature of God in the *first* category, emphasizing that they believe that there is only "one" god. The explanations presented herein are focused on the *second* of Cruden's categories: *sameness and unity of belief and purpose, held by more than a single entity.*

Believers in "trinitarianism" are at a loss to show any Bible passages where the word "one" means that separate beings are united into some metaphysical "substance." On the other hand, there are numerous biblical passages in which the word "one" clearly indicates that people or things are "united" in some way, as opposed to meaning that various individuals together constitute only one individual. For instance, from the **Old Testament**: • [1] When He came to observe the people of Babel who were building a tower to heaven, "the LORD said, Behold, the people is *one*, and they have all one language" (Gen. 11:6). • [2] When Ahab, king of Israel, conferred with Jehoshaphat, king of Judah, as to whether they should unite and wage war against Syria, four hundred of Ahab's false prophets prophesied that God would deliver Syria into Ahab's hand. Jehoshaphat, however, wanted to hear what a prophet of the LORD would prophesy. So Ahab sent for Micaiah, a prophet of Jehovah, whom he despised because he never would prophesy to Ahab's advantage. The messenger sent to Micaiah tried to influence him to prophesy the same outcome as the four hundred false prophets had foretold, by saying the four hundred were united in their message: "The messenger that was gone to call Micaiah spake unto him, saying, Behold now, the words of the prophets declare good unto the king with *one* mouth" (1 Kgs. 22:13). • [3] In the book of Proverbs, counsel is given against peer pressure from others who will want the targeted person to join with them in their evil ways, saying, "Cast in thy lot among us; let us all have *one* purse" (Prov. 1:14). • [4] After King Solomon completed the construction of his temple, a great celebration was held. During the festivities, the trumpeters and singers performed in unison: "the trumpeters and singers were as *one*, to make *one* sound to be heard in praising and thanking the LORD" (2 Chr. 5:13). • [5] Ezekiel prophesied of two books (representing Judah and Joseph), and two peoples (Ephraim and Judah), being united in the last days, by saying: "join them one to another into *one* stick; and they shall become *one* in thine hand" (Ezek. 37:17).

New Testament passages also use the term "one" in a sense of "unity." • [6] For instance, the book of Acts indicates that "the multitude of them that believed were of *one* heart and of *one* soul: neither said any of them that ought of the things which he possessed was his own; but they had all things common" (Acts 4:32). • [7] Paul, in his sermon on Mars Hill, spoke of the unity of mankind, saying that God "hath made of *one* blood all nations of men for to dwell on all the face of the earth" (Acts 17:26). • [8] In his first epistle to the Corinthians, Paul spoke of divisions in the church there, with some saying that they were of Paul (who planted the seeds of faith), and others of Apollos (who later nourished the church and helped it grow). He emphasized the need for unity in the church, saying, "Now he that planteth and he that watereth are *one*" (1 Cor. 3:8). • [9] In that same vein, Paul wrote to the Corinthians about the sacramental emblems, again emphasizing the unity of those who partake of them: "For we being many are *one* bread, and *one* body" (1 Cor. 10:17). • [10] Then, Paul emphasized that though the saints have many diverse gifts, offices and callings, they all are united in their membership in one church: "For we being many are *one* bread, and *one* body, . . . *the body is not one member, but many*. . . . now are they many members, yet but *one* body" (1 Cor. 10:12, 14, 20). • [11] As he closed his second epistle to the Corinthians, Paul reverted to the same theme, counseling them to "Be perfect, be of good comfort, be of *one* mind, live in peace" (2 Cor. 13:11). • [12] When warning of the evils of fornication, Paul admonished them: "know ye not that he which is joined to an harlot is *one* body? for two, saith he, shall be *one* flesh" (1 Cor. 6:16). • [13] To the saints in Galatia, Paul wrote: "There is neither Jew nor Greek, there is neither bond nor free, there is neither male nor female: for ye are all *one* in Christ Jesus" (Gal. 3:28). • [14] Paul prophesied to the Ephesians of a last-days event, writing that "in the dispensation of the fulness of times [God the Father] might gather together in *one* all things in Christ, both which are in heaven, and which are on earth; even in him" (Eph. 1:10). • [15] He also wrote to them concerning the enmity between Jews and Gentiles, asserting that Christ would "reconcile both unto God in *one* body by the cross" (Eph. 2:16). • [16] Paul counseled the saints in Philippi to "stand fast in *one* spirit, with *one* mind striving together for the faith of the gospel" (Phil. 1:27) • [17] and to "be likeminded, having the same love, being of *one* accord, of *one* mind" (Phil. 2:2).

Other Apostles wrote in like manner, using the term "one" to mean "unity," or "united." • [18] The Apostle Peter, for instance, wrote, in his first epistle: "be ye all of *one* mind, having compassion one of another, love as brethren, be pitiful, be courteous" (1 Pet. 3:8). • [19] The Apostle John, in a similar vein, used the term "one" to mean "united." He wrote, in his great apocalypse, of ten future kings who will be united: "These have *one* mind, and shall give their power and strength unto the beast" (Rev. 17:13).

Early Christian Fathers: *Unum*—A Unity of Harmony and Disposition

The early Christian Fathers, writing prior to the Council of Nicæa in AD 325, most certainly were not of the belief that the "oneness" of the Father, Son and Holy Ghost had anything to do with any type of metaphysical "substance." Rather, they perceived it to be a "harmony of disposition only," an "agreement of society, not a unity of person." Summarized concisely in this extract from Priestley's *A History of the Corruptions of Christianity* (Vol. 1, pp. 53–54), are statements from Tertullian, Origen, and Novatian, three of the most notable Christian "Fathers":

> Notwithstanding the supposed derivation of the Son from the Father, and therefore their being of the same substance, *most of the early Christian writers thought the text "I and my Father are one," was to be understood of an unity or harmony of disposition only.* Thus **Tertullian** observes that the expression is *unum*, one thing, not one person; and he explains it to mean *unity, likeness, conjunction, and of the love that the Father bore to the Son.* (Ad Praxeam, cap. 22. p. 513) **Origen** says, let him consider the text, *"All that believe were of one* (unum) *heart and of one* (unum) *soul," and then he will understand this, "I and my Father are one,"* (unum; Contra Celsum, Lib. 8, p. 386) **Novatian** says, "One thing (*unum*) being in the neutral gender, *signifies an agreement of society, not a unity of person,"* and he explains it by this passage in Paul: "He that planteth and he that watereth are both one (*unum*; cap. 27, p. 99). (Priestly, *A History of the Corruptions of Christianity*, as quoted in Roberts, *Mormon Doctrine of Deity*, 151)

A Priesthood Quorum: Basis for the Unity and "Oneness" of the Godhead

Believers in the ancient creeds of Christianity have stumbled and struggled for almost two millennia trying to reconcile the mathematical impossibility of their contradictory assertion that the Godhead is "one God in three persons." Their proof-texting of certain limiting passages, rather than interpreting based on all the pertinent scriptural passages and information available, has led them farther astray. Their functioning without the understandings revealed in latter-day scriptures, and by inspired statements made by prophets since the restoration of the gospel of Jesus Christ in 1830, has led them off into theological tangents from which they cannot extricate themselves.

Members of The Church of Jesus Christ of Latter-day Saints, on the other hand, have additional information that illuminates the darkness with which "trinitarians" have shrouded their teachings concerning the nature of God. They understand the patterns of priesthood organization by which the Godhead functions and governs.

President Joseph F. Smith, speaking in general conference of the Church in April, 1898, made reference to the Godhead as that *"matchless governing quorum over all the creations of the Father"* (*Conference Report*, April 1898, 69).

In commenting on this statement, Truman G. Madsen remarked, "That one word, quorum, helps explain what we mean when we talk about the three persons in the one Godhead. *It's a quorum—three persons—who nevertheless are at one with each other in mind and in will"* (Madsen, *The Presidents of The Church*, 168–69).

Latter-day Saints are long accustomed to seeing priesthood quorums in action. They see elders quorums functioning smoothly and effectively, governed by a president and two counselors. They observe ward bishoprics functioning under the guidance of an inspired bishop, called of God by revelation, with the assistance of his two counselors. They see stake presidencies, all led by a president and his two counselors, guiding stakes where the saints are functioning in unity and harmony. They understand the organization and leadership of the Quorum of the Twelve Apostles, and they also recognize that the entire Church, here on earth, is led by a divinely selected president and the counselors which he, through inspiration, has chosen to serve with him.

They see the same pattern with auxiliary organizations on the ward and stake levels: Sunday School presidencies, Young Men and Young Women presidencies, Relief Society and Primary presidencies. Each is functioning with a president, called by inspiration received by those in authority, governing in their sphere of responsibility with the aid of counselors whom they have selected through inspiration granted to them through prayerful communications with God. *They recognize that priesthood church organization is how the Lord enables His disciples and His entire church to be one with God in unity and purpose,* as He prayed to His father: *"that they all may be one; as thou, Father, art in me, and I in thee, that they also may be one in us"* (John 17:21).

A Larger Quorum: The Body of the Church

As previously seen, many scriptures speak of the Church of Jesus Christ as a body and emphasize that Christ is the head of that body. The Apostle Paul wrote to the wives of church members in Ephesus: "Wives, submit yourselves unto your own husbands, as unto the Lord. For the husband is the head of the wife, *even as Christ is the head of the church: and he is the saviour of the body"* (Eph. 5:22–23).

To the Colossians, Paul gave a more detailed explanation of the Lord's church being a body and of Christ's role as the head of that body:

> [Christ] "Who is the image of the invisible God, the firstborn of every creature:
> For by him were all things created, that are in heaven, and that are in earth,
> visible and invisible, whether they be thrones, or dominions, or principalities, or
> powers: all things were created by him, and for him:

And he is before all things, and by him all things consist.

And he is the head of the body, the church: who is the beginning, the firstborn from the dead; that in all things he might have the preeminence.

For it pleased the Father that in him should all fulness dwell. (Col. 1:15–19)

In that same chapter Paul also wrote:

be not moved away from the hope of the gospel, which ye have heard, and which was preached to every creature which is under heaven; whereof I Paul am made a minister;

Who now rejoice in my sufferings for you, and fill up that which is behind of the afflictions of Christ in my flesh *for his body's sake, which is the church.* (Col. 1:23–24)

But the most explicit scriptural passage that portrays Christ's church as a body is found in Paul's first epistle to the Corinthian saints:

For as the body is one, and hath many members, and all the members of that one body, being many, are one body: so also is Christ.

For by one Spirit *are we all baptized into one body,* whether we be Jews or Gentiles, whether we be bond or free; and have been all made to drink into one Spirit.

For the body is not one member, but many.

If the foot shall say, Because I am not the hand, I am not of the body; is it therefore not of the body?

And if the ear shall say, Because I am not the eye, I am not of the body; is it therefore not of the body?

If the whole body were an eye, where were the hearing? If the whole were hearing, where were the smelling?

But now hath God set the members every one of them in the body, as it hath pleased him.

And if they were all one member, where were the body?

But now are they many members, yet but one body.

And the eye cannot say unto the hand, I have no need of thee: nor again the head to the feet, I have no need of you.

Nay, much more those members of the body, which seem to be more feeble, are necessary:

And those members of the body, which we think to be less honourable, upon these we bestow more abundant honour; and our uncomely parts have more abundant comeliness.

For our comely parts have no need: but God hath tempered the body together, having given more abundant honour to that part which lacked:

That there should be no schism in the body; but that the members should have the same care one for another.

And whether one member suffer, all the members suffer with it; or one member be honoured, all the members rejoice with it.

Now ye are the body of Christ, and members in particular. (1 Cor. 12:12–27)

Several latter-day scriptures, found in the Doctrine and Covenants, also refer to Christ's church as being a body. For instance, section 84 states: "Therefore, let every man stand in his own office, and labor in his own calling; and let not the head say unto the feet it hath no need of the feet; for without the feet how shall the body be able to stand? *Also the body hath need of every member, that all may be edified together, that the system may be kept perfect*" (D&C 84:109–110). And section 107 contains the information that "Of the Melchizedek Priesthood, three Presiding High Priests, *chosen by the body*, appointed and ordained to that office, and *upheld by the confidence, faith, and prayer of the church*, form a *quorum of the Presidency* of the Church" (D&C 107:22).

One Fold and One Shepherd

Key understandings can be gained by reviewing what the Lord Jesus Christ said about His role as the "Lamb of God" and as the "good shepherd" and about "His sheep" (His followers which He seeks to combine into His church, which He calls His "fold"). The tenth chapter of John records a lengthy dialog between the Savior and some very critical Pharisees while Jesus attended the feast of the dedication in Jerusalem. The Savior told them: "I am the good shepherd, and know my sheep, and am known of mine. *As the Father knoweth me, even so know I the Father*: and I lay down my life for the sheep. And other sheep I have, which are not of this fold: them also I must bring, and they shall hear my voice; and *there shall be one fold, and one shepherd*" (John 10:14–16).

This "good shepherd" theme spills over into other scriptural passages. It occurs in several places in the Book of Mormon. For instance, the angel explaining Lehi's vision to Nephi indicated to him that "the words of *the Lamb* shall be made known in the records of thy seed, as well as in the records of the twelve Apostles of the Lamb; wherefore they both shall be established in one; for **there is one God and one Shepherd over all the earth**" (1 Ne. 13:41).

Nephi later utilized the same theme as he expounded various prophecies of the last days. He said, "the time cometh speedily that the righteous must be led up as calves of the stall, and the Holy One of Israel must reign in dominion, and might, and power, and great glory. And he gathereth his children from the four quarters of the earth; and he numbereth his sheep, and they know him; and *there shall be **one fold and one shepherd; and he shall feed his sheep,*** and in him they shall find pasture" (1 Ne. 22:24–25).

When Christ appeared to the believers in the land of Bountiful, shortly after His resurrection, He told them "other sheep I have which are not of this fold; them also I must bring, and they shall hear my voice; and there shall be one fold, and one shepherd. . . . And verily I say unto you, that ye are they of whom I said: Other sheep I have which are not of this fold; them also I must bring, and they shall hear my voice; and *there shall be one fold, and one shepherd*" (3 Ne. 15:17, 21).

While speaking of still other sheep than those in Palestine and in the Americas, He said, "I have received a commandment of the Father that I shall go unto them, and that they shall hear my voice, and shall be numbered among my sheep, that *there may be one fold and one shepherd*; therefore I go to show myself unto them" (3 Ne. 16:3).

God the Father in the Son, and the Son in the Father

The concept of members of the Godhead being "in" each other needs to be addressed, as well as the concepts that members of the Godhead are "in man" and that "man" may be "in" God. Various phrases from several of the passages previously cited in this chapter need to be recalled in this context. *Jesus said, concerning himself and God the Father:*
- "the Father is in me, and I in him" (John 10:38).
- "thou, Father, art in me, and I in thee" (John 17:21).
- "thou in me" (John 17:23).

- "I am in the Father, and the Father in me" (3 Ne. 11:27).
- "as thou, Father, art in me" (3 Ne. 19:23).
- "I am one in the Father, as the Father is one in me" (D&C 35:2).
- "I am in the Father and the Father in me" (D&C 50:43).

Much of this book is devoted to discussions of how the Father and the Son and Holy Spirit interact together, and how **they are united in thought, purpose, and actions as they strive to accomplish their holy and eternal purposes.** Some of those links will be briefly listed here, but this list will reach beyond scriptural texts in a few places, and will propose some "theories" which deserve consideration, though they do not stand as "doctrine." **Ponder these possibilities**, while **striving to segregate doctrine from theory:**

1. The Father and the Son are linked genetically, with the Son carrying His Father's genes. *If* spirit beings have spirit DNAs or their equivalents, as mortal beings have, these genes may be on both the spiritual and physical level.
2. Both the Father and the Son are holy, and without sin.
3. Both the Father and the Son have achieved perfection, with all its ramifications.
4. Both the Father and the Son are immersed in the same works: the creating of worlds without end, populating them, directing the worlds' populations in their progress and actions, judging them, and leading them toward immortality and eternal life.
5. Both of them have "all things," "all power," and "the fulness."
6. Both of them have "honor," "glory," and "dominions."
7. Both have unlimited communications and travel capacities, including the ability to know and read each other's and everyone else's minds and hearts.
8. Both have complete knowledge of all things past and present and foreknowledge of all things future, on all levels: from individuals' actions to national and international events to intergalactic happenings and creations.
9. Both have infinite wisdom and use it continually for the benefit of all their creations and offspring.
10. Both function in the role of "Father."
11. Both have intimate acquaintanceship and knowledge of every individual who has or will come to this earth, based on their eternal parental and/or sibling relationships.
12. Both are filled with love beyond the level of mortal comprehension, and that love emanates from their very beings.
13. Both are continually progressing, by accomplishing creative and governance goals which add to their own glory and which also, directly or indirectly, add to the other's glory and dominions.
14. Both collaborate with, give direction to, and are aided by the workings of the third member of their Godhead: the Holy Ghost, who may himself possess most, if not all, of the qualities listed here.
15. Both give commandments, revelations, statutes, ordinances, and covenants which guide their eternal families as they progress through their mortal probations and continue along the paths to eternal joy and association with the Godhead members.
16. Both collaborate, continually, in their self-assigned roles as supreme executives, administrators, judges, advocates, mediators, and personal confidants to all who offer up their prayers to them.

17. Both are beings of light. And since this list of generalities (of how the members of the Godhead are linked to and "in" one another's thoughts, plans, goals, interactions with their children and siblings, church members, priesthood leaders, and other divine administrators) could continue for infinity, it will return to the scriptures at this point and conclude with their roles as beings of light. *D&C 88:3–13 has much to say about how the Godhead intermingles,* and how they are "in" all things:

> I now send upon you *another Comforter,* even upon you my friends, *that it may abide in your hearts, even the Holy Spirit of promise;* which other Comforter is the same that I promised unto my disciples, as is recorded in the testimony of John.
>
> This Comforter is the promise which I give unto you of eternal life, even the glory of the celestial kingdom;
>
> Which glory is that of the church of the Firstborn, *even of God, the holiest of all, through Jesus Christ his Son—*
>
> He that *ascended up on high,* as also *he descended below all things,* in that *he comprehended all things, that he might be in all and through all things, the light of truth;*
>
> Which truth shineth. *This is the light of Christ.* As also *he is in the sun,* and the *light* of the sun, and the *power* thereof by which it was made.
>
> As also *he is in the moon,* and is the light of the moon, and the power thereof by which it was made;
>
> As also *the light of the stars,* and the power thereof by which they were made;
>
> And *the earth also, and the power thereof,* even the earth upon which you stand.
>
> And *the light which shineth, which giveth you light, is through him who enlighteneth your eyes, which is the same light that quickeneth your understandings;*
>
> *Which light proceedeth forth from the presence of God to fill the immensity of space—*
>
> *The light which is in all things, which giveth life to all things, which is the law by which all things are governed, even the power of God who sitteth upon his throne,* who is in the bosom of eternity, *who is in the midst of all things.* (D&C 88:3–13)

But lest this immense source of power be confused with the shapeless, formless, everywhere-but-invisible blob of undefined substance envisioned in "trinitarian" writings as their three-in-one only-a-spirit deity, the following key passage is repeated: "The Father has a body of flesh and bones as tangible as man's; the Son also; but the Holy Ghost has not a body of flesh and bones, but is a personage of Spirit. Were it not so, the Holy Ghost could not dwell in us. A man may receive the Holy Ghost, and it may descend upon him and not tarry with him" (D&C 130:22–23).

God in Man, and Man United with Members of the Godhead

Just as the scriptures assert that the Father, the Son, and the Holy Spirit are "in" each other and are "one" with each other in their all-encompassing unity of purpose, *the scriptures also speak of how the true followers of Christ will be "one" with the Godhead,* if they are obedient and endure to the end. Those passages include the following phrases, drawn from passages cited earlier in this chapter:

• "That they all may be one; as thou, Father, art in me, and I in thee, *that they also may be one in us:* that the world may believe that thou hast sent me" (John 17:21).

• "the glory which thou gavest me I have given them; *that they may be one, even as we are one: I in them, and thou in me*" (John 17:22–23).

• "*I in them, and thou in me,* that they may be made perfect in one" (John 17:23).

• *"I in them, and thou in me,* . . . that the world may know that thou hast sent me, and hast loved them, as thou hast loved me" (John 17:23).

• "now Father, I pray unto thee for them, and also for all those who shall believe on their words, that they may believe in me, *that I may be in them as thou, Father, art in me,* that we may be one" (3 Ne. 19:23).

• "Father, I thank thee that thou hast purified those whom I have chosen [the Nephite twelve], because of their faith, and I pray for them, and also for them who shall believe on their words, *that they may be purified in me,* through faith on their words, even as they are purified in me" (3 Ne. 19:28).

• "that they may be purified in me, *that I may be in them as thou, Father, art in me, that we may be one,* that I may be glorified in them" (3 Ne. 19:29).

• "that they may become the sons of God, *even one in me as I am one in the Father, as the Father is one in me, that we may be one*" (D&C 35:1–2).

• "I am in the Father and the Father in me; and inasmuch as ye have received me, *ye are in me and I in you*" (D&C 50:43).

These are some of the passages that make it clear that the unity of the Godhead is not some mysterious "substance" that is unique to the Father, Son, and Holy Ghost. Why? Because the scriptures continually specify that **the faithful followers will become one with the Godhead for the eternities.** So, **another brainstorming list** is offered here—"theories" dealing with, and suggesting, how millions of followers may become one with the Godhead.

1. The mortal inhabitants of this earth are all spirit children of God the Father. They, like His firstborn Son Jesus, have His genes and DNA, though it obviously reaches farther back into time than scientists as yet have been able to trace and identify.

2. They all are part of a vast family, with God the Father as their parent, and presumably (possibly?) He has an eternal mate who has assisted him in the vast responsibilities of parenting.

3. All who came to this earth are among those whom the Father "gave" to His Son, Jesus, and entrusted into His safekeeping.

4. The Son was given the responsibility to function as the Father of those who come into His Church—he is the Father of all who accept and live His gospel and functions as such.

5. All His righteous followers who become "one" with the Savior continue to be benefitted by the light of Christ. To continue with that theme presented scripturally above: • "the word of the Lord is truth, and whatsoever is truth is light, and whatsoever is light is Spirit, even the Spirit of Jesus Christ. And the *Spirit giveth light to every man that cometh into the world; and the Spirit enlighteneth every man through the world, that hearkeneth to the voice of the Spirit. And every one that hearkeneth to the voice of the Spirit cometh unto God, even the Father*" (D&C 84:45–47).

6. They are members of the Lord's church—that body of believers led by Jesus Christ himself which serves • "for the perfecting of the saints, for the work of the ministry, for the edifying of the body of Christ: Till we all come in the unity of the faith, and of the knowledge of the Son of God, unto a perfect man, unto the measure of the stature of the fulness of Christ" (Eph. 4:12–13).

7. They are entitled to the constant companionship of the Holy Ghost, based on their personal righteousness.

8. As pointed out in the scriptural passages cited above, they serve as living proof that the Father sent His Son into the world, so that • "the world may believe that thou hast sent me" (John 17:21).

9. They are to serve as witnesses that the Father • "hast loved them," just as He loved His Son Jesus (John 17:23).

10. They are those who will be purified in and by Christ so • "they may be made perfect in one" (John 17:23; 3 Ne. 19:28).

11. Those faithful followers who • "come unto Christ" to "be perfected in him," and who "deny [themselves] of all ungodliness" and "love God with all [their] might, mind and strength," will receive the benefits of the Savior's atoning sacrifice, and "by his grace" be made "perfect in Christ" (Moro. 10:32).

12. They are to be the recipients of Christ's glory, which He will give unto them (John 17:22–23).

13. Because of their righteousness, Christ will be glorified in them (3 Ne. 19:29).

14. They will eventually join the Father and the Son in the ranks of those who have achieved perfection and have become and been made • "holy, without spot" (Moro. 10:33).

15. They will be counted as the sons of God on the eternal, exalted level (D&C 35:2).

16. They are invited to join that unique community of beings who will be allowed to dwell in the Father's kingdom, and be "one" with all those found worthy to be there.

17. They are recipients of the • "promise . . . of eternal life, even the glory of the celestial kingdom" (D&C 88:4).

Perhaps the best summary of the eventual results that come to those who become "one" with God and immerse themselves "in" God's work and glory as they strive for the ultimate blessings of "immortality and eternal life" (Moses 1:39) is found in section 76 of the Doctrine and Covenants:

> this is the testimony of the gospel of Christ concerning them who shall come forth in the resurrection of the just—
>
> They are they who *received the testimony of Jesus*, and *believed on his name* and were *baptized* after the manner of his burial, being buried in the water in his name, and this according to the commandment which he has given—
>
> That by keeping the commandments they might be washed and cleansed from all their sins, and *receive the Holy Spirit* by the laying on of the hands of him who is ordained and sealed unto this power;
>
> And who *overcome by faith*, and *are sealed by the Holy Spirit of promise*, which the Father sheds forth upon all those who are just and true.
>
> They are they who are *the church of the Firstborn*.
>
> They are *they into whose hands the Father has given all things*—
>
> They are they who are *priests and kings*, who have received of his fulness, and of his glory;
>
> And are *priests of the Most High*, after the order of Melchizedek, which was after the order of Enoch, which was after the order of the Only Begotten Son.
>
> Wherefore, as it is written, *they are gods*, even *the sons of God*—
>
> Wherefore, *all things are theirs*, whether *life or death*, or *things present*, or *things to come*, all are theirs and *they are Christ's*, and *Christ is God's*.
>
> And *they shall overcome all things*. (D&C 76:50–60)

Other Insights About Oneness with God, from Beyond the Veil

During the past four decades, God has seen fit to open vast resources of knowledge concerning life beyond the veil to people of all races, faiths, and cultures throughout the world.

Within two decades, beginning in 1967, books such as *Life Everlasting, On Death and Dying, Life After Life, Return from Tomorrow, Beyond Death's Door, Life at Death, Adventures in Immortality, A Collection of Near-death Research Readings, Recollections of Death, Heading Toward Omega, On the Other Side of Life, The After Death Experience,* and *Otherworld Journeys* were published, with many of them gaining worldwide distribution.

The third and fourth decades, beginning in 1987 and continuing through the time of this writing, brought *Coming Back to Life; Beyond the Veil, volumes 1 & 2; Closer to the Light; Heaven and Hell; My Life After Dying; Glimpses of Eternity, Transformed by the Light; Echos from Eternity, Beyond Death's Door, Coming from the Light; The Burning Within; After the Light; Reborn in the Light; Children of the Light; Beyond the Darkness; Experiences Near Death; Absent From the Body; I Saw Heaven!; The Eternal Journey, Heavenly Answers for Earthly Challenges, Lessons from the Light, The LDS Gospel of Light; I Stand All Amazed; Fingerprints of God; Mindsight; The Soul's Remembrance; Blessing in Disguise; My Descent into Death; Nothing Better than Death; Religion, Spirituality and the Near-death Experience; If Morning Never Comes; Trailing Clouds of Glory; They Saw Beyond Death,* and hundreds of others. A significant number of the above research studies were written by Latter-day Saint authors.

It is clear that verge-of-death experiences, near-death experiences, and life-after-death experiences happen worldwide. It is equally clear that many such experiences provide valuable insights concerning the workings of God's eternal plan in the spirit world, beyond the end of man's mortal experience.

Are they revelations from God? A few are; most are not. But that by no means indicates that they come from Satan or from his evil dominions. Are they doctrine? Of course not. Are they true? Almost all are, but *the methods for determining "truth" differ from the methodologies for determining "scripture" and "doctrine."*

This book is not a book about life-after-death experiences, but it is deemed appropriate to alert readers to the existence of valuable insights concerning how man continues in his course toward oneness with God beyond the veil. A few subjects of interest are mentioned here, with page numbers indicated for my book, *Life Everlasting* (second revised edition, 2005).

Chapter 6, "The Amazing Capabilities of Spirit-world Beings," (pp. 194–212) presents enlightening, carefully documented evidences concerning the nature of spirit beings, telepathic mind communication, spirit-bodies filled with light, matter existing at different vibrational frequencies, and insights on the nature of time beyond the veil.

Chapter 7, "The Quest for Knowledge in the Spirit World," (pp. 213–228) presents documented citations on preparing to administer the affairs of Father's kingdom, increased ability to learn, recalling previously learned knowledge, learning from all parts of the body and other senses, advanced methods of learning, and learning centers in the spirit world.

Chapter 9, "The Spirit Prison—Temporary Realm of the Uncommitted," (pp. 275–298) explains the privilege of the righteous to preach to their forefathers beyond the veil, and shows that the power of the evil ones to tempt spirit beings who have not yet heard nor accepted the gospel continues in the spirit world.

Chapter 10, *"Eternal Family Relationships and Vicarious Work for the Dead,"* (pp. 299–326) contains documented quotations which explain that everyone must have opportunity to accept the gospel plan, the power of family genealogical links, spirit-world genealogical research centers, and evidences how spirit beings sometimes take actions to correct genealogical errors and omissions.

And finally, *chapter 16, "Exaltation,"* (pp. 449–83) documents in detail the various abilities and blessings that are acquired by, or bestowed upon, those who become one with God through participation in the ordinances and activities of His Church, both on earth and in the hereafter.

Occasionally, people are given experiences that enable them to taste and temporarily comprehend what becoming "one with God" actually means. The two experiences cited here are both quoted from original non-Latter-day Saint sources, and happened with individuals who were not Latter-day Saints. The first is part of a near-death experience of a woman who was injured in a 1970 motorcycle accident. She recorded that,

> *[As] I was given the answers,* my own awakening mind . . . responded, "Of course," I would think, "I already know that. How could I ever have forgotten!" . . . All that happens is for a purpose, and that purpose is already known to our eternal self.
>
> In time the questions ceased because *I suddenly was filled with all the Being's wisdom.* I was given more than just the answers to my questions; *all knowledge unfolded to me,* like the instant blooming of an infinite number of flowers all at once. *I was filled with God's knowledge, and in that precious aspect of his Beingness, I was one with him.* But my journey was just beginning.
>
> *Now I was treated to an extraordinary voyage through the universe.* Instantly we traveled to the center of stars being born, supernovas exploding, and many other glorious celestial events for which I have no name. The impression I have now of this trip is that *it felt like the universe is all one grand object, woven from the same fabric. Space and time are illusions that hold us to our plane; out there all is present simultaneously.* I was a passenger on a divine spaceship in which *the Creator showed me the fullness and beauty of all his Creations.* (Gibson, *They Saw Beyond Death,* 229)

The second, extracted from a report published in the *Vital Signs* publication of the International Association for Near-Death Studies (IANDS), tells of an individual experiencing his personal "life review" beyond the veil:

> Everything is going on at once, all around me . . . left, right, up, down . . . wherever I look I see my life. I can not only see it, but I can also hear, feel and experience every event [of] my life . . . past, present and future. *There is no beginning! There is no end! I can see all the movements of my life all at the same time, all around me.* Strange, there is no fear or judgment, it's just my life experiences as they are occurring. What incredible feelings. *I can feel each and every thought, word and action all at once . . . I am in the Light!* Oh, God, *I am actually in the Light. I am the Light!* . . . The Light says, 'Andy, do not be afraid. Everything is OK.' Then the Light says, 'Andy, I love you.' . . . *I am in the Light. The Light is in me. I can see me in the unending Light. But I am still 'Andy.' I'm everywhere and I am here, I can see me as a person and I can see me in the infinite, warm and loving Light.* I become the Light. . . . *I'm home!* I feel the unbelievable warmth, love, joy and completeness of the Light! . . . *I'm truly home!* (Gibson, *They Saw Beyond Death,* 230)

These two intriguing reports of near-death experiences, hopefully, are sufficient to whet their appetite sufficiently that readers will recognize that what we presently see and comprehend is only the "tip of the iceberg," as the cliché says. ***Suffice it to say that it truly is possible for man to become "one with God" and to have "God within him" and to be "in God,"*** though there is much to learn about how that happens, both figuratively and in reality. I, for one, am anxious to move beyond the veil of death, regain my lost memories of eternal and infinite verities, and to press on toward the goal of being "one with God" eternally!

Grammar-School First Grade: A Review of Basic Addition

So, as this "threeness and oneness" chapter comes to its conclusion, it's time to review a bit of basic math. Several of my grandchildren are presently leaping the hurdles and scaling the lofty curriculum peaks of kindergarten and first grade, and they take great pride in showing off their numbers and reading skills to their grandparents. The questioning goes something like this:

"Calvin, in your family there are you and your brothers Landon and Charlie. So how many boys are there in your family?"

"Three!"

"Good. And then there are your mom and dad and your sister Abby. So, what are all of you together called?"

"A family!"

"Very good! Are you a bunch of families, or just one? How many families are you?"

"Just one!"

"All right! Why do you call yourselves a family?"

"'Cause we live together and love each other a lot."

"Do you all get together for weekly family home evenings and family birthday parties, and do you kids pitch in to help your mom clean the house when company's coming to visit you?"

"Yeah, we work together to do our chores, and sometimes mom makes us cookies 'cause we worked so well together."

"You know, there's a special name for families like yours. People can say your family is 'united in purpose.' Do you understand what that means?"

"Uh huh. It means we're all trying to be happy together and that we help each other get things done."

"That's a good answer! But if there's a lot of you living in your house that are united in working together, aren't you more than just one family?"

"Nope, we're just one family."

"But how many boys are there, once again?"

"Three!"

"So you can be three boys, but just one family, all at the same time?"

"That's right."

"You know, you boys all look a lot like your Dad. Is it possible that you boys and your Dad could all be the same person?"

"Nah, Grandpa, that doesn't make sense!"

"Why not?"

"'Cause each one of us is a different person. There's no way my Dad could be me, or me be him. We can't get inside each other's bodies—I'm just me! I'm the only one I can be!"

"Well, let me ask you another question. You've learned to add numbers in school, so you were able to figure out that you and Landon and Charlie add up to be three boys. Is that right?"

"Yep. One plus one plus one makes three!"

"And you have a really smart teacher at school, you've told me. Do you still think she's super smart?"

"Yeah, she really knows a lot about a whole bunch of things."

"What if she decided that one plus one plus one didn't really add up to three, so she taught your class that one plus one plus one only added up to be *one*? What would everyone say?"

"They'd say that even though she's really smart, she was *wrong*. One plus one plus one *has* to add up to three. There isn't any other right answer! The answer always has to be *three*!"

"But say someone with more authority, like your school principal, said that one plus one plus one only equals one. Wouldn't *that* make it so?"

"C'mon, Grandpa, yer teasin' me! Even though he said one plus one plus one only equals *one*, that wouldn't make it so! And even if someone that was the boss of all the schools in the state, or even in the whole country or the whole world said the answer is *one*, he'd be *wrong*! The real answer is *three*, no matter what!"

Out of the mouths of babes . . . Don't you think he'd do well with the folk tale of "the Emperor's invisible new clothes"?

Summary

1. This chapter addresses the mathematical conundrum raised when the Catholic Church, in the Second Council of Constantinople (AD 553), adopted the anathema that "If anyone does not confess that the Father and the Son and the Holy Spirit are *one nature or essence*, one power or authority, worshipped as *a trinity of the same essence, one deity in three hypostases or persons, let him be anathema.*" The later Creed of Athanasius (Symbolum Quicunque) also made it anathema for Catholics to believe anything else than that their "trinity" God was *one* God, not three Gods. These "trinitarian" concepts remain inbedded in both Catholic and various Protestant churches today.

2. Recent research is unearthing extensive evidence that "Deuteronomists," following the time of the Old Testament religious leader Ezra, made extensive historical, scriptural and doctrinal revisions in the Jewish scriptures and practices which were intended, in part, to portray ancient Judaism as being monotheistic.

3. The handful of "only one God" scriptures typically used as proof-texts by believers in the "trinity" concept of God were examined. Each was cited, and it was shown that in *every* instance, the context indicated it was a passage warning the Israelites to avoid the worshiping of the false pagan gods that were tempting them. Hermeneutically, they were brief statements based on telling their unschooled recipients only what they needed to know at that time. None of the passages were intended as a deep theological explanation of the nature of God. Information concerning the other members of the Godhead was to be withheld until the New Testament era, when Christ would come to earth in the flesh.

4. The two statements made by Christ that seem to form the basis for the "three gods in one" concept of the trinity were cited and examined: John 10:25–30 and John 17:20–23.

5. The pivotal doctrinal choice concerning the "oneness" versus "threeness" of the Godhead comes down to the question: Are the three members of the Godhead one in "substance" or one in "unity of purpose"?

6. The Creed of Athanasius was cited, with the anathema phrases "*So are we forbidden by the Catholic Religion: to say, There be three Gods, or three Lords*" and "*He therefore that will be saved must thus think of the Trinity*" highlighted.

7. The concept that indicates the fallacy of the "trinitarian" concept of the "oneness" of God is that the scriptures repeatedly assert that the faithful followers of Christ will also be "one" with the Godhead members, in the same way as they are "one" among themselves. The ancient "trinitarian" concept of the unique but never-defined "substance" of God doesn't allow for this scriptural assertion.

8. Not only the New Testament speaks of the members of the Godhead being "one." Various Latter-day Saint scriptures, which convey the same teaching, are cited.

9. Numerous Bible passages where "one" means "unity," not "substance," are cited.

10. Statements from early Christian "Fathers" Tertullian, Origen, and Novatian are cited showing that they, in their day, believed that the "oneness" of the Godhead meant "unity or harmony of disposition only" rather than "substance." As Novatian observed concerning the pivotal word *unum*, "One thing (unum) being in the neutral gender, signifies an agreement of society, not a unity of person."

11. Many Latter-day Saints regard the Godhead as being united in a highest-level priesthood quorum. President Joseph F. Smith spoke of it as being a "matchless governing quorum over all the creations of the Father." The entire "body" of the Church is also viewed as a quorum. The Savior spoke of "one fold" and "one shepherd."

12. Passages referring to the Father being "in" the Son, and the Son being "in" the Father are listed, with the interpretive conclusion drawn that "they are united in thought, purpose, and actions as they strive to accomplish their holy and eternal purposes." The list is culminated by citing D&C 88:3–13.

13. A "brain-stormed" list of doctrines and theories is presented suggesting many ways in which the Godhead share functions and abilities. A similar "brain-stormed" list of how God is "in" man and how man is united with the Godhead is also presented. The list is culminated by citing D&C 76:50–60.

14. Other insights pertinent to various abilities of God, which man is in the process of acquiring in the spirit world, are alluded to from *Life Everlasting*. Two unique near-death accounts in which the recipients experienced becoming "one" with God also are cited.

15. The chapter ends with a short account of a young child who comments about the mathematical realities of "three" and "one."

CHAPTER 6

THE PHYSICAL ATTRIBUTES
OF GODHEAD MEMBERS

A Landmark Revelation: The Appearance of Jesus Christ to the Brother of Jared

One of the most significant revelations ever granted to mortal man occurred when the brother of Jared pled with the Lord to provide light for the barges they had built to cross the great ocean. In response to his plea, the Lord stretched forth His hand and touched 16 small stones, causing them to emit light. Astounded that he actually saw a finger touching the stones, the brother of Jared fell to the earth, but the Lord instructed him to arise and asked why he had fallen. His response was, "*I saw the finger of the Lord, and I feared lest he should smite me.*" When the Master inquired if the brother of Jared saw more than His finger, the man pled for further knowledge and insight, saying:

> Lord, show thyself unto me.
> And the Lord said unto him: Believest thou the words which I shall speak?
> And he answered: *Yea, Lord, I know that thou speakest the truth, for thou art a God of truth, and canst not lie.*
> And when he had said these words, behold, the Lord showed himself unto him, and said: *Because thou knowest these things ye are redeemed from the fall; therefore ye are brought back into my presence; therefore I show myself unto you.*
> Behold, *I am he who was prepared from the foundation of the world to redeem my people. Behold, I am Jesus Christ.* I am the Father and the Son. In me shall all mankind have life, and that eternally, even they who shall believe on my name; and *they shall become my sons and my daughters.*
> And never have I showed myself unto man whom I have created, for never has man believed in me as thou hast. *Seest thou that ye are created after mine own image? Yea, even all men were created in the beginning after mine own image.*
> *Behold, this body, which ye now behold, is the body of my spirit; and man have I created after the body of my spirit; and even as I appear unto thee to be in the spirit will I appear unto my people in the flesh.*
> And now, as I, Moroni, said I could not make a full account of these things which are written, therefore it sufficeth me to say that *Jesus showed himself unto this*

man in the spirit, even after the manner and in the likeness of the same body even as he showed himself unto the Nephites.

And he ministered unto him even as he ministered unto the Nephites; and *all this, that this man might know that he was God, because of the many great works which the Lord had showed unto him.*

And because of the knowledge of this man he could not be kept from beholding within the veil; and he saw the finger of Jesus, which, when he saw, he fell with fear; for he knew that it was the finger of the Lord; and he had faith no longer, for he knew, nothing doubting.

Wherefore, having this perfect knowledge of God, he could not be kept from within the veil; therefore he saw Jesus; and he did minister unto him. (Eth. 3:10–20)

This one-on-one encounter with the premortal Christ most certainly is one of the most informative and inspirational visitations of God with man. Because of this experience, the brother of Jared acquired more knowledge concerning the nature of God than was possessed by noted theologians for many centuries of the earth's history. It remains a guiding pillar of knowledge shared by those who have the blessing of the additional information available through The Church of Jesus Christ of Latter-day Saints to all mankind today.

Jesus, when praying to His Father just prior to undergoing His all-encompassing atoning sacrifice, observed that *"this is life eternal, that they might know thee the only true God, and Jesus Christ, whom thou hast sent"* (John 17:3). A knowledge of the physical nature of the members of the Godhead most certainly is a key beginning to knowing them. This chapter is devoted to the assembling and classifying of specific revealed insights concerning the physical nature of Godhood members as they are recorded in the standard works of the Church.

But before presenting this assembled information, another related matter should first be considered. There are vast differences in understanding of the nature of God between those who follow two schools of scriptural interpretation. There are those who believe that the Bible and other modern-day scriptural references contain hundreds of *literal* descriptions of God's physical nature. In contrast, there are those who believe that the many hundreds of scriptural references concerning the physical nature of God are only *figurative poetic language* and *not literal* descriptions. These differences must be addressed.

Many of these interpretational differences are related to *theological terminologies*; others are related to *dogmas* resulting from decisions made in early Christian councils beginning in the fourth century AD Comments on these differences follow.

Lessons Learned from the History of Hermeneutics

The dictionary defines the term *hermeneutic* as *"the study of the methodological principles of interpretation (as of the Bible)"* (*Merriam-Webster's Collegiate Dictionary*, 11th Edition, 582).

Another definition, by a doctor of Biblical Studies, is: *"Hermeneutics is the science that teaches us the principles, laws, and methods of interpretation. . . . Hermeneutics and Exegesis are related to each other as theory and practice. The one is a science, the other an art"* (Berkhof, *Principles of Biblical Interpretation*, 11, 13).

In the sub-sections that follow, valuable insights are cited from two noted scholars who have written extensively on the history of scriptural interpretation: Frederic W. Farrar and Louis Berkhof. (Note that many of the changes identified by Dr. Farrar, below, are part of the numerous revisions referred to in Margaret Barker's statements cited in chapter 5, "Deuteronomists Efforts to Assert Monotheism. . . .")

Allegorical Interpretation before the Time of Christ

More than a century ago, Frederic Farrar gave a monumental series of eight lectures on the history of scriptural interpretation which were later printed as the book *History of Interpretation.* In his second lecture, "Rabbinic Exegesis," he furnished many dozens of examples of the allegorical interpretations concocted by Jewish scholars located in Alexandria, Egypt.

Before doing so, he laid a historical background. He told how in ancient Judea, just before the Babylonian Captivity, the Mosaic law had fallen into such disuse that a discovery of the Book of the Law in the days of Jewish King Josiah (reigned c. 640–609 BC) caused great astonishment (2 Kgs. 22:8–20, 23:1–3). During the Babylonian exile, the Mosaic law again fell into widespread disuse. When Ezra was commissioned by the Persian king Artaxerxes to help rebuild Jerusalem (c. 458 BC), he again had to reintroduce the Mosaic law to the Jews (Neh. 8, 9, 13). Of the tremendous impact on Jewish history exerted by Ezra, Farrar wrote:

> [He was] *the founder of Judaism* as distinct from Mosaism; he who *transformed the theocracy into a nomocracy;* he who *changed Israel from a people into a church,* and *from a political power into an international sect;* he who *established a system under which Prophecy ceased* because it was no longer esteemed a necessity; he who *based the influence of the Scribe on so strong a foundation* that it overshadowed the authority of Princes, and *caused even the influence of Priests to dwindle* into gradual insignificance; he who was *the first to inaugurate the Midrash,* and the *Targum,* he who was the traditional *propounder of the decisions which form the earliest nucleus of the Mishna,* the *first author of liturgical forms;* and the *first authoriser of local synagogues;* the *first collector and editor of the Canon,* the *initiator of the long subsequent toil of the Massorets;* the *historic originator of the Oral Law*—*that man was Ezra, the priestly Scribe.* (Farrar, 51–52)

Concerning **the radical changing of the law of Moses which was engineered by Ezra's scholarly followers,** Farrar listed as examples numerous alterations that occurred, specifying a radical change of scriptural exegesis as the causing instrument:

> Alas! the Evil Impulse was so far from being exterminated that it found its stronghold in the spirit of the Scribe. The Law—not the Law in its simplicity but *the Law modified, transformed, distorted by Tradition—the Law robbed of its essential significance* by the blind zeal which professed to defend it—became the centre of an abject servility. It came to be regarded as *the only means of intercourse with God,* and almost as *the substitute for God.* Immeasurable evils ensued. *Piety dwindled into legalism.* Salvation was identified with *outward conformity.* A torturing *scrupulosity* was substituted for a glad obedience. God's righteous faithfulness was treated as a *forensic covenant.* For prophecy there was only the miserable substitute of the "Daughter of a Voice"; for faith the sense of *merit acquired by legal exactitude.* The "pious" were hopelessly identified with *the party of the Scribes. The Synagogues became schools.* Ethics were subordinated to *Liturgiology.* . . . This was the ultimate result of that *recrudescence of ceremonial,* which was the special work of the Scholars of Ezra. And of this work the basis was a *perverted Bibliolatry,* and **the instrument an elaborate exegesis.** . . .
> This tremendous *tyranny of Rabbinism* was built upon superstition and exclusiveness. The *Scribes were declared to be the successors of Moses.* The scholastic lecture-room

was the heir of *the political Sanhedrin.* The Patriarchs of the *House of Hillel* combined *for fourteen generations* the powers of Davidic king and Aaronic pontiff. *The casuists of Tradition completely superseded the Levitic Priests.* All liberty of thought was abrogated. (Farrar, 58–60)

A significant aspect of the broad exegetical changes that occurred in Judaism was the "whitewashing" of their scriptural history. Dr. Farrar listed many of those changes:

> For Scripture History we find the **gross substitution of the fictions** that *Israel is sinless, and holy, and never committed idolatry;* that *Rebecca,* and *Rachel,* and *Leah* were never actuated by any but the purest motives; that *Reuben* never committed incest; that *Judah* took the daughter of "a merchant," not of a "Canaanite"; that the *twelve Patriarchs* were all immaculate; that they never meant to murder their brother Joseph until he tried to lead them into Baal-worship; that *Tamar* was a daughter of Shem, and was perfectly innocent; that it was *only the Proselytes,* not the Israelites, who worshipped the golden calf; that neither *Aaron's sons,* nor *Samuel's sons,* nor *Eli's sons,* were really guilty. *David, Bathsheba, Josiah,* are all excused from blame, and so **step by step by the aid of an exegesis** which began in fetish worship and ended in casuistry, **Scripture was first placed upon an idol's pedestal and then treated with contumely by its own familiar priests.** (Farrar, 63)

Not only was Jewish history "whitewashed," but also numerous aspects of Mosaic law were "softened" or circumvented. Farrar wrote:

> Nor is this all: **the exegesis of the Scribes not only reversed the history of Scripture, but, as the Lord said, deliberately set aside the plain meaning of the laws which they professed to deify.** We have already noticed how they abolished *the humane provision of Moses* for the slave who did not wish to be separated from his family. In the same way Hillel by his legal fiction of "the Prosbol," found it easy to *nullify the fundamental Mosaic provision of the Sabbatic year.* "He did it," says the Talmud, "for the good order of the world;" and by a still more transparent collusion *he set aside the Levitical law about the sale of houses.* The Pharisees by their rule of "Mixtures" managed in a similar way to *get rid of everything which was inconvenient in the Sabbath observances.* These accommodations may have been in themselves excusable; but thus to violate a Law which they pretended all the while to regard as infinitely sacred, was *an encouragement to the grossest hypocrisy, and can only be classed with the transparent frauds of an ignorant Paganism. . . .*
>
> The builders of this vast inverted pyramid of exegesis, which so seldom explained and so often explained away, were many in number. The most eminent among them were *Hillel; Shammai; Rabbi Johanan ben Zakkai; Rabbi Aquiba;* and *Rabbi Juda the Holy.* (Farrar, 64–65)

Allegorical Interpretation Was Embraced by the Jews in Alexandria

There were two streams of Judaic revisionism that functioned in the centuries between Ezra and the meridian of time. One was *the scribes in Judea* and various areas of the diaspora. Of more significance in this chapter were *the Jews in Alexandria, Egypt, who embraced the Greek concepts of Platonism and adopted the erroneous concepts and warped techniques of allegorical interpretation.* These beliefs and techniques were operative among the Alexandrian Jews for at least three centuries before the time of Christ. They continued throughout the early centuries of the Christian church.

Many of them still linger today in the hermeneutics of modern Catholic and Protestant scholars. Wrote Farrar:

> *Alexandrian Judaism was Judaism tinged with Hellenic culture, and from Alexandrian Judaism were developed the learned schools of Alexandrian Christianity.* For it was almost exclusively in the splendid city of Alexandria that *the fusion of Greek philosophy and Jewish religion took place.* Egypt had been the House of Bondage for the fathers, but it became, as a Jewish historian had expressed it, a School of Wisdom for the children. (Farrar, 114)

Farrar told how the Jews saw, admired, and then copied the allegorical interpretative techniques of the Stoics, who were strongly entrenched in Alexandria. They were already using these techniques in their analyses of Greek poetry. He also commented on several driving forces which motivated the Alexandrian Jews in copying these techniques:

> *The Stoic Allegorists . . . set themselves to explain away all such passages as containing myths, and sacred enigmas, and adorable mysteries.* In carrying out their object they had recourse to *etymologies,* to *plays on words,* to the *juxtaposition of other passages,* to *physical allusions,* to the *symbolism of numbers,* to the *emphasizing of separate expressions,* to *inordinate developments of metaphor,* and interminable *inferences from incidental phrases.* By these means there was no sort of difficulty in making Homer speak the language of Pythagoras, of Plato, of Anaxagoras; or of Zeno; and *borrowing from them the very same methods the Alexandrian Jews made the Bible express and anticipate the doctrines of the same philosophers.*
>
> But the Jews were driven to allegory by a far more imperious necessity than the Stoics, because *their books were the constant butt for Gentile ridicule,* and *their persons for Gentile persecution.* And it was all the more easy for the Alexandrian Hellenists to adopt this method because, in Scripture itself, they found much importance attached to etymology and to symbolic numbers. *They not only embraced the allegoric system, but they gave it an immense and wholly unwarrantable development.* (Farrar, 136)

The Impact of Allegorical Interpretation on the Jewish Concept of God

The allegorical method of interpretation had significant impact on the Jewish concept of God that (as previous citations from the works of Margaret Barker have already indicated) was undergoing significant changes during this period. Greek philosophical concepts inherited from Plato and the other Greek philosophers—that *(1) God has no bodily form but is everywhere, (2) all matter is immaterial, (3) the human body is a vile form, the seat of all sin, which serves only to house an immortal soul, (4) mortals can never ascend to Godhood nor dwell among divine beings, and (5) it is impossible for man to understand the nature of God*—all played a significant role when they were integrated into Jewish thought. That integration spilled over to the post–New Testament formulation of creeds which shaped the "trinitarian" doctrines of today. *Of special note is the allegorical-interpretation concept that a scriptural passage is to be "allegorized" if the interpreter, for any reason, considers the passage to be "unworthy of God." Such a caveat, obviously, gives an interpreter free reign to foist his personal views without inhibition upon those who read his scriptural exegesis.* Farrar commented on this erroneous caveat as he gave an example of its application:

When once the Jews had embraced the allegorical method it was easy to support it by Scriptural arguments. Philo proves as follows that Scripture must have a mystic sense. In Num. xxiii. 19, we find *God is not a man;* in Deut. i. 31, we find, *The Lord thy God bare thee as a man doth bear his son.* Philo sees in these two passages indications *of the two methods of divine legislation, the literal and the allegorical. The former is the body of Scripture, the latter the soul, which like a fine fluid pervades the whole law. The former is only for the vulgar, the latter for the enlightened, the few, the men of vision and faculty, the initiated who can perceive and see.* . . . All this "madness" is reduced to "method" by a set of rules, half Haggadistic, half Stoic, but entirely inapplicable. By some of them the literal sense is positively excluded; by others, the allegoric sense is indicated as existing with the literal side by side. The rules by which the literal sense is excluded are chiefly Stoic. *It is excluded when the statement is unworthy of God; when there is any contradiction; when the allegory is obvious. If Scripture says that Adam "hid himself from God," the expression dishonors God who sees all things—and therefore it must be allegory.* (Farrar, 149–50)

Dr. Farrar speaks of "the special tendency of Alexandrian exegesis, namely, the method of allegory," and refers to *"its references to ritual and to legend, and its avoidance of anthropomorphism"* (Farrar, 126). In the same context he also wrote of other examples of their allegorical exegesis:

Greek influences produced far more decisive effects on the Book of Wisdom. In that book, side by side with traditions of the utmost extravagance, *we have a direct incorporation of views borrowed from Plato and the Stoics.* The unknown author who took the name of Solomon *derives from Plato his doctrine of ideas, from the Stoics their systems of ethics.* From Plato he had learnt the Immortality and prae-existence [sic] of souls; the coeval [sic] *existence of formless matter*; and *the view that the body is the seat of all sin.* From the Stoics he had learnt about the Four Cardinal Virtues and the Intelligential Spirit which pervades the world. The most remarkable instance of allegory in this book is the allusion to the High Priest's robes as an image of the whole world. (Farrar, 126)

The Influence of Greek Philosophy on the Septuagint

The Septuagint is a Greek translation of the Jewish scriptures redacted in the third and second centuries BC by Jewish scholars in Alexandria. (Since it supposedly was translated by seventy Jewish scholars, it is sometimes referred to as the LXX.) Of this translation, Farrar said:

The Seventy [translators of the Septuagint] had not realized that necessity for absolute faithfulness which we now regard as the first duty of every translator. Excellent as their version is, as a whole, it is in many details faulty, and it is full of intentional as well as of unintentional departures from the meaning of the original. . . . *The Seventy do not scruple to prefer the current view of their day to the literal and natural sense.* . . . *They feel so philosophical repugnance to the simple anthropomorphism of the sacred writers*, that in the earlier books—before the age in which such expressions no longer shocked a refined culture because they were explained away by allegory—*they deliberately soften or alter the phrases of the original.* . . . *They do not abstain from many alterations—historical, aesthetic, and even doctrinal*—of which some are not a little arbitrary. . . . In Ex. xii. 40, the words "and in the land of Canaan" seem to have been inserted to get rid of a chronological difficulty. It is a far more serious matter that *in the very second verse of Genesis the translators have rendered "without form" by "unseen," and have thus introduced the Platonic conception of a distinction between the material . . . and the ideal world . . .* and that *in Isa. ix. 6, in accordance with the Alexandrian theosophy, they substitute "an Angel of mighty counsel" for "the mighty God."* (Farrar, 119–21)

A forged letter written by Aristeas to Philocrates, (probably written near the end of the second century BC) falsely asserted that the 70 (or 72) translators (supposedly six from each of the twelve tribes) worked in separate cells, translating the whole, and in the end all their translations were found to be identical. This led to the belief that the entire translation was inspired, correct, and infallible. Concerning this belief, and the comparative value and weaknesses of the LXX, Farrar wrote:

> That famous translation became "the first Apostle of the Gentiles." As regards Judaism, it kept millions in the faith of their fathers, so that they neither became Macedonians in Philippi nor Spaniards in Gades. As regards Christianity, it exercised a powerful influence over the language, and therefore also inevitably over the thoughts, of the Apostles and the Evangelists. Further than this its effects upon the exegesis of Christendom can hardly be exaggerated. . . . *The Greek version is quoted to a very large extent by the writers of the New Testament, even in passages where it diverges widely from the original,* and it furnished them with not a few of the technical terms of Christian Theology. It was partly on this account that the belief in its inspiration, asserted by Philo and by the forged letter of Aristeas, was eagerly adopted by Irenaeus, Clemens of Alexandria, Epiphanius and Augustine, and opposed in vain by the better sense and more critical knowledge of Jerome. . . . *Out of 275 passages quoted from the O.T. in the New, there are 37 in which the LXX. differs materially from the Hebrew.* (Farrar, 116–17)

Aristobulus and Philo: Pre-Christ Proponents of Allegorical Interpretation

Farrar wrote of the impact of many Jews who utilized allegorical interpretation in the centuries prior to the birth of the Savior. Cited below are his observations on two of the more prominent among them: Aristobulus and Philo. Concerning *Aristobulus* (an Alexandrian Jew and a Peripatetic philosopher, BC 160), Farrar writes:

> He is one of the precursors whom Philo used though he did not name, and *he is the first to ennunciate two theses which were destined to find wide acceptance, and to lead to many false conclusions in the sphere of exegesis.* The first of these is the statement that Greek philosophy is borrowed from the Old Testament, and especially from the Law of Moses; the other that *all the tenets of the Greek philosophers, and especially of Aristotle, are to be found in Moses and the Prophets* by those who use the right method of inquiry. . . . *Such statements are destitute of every particle of historical foundation.*
>
> As to the second point—the possibility of extorting Greek philosophy out of the Pentateuch–it is maintained partly *by the modification of anthropomorphic expressions, partly by reading new conceptions between the lines of the ancient documents.* In answer to a question of Ptolemy, *Aristobulus told him that Scripture was not to be literally understood.* The *"hand" of God* means His might; the *"speech" of God* implies only an influence on the soul of man. The *"standing" of God* means the organization and immovable stability of the world. The *"coming down" of God* has nothing to do with time or space. The *"fire" and the "trumpet" of Sinai* are pure metaphors corresponding to nothing external. The *six days'*

creation merely implies continuous development. The *seventh day* indicates the cycle of hebdomads which prevails among all living things—whatever that piece of Pythagorean mysticism may chance to mean. . . . *Here then we trace to its source one of the tiny rills of exegesis, which afterwards swelled the mighty stream of Philonian and Christian allegory. . . .*

Allegory arose from the deeply felt necessity for finding some borderland for the harmonious junction of Greek philosophy with Jewish legislation. While *the Rabbinic casuists were spinning cobwebs of ceremonial inferences out of the letter of the Law, allegory was used by the Hellenists for the totally different object of developing out of Moses the attenuated semblance of an alien philosophy.* To the Rabbis the Pentateuch was the germ of all ritualism, *to the Hellenists it was the veil of all gnosis.* Ezra and the Pharisees were the masters of the Rabbis; Plato and the philosophers of the Alexandrians. *But both schools went widely astray.* (Farrar, 129–31)

Dr. Farrar had much more to say concerning *Philo*, who is universally accepted as the pinnacle of pre-Christ allegoric interpretation methodology. Concerning what may have been Philo's short-term objective, Dr. Farrar wrote:

Mingling daily with subtle thinkers of all schools from Egyptian priests to Greek atheists—talking one day on the mole or in the marketplace to some Eastern theosophist from the centre of Asia, and on the next to some bright Greek fresh from the Lyceum or the Academe, and trained in the encyclopaedic superficiality of that epoch—*no gifted Jew could remain spellbound in the narrow self-assertion of his race. . . .* On the other hand an Alexandrian of the school of Philo had no desire to apostatize. . . . *The Mosaic law was sacred and eternal; Greek philosophy was inspiring, noble irresistible. There must, he fancied, be some middle term by which the two could be united.* Such middle term could not be found in the trivial and hair-splitting casuistry of the Palestinian schools. *He felt himself driven by an imperious necessity to show that nothing in his ancestral faith shut him out from the charm of classical antiquity and the splendour of philosophic truth. His object was to defend the cause of Judaism alike against sneering Greeks, wavering Jews, and narrow-minded Pharisees, by harmonising the dogmas of divine revelation with the discoveries of speculative thought.* (Farrar, 132–33)

According to Farrar, there can be no doubt that Philo's methodologies were ultimately based on the mystic rationalizations of Plato and the other ancient Greek philosophers:

Philo's works are the epitome and the development of the principles of the Allegorists. To them—though not by name—he constantly refers; and *on allegory the whole Philonian philosophy entirely depends.* Eclecticism without originality usually has a chilling influence upon belief, but *by the aid of allegory Philo was able to regard himself as a Stoic philosopher and yet at the same time as a faithful Jew. . . . He believed in the strange methods which his predecessors had borrowed from the heathen.* This belief enabled him to combine *the mystic rationalism which he had learnt from Plato* with the supernaturalism which he owed to his Jewish training. It was, however, impossible that the deep self-delusion thus induced could long continue. The "sophists of the literal sense," as Philo calls them, *had good grounds for looking with suspicion on the religious philosophy which tried to turn Mosaism into a Platonic religion.* Events proved that *the God of Philo was but a vague abstraction, not the living God of Israel;* that when the Law was explained away into vaporous commonplace it ceased to be a national power; that the history of Israel lost all its beauty and all its interest when it was turned into didactic allegory and poetic mist. (Farrar, 136–38)

Philo was rarely content with the literal sense of the scriptures, and he almost always sought to amplify them—to read what he regarded as "higher thoughts" into them:

> Philo professes to respect the literal sense. It is, however, clear from the tenor of his works, as well as from his special observations, that *he regards the literal sense as a sort of concession to the weak and ignorant.* To him the Bible furnished not so much a text for criticism as a pretext for theory. *Instead of elucidating the literal sense he transforms it into a philosophic symbol.* To him the literal compared with the allegorical sense is but as the body to the soul. *The passages which he refracts through the distorting medium of his exegetic system may be counted by hundreds, whereas it is very rarely that he abides by the plain meaning of even the simplest narratives....* "For, he says, "the whole, or the greatest part of the legislation is allegorical." "Most things in the law are manifest symbols of the unmanifest, and uttered symbols of things unutterable." Intercourse with alien races is a powerful solvent of fixed beliefs. *As the earlier contact of the Jews with Greek life had been the parent of Sadduceeism,* so their later contact in Alexandria was the parent of an esoteric and mysticising allegory, and finally *Alexandrianism in its dazzling unreality was the precursor of the Gnostic systems* which were the later offspring of a combination of Eastern with Western thought.
>
> *The complete perversion of Scripture which results from Philo's method* can only be adequately measured by those who are familiar with his writings.... In the hands of Philo, the poetry, the prophecy, the narratives, even the simplest legal ordinances of Scripture are evaporated into commonplaces of philosophy, or turned into a vehicle for the rhetorical expansion of moral platitudes.... *Philo adopted the absurd thesis of Aristobulus, that Greek philosophy was a mere plagiarism from Moses and the Prophets.* (Farrar, 138–40)

Perhaps the greatest error of those who foisted upon the world their allegorical method of interpretation was their lack of understanding of the nature of God. Though many hundreds of scriptural passages reveal who and what He is, their allegorical methodology systematically skirted almost all of them—they most certainly couldn't "see the forest for the trees." Thus Philo's God remained incomprehensible to him:

> The old proverb said rightly, *"Either Plato philonises, or Philo platonises."* His dualism, his belief in the eternity of matter, *his assertion of the incognisable nature of God,* his "intermediate Words," his Platonic idealism, his theory of the primeval androgyne, *his contempt for the body,* were not learnt from Moses but from the Stoics, and "the holy Plat" and "the holy community of the Pythagoreans." He only reads his opinions into the Pentateuch by impossible processes supported by the self-delusion of his own infallibility. *His God is a philosophical abstraction—"a Place" rather than a Person*—and the message of that God becomes in Philo's hands a tedious, vague, and ill-constructed enigma. His whole system is a frozen sea of generalities, a "death kingdom of abstract thought." (Farrar, 142)

Added to Philo's confusion was his adoption of Plato's "condition of ecstasy" concept of how revelation is granted to man:

> Philo held the most rigid views of inspiration, though *when he deals with them practically he becomes vague and self-contradictory.* To him Scripture is "the holy word," "the divine word," "the right word;" and its utterances are "sacred oracles." *Borrowing a theory from Plato, he imagines that the sacred books were written in a condition*

> *of ecstasy, which wholly obliterated the human powers. The vocal organs of the prophets, without any co-operation of their part, were but used by a divine ventriloquism.* These views are the issue of nothing better than the pseudo-philosophic postulate, that "the mortal cannot dwell together with the immortal." (Farrar, 147)

He added centuries of confusion by taking sweeping liberties when quoting the revealed words of deity:

> Philo . . . indignantly repudiates the notion of mere narrative as such being worthy of the dignity of Scripture. *He considers that the Scriptures were verbally dictated, yet quotes them with careless variations and in the freest possible paraphrases; mingles them with traditional details; combines them with views borrowed from Greek poets and philosophers* whom he also reverences as inspired; and treats them in a manner purely arbitrary, derived from his own individual genius. (Farrar, 148)

Concerning the long-lasting effects of the allegorical-interpretation impact of the Alexandrian Jews, Dr. Farrar wrote:

> *The most essential contribution of Alexandrian Judaism to the history of exegesis is the allegorical method.* . . . It culminated in Philo, and through Philo—mainly on the strength of a passing instance in which it was used as an illustration by St. Paul—*it was transmitted to at least fifteen centuries of Christian exegetes.* (Farrar, 127–28)

And also,

> *The Apocraphal writers and Aristeas, and Aristobulus, and Philo, did but adapt to Scripture a method which had been developed by their heathen neighbours*—a method which had long been applied, and was under their own eyes being applied by contemporary thinkers to the poems of Homer. By a singular concurrence of circumstances the Homeric studies of Pagan philosophers suggested first to Jews and then, through them, to Christians, *a method of Scriptural interpretation before unheard of which remained unshaken for more than fifteen hundred years.* . . . (Farrar, 134–35)

And finally,

> *Centuries had to elapse before men ceased to explain Scripture in non-natural senses;* before they ceased to *isolate and distort* its separate expressions; before they ceased to *rely on purely verbal and accidental parallels;* before they saw that *Semitic literature was not to be interpreted by the rigid syllogisms of Western logic;* before they *ceased to bring to Scripture what they could never have fairly deduced* from it; *before they dreamed of applying to Holy Writ the verifying faculties of a reason and conscience informed by the Gospel and illuminated by the Spirit of God Himself;* before they suspected *the absurdity of rationalizing here and spiritualizing there* in accordance with *rules which had no foundation;* before they thought it in the least necessary to *master the original languages* in which the Scriptures were written; before they ceased to *quote it in defense of their own worst passions* and their own least venial ignorance; before they attained any *conception of it, as being composed of books of very unequal value,* the *far from homogeneous literature of two millenniums—as being a progressive revelation,* fragmentary and multifarious, though from the first dimly prophesying of a final perfection. (Farrar, 156–57)

Allegorical Interpretation in and Following the New Testament Era

In the interest of variety, the explanation of the aberrations of the allegorical interpretation methodologies in the early years after the birth of Jesus Christ is passed to another eminent, but more recent, authority on the science of hermeneutics: Louis Berkhof.

In his informative chapter titled "History of Hermeneutical Principles Among the Jews," Dr. Louis Berkhof gives a valuable overview of the development of biblical hermeneutics from the very beginning of the Christian era. In his historical overview, *he first discusses the Palestinian Jews at the time of Christ*, indicating that they "carefully distinguished between the mere literal sense of the Bible (technically called *peshat*) and its exposition of exegesis (*midrash*). . . . In a broad sense, the Midrashic literature may be divided into two classes: (a) interpretations of a legal character, dealing with matters of binding law in a strict legalistic sense (*Halakhah*) and (b) interpretations of a free and more edifying tendency, covering all the non-legal parts of scripture (*Haggadah*). The latter were homiletical and illustrative rather than exegetical."

He then pointed out that "One of the great weaknesses of the interpretation of the Scribes is due to the fact that *it exalted the Oral Law, which is, in the last analysis, identical with the inferences of the rabbis, as a necessary support of the Written Law, and finally used it as a means to set the Written Law aside. This gave rise to all manner of arbitrary interpretation.*" (Berkhof, *Principles of Biblical Interpretation*, 15)

At this point he calls attention to the Savior's criticism of the scribes of His day, who were ignoring or negating key points of His gospel through their interpretations. His criticism is recorded in the gospel of Mark: • Christ told them, you are "*Making the word of God of none effect through your tradition*, which ye have delivered" (Mark 7:13).

The "Authority of Tradition" Concept Advanced by the School of Antioch

Then Dr. Burkhof moves back a couple of centuries earlier to discuss the Jews in Alexandria, and the serious interpretational errors they adopted—errors which still affect biblical interpretation to this day:

> THE ALEXANDRIAN JEWS. Their interpretation was determined more or less by the philosophy of Alexandria. *They adopted the fundamental principle of Plato that one should not believe anything that is unworthy of God.* **And whenever they found things in the Old Testament that did not agree with their philosophy and that offended their sense of propriety, they resorted to allegorical interpretations.** Philo was the great master of this method of interpretation among the Jews. He did not altogether reject the literal sense of Scripture, but regarded it as a concession to the weak. For him, it was merely a symbol of far deeper things. The hidden meaning of Scripture was the all-important one. He, too, left us some principles of interpretation. "*Negatively*, he says that **the literal sense must be excluded when anything is stated that is unworthy of God;—when otherwise a contradiction would be involved;—and when Scripture itself allegorizes.** Positively, **the text is to be allegorized**, when **expressions are doubled**; when **superfluous words are used**; when there is a **repetition of facts** already known; when **an expression is varied**; when **synonyms are employed**; when **a play of words is possible** in any of its varieties;

when *words admit of a slight alteration*; when the *expression is unusual*; when there is *anything abnormal in the number or tense*" (Farrar, *History of Interpretation*, p. 22). *These rules naturally opened the way for all kinds of misinterpretations*. For examples, cf. Farrar, *History*, p. 139 ff.; Gilbert, *Interpretation of the Bible*, pp. 44–54. (Berkhof, *Principles of Biblical Interpretation*, 16; italics in the original; **bold italics** are added)

After following down through Jewish history, Dr. Berkhof devoted his third chapter to the "History of Hermeneutical Principles in the Christian Church," and again focused on what was going on in Alexandria in the third century, showing that Alexandria still remained the heart of allegorical interpretation methods more than two centuries after Philo:

THE SCHOOL OF ALEXANDRIA. At the beginning of the third century AD, *biblical interpretation was influenced especially by the catechetical school of Alexandria*. This city was an important seat of learning, where Jewish religion and Greek philosophy met and influenced each other. *The Platonic philosophy was still current there in the forms of Neo-Platonism and Gnosticism*. And it is no wonder that the famous catechetical school of this city came under the spell of the popular philosophy and accommodated itself to it in its interpretation of the Bible. *It found the natural method for harmonizing religion and philosophy at hand in the allegorical interpretation*, for (a) Pagan philosophers (Stoics) had already for a long time applied that method in the interpretation of Homer, and thereby pointed out the way; and (b) *Philo*, who was also an Alexandrian, lent to this method the weight of his authority, reduced it to a system, and *applied it even to the simplest narratives*.

The chief representatives of this school were *Clement of Alexandria* and his disciple, *Origen*. They both regarded the Bible as the inspired word of God, in the strictest sense, and shared the opinion of the day that special rules had to be applied in the interpretation of divine communications. And while they recognized the literal sense of the Bible, *they were of the opinion that only the allegorical interpretation contributed to real knowledge*.

Clement of Alexandria was the first one to apply the allegorical method to the interpretation of the New Testament as well as to that of the Old. He propounded the principle that all scripture must be understood **allegorically**. This was a step in advance of other Christian interpreters, and constitutes the chief characteristic of Clement's position. *According to him, the literal sense could only furnish an elementary faith, while the allegorical sense led on to true knowledge*.

His disciple, *Origen*, surpassed him in both learning and influence. He was, no doubt, *the greatest theologian of his age*. But his abiding merit lies in his work in textual criticism rather than in biblical interpretation. *"As an interpreter, he illustrated the Alexandrian type of exegesis most systematically and extensively"* (Gilbert). In one of his works, he furnished a detailed theory of interpretation. *The fundamental principle* of this work *is, that the meaning of the Holy Spirit is always simple and clear and worthy of God. All that seems dark and immoral and unbecoming in the Bible simply serves as an incentive to transcend or pass beyond the literal sense*. Origin regarded the Bible as a means for the salvation of man; and because, according to Plato, man consists of three parts—body, soul, and spirit—*he accepted a threefold sense, namely the literal, the moral, and the mystical or allegorical sense*. In his exegetical praxis, *he rather disparaged the literal sense of Scripture, referred but seldom to the moral sense, and constantly employed allegory—since only it yielded true knowledge*. (Berkhof, 19–20; italics in the original, **bold italics** are added.)

Dr. Berkhof then covered the *school of Antioch* with *Theodore of Mopsuestia* and *John Chrysostom,* and then moved on to the Western Type of Exegesis, observing that "A mediating type of exegesis made its appearance in the West. It harbored some elements of the allegorical school of Alexandria, but also recognized some of the principles of the Syrian school. Its most characteristic feature, however, is found in the fact that *it advanced another element, which had not asserted itself up to that time, namely, the authority of tradition and of the Church in the interpretation of the Bible.* Normative value was ascribed to the teaching of the Church in the sphere of exegesis. This type of exegesis was represented by *Hilary* and *Ambrose*; but especially by *Jerome* and *Augustine*" (Berkhof, 21–22; *italics in the original*). After briefly discussing the contributions of Jerome in his translation of the Vulgate, he focused on Augustine:

> *Augustine* differed from Jerome in that his knowledge of the original languages was *very deficient.* This is equivalent to saying that *he was not primarily an exegete.* He was great in systematizing the truths of the Bible, but not in the interpretation of Scripture. His Hermeneutical principles, which he worked out in his *De Doctrina Christiana,* were better than his exegesis. He demands that *an interpreter shall be philologically, critically, and historically equipped for his task, and shall, above all, have love for his author.* He stressed the necessity of *having regard for the literal sense,* and of basing the allegorical upon it; but, at the same time, *he indulged rather freely in allegorical interpretation.* Moreover, in cases where the sense of Scripture was doubtful, he gave a deciding voice to the *regula fidei* by which he meant a compendious statement of the faith of the Church. Sad to say, Augustine also adopted a fourfold sense of Scripture: *a historical, an aetiological, an analogical, and an allegorical sense.* And *it was particularly in this respect that he influenced the interpretation of the Middle Ages.* (Berkhof, 21–22; *italics in the original,* **bold italics** are added.)

Others have written concerning the works of many of those summarized above by Dr. Berkhof. For instance, Walker, et al., in their book *A History of the Christian Church,* wrote concerning Philo, one of the originators of the tendency to "allegorize" doctrines, in this manner:

> This dialogue [between Jews scattered about the Roman world because of the Diaspora] produced its most remarkable fruit in the Jewish community at Alexandria in Egypt, where, in the work of Philo (d. ca. 42 AD), *themes from the Jewish scriptures were combined in a remarkable syncretism with Stoic and Platonist philosophical ideas.* A faithful Jew, Philo sought to show that the law—that is, the Pentateuch—intimated a wisdom which agreed with the best in the teaching of the philosophical tradition. To do this, *he used the method of allegorical interpretation* well known to Hellenistic exegetes of Homer, and by this means uncovered in the pages of Moses not only an ethic but also *a philosophical doctrine of God and of creation.* According to Philo, the cosmos is the product of God's outflowing goodness. Incomprehensible in his transcendence, God is linked to the world by the divine powers. Of these, the highest is the Logos, which flows out of the being of God himself and is not only the agent through whom God created the world but also the source of all other powers and the ultimate model of the spiritual and visible creations. *Philo's picture of the Logos thus fuses together elements from many sources: from Jewish Wisdom speculation, from Platonist ideas about an intelligible realm of Forms, and from the scriptural notion that God creates by His Word (Logos).* This kind of thinking,

which has less sophisticated parallels in New Testament ideas of God's Word and Wisdom, *was to prove a fertile model in the development of later Christian theology.* (Williston Walker, et al., *A History of the Christian Church*, 4th edition, 19)

How "Allegorical Interpretation" Was Applied Concerning the Nature of God

A quick summary of these extracts cited from Dr. Berkhof's chapters on the history of hermeneutics may prove valuable at this point.

1. Already, in the time of Christ, the Jewish scribes were supplanting the written law of the Old Testament with their oral traditions, which changed the emphasis and direction of so many principles that Christ rebuked them, saying they were "making the word of God of none effect" through their doctrinally altered oral traditions.

2. Both the Jews and the early Christian leaders ("fathers") were heavily influenced by Greek thought in their day, especially the teachings of Plato and Neo-Platonism.

3. Greek methods of analyzing literature minimized its literal nature and constantly sought to find deeper, "allegorical" meanings that extended beyond what was written. The messages of the written word was typically changed to what the thinkers perceived to be deeper, more profound thoughts and understandings.

4. Philo, a Jewish scholar at Alexandria, was an early leader in utilizing "allegorical interpretation." Clement of Alexandria (?–ca. 215), Origen (182/185–251/254), and Augustine, Bishop of Hippo (354–430) were other major figures in utilizing and solidifying the use of this interpretive approach in New Testament times.

5. Key phrases which exemplify this allegorical interpretive philosophy, drawn from the above historical summaries, include:

   A. They adopted the fundamental principle of Plato that one should not believe anything that is unworthy of God.

   B. Whenever they found things in the Old Testament that did not agree with their philosophy and that offended their sense of propriety, they resorted to allegorical interpretations.

   C. The literal sense must be excluded when anything is stated that is unworthy of God or when otherwise a contradiction would be involved.

   D. He propounded the principle that all scripture must be understood allegorically.

   E. All that seems dark and immoral and unbecoming in the Bible simply serves as an incentive to transcend or pass beyond the literal sense.

   F. The Western type of exegesis advanced another element, which had not asserted itself up to that time, namely, the authority of tradition and of the Roman Catholic Church in the interpretation of the Bible.

Using "Allegorical Interpretation" as an Instrument of Ancient Church Policy: The Copernicus/Galileo Incident

Nicolaus Copernicus (1473–1543), a Polish astronomer, was a well-educated man who had earned the degree of doctor of canon law and was said to have "been in possession of all the knowledge of the day in mathematics, astronomy, medicine and theology." It was he who propounded the "Copernican theory" that the earth and other planets revolved around the sun.

His idea that the sun was the center of the universe, not the earth, was considered radical in his day because it was in direct opposition to the long-accepted astronomical theories of Ptolemy. Indeed, by the sixteenth century Ptolemy's concept that the earth was the center of the universe had become not only firmly entrenched in astronomical thought; it also had the virtual standing within Catholicism of being a religious doctrine, so Copernicus was cautious not to offend the church because of his astronomical calculations. When he died, his "Copernican theory" remained an unproven but much discussed astronomical theory.

Galileo Galilei (1564–1642) was born 21 years after Copernicus' death. He was an Italian mathematician, astronomer, and physicist. Early in life he became convinced the Copernican theory was true but was reluctant to embrace it openly for fear of ridicule.

When the telescope was first invented in 1609, Galileo began using and improving it. He invented methods for checking the curvature of lenses, which enabled him to develop telescopes powerful enough to make astronomical observations. He began observing the skies and in early 1610 announced several very significant astronomical discoveries. In particular, he observed sunspots and recorded their movements across the sun, which convinced him that Copernicus was right: the earth, not the sun, was rotating. With this evidence, he deduced that the sun, not the earth, was the center of this earth's solar system.

In 1611 he visited Rome and demonstrated his telescopes to the most eminent personages at the pontifical court. Flattered by his reception, he grew bold and published his support for the "Copernican theory" in 1613. This stirred up a "hornet's nest" of Catholic opposition because the church had long believed that the earth was the center of the universe. It's what happened next that causes the matter to be cited in this context. This quote from the *Encyclopedia Britannica* is typical of the various sources which report the interesting historical saga:

> The great expository gifts of Galileo and his choice of Italian, in which he was an acknowledged master of style, made his thoughts popular beyond the confines of the universities and created a powerful movement of opinion. *The Aristotelian professors, seeing their vested interests threatened, united against him. They strove to cast suspicion upon him in the eyes of ecclesiastical authorities because of contradictions between the Copernican theory and the Scriptures.* They obtained the cooperation of the Dominican preachers, who fulminated from the pulpit against the new impiety of "mathematicians" and *secretly denounced Galileo to the Inquisition for blasphemous utterances which had been freely invented.* Galileo, gravely alarmed, agreed with one of his pupils, B. Castelli, a Benedictine monk, that something should be done to forestall a crisis. He accordingly wrote letters meant for the grand duke and for the Roman authorities . . . in which *he pointed out the danger,* **reminding the church of its standing practice of interpreting scripture allegorically whenever it came into conflict with scientific truth,** quoting patristic authorities and warning that it would be *"a terrible detriment for the souls if the people found themselves convinced by proof of something that it was made then a sin to believe."* He even went to Rome in person to beg the authorities to leave the way open for a change. A number of ecclesiastical experts were on his side. Unfortunately, Cardinal Bellarmine, the chief theologian of the church, was unable to appreciate the importance of the new theories. He clung to the time-honoured belief that "mathematical hypotheses" have nothing to do with physical reality. *He only saw the danger of a "scandal" which might undermine Catholicity* in its fight with Protestantism. He

accordingly decided that the best thing would be to check the whole issue by *having Copernicanism declared "false and erroneous"* and the book of Copernicus suspended by the congregation of the Index. The decree came out on March 5, 1616. On the previous Feb. 26, however, as an act of personal consideration, Cardinal Bellarmine had granted an audience to Galileo and informed him of the forthcoming decree, *warning him that he must henceforth neither "hold nor defend" the doctrine,* although it could still be discussed as a mere "mathematical supposition."

Galileo went into a period of "studious retirement," but later began again to write about and advocate the concept that the sun, not the earth, is the center of this universe. In 1632 he wrote a noncommital book on the subject, but *the Jesuits insisted that it could have worse consequences on the established system of teaching "than Luther and Calvin put together." The decision was made to prosecute Galileo for "vehement suspicion of heresy."* He was found guilty of having "held and taught" the Copernican doctrine and was ordered to recant, being compelled to recite a formula in which he "abjured, cursed and detested" his past errors. He was placed under house arrest for the last eight years of his life ("Copernicus, Nicolaus," in *Britannica Encyclopedia* 6:462–63; and "Galileo Galilei" in 9:1088–90).

Time and history have long since shown that Copernicus and Galileo were right and the church was wrong: the sun, not the earth, is the center of this earth's solar system. What is instructional here is the history of how conflicts were handled: (1) in-church politics played a major role; (2) it was acknowledged that *the church followed the practice of using allegorical interpretation to circumvent facts when doctrinal or scientific conflicts occurred*; and (3) the major strategic objective was to spare the church from scandal and embarrassment.

The scripturally weak and doctrinally incorrect doctrine of the "trinity" has the potential to be as great a dilemma for "trinitarian" churches and theologians today as the issue of whether the earth or the sun was the center of the solar system back in the seventeenth century. It may someday suffer its own "big bang."

A Caution Concerning "Loaded Terminology" Used by Theologians

Latter-day Saints would do well to become more aware that various terms frequently used by non-Latter-day Saint theologians have far-different meanings than Latter-day Saint members perceive. For instance, some Latter-day Saints erroneously say "we believe in an **anthropomorphic God**" when they attempt to convey the Latter-day Saint doctrine that "The Father has a body of flesh and bones as tangible as man's; the Son also" (D&C 130:22). Some of them do not realize that the term has the generally understood non-Latter-day Saint meaning of making an "*interpretation of what is not human or personal in terms of human or personal characteristics.*" So when they use the word "anthropomorphic" to assert that God the Father and God the Son have physical, tangible bodies, they're unwittingly conveying the opposite meaning. They're inadvertently making the untrue statement that "we believe that God *does not* have human or personal characteristics such as a tangible body; we're just trying to describe it in human terms." It's time to reach for the dictionary! The *Merriam-Webster's Collegiate Dictionary* provides definitions for this and several other related words as follows:

> **Anthropomorphism**: "an interpretation of what is not human or personal in terms of human or personal characteristics." **Anthropomorphic**: "1. described or thought of as having a human form or human attributes (deities) 2. ascribing human

characteristics to nonhuman things (supernaturalism)." ***Anthropomorphize***: "to attribute human form or personality to things not human." ***Anthropopathism***: "the ascription of human feelings to something not human." (11th edition, 2003:53)

How do various theological dictionaries define these terms? Here are other examples:

> ***Anthropomorphism.*** The representation of something other than man—e.g. the sea, an animal, a computer, or God—as possessing quasi-human characteristics. In its wider use, this is a matter of attributing not only something like human form or shape, but also something like human attitudes, feelings, characteristics, actions and intentions to non-human entities. In the case of talk about God, many such uses are *clearly metaphorical*, as indeed is the use of inanimate or animal imagery such as 'rock' or 'lion'. *To speak of the 'hand' or 'eye' of God or of God 'walking in the garden in the cool of the day' is metaphorical talk.* (Richardson & Bowden [eds.], *The Westminster Dictionary of Christian Theology*, 26)

Another theological definition:

> ***Attributes of Greatness: Spirituality.*** *God is spirit; that is, he is not composed of matter and does not possess a physical nature.* This is most clearly stated by Jesus in John 4:24, "God is spirit, and those who worship him must worship in spirit and truth." It is also implied in various references to his invisibility (John 1:18; 1 Tim. 1:17; 6:15–16).
>
> One consequence of God's spirituality is that *he does not have the limitations involved with a physical body. For one thing, he is not limited to a particular geographical or spatial location.* This is implicit in Jesus' statement, "the hour is coming when neither on this mountain nor in Jerusalem will you worship the Father" (John 4:21). Consider also Paul's statement made in Acts 17:24: "The God who made the world and everything in it, being Lord of heaven and earth, does not live in shrines made by man." Furthermore, he is not destructible, as is material nature.
>
> *There are, of course, numerous passages which suggest that God has physical features* such as hands or feet. How are we to regard these references? It seems most helpful to treat *them as anthropomorphisms, attempts to express the truth about God through human analogies.* There also are cases where God appeared in physical form, particularly in the Old Testament. *These should be understood as theophanies, or temporary manifestations of God.* **It seems best to take the clear statements about the spirituality and invisibility of God at face value and interpret the anthropomorphisms and theophanies in the light of them.** Indeed, Jesus himself clearly indicated that a spirit does not have flesh and bones (Luke 24:39)." (Erickson, *Christian Theology*, 267–68)

Here is another example from a typical Bible dictionary:

> ***Anthropomorphism.*** A literary device that speaks of God, animals, or objects in human terms. The Bible speaks of God's hand, of his face, of God feeling jealousy, etc. *The biblical language, however, is clearly figurative.* Moses quotes God in Ex. 33:20, "You cannot see my face, for no one may see me and live," and 1 Tim. 6:16 describes the Lord as one "who lives in unapproachable light, whom no one has seen or can see."
>
> *Why then the use of anthropomorphic language for God?* On the one hand, if we could not use language which described God in ways human beings can understand, very little could be said about him. But more importantly, the God of Scripture is personal rather than impersonal, a living being rather than an abstract force. *We properly speak of God's eyes, not because he has two giant physical eyes, but because it*

is inconceivable that the one who formed the eye cannot see. The Hebrew people properly spoke of God's right hand, not because a giant arm appeared in the sky when God acted, but because the right hand in that culture symbolized power, and God's people knew the Lord as a living being who exerted his power on their behalf.

The anthropomorphic language of the Bible does not reflect a crude or primitive view of God. Instead it expresses an exalted concept, which honors God as a personal being, and which maintains the necessary balance between God's transcendence and his active involvement in the affairs of this world. ("Anthropomorphism," *The Revell Bible Dictionary*, Deluxe Color Edition, p. 72)

Yet another typical example:

Anthropomorphism—*the practice of describing God in human terms,* as if He has feet (Ex. 24:10), hands (John 10:29), a face (Matt. 18:10), a heart (Hos. 11:8), and so forth. Although the Old and New Testaments deny any literal similarity of form between God and His creatures (Job 9:32; John 4:24), the Bible frequently uses such human language to affirm that God is personal and active in His creation.

The appearance of Jesus, God's Son, in a human body is a literal revelation of God in the form of man. Jesus was "in the form of God," but He took "the form of a servant," the "likeness" and "appearance" of man (Phil. 2:6–8), to save us and to reveal the depth of God's love (John 14:9; 1 John 1:1–2). Therefore, with respect to Jesus, we can literally speak of God in human form. (Lockyer, Herbert Sr., [Gen. Ed.], *Nelson's Illustrated Bible Dictionary*, p. 67)

Another example of "loaded terminology" is the use of the term "**theophany**." Latter-day Saints tend to use it as a reference to an actual appearance of God. Non-Latter-day Saint theologians use the word to represent "*temporary manifestations of God*" (see Erickson, *Christian Theology*, p. 268, cited below).

The *Merriam Webster's Collegiate Dictionary* (11th Edition, 1296) defines "theophany" as "a visible manifestation of a deity"—a non-committal definition. It's what it means to non-Latter-day Saint theologians that is operative in this situation:

R.A. Torrey puts the Protestant "spin" on it in *What the Bible Teaches*. In his chapter 1: *God as Spirit*, he moves through a series of propositions, as follows: "First Proposition: *God is Spirit.*" "Second Proposition: *That which is spirit may manifest itself in visible form.*" "Third Proposition: *God has in times past manifested Himself in visible form.*" Fourth Proposition: *That which was seen in these manifestations of God **was not** God Himself—God in His invisible essence—but a **manifestation** of God.*" (pp. 13–14). In other words, in his view, the various Old Testament appearances of God weren't really God, because in Catholic-Protestant theology God is an invisible, shapeless spirit. Rather, in his view, *these appearances were temporary manifestations in which God for a few moments made himself "look like" a physical being.*

Shades of science fiction in all its glory! Latter-day Saints believe that contrasting that weakly supported supposition with the hundreds of scriptural passages in which God forthrightly describes himself as having numerous body parts clearly leads to the conclusion that *God has a physical body.*

"**Tritheism**" is another term which needs consideration. According to Merriam-Webster's Collegiate Dictionary, tritheism is "the doctrine that the Father, Son, and Holy Ghost are three distinct Gods" (Eleventh edition, 2003, 1340). However, Van Harvey's *A Handbook of Theological Terms* reveals the typical "trinitarinan spin"on the term: "*Tritheism is an extreme form of Trinitarianism.* It asserts the existence of three separate and distinct centers of consciousness sharing the *abstract and common* nature of deity. *It denies the unity of deity as it has been conceived in orthodox Trinitarian theology"* (Harvey, 247). The same *Handbook's* related definition of the term *existence* in this context is also of interest: "In classical theology, *E. is usually contrasted with essence* and *refers to the actuality in time and space of any subject,* in contrast to its mere possibility or potentiality. For example, after having defined the essential characteristics of a thing (what it is), *to assert its E. is to say that there is such a thing so defined"* (Harvey, 91).

So, according to these definitions, are Latter-day Saints "trithestic"? Most certainly, they believe the Father, Son, and Holy Spirit are three separate individuals, or "separate and distinct centers of consciousness," as the *Handbook* refers to them. With equal certainty, the Latter-day Saints believe in their "actuality in time and space," as alluded to in the "existence" definition. **But the term "tritheistic" does not appropriately fit Latter-day Saint beliefs.** *Latter-day Saints most certainly don't believe that the Father, Son, and Holy Spirit share the "abstract and common nature of deity" defined in "trinitarian" creeds.* Likewise, Latter-day Saints **do not** *"deny the unity of deity as it has been conceived in orthodox Trinitarian theology"*—they are not a break-off from ancient Catholic beliefs, as are the numerous Protestant denominations. In modern theological terminology, the term "tritheism" implies that break-off aspect.

Latter-day Saint beliefs concerning the nature of God most definitely are not *"an extreme form of Trinitarianism"*—they never have accepted the validity of "trinitarian" doctrines. Rather, they regard them as early fruits of the Great Apostasy which was clearly prophesied in numerous Old and New Testament passages.

In summation, when applied to Latter-day Saint beliefs, the term "tritheism" is another "theologically loaded" term. Latter-day Saints should not fall into the error of referring to their belief that the Godhead consists of three separate beings as being "tritheism."

Two other examples of "loaded terminology" are the terms "**transcendence**" and "**immanence**" because of the misleading conclusions theologians draw from them. Though they are terms Latter-day Saints rarely use, they form major cogs in the thought-processes which non-Latter-day Saint theologians have used for centuries in their efforts to define God.

The dictionary definition of "transcendence" is "the quality or state of being transcendent," which leads to its definition of "transcendent":

> **Transcendent: 1a**: exceeding usual limits: surpassing; **b:** extending or lying beyond the limits of ordinary experience; **c**: *in Kantian philosophy*: being beyond the limits of all possible experience and knowledge. **2**: being beyond comprehension; **3**: transcending the universe or material existence—compare IMMANENT 2. **4**: universally applicable or significant. (*Merriam Webster's Collegiate Dictionary*, 11th Edition, 1327)

The dictionary definition of "immanent" and its companion word, "immanentism":

> **Imminent: 1**: indwelling, inherent; **2**: being within the limits of possible experience—compare transcendent.
> **Immanentism**: any of several theories according to which God or an abstract mind or spirit pervades the world. (*Merriam Webster's Collegiate Dictionary*, 11th Edition, 620)

Notice the chain of logic utilized when the terms "transcendence" and "imminence" are used in a typical Bible dictionary:

> **God is Holy.** One of the most fundamental features of God's being is expressed
> by the word "holy." He is the incomparable God, "the Holy One" (Isa. 40:25, cf.
> Hab. 3:3). The word "holy," which in both Hebrew and Greek *has the root meaning of
> separateness*, is used predominantly in Scripture for a separateness from sin. *But this
> is only a secondary meaning derived from the primary application to God's separateness
> from all creation, i.e., his transcendence.* "He is exalted above all the peoples." There-
> fore, "holy is he" (Ps. 99:2–3). He is "the high and exalted One . . . whose name is
> Holy," and he lives "on a high and holy place" (Isa. 57:15). In his holiness God is the
> transcendent Deity.
>
> *The transcendence of God expresses the truth that God in himself is infinitely exalted
> above all creation. The concept of revelation presupposes a transcendent God who must
> unveil himself to be known.* Transcendence is further seen in God's position as Creator
> and Sovereign Lord of the universe. As the former he distinguishes himself from all cre-
> ation (Rom. 1:25), and in his sovereignty he evidences his transcendent supremacy.
>
> The transcendence of God is frequently expressed biblically in terms of time and
> space. He exists before all creation (Ps. 90:2), and neither the earth nor the highest
> heavens can contain him (1 Kings 8:27). *A certain anthropomorphic sense must be
> recognized in such expressions* lest God's transcendence be conceived in terms of our
> time and space, as though he lives in a time and space like ours only beyond that
> of creation. On the other hand, it is biblically incorrect to conceive of God in his
> transcendence as existing in a realm of timeless nowhereness outside of creation. In
> a manner that exceeds our finite understanding God exists in his own infinite realm
> as transcendent Lord over all creaturely time and space.
>
> God's transcendent holiness is biblically balanced with *the teaching of his imma-
> nence*, which signifies that *he is wholly present in his being* and power in every part and
> movement of the created universe. He is "over all and through all and in all" (Eph.
> 4:6). Not only does everything exist in him (Acts 17:28), but there is no place where
> his presence is absent (Ps. 139:1–10). His immanence is seen especially in relation to
> man. The Holy One who lives in a high and holy place also dwells with the "contrite
> and lowly of spirit" (Isa. 57:15). This dual dimension of God is seen clearly in the
> description "the Holy One of Israel" as well as in the name Yahweh, which describes
> both his transcendent power and his personal presence with and for his people.
>
> The biblical teaching of both God's transcendence and immanence counters
> the human tendency through history to emphasize one or the other. *A one-sided
> transcendence is seen in the Greek philosophers' concept of the ultimate ground of being
> as well as the later deists of the seventeenth and eighteenth centuries. The various forms of
> pantheism throughout history give evidence of the opposite emphasis on immanence.* The
> attractiveness of these exaggerations to sinful man is in the fact that in both man
> no longer stands before God in any practical sense as a responsible creature. (Elwell,
> Walter A. [editor], *Evangelical Dictionary of Theology*, 461–62)

The doctrines of Catholic and Evangelical theology deny (1) the premortal existence of mankind, (2) the knowledge that God the Father is the father of the spirits
of all mankind, and (3) the realization that God the Father, God the Son, and God
the Holy Spirit are three separate beings united in purpose but not in "substance."
Thus, they are severely limited in their understanding of the principles of what they
label transcendence and immanence. Likewise, (4) they have no or little grasp that it
is God's work and glory to bring to pass the immortality, eternal life and exaltation
of His children, nor of (5) His personal, father-based parental love for each and all of

His children. (6) They have no knowledge or concept of the special tools created for the use of exalted beings in obtaining knowledge of and communicating with all their creations (D&C 130:3–11; 77:1; Rev. 4:6; 21:11). In short, with only biblical scripture without the enriching, extending, and clarifying influence of the other volumes of latter-day scripture, they are severely limited in many key understandings concerning the true nature of God and the Godhead.

The Use of "Anthropomorphic," "Theophanies," and "Metaphors" as Discrediting Labels

The statement cited above, from Erickson's *Christian Theology*, typifies the usual "trinitarian" treatment of the hundreds of scriptural statements which make clear reference to the physical nature of God. They attempt to sidestep these statements, which in the aggregate powerfully refute their definition of God's nature (only a spirit) and of the relationship of the members of the Godhead (their three-persons-in-one-substance trinity). Their sidestepping typically is accomplished by labeling these hundreds of scriptural references as "anthropomorphisms," "theophanies," or "metaphors." The *Christian Theology* statement is repeated here:

> There are, of course, numerous passages which suggest that God has physical features such as hands or feet. How are we to regard these references? It seems most helpful to *treat them as anthropomorphisms, attempts to express the truth about God through human analogies.* There also are cases where God appeared in physical form, particularly in the Old Testament. *These should be understood as theophanies, or temporary manifestations of God.* It seems best to *take the clear statements about the spirituality and invisibility of God at face value* and *interpret the anthropomorphisms and theophanies in the light of them.*" (Erickson, *Christian Theology*, 268)

The counsel Erickson expresses, of *interpreting conflicting scriptural passages as anthropomorphisms* or *theophanies*, is an approach sometimes used by prominent theologians, and more so by not-so-prominent theologians who fancy themselves as apologists for their faiths. The approach is frequently encountered when they are dealing with individuals and writings from other faiths.

These deflecting (and sometimes derisive) terms are sometimes used by "trinitarian" theologians because of the innate doctrinal problems which they have inherited from ages past. What problems?

1. **On the subjects of the spirituality and invisibility of God,** they typically assert that there are no clear (not vague), fully definitive (not subject to various other definitions) scriptural statements which together join in a broad, clear pattern of doctrinal exposition (without being contradicted by dozens of other scriptural passages). To the contrary, the reality is that there are hundreds of passages that indicate with clarity that God is not *just* a spirit, he also has a physical body.

2. **On the subject of the three-in-one trinity,** they typically assert that there also are no clear (not vague), fully definitive (not subject to various other definitions) scriptural statements which together join in a broad, clear pattern of doctrinal exposition (without being contradicted by dozens of other scriptural passages). To the contrary, there are hundreds of passages which indicate with clarity that the Father, Son, and Holy Spirit are three separate beings, and that they are not three different manifestations of the same "physical but not-physical substance" (such as ice, water, and steam being three different manifestations of water).

Those who are not based in the Catholic/Protestant doctrinal perspective look in vain for competent doctrinal expositions from them which are not founded in what they regard as the highly flawed assumptions of "trinitarian" dogmas. In place of finding doctrinal expositions with a carefully assembled, broad array of inter-connected and mutually supporting scriptural citations, they find scholarly writings in which the authors, knowingly or unknowingly, appear to make broad leaps of logic which circumvent key concepts and principles.

Other, less-skillful authors, are sometimes content to offer a few extremely vague proof-texts about "the spirituality and invisibility of God." Often, the passages they cite are out of context or have no meaningful related context that clarifies them or are refuted by other related scriptures. (For instance, John 1:18 "No man hath seen God at any time" is clarified, and its meaning reversed, by John 6:46—"Not that any man hath seen the Father, save *he which is of God, he hath seen the Father.*" And the typical Catholic/Protestant interpretation of John 1:18 is further refuted by Acts 7:55–56, when Stephen, "being full of the Holy Ghost, looked up stedfastly into heaven, and *saw the glory of God,* and Jesus standing on the right hand of God, And said, Behold, I see the heavens opened, and the Son of man *standing on the right hand of God.*")

The Intended Plainness and Clarity of the Scriptures

A Book of Mormon Prophet, Nephi, commented several times about the clarity of the scriptures. He wrote that "*I shall speak unto you plainly,* according to the plainness of my prophesying. *For my soul delighteth in plainness*; for *after this manner doth the Lord God work among the children of men.* For *the Lord God giveth light unto the understanding; for he speaketh unto men according to their language, unto their understanding*" (2 Ne. 31:2–3).

It was Nephi who was commanded to begin making the metal plates upon which the Book of Mormon was recorded. As he began that process, he recorded that "after I had made these plates by way of commandment, I, Nephi, received a commandment that the ministry and the prophecies, *the more plain and precious parts of them, should be written upon these plates*; and that the things which were written should be kept for the instruction of my people" (1 Ne. 19:3; see also 1 Ne. 4:14–16).

It was this Nephi who, in vision, saw the coming forth of the Bible, and that in its transmission, key elements were lost:

> And the angel of the Lord said unto me: Thou hast beheld that the book proceeded forth from the mouth of a Jew; and *when it proceeded forth from the mouth of a Jew it contained the fulness of the gospel of the Lord, of whom the twelve apostles bear record*; and they bear record according to the truth which is in the Lamb of God.
> Wherefore, *these things go forth from the Jews in purity unto the Gentiles, according to the truth which is in God.* (1 Ne. 13:24–25)

But then he saw that in the time when the early Bible manuscripts were being transmitted "from the Jews unto the Gentiles," that "***they have taken away from the gospel of the Lamb many parts which are plain and most precious; and also many covenants of the Lord have they taken away.*** And all this have they done that they might pervert the right ways of the Lord, that they might blind the eyes and harden the hearts of the children of men" (1 Ne. 13:26–27). And "because of the *many plain and precious things which have been taken out of the book,* which were *plain* unto the understanding of the children of men, according to *the plainness which is in the Lamb* *of God*—because of *these things which are taken away out of the gospel of the Lamb,* an exceedingly great many do stumble" (1 Ne. 13:29).

However, later in the vision, Nephi saw "other books, which came forth by the power of the Lamb." And the angel who was showing Nephi the vision bore witness that "*These last records, which thou hast seen among the Gentiles, shall establish the truth of the first,* which are of the twelve apostles of the Lamb, and *shall make known the plain and precious things which have been taken away from them*; and shall make known to all kindreds, tongues, and people, that the Lamb of God is the Son of the Eternal Father, and the Savior of the world; and that all men must come unto him, or they cannot be saved" (1 Ne. 13:39–40).

Thus, Latter-day Saints believe (1) "*that which may be known of God is manifest*" in the Bible, that God showed unto them "the invisible things of him from the creation of the world," and that they were clearly seen and understood" at that time. (Rom. 1:18–20). However, (2) in the transmission of the Bible from the Jews to the Gentiles (presumably prior to the canonization of the New Testament in the fourth century), many parts which were "*plain and most precious*" were lost (1 Ne. 13:26–27), causing serious difficulties in defining essential doctrines correctly.

Most Scriptural Descriptions of the Physical Nature of God Are Forthright Statements, Not Metaphorical Allusions

The Apostle Paul wrote an amazing testimony concerning the gospel of Jesus Christ; this testimony is known and loved the world over: "I am not ashamed of the gospel of Christ: for it is the power of God unto salvation to every one that believeth; to the Jew first, and also to the Greek. For therein is the righteousness of God revealed from faith to faith: as it is written, The just shall live by faith" (Rom. 1:16–17). But then, he wrote his testimony concerning the clarity of the revealed scriptures concerning the nature of God: "For *the wrath of God is revealed from heaven* against all ungodliness and unrighteousness of men, who hold the truth in unrighteousness; Because *that which may be known of God is manifest in them; for God hath shewed it unto them. For the invisible things of him from the creation of the world are clearly seen, being understood by the things that are made, even his eternal power and Godhead;* so that they are without excuse" (Rom. 1:18–20).

Latter-day Saints believe Paul. When he wrote that "*that which may be known of God is manifest*" and that "the invisible things of him from the creation of the world are *clearly seen, being understood* by the things that are made, even his eternal power and Godhead," they believe it to be true!

However, there certainly are various metaphorical allusions included among the references cited concerning the physical attributes in the chapter sections that follow. The interpretational problem arises when "trinitarian" interpreters attempt to "throw out the baby with the bath water." *They incorrectly make the false assumption that if any part of a passage is metaphorical, then the whole passage is metaphorical.* That certainly is an invalid assumption. This can be illustrated by commenting on a metaphorical, or comparative, passage written by the author of Hebrews. It is found in Hebrews 6:7–8. Its context, found in Hebrews 6:4–6, shows that the metaphor is contrasting those who remain true to the faith with those who fall away into apostasy or sin, and emphasizing that some who fall away will be rejected by God because they can't manage to "renew them again unto repentance." This is the two-verse metaphor:

> For the *earth* which drinketh in the *rain* that cometh oft upon it, and bringeth forth *herbs* meet for them *by whom it is dressed*, receiveth blessing from God:
>
> But that which beareth *thorns* and *briers* is rejected, and is nigh unto cursing; whose end is to be burned. (Heb. 6:7–8)

What elements are metaphorical in this passage? (1) The earth doesn't "drink." (2) The earth doesn't literally bring forth herbs; seeds have to be planted which grow into the herbs. (3) The earth doesn't literally make plants "meet" for "them by whom it is dressed." (4) The earth doesn't of itself reject thorns and briers. All these elements are metaphorical allusions to what other beings and entities do.

But, the basic nouns upon which the metaphor is constructed are, of necessity, literal objects: (1) earth, (2) rain, (3) herbs, (4) people who plant the herbs and nurture their growth, (5) thorns, (6) briars, and of necessity: (7) God. The fact that physical entities are part of a scriptural metaphor doesn't, by any means, mean that they are nonexistent, even though metaphorical concepts are woven around them.

Again, one shouldn't "throw out the baby with the bath water."

Again, metaphors are almost always woven around known, recognizable physical objects.

Again, *there is no well-founded, scriptural basis for assertions that the many hundreds of scriptural references to the physical parts and physical form of God are only "anthropomorphisms,"* which "trinitarians" define as attempts to describe what they believe is a non-physical, formless god through human analogies (meaning: attempts to describe God using references to human body parts). That assertion is a long-practiced rationalization designed to skirt around an overwhelming amount of contrary scriptural evidence.

Again, *there is no well-founded, scriptural basis for assertions that "theophanies" are only "temporary manifestations," in physical form, of a non-physical, formless God.* That assertion is also a long-practiced rationalization designed to skirt around an overwhelming amount of contrary scriptural evidence.

An Example: Separating Scriptural Realities from "Spiritualized," "Metaphorical" Interpretations

Cited in chapter 2 was the Episcopalian comment concerning wording in the early Christian creeds (in this case speaking of the Apostles' Creed which cites Colossians 3:1)—*"Some of the phrases are clearly "symbolic" (as, "sitteth on the right hand of God the Father," which, of course, could not be literally true)."*

The individual expressing that opinion obviously was an adherent of the "trinitarian" concepts that God is a non-material, shapeless "spirit" which is everywhere present at the same time. In other words, he embraces the "trinitarian" belief that God has no human-like form, and thus one can't sit or stand beside him, nor be positioned beside him. Also, that belief orientation would assert that God can neither walk, nor raise His hand, nor hold tangible objects since he doesn't have feet, legs, hands, and other body parts.

A *"spiritualized" interpreter*, believing that a spirit is a formless entity, would thus reject any literal interpretation of someone actually being positioned beside God or situated in any directional proximity to God. He would, perhaps, express an opinion such as "I know the scripture says that, but it can't literally be true," and he would typically ignore such passages as would conflict with his spiritualized interpretation.

A *"metaphorical" interpreter* would similarly reject any concept of actual physical positioning relationships related to God's presence but might perceive that one's being on the right side of God could mean that he has God's acceptance and approbation. In modern vernacular, a metaphorical interpreter would say that being on the right hand of God only means that "one can be on His good side," or one is part of God's "in crowd." He would accept this "higher meaning" of the passages but reject the literal insights concerning the physical nature of God that the passages clearly state.

A *"literal" interpreter* would accept both the physical aspects of the passage and also seek to perceive the higher-level meaning(s) as well. He would recognize and accept both (1) the physical-level assertion that God has a tangible form, is in a specific place, and that others can be geographically situated beside him and (2) the higher concept that literally being positioned by God's side represents one's having God's acceptance and approbation.

A careful literal interpreter would also look for a broad pattern of scripture that guides and confirms his interpretational understanding. In this case, such a broad pattern of scripture exists. Both the Old and New Testaments contribute to it, as follows:

Principle #1: *sitting near a king's throne, especially to the right of a king's throne, is a symbol of the king's acceptance and honoring of an individual:* • "Bathsheba therefore went unto king Solomon, to speak unto him for Adonijah. And the king rose up to meet her, and bowed himself unto her, and sat down on his throne, and *caused a seat to be set for the king's mother; and she sat on his right hand"* (1 Kgs. 2:19).

Principle #2: *The right hand, itself, is a symbol of honor.* See, for instance, Jacob's crossing his hands and placing his right hand on the head of Ephraim while blessing the sons of Joseph (Gen. 48:8–19).

Principle #3: *Jesus' Apostles believed that sitting near God and His throne in the afterlife is both physically possible and highly desirable:* • "And *James and John,* the sons of Zebedee, come unto him, saying, Master, we would that thou shouldest do for us whatsoever we shall desire. . . . *Grant unto us that we may sit, one on thy right hand, and the other on thy left hand, in thy glory"* (Mark 10:35, 37; see Matt. 20:20–23).

4. Scriptural Evidence: *Old Testament, New Testament, and modern prophets and Church leaders have testified of seeing Godhood members in the form of a man and located in a specific place:* • [1] "Hear thou therefore the word of the LORD: *I saw the LORD sitting on his throne, and all the host of heaven standing by him on his right hand and on his left"* (1 Kgs. 22:19; see also 2 Chr. 18:18). • [2] "But he, being full of the Holy Ghost, looked up stedfastly into heaven, and saw the glory of God, and *Jesus standing on the right hand of God,* And said, Behold, I see the heavens opened, and *the Son of man standing on the right hand of God"* (Acts 7:55–56). • [3] *"I saw in the right hand of him that sat on the throne* a book written within and on the backside, sealed with seven seals" (Rev. 5:1). • [4] "And he came and *took the book out of the right hand of him that sat upon the throne"* (Rev. 5:7). • [5] "the Lord touched the eyes of our understandings and they were opened, and the glory of the Lord shone round about. And *we beheld the glory of the Son, on the right hand of the Father,* and received of his fulness" (D&C 76:19–20). • [6] *"For we saw him, even on the right hand of God;* and we heard the voice bearing record that he is the Only Begotten of the Father" (D&C 76:23–24).

5. Scriptural Evidence: *Jesus Christ himself emphatically proclaimed that he would sit on the right hand of God's power* (to the Jewish Sanhedrin, which was seeking grounds to accuse him of blasphemy): • "Hereafter shall the *Son of man sit on the right hand of the power of God"* (Luke 22:69).

6. Scriptural Evidence: *Eight New Testament passages specifically assert that Jesus Christ rose and is positioned on the right-hand side of God the Father.* These passages, then, clearly and unequivocally indicate that God the Father exists in a specific location, has a throne upon which he sits, and that Jesus' position is one of honor, geographically situated to the right-hand side of God the Father's throne: • [1] "So then after the Lord had spoken unto them, *he was received up into heaven, and sat on the right hand of God"* (Mark 16:19). • [2] *"It is Christ that died, yea rather, that is risen again, who is even at the right hand of God,* who also maketh intercession for us" (Rom. 8:34). • [3] "If ye then be risen with Christ, seek those things which are above, where *Christ sitteth on the right hand of God"* (Col. 3:1). • [4] "But this man, after he had offered one sacrifice for sins for ever, *sat down on the right hand of God"* (Heb. 10:12). • [5] "Looking unto Jesus the author and finisher of our faith; who for the joy that was set before him endured the cross, despising the shame, and *is set down at the right hand of the throne of God"* (Heb. 12:2). • [6] *"Jesus Christ: Who is gone into heaven, and is on the right hand of God;* angels and authorities and powers being made subject unto him" (1 Pet. 3:21–22). • [7] "We have such an high priest, *who is set on the right hand of the throne of the Majesty in the heavens"* (Heb. 8:1). • [8] "Looking unto *Jesus* the author and finisher of our faith; who for the joy that was set before him endured the cross, despising the shame, and *is set down at the right hand of the throne of God"* (Heb. 12:2).

7. Scriptural Evidence: *Two other New Testament passages speak specifically of God the Father's right hand, indicating both that he has a right hand and that Jesus has been exalted to a place of honor:* • [1] "This Jesus hath God raised up, whereof we all are witnesses. Therefore *being by the right hand of God exalted"* (Acts 2:32–33). • [2] "The God of our fathers raised up Jesus, whom ye slew and hanged on a tree. *Him hath God exalted with his right hand to be a Prince and a Saviour"* (Acts 5:30–31).

8. Scriptural Evidence: *Latter-day Saint scriptures also specifically indicate that Jesus rose and is positioned on the right-hand side of God the Father:* • [1] *"Christ hath ascended into heaven, and hath sat down on the right hand of God,* to claim of the Father his rights of mercy which he hath upon the children of men?" (Moro. 7:27) • [2] "may the grace of God the Father, whose *throne* is high in the heavens, and *our Lord Jesus Christ, who sitteth on the right hand of his power,* until all things shall become subject unto him, be, and abide with you forever. Amen" (Moro. 9:26). • [3] "He was crucified, died, and rose again the third day; *And ascended into heaven, to sit down on the right hand of the Father,* to reign with almighty power according to the will of the Father" (D&C 20:23–24).

Conclusion: The commonly held "trinitarian" assumption that the Colossians 3:1 statement that Christ sitteth on the right hand of God *"could not be literally true"* stands in direct contradiction to a strong, many-scriptural-passage array of forthrightly stated contrary evidence. That evidence specifically asserts that the resurrected Christ literally has a seat of honor geographically located to the right of the literal throne of God the Father, upon which the Father literally sits.

Every one of the evidentiary passages cited are straightforward and specific; there is no intimation of metaphorical or allegorical language utilized in any of them. There is not the slightest indication that the cited passages refer to imagined "theophanies" in which God the Father and God the Son temporarily change themselves so they appear to be in specific geographical locations. To the contrary, the passages clearly indicate that the New Testament Apostles who recorded them knew that both the Father and the Son (1) are two separate beings, not two different manifestations of the same being; (2) are not formless entities devoid of body parts and shapes; rather, (3) they are beings who have definite body shapes that occupy specific geographical locations.

This "cannot be literally true" assumption, like every element of the erroneous "trinitarian" concept of God, literally hits a brick wall every time it is compared to broad patterns of scriptural documentation.

Two Levels of Scriptural Evidence and 419 Passages Asserting the Physical Nature of God

When considering the physical natures and attributes of the members of the Godhead, it is important to note that there are two levels of evidence found in the canonical scriptures.

The first and highest level is *words spoken in first person by members of the Godhead concerning some portion of their physical anatomy*. These could be statements by God the Father, by Jehovah/Jesus Christ, and by The Holy Ghost, and they are to be regarded as *direct quotations of the words of deity*.

A fundamental belief in the Bible, especially by the millions who regard the Bible as being inerrant, is that it is truly the word of God, and that God speaks only the truth. Thus, the scriptures repeatedly assert that *God* truly is • "a *God of truth* and without iniquity" (Deut. 32:4). • "God is *not* a man, *that he should lie*" (Num.23:19). [It is interesting when individuals try to twist this passage out of its expressed meaning: that God does not lie, and they instead attempt to make it appear as a passage that is talking about the physical form of God!] • "thou hast redeemed me, O LORD *God of truth*" (Ps. 31:5). • "he who blesseth himself in the earth shall bless himself in the *God of truth*" (Isa. 65:16). • "I, Enos, knew that *God could not lie*" (Enos 1:6).

Scriptural passages also specifically assert that God the Son is a God of truth: • "his glory shall be the glory of the Only Begotten of the Father, *full of grace, equity, and truth*" (Alma 9:26). • "Yea, Lord, I know that thou speakest the truth, for *thou art a God of truth*, and *canst not lie*" (Eth. 3:12). The same assertion is also made for *the Holy Ghost*: • "*the Spirit speaketh the truth and lieth not*" (Jacob 4:13).

What does the truthfulness of God mean in this context? It means that if God says that He has a face, eyes, ears, mouth, shoulders, arms, hands, fingers, a bosom, a heart, bowels, sides, a seat, feet, and other tangible body parts, *He really has them*! He is not deceiving those who read His forthright, unambiguous first-person statements in the scriptures!

Likewise, it means that if God says that He breathes, can cast a shadow, walks, stands, sits, occupies a space so others can stand or sit beside or around him, and wears clothes and wears or handles other tangible objects, *He really does these things*! He is not speaking "metaphorically," "allegorically," or "spiritually." When many dozens of first-person statements are made by members of the Godhead concerning their physical nature, no amount of scripture-twisting can alter their truthfulness.

The second level consists of *words spoken or written by other individuals in the scriptures about the physical natures of the divine beings*. These statements usually are recorded by inspired prophets and Apostles who have eyewitness knowledge and who are usually regarded as writing under divine inspiration. (See 2 Tim. 3:16: "*All scripture is given by inspiration of God, and is profitable for doctrine*, for reproof, for correction, for instruction in righteousness.")

In the numerous scriptural texts cited in this chapter concerning the various physical body parts of members of deity, the statements for each body part are divided into these two levels. **Level-one quotations** are *Scriptural first-person statements made by members of the Godhead*, reduced to the abbreviated form **First-person statements**. **Level-two quotations** are *Scriptural second-person statements made by knowledgeable observers about God*, reduced to the abbreviated form **Second-person statements**.

Numerous pertinent passages concerning many of the body parts of God, certainly *several hundred others*, have not been cited in this context. Obviously, some of the "better" scriptural verses have been selected—enough to make an extremely convincing case that God literally has the body parts mentioned. To aid the reader in keeping track of those quoted herein, the cited subjects, and passages concerning them, have been numbered, with separate numbering systems used for first-person and second-person levels.

Frequently, verses mentioning one anatomical part also refer to other body parts as well. Those additional parts have been italicized but not included in the running counts for those additional body parts unless the passage is repeated under another heading.

By definition, the passages cited below are spoken by or are references to God the Father; Jehovah [the LORD]; Jesus Christ as a premortal or postmortal being; and the Holy Ghost. Statements made by the above beings, whether referring to Himself or to one of the other divine beings (since they are all Gods of truth), are always considered **First-person statements**.

At this point, no specific effort is being made in this chapter to fully differentiate between members of the Godhead, since believers in "trinitarian" doctrines believe that God the Father and God the Son are two different manifestations of the same "substance." They also believe that Jehovah is God the Father, so most of the passages to be cited would be references to the physical nature of the same being. Those beliefs, of course, are not the doctrinal beliefs of Latter-day Saints, so the characteristics of the individual members of the Godhead will be identified and separated further in other chapters. Presented below are *24 categories of physical descriptions of God, organized into nine groups.*

Group A: Male Beings

I. Members of the Godhead Are Male Beings

The scriptures consistently speak of God the Father, God the Son Jesus Christ, and God the Holy Ghost as male beings and never refer to them in the feminine gender. Gender, in the English language, requires that its possessor be a living entity, and it requires that its possessor have a physical shape, with gender-specific body parts.

First-person statements: **God the Father** is referred to and described by Jesus Christ as being male. Jesus called him Father (not mother or just a parent), and referred to him with male nouns (*Father, Son*, etc.) or pronouns (*he, him, his, himself*, etc.). For instance, He told His disciples, • [1] "In *my Father's house* are many mansions" (John 14:2), and told them • [2] "I will pray the Father, and *he* shall give you another Comforter" (John 14:16). Dozens of passages are consistent in this usage. See • [3] "*your Father* which is in heaven: for *he* maketh his sun to rise on the evil and on the good" (Matt. 5:45). • [4] "the Son of man shall come in the glory of his Father with his angels; and then *he* shall reward every man according to his works"

(Matt. 16:27). • [5] "Thinkest thou that I cannot now pray to my Father, and *he* shall presently give me more than twelve legions of angels?" (Matt. 26:53). • [6] "the Father loveth the Son, and sheweth him all things that *himself* doeth" (John 5:20). • [7] "as the Father hath life in himself; so hath *he* given to the Son to have life in himself" (John 5:26). • [8] "When ye have lifted up the Son of man, then shall ye know that I am *he,* and that I do nothing of myself" (John 8:28). • [9] "Jesus said . . . I proceeded forth and came from God; neither came I of myself, but *he* sent me" (John 8:42). • [10] "it is *my Father* that honoureth me; of whom ye say, that *he* is your God" (John 8:54). • [11] "the Father which sent me, *he* gave me a command- ment" (John 12:49). • [12] "the Father that dwelleth in me, *he* doeth the works" (John 14:10). • [13] "that whatsoever ye shall ask of the Father in my name, *he* may give it you" (John15:16). • [14] "Whatsoever ye shall ask the Father in my name, *he* will *give it you*" (John 16:23).

Second-person statements: **God the Father** • [1] "but wait for the promise of *the Father*, which, *saith he,* ye have heard of me" (Acts 1:4). • [2] "being by the right hand of God exalted, and having received of the *Father* the promise of the Holy Ghost, *he* hath shed forth this" (Acts 2:33). • [3] "I will be to him a *Father*, and *he* shall be to me a *Son*?" (Heb. 1:5). • [4] "the work of the *Father* shall commence, in preparing the way for the fulfilling of *his* covenants, which *he* hath made to *his* people" (1 Ne. 14:17). • [5] "the *Father* and the Son, unto the fulfilling of the promise which *he* hath made, that if ye entered in by the way ye should receive" (2 Ne. 31:18). • [6] "ye shall pray unto the *Father* in the name of Christ, that *he* will consecrate thy performance" (2 Ne. 32:9). • [7] "I had requested it of my *Father* who was in heaven; for *he* had heard my cry" (Jacob 7:22). • [8] "*he* is the beginning and the end, the first and the last" (Alma 11:39). • [9] "unto him will the *Father* bear record of me, for *he* will visit him with fire and with the Holy Ghost" (3 Ne. 11:35). • [10] "That ye may be the children of your *Father* who is in heaven; for *he* maketh his sun to rise on the evil and on the good" (3 Ne. 12:45; See also 3 Ne. 17:4; 18:27; 20:27, 34; 21:4, 6, 7; 27:7; Morm. 6:22; 9:31, 37; Eth. 4:15; Moro. 7:27, 31, 32, 48; 8:3; 10:4, 21).

First-person statements: **Jesus Christ.** God the Father, in turn, consistently referred to Jesus as a male being, saying • [1] "This is my beloved *Son,* in whom I am well pleased" (Matt. 3:17). • [2] "This is my beloved *Son,* in whom I am well pleased; hear ye *him*" (Matt. 17:5). • [3] "there came a voice from heaven, saying, Thou art my beloved *Son,* in whom I am well pleased" (Mark 1:11). • [4] "a voice came out of the cloud, saying, This is my beloved *Son*: hear *him*" (Mark 9:7). • [5] "a voice came from heaven, which said, Thou art my beloved *Son*; in thee I am well pleased" (Luke 3:22). • [6] "there came a voice out of the cloud, saying, This is my beloved *Son*: hear *him*" (Luke 9:35). • [7] "there came such a voice to him from the excellent glory, This is my beloved *Son,* in whom I am well pleased" (2 Pet. 1:17). • [8] "the Father said: Repent ye, repent ye, and be baptized in the name of my Beloved *Son*" (2 Ne. 31:11). • [9] "Behold my Beloved *Son,* in whom I am well pleased, in whom I have glorified my name—hear ye *him*" (3 Ne. 11:7). • [10] "saith the Father, that at that day whosoever will not repent and come unto my Beloved *Son,* them will I cut off from among my people, O house of Israel" (3 Ne. 21:20). • [11] "Jesus is the Christ, the *Son* of the living God; that the *Father* may bring about, through *his* most Beloved, *his* great and eternal purpose" (Morm. 5:14). • [12] "behold the blood of thy *Son* which was shed, the blood of *him* whom thou gavest that thyself might be glorified" (D&C 45:4).

• [13] "the Holy Ghost descended upon *him* in the form of a dove, and sat upon *him*, and there came a voice out of heaven saying: This is my beloved *Son*" (D&C 93:15). • [14] "behold, my Beloved *Son*, which was my Beloved and Chosen from the beginning" (Moses 4:2). • [15] "One of them spake unto me, calling me by name and said, pointing to the other—This is My Beloved *Son*. Hear *Him!*" (JS—H 1:17).

First-person statements: the Holy Ghost. Then, while speaking of the Holy Ghost, Jesus said, • [1] "But the Comforter, which is the *Holy Ghost*, . . . *he* shall teach you all things" (John 14:26). • [2] "The *Spirit of the Lord* is upon me, because *he* hath anointed me to preach the gospel to the poor" (Luke 4:18). • [3] "the Spirit of truth; . . . ye know him; for *he* dwelleth with you, and shall be in you" (John 14:17). • [4] "the Spirit of truth, which proceedeth from the Father, *he* shall testify of me" (John 15:26). • [5] "when *he*, the *Spirit of truth*, is come, *he* will guide you into all truth: for *he* shall not speak of *himself*" (John 16:13).

Second person statements: the Holy Ghost. • [1] "the *Holy Ghost* also is a witness to us: for after that *he* had said before" (Heb. 10:15). • [2] "I beheld that *he* was in the form of a man; yet nevertheless, I knew that it was the *Spirit of the Lord* (1 Ne. 11:11). • [3] "I beheld the Spirit of God, . . . and *he* went forth upon the many waters" (1 Ne. 13:12). • [4] "according to the . . . Spirit of the Lord which is in me. . . . *he* worketh in me to do according to his will" (W of M 1:7).

Group B: God's Face and Countenance, Head and Hair

2. God Has a Face and Countenance

First-person statements: • [1] "Thou canst not see *my face*: for there shall no man see me, and live" (Ex. 33:20; for further understanding see Moses 1:11, 31; Ex. 33:11). • [2] "thou shalt see *my back parts*: but *my face shall not be seen*" (Ex. 33:23). • [3] "*I will even set my face* against that soul that eateth blood, and will cut him off from among his people" (Lev. 17:10). • [4, 5] "*I will set my face* against that man, and will cut him off from among his people; because he hath given of his seed unto Molech, . . . And if the people of the land do any ways hide their eyes from the man, when he giveth of his seed unto Molech, and kill him not: Then I will *set my face* against that man, and against his family, and will cut him off" (Lev. 20:3–5). • [6] "And the soul that turneth after such as have familiar spirits, and after wizards, to go a whoring after them, *I will even set my face* against that soul, and will cut him off from among his people. Sanctify yourselves therefore, and be ye holy: for I am the LORD your God" (Lev. 20:6–7). • [7] "If my people, which are called by my name, shall humble themselves, and pray, and seek *my face*, and turn from their wicked ways; then will I hear from heaven, and will forgive their sin, and will heal their land. Now *mine eyes* shall be open, and *mine ears* attent unto the prayer that is made in this place" (2 Chr. 7:14–15). • [8, 9] "Hear, O LORD, when I cry with my voice: have mercy also upon me, and answer me. When thou saidst, *Seek ye my face*; my heart said unto thee, *Thy face*, LORD, will I seek" (Ps. 27:7–8). • [10] "In a little wrath *I hid my face from thee for a moment*; but with everlasting kindness will I have mercy on thee, saith the LORD thy Redeemer" (Isa. 54:8). • [11] "Behold, . . . saith the LORD, . . . they shall hunt them from every mountain, and from every hill, and out of the holes of the rocks. *For mine eyes are upon all their ways*: they are not hid from *my face*, neither is their iniquity hid *from mine eyes*" (Jer. 16:16–17). • [12] "Thus saith the LORD the maker thereof, the LORD that formed it, to establish it; the LORD is his name; . . . They come to fight with the Chaldeans, but it is to fill them with the dead bodies of men, whom I have slain in mine anger and in my fury, and for all whose wickedness *I have hid my face* from this city" (Jer. 33:2, 5). • [13] "Therefore thus saith the LORD of hosts, the God of Israel; Behold, *I will set my face* against you for evil, and to cut off all Judah" (Jer. 44:11). • [14, 15] "I will *set my face* against them; they shall go out from one fire, and another fire shall devour them; and ye shall know that I am the LORD, when I *set my face* against them" (Ezek. 15:7). • [16, 17] "So the house of Israel shall know that I am the LORD their God from that day and forward. And the heathen shall know that the house of Israel went into captivity for their iniquity: because they trespassed against me, therefore *hid I my face from them*, and gave them into the hand of their enemies: so fell they all by the sword. According to their uncleanness and according to their transgressions have I done unto them, and *hid my face from them*" (Ezek. 39:22–24). • [18] "Then shall they know that I am the LORD their God, which cause them to be led into captivity among the heathen: but I have gathered them unto their own land, and have left none of them any more there. *Neither will I hide my face* any more from them: for I have poured out my spirit upon the house of Israel, saith the Lord GOD" (Ezek. 39:28–29).

Second-person statements: • [1] Genesis 32 records that Jacob wrestled throughout the night with "a man" whom he perceived to be God. When daybreak dawned, the "man" said, "Let me go, for the day breaketh," but Jacob replied, "I will not let thee go, except thou bless me." The blessing was given: God changed his name from Jacob to Israel, and stated that "*as a prince hast thou power with God* and with men, and *hast prevailed.*" The scripture then records that "Jacob called the name of the place Peniel: for *I have seen God face to face*, and my life is preserved" (Gen. 32:30; see 32:24–32; also Gen. 33:10). • [2] Later, Moses saw the face of God at the door of the tabernacle, while the people of Israel worshiped Him: "*the LORD spake unto Moses face to face*, as a man speaketh unto his friend" (Ex.33:10; see Ex. 33:7–23). • [3] Moses and the people of Israel saw the face of God on Mount Sinai, as Moses later reminded the Israelite nation: "*The LORD talked with you face to face* in the mount out of the midst of the fire" (Deut. 5:4; see 5:1–22). • [4] "There arose not a prophet since in Israel like unto Moses, whom the LORD knew *face to face*" (Deut. 34:10). • [5] "Seek the LORD and his strength, seek *his face* continually" (1 Chr. 16:11). • [6] "For the righteous LORD loveth righteousness; *his countenance doth behold* the upright" (Ps. 11:7). • [7, 8] "When thou saidst, *Seek ye my face*; my heart said unto thee, *Thy face*, LORD, will I seek. *Hide not thy face* far from me; . . . (Ps. 27:8–9) • [9] "The *eyes* of the LORD are upon the righteous, and *his ears* are open unto their cry. The *face* of the LORD is against them that do evil" (Ps. 34:15–16). • [10] "They got not the land in possession by their own sword, . . . but *thy right hand*, and *thine arm*, and the *light of thy countenance*, because thou hadst a favour unto them" (Ps. 44:3). • [11] "And there shall be no more curse: but the *throne of God and of the Lamb* shall be in it; and his servants shall serve him: And they shall *see his face*" (Rev. 22:3–4).

Second-person statements: God's Face Can Shine. • [12, 13] "The LORD bless thee, and keep thee: The LORD *make his face shine* upon thee, and be gracious unto thee: The LORD lift up *his countenance* upon thee, and give thee peace" (Num. 6:24–26). • [14] "*LORD, lift thou up the light of thy countenance* upon us" (Ps. 4:6). • [15] "*Make thy face to shine* upon thy servant: save me for thy mercies' sake" (Ps. 31:160). • [16] "hope thou in God: for I shall yet praise him for *the help of his countenance*" (Ps. 42:5). • [17] "God be merciful unto us, and bless us; and *cause his face to shine upon us*" (Ps. 67:1). • [18] "Turn us again, O God, and *cause thy face to shine*" (Ps. 80:3; see also 80:7, 19).

• [19] "they shall walk, O LORD, in *the light of thy countenance*" (Ps. 89:15). • [20] "Thou hast set our iniquities before thee, our secret sins in *the light of thy countenance*" (Ps. 90:8). • [21] "*Make thy face to shine* upon thy servant; and teach me thy statutes" (Ps. 119:135). O our God, hear the prayer of thy servant, . . . and *cause thy face to shine* upon thy sanctuary" (Dan. 9:17). • [22, 23] "Jesus blessed them as they did pray unto him; and *his countenance* did smile upon them, and *the light of his countenance did shine upon them, and behold they were as white as the countenance and also the garments of Jesus*" (3 Ne. 190:25). • [24] "We saw the Lord *standing* upon the breastwork of the pulpit, before us; and under *his feet* was a paved work of pure gold, in color like amber. *His eyes* were as a flame of fire; the *hair of his head was white* like the pure snow; *his countenance* shone above the brightness of the sun" (D&C 110:2–3). • [25] "Their *countenances shone*, and the radiance from the presence of the Lord rested upon them" (D&C 138:24).

Compare: • [26] "After six days Jesus taketh Peter, James, and John his brother, and bringeth them up into an high mountain apart, And *was transfigured* before them: and *his face did shine* as the sun, and his raiment was white as the light" (Matt. 17:1–2). Compare that account with the report of when Moses came down from mount Sinai with the two tables of testimony in his hand: "When Aaron and all the children of Israel saw Moses, behold, *the skin of his face shone*; and they were afraid to come nigh him. . . . and Moses talked with them. . . . And till Moses had done speaking with them, *he put a vail on his face*" (Exodus 34:30–31, 33).

• [27] Other passages speak of the shining countenance of God. For instance, "We have heard with our ears, O God, our fathers have told us, what work thou didst in their days, in the times of old. How thou didst drive out the heathen with *thy hand*, and plantedst them; how thou didst afflict the people, and cast them out. For they got not the land in possession by their own sword, neither did their own arm save them: but *thy right hand*, and *thine arm*, and *the light of thy countenance*, because thou hadst a favour unto them" (Ps. 44:1–3). • [28] "They perish at the rebuke of *thy countenance*" (Ps. 80:16).

3. God's Head and Hair

Second-person statements: One passage, which most of the Christian world interprets as referring to God, deserves to be included in this context. (In contrast, Latter-day Saints believe the Ancient of Days is Michael, who is Adam [see D&C 116:1; 138:38].) But since Protestants, Evangelicals, Fundamentalists, Greek Orthodox, and Roman Catholics regard it as referring to God, it is pertinent to cite the passage in this context: • [1] "I beheld till the thrones were cast down, and the Ancient of days did sit, whose garment was white as snow, and *the hair of his head like the pure wool*: his *throne* was like the fiery flame" (Dan. 7:9). • [2] "I saw . . . in the midst of the seven candlesticks one like unto the Son of man, clothed with a garment down to *the foot*, and girt about *the paps* with a golden girdle. *His head* and *his hairs were white like wool*, as *white* as snow; and *his eyes* were as a flame of fire; And *his feet* like unto fine brass" (Rev. 1:12–15). • [3] "upon the cloud one *sat* like unto the Son of man, *having on his head a golden crown*, and *in his hand a sharp sickle*" (Rev. 14:14).

Another passage, which is a description of Jehovah's appearance in the Latter-day Saint Kirtland Temple on April 3, 1836, says: • [4] "We saw the Lord standing upon the breastwork of the pulpit, before us; and under *his feet* was a paved work of pure gold, in color like amber. His *eyes were as a flame of fire*; the *hair of his head was white like the pure snow*; his *countenance shone above the brightness of the sun*; and *his voice was as the sound of the rushing of great waters*, even the voice of Jehovah, saying: I am the first and the last; I am he who liveth, I am he who was slain; I am your advocate with the Father" (D&C 110:2–4).

Group C: God's Mind and Soul

4. God's Mind

First-person statements: • [1] "Wherefore the LORD God of Israel saith, . . . I will raise me up a faithful priest, that shall do according to that which is in *mine heart and in my mind*" (1 Sam. 2:30, 35). • [2] "Then said the LORD unto me, Though Moses and Samuel stood before me, yet *my mind could not be toward this people*" (Jer. 15:1). • [3, 4] "Wherefore the LORD God of Israel saith, . . . she discovered her whoredoms, and discovered her nakedness: then *my mind* was alienated from her, like as *my mind* was alienated from her sister" (Ezek. 23:1, 18).

Second-person statements: • [1] "they put him in ward, *that the mind of the LORD* might be shewed them" (Lev. 24:12). • [2] "Surely it is meet to be said unto God, . . . That which I see not teach thou me: if I have done iniquity, I will do no more. Should it be according to *thy mind*? (Job 34:31, 33). • [3] "did not the LORD remember them, and *came it not into his mind*?" (Jer. 44:21). • [4] "Who hath known *the mind of the Lord*? or who hath been his counsellor?" (Rom. 11:34). • [5, 6] "For *who hath known the mind of the Lord*, that he may instruct him? But we have *the mind of Christ*" (1 Cor. 2:16). • [7] "whatsoever they shall speak when moved upon by the Holy Ghost shall be scripture, shall be the will of the Lord, *shall be the mind of the Lord*" (D&C 68:4). • [8] "Now here is wisdom, and *the mind of the Lord*—let the house be built" (D&C 95:13). • [9] "the president may inquire and *obtain the mind of the Lord by revelation*" (D&C 102:23). • [10] "And this *according to the mind and will of the Lord*, who ruleth over all flesh" (D&C 133:61). • [11] "The Lord will never permit me or any other man who stands as President of this Church to lead you astray. It is not in the programme. It is not in *the mind of God*" (OD 1). • [12] "The Son of God felt disposed to have that thing presented to the Church and to the world for purposes *in his own mind*" (OD 1).

5. God's Soul

First-person statement: • [1] "Saith the LORD. . . . *My bowels, my bowels!* I am pained at *my very heart*; *my heart* maketh a noise in me; I cannot hold my peace, because thou hast heard, O *my soul*, the sound of the trumpet, the alarm of war" (Jer. 4:17, 19).

Second-person statements: • [1] "The children of Israel . . . put away the strange gods from among them, and served the LORD: and *his soul* was grieved for the misery of Israel" (Judg. 10:15–16). • [2] "The LORD trieth the righteous: but the wicked and him that loveth violence *his soul hateth*" (Ps. 11:5).

Group D: God's Facial Features, Smelling, and Breathing

6. God's Eyes and Eyelids

First-person statements: • [1] "Thus saith the LORD, the God of Israel, . . . they have forsaken me, . . . and have not walked in my ways, to do that which is right in *mine eyes*" (1 Kgs. 11:31, 33). • [2] "Thus saith the LORD God of Israel, . . . thou hast not been as my servant David, who kept my commandments, and who followed me with all his heart, to do that only which was right in *mine eyes*" (1 Kgs. 14:7–8). • [3] "Now *mine eyes* shall be open, and *mine ears* attent unto the prayer that is made in this place. For now have I chosen and sanctified this house, that my name may be there for ever: and *mine eyes* and *mine heart* shall be there perpetually" (2 Chr. 7:15–16). • [4] "I [the Lord] will instruct thee and teach thee in the way which thou shalt go: I will guide thee with *mine eye*" (Ps. 32:8). • [5, 6] "Behold, . . . saith the Lord, . . . they shall hunt them from every mountain, and from every hill, and out of the holes of the rocks. *For mine eyes are upon all their ways*: they are not hid from *my face*, neither is their iniquity hid *from mine eyes*" (Jer. 16:16–17). • [7] "I saw *the Lord standing* upon the altar: and he said, . . . I will *set mine eyes* upon them for evil, and not for good" (Amos 9:1, 4).

Second-person statements: • [1] "David did that which was right *in the eyes of the Lord*" (1 Kgs. 15:5; see also 1511; 16:25; 22:43). • [2] "Lord, bow down *thine ear*, and hear: *open, Lord, thine eyes, and see: and hear*" (2 Kgs. 19:16; see Isa. 37:17). • [3] "O Lord my God, hearken unto the cry and the prayer which thy servant prayeth before thee: *That thine eyes may be open* upon this house day and night" (2 Chr. 6:19–20; see Neh. 1:6). • [4] "Now, my God, let, I beseech thee, *thine eyes be open*, and *let thine ears be attent unto the prayer* that is made in this place" (2 Chr. 6:40). • [5] "The *eyes of the Lord* run to and fro throughout the whole earth, to shew himself strong in the behalf of them whose heart is perfect toward him" (2 Chr. 16:9). • [6] "*Hast thou eyes of flesh?* or *seest thou as man seeth?*" (Job. 10:4). • [7] "The *eyes* of the Lord are upon the righteous, and *his ears* are open unto their cry. The *face* of the Lord is against them that do evil" (Ps. 34:15–16). • [8] "Now, saith the Lord . . . shall I be glorious in *the eyes of the Lord*, and my God shall be my strength" (Isa. 49:5). • [9] "O Lord, are not *thine eyes* upon the truth?" (Jer. 5:3). • [10] "Lord, bow down thine *ear*, and hear: *open, Lord, thine eyes, and see*" (2 Kgs. 19:16). • [11, 12] "The Lord is in his holy temple, the Lord's throne is in heaven, *his eyes* behold, *his eyelids* try, the children of men" (Ps. 11:4). • [13] "The *eyes of the Lord* are upon the righteous, and *his ears* are open unto their cry. The *face of the Lord* is against them that do evil" (Ps. 34:15–16). • [14] "He that *planted the ear*, shall he not hear? he that *formed the eye*, shall he not see?" (Ps. 94:9). • [15] "Incline *thine ear*, O Lord, and hear; open *thine eyes*, O Lord, and see" (Isa. 37:17). • [16] "O my God, incline *thine ear*, and hear; open *thine eyes*, and behold our desolations" (Dan. 9:18). • [17] "I saw . . . in the midst of the seven candlesticks one like unto the Son of man, clothed with a garment down to *the foot*, and girt about *the paps* with a *golden girdle*. His head and *his hairs* were white like wool, as white as snow; and *his eyes* were as a flame of fire; And *his feet* like unto fine brass" (Rev. 1:12–15). • [18] "O Lord God Almighty, maker of heaven, earth, and seas, and of all things that in them are, and who controllest and subjectest the devil, and the dark and benighted dominion of Sheol—stretch forth *thy hand*; let *thine eye* pierce; let *thy pavilion* be taken up; let *thy hiding place* no longer be covered; let *thine ear* be inclined; let *thine heart* be softened, and *thy bowels* moved with compassion toward us" (D&C 121:4).

7. God's Ears

First-person statements: • [1] "The Lord said unto Moses, . . . say thou unto the people, Sanctify yourselves against to morrow, and ye shall eat flesh: for *ye have wept in the ears of the Lord* . . ." (Num. 11:16, 18). • [2] "And the Lord spake unto Moses and unto Aaron, saying, . . . Say unto them, As truly as I live, saith the Lord, *as ye have spoken in mine ears*, so will I do to you" (Num. 14:26, 28). • [3] "Thus saith the Lord God of Israel, . . . Because thy rage against me and thy tumult *is come up into* *mine ears*, therefore I will put my hook in thy nose, and my bridle in thy lips, and I will turn thee back by the way by which thou camest" (2 Kgs. 19:20, 28). • [4] "The LORD appeared to Solomon by night, and said unto him, I have heard thy prayer, . . . Now *mine eyes shall be open*, and *mine ears* attent unto the prayer that is made in this place" (2 Chr. 7:12, 15). • [5] "This is the word which the LORD hath spoken . . . Because thy rage against me, and thy tumult, *is come up into mine ears*, therefore will I put my hook in thy nose, and my bridle in thy lips" (Isa. 37:22, 29). • [6] "The glory of the God of Israel was there, according to the vision . . . Then said he unto me, . . . *though they cry in mine ears* with a loud voice, yet will I not *hear* them" (Ezek. 8:4–5, 18). • [7] "Thus saith the Lord, . . . thy prayers and the prayers of thy brethren have come up *into my ears*" (D&C 90:1). • [8] "Verily, thus saith the Lord unto you whom I love, . . . I gave unto you a commandment that you should call your solemn assembly, that your fastings and your mourning might come up *into the ears* of the Lord of Sabaoth" (D&C 95:1, 7). • [9] "Thus saith the Lord, verily, verily I say unto you my son, thy sins are forgiven thee, according to thy petition, for thy prayers and the prayers of thy brethren have come up into *my ears*" (D&C 90:1). • [10] "I, [the Lord] say unto you my friends, . . . your prayers have entered into *the ears of the Lord of Sabaoth*, and are recorded with this seal and testament" (D&C 98:1–2, 5).

Second-person statements: • [1] "I called upon the LORD, and cried unto my God: *he heard my voice* out of his temple, and my cry came before him, even *into his ears*" (Ps. 18:6). • [2] "*Bow down thine ear to me*; deliver me speedily: be thou my strong rock" (Ps. 31:2). • [3] "The *eyes* of the LORD are upon the righteous, and *his ears* are open unto their cry. The *face* of the LORD is against them that do evil" (Ps. 34:15–16). • [4] "Hear my prayer, O God; *give ear* to the words of my mouth" (Ps. 54:2; 55:1). • [5] "And say thou unto the people, Sanctify yourselves against to morrow, and ye shall eat flesh: for ye have wept in the *ears of the LORD*" (Num. 11:18). • [6] "Samuel heard all the words of the people, and he rehearsed them in *the ears of the LORD*" (1 Sam. 8:21). • [7] "Let thine *ear* now be attentive, and thine *eyes* open, that thou mayest *hear* the prayer of thy servant, which I pray before thee now, day and night" (Neh. 1:6). • [8] "*Give ear* to my words, O LORD, consider my meditation" (Ps. 5:1). • [9] "He that *planted the ear*, shall he not hear? he that *formed the eye*, shall he not see?" (Ps. 94:9). • [10] "Incline *thine ear*, O LORD, and hear; open *thine eyes*, O LORD, and see" (Isa. 37:17). • [11] "Thou hast *heard* my voice: hide not *thine ear* at my breathing, at my cry" (Lam. 3:56). • [12] "O my God, incline *thine ear*, and hear; open *thine eyes*, and behold our desolations" (Dan. 9:18). • [13] "O Lord God Almighty, maker of heaven, earth, and seas, and of all things that in them are, and who controllest and subjectest the devil, and the dark and benighted dominion of Sheol—stretch forth *thy hand*; let *thine eye* pierce; let *thy pavilion* be taken up; let *thy hiding place* no longer be covered; let *thine ear* be inclined; let *thine heart* be softened, and *thy bowels* moved with compassion toward us" (D&C 121:4).

8. God's Nostrils

Second-person statements: • [1] "*Thy right hand*, O LORD, is become glorious in power . . . And with the *blast of thy nostrils* the waters were gathered together, the floods stood upright as an heap" (Ex. 15:6–8). • [2] "I called upon the LORD, and cried to my God: . . . and my cry did enter into *his ears*. . . . There went up a smoke out of *his nostrils*, and fire out of *his mouth* . . . and darkness was under *his feet*" (2 Sam. 22:7, 9–10). • [3] "the channels of the sea appeared, the foundations of the world were discovered, at the rebuking of the LORD, at the blast *of the breath of his nostrils*" (2 Sam. 22:16). • [4] "By the blast of God they perish, and by *the breath of his nostrils* are they consumed" (Job 4:9). • [5] "The foundations of the world were discovered at thy rebuke, O LORD, at the blast of *the breath of thy nostrils*" (Ps. 18:15).

9. God Can Smell

First-person statements: • [1] "I am the LORD your God, . . . But if ye will not hearken unto me, . . . I will . . . bring your sanctuaries unto desolation, and *I will not smell the savour of your sweet odours*" (Lev. 26:13–14, 31). • [2] "My offering, and my bread for my sacrifices made by fire, *for a sweet savour unto me* . . . This is the offering made by fire which ye shall offer unto the LORD" (Num. 28:2–3). • [3] "*I will accept you with your sweet savour,* when I bring you out from the people, and gather you out of the countries wherein ye have been scattered . . . And ye shall know that I am the LORD" (Ezek. 20:41–42).

Second-person statement: • [1] "the LORD *smelled* a sweet savour; and the LORD said in *his heart,* I will not again curse the ground any more for man's sake" (Gen. 8:21). • [2] "make an offering by fire unto the LORD, a burnt offering, . . . *to make a sweet savour unto the LORD*" (Num. 15:3). • [3] "for a drink offering thou shalt offer the third part of an hin of wine, *for a sweet savour unto the LORD*" (Num. 15:7). • [4] "the firstling of a cow, or the firstling of a sheep, or the firstling of a goat, thou shalt not redeem; they are holy: thou shalt . . . burn their fat for an offering made by fire, *for a sweet savour unto the LORD*" (Num. 18:17). • [5] "It is a continual burnt offering, which was ordained in mount Sinai for *a sweet savour, a sacrifice made by fire unto the LORD*" (Num. 28:6). • [6] "ye shall offer the burnt offering *for a sweet savour unto the LORD;* two young bullocks, one ram, seven lambs of the first year" (Num. 28:27). • [7] "offer sacrifices of *sweet savours unto the God of heaven*" (Ezra 6:10).

10. God's Breath, Breathing and Blowing

First-person statements: • [1] "I, the Lord God, formed man from the dust of the ground, and *breathed* into his nostrils the breath of life; and man became a living soul" (Moses 3:7). • [2] "I, God, *breathed* into them the breath of life" (Moses 3:19).

Second-person statements: • [1] "The LORD God formed man of the dust of the ground, and *breathed* into his nostrils the breath of life; and man became a living soul" (Gen. 2:7). • [2] "Thy *right hand,* O LORD, is become glorious in power . . . And with the *blast of thy nostrils* the waters were gathered together, the floods stood upright as an heap" (Ex. 15:6–8). • [3] "the channels of the sea appeared, the foundations of the world were discovered, at the rebuking of the LORD, at the blast *of the breath of his nostrils*" (2 Sam. 22:16). • [4] "By the blast of God they perish, and by *the breath of his nostrils* are they consumed" (Job 4:9). • [5] "The Spirit of God hath made me, and *the breath of the Almighty* hath given me life" (Job 33:4). • [6] "Surely God will not do wickedly, . . . If he set *his heart* upon man, if he gather unto himself *his spirit* and *his breath*" (Job 34:12, 14). • [7] "By *the breath of God* frost is given" (Job 37:10). • [8] "The foundations of the world were discovered at thy rebuke, O LORD, at the blast of *the breath of thy nostrils*" (Ps. 18:15). • [9] "By the word of the LORD were the heavens made; and all the host of them by the *breath of his mouth* (Ps. 33:6). • [10] "He shall smite the earth with the rod of *his mouth,* and with the *breath of his lips* shall he slay the wicked" (Isa. 11:4). • [11] "Behold, the name of the LORD cometh from far, burning with anger, . . . *his lips* are full of indignation, and *his tongue* as a devouring fire:

And *his breath*, as an overflowing stream, shall reach to the midst of *the neck*" (Isa. 30:27–28). • [12] "For Tophet is ordained of old; . . . the pile thereof is fire and much wood; the *breath of the* LORD, like a stream of brimstone, doth kindle it" (Isa. 30:33). • [13] "And the Gods formed man from the dust of the ground, and took his spirit (that is, the man's spirit), and put it into him; and *breathed* into his nostrils the breath of life, and man became a living soul" (Abr. 5:7).

II. God's Mouth, Lips, Tongue and Neck

First-person statements: • [1] "The LORD came down in the pillar of the cloud, and stood in the door of the tabernacle, and called Aaron and Miriam: and they both came forth. And he said, . . . If there be a prophet among you, I the LORD will make myself known unto him in a vision, . . . My servant Moses is not so, . . . *With him will I speak mouth to mouth, even apparently*" (Num. 12:5–8). • [2] "The LORD appeared to Solomon by night, and said unto him, . . . If my people, which are called by my name, shall humble themselves, and pray, and *seek my face*, . . . then will I *hear* from heaven, . . . Now *mine eyes* shall be open, and *mine ears* attent unto the prayer that is made in this place" (2 Chr. 7:12, 14–15). • [3] "My covenant will I not break, nor alter the thing that is *gone out of my lips*" (Ps. 89:34).

Second-person statements: • [1] "I called upon the LORD, and cried to my God: . . . and my cry did enter into *his ears*. . . . There went up a smoke out of *his nostrils*, and fire out of *his mouth* . . . and darkness was under *his feet*" (2 Sam. 22:7, 9–10). • [2] "oh that God would speak, and *open his lips* against thee" (Job. 11:5). • [3] "Neither have I gone back from *the commandment of his lips*; I have esteemed *the words of his mouth* more than my necessary food. But he is in *one mind*, and who can turn him? and what *his soul desireth*, even that he doeth" (Job 23:12–13). • [4] "In *his neck* remaineth strength, and sorrow is turned into joy before him" (Job 41:22). • [5] "O LORD, attend unto my cry, . . . Concerning the works of men, by *the word of thy lips* I have kept me from the paths of the destroyer" (Ps. 17:1, 4). • [6] "The preparations of the heart in man, and *the answer of the tongue, is from the LORD*" (Prov. 16:1). • [7] "Hear the word of the LORD, O ye women, and let your ear receive the word of *his mouth*" (Jer. 9:20). • [8] "But with righteousness shall he judge the poor, . . . and with *the breath of his lips* shall he slay the wicked" (Isa. 11:4). • [9] "Behold, the name of the LORD cometh from far, burning with anger, . . . *his lips* are full of indignation, and *his tongue* as a devouring fire: And *his breath*, as an overflowing stream, shall reach to the midst of *the neck*" (Isa. 30:27–28).

Group E: God's Shoulders, Arms, Hands and Fingers

12. God's Shoulders, Arms and Arm Hair

First-person statements: • [1] "Then answered the LORD unto Job out of the whirlwind, and said, . . . Hast thou *an arm like God*?" (Job 40:6, 9). • [2, 3] "Hearken unto me, my people; and give ear unto me, O my nation: . . . My righteousness is near; my salvation is gone forth, and *mine arms* shall judge the people; . . . and on *mine arm* shall they trust" (Isa. 51:4–5). • [4] "Wo be unto the Gentiles, saith the Lord God of Hosts! For notwithstanding I shall *lengthen out mine arm* unto them from day to day, they will deny me" (2 Ne. 28:32). • [5] "Hearken, . . . saith the Lord your God; for behold, mine anger is kindled against the rebellious, and they shall know *mine arm* and mine indignation" (D&C 56:1).

Second-person statements: • [1] "Hath God assayed to go and take him a nation . . . by a *mighty hand*, and by a *stretched out arm*" (Deut. 4:34). • [2] "Remember that thou wast a servant in the land of Egypt, and that the LORD thy God brought thee out thence through a *mighty hand* and by a *stretched out arm*" (Deut. 5:15). • [3] "Remember what the LORD thy God did unto Pharaoh, and unto all Egypt; . . . the *mighty hand*, and the *stretched out arm*, whereby the LORD thy God brought thee out" (Deut. 7:18–19). • [4] "And of Benjamin he [Moses] said, The beloved of the LORD shall dwell in safety by him; and the LORD shall cover him all the day long, and he shall dwell between *his shoulders*" (Deut. 33:12). • [5] "I speak not with your children which have not known . . . the LORD your God, his greatness, his *mighty hand*, and his *stretched out arm*" (Deut. 11:2). • [6] "They got not the land in possession by their own sword, . . . but *thy right hand*, and *thine arm*, and the *light of thy countenance*, because thou hadst a favour unto them" (Ps. 44:3). • [7] "Behold, the Lord GOD will come with *strong hand*, and *his arm* shall rule for him" (Isa. 40:10). • [8] "They got not the land in possession by their own sword, . . . but *thy right hand*, and *thine arm*, and the *light of thy countenance*, because thou hadst a favour unto them" (Ps. 44:3). • [9, 10] "O LORD God of hosts, . . . Thou hast *a mighty arm*: strong is *thy hand*, and high is *thy right hand*" (Ps. 89:8, 13). • [11] "The LORD shall cause his *glorious voice* to be heard, and shall shew *the lighting down of his arm*" (Isa. 30:30). • [12] "I saw . . . in the midst of the seven candlesticks one like unto the Son of man, clothed with a garment down to *the foot*, and girt about *the paps* with a golden girdle. *His head* and *his hairs* were white like wool, as white as snow; and *his eyes* were as a flame of fire; And *his feet* like unto fine brass" (Rev. 1:12–15). • [13] "Wherefore, the Lord God will proceed to *make bare his arm* in the eyes of all the nations, in bringing about his covenants and his gospel" (1 Ne. 22:11). • [14] "The Lord God would preserve a record of my people, the Nephites; even if it so be by the *power of his holy arm*" (Enos 1:13). • [15] "The Lord hath *made bare his holy arm* in the eyes of all the nations, and all the ends of the earth shall see the salvation of our God" (Mosiah 12:24; 15:31).

13. God's Hands and Palms, Their Hollow and Span

First-person statements: • [1] "Thus saith the Lord, . . . Behold, I have graven thee upon *the palms of my hands*" (Ps. 49:8, 16). • [2, 3] "Thus saith the LORD, . . . Is *my hand* shortened at all, that it cannot redeem? . . . This ye shall have of *mine hand*; ye shall lie down in sorrow" (Isa. 50:1–2, 11).

Second-person statements: • [1] "Hath God assayed to go and take him a nation . . . by a *mighty hand*, and by a *stretched out arm*" (Deut. 4:34). • [2] "Remember that thou wast a servant in the land of Egypt, and that the LORD thy God brought thee out thence through a *mighty hand* and by a *stretched out arm*" (Deut. 5:15). • [3] "Remember what the LORD thy God did unto Pharaoh, and unto all Egypt; . . . the *mighty hand*, and the *stretched out arm*, whereby the LORD thy God brought thee out" (Deut. 7:18–19). • [4] "I speak not with your children which have not known . . . the LORD your God, his greatness, his *mighty hand*, and his *stretched out arm*" (Deut. 11:2). • [5, 6, 7] "Behold, the Lord GOD will come with strong *hand*, and *his arm* shall rule for him: . . . Who hath measured the waters in the *hollow of his hand*, and meted out heaven with *the span*" (Isa. 40:10, 12). • [8] "Behold, the Lord GOD will come with strong *hand*, and *his arm* shall rule for him: . . . He shall feed his flock like a shepherd: he shall gather the lambs with his arm, and *carry them in his bosom*" (Isa. 40:10–11). • [9] "Behold, *the LORD's hand* is not shortened, that it cannot save; neither *his ear* heavy, that it cannot hear" (Isa. 59:1). • [10] "upon the cloud one *sat* like unto the Son of man, *having on his head a golden crown,* and *in his hand a sharp sickle*" (Rev. 14:14). • [11] "O Lord God Almighty, maker of heaven, earth, and seas, and of all things that in them are, and who controllest and subjectest the devil, and the dark and benighted dominion of Sheol—stretch forth *thy hand;* let *thine eye* pierce; let *thy pavilion* be taken up; let *thy hiding place* no longer be covered; let *thine ear* be inclined; let *thine heart* be softened, and *thy bowels* moved with compassion toward us" (D&C 121:4).

14. God's Right and Left Hands

First-person statements: Note particularly the first statement, in which he refers to wearing a signet ring on his right hand: • [1] "As I live, saith the LORD, though Coniah the son of Jehoiakim king of Judah were *the signet upon my right hand,* yet would I pluck thee thence" (Jer. 22:24). • [2, 3] "I am he; I am the first, and I am also the last. Mine *hand* hath also laid the foundation of the earth, and *my right hand* hath spanned the heavens" (1 Ne. 20:12–13). • [4] The names of the righteous shall be written in the book of life, and unto them will I grant an inheritance *at my right hand*" (Alma 5:58). • [5, 6] "The righteous shall be gathered on *my right hand* unto eternal life; and the wicked on *my left hand* will I be ashamed to own before the Father" (D&C 29:27).

Second-person statements: • [1, 2] "Thy *right hand,* O LORD, is become glorious in power: thy *right hand,* O LORD, hath dashed in pieces the enemy" (Ex. 15:6). • [3] "O God, . . . thy *right hand* is full of righteousness" (Ps. 48:10). • [4, 5] "O God, . . . Why withdrawest thou *thy hand,* even *thy right hand?* pluck it out of *thy bosom*" (Ps. 74:11). • [6, 7] "O God of hosts: *look* down from heaven, and behold, and visit this vine; . . . Let *thy hand* be upon the man of *thy right hand,* upon the son of man whom thou madest strong for thyself" (Ps. 80:14, 17). • [8] "This Jesus hath God raised up, whereof we all are witnesses. Therefore being *by the right hand of God exalted,* and having received of the Father the promise of the Holy Ghost, he hath shed forth this, which ye now see and hear" (Acts 2:32–33). • [9] The God of our fathers raised up Jesus, . . . Him hath God exalted *with his right hand* to be a Prince and a Saviour" (Acts 5:30–31). • [10] "But to which of the angels said he at any time, Sit on my *right hand,* until I make thine enemies thy footstool?" (Heb. 1:13; see 1:4–12).

The terms "right hand" and "left hand" also are used in positioning statements, indicating the relative locations of two or more individuals or groups. Of course, the literal, physical existence of the Father and the Son, and especially their right and left hands, are essential for these position explanations to be understood: • [11, 12] "I saw the LORD sitting upon his throne, and all the host of heaven standing on his *right hand* and on his *left*" (2 Chr. 18:18). • [13] "O God, . . . Why withdrawest thou *thy hand,* even *thy right hand?* pluck it out of *thy bosom*" (Ps. 74:10–11). • [14] "The LORD said unto my Lord, Sit thou at *my right hand*" (Ps. 110:1; see Matt. 22:44). • [15] "Jesus saith . . . Hereafter shall ye see the Son of man *sitting on the right hand of power,* and coming in the clouds of heaven" (Matt. 26:64; see Luke 22:69). • [16] "After the Lord had spoken unto them, he was received up into heaven, and *sat on the right hand of God*" (Mark 16:19). • [17, 18] "But he [Stephen], being full of the Holy Ghost, looked up stedfastly into heaven, and saw the glory of God, and Jesus standing on the *right hand of God,* And said, Behold, I see the heavens opened, and *the Son of man standing on the right hand of God*" (Acts 7:55–56). • [19] "It is Christ . . . who is even *at the right hand of God,* who also maketh intercession for us" (Rom. 8:34). • [20]

"The God of our Lord Jesus Christ, the Father of glory, . . . according to the working of his mighty power, Which he wrought in Christ, when he raised him from the dead, and *set him at his own right hand in the heavenly places"* (Eph. 1:17, 19–20). • [21] "Seek those things which are above, where *Christ sitteth on the right hand of God"* (Col. 3:1). • [22] [Christ] "Sat down on the *right hand* of the Majesty on high" (Heb. 1:3). • [23] "We have such an high priest [Christ], who is *set on the right hand of the throne of the Majesty in the heavens"* (Heb. 8:1). • [24] "But this man [Christ], after he had offered one sacrifice for sins for ever, *sat down on the right hand of God"* (Heb. 10:12). • [25] "Jesus . . . *is set down at the right hand of the throne of God"* (Heb. 12:2). • [26] "Jesus Christ . . . is gone into heaven, and is on the *right hand* of God" (1 Pet. 3:21–22). • [27, 28] "Whosoever doeth this shall be found at *the right hand of God*; . . . whosoever shall not take upon him the name of Christ . . . findeth himself on *the left hand of God"* (Mosiah 5:9–10). • [29, 30] "It is I that taketh upon me the sins of the world; for it is I that hath created them; and it is I that granteth unto him that believeth unto the end a *place at my right hand*. . . . a place eternally at my *right hand"* (Mosiah 26:23–24). • [31] "The names of the righteous shall be written in the book of life, and unto them will I grant an inheritance at *my right hand"* (Alma 5:58). • [32] "May the grace of God the Father, whose throne is high in the heavens, and our Lord Jesus Christ, who *sitteth on the right hand of his power*, until all things shall become subject unto him, be, and abide with you forever" (Moro. 9:26). • [33] "Have miracles ceased because Christ hath ascended into heaven, and hath sat down on the *right hand of God*, to claim of the Father his rights of mercy which he hath upon the children of men?" (Moro. 7:27) • [34] [Christ] "ascended into heaven, to sit down on the *right hand of the Father"* (D&C 20:24; see 49:6; Alma 28:12; Hel. 3:30; Eth. 12:4). • [35] "You shall have a crown of eternal life at the *right hand of my* [Christ's] *Father"* (D&C 66:12). • [36, 37] "We beheld the glory of the Son, *on the right hand of the Father*, and received of his fulness; . . . For we saw him, even *on the right hand of God"* (D&C 76:20, 23). • [38] "I, the Lord, have promised unto you a crown of glory at *my right hand"* (D&C 104:7). • [39] "The graves of the saints shall be opened; and they shall come forth and *stand on the right hand of the Lamb"* (D&C 133:56). • [40, 41] "The rocks were rent; and the saints arose, and were crowned *at the right hand of the Son of Man*, with crowns of glory; And as many of the spirits as were in prison came forth, and *stood on the right hand of God"* (Moses 7:56–57).

15. The Shadow of God's Hand

First-person statement: Note that there even is a first-person statement by God referring specifically to the shadow cast by his hands: • [1] "I have put my words in thy mouth, and I have covered thee *in the shadow of mine hand"* (Isa. 51:16; 2 Ne. 8:16).

Second-person statements: Note that these passages, which refer to the shadow of God's hand, also imply God's overall physical presence casting a shadow: • [1] "The LORD hath called me from the womb; . . . in the *shadow of his hand* hath he hid me, and made me a polished shaft" (Isa. 49:1–2). • [2] "He that dwelleth in the secret place of the most High shall abide under *the shadow of the Almighty"* (Ps. 91:1). • [3] "O Israel, return unto the LORD thy God; . . . They that dwell under *his shadow* shall return" (Hos. 14:1, 7). • [4] "in the *shadow of his hand* hath he hid me, and made me a polished shaft" (1 Ne. 21:2).

16. God's Fingers

First-person statements: • [1] "The Lord hath said: I will raise up a Moses; . . . I will write unto him my law, *by the finger of mine own hand*" (2 Ne. 3:17). • [2] "The Lord said unto him [the brother of Jared]: Because of thy faith thou hast seen that I shall take upon me flesh and blood; and never has man come before me with such exceeding faith as thou hast; for were it not so ye could not have seen *my finger* (Eth. 3:9).

Second-person statements: • [1] "He gave unto Moses, when he had made an end of communing with him upon mount Sinai, two tables of testimony, tables of stone, *written with the finger of God*" (Ex. 31:18). • [2] "The LORD delivered unto me two tables of stone *written with the finger of God*; and on them was written according to all the words, which the LORD spake with you in the mount" (Deut. 9:10). • [3] "O LORD our Lord, . . . When I consider thy heavens, the work of *thy fingers*, the moon and the stars, which thou hast ordained; . . ." (Ps. 8:1, 3). • [4] "But if I [the mortal Jesus] *with the finger of God* cast out devils, no doubt the kingdom of God is come upon you (Luke 11:20). • [5] "It was the same Aminadi who interpreted the writing which was upon the wall of the temple, which was *written by the finger of God* (Alma 10:2). • [6, 7] "When the brother of Jared had said these words, behold, the Lord stretched forth *his hand* and *touched the stones one by one with his finger*. And the veil was taken from off the eyes of the brother of Jared, and *he saw the finger of the Lord*; and *it was as the finger of a man, like unto flesh and blood*" (Eth. 3:6). • [8, 9] "We have seen in this record that one of these was the brother of Jared; for so great was his faith in God, that when *God put forth his finger* he could not hide it from the sight of the brother of Jared, . . . And after the brother of Jared had beheld the *finger of the Lord*, because of the promise which the brother of Jared had obtained by faith, the Lord could not withhold anything from his sight; wherefore he showed him all things, for he could no longer be kept without the veil" (Eth. 12:20–21). • [10] "The city of New Jerusalem. Which city shall be built, beginning at the temple lot, which is appointed by *the finger of the Lord*, in the western boundaries of the State of Missouri" (D&C 84:2–3) • [11] "A book of remembrance we have written among us, according to the pattern given by the *finger of God*" (Moses 6:46).

Group F: God's Bosom, Heart and Bowels

17. God's Bosom

First-person statements: • [1] I am God, and *mine arm* is not shortened; . . . and the scriptures shall be given, even as they are *in mine own bosom*, to the salvation of mine own elect; For they will hear my voice, and *shall see me*" (D&C 35:8, 20–21) • [2] "I am the same which have taken the Zion of Enoch into *mine own bosom*; . . . for I am Christ" (D&C 38:4). • [3] "The redemption of the soul is through him that quickeneth all things, *in whose bosom* it is decreed that the poor and the meek of the earth shall inherit it" (D&C 88:17).

Second-person statements: • [1] "O God, . . . Why withdrawest thou *thy hand*, even *thy right hand*? pluck it out of *thy bosom*" (Ps. 74:10–11). • [2] "Behold, the Lord GOD will come with strong *hand*, and *his arm* shall rule for him: . . . He shall feed his flock like a shepherd: he shall gather the lambs with his arm, and *carry them in his bosom*" (Isa. 40:10–11). • [3] "No man hath seen God at any time; the only begotten Son, which is in *the bosom of the Father*, he hath declared him" (John 1:18; see Moses

1:11, 31, Ex. 33:11). • [4] "Those things which were from the beginning before the world was, which were ordained of the Father, through his Only Begotten Son, who was in *the bosom of the Father*, even from the beginning" (D&C 76:13). • [5] "An angel of God who was in authority in the presence of God, who rebelled against the Only Begotten Son whom the Father loved and *who was in the bosom of the Father*, was thrust down from the presence of God and the Son" (D&C 76:25). • [6] "For all the rest shall be brought forth by the resurrection of the dead, through the triumph and the glory of the Lamb, who was slain, who was *in the bosom of the Father* before the worlds were made" (D&C 76:39). • [7] "We ask thee, Holy Father, in the name of Jesus Christ, *the Son of thy bosom*, in whose name alone salvation can be administered to the children of men" (D&C 109:4). • [8] "Were it possible that man could number the particles of the earth, yea, millions of earths like this, it would not be a beginning to the number of thy creations; . . . and *thy bosom is there*" (Moses 7:30). • [9] "thou hast taken Zion *to thine own bosom*, from all thy creations, from all eternity to all eternity" (Moses 7:31). • [10] "Enoch and all his people walked with God, . . . and it came to pass that Zion was not, for God received it up into *his own bosom*" (Moses 7:69).

18. God's Heart

First-person statements: • [1] "The LORD said in *his heart*, I will not again curse the ground any more for man's sake" (Gen. 8:21). • [2] "Wherefore the LORD God of Israel saith, . . . I will raise me up a faithful priest, that shall do according to that which is in *mine heart* and in *my mind*" (1 Sam. 2:30, 35). • [3] "The LORD said unto him, . . . I have hallowed this house, which thou hast built, to put my name there for ever; and *mine eyes* and *mine heart* shall be there perpetually (1 Kgs. 9:3). • [4] "The LORD said unto Jehu, Because thou hast done well in executing that which is right in *mine eyes*, and hast done unto the house of Ahab according to all that was in *mine heart*, thy children of the fourth generation shall sit on the throne of Israel" (2 Kgs. 10:30). • [5] "the LORD appeared to Solomon by night, and said unto him, . . . now have I chosen and sanctified this house, . . . and *mine eyes* and *mine heart* shall be there perpetually" (2 Chr. 7:12, 16). • [6] "I have trodden the winepress alone; . . . I will tread them in mine anger, and trample them in my fury; . . . For the day of vengeance is in *mine heart*" (Isa. 63:3–4). • [7, 8] "Saith the LORD. . . . *My bowels, my bowels!* I am pained at *my very heart*; *my heart* maketh a noise in me; I cannot hold my peace" (Jer. 4:17, 19). • [9] "I have decreed in *my heart*, saith the Lord, that I will prove you in all things" (D&C 98:14). • [10] "I, the Lord, have decreed in *my heart*, that inasmuch as any man belonging to the order shall be found a transgressor, . . . he shall be cursed in his life" (D&C 104:5).

Second-person statements: • [1] "O Lord, how long shall they suffer these wrongs and unlawful oppressions, before *thine heart* shall be softened toward them, and *thy bowels* be moved with compassion toward them? (D&C 121:3). • [2] "O Lord God Almighty, maker of heaven, earth, and seas, and of all things that in them are, and who controllest and subjectest the devil, and the dark and benighted dominion of Sheol—stretch forth *thy hand*; let *thine eye* pierce; let *thy pavilion* be taken up; let *thy hiding place* no longer be covered; let *thine ear* be inclined; let *thine heart* be softened, and *thy bowels* moved with compassion toward us" (D&C 121:4). • [3] "I did tread upon them in mine anger, and their blood have I sprinkled upon *my garments*, and stained all *my raiment*; for this was the day of vengeance which was in *my heart* (D&C 133:51). • [4] "The Lord said unto me: . . . there is nothing that the Lord thy God shall take in *his heart* to do but what he will do it" (Abr. 3:15, 17).

19. God's Bowels

First-person statements: • [1] "Thus saith the LORD to the men of Judah and Jerusalem, . . . *My bowels, my bowels*! I am pained at *my very heart; my heart maketh a noise in me*; I cannot hold my peace (Jer. 4:3, 19). • [2] "Is Ephraim my dear son? . . . I do earnestly remember him still: therefore *my bowels* are troubled for him; I will surely have mercy upon him, saith the LORD" (Jer. 31:20). • [3] "The Lord their God . . . Verily I say unto you, notwithstanding their sins, *my bowels* are filled with compassion towards them" (D&C 101:7, 9).

Second-person statements: • [1] "Look down from heaven, and behold from the habitation of thy holiness and of thy glory: where is thy zeal and thy strength, the sounding of *thy bowels* and of thy mercies toward me?" (Isa. 63:15). • [2] "Thus God breaketh the bands of death, having gained the victory over death; giving the Son power to make intercession for the children of men—Having ascended into heaven, having the *bowels* of mercy" (Mosiah 15:8–9). • [3] "And he will take upon him death, . . . and he will take upon him their infirmities, that *his bowels* may be filled with mercy, according to the flesh, that he may know according to the flesh how to succor his people according to their infirmities" (Alma 7:12). • [4] "God is mindful of every people, . . . yea, he numbereth his people, and *his bowels of mercy* are over all the earth" (Alma 26:37). • [5] "O Lord God Almighty, . . . stretch forth *thy hand*; let thine *eye pierce*; let thy *pavilion* be taken up; let thy *hiding place* no longer be covered; let *thine ear* be inclined; let *thine heart* be softened, and *thy bowels* moved with compassion toward us" (D&C 121:4).

Group G: God's Waist, Thighs, and Back Parts

20. God's Body, Waist, Loins, Thighs, Paps, Back Parts, and Sides

First-person statements: • [1] "thou shalt see *my back parts*: but *my face shall not be seen*" (Ex. 33:23). • [2] "Behold the wounds which pierced *my side*, and also the prints of the nails in *my hands* and *feet*" (D&C 6:37).

Second-person statements: • [1] "Jacob was left alone; and there wrestled a man with him until the breaking of the day. And when he saw that he prevailed not against him, *he touched the hollow of his thigh;* and the hollow of Jacob's thigh was out of joint, as he wrestled with him. . . . And he blessed him there. And Jacob called the name of the place Peniel: for *I have seen God face to face,* and my life is preserved" (Gen. 32:24–25, 29–30). • [2] "Gird thy sword upon *thy thigh,* O most mighty, with thy glory and thy majesty. . . . Thy *throne,* O God, is for ever and ever: the *sceptre* of thy kingdom is a right sceptre" (Ps. 45:3, 6). • [3, 4] "I saw as the colour of amber, as the appearance of fire round about within it, from the appearance of *his loins* even upward, and from the appearance of *his loins* even downward, . . . This was the appearance of the likeness of the glory of the LORD" (Ezek. 1:27–28). • [5, 6] "I beheld, and lo a likeness as the appearance of fire: from the appearance of *his loins* even downward, fire; and from *his loins* even upward, . . . And, behold, the glory of the God of Israel was there" (Ezek. 8:2, 4). • [7] "Who shall change our vile body, that it may be fashioned like unto *his glorious body,* according to the working whereby he is able even to subdue all things unto himself" (Phil. 3:21). • [8] "I saw . . . in the midst of the seven candlesticks one like unto the Son of man, clothed with a garment down to *the foot,* and girt about *the paps* with a golden girdle. *His head* and *his hairs* were white like wool, as white as snow; and *his eyes* were as a flame of fire; And *his feet* like unto fine brass" (Rev. 1:12–15). • [9] "I saw heaven opened, and behold a white horse; and he that sat upon him was called Faithful and True, . . . And he hath on *his vesture* and on *his thigh* a name written, KING OF

KINGS, and LORD OF LORDS" (Rev. 19:11, 16). • [10] "The Lord spake unto them saying: Arise and come forth unto me, that ye may thrust your hands into *my side*, and also that ye may feel the prints of the nails in *my hands* and in *my feet*" (3 Ne. 11:13–14).

21. God Sits, Has a Seat and Throne

First-person statements: • [1] "The Son of man shall *sit in the throne* of his glory, ye also shall sit upon twelve thrones" (Matt. 19:28). • [2] "He that shall swear by heaven, sweareth by the *throne of God*, and by him that *sitteth* thereon" (Matt. 23:22). • [3] "When the Son of man shall come in his glory, and all the holy angels with him, then shall *he sit upon the throne of his glory*" (Matt. 25:31). • [4, 5] "To him that overcometh will I grant to *sit with me in my throne*, even as I also overcame, and am *set down with my Father in his throne*" (Rev. 3:21).

Second-person statements: • [1, 2] "The LORD *sitteth* upon the flood; yea, the LORD *sitteth* King for ever" (Ps. 29:10). • [3] "Hear thou therefore the word of the LORD: I saw the LORD *sitting on his throne*, and all the host of heaven standing by him on his *right hand* and on *his left*" (1 Kgs. 22:19). • [4] "Therefore hear the word of the LORD; I saw the LORD *sitting upon his throne*, and all the host of heaven standing on his *right hand* and on *his left*" (2 Chr. 18:18). • [5] "*Thy throne*, O God, is for ever and ever: the *sceptre* of thy kingdom is a right *sceptre*" (Ps. 45:6). • [6] "In the year that king Uzziah died, I saw also the Lord *sitting upon a throne*, high and lifted up, and his train filled the temple" (Isa. 6:1; 2 Ne. 16:1). • [7] "Son of man, say unto the prince of Tyrus, Thus saith the Lord GOD; Because thine heart is lifted up, and thou hast said, I am a God, I sit in *the seat of God . . .*" (Ezek. 28:2). • [8, 9] "I was in the spirit: and, behold, a throne was set in heaven, and one *sat* on the throne. And he that *sat* was to look upon like a jasper and a sardine stone . . . And round about the throne were four and twenty *seats*: and upon the *seats* I saw four and twenty elders *sitting*" (Rev. 4:2–4, 9–10). • [10, 11] "I saw *in the right hand* of him that *sat on the throne* a book . . . And he came and took the book *out of the right hand* of him that sat upon the throne. And when he had taken the book, the four beasts and four and twenty elders fell down before the Lamb" (Rev. 5:1, 7–8). • [12] "Salvation to our God which *sitteth upon the throne*, and unto the Lamb" (Rev. 7:10). • [13] "Therefore are they before the throne of God, and serve him day and night in his temple: and *he that sitteth on the throne* shall dwell among them" (Rev. 7:15). • [14, 15] "I saw a *great white throne*, and him that *sat* on it, from whose *face* the earth and the heaven fled away; and there was found no place for them. And I saw the dead, small and great, *stand before God*" (Rev. 20:11–12). • [16] "God had sworn with an oath to him, that of the fruit of his [King David's] loins, according to the flesh, he would raise up Christ to *sit on his throne*" (Acts 2:30). • [17] "He saw *God sitting upon his throne*, surrounded with numberless concourses of angels in the attitude of singing and praising their God" (1 Ne. 1:8). • [18] "I saw, even as our father Lehi saw, *God sitting upon his throne*, surrounded with numberless concourses of angels" (2 Ne. 16:1). • [19] "May the grace of God the Father, whose *throne* is high in the heavens, and our Lord *Jesus Christ, who sitteth on the right hand of his power*" (Moro. 9:26). • [20] "Let no man think he is ruler; but let God rule him that judgeth, according to the counsel of his own will, or, in other words, him that counseleth or *sitteth* upon the judgment seat" (D&C.58:20). • [21] "These all shall bow the knee, and every tongue shall confess *to him who sits upon the throne* forever and ever" (D&C 76:110).

Group H: God's Walking, Standing, and Feet

22. God Walks and Stands

Second-person statements: • [1] "And they heard the *voice* of the LORD God *walking in the garden* in the cool of the day: and Adam and his wife hid themselves from the presence of the LORD God amongst the trees of the garden" (Gen. 3:8). • [2] "Thus hath the Lord GOD shewed unto me [Amos] . . . the Lord *stood* upon a wall made by a plumbline, with a plumbline in *his hand* (Amos 7:1, 7). • [3] "I saw the Lord *standing* upon the altar" (Amos 9:1). • [4, 5] "But he [Stephen], being full of the Holy Ghost, looked up stedfastly into heaven, and *saw the glory of God, and Jesus standing on the right hand of God*, And said, Behold, *I see the heavens opened, and the Son of man standing on the right hand of God*" (Acts 7:55–56).

23. God's Feet and the Soles of His Feet

First-person statements: • [1] "Thus saith the LORD God of Israel, . . . I have *digged* and *drunk* strange waters, and with the *sole of my feet* have I dried up all the rivers of besieged places" (2 Kgs. 19:20–24). • [2] "The glory of the LORD is risen upon thee. . . . The glory of Lebanon shall come unto thee, the fir tree, the pine tree, and the box together, to beautify the place of *my sanctuary*; and I will make the place of *my feet* glorious" (Isa. 60:1, 13). • [3] "Behold, the glory of the LORD filled the house. . . . And he said unto me, Son of man, the place of *my throne*, and the place of the *soles of my feet*, . . . shall the house of Israel no more defile" (Ezek. 43:5, 7). • [4] "The Lord spake unto them saying: Arise and come forth unto me, that ye may thrust your hands into *my side*, and also that ye may feel the prints of the nails in *my hands* and in *my feet*" (3 Ne. 11:13–14). • [5] "Behold the wounds which pierced *my side*, and also the prints of the nails in *my hands* and *feet*" (D&C 6:37).

Second-person statements: • [1] "Then went up Moses, and Aaron, Nadab, and Abihu, and seventy of the elders of Israel: And they saw the God of Israel: and there was under *his feet* as it were a paved work of a sapphire stone" (Ex. 24:9–10). • [2] "In my distress I called upon the LORD, . . . and fire out of *his mouth* devoured: . . . He . . . came down; and darkness was under *his feet*" (2 Sam. 22:7, 10). • [3] "For the Lord will not cast off for ever: . . . For he doth not afflict willingly nor grieve the children of men. To crush under *his feet* all the prisoners of the earth" (Lam. 3:31, 33–34). • [4] "God came from Teman, . . . his brightness was as the light; . . . and burning coals went forth at *his feet*" (Hab. 3:3–5). • [5] "Then shall the LORD go forth, . . . And *his feet* shall stand in that day upon the mount of Olives" (Zech. 14:3–4). • [6, 7] "Behold *my hands* and *my feet*, that it is I myself: handle me, and see; for a spirit hath not flesh and bones, as ye see me have. And when he had thus spoken, he shewed them *his hands* and *his feet*" (Luke 24:39–40). • [8] "Then cometh the end, when he shall have delivered up the kingdom to God, even the Father; when he shall have put down all rule and all authority and power. For he must reign, till he hath put all enemies under *his feet* (1 Cor. 15, 24–25, 27). • [9] "That the God of our Lord Jesus Christ, the Father of glory, may give unto you the spirit of wisdom and revelation in the knowledge of him: . . . the exceeding greatness of his power . . . Which he wrought in Christ, when he raised him from the dead, and set him at *his own right hand* in the heavenly places, . . . And hath put all things under *his feet*" (Eph. 1:17, 19–20, 22). • [10] "I saw . . . in the midst of the seven candlesticks one like unto the Son of man, *clothed with a garment* down to *the foot*, and girt about *the paps* with a *golden girdle*. *His head* and *his hairs* were white like wool, as white as snow; and *his eyes* were as a flame of fire; And *his feet* like unto fine brass" (Rev. 1:12–15). • [11] "These things saith the Son of God, who hath *his eyes* like unto a flame of fire, and *his feet* are like fine brass" (Rev. 2:18). • "Then shall the Lord set *his foot* upon this mount, and it shall cleave in twain . . . And then shall the Jews look upon me and say: What are these wounds in *thine hands* and in *thy feet?*" (D&C 45:48, 51). • [12] "We saw the Lord *standing* upon the breastwork of the pulpit, before us; and under *his feet* was a paved work of pure gold, in color like amber. *His eyes* were as a flame of fire; the *hair of his head* was white like the pure snow; *his countenance* shone above the brightness of the sun" (D&C 110:2–3).

Group I: God's Clothing, and Objects He Owns and Uses

24. God Owns, Holds, or Wears Tangible Objects

Second-person statements: • [1] *"Gird thy sword upon thy thigh,* O most mighty, with thy glory and thy majesty" (Ps. 45:3). • [2] "Thy *throne,* O God, is for ever and ever: *the sceptre of thy kingdom* is a right sceptre . . . *All thy garments* smell of myrrh, and aloes, and cassia" (Ps. 45:6, 8). • [3] Note particularly the next statement in which Jehovah refers to wearing a signet ring on his right hand: "As I live, saith the LORD, though Coniah the son of Jehoiakim king of Judah were *the signet upon my right hand,* yet would I pluck thee thence" (Jer. 22:24). • [4] "The LORD hath called me from the womb; . . . in the *shadow of his hand* hath he hid me, and made me a polished shaft; *in his quiver* hath he hid me" (Isa. 49:1–2; 1 Ne. 21:1–2). • [5] "O LORD, . . . Wherefore *art thou red in thine apparel,* and *thy garments* like him that treadeth in the winefat" (Isa. 63:17, 2). • [6, 7] "unto the Son he saith, Thy *throne,* O God, is for ever and ever: *a sceptre of righteousness* is the *sceptre* of thy kingdom" (Heb. 1:8). • [8, 9] "I saw . . . in the midst of the seven candlesticks one like unto the Son of man, *clothed with a garment* down to *the foot,* and girt about *the paps* with *a golden girdle. His head* and *his hairs* were white like wool, as white as snow; and *his eyes* were a flame of fire; And *his feet* like unto fine brass" (Rev. 1:12–15). • [10] "upon the cloud one *sat* like unto the Son of man, *having on his head a golden crown,* and *in his hand a sharp sickle*" (Rev. 14:14). • [11] "And he hath on *his vesture* and on *his thigh* a name written, KING OF KINGS, AND LORD OF LORDS" (Rev. 19:16). • [12] "The Holy Ghost shall be thy constant companion, and *thy scepter* an unchanging *scepter* of righteousness and truth; and thy dominion shall be an everlasting dominion" (D&C 121:46). • [13] "And *the Lord shall be red in his apparel,* and *his garments* like him that treadeth in the wine-vat" (D&C 133:48). • [14, 15] "I did *tread upon them* in mine anger, and their blood have I sprinkled upon *my garments,* and stained all *my raiment*; for this was the day of vengeance which was in *my heart*" (D&C 133:51).

How Many Scriptural Passages Does It Take to Show God Actually Means What He Says?

The above collection of quoted passages contain 129 first-person statements referring to specific parts or operations of His physical nature, made by a member of the Godhead. It also contains 290 other, second-person statements referring to specific parts or operations of God's physical nature, recorded by other authorized individuals whose statements are contained in canonized scriptures. They combine for a total of **419** specific references. In addition, there are hundreds of other second-person citations concerning God's physical body in the Bible and the other Latter-day Saint scriptures that are not cited herein.

It seems appropriate, at this juncture, to pose the question, "How many scriptural passages does it take to show that *God is a God of truth, and that He actually means what He says*, and that *"allegorizing" these 129 first-person statements uttered by God's lips, and the additional 290 other, second-person statements is incorrect and inappropriate scriptural hermeneutics and exegesis?* Will the "trinitarians" ever face up to reality?

Genesis 18:22–32 is the interesting account of Abraham bargaining with God for the lives of the inhabitants of Sodom and Gomorrah. In this account, "Abraham stood yet before the LORD" (which, of course, would be impossible if God was a shapeless being and was not situated in a specific space), and pled with him, saying, "Wilt thou also destroy the righteous with the wicked?" (Gen. 18:23). God said He would spare them if 50 righteous people could be found in the cities. Abraham queried concerning 45 righteous individuals, then 40, then 30, then 20, and finally, 10 righteous people.

So, if God is willing to barter, why not the "God is an incorporeal being" people? If God, himself, says 50 times that He has tangible body parts, shouldn't that be enough to convince them that a spirit can also have a body? Perhaps 60 times? 70? 80? 90? 100?

Presented here are 129 first-person statements, plus another 290 second-person statements. At some point, they who attempt to "allegorize" these statements, intentionally mistreating them as "anthropomorphisms" rather than as actual statements of fact which clearly establish the physical nature of God—the most central doctrine of Christianity—they are going to have to square themselves with the truth. Who knows whether it will be here on earth or at the judgment seat of God? Most certainly, the eternal stakes will be high for them!

Summary

1. The appearance of the premortal Jesus Christ to the brother of Jared is one of the most significant revelations in all scripture. It contains key insights on spirit bodies, tells us that mortal bodies were created in the image of Christ's spirit body, and indicates that Christ was prepared from the foundation of the world to redeem His people.

2. Ezra, who helped rebuild the Jerusalem temple, made significant changes that altered the entire course of Judaism. Later, Jewish scribes made radical changes to Jewish scriptures, doctrines, and religious procedures.

3. The history of hermeneutics clearly indicates that "allegorical interpretation," founded on Greek philosophical thought (particularly Plato's), was adopted by the Jews in Alexandria, Egypt several centuries before Christ "allegorical interpretation" continued through the time of Christ and strongly influenced the doctrinal creeds formulated in the fourth century after Christ and in later centuries.

4. Elements of Greek thought embodied in Jewish and early-Christian "allegorical interpretation" included the erroneous concepts that (a) God has no bodily form but is everywhere, (b) all matter is immaterial, (c) the human body is a vile form, the seat of all sin, which serves only to house an immortal soul, (d) mortals can never ascend to Godhood nor dwell among divine beings, and (e) it is impossible for man to understand the nature of God. These early Greek beliefs all played a significant role when they were integrated into Jewish thought.

5. Terms such as "anthropomorphisms," "theophanies," "tritheism," "transcendence," and "immanence" were identified as words often misunderstood and misused by Latter-day Saints.

6. Non-Latter-day Saint theologians, grounded in "god-is-a-shapeless-spirit" and "three-gods-in-one-substance" dogmas formulated in early Catholic councils, typically regard scriptural statements asserting and demonstrating the physical nature of God as "anthropomorphisms" (which they define as statements interpreting non-human beings or objects in terms of human terms and feelings), "theophanies" (which they define as God temporarily manifesting himself in human form though not actually having that form or appearance), or "metaphors" (figurative language in which words literally denoting some kinds of objects or ideas are used in place of different objects or ideas to suggest a likeness or analogy between them).

7. Some theologians and apologists for non-Latter-day Saint concepts have attempted to use the terms "anthropomorphic," "theophanies," and "metaphors" as doctrine-discrediting labels against believers of the doctrines of The Church of Jesus Christ of Latter-day Saints.

8. A major objective of this chapter is to demonstrate that scriptural descriptions of the physical nature of God are forthright statements, not metaphorical allusions.

9. Bible and Book of Mormon passages assert the original plainness and clarity of ancient scriptures. These passages indicate that such clarity is what God desires.

10. Book of Mormon passages assert that when the early Bible manuscripts were being transmitted from the Jews to the Gentiles (probably prior to the fourth-century canonization of the New Testament), some plain and precious parts were taken away, thus blinding the eyes and hardening the hearts of many.

11. Book of Mormon passages prophesy that scriptures revealed in the latter days would bear witness of the truthfulness of the Bible and would illuminate previously unclear biblical teachings. Latter-day Saints believe that the **Book of Mormon**, **Pearl of Great Price**, and **Doctrine and Covenants** have added much doctrinal understanding and clarity.

12. It is a fundamental doctrine of the scriptures that God is a God of truth and that all the members of the Godhead are characterized by complete truthfulness and absence of guile or falsehoods.

13. Thus, if God, in a first-person clear and unambiguous scriptural statement, asserts that He has a particular body part, that statement should be regarded as truth and not be interpreted otherwise.

14. Hundreds of scriptural statements concerning various aspects of God's physical nature are assembled in this chapter. They are classified as having two levels of significance. Of highest-level significance are first-person statements by members of the Godhead concerning their personal physical characteristics. A lower level of significance is attributed to second-person scriptural statements alluding to or attributing to physical aspects of the natures of Godhead members.

15. No specific effort is being made in this chapter to fully differentiate between members of the Godhead, since advocates of "trinitarian" doctrines believe that God the Father and God the Son are two different manifestations of the same "substance," and they also believe that Jehovah is God the Father, two beliefs not held by Latter-day Saint theologians.

16. In this chapter, 419 scriptural statements concerning many physical aspects of God's nature are briefly quoted. Of the 419 statements, 129 are first-person scriptural statements made by members of the Godhead; 290 are second-person scriptural statements that amplify and elucidate the higher-level passages.

17. Evidence is presented that God the Father, Jehovah/Jesus Christ, and the Holy Ghost are all male beings.

18. Two areas of scriptural statements indicate that God has a mind and a soul.

19. Eight areas of scriptural statements indicate that God has a head with hair, a face and a countenance that shines, with eyes, ears, nostrils (with ability to smell, breath, and blow), and a mouth.

20. Six areas of scriptural statements indicate that God has a torso with shoulders, a heart, a bosom, bowels, and a seat.

21. Four areas of scriptural statements indicate that God has arms, right and left hands, fingers, and can cast a shadow.

22. Four areas of scriptural statements indicate that God has thighs, loins, paps, legs, feet, and soles, and that He stands, sits, walks, and performs other visible movements.

23. A final area of scriptural statements indicates that God wears clothes, may wear jewelry, and holds and handles physical objects.

24. These extensive descriptions clearly indicate that God has a physical form that occupies a specific area. Others stand and sit beside him, gather around him, etc.

25. The scriptures indicate that God is a spirit, just as all human beings are spirits, and that God's and man's physical bodies are in the shape of, and have the appearance of, their spirit bodies.

26. The concept that God is a formless spirit that is everywhere and yet is invisible and without tangible substance cannot be substantiated from the scriptures and is in direct contradiction with the 419 scriptural passages cited concerning His physical nature in this chapter.

PART THREE

PREMORTAL EVENTS AND THE CREATION OF PLANET EARTH

CHAPTER 7

"IN THE BEGINNING": EVENTS PRIOR TO THE CREATION OF THIS PLANET EARTH

"In the Beginning . . ." of What?

For centuries, the scriptures have tantalized man with the phrase "in the beginning." The Bible begins with the words • *"In the beginning God* created the heaven and the earth" (Gen. 1:1). The Gospel of John commences with the same phrase: • *"In the beginning* was the Word, and the Word was with God, and the Word was God. The same was *in the beginning* with God" (John 1:1–2).

It is modern revelation, however, that gives us definition of what that point of beginning is to which these Bible verses make reference. Doctrine and Covenants section 93 records a testimony of John the Baptist which begins: "I saw his glory, that he was *in the beginning, before the world was*" (D&C 93:7). That revelation furnishes the pivotal clue: the biblical term "in the beginning" uses the creation of *this* earth as a marker—a dividing point. Any of the many scriptural events which took place prior to the creation of *this particular earth* are considered to be "in" the beginning.

The Book of Moses, in the Pearl of Great Price, provides a key insight concerning God's revelations to mankind as they currently stand. God told Moses, • *"only an account of this earth, and the inhabitants thereof,* give I unto you" (Moses 1:35). As will be seen, many great and glorious things transpired before the creation of this planet—present-day mankind are latecomers in the eternal flow of events. But the members of the Godhead, in their wisdom, have seen fit to withhold most of the information concerning those wondrous premortal events from man at the present time; *only glimpses of the eternal scheme of things* have been granted.

Passages about "in the beginning," as presently available in the scriptures, don't answer all those nagging questions about "the great first cause," "where God the Father came from," the "big bang," "time as related to eternity," and so on. Faithful Latter-day Saints do have the promise that there is to be,

> A time to come in the which *nothing shall be withheld*, whether there be *one God or many gods*, they shall be manifest.
>
> *All thrones and dominions, principalities and powers, shall be revealed* and set

forth upon all who have endured valiantly for the gospel of Jesus Christ.

And also, *if there be bounds set to the heavens or to the seas, or to the dry land, or to the sun, moon, or stars—*

All the times of their revolutions, all the *appointed days*, months, and years, and all *the days of their days*, months, and years, and *all their glories*, laws, and set times, shall be revealed in the days of the dispensation of the fulness of times—

According to that which was ordained in the midst of *the Council of the Eternal God of all other gods before this world was*, that should be *reserved unto the finishing and the end thereof, when every man shall enter into his eternal presence and into his immortal rest.* (D&C 121:28–32)

In the Beginning . . . Was God

That phrase "the Council of the Eternal God of all other gods before this world was" (D&C 121:32) is an intriguing clue—a single passage which indicates that (1) there is an Eternal God of all other Gods and (2) there was a Council of the Eternal God of all other Gods which existed before this particular world was created. Without further information being revealed, the Saints here on earth are left to ponder if that term refers to (A) a group of beings who had attained Godhood or (B) a glorious council meeting that those included in that glorified group held.

The Latter-day Saints also don't know what role, if any, God their Heavenly Father, played in that council. Is He the Eternal God of all other Gods? One of the other Gods? A God who was not a member of that supreme council? We assume the answers to those and many other questions will be common knowledge when we move past the veil of forgetfulness that has been imposed upon all mankind as part of their mortal probation.

What is known is that God the Father, an eternal being as are all mankind, existed and at some point in that timeless existence He attained Godhood. How and when this was accomplished is not defined in the scriptures as they presently exist.

How God the Father and Jesus Christ Attained Godhood: Joseph Smith's Explanation

An oft-quoted discourse delivered by the Prophet Joseph Smith provides profound insights. This explanation of the origin of God was delivered on Sunday, April 7, 1844, in Nauvoo, Illinois, in the afternoon session of a general conference of the Church, before about twenty thousand Saints. It was given, in part, as a funeral tribute to Elder King Follett, who was killed on March 8 while walling up a well. (The entire sermon, recorded in *History of the Church*, Vol. VI, pp. 302–317, covers a range of 13 subjects, according to subheadings supplied by later historians. Cited here are excerpts from three of those sections: "God An Exalted Man," "Eternal Life to Know God and Jesus Christ," and "The Righteous to Dwell in Everlasting Burnings," found on pp. 305–307.)

> *I will go back to the beginning before the world was,* to show what kind of a being God is. What sort of a being was God in the beginning? . . .
>
> *God himself was once as we are now, and is an exalted man, and sits enthroned in yonder heavens!* That is the great secret. If the vail were rent today, and the great God who holds this world in its orbit, and who upholds all worlds and all things by his power, was to make himself visible,—I say, if you were to see him today, *you would see him like a man in form—like yourselves in all the person, image, and very form as a man:*

for Adam was created in the very fashion, image and likeness of God, and received instruction from, and walked, talked and conversed with him, as one man talks and communes with another. . . .

The scriptures inform us that Jesus said, As the Father hath power in himself, even so hath the Son power—to do what? Why, what the Father did. The answer is obvious—in a manner, *to lay down his body and take it up again. Jesus, what are you going to do? To lay down my life as my Father did, and take it up again.* Do you believe it? If you do not believe it, you do not believe the Bible. [See John 5:19.] . . .

Here, then, is eternal life—to know the only wise and true God; and *you have got to learn how to be Gods yourselves, and to be kings and priests to God, the same as all Gods have done before you, namely, by going from one small degree to another, and from a small capacity to a great one: from grace to grace, from exaltation to exaltation,* until you attain to the resurrection of the dead, and are able to dwell in everlasting burnings, and to sit in glory, as do those who sit enthroned in everlasting power. . . .

How consoling to the mourners when they are called to part with a husband, wife, father, mother, child, or dear relative, to know that, although the earthly tabernacle is laid down and dissolved, *they shall rise again to dwell in everlasting burnings in immortal glory, not to sorrow, suffer, or die any more; but they shall be heirs of God and joint heirs with Jesus Christ. What is it? To inherit the same power, the same glory and the same exaltation, until you arrive at the station of a God, and ascend the throne of eternal power, the same as those who have gone before.* What did Jesus do? Why; I do the things I saw my Father do when worlds came rolling into existence. *My Father worked out his kingdom with fear and trembling, and I must do the same; and when I get my kingdom, I shall present it to my Father, so that he may obtain kingdom upon kingdom, and it will exalt him in glory. He will then take a higher exaltation, and I will take his place, and thereby become exalted myself. So that Jesus treads in the tracks of his Father, and inherits what God did before; and God is thus glorified and exalted in the salvation and exaltation of all his children.* It is plain beyond disputation, and you thus learn some of the first principles of the gospel, about which so much hath been said.

When you climb up a ladder, you must begin at the bottom, and ascend step by step, until you arrive at the top; and so it is with the principles of the *gospel—you must begin with the first, and go on until you learn all the principles of exaltation.* But it will be a great while after you have passed through the veil before you will have learned them. It is not all to be comprehended in this world; it will be a great work to learn our salvation and exaltation even beyond the grave.

This statement is so full of profound teachings that it is appropriate to briefly outline its messages so they won't be overlooked.

1. "God himself was once as we are now, and is an exalted man."
2. God has a physical body; He is "like a man in form . . . in all the person, image, and very form as a man."
3. God now "sits enthroned in yonder heavens."
4. "Adam was created in the very fashion, image and likeness of God."
5. "The Father hath power in himself, . . . to lay down his body and take it up again."
6. The Father laid down His life and took it up again. (However, this statement gives no implication that the Father atoned for the sins of others as he died and was resurrected.)
7. Jesus Christ also had power "to lay down his body and take it up again."
8. Men "have got to learn how to be Gods . . . and to be kings and priests to God."

9. Learning how to be Gods is the same task "as all Gods have done before you."
10. The path to exaltation is to progress "from one small degree to another, and from a small capacity to a great one: from grace to grace, from exaltation to exaltation."
11. Exalted beings don't just arrive at exaltation; they progress "from exaltation to exaltation."
12. Attaining "to the resurrection of the dead" enables a being to be "able to dwell in everlasting burnings, and to sit in glory, as do those who sit enthroned in everlasting power."
13. Exalted beings are able to "sit enthroned in everlasting power."
14. Righteous beings "shall rise again to dwell in everlasting burnings in immortal glory, not to sorrow, suffer, or die any more."
15. Righteous resurrected beings "shall be heirs of God and joint heirs with Jesus Christ."
16. Righteous beings will "inherit the same power, the same glory and the same exaltation" "as those who have gone before."
17. Righteous beings will progress by receiving power, glory, and exaltation until they "arrive at the station of a God, and ascend the throne of eternal power." Receiving Godhood comes long after receiving power, glory, and exaltation.
18. Jesus was with His Father and observed His Father as His Father was creating worlds: "I do the things I saw my Father do when worlds came rolling into existence."
19. God the Father "worked out his kingdom with fear and trembling." Jesus had to "do the same."
20. When Jesus received His kingdom, he presented it to His Father, "so that he may obtain kingdom upon kingdom, and it will exalt him [the Father] in glory."
21. "Jesus treads in the tracks of his Father, and inherits what God did before; and God is thus glorified and exalted in the salvation and exaltation of all his children." Thus an exalted being moves from exaltation to exaltation; this is the process of eternal progression.
22. Gospel progression is like climbing up a ladder: "you must begin with the first, and go on until you learn all the principles of exaltation."
23. "It will be a great while after you have passed through the veil before you will have learned" the principles of exaltation. "It is not all to be comprehended in this world."
24. "It will be a great work to learn our salvation and exaltation even beyond the grave."

Thus the Prophet Joseph Smith described the role of God the Father as one in a continuing series of other beings who are in the process of working out their own salvation and then progressing from exaltation to exaltation. Jesus, the firstborn son, was with His Father while He was working out His own salvation, and entered into the same process by emulating the lessons He learned by observing His Father's activities. However, the scriptures repeatedly assert that Jesus is the only Savior and Redeemer for all of Heavenly Father's children and creations.

The many profound concepts summarized by Joseph Smith in his King Follett discourse will be substantiated by the numerous scriptural passages cited in the remainder of this chapter.

It should be noted, however, that Joseph Smith's concepts of the eternal plan are far different from the concept of "the beginning" adopted almost two millennia ago by the early Christian Fathers as they attempted to define their beliefs in that era when revelation had ceased and the Apostasy was in full blossom. Many of them, at that time adopted a number of premises which latter-day revelation has indicated to be *incorrect*, such as:

1. God the Father was the very, very, very beginning of everything. Nothing existed prior to him.
2. God the Father was, and is, a being without shape or form.
3. God the Father was alone in the very, very, very beginning of everything. He created everyone and everything besides Him that exists or ever has existed.
4. This earth, and everything God has personally created or directed others to create, was created out of nothing.
5. Jesus Christ was the only Son and child of God the Father. No mention is even considered or made that all mankind are his brothers and sisters.
6. Man, and all the animal and plant inhabitants of this earth, did not exist prior to the creation of this earth.

So, with all these preliminary insights gleaned from the Prophet Joseph's discourse, this chapter returns to the scriptures.

Intelligences and Spirit Beings Existed "In the Beginning"

It is revealed in the Doctrine and Covenants that man, in the form of "intelligence," also existed prior to the beginning of this earth: • "Man was also in the beginning with God. *Intelligence, or the light of truth, was not created or made, neither indeed can be.* All truth is independent in that sphere in which God has placed it, to act for itself, as all intelligence also; otherwise there is no existence" (D&C 93:29–30).

Premortal intelligences were shown in vision to Abraham, and God told him that from the very beginning, intelligences differed one from another, and that all of them were and are eternal beings: "if there be two spirits, and *one shall be more intelligent than the other*, yet these two spirits, notwithstanding one is more intelligent than the other, *have no beginning*; they existed before, they shall have no end, they shall exist after, for they are gnolaum, or eternal. And the Lord said unto me: These two facts do exist, that there are two spirits, one being more intelligent than the other; there shall be another more intelligent than they; *I am the Lord thy God, I am more intelligent than they all*" (Abr. 3:18–19; For more insights on intelligences, see "Visions of Premortal Events" in *Life Everlasting*, 2nd revised edition [Springville, UT: Horizon Publishers, 2005], pp. 91–98).

Latter-day Saints believe that in some manner not fully explained in the scriptures, an intelligence is transformed or born as a spirit child of more advanced (resurrected and sanctified?) beings. Doctrine and Covenants 93 lends additional insight on this matter as the words of Jesus are recorded. He indicates that at some point "in the beginning," spirit beings existed, and that they each had specific identities and personal agency with the ability to choose between good and evil: "I was in the beginning with the Father, and am the Firstborn; . . . *Ye were also in the beginning with the Father; that which is Spirit, even the Spirit of truth;* . . . Behold, here is the agency of man, and here is the condemnation of man; because that which was from the beginning is plainly manifest unto them, and they receive not the light. . . . And every man whose spirit receiveth not the light is under condemnation. *For man is spirit*" (D&C 93:21, 23, 31–33).

In the same revelation, the Lord reveals that premortal spirit beings were without sin, and guiltless in the sight of God: *"Every spirit of man was innocent in the beginning;* . . . in their infant state, innocent before God"* (D&C 93:38).

God the Father Is the Father of All Spirit Beings Who Come to This Earth

A fundamental tenant of Latter-day Saint doctrine is that those righteous beings who have been sealed together in eternal marriage and have progressed sufficiently that they have attained to the highest level of the celestial kingdom are permitted to have eternal increase. Doctrine and Covenants contains the promise that,

> if a man marry a wife by my word, which is my law, and by the new and everlasting covenant, and it is sealed unto them by the Holy Spirit of promise, by him who is anointed, unto whom I have appointed this power and the keys of this priesthood; and it shall be said unto them—Ye shall come forth in the first resurrection; and if it be after the first resurrection, in the next resurrection; and shall inherit thrones, kingdoms, principalities, and powers, dominions, all heights and depths—then shall it be written in the Lamb's Book of Life, . . .it shall be done unto them in all things whatsoever my servant hath put upon them, in time, and through all eternity; and shall be of full force when they are out of the world; and they shall pass by the angels, and the gods, which are set there, to their exaltation and glory in all things, as hath been sealed upon their heads, *which glory shall be a fulness and a continuation of the seeds forever and ever.*
>
> *Then shall they be gods, because they have no end; therefore shall they be from everlasting to everlasting, because they continue*; then shall they be above all, because all things are subject unto them. *Then shall they be gods, because they have all power,* and the angels are subject unto them. (D&C 132:19–20)

Doctrine and Covenants section 131 adds further insight: "*In the celestial glory there are three heavens or degrees; And in order to obtain the highest, a man must enter into this order of the priesthood* [meaning the new and everlasting covenant of marriage]; *And if he does not, he cannot obtain it. He may enter into the other, but that is the end of his kingdom; he cannot have an increase*" (D&C 131:1–4).

Based on the insights concerning eternal marriage found in D&C sections 131 and 132, many Latter-day Saints conclude that God the Father and His spouse had attained to this level, and they were entitled to the blessing of "the continuation of the[ir] seeds forever and ever." Thus they were able to bring forth intelligences who were born in the form of spirit children. This, however, is not asserted as being a doctrine of the Church.

The Prophet Enoch was allowed to see these premortal beings on one occasion: "*he beheld the spirits that God had created;* and he beheld also things which were not visible to the natural eye" (Moses 6:36). Thus, God the Father is known as the father of spirits in the scriptures.

It apparently is this spiritual birth to which the Prophet Malachi made reference when he wrote, "*Have we not all one father? hath not one God created us?*" (Mal. 2:10). God the Father is the being referred to by the author of the Book of Hebrews when he contrasted mortal fathers with God, the Father of our spirits, saying that since reverence is given unto the fathers of our flesh, "*shall we not much rather be in subjection unto the Father of spirits, and live?*" (Heb. 12:9). Moses and Aaron prayed to "*the God of the spirits of all flesh*" (Num. 16:22), and Moses in another setting prayed to "*the God of the spirits of all flesh*" (Num. 27:16). Paul, in his discourse on Mars Hill, spoke about man's relationship to deity, and taught that "*we are the offspring of God*" (Acts 17:29). When on the earth, Jesus Christ regarded those around him as children of God the Father, who was also His Father. He taught them to pray to *"Our Father* which art in heaven"* (Matt. 6:9). Following His resurrection, he told Mary to "Touch me not; for I am not yet ascended to my Father, but go to your brethren, and say to them, *I ascend unto my Father, and your Father; and to my God, and your God"* (John 20:17).

Knowing what the scriptures say about the essential nature of eternal marriage, some Latter-day Saints draw the conclusion that all mankind also have a Heavenly Mother, the spouse of Father in Heaven, though the scriptures are mute as to her existence and status. Clearly implied, also, is the conclusion that God the Father is the offspring of parents who together had merited and attained exaltation, with the privilege of the continuing of their seeds forever and ever (see D&C 131, 132).

Jehovah/Jesus Christ Is the Firstborn Child and Son of God the Father in the Premortal Spirit World

The Apostle Paul, writing of how other individuals existed prior to the foundation of this earth, indicates that God knew them, and that • "whom he did foreknow, he also did predestinate to be *conformed to the image of his Son* [Jesus Christ], that *he might be the firstborn* among many brethren" (Rom. 8:29). Paul wrote to the Colossians that Christ is *"the firstborn of every creature*: . . . and he is before all things, and by him all things consist"* (Col. 1:15–17). Since he is the firstborn of God the Father's spirit children, he holds the title of *Alpha*, as is found in Rev. 1:11, 22:13, 3 Ne. 9:18, D&C 38:1, 107:9. Thus, he is able to refer to himself as *"the beginning of the creation of God"* (Rev. 3:14). Christ's words in the D&C clearly assert His position among all the children of God. He revealed that "I was in the beginning with the Father, *and am the Firstborn"* (D&C 93:21). During His earthly ministry Jesus taught that *"I proceeded forth and came from God*; neither came I of myself, but he sent me" (John 8:42). Also during his mortal ministry in the meridian of time, the Prophet John the Baptist bore witness of him, saying that "This was he of whom I spake, He that cometh after me is preferred before me: *for he was before me"* (John 1:15).

The Loving Premortal Relationship of God the Father and His Firstborn Son

The scriptures make it abundantly clear that during all of His premortal rearing and training, Jesus dwelt in an intimate, loving relationship with His father. They indicate that He was the *"Son, who was in the bosom of the Father*, even from the beginning" (D&C 76:13); the *"Son whom the Father loved* and who was in the bosom of the Father" (D&C 76:25). He *"was in the bosom of the Father before the worlds were made"* (D&C 76:39; see also D&C 109:4).

The scriptures speak repeatedly of the love between God the Father and His Son Jesus Christ: • *"The Father loveth the Son*, and hath given all things into his hand" (John 3:35). • *"the Father loveth the Son*, and sheweth him all things that himself doeth" (John 5:20). • *"Therefore doth my Father love me*, because I lay down my life, that I might take it again" (John 10:17). • *"As the Father hath loved me*, so have I loved you" (John 15:9). • "Father, . . . *thou lovedst me before the foundation of the world"* (John 17:24). • "the Only Begotten Son *whom the Father loved* and who was in the bosom of the Father" (D&C 76:25).

Even in this early father-son relationship, God the Father was issuing instructions through His Son, Jehovah/Jesus Christ, for the Doctrine and Covenants makes reference to • *"Those things which were from the beginning before the world was, which were ordained of the Father, through his Only Begotten Son,* who was in the bosom of the Father, even from the beginning" (D&C 76:13).

Scriptural passages repeatedly record the words of God the Father as he specifically refers to Jesus as His *"beloved son"* (see Matt. 3:17; 17:5; Mark 1:11; 9:7; Luke 3:22; 9:35; 2 Pet. 1:17; 2 Ne. 31:11; 3 Ne. 11:7; 21:20; D&C 93:15; Moses 4:2; JS—H 1:17).

The scriptures also make it clear that Jesus was God the Father's son • "who did no sin, in whom [he] wast *well pleased"* (D&C 45:4). In the several occasions during Christ's mortal ministry when the Father spoke from the heavens, He indicated that He was well pleased with His Son (see Matt. 3:17; 12:18; 17:5; Mark 1:11; Luke 3:22; 2 Pet. 1:17; 3 Ne. 11:7; D&C 45:4).

The Premortal Jehovah/Jesus Grew, Grace by Grace, until He Received a Fulness

The Doctrine and Covenants records a unique testimony of Christ's premortal life which was borne by John the Baptist. He said, in part:

> I saw his glory, that *he was in the beginning,* before the world was;
> Therefore, in the beginning the Word was, for he was the Word, even the messenger of salvation . . .
> And I, John, saw that *he received not of the fulness at the first, but received grace for grace;*
> And he received not of the fulness at first, but continued from grace to grace, until he received a fulness;
> And thus he was called the Son of God, because *he received not of the fulness at the first.* (D&C 93:7–8, 12–14)

This appears to be the same learning pattern the Lord uses when interacting with man upon the earth, as recorded in the Book of Mormon: • "thus saith the Lord God: I will give unto the children of men *line upon line, precept upon precept,* here a little and there a little; and blessed are those who hearken unto my precepts, and lend an ear unto my counsel, for they shall learn wisdom; for *unto him that receiveth I will give more"* (2 Ne. 28:30; see Isa. 28:9–13; D&C 98:12; 128:21). And the Savior, even after His immense accomplishments in the premortal realm, still had to progress in His physical growth and in His learning of mortal experiences when He came to dwell on this earth: "Jesus increased in wisdom and stature, and in favour with God and man" (Luke 2:52).

Like many others in the Christian world, Latter-day Saints believe that the mortal and postmortal Jesus Christ is the same individual who was known as Jehovah during His premortal existence, during the creation of this earth, and during the Old Testament era in the Bible. But since many of the scriptural passages cited in this chapter come from the Savior's own words while He experienced mortality, and since the name by which He was known while here on earth (as portrayed in the English King James Version of the Bible) is Jesus, the Christ, this chapter will identify Him as Jehovah/Jesus Christ, without further discussion on the matter.

God the Father Mentored His Son Jehovah/Jesus Christ

During His mortal ministry, the Savior made repeated references to the premortal training and instruction He received from His Father. Typical is His statement that • *"I do nothing of myself; but as my Father hath taught me, I speak these things"* (John 8:28).

However, little has been revealed about His premortal "childhood" period of experiences. Perhaps it was the relationship spoken of by the Apostle Paul in his epistle to the Galatians: • "Now I say, That *the heir, as long as he is a child, differeth nothing from a servant, though he be lord of all; But is under tutors and governors until the time appointed of the father*" (Gal. 4:1–2).

What is known, however, is that as Jehovah/Jesus Christ matured, he saw His father in action on many occasions during the eternities before "the beginning" of this earth, and learned to emulate His Father's example. During His mortal ministry, he repeatedly made comments such as: • *"The Son can do nothing of himself, but what he seeth the Father do: for what things soever he doeth, these also doeth the Son likewise"* (John 5:19). • "the Father loveth the Son, and *sheweth him all things that himself doeth*: and he will shew him greater works than these, that ye may marvel" (John 5:20). • "he that sent me is true; and *I speak to the world those things which I have heard of him*. They understood not that *he spake to them of the Father*" (John 8:26–27). • *"I do nothing of myself; but as my Father hath taught me, I speak these things"* (John 8:28). • *"I speak that which I have seen with my Father"* (John 8:38). • *"I must work the works of him that sent me"* (John 9:4). • "Many good works have I shewed you *from my Father*" (John 10:32). • "If I do not *the works of my Father*, believe me not. But if I do, though ye believe not me, believe the works: that ye may know, and believe" (John 10:37–38). • *"all things that I have heard of my Father I have made known unto you"* (John 15:15). • "I was in the world and received of my Father, *and the works of him were plainly manifest*" (D&C 93:5).

During His mortal ministry, Jesus frequently indicated that while here on earth, he was to follow the example and apply the teachings and instructions His Father had given him. He said, for instance: • *"My meat is to do the will of him that sent me, and to finish his work"* (John 4:34). • "My Father worketh hitherto, and I work" (John 5:17). • *"I seek not mine own will, but the will of the Father which hath sent me"* (John 5:30). • *"the works which the Father hath given me to finish, the same works that I do, bear witness of me*, that the Father hath sent me" (John 5:36). • "I came down from heaven, *not to do mine own will, but the will of him that sent me*" (John 6:38). • "the Father hath not left me alone; for I do always those things that please him" (John 8:29). • "the works that I do in my Father's name, they bear witness of me" (John 10:25). • *"The Father which sent me, he gave me a commandment, what I should say, and what I should speak. . . . even as the Father said unto me, so I speak"* (John 12:49–50). • "that the world may know that *I love the Father;* and *as the Father gave me commandment, even so I do*" (John 14:31). • "All things are delivered to me of my Father" (Luke 10:22). • [he that overcometh] "he shall rule them with a rod of iron; as the vessels of a potter shall they be broken to shivers: *even as I received of my Father*" (Rev. 2:27). • "Those things which were from the beginning before the world was, which were *ordained of the Father*, through his Only Begotten Son, who was in the bosom of the Father, even from the beginning" (D&C 76:13). • *"herein is the work of my Father continued, that he may be glorified"* (D&C 132:63).

Worlds Without Number Created by God the Father and Jehovah/Jesus Christ

One of the most remarkable passages in all scripture is the record of the glorious vision granted to the Prophet Moses concerning innumerable premortal creations. It shows that many, many worlds were created by the God the Father, using His "Only Begotten Son," Jesus Christ, as His builder.

The vision recorded in the book of Moses began when Moses was caught up into an exceedingly high mountain, and he saw God face to face, and he talked with him. The record states that • "the glory of God was upon Moses; therefore Moses could endure his presence. And God spake unto Moses, saying: . . . look, and I will show thee the workmanship of mine hands; but not all, for *my works are without end, and also my words*, for they never cease" (Moses 1:1–4). Moses was overcome by what he saw and learned, but then he regained his strength and again communed with God. This is the record of the glorious vision which he then received:

> And it came to pass, as the voice was still speaking, Moses cast his eyes and *beheld the earth, yea, even all of it; and there was not a particle of it which he did not behold, discerning it by the spirit of God.*
>
> *And he beheld also the inhabitants thereof,* and there was not a soul which he beheld not; and he discerned them by the Spirit of God; and their numbers were great, even numberless as the sand upon the sea shore.
>
> *And he beheld many lands; and each land was called earth, and there were inhabitants on the face thereof.*
>
> And it came to pass that Moses called upon God, saying: Tell me, I pray thee, why these things are so, and by what thou madest them?
>
> And behold, the glory of the Lord was upon Moses, so that Moses stood in the presence of God, and talked with him face to face. And the Lord God said unto Moses: *For mine own purpose have I made these things.* Here is wisdom and it remaineth in me.
>
> *And by the word of my power, have I created them, which is mine Only Begotten Son, who is full of grace and truth.*
>
> *And worlds without number have I created; and I also created them for mine own purpose; and by the Son I created them, which is mine Only Begotten.*
>
> *And the first man of all men have I called Adam, which is many.*
>
> But only an account of this earth, and the inhabitants thereof, give I unto you. *For behold, there are many worlds that have passed away by the word of my power. And there are many that now stand, and innumerable are they unto man; but all things are numbered unto me, for they are mine and I know them.*
>
> And it came to pass that Moses spake unto the Lord, saying: Be merciful unto thy servant, O God, and tell me concerning this earth, and the inhabitants thereof, and also the heavens, and then thy servant will be content.
>
> And the Lord God spake unto Moses, saying: *The heavens, they are many, and they cannot be numbered unto man; but they are numbered unto me, for they are mine.*
>
> *And as one earth shall pass away, and the heavens thereof even so shall another come, and there is no end to my works, neither to my words.*
>
> For behold, this is my work and my glory—to bring to pass the immortality and eternal life of man. (Moses 1:27–39)

So, who was the "creator" of these numberless worlds? Both God the Father and God the Son! This type of situation is frequently seen in today's construction projects, where many individuals are the "creator" of beautiful buildings and vast tracts of homes, stores, malls, parks, and thoroughfares. There is the *developer*, who envisions the project, defines it, and oversees the initial legal and developmental arrangements; the *architect*, who designs the details of the projected edifices and prepares the working drawings and blueprints; the *general contractor*, who coordinates and ramrods the actual construction; and *subcontractors* galore who handle the concrete, the bricklayers, the carpenters, the plumbing, the electrical work, etc. All of them, in their advertising, take credit for "creating" and "building" the project, and rightfully so.

Perhaps envisioning *God the Father as the developer and architect* and *God the Son as the general contractor* provides as good an insight as is available based on the limited knowledge at present available. Both reveal themselves as the creator of this earth and numberless other worlds. *Other scriptural passages speak of "worlds":* some speak of their being created by the Father and the Son; others attribute their creation to the Son, Jesus Christ; still others speak of future worlds: • "God . . . Hath in these last days spoken unto us by his Son, whom he hath appointed heir of all things, *by whom also he made the worlds"* (Heb. 1:1–2). • "*Through faith we understand that the worlds were framed by the word of God"* (Heb. 11:3). • "*he is the Only Begotten of the Father—That by him, and through him, and of him, the worlds are and were created, and the inhabitants thereof are begotten sons and daughters unto God"* (D&C 76:23–24). • "*all the rest shall be brought forth by the resurrection of the dead, through the triumph and the glory of the Lamb,* who was slain, who was in the bosom of the Father before the worlds were made" (D&C 76:39). • "where God and Christ dwell they cannot come, worlds without end" (D&C 76:112). • "The light and the Redeemer of the world; . . . *The worlds were made by him; men were made by him;* all things were made by him, and through him, and of him" (D&C 93:9–10). • "*and crowns of eternal lives in the eternal worlds"* (D&C 132:55). • "to fulfil the promise which was given by my Father before the foundation of the world, and *for their exaltation in the eternal worlds, that they may bear the souls of men; for herein is the work of my Father continued, that he may be glorified"* (D&C 132:63).

How many worlds have the Father and Son together created? How many is "worlds without number"? The only scriptural passage that even begins to quantify that number is found in the book of Moses, where the Prophet Enoch is conversing with the Lord. He says, "*were it possible that man could number the particles of the earth, yea, millions of earths like this, it would not be a beginning to the number of thy creations;* and thy curtains are stretched out still" (Moses 7:30).

As has been seen, worlds without number already have been created; many have fulfilled their purpose and have been allowed to pass away; innumerable others remain and are active at the present time. The question can be posed: **are these earths visited by their Creator?** An intriguing parable in the Doctrine and Covenants addresses this query as it describes their administrations and their visitations:

> Judgment goeth before the face of him who sitteth upon the throne and governeth and executeth all things.
> *He comprehendeth all things, and all things are before him, and all things are round about him; and he is above all things, and in all things, and is through all things, and is round about all things; and all things are by him, and of him, even God, forever and ever.*
> And again, verily I say unto you, *he hath given a law unto all things, by which they move in their times and their seasons;*
> *And their courses are fixed, even the courses of the heavens and the earth, which comprehend the earth and all the planets.*
> *And they give light to each other in their times and in their seasons, in their minutes, in their hours, in their days, in their weeks, in their months, in their years—all these are one year with God, but not with man.*
> The earth rolls upon her wings, and the sun giveth his light by day, and the moon giveth her light by night, and the stars also give their light, as they roll upon their wings in their glory, in the midst of the power of God.
> Unto what shall I liken these kingdoms, that ye may understand?
> *Behold, all these are kingdoms, and any man who hath seen any or the least of these*

hath seen God moving in his majesty and power.

I say unto you, he hath seen him; nevertheless, he who came unto his own was not comprehended.

The light shineth in darkness, and the darkness comprehendeth it not; nevertheless, **the day shall come when you shall comprehend even God, being quickened in him and by him.**

Then shall ye know that ye have seen me, that I am, and that I am the true light that is in you, and that you are in me; otherwise ye could not abound.

Behold, I will liken these kingdoms unto a man having a field, and he sent forth his servants into the field to dig in the field.

And he said unto the first: Go ye and labor in the field, and *in the first hour I will come unto you, and ye shall behold the joy of my countenance.*

And he said unto the second: Go ye also into the field, and *in the second hour I will visit you with the joy of my countenance.*

And also unto the *third,* saying: I will visit you;

And unto the *fourth,* and so on unto the *twelfth.*

And the lord of the field went unto the first in the first hour, and tarried with him all that hour, and he was made glad with the light of the countenance of his lord.

And then he withdrew from the first that he might visit the second also, and the third, and the fourth, and so on unto the twelfth.

And thus they all received the light of the countenance of their lord, every man in his hour, and in his time, and in his season—

Beginning at the first, and so on unto the last, and from the last unto the first, and from the first unto the last;

Every man in his own order, until his hour was finished, even according as his lord had commanded him, *that his lord might be glorified in him, and he in his lord, that they all might be glorified.*

Therefore, unto this parable I will liken all these kingdoms, and the inhabitants thereof—every kingdom in its hour, and in its time, and in its season, even according to the decree which God hath made.

And again, verily I say unto you, my friends, I leave these sayings with you to ponder in your hearts, with this commandment which I give unto you, that ye shall call upon me while I am near. (D&C 88:40–62)

Is this what will be occurring when the Savior comes to dwell on this earth for the thousand years following his glorious Second Coming? (see Rev. 20:2–6; D&C 29:11, 22; 77:12; Moses 7:64–65; Ps. 90:2–4).

The Astronomy of Many of God's Creations

Significant knowledge and understanding of many of the key creations of God established prior to "in the beginning" were revealed to the prophet Abraham through the Urim and Thummin, given to him when he was still in Ur of the Chaldees. This is what is recorded in the third chapter of the book of Abraham in the Pearl of Great Price:

I saw the stars, that they were very great, and that *one of them was nearest unto the throne of God; and there were many great ones which were near unto it;*

And the Lord said unto me: These are the governing ones; and *the name of the great one is **Kolob,** because it is near unto me, for I am the Lord thy God: I have set this one to govern all those which belong to the same order as that upon which thou standest.*

And the Lord said unto me, by the Urim and Thummim, that *Kolob was after the manner of the Lord, according to its times and seasons in the revolutions thereof; that one revolution was a day unto the Lord, after his manner of reckoning, it being one thou-*

sand years according to the time appointed unto that whereon thou standest. **This is the reckoning of the Lord's time, according to the reckoning of Kolob.**

And the Lord said unto me: *The planet which is the lesser light, lesser than that which is to rule the day, even the night, is above or greater than that upon which thou standest in point of reckoning, for it moveth in order more slow; this is in order because it standeth above the earth upon which thou standest, therefore the reckoning of its time is not so many as to its number of days, and of months, and of years.*

And the Lord said unto me: Now, Abraham, these two facts exist, behold thine eyes see it; *it is given unto thee to know the times of reckoning, and the set time, yea, the set time of the earth upon which thou standest, and the set time of the greater light which is set to rule the day, and the set time of the lesser light which is set to rule the night.*

Now the set time of the lesser light is a longer time as to its reckoning than the reckoning of the time of the earth upon which thou standest.

And where these two facts exist, there shall be another fact above them, that is, there shall be another planet whose reckoning of time shall be longer still;

And thus there shall be the reckoning of the time of one planet above another, until thou come nigh unto Kolob, which Kolob is after the reckoning of the Lord's time; **which Kolob is set nigh unto the throne of God,** *to govern all those planets which belong to the same order as that upon which thou standest.*

And it is given unto thee to know *the set time of all the stars that are set to give light,* until thou come near unto the throne of God. . . .

Thus I, Abraham, talked with the Lord, face to face, as one man talketh with another; and he told me of the works which his hands had made;

And he said unto me: My son, my son (and his hand was stretched out), behold I will show you all these. And *he put his hand upon mine eyes, and I saw* those things which his hands had made, which were many; and they multiplied before mine eyes, and *I could not see the end thereof.*

And he said unto me: This is **Shinehah,** *which is the sun.* And he said unto me: **Kokob,** *which is star.* And he said unto me: **Olea,** *which is the moon.* And he said unto me: **Kokaubeam,** *which signifies stars, or all the great lights, which were in the firmament of heaven.*

And it was in the night time when the Lord spake these words unto me: I will multiply thee, and thy seed after thee, like unto these; and if thou canst count the number of sands, so shall be the number of thy seeds.

And the Lord said unto me: Abraham, I show these things unto thee before ye go into Egypt, that ye may declare all these words.

If two things exist, and there be one above the other, there shall be greater things above them; *therefore Kolob is the greatest of all the Kokaubeam that thou hast seen, because it is nearest unto me.*

Now, if there be two things, one above the other, and the moon be above the earth, then it may be that a planet or a star may exist above it; and *there is nothing that the Lord thy God shall take in his heart to do but what he will do it.*

Howbeit that *he made the greater star;* as, also, if there be two spirits, and one shall be more intelligent than the other, yet *these two spirits, notwithstanding one is more intelligent than the other, have no beginning; they existed before, they shall have no end, they shall exist after, for they are gnolaum, or eternal.*

And the Lord said unto me: These two facts do exist, that there are two spirits, one being more intelligent than the other; there shall be another more intelligent than they; *I am the Lord thy God, I am more intelligent than they all.*

The Lord thy God sent his angel to deliver thee from the hands of the priest of Elkenah.

I dwell in the midst of them all; I now, therefore, have come down unto thee to declare unto thee the works which my hands have made, wherein *my wisdom excelleth them all, for I rule in the heavens above, and in the earth beneath, in all wisdom and prudence, over all the intelligences thine eyes have seen from the beginning; I came down in the beginning in the midst of all the intelligences thou hast seen.* (Abr. 3:2–21)

Note that in the revelation given to Abraham, reference is repeatedly to "the order . . . upon which thou standest," which implies that God (or other Gods) has/have created other planetary orders; Abraham apparently was not shown all of God's creations.

The book of Abraham contains a hieroglyphic presentation which apparently depicts what was shown to Abraham in greater detail. Several of *the explanations given for Facsimile 2* provide interesting insights concerning the planets near the residence of God. It appears that the planets described were created and in place prior to "in the beginning" when the creation of this earth was begun:

Fig. 1. **Kolob,** *signifying the first creation, nearest to the celestial, or the residence of God. First in government, the last pertaining to the measurement of time. The measurement according to celestial time, which celestial time signifies one day to a cubit. One day in Kolob is equal to a thousand years according to the measurement of this earth . . .*

Fig. 2. *Stands next to Kolob, called by the Egyptians* **Oliblish,** *which is the next grand governing creation near to the celestial or the place where God resides; holding the key of power also, pertaining to other planets . . .*

Fig. 4. Answers to the Hebrew word **Raukeeyang,** signifying *expanse, or the firmament of the heavens;* also a numerical figure, in Egyptian signifying one thousand; answering to *the measuring of the time of Oliblish, which is equal with Kolob in its revolution and in its measuring of time.*

Fig. 5. Is called in Egyptian **Enish-go-on-dosh;** this is *one of the governing planets also,* and is said by the Egyptians to be *the Sun, and to borrow its light from Kolob* through the medium of **Kae-e-vanrash,** *which is the grand Key, or, in other words, the governing power, which governs fifteen other fixed planets or stars, as also* **Floeese** *or the Moon, the Earth and the Sun in their annual revolutions. This planet receives its power through the medium of* **Kli-flos-is-es,** *or* **Hah-ko-kau-beam,** *the stars represented by numbers 22 and 23, receiving light from the revolutions of Kolob.*

The above translation is given as far as we have any right to give at the present time. (Abr. 2, Facsimile 2:1–13)

The interpretation of these explanations is beyond the scope of this book, though interesting relations and conclusions can be drawn from them. Suffice it to say that prior to the creation of this earth, a vast number of other earths and planets had been created by God the Father with and through the implementation of His Son, Jehovah, who is referred to in this chapter by the name given to Him in preparation for His mortality: Jesus, the Christ.

Summary

1. The many scriptural events that took place prior to the creation of this particular earth are considered to be "in" the beginning.

2. God told Moses, "only an account of this earth, and the inhabitants thereof, give I unto you" (Moses 1:35).

3. There will come a time when no information from God will be withheld (D&C 121:28).

4. The Doctrine and Covenants alludes to "the Council of the Eternal God of all

other gods before this world was" (D&C 121:32), but no other information is furnished to help in the interpretation of the passage.

5. Joseph Smith's explanation of how God the Father and Jesus Christ attained Godhood was cited from his King Follett Discourse, and a 25-point analysis list was provided.

6. A brief list of incorrect doctrines which came out of the Great Apostasy was provided.

7. Passages from the Doctrine and Covenants and the book of Abraham are the only scriptural sources on the nature of intelligences (D&C 93 and Abr. 3).

8. God the Father is believed to be the Father of all the spirit beings who come to this earth. Doctrine and Covenants sections 131 and 132 lead to speculation and theories concerning mankind's mother or mothers in heaven.

9. Jehovah, who is Jesus Christ, is the firstborn spirit child and son of God the Father in the premortal spirit world.

10. Various passages speaking of the mutual love of God the Father and His son are listed.

11. Several passages alluding to the childhood of Jehovah in the premortal spirit world are cited. It is clear that God the Father mentored and prepared His Son.

12. Worlds "without number," at least "millions" of them, were created by God the Father and Jehovah/Jesus Christ prior to the creation of this earth.

13. A comparison to modern home builders suggests that perhaps the creative role of God the Father is similar to the "developer" of creation projects, while Jehovah/Jesus Christ may function in the role of "general contractor."

14. A parable in the Doctrine and Covenants (D&C 88:51–62) speaking of the man having various fields and visiting them hour by hour may be an explanation of how and why the Lord Jesus Christ will dwell on this earth for the millennium.

15. The astronomy of God's creations, as revealed in the book of Abraham, is cited but not explained in depth (Abr. 3:2–21; Facsimile 2:1–13).

CHAPTER 8

JEHOVAH/JESUS CHRIST ATTAINED GODHOOD IN PREMORTALITY

Differing Views Concerning the Nature of Godhood

Just what constitutes being a God, and of what attributes does Godhood consist? In the centuries following the death and resurrection of Jesus, church fathers struggled mightily to define the nature of God. Heavily influenced by the Greek philosophers who preceded them and increasingly cut off from the guidance of the Holy Spirit as the Apostasy grew in influence, they concocted definitions and explanations that ranged farther and farther away from the revealed truths found in the scriptures. Because of their background in Greek thought, they typically envisioned God the Father and God the Son as uncreated, self-existent beings, without beginning or ending, who always possessed all the attributes of Godhood. No element of progression was attributed to them.

In contrast, Latter-day Saints view Godhood as a priesthood office, received by sacred ordinances after the individual has progressed unto perfection. Statements by Latter-day Saint Church President Lorenzo Snow are characteristic of Latter-day Saint beliefs: *"Man may become like his Father, doing the works which his Father did before him, and he cannot be deprived of the opportunity of reaching this exalted state. . . . The* destiny of man is to be like his Father—a God in eternity. This should be a bright, illuminating star before him all the time—in his heart, in his soul, and all through him." It is President Snow who received, by inspiration, the profound couplets:

As man now is, God once was:
As God now is, man may be.
A son of God, like God to be,
Would not be robbing Deity.

He also said that *"Godliness cannot be conferred, but must be acquired. . . . We approach godliness as fast as we approach perfection. . . . The* reward for righteousness is exaltation. . . . If we are faithful, we shall at some time do our own work, but now we are doing the work of our Father" ("Characteristic Sayings of President Lorenzo Snow," *Improvement Era*, June 1919, Vol. XXII, No. 8, p. 651).

Was Jehovah/Jesus Christ Ready and Worthy to Be Granted Godhood?

Was Jehovah/Jesus Christ properly prepared and ready to receive Godhood in the premortal realms? What were His qualifications, if godliness must be acquired through personal worthiness and development? The scriptures summarize and emphasize His supreme readiness in two essential, all-encompassing areas:

1. **Jehovah/Jesus Christ was pure, free from sin, and spotless:** • "*The words of the* Lord *are pure words*: as silver tried in a furnace of earth, purified seven times" (Ps. 12:6). • The statutes of the Lord are right, rejoicing the heart: *the commandment of the* Lord *is pure*, enlightening the eyes. *The fear of the* Lord *is clean*" (Ps. 19:8–9). • "Jesus the Son of God . . . was in all points tempted like as we are, *yet without sin*" (Heb. 4:14–15). • "For such an high priest became us, *who is holy, harmless, undefiled, separate from sinners*, and made higher than the heavens" (Heb. 7:26). • "Christ, . . . offered himself *without spot* to God" (Heb. 9:14). • "*God cannot be tempted with evil*, neither tempteth he any man" (James 1:13). • "Christ, as of a lamb *without blemish and without spot*" (1 Pet. 1:19). • "Christ . . . *did no sin*, neither was guile found in his mouth" (1 Pet. 2:21–22).

An essential principle of the gospel is that Christ's atoning sacrifice had to be an infinite atonement; another way of saying that Jesus had to be completely without sin to be able to break the bands of sin and death. Hence, • "it must needs be an infinite atonement—*save it should be an infinite atonement this corruption could not put on incorruption*" (2 Ne. 9:7). • "until they shall be persuaded to believe in Christ, the Son of God, and *the atonement, which is infinite for all mankind*" (2 Ne. 25:16). • "therefore there can be nothing which is short of an infinite atonement which will suffice for the sins of the world" (Alma 34:12).

It is because He was entirely free from sin that the Redeemer was able to present Himself as an example in statements such as • "what manner of men ought ye to be? Verily I say unto you, *even as I am*" (3 Ne. 27:27). • "Behold I am the light; *I have set an example for you*" (3 Ne. 18:16). • "*that which ye have seen me do even that shall ye do*" (3 Ne. 27:21). In the same vein, if Jesus Christ was not, and is not, completely sinless, others could not be cleansed through Him and through His atoning blood. It is only through His being clean that the scriptures can repeatedly speak of man being cleansed and becoming purified through Christ: • "turn ye unto the Lord; cry mightily unto the Father in the name of Jesus, that perhaps ye may be found spotless, pure, fair, and white, *having been cleansed by the blood of the Lamb*" (Morm. 9:6). • "that we may have this hope; that we may *be purified even as he is pure*" (Moro. 7:48).

2. **Jehovah/Jesus Christ achieved personal perfection:** Though man cannot as yet fully comprehend the infinite aspects of being perfect, the scriptures repeatedly assert that Jehovah/Jesus Christ achieved that level: • "I would that ye should *be perfect even as I, or your Father who is in heaven is perfect*" (3 Ne. 12:48). • "As for God, *his way is perfect*; the word of the Lord is tried" (2 Sam. 22:31; Ps. 18:30). • "God himself atoneth for the sins of the world, to bring about the plan of mercy, to appease the demands of justice, *that God might be a perfect, just God*, and a merciful God also" (Alma 42:15). • "Though he were a Son, yet learned he obedience . . . And *being made perfect*, he became the author of eternal salvation unto all them that obey him" (Heb. 5:8–9).

Just as man's becoming cleansed and sinless is seen as being achieved through Jesus Christ, the achieving of personal perfection is also perceived as being achieved through him, which wouldn't in any way be feasible unless he, himself, had become a perfect being: • "let patience have *her perfect work, that ye may be perfect and entire, wanting nothing.* If any of you lack wisdom, let him ask of God, that giveth to all men liberally, and upbraideth not; and it shall be given him" (James 1:4–5). • "Till we all come in the unity of the faith, and of the knowledge of the Son of God, *unto a perfect man,* unto the measure of the stature of the fulness of Christ" (Eph. 4:13). • "that we may *present every man perfect in Christ Jesus*" (Col. 1:28). • "Therefore [not] leaving the principles of the doctrine of Christ, *let us go on unto perfection*" (Heb. 6:1). • "Christ being come an high priest of good things to come, *by a greater and more perfect tabernacle,* . . . by his own blood he entered in once into the holy place, having obtained eternal redemption for us" (Heb. 9:11–12). • "the God of peace, that brought again from the dead our Lord Jesus, . . . *Make you perfect . . . through Jesus Christ*" (Heb. 13:20–21). • "the God of all grace, who hath called us unto his eternal glory *by Christ Jesus,* . . . *make you perfect*" (1 Pet. 5:10). • "come *unto Christ, and be perfected in him*" (Moro. 10:32). • "*if* ye by the grace of God *are perfect in Christ,* and deny not his power, then are ye sanctified in Christ" (Moro. 10:33). • "until the fulness of times, when *Christ shall have subdued all enemies under his feet, and shall have perfected his work*" (D&C 76:106). • "*Be ye therefore perfect, even as your Father which is in heaven is perfect*" (Matt. 5:48).

Scriptural Allusions to Priesthood Ordinances and Procedures Concerning the Elevation to Godhood of Jehovah/Jesus Christ

The scriptures do not convey with exactness the process and events by which the title and status of "God" is conveyed to a worthy individual, though it can be surmised that the process will be regarded as common knowledge to those who pass beyond death and have their memory of past events restored to them. It seems appropriate to assume that the process is a continuance and extension of what is required as priesthood ordinations and temple rites take place here on earth.

Concerning Jehovah/Jesus Christ, the scriptures relate that he was or has been **sanctified, anointed, ordained, sealed, appointed heir, crowned, made a king,** and **given a throne**:

1. **Jehovah/Jesus Christ was sanctified:** • "Say ye of *him whom the Father hath sanctified, and sent into the world,* Thou blasphemest; because I said, I am the Son of God?" (John 10:36). • "Christ Jesus, who of God is made unto us wisdom, and righteousness, and *sanctification,* and redemption" (1 Cor. 1:30). • "Jesus also, *that he might sanctify the people with his own blood,* suffered" (Heb. 13:12). • "*that they may become sanctified in me,* . . . saith Jesus Christ" (Eth. 4:7). • "we know also, that *sanctification through the grace of our Lord and Savior Jesus Christ* is just and true" (D&C 20:31). • "he came into the world, even Jesus, to be crucified for the world, and to bear the sins of the world, and to *sanctify the world*" (D&C 76:41).

2. **Jehovah/Jesus Christ was anointed:** • "The Spirit of the Lord is upon me, because *he hath anointed me* to preach the gospel . . . This day is this scripture fulfilled in your ears" (Luke 4:18, 21). • "thy holy child Jesus, *whom thou hast anointed*" (Acts 4:27). • "*God anointed Jesus* of Nazareth with the Holy Ghost and with power" (Acts 10:38). • "the LORD of hosts shall stir up a scourge for him . . . *and the yoke shall be destroyed because of the anointing*" (Isa. 10:26–27; 2 Ne. 20:26–27). • "the LORD hath said unto me, Thou art my Son; this day have I begotten thee. . . . the rulers take counsel together, *against the LORD, and against his anointed*" (Ps. 2:2).

3. *Jehovah/Jesus Christ was* **ordained:** • "it is *he which was ordained of God* to be the Judge of quick and dead" (Acts 10:42). • "he will judge the world in righteousness by *that man whom he hath ordained*" (Acts 17:31). • "we are his workmanship, created in Christ Jesus unto good works, *which God hath before ordained*" (Eph. 2:10). • "*Called of God* an high priest" (Heb. 5:10). • "the Son of God; *abideth a priest continually*" (Heb. 7:3). • "*Thou art a priest for ever after the order of Melchisedec*" (Heb. 7:17, 21). • "*We have such an high priest,* who is set on the right hand of the throne of the Majesty in the heavens" (Heb. 8:1). • "Christ, . . . *was foreordained before the foundation of the world*" (1 Pet. 1:19–20).

4. *Jehovah/Jesus Christ was* **sealed:** "Labour not for the meat which perisheth, but for that meat which endureth unto everlasting life, which the Son of man shall give unto you: *for him hath God the Father sealed*" (John 6:27). • "the foundation of God standeth sure, *having this seal, The Lord knoweth them that are his*" (2 Tim. 2:19). • "that Christ, the Lord God Omnipotent, *may seal you his, that you may be brought to heaven,* that ye may have everlasting salvation and eternal life, through the wisdom, and power, and justice, and mercy of him who created all things, in heaven and in earth, who is God above all" (Mosiah 5:15). • "the angel ascending from the east is *he to whom is given the seal of the living God*" (D&C 77:9).

5. *Jehovah/Jesus Christ was* **appointed heir:** • "GOD, . . . Hath . . . spoken unto us by his Son, *whom he hath appointed heir of all things*" (Heb. 1:1–2). • "we are the children of God: And if children, then heirs; *heirs of God, and joint-heirs with Christ*" (Rom. 8:16–17). • "ye are all one in Christ Jesus. And if ye be Christ's, then are ye Abraham's seed, and *heirs according to the promise*" (Gal. 3:28–29). • "thou art no more a servant, but a son; and if a son, then *an heir of God through Christ*" (Gal. 4:7). • "the children of Christ, *and heirs to the kingdom of God*" (4 Ne. 1:17).

6. *Jehovah/Jesus Christ was* **crowned:** *"thou hast . . . crowned him with glory and honour."* (Ps. 8:5). • "we see Jesus, who was made a little lower than the angels for the suffering of death, *crowned with glory and honour*" (Heb. 2:9).

7. *Jehovah/Jesus Christ was* **made a King:** • *"Blessed be the King* that cometh in the name of the Lord: peace in heaven, and glory in the highest" (Luke 19:38). • *"Let Christ the King of Israel* descend now from the cross, that we may see and believe" (Mark 15:32). • "they began to accuse him, saying, We found this fellow . . . *saying that he himself is Christ a King.* And Pilate asked him, saying, *Art thou the King of the Jews?* And he answered him and said, *Thou sayest it*" (Luke 23:2–3). • *"I, the Lord, the king of heaven,* will be their king" (2 Ne. 10:14). • "the glory of *the King of all the earth;* and also *the King of heaven* shall very soon shine forth among all the children of men" (Alma 5:50).

8. *Jehovah/Jesus Christ was* **given a throne** *beside the throne of His Father:* • "in the regeneration *when the Son of man shall sit in the throne of his glory,* ye also shall sit upon twelve thrones, judging the twelve tribes of Israel" (Matt. 19:28). • "he was received up into heaven, and *sat on the right hand of God*" (Mark 16:19). • *"Hereafter shall the Son of man sit on the right hand of the power of God*" (Luke 22:69). • *"the Lord God shall give unto him the throne* of his father David" (Luke 1:32). • *"Jesus . . . is set down at the right hand of the throne of God*" (Heb. 12:2). • *"I saw thrones,* and they sat upon them" (Rev. 20:4). • "God the Father, whose *throne* is high in the heavens, and *our Lord Jesus Christ, who sitteth on the right hand of his power,* until all things shall become subject unto him" (Moro. 9:26).

Specific Powers and Blessings Conveyed to Jehovah/Jesus Christ

According to a broad pattern of scriptures, certain very specific powers and blessings were given or granted to Jehovah/Jesus Christ. Some, very specifically, are identified as being conferred upon Him by His Father, God the Father. What follows is a list of 20 such blessings and powers, with supporting scriptural passages accompanying them. These include:

1. *Jehovah/Jesus Christ was given* all things: • *"All things are delivered unto me of my Father"* (Matt. 11:27; Luke 10:22). • *"The Father loveth the Son, and hath given all things into his hand"* (John 3:35). • *"the Father loveth the Son, and sheweth him all things that himself doeth*: and he will shew him greater works than these" (John 5:20). • *"All that the Father giveth me shall come to me"* (John 6:37). • "Jesus knowing that *the Father had given all things into his hands*, and that he was come from God" (John 13:3). • *"all things that I have heard of my Father* I have made known unto you" (John 15:15). • *"All things that the Father hath are mine"* (John 16:15). • "God, the Father, *of whom are all things*, and we in him; and *one Lord Jesus Christ, by whom are all things, and we by him"* (1 Cor. 8:6).

2. *Jehovah/Jesus Christ was given* all power: • "Jesus came and spake unto them, saying, *All power is given unto me in heaven and in earth"* (Matt. 28:18). • *"with God all things are possible"* (Mark 10:27). • *"with God nothing shall be impossible"* (Luke 1:37). • "Worthy is the Lamb that was slain *to receive power*, and riches, and wisdom, and strength, and honour, and glory, and blessing" (Rev. 5:12). • "Now is come salvation, and strength, and the kingdom of our God, and *the power of his Christ"* (Rev. 12:10). • *"with power, the Lord Omnipotent who reigneth,* who was, and is from all eternity to all eternity, shall come down from heaven among the children of men" (Mosiah 3:5). • *"he received all power, both in heaven and on earth,* and the glory of the Father was with him" (D&C 93:17).

3. *Jehovah/Jesus Christ was given* dominion *over all God the Father's works:* • "What is man, that thou art mindful of him? and the son of man, that thou visitest him? For thou hast made him a little lower than the angels, and hast crowned him with glory and honour. *Thou madest him to have dominion over the works of thy hands; thou hast put all things under his feet"* (Ps. 8:4–6). • *"Thou . . . didst set him over the works of thy hands: Thou hast put all things in subjection under his feet.* For in that he put all in subjection under him, *he left nothing that is not put under him"* (Heb. 2:7–8). • *"Bless the LORD, all his works in all places of his dominion*: bless the LORD, O my soul" (Ps. 103:22). • *"Thy kingdom is an everlasting kingdom, and thy dominion endureth throughout all generations"* (Ps. 145:13). • "the high God . . . his kingdom is an everlasting kingdom, and *his dominion is from generation to generation"* (Dan. 4:2–3). • "I blessed the most High, and I praised and honoured him that liveth for ever, *whose dominion is an everlasting dominion*, and his kingdom is from generation to generation" (Dan. 4:34). • "the God of Daniel: for he is the living God, and stedfast for ever, and his kingdom that which shall not be destroyed, and *his dominion shall be even unto the end"* (Dan. 6:26). • *"the kingdom and dominion*, and the greatness of the kingdom under the whole heaven, shall be given to the people of the saints of the most High, whose kingdom is an everlasting kingdom, *and all dominions shall serve and obey him"* (Dan. 7:27). • "that God in all things may be glorified through Jesus Christ, *to whom be praise and dominion for ever and ever"* (1 Pet. 4:11). • "To the only wise God our Saviour, be glory and majesty, *dominion and power*, both now and ever" (Jude 1:25).

• *"the Holy One of Israel must reign in dominion, and might,* and power, and great glory" (1 Ne. 22:24). • "the Son of God cometh in his glory, *in his might, majesty, power, and dominion"* (Alma 5:50).

4. *Jehovah/Jesus Christ was given* **the fulness:** • "I, John, bear record that *he received a fulness of the glory of the Father"* (D&C 93:16). • "he is the head of the body, the church: who is the beginning, the firstborn from the dead; that in all things he might have the preeminence. *For it pleased the Father that in him should all fulness dwell"* (Col. 1:18–19). • "your joy shall be full, even as *the Father hath given me fulness of joy"* (3 Ne. 28:10). • "we beheld the glory of the Son, on the right hand of the Father, *and received of his fulness"* (D&C 76:20). • "The Father because *he gave me of his fulness"* (D&C 93:4). • "I, John, bear record that *he received a fulness of the glory of the Father"* (D&C 93:16).

5. *Jehovah/Jesus Christ was given* **honor:** • "the Egyptians shall know that I am the LORD, *when I have gotten me honour upon Pharaoh"* (Ex. 14:18). • "the LORD God of Israel saith, . . . *them that honour me I will honour"* (1 Sam. 2:30). • "His glory is great in thy salvation: *honour and majesty hast thou laid upon him"* (Ps. 21:5). • "the LORD made the heavens. *Honour and majesty are before him:* strength and beauty are in his sanctuary" (Ps. 96:5–6). • "call the sabbath a delight, the holy of the LORD, honourable; and *shalt honour him"* (Isa. 58:13). • "I blessed the most High, and *I praised and honoured him* that liveth for ever" (Dan. 4:34). • "But Jesus said unto them, *A prophet is not without honour,* save in his own country" (Matt. 13:37; Mark 6:4; John 4:44). • "the Father . . . hath committed all judgment unto the Son: *That all men should honour the Son"* (John 5:22–23). • "Jesus answered, If I honour myself, my honour is nothing: *it is my Father that honoureth me"* (John 8:54). • "we see Jesus, who was made a little lower than the angels for the suffering of death, *crowned with glory and honour"* (Heb. 2:9). • *"praise and honour and glory* at the appearing of Jesus Christ" (1 Pet. 1:7). • "For *he received from God the Father honour and glory,* when there came such a voice to him from the excellent glory, This is my beloved Son, *in whom I am well pleased"* (2 Pet. 1:17). • "Worthy is the Lamb that was slain to receive power, and riches, and wisdom, and strength, *and honour, and glory,* and blessing" (Rev. 5:12). • "the Lord God has spoken it; *and honor, power and glory* be rendered to his holy name" (D&C 20:36).

6. *Jehovah/Jesus Christ was given* **glory:** • *"thou . . . hast crowned him with glory and honour."* (Ps. 8:5) • *"he shall come in his own glory,* and in his Father's, and of the holy angels" (Luke 9:26). • "and the Word was made flesh, and dwelt among us, (and *we beheld his glory,* the glory as of the only begotten of the Father, full of grace and truth" (John 1:14). • "O Father, *glorify thou me with thine own self with the glory which I had with thee before the world was"* (John 17:5). • "Father, I will that they also, whom thou hast given me, be with me where I am; *that they may behold my glory, which thou has given me*: for thou lovedst me before the foundation of the world" (John 17:24). • "I, John, bear record that *he received a fulness of the glory of the Father"* (D&C 93:16). • "He received all power, both in heaven and on earth, and *the glory of the Father was with him"* (D&C 93:17).

7. *Jehovah/Jesus Christ received* **grace:** *"the grace of God was upon him"* (Luke 2:40). • "the Son of God shall come in his glory; and his glory shall be the glory of the Only Begotten of the Father, *full of grace"* (Alma 9:26). • "the Only Begotten of the Father, who is without beginning of days or end of years, *who is full of grace"* (Alma

13:9). • "the Only Begotten of the Father, which is *full of grace and truth*" (Moses 5:7). • "I should baptize in the name of the Father, and of the Son, *which is full of grace and truth*" (Moses 7:11).

8. *Jehovah/Jesus Christ acquired* knowledge of all things: • "Now are we sure that *thou knowest all things*" (John 16:30). • *"the Lord knoweth all things* from the beginning; wherefore, he prepareth a way to accomplish all his works among the children of men" (1 Ne. 9:6). • "his Son, which order was from the foundation of the world; . . . being prepared from eternity to all eternity, according to *his foreknowledge of all things*" (Alma 13:7). • "Thus saith the Lord your God, even Jesus Christ . . . *The same which knoweth all things,* for all things are present before mine eyes" (D&C 38:1–2). • "through Jesus Christ his Son—He that ascended up on high, as also he descended below all things, in that *he comprehended all things*" (D&C 88:5–6). • *"He comprehendeth all things,* and all things are before him, and all things are round about him; and he is above all things, and in all things, and is through all things, and is round about all things" (D&C 88:41). • *"God knoweth all these things,* whether it be good or bad" (D&C 127:2).

9. *Jehovah/Jesus Christ was given the* power of creation: • *"by him were all things created,* that are in heaven, and that are in earth, visible and invisible, whether they be thrones, or dominions, or principalities, or powers: *all things were created by him, and for him:* And he is before all things, and *by him all things consist"* (Col. 1:16–17). • "he shall be called Jesus Christ, the Son of God, the Father of heaven and earth, *the Creator of all things from the beginning"* (Mosiah 3:8). • "he said unto them that Christ was the God, *the Father of all things"* (Mosiah 7:27). • "the coming of Jesus Christ, the Son of God, the Father of heaven and of earth, *the Creator of all things from the beginning"* (Hel. 14:12). • "I am Jesus Christ the Son of God. *I created the heavens and the earth, and all things that in them are.* I was with the Father from the beginning" (3 Ne. 9:15). • "saith Jesus Christ, the Son of God, *the Father of the heavens and of the earth, and all things that in them are"* (Eth. 4:7). • "Thus saith the Lord your God, even Jesus Christ . . . the beginning and the end, the same which looked upon the wide expanse of eternity, and all the seraphic hosts of heaven, before the world was made; . . . *I am the same which spake, and the world was made, and all things came by me"* (D&C 38:1, 3). • *"all things are by him, and of him,* even God, forever and ever" (D&C 88:41).

10. *Jehovah/Jesus Christ was given* life in himself: • "For as the Father raiseth up the dead, and quickeneth them; even so *the Son quickeneth whom he will"* (John 5:21). • "as the Father hath life in himself; so hath *he given to the Son to have life in himself"* (John 5:26). • "Therefore doth my Father love me, because I lay down my life, that I might take it again. No man taketh it from me, but I lay it down of myself. *I have power to lay it down, and I have power to take it again.* This commandment have I received of my Father" (John 10:17–18).

11. *Jesus Christ was given the* power to live eternally: • "having neither beginning of days, *nor end of life"* (Heb. 7:3). • "Who is made, . . . [with] the power of *an endless life* (Heb. 7:16). • "The Lord sware and will not repent, *Thou art a priest for ever"* (Heb. 7:21). • "this man, because *he continueth ever, hath an unchangeable priesthood"* (Heb. 7:24). "I am he that liveth, and was dead; and, behold, *I am alive for evermore"* Rev. 1:18).

12. *Jehovah/Jesus Christ was given* power over death: • "Christ being raised from the dead dieth no more; *death hath no more dominion over him"* (Rom. 6:9). • "our

Saviour Jesus Christ, *who hath abolished death,* and hath brought life and immortality to light through the gospel" (2 Tim. 1:10). • *"I am he that liveth, and was dead;* and, behold, *I am alive for evermore,* . . . and have the keys of hell and of death" (Rev. 1:18). • "they have eternal life through *Christ, who has broken the bands of death"* (Mosiah 15:23). • "if Christ had not risen from the dead, or have *broken the bands of death* that the grave should have no victory, and that death should have no sting, there could have been no resurrection" (Mosiah 16:7). • "there is a resurrection, therefore the grave hath no victory, and *the sting of death is swallowed up in Christ"* (Mosiah 16:8). • "the will and power and *deliverance of Jesus Christ from the bands of death"* (Alma 4:14). • "the death of Christ *shall loose the bands of this temporal death"* (Alma 11:42). • "their hope and views of Christ and the resurrection; therefore, *death was swallowed up to them by the victory of Christ over it"* (Alma 27:28). • "believe in Jesus Christ, that he is the Son of God, . . . *he hath gained the victory over the grave;* and also *in him is the sting of death swallowed up"* (Morm. 7:5).

13. *Jesus Christ was given* the **power of resurrection:** • "the hour is coming, in the which *all that are in the graves shall hear his voice,* And shall come forth; they that have done good, *unto the resurrection of life;* and they that have done evil, unto the resurrection of damnation" (John 5:28–29). • "Therefore doth my Father love me, because *I lay down my life, that I might take it again.* No man taketh it from me, but I lay it down of myself. *I have power to lay it down, and I have power to take it again.* This commandment have I received of my Father" (John 10:17–18). • "all these had departed the mortal life, firm in the hope of *a glorious resurrection, through the grace of God the Father and his Only Begotten Son, Jesus Christ"* (D&C 138:14).

14. *Jehovah/Jesus Christ was given* **power over all flesh:** • "Father, the hour is come; glorify thy Son, that thy Son also may glorify thee: *As thou hast given him power over all flesh"* (John 17:1–2). • "to this end Christ both died, and rose, and revived, that *he might be Lord both of the dead and living"* (Rom. 14:9). • *"the Lord knoweth all things from the beginning;* wherefore, he prepareth a way to accomplish all his works among the children of men; for behold, *he hath all power unto the fulfilling of all his words"* (1 Ne. 9:6).

15. *Jehovah/Jesus Christ was given* **authority to judge mankind:** • "For the Father judgeth no man, but *hath committed all judgment unto the Son:* That all men should honour the Son, even as they honour the Father" (John 5:22–23). • *"[the Father] hath given him authority to execute judgment* also, because he is the Son of man" (John 5:27). • "it is *he which was ordained of God to be the Judge* of quick and dead" (Acts 10:42). • "we shall all stand before *the judgment seat of Christ.* . . . every one of us shall give account of himself to God" (Rom. 14:10, 12). • "the Lord cometh with ten thousands of his saints, *To execute judgment upon all"* (Jude 1:14–15). • "we must come forth and stand before him in his glory, and in his power, and in his might, majesty, and dominion, and acknowledge to our everlasting shame that *all his judgments are just"* (Alma 12:15).

16. *Jehovah/Jesus Christ was given* **priesthood keys:** • "I am he that liveth, and was dead; and, behold, I am alive for evermore, Amen; and *have the keys of hell and of death"* (Rev. 1:18). • "thou art Peter, . . . *I will give unto thee the keys of the kingdom* of heaven: and whatsoever thou shalt bind on earth shall be bound in heaven: and whatsoever thou shalt loose on earth shall be loosed in heaven" (Matt. 16:18–19; D&C 128:10; JS—H 1:72). • "unto you three *I will give this power and the keys of this minis-*

try until I come" (D&C 7:7). • *"in the name of Messiah I confer the Priesthood of Aaron, which holds the keys* of the ministering of angels, and of the gospel of repentance, and of baptism by immersion" (D&C 13:1). • "Elias, to whom *I have committed the keys* of bringing to pass the restoration of all things" (D&C 27:6). • "Elijah, *unto whom I have committed the keys* of the power of turning the hearts of the fathers to the children" (D&C 27:9). • "Peter, and James, and John, *Unto whom I have committed the keys* of my kingdom, and a dispensation of the gospel for the last times" (D&C 27:12–13). • "Israel shall be saved in mine own due time; and *by the keys which I have given* shall they be led" (D&C 35:25). • "rejoice, for unto you the kingdom, or in other words, *the keys of the church* have been given" (D&C 42:69). • "Joseph Smith, Jun.; *Unto whom I have given the keys* of the kingdom, which belong always unto the Presidency of the High Priesthood" (D&C 81:1–2). • "this greater priesthood . . . *holdeth the key* of the mysteries of the kingdom, even *the key of the knowledge of God*" (D&C 84:19–20). • *"For I have conferred upon you the keys* and power of the priesthood, wherein I restore all things, and make known unto you all things in due time" (D&C 132:45). • "if a man be called of my Father, as was Aaron, by mine own voice, and by the voice of him that sent me, and *I have endowed him with the keys* of the power of this priesthood, if he do anything in my name . . . I will justify him" (D&C 132:59).

17. *Jehovah/Jesus Christ was given a* **Priesthood Order:** • "I, Jacob, having been called of God, and ordained after the manner of *his holy order"* (2 Ne. 6:2). • "according to the testimony of Jesus Christ, the Son of God, who should come to redeem his people from their sins, and the *holy order* by which he [Alma] was called" (Alma 6:8). • "Thus they become high priests forever, *after the order of the Son,* the Only Begotten of the Father" (Alma 13:9). • "And are priests of the Most High, after the order of Melchizedek, which was after the order of Enoch, which was after *the order of the Only Begotten Son"* (D&C 76:57). • "Before his day it was called *the Holy Priesthood, after the Order of the Son of God"* (D&C 107:3). • "that ye may hold the keys thereof, even the Priesthood which is after the order of Melchizedek, which is after *the order of mine Only Begotten Son"* (D&C 124:123). • "I am the Lord thy God, and will give unto thee the law of *my Holy Priesthood,* as was ordained by me and my Father before the world was" (D&C 132:28).

18. *Jehovah/Jesus Christ was given a* **Church:** • "his mighty power, Which he wrought in Christ, when he raised him from the dead, and set him at his own right hand in the heavenly places, . . . not only in this world, but also in that which is to come: And hath put all things under his feet, and *gave him to be the head over all things to the church"* (Eph. 1:19–22). • *"he is the head of the body, the church:* who is the beginning, the firstborn from the dead; that in all things he might have the preeminence. For it pleased the Father that in him should all fulness dwell" (Col. 1:18–19). • "To the general assembly and *church of the firstborn,* which are written in heaven" (Heb. 12:23). • "They are they who are the *church of the Firstborn"* (D&C 76:54). • "These are they who have come to an innumerable company of angels, to the general assembly and *church of Enoch, and of the Firstborn"* (D&C 76:67). • "these are they who are of the terrestrial, whose glory differs from that of the *church of the Firstborn"* (D&C 76:71). • "They who dwell in his presence are *the church of the Firstborn"* (D&C 76:94). • "these all are they who will not be gathered with the saints, *to be caught up unto the church of the Firstborn,* and received into the cloud" (D&C 76:102). • "they who are ordained . . . by the angels to whom is given power over the nations of the earth, to bring as many as will come to *the church of the Firstborn"* (D&C 77:11). • *"ye*

are the church of the Firstborn, and he will take you up in a cloud, and appoint every man his portion" (D&C 78:21). • "the celestial kingdom; Which glory is that of the *church of the Firstborn,* even of God, the holiest of all, *through Jesus Christ his Son*" (D&C 88:4–5). • "I was in the beginning with the Father, and am the Firstborn; And all those who are begotten through me are partakers of the glory of the same, and are *the church of the Firstborn*" (D&C 93:21–22). • "to commune with the general assembly and *church of the Firstborn*" (D&C 107:19).

19. *Jehovah/Jesus Christ received a* **kingdom:** "I appoint unto you *a kingdom, as my Father hath appointed unto me*" (Luke 22:29). • "they believed Philip preaching *the things concerning the kingdom of God,* and the name of Jesus Christ" (Acts 8:12). • "Paul . . . received all that came in unto him, *Preaching the kingdom of God,* and teaching those things which concern the Lord Jesus Christ" (Acts 28:30–31). • "no . . . unclean person . . . hath any inheritance *in the kingdom of Christ*" (Eph. 5:5). • "an entrance shall be ministered unto you abundantly into *the everlasting kingdom of our Lord and Saviour Jesus Christ*" (2 Pet. 1:11). • "The kingdoms of this world are become *the kingdoms of our Lord, and of his Christ;* and he shall reign for ever and ever" (Rev. 11:15). • "we knew of *Christ and his kingdom,* which should come" (Jacob 1:6). • "This earth, in its sanctified and immortal state, will be made like unto crystal and will be a Urim and Thummim to the inhabitants who dwell thereon, whereby all things pertaining to an inferior kingdom, or all kingdoms of a lower order, will be manifest to those who dwell on it; and *this earth will be Christ's*" (D&C 130:9). • "behold, one like the Son of man came with the clouds of heaven, and came to the Ancient of days, and they brought him near before him. And there was given him dominion, and glory, and a *kingdom*" (Dan. 7:13–14).

20. *Jehovah/Jesus Christ was given a* **people:** He was assigned to rule over the house of Jacob forever: • "let us go up to the mountain of the LORD, to the house of *the God of Jacob;* and he will teach us of his ways, and we will walk in his paths" (Isa. 2:3; Mic. 4:2). • *"O house of Jacob, come ye,* and let us walk in the light of the LORD" (Isa. 2:5). • *"the remnant of Israel,* and such as are escaped of the house of Jacob, shall . . . *stay upon the LORD,* the Holy One of Israel, in truth. The remnant shall return, even *the remnant of Jacob, unto the mighty God*" (Isa. 10:20–21). • "thus saith the LORD, who redeemed Abraham, *concerning the house of Jacob*" (Isa. 29:22). • "Hear ye the word of the LORD, O house of Jacob, and *all the families of the house of Israel*" (Jer. 2:4). • "Thus saith the Lord GOD; In the day when *I chose Israel,* and *lifted up mine hand unto the seed of the house of Jacob,* and made myself known unto them in the land of Egypt, when I lifted up mine hand unto them, saying, I am the LORD your God" (Ezek. 20:5). • "thus saith the Lord GOD; *Now will I bring again the captivity of Jacob,* and have mercy upon the whole house of Israel" (Ezek. 39:25). • "He shall be great, and shall be called the Son of the Highest: and the Lord God shall give unto him the throne of his father David: And *he shall reign over the house of Jacob for ever*" (Luke 1:32–33). • *"the God of Abraham, and of Isaac, and the God of Jacob,* yieldeth himself, . . . as a man, into the hands of wicked men, to be lifted up, . . . and to be crucified" (1 Ne. 19:10).

Scriptural References to Jehovah/Jesus Christ Being a God in Premortality

• "These are the generations of the heavens and of the earth when they were created, in the day that *the LORD God made the earth and the heavens,* And every plant of the field before it was in the earth, and every herb of the field before it grew: for *the*

LORD *God had not caused it to rain upon the earth,* and there was not a man to till the ground (Gen. 2:4–5). • "(For the LORD thy God is a merciful God;) he will not forsake thee, neither destroy thee, nor forget the covenant of thy fathers which he sware unto them. For ask now of the days that are past, which were before thee, *since the day that God created man upon the earth,* and ask from the one side of heaven unto the other, whether there hath been any such thing as this great thing is, or hath been heard like it?" (Deut. 4:31–32). • *"For we are his workmanship, created in Christ Jesus* unto good works, which God hath before ordained that we should walk in them" (Eph. 2:10). • "And also to the convincing of the Jew and Gentile that JESUS is the CHRIST, *the ETERNAL GOD"* (BoM Preface, Title Page: 2). • "the Lord Omnipotent who reigneth, *who was, and is from all eternity to all eternity,"* (Mosiah 3:5). • "Teach them that redemption cometh through Christ the Lord, *who is the very Eternal Father"* (Mosiah 16:15). • *"thus did I, the Lord God, appoint unto man the days of his probation*—that by his natural death he might be raised in immortality unto eternal life, even as many as would believe" (D&C 29:43). • "Thus saith the Lord your God, even Jesus Christ, the Great I AM, Alpha and Omega, the beginning and the end, *the same which looked upon the wide expanse of eternity, and all the seraphic hosts of heaven, before the world was made"* (D&C 38:1). • "it is only to answer the will of God, by conforming to *the ordinance and preparation that the Lord ordained and prepared before the foundation of the world,* for the salvation of the dead who should die without a knowledge of the gospel" (D&C 128:5). • *"I, the Lord God, created all things,* of which I have spoken, spiritually, before they were naturally upon the face of the earth. For I, the Lord God, had not caused it to rain upon the face of the earth. And *I, the Lord God, had created all the children of men;* and not yet a man to till the ground; for *in heaven created I them;* and there was not yet flesh upon the earth, neither in the water, neither in the air" (Moses 3:5). • *"I, the Lord God, formed man from the dust of the ground,* and breathed into his nostrils the breath of life; and man became a living soul, the first flesh upon the earth, the first man also; nevertheless, all things were before created; but *spiritually were they created and made according to my word"* (Moses 3:7).

Summary
1. Latter-day Saints view Godhood as a priesthood office, received through sacred ordinances.
2. President Lorenzo Snow is quoted with various statements he made concerning man's potential to achieve Godhood, such as "As man now is, God once was: As God now is, man may be."
3. Jehovah/Jesus Christ had two supreme qualifications that made Him ready and worthy to be granted Godhood: (a) He was pure, free from sin, and spotless and (b) He achieved personal perfection. Scriptures were cited illustrating both qualifications.
4. Scriptural allusions were cited to eight priesthood and other sacred procedures that may pertain in some way to Jehovah/Jesus Christ's elevation to Godhood: Jehovah was (a) sanctified, (b) anointed, (c) ordained, (d) sealed, (e) appointed heir, (f) crowned, (g) made a King, and (h) given a throne.
5. Scriptural allusions were cited concerning 20 specific powers and blessings which were conveyed to Jehovah/Jesus Christ: (a) all things, (b) all power, (c) dominion, (d) the fulness, (e) honor, (f) glory, (g) grace, (h) knowledge of all things, (i) power of creation, (j) life in Himself, (k) power to live eternally, (l) power over death, (m) power of resurrection, (n) power over all flesh, (o) authority to judge

mankind, (p) priesthood keys, (q) a priesthood order, (r) a church, (s) a kingdom, and (t) a people.

6. Various scriptures were cited that indicate that Jehovah/Jesus Christ had achieved Godhood prior to the creation of this earth.

CHAPTER 9

PREMORTAL PREPARATIONS AND THE CREATION

Many Leaders Were Chosen in the Premortal Era

Latter-day Saint scriptures indicate that prior to the creation of this earth, various spirit beings (intelligences that were organized), in the course of events, progressed until they became "noble and great ones." God, recognizing their progress, designated them to be leaders in the spirit realm. They apparently were trained and prepared to fulfill positions of responsibility on this or other earths. The book of Abraham, in the Pearl of Great Price, records a vision granted to Abraham (in his mortal state), in which he was shown significant aspects of premortal life, prior to "the beginning" of this earth:

> Now the Lord had shown unto me, Abraham, the intelligences that were organized before the world was; and among all these there were many of the noble and great ones;
> And God saw these souls that they were good, and he stood in the midst of them, and he said: *These I will make my rulers; for he stood among those that were spirits, and he saw that they were good*; and he said unto me: Abraham, thou art one of them; thou wast chosen before thou wast born. (Abr. 3:22–23)

Chapter 13 of the book of Alma also tells of individuals given the priesthood (the power and authority to act in the name of God) prior to the creation of this earth. Notice that certain chronological clues are provided in this passage. Before this takes place, a priesthood organization (a holy order, which was after the order of God's Son, Jesus Christ, Alma 13:1–3) already has been established. Notice, also, that this organization is established "from the foundation of the world," so "the beginning"—the creation of this earth—is imminent. The planning and preparations are in process.

Be aware, also, of the "***preparatory redemption***" which had already been made (Alma 13:3), though it was before the creation of this earth and therefore long prior to the mortal atonement of Jesus Christ. *Yet they were eligible to be "sanctified" and to have their garments washed white "through the* [as-yet-unshed] *blood of the Lamb"* (Alma 13:12). Though little is known about this "preparatory redemption," it may be the key to understanding how people who lived and died on previously created earths, may have been saved through the Atonement of Christ before He actually gave His life on this earth for all mankind (everywhere, on worlds without number!) through His infinite Atonement. This is what Alma recorded:

> And again, my brethren, I would cite your minds forward to the time when the Lord God gave these commandments unto his children; and I *would that ye should remember that the Lord God ordained priests, after his holy order, which was after the order of his Son, to teach these things unto the people.*
>
> *And those priests were ordained after the order of his Son, in a manner that thereby the people might know in what manner to look forward to his Son for redemption.*
>
> And this is the manner after which they were *ordained—being called and prepared from the foundation of the world according to the foreknowledge of God, on account of their exceeding faith and good works; in the first place being left to choose good or evil; therefore they having chosen good, and exercising exceedingly great faith, are called with a holy calling, yea, with that holy calling which was prepared with, and according to, a* **preparatory redemption** *for such.*
>
> And thus they have been called to this holy calling on account of their faith, while others would reject the Spirit of God on account of the hardness of their hearts and blindness of their minds, while, if it had not been for this they might have had as great privilege as their brethren.
>
> Or in fine, *in the first place they were on the same standing with their brethren; thus this holy calling being prepared from the foundation of the world for such as would not harden their hearts, being in and through the atonement of the Only Begotten Son, who was prepared—*
>
> And thus being called by this holy calling, and *ordained unto the high priesthood of the holy order of God,* to teach his commandments unto the children of men, that they also might enter into his rest—
>
> *This high priesthood being after the order of his Son, which order was from the foundation of the world;* or in other words, being without beginning of days or end of years, being prepared from eternity to all eternity, *according to his foreknowledge of all things—*
>
> Now they were ordained after this manner—being called with a holy calling, and ordained with a holy ordinance, and taking upon them the high priesthood of the holy order, which calling, and ordinance, and high priesthood, is without beginning or end—
>
> *Thus they become high priests forever, after the order of the Son, the Only Begotten of the Father,* who is without beginning of days or end of years, who is full of grace, equity, and truth. And thus it is. Amen.
>
> Now, as I said concerning the holy order, or this high priesthood, *there were many who were ordained and became high priests of God;* and it was on account of their exceeding faith and repentance, and their righteousness before God, they choosing to repent and work righteousness rather than to perish;
>
> Therefore they were called after this holy order, and *were sanctified, and their* **garments were washed white through the blood of the Lamb.** (Alma 13:1–12)

When he received his glorious **Vision of the Redemption of the Dead**, President Joseph F. Smith observed the calling of some of these premortal leaders, and learned of the special premortal training they received to prepare them for their mortal experiences and responsibilities. He wrote: • "I observed that they were also among the noble and great ones who were *chosen in the beginning to be rulers in the Church of God. Even before they were born, they, with many others, received their first lessons in the world of* *spirits and were prepared to come forth in the due time of the Lord to labor in his vineyard for the salvation of the souls of men"* (D&C 138:55–56).

Some individuals receiving near-death experiences have been shown snatches of their premortal training. Examples are recorded in **Life Everlasting** (2nd revised edition, 93–100).

Laying the Foundation: Strategic Planning for This Earth's Creation

It is interesting to examine the unique group of scriptural passages which, by definition, speak specifically of planning and actions taken "from the foundation of the world" or "from before the world was." Together, they provide a unique outline of strategic world-formulation steps taken by those entitled to function on the level of deity.

Significance is seen in the source of these passages: all but one passage in the New Testament (an allusion in one of the Savior's end-of-his-ministry parables) come from Latter-day Saint scriptures. Together, they stand as another example of significant doctrinal insights granted to the Saints in these latter days to be carried to the rest of the world. It is possible that these teachings may be some of the plain and precious truths lost from the Bible during its transmission to the gentiles during the first three centuries following the ministry of Christ (see 1 Ne. 13:23–42).

1. *God defined His great and eternal purposes:*
    *   When explaining the gospel to his son, Corianton, the prophet **Alma** summed up his explanation by saying, "And thus *God bringeth about his great and eternal purposes, which were prepared from the foundation of the world.* And thus cometh about the salvation and the redemption of men, and also their destruction and misery" (Alma 42:26).

2. *The plan of redemption was formulated:*
    *   **Abinadi,** the missionary who converted the prophet Alma while prophecying of the future coming of the Lord, said, • "O how beautiful upon the mountains are the feet of him that bringeth good tidings, that is the founder of peace, yea, even the Lord, who has redeemed his people; yea, him who has granted salvation unto his people; For were it not for *the redemption which he hath made for his people, which was prepared from the foundation of the world,* I say unto you, were it not for this, *all mankind must have perished"* (Mosiah 15:18–19).
    *   **Amulek,** Alma's missionary companion, explained that • "they began from that time forth to call on his name; therefore God conversed with men, and *made known unto them the plan of redemption, which had been prepared from the foundation of the world*; and this he made known unto them according to their faith and repentance and their holy works" (Alma 12:30).
    *   **Ammon,** the great missionary son of King Mosiah, while laboring among the Lamanites, • "expounded unto them *the plan of redemption, which was prepared from the foundation of the world"* (Alma 18:39).
    *   **Aaron,** while teaching the father of Lamoni, the great Lamanite king, • "did expound unto him the scriptures from the creation of Adam, laying the fall of man before him, and their carnal state and also *the plan of redemption, which was prepared from the foundation of the world, through Christ,* for all whosoever would believe on his name" (Alma 22:13).

3. *The need for an atoning sacrifice was recognized, and that sacrifice was made an integral part of the plan:*

- **King Benjamin** preached of • *"the atonement which has been prepared from the foundation of the world,* that thereby salvation might come to him that should put his trust in the Lord" (Mosiah 4:6).

- **King Benjamin** also described the righteous as those who • "should be diligent in keeping his commandments, and continue in the faith even unto the end of his life, I mean the life of the mortal body—I say, that this is the man who receiveth salvation, *through the atonement which was prepared from the foundation of the world for all mankind,* which ever were since the fall of Adam, or who are, or who ever shall be, even unto the end of the world" (Mosiah 4:6–7).

4. *Jehovah/Jesus Christ, the Son of God, was selected to be the Messiah and Redeemer:*

- The prophet **Nephi** wrote that • *"the Son of God was the Messiah who should come"* and stressed that "he is the same yesterday, to-day, and forever; and *the way is prepared for all men from the foundation of the world, if it so be that they repent and come unto him"* (1 Ne. 10:17–18).

5. *Jehovah/Jesus Christ was prepared from the foundation of the world for His redemptive role:*

- The prophet **Alma,** when baptizing at the Waters of Mormon, alluded to the premortal planning of "the Almighty God," which paved the way for the granting of • *"eternal life, through the redemption of Christ, whom he has prepared from the foundation of the world"* (Mosiah 18:13).

- The book of **Moses** speaks of God's • "Only Begotten Son, *even him whom he declared should come in the meridian of time, who was prepared from before the foundation of the world"* (Moses 5:57).

- The premortal **Savior,** when He revealed Himself to the brother of Jared, told him that • *"I am he who was prepared from the foundation of the world to redeem my people. Behold, I am Jesus Christ"* (Eth. 3:14).

6. *An entire priesthood order, under the founding leadership of God the Son, was organized:*

- **Alma** taught that the priesthood which these chosen individuals received was established in premortality, based on the foreknowledge of God: • *"This high priesthood being after the order of his Son, which order was from the foundation of the world;* or in other words, being without beginning of days or end of years, being prepared from eternity to all eternity, *according to his foreknowledge of all things"* (Alma 13:7).

7. *Priesthood leaders were called and prepared for mortal service, based on the foreknowledge of God, and were given a preparatory redemption:*

- **Alma** taught, concerning those called to priesthood positions of authority in premortality in preparation for their service on this earth in mortality, that: • *"this is the manner after which they were ordained—being called and prepared from the foundation of the world according to the foreknowledge of God,* . . . are called with a holy calling, yea, with that holy calling which was prepared with, and according to, a *preparatory redemption* for such" (Alma 13:3).

- **Alma** spoke, in addition, of • *"this holy calling being prepared from the foundation of the world for such as would not harden their hearts, being in and through the atonement of the Only Begotten Son"* (Alma 13:5).

8. *A postmortality kingdom was designed as a reward for those who would merit eternal rewards as a result of their righteousness in mortality:*
   - Nephi's brother *Jacob* wrote that • "the righteous, the saints of the Holy One of Israel". . . *shall inherit the kingdom of God, which was prepared for them from the foundation of the world*" (2 Ne. 9:18).
   - *Jesus,* during His mortal ministry, spoke of the final reward for the righteous in His Parable of the Talents: • "Then shall the King say unto them on his right hand, Come, ye blessed of my Father, *inherit the kingdom prepared for you from the foundation of the world*" (Matt. 25:34).
   - *Moroni,* in his translation of the book of Ether, observed that • "blessed is he that is found faithful unto my name at the last day, for *he shall be lifted up to dwell in the kingdom prepared for him from the foundation of the world*" (Eth. 4:19).

9. *Provisions for eternal marriage and the procreating of children were made:*
   - "And will I appoint unto you, saith the Lord, except it be by law, *even as I and my Father ordained unto you, before the world was?* I am the Lord thy God; and I give unto you this commandment—that *no man shall come unto the Father but by me or by my word, which is my law,* saith the Lord" (D&C 132:11–12; speaking of the law of eternal marriage).
   - "I am the Lord thy God, and will give unto thee the law of my Holy Priesthood, *as was ordained by me and my Father before the world was*" (D&C 132:28; speaking of the law of eternal marriage).
   - "and to fulfil *the promise which was given by my Father before the foundation of the world,* and for their [women's] exaltation in the eternal worlds, *that they may bear the souls of men; for herein is the work of my Father continued, that he may be glorified*" (D&C 132:63).

10. *Temple ordinances for the dead were ordained and prepared:*
    - *Joseph Smith,* in his great epistle concerning baptism for the dead, wrote that • "You may think this order of things to be very particular; but let me tell you that it is only to answer the will of God, *by conforming to the ordinance and preparation that the Lord ordained and prepared before the foundation of the world, for the salvation of the dead who should die without a knowledge of the gospel*" (D&C 128:5).
    - *Joseph* also revealed, in his epistle, that even temple ordinances for the dead were part of the premortal planning: • "it is granted that whatsoever you bind on earth shall be bound in heaven, and whatsoever you loose on earth shall be loosed in heaven. . . . *according to the ordinance which God has prepared for their salvation from before the foundation of the world*" (D&C 128:8).

Specific Instructions Concerning This Earth Were Given by God the Father to His Son Jehovah/Jesus Christ

Several patterns of scripture emerge which describe the relationships between the Father and the Son during this premortal planning stage.

First, *Jehovah/Jesus Christ was literally sent to this earth by God the Father:* Several of the passages express the specific purposes which He was to accomplish here on earth: (1) to be the Savior and to save the world, (2) to finish the works that His Father had assigned to Him, (3) to do the Father's will, (4) to perform His atoning sacrifice, (5) to unite His followers so they might be "one" with the Father and the

Son, (6) to convince the world that the Father sent Him to earth, and (7) for Christ to subdue all things unto Himself. These are some of the representative "sent" passages:

• "For God so loved the world, that he gave his only begotten Son, that whosoever believeth in him should not perish, but have everlasting life. *For God sent not his Son into the world to condemn the world; but that the world through him might be saved"* (John 3:16–17). • *"the works which the Father hath given me to finish,* the same works that I do, bear witness of me, *that the Father hath sent me"* (John 5:36). • "For *I came down from heaven, not to do mine own will, but the will of him that sent me"* (John 6:38). • "Father, save me from this hour: but *for this cause came I unto this hour"* (John 12:27). • "That they all may be one; as thou, Father, [art] in me, and I in thee, that they also may be one in us: that the world may believe that *thou hast sent me"* (John 17:21). • "O righteous Father, the world hath not known thee: but I have known thee, and *these have known that thou hast sent me"* (John 17:25). • "Then said Jesus unto Peter, Put up thy sword into the sheath: *the cup which my Father hath given me, shall I not drink it?"* (John 18:11). • "Then said Jesus to them again, Peace be unto you: *as my Father hath sent me,* even so send I you" (John 20:21). • "We have seen and do testify that *the Father sent the Son to be the Saviour of the world"* (1 Jn. 4:14). • "I am the light and the life of the world; and *I have drunk out of that bitter cup which the Father hath given me,* and have glorified the Father in taking upon me the sins of the world, *in the which I have suffered the will of the Father in all things from the beginning"* (3 Ne. 11:11). • *"I, having accomplished and finished the will of him whose I am, even the Father,* concerning me—having done this *that I might subdue all things unto myself"* (D&C 19:2). • "I am Jesus Christ; *I came by the will of the Father, and I do his will"* (D&C 19:24).

Second, **the future role of Jesus Christ as the "only begotten Son" of God the Father was clearly prefigured and understood in the premortal realms prior to "the beginning" of this earth.** Though Jehovah/Jesus Christ had been involved in the creation and administration of "worlds without number," His coming to *this* earth was to be distinctly different. On this earth He was to be born as a mortal, as a child of God the Father, an immortal being, and the virgin Mary, a mortal mother, thus giving Him both the power to live forever (from His Father) and the power to die (from His mother)—the only mortal being ever to have had the two powers within Himself. Thus Jesus was to become the "Only Begotten Son" of the Father. What is significant in this context is that long before His mortal birth on this earth, Jesus Christ had already been designated to be the Father's only begotten Son:

• "Wherefore, beloved brethren, be reconciled unto him through the atonement of Christ, his *Only Begotten Son,* and ye may obtain a resurrection" (Jacob 4:11; between 544 & 421 BC). • "But God did call on men, in the name of his Son, (this being the plan of redemption which was laid) saying: If ye will repent and harden not your hearts, then will I have mercy upon you, through mine *Only Begotten Son;* Therefore, whosoever repenteth, and hardeneth not his heart, he shall have claim on mercy through mine *Only Begotten Son,* unto a remission of his sins; and these shall enter into my rest" (Alma 12:33–34; about 82 BC). • "thus this holy calling being prepared from the foundation of the world for such as would not harden their hearts, being in and through the atonement of the *Only Begotten Son,* who was prepared" (Alma 13:5, about 82 BC). • "I, the Lord God, gave unto Adam and unto his seed, that they should not die as to the temporal death, until I, the Lord God, should send forth angels to declare unto them repentance and redemption, through faith on the name of mine

Only Begotten Son" (D&C 29:42; about 4000 BC). • "Even those things which were *from the beginning before the world was*, which were ordained of the Father, through his *Only Begotten Son*, who was in the bosom of the Father, even from the beginning" (D&C 76:13; premortality). • "by the word of my power, have I created them, which is mine *Only Begotten Son*, who is full of grace and truth. And worlds without number have I created; and I also created them for mine own purpose; and *by the Son I created them, which is mine Only Begotten*" (Moses 1:32–33; premortality). • "For they would not hearken unto his voice, nor believe on his *Only Begotten Son*, even him whom he declared should come in the meridian of time, *who was prepared from before the foundation of the world*" (Moses 5:57; premortality). • "he also said unto him: If thou wilt turn unto me, and hearken unto my voice, and believe, and repent of all thy transgressions, and be baptized, even in water, in the name of mine *Only Begotten Son*, who is full of grace and truth, *which is Jesus Christ, the only name which shall be given under heaven, whereby salvation shall come unto the children of men*" (Moses 6:52; about 4000 BC).

Third, **both God the Father and the Son were able to anticipate all earth events because of their foreknowledge of all things:**

• "Jesus *knowing that the Father had given all things into his hands*, and that he was come from God, and went to God" (John 13:3). • "Now are we sure that *thou knowest all things*, . . . by this we believe that thou camest forth from God" (John 16:30). • "God is greater than our heart, and *knoweth all things*" (1 Jn. 3:20). • "Jesus of Nazareth, a man approved of God among you by miracles and wonders and signs, which God did by him in the midst of you, as ye yourselves also know: Him, being *delivered by the determinate counsel and foreknowledge of God*, ye have taken" (Acts 2:22–23). • "all things work together for good to them that love God, to them who are the called according to his purpose. For *whom he did foreknow*, he also did predestinate to be conformed to the image of his Son" (Rom. 8:28–29). • "Hath God cast away his people? God forbid. For I also am an Israelite, of the seed of Abraham, of the tribe of Benjamin. God hath not cast away *his people which he foreknew*" (Rom. 11:1–2; see Abr. 3:23). • "Peter, an Apostle of Jesus Christ, to the strangers scattered throughout Pontus, Galatia, Cappadocia, Asia, and Bithynia, *Elect according to the foreknowledge of God the Father*, through sanctification of the Spirit, unto obedience and sprinkling of the blood of Jesus Christ" (1 Pet. 1:1–2). • "O how great the holiness of our God! *For he knoweth all things, and there is not anything save he knows it*. And he cometh into the world that he may save all men if they will hearken unto his voice" (2 Ne. 9:20–21). • "this is the manner after which they were ordained—being called and *prepared from the foundation of the world according to the foreknowledge of God*" (Alma 13:3). • "the order of his Son, which order was from the foundation of the world; or in other words, being without beginning of days or end of years, being prepared from eternity to all eternity, *according to his foreknowledge of all things*" (Alma 13:7). • "*God knowing all things*, being from everlasting to everlasting" (Moro. 7:22). • "I am the Lord thy God . . . My name is Jehovah, and *I know the end from the beginning*; therefore my hand shall be over thee" (Abr. 2:7–8).

Fourth, **based on His/their foreknowledge, God apportioned the times and bounds of all the people who would be sent to dwell on this planet earth:**

• "Remember the days of old, . . . When *the most High divided to the nations their inheritance, when he separated the sons of Adam, he set the bounds of the people according to the number of the children of Israel. For the* LORD's *portion is his people;* Jacob is the lot of his inheritance" (Deut. 32:7–9). • "Man that is born of a woman is of few days, . . . *his daysare determined, the number of his months are with thee, thou hast appointed his bounds that he cannot pass"* (Job 14:1, 5; see Job 7:1). • *"To every thing there is a season, and a time to every purpose under the heaven:* A time to be born, and a time to die; a time to plant, and a time to pluck up that which is planted; A time to kill, and a time to heal; a time to break down, and a time to build up" (Eccl. 3:1–3). • "God that made the world and all things therein . . . hath made of one blood all nations of men for to dwell on all the face of the earth, and *hath determined the times before appointed, and the bounds of their habitation"* (Acts 17:24, 26). • "thus did I, the Lord God, *appoint unto man the days of his probation*—that by his natural death he might be raised in immortality unto eternal life, even as many as would believe; And they that believe not unto eternal damnation" (D&C 29:43–44).

Thus, it is obvious that the creation of this earth involved detailed planning and the anticipating of all the earth's events, needs, problems, challenges, and opportunities. This planning involved both the Father and the Son, and who knows how many other participants?

The Spirit Creation of This Planet Earth

The account of the Gods creating this earth is provided in thorough detail in chapters 4 and 5 of the book of Abraham, chapters 2 and 3 of the book of Moses, and chapters 1 and 2 of the book of Genesis. These chapters are too long to be quoted in their entirety in this context. The summary of the creation of this planet presented here is based primarily on the book of Abraham account. As will be seen later in this chapter, in the section which considers the premortal councils, the council of the Gods as they created this earth is there labeled as **Council Number Three.**

When reading the Abraham account, it immediately becomes apparent that this gathering of Gods was a working council, a get-it-done activity. Day one of the great creative process is recounted in this manner:

> And then *the Lord said*: Let us go down. And they went down at the beginning, and *they, that is the Gods, organized and formed the heavens and the earth.*
> And the earth, after it was formed, was empty and desolate, because they had not formed anything but the earth; and darkness reigned upon the face of the deep, and *the Spirit of the Gods was brooding upon the face of the waters.*
> *And they (the Gods) said: Let there be light; and there was light.*
> *And they (the Gods) comprehended the light,* for it was bright; and they divided the light, or caused it to be divided, from the darkness.
> *And the Gods called the light Day, and the darkness they called Night.* And it came to pass that from the evening until morning they called night; and from the morning until the evening they called day; and this was the first, or the beginning, of that which they called day and night. (Abr. 4:1–5)

Note that it is "the Lord" who is leading the creation activities and that the Holy Ghost (the Spirit of the Gods) is present and active. Abraham chapter 4 goes through the various days of creation:

• Abraham 4:1–5 covers **Day One** (compare Moses 2:1–5; Gen. 1:1–5): light, day and night;

• Abraham 4:6–8, **Day Two** (compare Moses 2:6–8; Gen. 1:6–8): heaven (the expanse), with waters above and beneath it;

• Abraham 4:9–13, **Day Three** (compare Moses 2:9–13; Gen. 1:9–13): waters under the heavens gathered together, the earth appears, plant life;

• Abraham 4:14–19, **Day Four** (compare Moses 2:14–19; Gen. 1:14–19): lights in the heavens were created and organized for signs and for seasons, great lights were created to rule the day and the night;

• Abraham 4:20–23, **Day Five** (compare Moses 2:20–23; Gen. 1:20–23): water creatures and winged fowl were created;

• Abraham 4:24–31, **Day Six** (compare Moses 2:24–31; Gen. 1:24–31): land animals were created, male and female spirits who were to become humans were created and given dominion.

• Abraham 5:1–4 covers **Day Seven**, as follows:

> *And the Gods said among themselves: On the seventh time we will end our work, which we have counseled; and we will rest on the seventh time from all our work which we have counseled.*
>
> *And the Gods concluded upon the seventh time, because that on the seventh time they would rest from all their works which they (the Gods) counseled among themselves to form; and sanctified it. And thus were their decisions at the time that they counseled among themselves to form the heavens and the earth.*
>
> *And the Gods came down and formed these the generations of the heavens and of the earth*, when they were formed in the day that the Gods formed the earth and the heavens. (Abr. 5:1–3)

Note, however, that the above listing is actually ***describing the spiritual creation*** of this earth—a kind of spirit modeling of what was about to become a tangible, physical earth as man encounters it even in this day. Moses 3:5–6 makes it clear that this earth was created as only a spirit entity, at first:

> *I, the Lord God, created all things, of which I have spoken, spiritually, before they were naturally upon the face of the earth.* For I, the Lord God, had not caused it to rain upon the face of the earth. *And I, the Lord God, had created all the children of men; and not yet a man to till the ground; for in heaven created I them; and there was not yet flesh upon the earth*, neither in the water, neither in the air. (Moses 3:5)

The Transformation of This Planet Earth into a Physical Entity

Then, in one day (apparently on the ***seventh day***, before they rested), the Gods caused moisture to come upon the spiritual earth; they created man by taking his premortal spirit and putting it into a physical body which they created, so man became a living soul (Abr. 5:7, see D&C 88:15: "the spirit and the body are the soul of man"). The Garden of Eden was planted, and plants were brought forth (Abr. 5:5:4–9; Moses 3:6–9; Gen. 2:5–9).

Thus, in just a few short verses, the actual physical creation of this planet, earth, is described. What a momentous occasion!

Where Was This Earth Created?

The book of Moses repeats the assertion that "*all things were before created; but spiritually were they created and made*" (Moses 3:7), and also, "*it was spiritual in the day that I created it; for it remaineth in the sphere in which I, God, created it*" (Moses 3:9).

So, where was this earth created, and what does the creation location have to do with the time involved in the creation?

Note again the assertion in Moses 3:5 that "in heaven created I them." The book of Abraham states that "I, Abraham, saw that *it was after the Lord's time, which was after the time of Kolob*; for as yet the Gods had not appointed unto Adam his reckoning" (Abr. 5:13). So this earth was created on or near the planet Kolob, in a completely different time environment. (See again statements from the explanation of Facsimile 2 of Abraham, cited in chapter 7.)

Latter-day Saint Apostle (later President) John Taylor wrote (to women of the Church): "Thou longed, thou sighed and thou prayed to thy Father in heaven for the time to arrive when thou couldst come to this earth, **which had fled and fallen from where it was first organized, near the planet Kolob**" (John Taylor, "The Mormon," as cited in **Life Everlasting**, 2nd revised edition, 106).

Another significant insight, which often is overlooked, is the verse in the sixth chapter of Moses, in which God told Adam that "all things have their likeness, and *all things are created and made to bear record of me, both things which are temporal, and things which are spiritual*; things which are in the heavens above, and things which are on the earth, and things which are in the earth, and things which are under the earth, both above and beneath: *all things bear record of me*" (Moses 6:63). Thus, all things on this earth, both temporal and spiritual, have been created with the express purpose of bearing record of the God specifically responsible for this earth's creation.

Who Is the Specific Creator of This Earth?

The scriptures, in numerous passages, assert that the Old Testament Jehovah, who is the same person as the New Testament Jesus Christ, is He who created this earth and who rules over it throughout its mortal sojourn. In the next three sections: (1) Old Testament passages which speak of *Jehovah* being the creator of this earth will first be presented. Then, (2) numerous passages from the New Testament, Book of Mormon, and Doctrine and Covenants which clearly state that *Jesus Christ* is the Creator of this earth will be listed. Together, these passages clearly indicate that the premortal Jehovah is the same divine being as the mortal Jesus, the Christ and the Messiah. Finally, (3) the few passages indicating that *God the Father created the earth through Jesus Christ* are cited, which among other things make it clear that *God the Father did not come to earth in the form of Jesus Christ* (as another manifestation of the "trinitarian" three-in-one God), and also that *God the Father is **not** Jehovah*. Perhaps it can be said that He was the original designer of this earth's creation, but Jesus Christ was the Father's executive, the "chief contractor" who supervised and managed the actual creation process. (It will be interesting, when one passes death and returns to the spirit world, to gain or regain a clearer understanding of this working relationship, won't it?)

Passages That Identify Jehovah as the Creator of This Earth

1. • "These are the generations of the heavens and of the earth when they were created, *in the day that the* LORD *God made the earth and the heavens*, . . . for the LORD God had not caused it to rain upon the earth, and there was not a man to till the ground. But there went up a mist from the earth, and watered the whole face of the ground. *And the* LORD *God formed man of the dust of the ground, and breathed into his nostrils the breath of life; and man became a living soul*" (Gen. 2:4–7).

2. • "*the* LORD *said, I will destroy man whom I have created from the face of the earth*;

both man, and beast, and the creeping thing, and the fowls of the air; for it repenteth me that I have made them" (Gen. 6:7).

3. • "Then the Lord answered Job out of the whirlwind, and said, . . . *Where wast thou when I laid the foundations of the earth?* declare, if thou hast understanding" (Job 38:1, 4).

4. Some passages, such as Psalm 102, speak of Jehovah (the Lord) but refer to Him both in the past and in future last-days events such as "when the Lord shall build up Zion, he shall appear in his glory":

> *But thou, O Lord, shalt endure for ever; and thy remembrance unto all generations.* . . .
> When the Lord shall build up Zion, he shall appear in his glory.
> This shall be written for the generation to come: and the people which shall be created shall praise the Lord.
> *For he hath looked down from the height of his sanctuary; from heaven did the Lord behold the earth;* . . .
> To declare the name of the Lord in Zion, and his praise in Jerusalem;
> When the people are gathered together, and the kingdoms, to serve the Lord.
> He weakened my strength in the way; he shortened my days.
> I said, O my God, take me not away in the midst of my days: thy years are throughout all generations.
> *Of old hast thou laid the foundation of the earth: and the heavens are the work of thy hands.* (Ps. 102:12, 16, 18–19, 21–25)

5. Psalm 104 is a glorious tribute to Jehovah for his creation of this earth. It speaks in detail of various geographical and botanical parts of that creation. It is also one of the passages which allude to the participation of the Holy Spirit in the creation process. The verses cited here are an abbreviation of the entire psalm:

> Bless the Lord, O my soul. O Lord my God, thou art very great; thou art clothed with honour and majesty.
> Who coverest thyself with light as with a garment: *who stretchest out the heavens like a curtain* . . .
> *Who laid the foundations of the earth,* that it should not be removed for ever. . . .
> O Lord, how manifold are thy works! *in wisdom hast thou made them all: the earth is full of thy riches.* . . .
> *Thou sendest forth thy spirit, they are created*: and thou renewest the face of the earth. (Ps. 104:1–2, 5, 24, 30)

6. The eighth chapter of Proverbs harks back to premortality, prior to the creation of this earth. It asserts that the quality of wisdom was possessed by Jehovah "in the beginning of his way, before his works of old," and that He used wisdom abundantly when He enacted this earth's creation:

> Wisdom is better than rubies; and all the things that may be desired are not to be compared to it.
> I wisdom dwell with prudence, and find out knowledge of witty inventions.
> The fear of the Lord is to hate evil: pride, and arrogancy, and the evil way, and the froward mouth, do I hate. . . .
> *The Lord possessed me in the beginning of his way, before his works of old.*
> *I was set up from everlasting, from the beginning, or ever the earth was.*

When there were no depths, I was brought forth; when there were no fountains abounding with water.

Before the mountains were settled, before the hills was I brought forth:

While as yet he had not made the earth, nor the fields, nor the highest part of the dust of the world.

When he prepared the heavens, I was there: when he set a compass upon the face of the depth:

When he established the clouds above: when he strengthened the fountains of the deep:

When he gave to the sea his decree, that the waters should not pass his commandment: when he appointed the foundations of the earth:

Then I was by him, as one brought up with him: and I was daily his delight, rejoicing always before him; . . .

Now therefore hearken unto me, O ye children: for blessed are they that keep my ways.

Hear instruction, and be wise, and refuse it not. . . .

For whoso findeth me findeth life, and shall obtain favour of the LORD. (Prov. 8:11–13, 22–30, 32–33, 35)

7. Chapter 40 of Isaiah is another chapter that glances back to premortality and tells, in part, of the creation of this earth. It shows with clarity that Jehovah is Jesus Christ, for it alludes to the LORD's being preceded by a "voice crying in the wilderness, Prepare ye the way of the Lord," a prophecy which was fulfilled by John the Baptist's ministry preparing the way for Jesus (see Matt. 3:1–3; Mark 1:2–5; Luke 3:1–6; John 1:23). It speaks of the LORD's future coming in glory, a clear allusion to the second advent of Jesus Christ. But of greater significance in this context are the various verses which refer to Jehovah's creating this earth, while inquiring who taught him knowledge, and showed him the way of understanding. It emphasizes that when He created the earth and set man upon it, "he calleth them all by names," obviously emphasizing that ***He knows, personally, every individual who has dwelt upon this earth in mortality***:

Comfort ye, comfort ye my people, saith your God.

Speak ye comfortably to Jerusalem, and cry unto her, that her warfare is accomplished, that her iniquity is pardoned: for she hath received of the LORD's hand double for all her sins.

The voice of him that crieth in the wilderness, Prepare ye the way of the LORD, make straight in the desert a highway for our God.

Every valley shall be exalted, and every mountain and hill shall be made low: and the crooked shall be made straight, and the rough places plain:

And the glory of the LORD shall be revealed, and all flesh shall see it together: for the mouth of the LORD hath spoken it. . . .

Who hath measured the waters in the hollow of his hand, and meted out heaven with the span, and comprehended the dust of the earth in a measure, and weighed the mountains in scales, and the hills in a balance?

Who hath directed the Spirit of the LORD, or being his counsellor hath taught him?

With whom took he counsel, and who instructed him, and taught him in the path of judgment, and taught him knowledge, and shewed to him the way of understanding? . . .

To whom then will ye liken God? or what likeness will ye compare unto him? . . .

Have ye not known? have ye not heard? hath it not been told you from the beginning? have ye not understood from the foundations of the earth?

It is he that sitteth upon the circle of the earth, and the inhabitants thereof are as grasshoppers; that stretcheth out the heavens as a curtain, and spreadeth them out as a tent to dwell in . . .

To whom then will ye liken me, or shall I be equal? saith *the Holy One.*

Lift up your eyes on high, and *behold who hath created these things, that bringeth out their host by number: he calleth them all by names by the greatness of his might, for that he is strong in power; not one faileth.*

Hast thou not known? hast thou not heard, that *the everlasting God, the* LORD, *the Creator of the ends of the earth, fainteth not, neither is weary? there is no searching of his understanding.* . . .

But they that wait upon the LORD shall renew their strength; they shall mount up with wings as eagles; they shall run, and not be weary; and they shall walk, and not faint. (Isa. 40:1–5, 12–14, 18, 21–22, 25–26, 28, 31)

8. • *"Thus saith God the* LORD, *he that created the heavens, and stretched them out; he that spread forth the earth, and that which cometh out of it; he that giveth breath unto the people upon it, and spirit to them that walk therein"* (Isa. 42:5).

9. • *"let the earth open, and let them bring forth salvation, and let righteousness spring up together; I the* LORD *have created it"* (Isa. 45:8).

10. • *"Thus saith the* LORD, *the Holy One of Israel,* . . . *I have made the earth, and created man upon it: I, even my hands, have stretched out the heavens,* and all their host have I commanded" (Isa. 45:11–12).

11. • *"For thus saith the* LORD *that created the heavens; God himself that formed the earth and made it; he hath established it, he created it not in vain, he formed it to be inhabited*: I am the LORD; and there is none else (Isa. 45:18).

12. • "Hearken unto me, O Jacob and Israel, my called; *I am he; I am the first, I also am the last. Mine hand also hath laid the foundation of the earth, and my right hand hath spanned the heavens* . . . *Thus saith the* LORD, *thy Redeemer,* the Holy One of Israel; I am the LORD thy God" (Isa. 48:12–13, 17; 1 Ne. 20:12–13, 17).

13. Chapter 51 of Isaiah clearly indicates that it was Jehovah who created the heavens and lay the foundation of the earth, but also depicts Him functioning in the last days as the God who will gather the redeemed of Israel and say to Zion: "Thou art my people"—last-days functions which other scriptures assert will be fulfilled by Jesus Christ: "Awake, awake, put on strength, O arm of the LORD; awake . . . the redeemed of the LORD shall return, and come with singing unto Zion; and everlasting joy shall be upon their head: they shall obtain gladness and joy; and sorrow and mourning shall flee away. I, even I, am he that comforteth you . . . *forgettest the* LORD *thy maker, that hath stretched forth the heavens, and laid the foundations of the earth* . . . *I am the* LORD *thy God, that divided the sea, whose waves roared* . . . *that I may plant the heavens, and lay the foundations of the earth,* and say unto Zion, Thou art my people. (Isa. 51:9, 11–13, 15–16; 2 Ne. 8:9, 11–13, 15–16).

14. • *"For, lo, he that formeth the mountains, and createth the wind, and declareth unto man what is his thought,* that maketh the morning darkness, and treadeth upon the high places of the earth, *The* LORD, *The God of hosts, is his name"* (Amos 4:13).

15. • *"The burden of the word of the* LORD for Israel, *saith the* LORD, *which stretcheth forth the heavens, and layeth the foundation of the earth, and formeth the spirit of man within him"* (Zech. 12:1).

Passages That Identify God the Son, Jesus Christ, as the Creator of This Earth

As will be clearly shown in chapter 10, Jehovah of the Old Testament is Jesus Christ of the New Testament. The passages cited in the above section indicate Jehovah is the Creator; this section cites passages which indicate that the same individual is the Creator, but in these passages the Creator is described or referred to by His New Testament, Book of Mormon, and Doctrine and Covenants name: Jesus Christ.

1. • "*his dear Son* [Jesus Christ]: *In whom we have redemption through his blood, . . . by him were all things created, that are in heaven, and that are in earth, visible and invisible, whether they be thrones, or dominions, or principalities, or powers: all things were created by him, and for him: And he is before all things, and by him all things consist*" (Col. 1:13–14, 16–17).

2. • "unto the Son [Jesus Christ] he [God the Father] saith, Thy throne, O God, is for ever and ever: a sceptre of righteousness is the sceptre of thy kingdom. Thou hast loved righteousness, and hated iniquity; therefore God [God the Father], even *thy God, hath anointed thee with the oil of gladness* above thy fellows. And, *Thou, Lord* [Jesus Christ], *in the beginning hast laid the foundation of the earth; and the heavens are the works of thine hands*" (Heb. 1:8–10).

3. • "*he shall be called Jesus Christ, the Son of God, the Father of heaven and earth, the Creator of all things from the beginning*; and his mother shall be called Mary" (Mosiah 3:8).

4. • "we believe in *Jesus Christ, the Son of God, who created heaven and earth, and all things*; who shall come down among the children of men" (Mosiah 4:2).

5. • "*that Christ, the Lord God Omnipotent,* may seal you his, that you may be brought to heaven, that ye may have everlasting salvation and eternal life, through the wisdom, and power, and justice, and mercy *of him who created all things, in heaven and in earth, who is* **God above all**" (Mosiah 5:15).

6. • "he said unto them that *Christ was the God, the Father of all things*, and said that he should take upon him the image of man, and it should be the image after which man was created in the beginning; or in other words, *he said that man was created after the image of God, and that God should come down among the children of men, and take upon him flesh and blood*, and go forth upon the face of the earth" (Mosiah 7:27).

7. • "I rejected *my Redeemer*, and denied that which had been spoken of by our fathers; but now that they may foresee that he will come, and that *he remembereth every creature of his creating*, he will make himself manifest unto all" (Mosiah 27:30).

8. • "*Jesus Christ, the Son of God, the Father of heaven and of earth, the Creator of all things from the beginning*; and that ye might know of the signs of his coming, to the intent that ye might believe on his name" (Hel. 14:12).

9. • "*I am Jesus Christ the Son of God. I created the heavens and the earth, and all things that in them are. I was with the Father from the beginning.* I am in the Father, and the Father in me; and in me hath the Father glorified his name" (3 Ne. 9:15).

10. • "Who shall say that it was not a miracle that *by his word the heaven and the earth should be; and by the power of his word man was created of the dust of the earth*; and by the power of his word have miracles been wrought? And who shall say that *Jesus Christ* did not do many mighty miracles?" (Morm. 9:17–18).

11. • *"I am Jesus Christ, the Son of the living God, who created the heavens and the earth,* a light which cannot be hid in darkness" (D&C 14:9).

12. Doctrine and Covenants 29 adds numerous additional insights:

> Listen to the voice of *Jesus Christ, your Redeemer, the Great I AM,* whose arm of mercy hath atoned for your sins; . . . as the words have gone forth out of my mouth even so shall they be fulfilled, that the first shall be last, and that the last shall be first *in all things whatsoever I have created by the word of my power, which is the power of my Spirit.*
>
> *For by the power of my Spirit created I them; yea, all things both spiritual and temporal—*
>
> *First spiritual, secondly temporal, which is the beginning of my work; and again, first temporal, and secondly spiritual, which is the last of my work—*
>
> Speaking unto you that you may naturally understand; but *unto myself my works have no end, neither beginning;* but it is given unto you that ye may understand, because ye have asked it of me and are agreed.
>
> Wherefore, verily I say unto you that *all things unto me are spiritual,* and not at any time have I given unto you a law which was temporal; neither any man, nor the children of men; *neither Adam, your father, whom I created.* (D&C 29:1, 30–34; see Moses 6:27–28)

13. • "Hearken, O ye people of my church, . . . *hearken ye and give ear to him who laid the foundation of the earth, who made the heavens and all the hosts thereof, and by whom all things were made which live, and move, and have a being.* . . . Listen to him who is *the advocate with the Father,* who is pleading your cause before him" (D&C 45:1–3).

Passages that Assert God the Father's Creation Role through the Labors of Jesus Christ

1. • "to us there is but one God, the Father, **of** *whom are all things,* and we in him; and one Lord Jesus Christ, **by** *whom are all things,* and we by him" (1 Cor. 8:6).

2. • "the mystery, which from the beginning of the world hath been hid in God, who created all things by Jesus Christ" (Eph. 3:9).

3. • "despise not the revelations of God. For behold, *by the power of his word man came upon the face of the earth, which earth was created by the power of his word.* Wherefore, if God being able to speak and the world was, and to speak and man was created, O then, *why not able to command the earth, or the workmanship of his hands upon the face of it,* according to his will and pleasure?" (Jacob 4:8–9; see John 1:1–10).

4. • "Those things which were from the beginning before the world was, *which were ordained of the Father, through his Only Begotten Son,* who was in the bosom of the Father, even from the beginning" (D&C 76:13).

5. • *"I am the Beginning and the End, the Almighty God; by mine Only Begotten I cre-ated these things;* yea, in the beginning I created the heaven, and the earth upon which thou standest" (Moses 2:1).

Other Passages that Describe "God" (Not Clearly Identified) as Creating This Earth

There are other passages that speak of God in the creation process, but the specific identity of who that being is may be subject to varying interpretations. But certainly, they should not be omitted from consideration in this context, so they are included here. (In some instances, interpretative clues are cross-referenced.)

1. • "In the beginning God created the heaven and the earth" (Gen. 1:1).

2. • "And God said, *Let us make man in our image, after our likeness*: and let them have dominion over the fish of the sea, and over the fowl of the air, and over the cattle, and over all the earth, and over every creeping thing that creepeth upon the earth. So *God created man in his own image, in the image of God created he him; male and female created he them*" (Gen. 1:26–27; see Gen. 5:1, 5; Luke 3:38).

3. • "God that made the world and all things therein, seeing he is Lord of heaven and earth, . . . hath appointed a day, in the which he will judge the world in righteousness by that man whom he hath ordained; whereof he hath given assurance unto all men, in that he hath raised him from the dead" (Acts 17:24, 31).

4. • "Behold, *the Lord hath created the earth* that it should be inhabited; and *he hath created his children that they should possess it*" (1 Ne. 17:36).

5. • for *there is a God, and he hath created all things, both the heavens and the earth, and all things that in them are, both things to act and things to be acted upon.* And to bring about his eternal purposes in the end of man, after He had created our first parents, and the beasts of the field and the fowls of the air, and in fine, all things which are created, it must needs be that there was an opposition; even the forbidden fruit in opposition to the tree of life; the one being sweet and the other bitter. Wherefore, *the Lord God gave unto man that he should act for himself.* Wherefore, man could not act for himself save it should be that he was enticed by the one or the other (2 Ne. 2:14–16).

6. • "Know ye not that *I, the Lord your God, have created all men*, and that *I remember* those who are upon the isles of the sea; and that *I rule* in the heavens above and in the earth beneath; and *I bring forth my word* unto the children of men, yea, even upon all the nations of the earth?" (2 Ne. 29:7).

7. • "Believe in God; believe that he is, and that *he created all things, both in heaven and in earth*; believe that *he has all wisdom, and all power, both in heaven and in earth*; believe that man doth not comprehend all the things which the Lord can comprehend" (Mosiah 4:9).

8. • "all things denote there is a God; yea, even the earth, and all things that are upon the face of it, yea, and its motion, yea, and also all the planets which move in their regular form do witness that there is a Supreme Creator" (Alma 30:44).

9. • "I will show unto you a God of miracles, even *the God of Abraham, and the God of Isaac, and the God of Jacob*; and *it is that same God who created the heavens and the earth, and all things that in them are.* Behold, *he created Adam*, and by Adam came the fall of man. And *because of the fall of man came Jesus Christ*" (Morm. 9:11–12; see D&C 29:1, 30–34; Moses 6:27–28).

The Premortal and New-Earth Councils in Heaven

Council 1: the Council of the Eternal God of all other gods. Reference has already been made to D&C 121:32, which alludes to "that which was ordained in the midst of *the Council of the Eternal God of all other gods before this world was.*" For purposes of clarity, that council gathering is arbitrarily labeled **Council Number 1** in this chapter.

It appears that it was a top-level gathering, though nothing is known beyond what meanings those 13 words convey. Perhaps, rather than actively participating in the creation of this earth, they may have functioned as some sort of heavenly "Planning and Zoning Commission." Someday more will be known on this intriguing subject.

Council 2: the Choosing of Christ and the Rebellion of Satan Council. The focus of this next sub-section is on a different council, one which appears to have dealt with specific issues more related to the governance of this and other earths. This council is arbitrarily labeled **Council Number 2** in this chapter.

Four major events characterize this council:

1. The selection of various individuals to be leaders.
2. The proposal, made by one "like unto God," that a new earth be created upon which the assembled participants could experience their mortal probation.
3. The attempt made by Lucifer to usurp the responsibilities intended for Jesus the Christ in connection with the creation and administration of the new earth.
4. Because of his rejection, Lucifer rebelled against God. There was war in heaven, and Lucifer and the third of all the spirit beings, they who followed him, were cast out.

Two key Pearl of Great Price passages describe this council. The first is from the book of Abraham. In this passage, the "first estate" spoken of apparently is their pre-mortal life; their "second estate" refers to man's mortal experience here on this earth (and perhaps on other earths as well):

> Now the Lord had shown unto me, Abraham, *the intelligences that were organized before the world was; and among all these there were many of the noble and great ones;*
>
> *And God saw these souls that they were good, and he stood in the midst of them, and he said: These I will make my rulers;* for he stood among those that were spirits, and he saw that they were good; and he said unto me: Abraham, thou art one of them; thou wast chosen before thou wast born.
>
> *And there stood one among them that was **like unto God**, and he said unto those who were with him: We will go down, for there is space there, and we will take of these materials, and we will make an earth whereon these may dwell;*
>
> *And we will prove them herewith, to see if they will do all things whatsoever the Lord their God shall command them;*
>
> And they who keep their first estate shall be added upon; and they who keep not their first estate shall not have glory in the same kingdom with those who keep their first estate; and *they who keep their second estate shall have glory added upon their heads for ever and ever.*
>
> And the Lord said: Whom shall I send? *And one answered **like unto the Son of Man**: Here am I, send me. And **another answered** and said: Here am I, send me. And the Lord said: I will send the first.*
>
> And the second was angry, and kept not his first estate; and, at that day, many followed after him. (Abr. 3:22–28)

The second Pearl of Great Price passage telling of this premortal council is found in Moses 4:1–4. It is more specific and identifies the central messages of both Jesus and Lucifer. The dividing issues became (1) the agency of man and (2) who would receive the honor for providing the earth experience.

> And I, the Lord God, spake unto Moses, saying: That **Satan**, whom thou hast commanded in the name of mine Only Begotten, is the same which was from the beginning, and he came before me, *saying—Behold, here am I, send me, I will be thy son, and I will redeem all mankind, that one soul shall not be lost, and surely I will do it; wherefore give me thine honor.*

But, behold, *my **Beloved Son**, which was my Beloved and Chosen from the beginning, said unto me—Father, thy will be done, and the glory be thine forever.*

Wherefore, *because that Satan rebelled against me*, and sought to destroy the agency of man, which I, the Lord God, had given him, and also, that I should give unto him mine own power; *by the power of mine Only Begotten, I caused that he should be cast down;*

And he became Satan, yea, even the devil, the father of all lies, to deceive and to blind men, and to lead them captive at his will, even as many as would not hearken unto my voice. (Moses 4:1–4)

When Jesus was chosen to come to earth as its Savior, and Lucifer was not selected for that responsibility, Lucifer rebelled against God and was cast out of the spirit world. In section 29 of the Doctrine and Covenants, the Lord revealed that • "*behold, the devil was before Adam, for he rebelled against me, saying, Give me thine honor, which is my power; and also a third part of the hosts of heaven turned he away from me because of their agency; And they were thrust down, and thus came the devil and his angels; And, behold, there is a place prepared for them from the beginning, which place is hell*" (D&C 29:36–38).

Greater detail is found in D&C 76:

An angel of God who was in authority in the presence of God, who rebelled against the Only Begotten Son whom the Father loved and who was in the bosom of the Father, was thrust down from the presence of God and the Son,

And was called Perdition, for the heavens wept over him—he was Lucifer, a son of the morning.

And we beheld, and lo, he is fallen! is fallen, even a son of the morning! (D&C 76:25–27)

An allusion to the great battle which ensued as part of this rebellion is found in the book of Revelation:

There appeared another wonder in heaven; and behold a great red dragon, having seven heads and ten horns, and seven crowns upon his heads.

And his tail drew the third part of the stars of heaven, and did cast them to the earth . . .

And there was war in heaven: Michael [Adam] and his angels fought against the dragon; and the dragon fought and his angels,

And prevailed not; neither was their place found any more in heaven.

And the great dragon was cast out, that old serpent, called the Devil, and Satan, which deceiveth the whole world: *he was cast out into the earth, and his angels were cast out with him.* (Rev. 12:3–4, 7–9; see D&C 107:34)

It is difficult to determine the chronological relationships of the various premortal councils, but Rev. 12:4 indicates that Satan and his followers were cast down "to the earth." It doesn't specify what earth, but *if* it was *this* earth, then the council probably didn't take place until after "the beginning" had ended and this earth had been created.

An allusion in the fourteenth chapter of Isaiah, in which a taunt against the king of Babylon is being recorded, harks back to the outcome of this council as the Babylonian king is compared to Lucifer:

How art thou fallen from heaven, O Lucifer, son of the morning! how art thou cut down to the ground, which didst weaken the nations!

For thou hast said in thine heart, *I will ascend into heaven, I will exalt my throne above the stars of God: I will sit also upon the mount of the congregation, in the sides of the north:*

I will ascend above the heights of the clouds; I will be like the most High.

Yet thou shalt be brought down to hell, to the sides of the pit. (Isa. 14:12–15)

This passage is interesting because it depicts a mount or mountain setting for heavenly gatherings, with the "privileged" seating on the north side of the arena or conference setting.

Council 3: *The Council of the Gods Who United in Creating This Planet: Earth.* A third premortal gathering of the Gods is reported in detail in the book of Abraham. It is arbitrarily labeled **Council Number 3** in this chapter. The "minutes" of this Council were previously reviewed in this chapter, as the spritual and physical creations of this earth were summarized. Again, this Council of the Gods as they created this earth (first spiritually, then physically) is arbitrarily termed **Council Number 3** in this chapter.

Council 4: *The "Sons of God Shouted for Joy" Council.* Another allusion that harks back to a premortal (or early-mortal) activity is found in the book of Job. It is arbitrarily labeled **Council Number 4** in this chapter. It seems to speak of happier events than those associated with Council Number 2, (the choosing of Christ and the rebellion of Satan council) referenced above. Many, however, not realizing that the scriptures speak of several premortal councils, assume that it is just another scriptural passage referring to Council Number 2. The Job allusion speaks of when God laid the foundations of the earth, saying that it was during that event that "*the morning stars sang together, and all the sons of God shouted for joy.*" The context of the passage seems to indicate that this is a later event than Council 2 depicts. Note that the physical foundations of the new earth have been laid, measurements have been taken, and a cornerstone has been installed:

Where wast thou *when I laid the foundations of the earth?* declare, if thou hast understanding.

Who hath *laid the measures thereof,* if thou knowest? or who hath *stretched the line* upon it?

Whereupon are *the foundations* thereof fastened? or who *laid the corner stone* thereof;

When the morning stars sang together, and all the sons of God shouted for joy? (Job 38:4–7)

Later verses in Job 38 indicate further construction and early temporal events on the earth: (1) the sea has broken out of its bounds and had to be shut up (v. 8–11); (2) mornings have occurred (v. 12); wicked influences have been "shaken" and have had light "withholden" from them (v. 13, 15); death has occurred on the earth (v. 17); snow and hail have occurred there (v. 22); there has been an east wind (v. 24); there has been lightening and thunder (v. 25); rain has fallen (v. 26–28); there have been frost and ice (v. 29–30); the star constellations are in place (v. 31–32); there are clouds (v. 37); there is dust and clods of dirt (v. 38); lions and ravens are present and seek their food (v. 39–41). It seems clear that this gathering "*when the morning stars sang together, and all the sons of God shouted for joy*" is later than Councils numbers 2 and 3. Perhaps it is an allusion to a dedicatory celebration in honor of the completion of the newly formed earth.

God the Father Gave the Mortal Inhabitants of This Earth to His Son Jehovah/Jesus Christ for His Care and Responsibility

Throughout His mortal ministry, Jesus Christ made repeated references to His Father's "giving him" the people of this earth. When God the Father "gave" all the spirits who were to become mortal beings on this earth to His Son, the Savior received the charge that He was to save as many as would come unto him and bring them back into the Father's presence. Both the Father and the Son entertained the desire "that *none of them that my Father hath given me* shall be lost" (D&C 50:41–42).

• *"All that the Father giveth me shall come to me; and him that cometh to me I will in no wise cast out.* . . . And this is the Father's will which hath sent me, *that of all which he hath given me I should lose nothing, but should raise it up again at the last day.* And this is the will of him that sent me, that *every one which seeth the Son, and believeth on him, may have everlasting life: and I will raise him up at the last day*" (John 6:37, 39–40).

• "My Father, *which gave them me,* is greater than all; and no man is able to pluck them out of my Father's hand" (John 10:29).

• "I have manifested thy name unto *the men which thou gavest me out of the world: thine they were, and thou gavest them me*; and they have kept thy word. Now they have known that all things whatsoever thou hast given me are of thee" (John 17:6–7).

• I pray for them: I pray not for the world, but *for them which thou hast given me; for they are thine. And all mine are thine, and thine are mine; and I am glorified in them*" (John 17:9–10).

• "While I was with them in the world, I kept them in thy name: *those that thou gavest me I have kept, and none of them is lost, but the son of perdition*; that the scripture might be fulfilled" (John 17:12).

• "Father, *I will that they also, whom thou hast given me, be with me where I am; that they may behold my glory, which thou has given me*: for thou lovedst me before the foundation of the world" (John 17:24).

• "behold, ye have both heard my voice, and seen me; and ye are my sheep, and *ye are numbered among those whom the Father hath given me*" (3 Ne. 15:24).

• "with all *those whom my Father hath given me* out of the world" (D&C 27:14).

• "Fear not, little children, for you are mine, . . . and *you are of them that my Father hath given me; and none of them that my Father hath given me shall be lost*" (D&C 50:41–42).

• "that through him all might be saved *whom the Father had put into his power and made by him*" (D&C 76:42).

• "You are mine apostles, . . . *ye are they whom my Father hath given me*" (D&C 84:63).

• "Giving thanks unto the Father, which hath made us meet to be partakers of the inheritance of the saints in light" (Col. 1:12).

• "And who shall be his seed? . . . all those who have hearkened unto their [the prophets'] words, and believed that the Lord would redeem his people, and have looked forward to that day for a remission of their sins, I say unto you, that *these are his seed, or they are the heirs of the kingdom of God*" (Mosiah 15:10–11).

Jesus Christ Was Designated as the "Father" of Those Who Would Abide in His Gospel

It appears that with God the Father giving Christ the responsibility for bringing all mankind who will believe in Him and accept His gospel back into the Father's presence, the Father saw fit that Christ should function in a parental relationship with them. Thus came to pass the inspired arrangement that Christ "adopts" those who believe in Him, and He assumes the role of Father to them. This doesn't change the reality that *God the Father remains the literal father of their spirits; but it makes the Savior their Father in the gospel.* It is through Christ, by becoming an heir, that man will be able to inherit the richest blessings of heaven. *Many passages speak of this Father-child relationship, with Jesus and those who believe in Him*, and their subsequent right as heirs in the heavenly kingdom. The following are examples:

• "The Spirit itself beareth witness with our spirit, that we are the children of God: And *if children, then heirs; heirs of God, and joint-heirs with Christ"* (Rom. 8:16–17).

• "in Christ Jesus *I have begotten you through the gospel"* (1 Cor. 4:15).

• "for ye are all one in Christ Jesus. And if ye *be* Christ's, then are ye Abraham's seed, and *heirs according to the promise"* (Gal. 3:28–29).

• "God sent forth his Son, . . . To redeem them that were under the law, that we might *receive the adoption of sons.* And because ye are sons, God hath sent forth the Spirit of his Son into your hearts, crying, Abba, Father. Wherefore *thou art no more a servant, but a son; and if a son, then an heir of God through Christ"* (Gal. 4:4–7).

• "Having predestinated us unto *the adoption of children by Jesus Christ to himself, according to the good pleasure of his will,* To the praise of the glory of his grace, wherein he hath made us accepted in the beloved" (Eph. 1:5–6).

• "what manner of love the Father hath bestowed upon us, that we should be called the sons of God . . . Beloved, *now are we the sons of God,* and it doth not yet appear what we shall be: but we know that, *when he shall appear, we shall be like him*; for we shall see him as he is" (1 Jn. 3:1–2).

• "Whosoever believeth that Jesus is the Christ is born of God: and *every one that loveth him that begat loveth him also that is begotten of him"* (1 Jn. 5:1).

• "they were in one, *the children of Christ, and heirs to the kingdom of God.* And how blessed were they!" (4 Ne. 1:17–18).

• "now, because of the covenant which ye have made *ye shall be called the children of Christ, his sons, and his daughters*; for behold, this day *he hath spiritually begotten you"* (Mosiah 5:7).

• "Behold, I am Jesus Christ, the Son of God. I am the life and the light of the world. . . . I say unto you, that *as many as receive me, to them will I give power to become the sons of God,* even to them that believe on my name" (D&C 11:28, 30).

• "Jesus Christ your Redeemer . . . Who so loved the world that he gave his own life, *that as many as would believe might become the sons of God"* (D&C 34:1, 3).

• "I am Jesus Christ, the Son of God, who was crucified for the sins of the world, even *as many as will believe on my name, that they may become the sons of God"* (D&C 35:2).

• "Jesus Christ—to as many as received me, *gave I power to become my sons*; and even so will I give unto as many as will receive me, *power to become my sons"* (D&C 39:1, 4).

• "I am Alpha and Omega, . . . unto as many as received me *gave I power to do many miracles, and to become the sons of God"* (D&C 45:7–8).

• "they are gods, *even the sons of God*—Wherefore, all things are theirs, whether life or death, or things present, or things to come, all are theirs and *they are Christ's, and Christ is God's"* (D&C 76:58–59).

• "I was in the beginning with the Father, and am the Firstborn; And *all those who are begotten through me* are partakers of the glory of the same, and *are the church of the Firstborn"* (D&C 93:21–22).

Thus it is proper to speak of Christ as the Father of the righteous, for they have become His children, and He has been made their Father through the regeneration of baptism and their having been born again.

Summary

1. Many were called to priesthood positions prior to the creation of this earth. They were taught and prepared to serve in various positions of leadership in mortality. Through a "preparatory redemption," they were able to partake of Christ's atoning sacrifice prior to His atonement occurring here on this earth.

2. Extensive strategic planning took place prior to this earth's physical creation. Ten specific planning areas were identified.

3. Specific instructions concerning this earth were given by God the Father to Jehovah. Four patterns of scripture concerning the relationships between the Father and the Son during the premortal planning stage were explored.

4. The spirit creation of this earth was summarized and outlined in detail, comparing references in Genesis, Moses, and Abraham. Then, the transformation of this planet earth into a physical entity was explained.

5. This earth first was created, spiritually, on or near the planet Kolob.

6. Numerous scriptural passages specifically identify Jehovah as the creator of this earth. Many other passages identify God the Son, Jesus Christ as the creator of this earth. Together, they show that Jehovah *is* Jesus Christ. Several passages make reference to God the Father creating the earth *through* Jesus Christ, but clearly, it is Jesus, not the Father, whom almost all scriptures identify and laud as this earth's creator.

7. Four separate premortal or new-earth councils are alluded to in the scriptures:
   A. The council of the Eternal God of all other gods.
   B. The choosing of Christ and the rebellion of Satan council.
   C. The council of the Gods who united in creating this planet: earth.
   D. The "sons of God shouted for joy" council, which appears to have taken place *after* the creation of this earth.

8. God the Father gave the mortal inhabitants of this earth to Jehovah/Jesus Christ for His care and responsibility.

9. Jesus Christ was designated as the "Father" of all those will abide in His gospel.

PART FOUR

JESUS THE CHRIST AS JEHOVAH AND AS THE FATHER

CHAPTER 10

JEHOVAH IS JESUS THE CHRIST

The Name "Jehovah" in the Scriptures

The name "Jehovah" appears 14 times in the four standard works of The Church of Jesus Christ of Latter-day Saints. It appears four times in the King James Version Old Testament: once when the LORD appeared to Moses, once in a Psalm, and twice in the writings of Isaiah.

It is found twice in the Book of Mormon: once when the writings of Isaiah are being quoted, and in the very last verse of the entire Book of Mormon as Moroni bids farewell to his future readers.

The sacred name "Jehovah" is used six times in the Doctrine and Covenants; four of those usages are in the dedicatory prayer of the Kirtland temple, which the *History of the Church* specifically states "was given by Revelation to Joseph, the Seer" (Vol. 2, p. 420). Doctrine and Covenants 110:2–4 is the record of Christ's appearance in the Kirtland Temple on April 3, 1836, a week after the temple dedicatory prayer was given; at this time the Lord accepted the temple. Doctrine and Covenants 128:1 is a letter written by Joseph Smith to the Church members containing further directions on baptism for the dead.

The two appearances of the name Jehovah in the Pearl of Great Price are both in the book of Abraham, and recount the saving of Abraham's life when he was about to be sacrificed on a pagan altar and then the LORD's appearance to Abraham when He first made the Abrahamic covenant with him. (See Gen. 11:31–12:5.) These 14 passages are cited below, occasionally with their contexts indicated in braces {} following them:

Bible (Old Testament)

1. "And God spake unto Moses, and said unto him, I am the LORD: And I appeared unto Abraham, unto Isaac, and unto Jacob, by the name of God Almighty, but by my name JEHOVAH was I not known to them" (Ex. 6:2–3).
2. "That men may know that thou, whose name alone is JEHOVAH, art the most high over all the earth" (Ps. 83:18 {1–18}).

3. "Behold, God is my salvation; I will trust, and not be afraid: for the LORD JEHOVAH is my strength and my song; he also is become my salvation" (Isa. 12:2; compare with 2 Ne. 22:2).
4. "Trust ye in the LORD for ever: for in the LORD JEHOVAH is everlasting strength" (Isa. 26:4).

Book of Mormon

5. "Behold, God is my salvation; I will trust, and not be afraid; for the Lord JEHOVAH is my strength and my song; he also has become my salvation" (2 Ne. 22:2; compare with Isa. 12:2).
6. "And now I bid unto all, farewell. I soon go to rest in the paradise of God, until my spirit and body shall again reunite, and I am brought forth triumphant through the air, to meet you before the pleasing bar of the great *Jehovah*, the Eternal Judge of both quick and dead. Amen" (Moro. 10:34).

Doctrine and Covenants

7. "O *Jehovah*, have mercy upon this people, and as all men sin forgive the transgressions of thy people, and let them be blotted out forever" (D&C 109:34).
8. "But deliver thou, O *Jehovah*, we beseech thee, thy servants from their hands, and cleanse them from their blood" (D&C 109:42).
9. "That their hearts may be softened when thy servants shall go out from thy house, O *Jehovah*, to bear testimony of thy name; that their prejudices may give way before the truth, and thy people may obtain favor in the sight of all" (D&C 109:56).
10. "O Lord, remember thy servant, Joseph Smith, Jun., and all his afflictions and persecutions—how he has covenanted with *Jehovah*, and vowed to thee, O Mighty God of Jacob—and the commandments which thou hast given unto him, and that he hath sincerely striven to do thy will" (D&C 109:68).
11. "We saw the Lord standing upon the breastwork of the pulpit, before us; and under his feet was a paved work of pure gold, in color like amber. His eyes were as a flame of fire; the hair of his head was white like the pure snow; his countenance shone above the brightness of the sun; and his voice was as the sound of the rushing of great waters, even the voice of *Jehovah*, saying: I am the first and the last; I am he who liveth, I am he who was slain; I am your advocate with the Father" (D&C 110:2–4).
12. "It may seem to some to be a very bold doctrine that we talk of—a power which records or binds on earth and binds in heaven. Nevertheless, in all ages of the world, whenever the Lord has given a dispensation of the priesthood to any man by actual revelation, or any set of men, this power has always been given. Hence, whatsoever those men did in authority, in the name of the Lord, and did it truly and faithfully, and kept a proper and faithful record of the same, it became a law on earth and in heaven, and could not be annulled, according to the decrees of the great *Jehovah*. This is a faithful saying. Who can hear it?" (D&C 128:9).

Pearl of Great Price

13. "And his voice was unto me: Abraham, Abraham, behold, my name is *Jehovah*, and I have heard thee, and have come down to deliver thee, and to take thee away from thy father's house, and from all thy kinsfolk, into a strange land which thou knowest not of" (Abr. 1:16 {1–19}. See Ex. 6:2–3, but in the light of Abr. 1:15; Moses 1:2; 1:25; 2:1; 7:66; JS—H 1:29; A of F 1:11).

14. "My name is *Jehovah*, and I know the end from the beginning; therefore my hand shall be over thee" (Abr. 2:8 {1–20}).

How Jesus Is Shown to be Jehovah in Modern Latter-day Saint Scriptures

Latter-day Saints have a sure knowledge that Jesus Christ is Jehovah from modern scripture, which clearly indicates that **the New Testament Jesus Christ, not God the Father, is the Jehovah of the Old Testament.** Most specifically, this knowledge is ascertained from the April 3, 1836 appearance of the Savior to Joseph Smith and Oliver Cowdery as he accepted the newly dedicated Kirtland Temple as His house, the place where He would manifest himself to His people and where His name would reside:

The veil was taken from our minds, and the eyes of our understanding were opened.

We saw the Lord standing upon the breastwork of the pulpit, before us; and under his feet was a paved work of pure gold, in color like amber.

His eyes were as a flame of fire; the hair of his head was white like the pure snow; his countenance shone above the brightness of the sun; and his voice was as the sound of the rushing of great waters, *even the voice of Jehovah,* saying:

I am the first and the last; I am he who liveth, I am he who was slain; I am your advocate with the Father.

Behold, your sins are forgiven you; you are clean before me; therefore, lift up your heads and rejoice.

Let the hearts of your brethren rejoice, and let the hearts of all *my people* rejoice, who have, with their might, built this house to my name.

For behold, I have accepted this house, and *my name* shall be here; and I will manifest myself to my people in mercy in this house.

Yea, I will appear unto *my servants*, and speak unto them with mine own voice, if my people will keep *my commandments*, and do not pollute this holy house.

Yea the hearts of thousands and tens of thousands shall greatly rejoice in consequence of the blessings which shall be poured out, and the endowment with which *my servants* have been endowed in this house.

And the fame of this house shall spread to foreign lands; and this is the beginning of the blessing which shall be poured out upon the heads of *my people*. Even so. Amen. (D&C 110:1–10)

Numerous clues in this revelation make it certain that it was Jesus Christ who appeared in this glorious manifestation and was recognized as being Jehovah:

1. *In this passage Jehovah specifically identifies Himself as being "the first and the last."* The last book of the New Testament, the book of Revelation, is clearly defined as being • "The Revelation of Jesus Christ" (Rev. 1:1). In this revelation Jesus is identified as saying: • "I am Alpha and Omega, *the beginning and the ending*, saith the Lord, which is, and which was, and which is to come, the Almighty" (Rev. 1:8 {5–8}). A few verses later, when John hears a voice saying • "I am Alpha and Omega, *the first and the last*" (Rev. 1:11), he turns to see who is speaking and is shown *"the Son of man,"* a very common New Testament name for Jesus Christ (see Matt. 8:20; 9:6; 10:23; 11:19; 12:8, 32, 40; 13:37, 41; 16:13, 27, 28; etc.). When John kneels to worship Him, the Savior says: • "Fear not; *I am the first and the last: I am he that liveth, and was dead; and, behold, I am alive for evermore"* (Rev. 1:17–18 {12–20}). As Jesus gives instructions to John concerning

letters to the seven churches, He said, • "unto the angel of the church in Smyrna write; These things saith *the first and the last*, which was dead, and is alive" (Rev. 2:8). Near the end of the book of Revelation an angel comes to John, speaking in first person as if he is the Lord Jesus Christ, and says, • "I am Alpha and Omega, the beginning and the end, *the first and the last*" (Rev. 22:13).

2. *Another identifying phrase which Jehovah uses to identify Himself as being the Lord Jesus Christ in D&C 110:1–10 is, "I am he who liveth, I am he who was slain"* (verse 4). In Revelation 1:18, Jesus identifies Himself with the words • *"I am he that liveth, and was dead; and, behold, I am alive for evermore."* The theme that Jesus Christ was slain, but then was resurrected and thus restored to life, is a common theme throughout the scriptures. Even before His crucifixion, Jesus used the concept in reference to Himself. For instance, as He was descending from the Mount of Transfiguration with Peter, James and John, He told them, • *"Tell the vision to no man, until the Son of man be risen again from the dead"* (Matt. 17:9). The angel who greeted Christ's followers as they sought for Him in the sepulcher told them, • "He is not here: for he is risen, . . . go quickly, and tell his disciples that he is risen from the dead" (Matt. 28:6–7). Shortly after the Savior's resurrection, the Apostle Peter reprimanded a group of the Jews who challenged Him on Solomon's porch, saying that they • *"killed the Prince of life, whom God hath raised from the dead;* whereof we are witnesses" (Acts 3:15). Paul, in his epistle to the Romans, used the theme as a metaphor for the process of baptism: • "Therefore *we are buried with him* by baptism into death: that *like as Christ was raised up from the dead by the glory of the Father,* even so we also should walk in newness of life" (Rom. 6:4). Numerous other scriptural passages speak of Christ's being dead and then alive. See, for example: Luke 24:46, John 20:9; 21:14; Acts 10:40–41; Rom. 14:9, 1 Cor. 15:12–17; Col. 2:12; 2 Tim. 2:11; 1 Ne. 10:11; 2 Ne. 2:8; 25:13–14; 26:1; Alma 33:22; Hel. 14:20; D&C 1:19; 18:12; etc.

3. *In D&C 110:1–10 the Lord Jesus Christ uses several of the "my" terms which serve as identifying phrases and which characterize His revelations* throughout the Doctrine and Covenants. These include *"my people"* (cf. D&C 3:16; 10:52; 39:11; 41:1; 42:9; etc.), *"my servants"* (cf. D&C 1:6; 5:11; 27:8; 32:2; 33:1; etc.), *"my commandments"* (cf. D&C 11:9; 12:6; 14:6; 15:5; 18:8; etc.) and *"my name"* (cf. D&C 6:32; 10:61; 11:30; 14:8; 18:18; etc.).

4. *But even more specific is the identifying phrase: "I am your advocate with the Father"* (D&C 110:4). Obviously, if Jehovah, that Holy individual who appeared in D&C 110, functions as man's advocate with God the Father, then He is not God the Father Himself. He is not His own father, whom all the world knows as God the Father—that being whom others erroneously teach is Jehovah. The Apostle John wrote that • "if any man sin, *we have an advocate with the Father, Jesus Christ* the righteous" (1 Jn. 2:1). In the Doctrine and Covenants, • "Jesus Christ, your Redeemer, the Great I AM" says that • "I am in your midst, and am your advocate with the Father" (D&C 29:1–5; see also D&C 32:3 and 45:3–5). To be an advocate means that He is speaking in behalf of the righteous and pleading their acceptance and grace before God the Father, so that they can be saved and allowed to enter into the Father's kingdom. See also D&C 62:1 and Moro. 7:28. He is also known as "Jesus the mediator of the new covenant," who stands in the • "presence of God the Father" (D&C 107:19).

All these clues found in this revelation make it abundantly clear that Jesus Christ, who appeared in this glorious manifestation, is literally Jehovah, as is announced in D&C 110:3.

The Challenge: Assembling Sufficient Evidence to Show That Jehovah Is Jesus Christ, Not God the Father

Unfortunately, almost all of the Christian denominations are under the misinformed impression that Jehovah is God the Father, not Jesus Christ. This reaches all the way back to the *Nicene Creed*, which begins: "*I Believe in one God, the Father Almighty, Maker of heaven and earth, And of all things visible and invisible.*" The *Apostle's Creed* echoes it: "*I believe in God the Father Almighty, Maker of heaven and earth.*"

As has already been shown (in chapter 9) numerous scripture passages indicate that Jehovah was the creator of this earth and all that is in it, so for almost two millennia they have made the assumption that God the Father is this earth's supreme creator and equated Him with being Jehovah. They've completely ignored the many passages (also listed in chapter 9) that show that Jesus Christ is this earth's creator. The concept has never even occurred to most "trinitarians" that Jehovah is Jesus rather than God the Father (though there are a few who have made that scriptural connection and teach the matter correctly). Jehovah's Witnesses, especially, are adamant in their belief that Jehovah is God the Father.

An objective of this chapter is to assemble sufficient scriptural proof that Jehovah is Jesus that no truth-loving Christian can ignore or challenge it. That's why I haven't been content to merely list a few scripture references without citing the central message of those scriptures.

Comparisons of (LORD) Jehovah and Jesus Passages

All four of the standard works of scripture contain passages which, when compared, show that the Old Testament "Jehovah" is the same person as the New Testament "Jesus." The approach used in the remainder of this chapter is to list numerous passages that describe an identifying title or characteristic of Jehovah and then list numerous passages about Jesus Christ that identify him as having the same characteristics and titles; thus showing that Jehovah and Jesus Christ are the same divine being.

In other words, the Old Testament passages, which usually have been changed to the small-capital-letters "LORD," state that Jehovah is or does something. Then passages from the New Testament and other scriptures indicate that Jesus is or does the same thing, indicating that "Jehovah" and "Jesus" is the same individual—the same divine entity. The remainder of this chapter is devoted to hundreds of passages which provide these comparisons and lead to the inescapable conclusion that "Jehovah" is "Jesus." In most cases, other examples typical of the cited passages exist. They can be located through the use of concordances or scripture word-search programs.

Twenty-two scriptural themes are cited below with passages that give clear indication that Jehovah *is* Jesus Christ.

I. The Great I AM

Jehovah Is I AM. When Moses was first called of God to return to Egypt and liberate his people Israel from the Egyptian yoke, Moses inquired of the LORD, "Behold, when I come unto the children of Israel, and shall say unto them, The God of your fathers hath sent me unto you; and they shall say to me, What is his name? what shall

I say unto them?" The answer he received, as recorded in Exodus, was that:

> God said unto Moses, *I AM THAT I AM*: and he said, Thus shalt thou say unto the children of Israel, *I AM hath sent me unto you.*
> And God said moreover unto Moses, Thus shalt thou say unto the children of Israel, *The LORD God of your fathers*, the God of Abraham, the God of Isaac, and the God of Jacob, hath sent me unto you: *this is my name for ever, and this is my memorial unto all generations.* (Ex. 3:13–15)

Jesus Christ Is I AM. During the Savior's late Judean ministry, about six months prior to His death, Jesus was accosted by a group of critical scribes and Pharisees as He taught in the temple at Jerusalem. After challenging Him to judge a woman taken in adultery, they began to challenge His authority, saying that He alone bore witness of Himself. The Master replied that His father, God the Father, also bore witness of Him. When the Pharisees sought to assert their righteousness as descendants of Abraham, their remarks resulted in this discussion in which Jesus asserted that He was, and is, the great I AM:

> Your father Abraham rejoiced to see my day: and he saw it, and was glad.
> Then said the Jews unto him, Thou art not yet fifty years old, and hast thou seen Abraham?
> Jesus said unto them, Verily, verily, I say unto you, *Before Abraham was, I am.* (John 8:56–58 {1–59})

It is obvious that they understood that Jesus was saying that He was Jehovah, the great I AM, which they considered to be blasphemy, because the next verse records that • "Then took they up stones to cast at him: but Jesus hid himself, and went out of the temple, going through the midst of them, and so passed by" (John 8:59). Many King James Version Bibles carry cross references that link John 8:58 with John 17:5, 24—verses in which Christ speaks of the glory His Father had given Him before the foundation of the world.

Modern revelation clarifies that Jesus Christ is the great I AM. D&C 29:1 begins with the Savior's identifying words: • "Listen to the voice of Jesus Christ, your Redeemer, *the Great I AM.*"

D&C 38:1 begins in a similar manner: • "Thus saith the Lord your God, even Jesus Christ, *the Great I AM*, Alpha and Omega, the beginning and the end." Similarly, D&C 39:1 begins with the words • "Hearken and listen to the voice of him who is from all eternity to all eternity, *the Great I AM*, even Jesus Christ."

2. The First and the Last

The LORD Jehovah Is the First and the Last. (This comparison is covered earlier in this chapter so it will not be covered in such depth here.) Several passages indicate that the LORD is the First and the Last: • "I the LORD, *the first, and with the last*; I am he" (Isa. 41:4). • "Thus saith . . . the LORD of hosts; *I am the first, and I am the last*" (Isa. 44:6). And also, • "Hearken unto me, O Jacob and Israel, my called; I am he; *I am the first, I also am the last*. . . . Thus saith the LORD, thy Redeemer, the Holy One of Israel" (Isa. 48:12, 17).

Jesus Christ Is the First and the Last. New Testament passages which show that Jesus is the first and the last include: • "I am Alpha and Omega, *the first and the last*" (Rev. 1:11). • "Fear not; *I am the first and the last*" (Rev. 1:17–18). • "These things saith *the first and the last,* which was dead, and is alive" (Rev. 2:8). And also, • "I am Alpha and Omega, the beginning and the end, *the first and the last*" (Rev. 22:13). The Book of Mormon adds: • "Hearken unto me, O Jacob, and Israel my called, for I am he; *I am the first, and I am also the last*" (1 Ne. 20:12). And the Doctrine and Covenants contains the words of Christ saying: • "*I am the first and the last*; I am he who liveth, I am he who was slain; I am your advocate with the Father" (D&C 110:4).

3. The Beginning and the End, Alpha and Omega

The LORD Jehovah Is the Beginning and the End. Two other parallel phrases to "the first and the last" are found in the scriptures: "*the beginning and the end*" and "*Alpha and Omega.*" All three have the same connotations: present prior to the beginning of the world, and its creator; and present at the end of the world, its finisher, and controller of end-days events. While the Isaiah passages cited above don't use the words "the beginning and the end," nor "Alpha and Omega," their use of "the first and the last" clearly assert the same meaning. And the scriptures clearly put the LORD present as the earth was created: • "These are the generations of the heavens and of the earth when they were created, in the day that the LORD God made the earth and the heavens" (Gen. 2:4. See also Gen. 1:26–27; 6:7; Ps. 148:5; Isa. 40:28; 41:20; 42:5; 45:18)

Jesus Christ Is the Beginning and the End and also Alpha and Omega. Many of the passages that say Christ is "the beginning and the end" also use the words "Alpha and Omega." For instance, • "*I am Alpha and Omega, the beginning and the ending,* saith the Lord" (Rev. 1:8). • "*I am Alpha and Omega, the beginning and the end*" (Rev. 21:6. See also Rev. 22:13; 3 Ne. 9:18; 19:1; 35:1; 38:1; 45:7; 54:1; 84:120). Other passages include: • "Believe on the name of the Lord Jesus, who was on the earth, and is to come, *the beginning and the end*" (D&C 49:12), also, • "Behold, and hearken unto the voice of him who has all power, who is from everlasting to everlasting, even *Alpha and Omega, the beginning and the end*" (D&C 61:1), and again, • ". . . that your fastings and your mourning might come up into the ears of the Lord of Sabaoth, which is by interpretation, the creator of the first day, *the beginning and the end*" (D&C 95:7).

4. The Savior

The LORD Jehovah Is the Savior. Old Testament passages repeatedly speak of the LORD as being a savior. • "The LORD is my rock, and my fortress, and my deliverer; The God of my rock; in him will I trust: he is my shield, and the horn of my salvation, my high tower, and my refuge, *my saviour*" (2 Sam. 22:2–3). • "Remember me, O LORD, . . . They forgat *God their saviour,* which had done great things in Egypt" (Ps. 106:4, 21). • "I am the LORD thy God, the Holy One of Israel, *thy Saviour*" (Isa. 43:3). • "I, even I, am the LORD; and *beside me there is no saviour*" (Isa. 43:11). • "Who hath told it from that time? have not I the LORD? and there is no God else beside me; a just God and a *Saviour;* there is none beside me" (Isa. 45:21). • "I the LORD am *thy Saviour* and thy *Redeemer,* the mighty One of Jacob" (Isa. 49:26; 60:16). • "Yet I am the LORD thy God from the land of Egypt, and thou shalt know no god but me: for *there is no saviour beside me*" (Hos. 13:4).

Jesus Christ Is the Savior. Numerous New Testament and Doctrine and Covenants passages clearly indicate that Jesus is the Savior: • "For unto you is born this day in the city of David *a Saviour, which is Christ the Lord*" (Luke 2:11). • "we have heard him ourselves, and know that this is indeed *the Christ, the Saviour of the world*" (John

4:42). • "Him hath God exalted with his right hand to be a Prince and *a Saviour,* for to give repentance to Israel, and forgiveness of sins" (Acts 5:31). • "Of this man's [King David's] seed hath God according to his promise raised unto Israel *a Saviour, Jesus*" (Acts 13:23). • "For the husband is the head of the wife, even as *Christ is the head of the church: and he is the saviour of the body*" (Eph. 5:23). • "For our conversation is in heaven; from whence also *we look for the Saviour, the Lord Jesus Christ*" (Phil. 3:20). • "But *is now made manifest by the appearing of our Saviour Jesus Christ,* who hath abolished death" (2 Tim. 1:10). • "Grace, mercy, and peace, from God the Father and *the Lord Jesus Christ our Saviour*" (Titus 1:4). • ". . . the Holy Ghost; Which he shed on us abundantly through *Jesus Christ our Saviour*" (Titus 3:5–6). • ". . . into the everlasting kingdom of *our Lord and Saviour Jesus Christ*" (2 Pet. 1:11). • "But grow in grace, and in the knowledge of *our Lord and Saviour Jesus Christ*" (2 Pet. 3:18). • "we have seen and do testify that the Father *sent the Son to be the Saviour of the world*" (1 Jn. 4:14). Latter-day Saint passages also indicate with clarity that Jesus Christ is the Savior: • "the Lamb of God is the Son of the Eternal Father, and *the Savior of the world*" (1 Ne. 13:40). • "witnessing unto the Father that ye are willing to take upon you the name of *Christ,* by baptism—yea, *by following your Lord and your Savior* down into the water" (2 Ne. 31:13). • "I have reason to bless my God and *my Savior Jesus Christ*" (3 Ne. 5:20). • "I am Alpha and Omega, Christ the Lord; . . . *come unto me thy Savior*" (D&C 19:1, 41). • "we know that justification through the grace of our Lord and *Savior Jesus Christ* is just and true" (D&C 20:30). • "even Jesus Christ the Son of the living God, *the Savior of the world*" (D&C 42:1). • "I know that this record is true, through the blessing of *our Lord and Savior, Jesus Christ*" (D&C 138:60).

5. The Redeemer

The LORD Jehovah Is the Redeemer. • "I will help thee, saith the LORD, and *thy redeemer,* the Holy One of Israel" (Isa. 41:14). • "Thus saith the LORD *thy redeemer,* and he that formed thee from the womb, I am the LORD that maketh all things" (Isa. 44:24). • "Thus saith *the LORD, thy Redeemer,* the Holy One of Israel; I am the LORD thy God which teacheth thee to profit" (Isa. 48:17). • "all flesh shall know that I the LORD am thy Saviour and *thy Redeemer,* the mighty One of Jacob" (Isa. 49:26).

Jesus Christ Is the Redeemer. • "Being justified freely by his grace through *the redemption that is in Christ Jesus*" (Rom. 3:24). • "in Christ Jesus, who of God is made unto us wisdom, and righteousness, and sanctification, and *redemption*" (1 Cor. 1:30). • "*Christ hath redeemed us* from the curse of the law" (Gal. 3:13). • "Jesus Christ . . . In whom *we have redemption through his blood,* the forgiveness of sins, according to the riches of his grace" (Eph. 1:5, 7). • ". . . his dear Son: In whom *we have redemption through his blood,* even the forgiveness of sins" (Col. 1:13–14). • "our Saviour Jesus Christ; Who gave himself for us, *that he might redeem us* from all iniquity" (Titus 2:13–14). • "Christ being come an high priest . . . entered in once into the holy place, having *obtained eternal redemption for us*" (Heb. 9:11–12). • "ye were not *redeemed* with corruptible things, . . . But with the precious blood of Christ" (1 Pet. 1:18–19). Latter-day Saint scripture also affirms that Jesus Christ is the Redeemer: • "they brought them to the knowledge of the Lord their God, and to rejoice in *Jesus Christ their Redeemer*" (Alma 37:9). • "And then shall they know *their Redeemer, who is Jesus Christ,* the Son of God" (3 Ne. 5:26). • "listen to the words of *Jesus Christ, your Lord and your Redeemer*" (D&C 15:1). • "Behold, I, Jesus Christ, your Lord and your God, and *your Redeemer,* by the power of my Spirit have spoken it" (D&C 18:47).

• "Listen to the voice of *Jesus Christ, your Redeemer,* the Great I AM" (D&C 29:1).

6. The Holy One of Israel

The LORD *Jehovah Is the Holy One of Israel.* • "For the LORD is our defence; and the *Holy One of Israel* is our king" (Ps. 89:18). • "the remnant of Israel, . . . shall stay upon *the* LORD, *the Holy One of Israel,* in truth" (Isa. 10:20). • "thus saith *the Lord* GOD, *the Holy One of Israel*" (Isa. 30:15). • "saith the LORD, and thy redeemer, *the Holy One of Israel*" (Isa. 41:14). • "I am the LORD thy God, *the Holy One of Israel,* thy Saviour" (Isa. 43:3). • "Thus saith the LORD, your redeemer, *the Holy One of Israel*" (Isa. 43:14). • "As for our redeemer, the LORD of hosts is his name, *the Holy One of Israel*" (Isa. 47:4). • "she hath been proud against the LORD, against *the Holy One of Israel*" (Jer. 50:29). • "the heathen shall know that I am the LORD, *the Holy One in Israel*" (Ezek. 39:7).

Jesus Christ Is the Holy One of Israel. In the New Testament the complete phrase "Holy One of Israel" is not used in reference to Jesus Christ. Rather, he is simply termed the "Holy One" or "the Holy One of God." For instance: • "a man with an unclean spirit . . . cried out, Saying, . . . I know thee who thou art, *the Holy One of God*" (Mark 1:23–24; Luke 4:33–34). • "the God of our fathers, hath glorified his Son Jesus; whom ye delivered up, and denied him in the presence of Pilate, when he was determined to let him go. . . . *ye denied the Holy One* and the Just" (Acts 3:13–14). • "God hath . . . raised up Jesus again; as it is also written in the second psalm, Thou art my Son, this day have I begotten thee. . . . Wherefore he saith also in another psalm, Thou shalt not suffer *thine Holy One* to see corruption" (Acts 13:33–35). • "we have an advocate with the Father, Jesus Christ the righteous: . . . ye have an unction from *the Holy One,* and ye know all things" (1 Jn. 2:1, 20). The Book of Mormon, however, refers repeatedly to Jesus Christ as the Holy One of Israel: • "they will reject *the Holy One of Israel, the true Messiah,* their Redeemer and their God" (2 Ne. 1:10). • "the Lord God, *the Holy One of Israel,* should manifest himself unto them in the flesh; and after he should manifest himself they should scourge him and crucify him" (2 Ne. 6:9). • "this prophet of whom Moses spake was *the Holy One of Israel;* wherefore, he shall execute judgment in righteousness" (1 Ne. 22:21). • "the righteous must be led up as calves of the stall, and *the Holy One of Israel must reign* in dominion, and might, and power, and great glory" (1 Ne. 22:24). • "if the day shall come that *they will reject the Holy One of Israel, the true Messiah,* their Redeemer and their God, behold, the judgments of him that is just shall rest upon them" (2 Ne. 1:10). • "the bodies and the spirits of men will be restored one to the other; and it is by the power of the resurrection of *the Holy One of Israel*" (2 Ne. 9:12). • "O the greatness of the mercy of *our God, the Holy One of Israel!* For he delivereth his saints from that awful monster the devil, and death, and hell" (2 Ne. 9:19). • "the right way is to believe in Christ, and deny him not; and *Christ is the Holy One of Israel*" (2 Ne. 25:29). • "For thy maker, thy husband, the Lord of Hosts is his name; and *thy Redeemer, the Holy One of Israel*—the God of the whole earth shall he be called" (3 Ne. 22:5; see Isa. 54:5).

7. The Mighty God of Jacob

The LORD *Jehovah Is the Mighty One of Jacob.* • "I have waited for thy salvation, O LORD. . . . the arms of his hands were made strong by the hands of the *mighty God of Jacob;* (from thence is the shepherd, the stone of Israel:)" (Gen. 49:18, 24). • "he [David] sware unto the LORD, and vowed unto *the mighty God of Jacob*" (Ps. 132:2).

• "Until I find out a place for the LORD, an habitation for the *mighty God of Jacob*" (Ps. 132:5). • "all flesh shall know that I the LORD am thy Saviour and thy Redeemer, *the mighty One of Jacob*" (Isa. 49:26). • "and thou shalt know that I the LORD am thy Saviour and thy Redeemer, *the mighty One of Jacob*" (Isa. 60:16).

Jesus Christ Is the Mighty One of Jacob. • "and all flesh shall know that I, the Lord, am thy Savior and thy Redeemer, *the Mighty One of Jacob*" (1 Ne. 21:26; see Isa. 49:26). • "the Messiah . . . all flesh shall know that I the Lord am thy Savior and thy Redeemer, *the Mighty One of Jacob*" (2 Ne. 6:14, 18). • "O Lord, remember thy servant, Joseph Smith, Jun. . . . how *he has covenanted with Jehovah, and vowed to thee, O Mighty God of Jacob*" (D&C 109:68).

8. The Rock

The LORD Jehovah Is the Rock. • "There is none holy as the LORD: for there is none beside thee: *neither is there any rock like our God*" (1 Sam. 2:2). • "*The LORD is my rock*, and my fortress, and my deliverer" (2 Sam. 22:2). • "For who is God, save the LORD? and *who is a rock, save our God?*" (2 Sam. 22:32). • "The LORD liveth; and *blessed be my rock*; and exalted be *the God of the rock of my salvation*" (2 Sam. 22:47). • "*The LORD is my rock*, and my fortress, and my deliverer; my God, my strength, in whom I will trust; my buckler, and the horn of my salvation, and my high tower" (Ps. 18:2). • "The LORD liveth; and *blessed be my rock*; and let the God of my salvation be exalted" (Ps. 18:46). • "the LORD is my defence; and my God is *the rock of my refuge*" (Ps. 94:22).

Jesus Christ Is the Rock. • "I would not that ye should be ignorant, how that all our fathers . . . did all drink the same spiritual drink: for they drank of that spiritual Rock that followed them: and *that Rock was Christ*" (1 Cor. 10:1, 4). • "acceptable to God by Jesus Christ. . . . *a stone of stumbling, and a rock of offence*, even to them which stumble at the word, being disobedient" (1 Pet. 2:5, 8). • "in them shall be written my gospel, saith the Lamb, and *my rock* and my salvation" (1 Ne. 13:36). • "Rejoice, O my heart, and cry unto the Lord, and say: O Lord, I will praise thee forever; yea, my soul will rejoice in thee, *my God, and the rock of my salvation*" (2 Ne. 4:30). • "I know that ye know that in the body he shall show himself unto those at Jerusalem, . . . O, my beloved brethren, . . . come unto that God who is *the rock* of your salvation" (2 Ne. 9:5, 45). • "remember that it is upon *the rock of our Redeemer, who is Christ*, the Son of God, that ye must build your foundation" (Hel. 5:12). • "I say unto you, ye must repent, and be baptized in my name, and become as a little child, . . . this is my doctrine, and whoso buildeth upon this *buildeth upon my rock*" (3 Ne. 11:38–39). • "Behold, I am Jesus Christ, . . . whosoever is of my church, and endureth of my church to the end, *him will I establish upon my rock*" (D&C 10:57, 69). • "Wait a little longer, until you shall have my word, *my rock*, my church, and my gospel . . . Behold, I am Jesus Christ, the Son of God" (D&C 11:16, 28). • "Build upon *my rock, which is my gospel*; . . . I am Jesus Christ, the Son of God" (D&C 11:24, 28). • "in them are all things written concerning the foundation of my church, my gospel, and *my rock*. . . . Behold, I, Jesus Christ, . . . have spoken it" (D&C 18:4, 47). • "I am the good shepherd, and *the stone of Israel*. He that buildeth upon *this rock* shall never fall" (D&C 50:44).

9. The Stone of Israel

The LORD Jehovah Is a Stone. • "O LORD. . . the shepherd, *the stone of Israel*" (Gen. 49:18, 24). • "Sanctify the LORD . . . he shall be for a sanctuary; but for *a stone of* *stumbling* and for *a rock of offence* to both the houses of Israel" (Isa. 8:13–14). • "Sanctify the Lord of Hosts himself, . . . he shall be for a sanctuary; but for *a stone of stumbling*, and for *a rock of offense* to both the houses of Israel" (2 Ne. 18:13–14).

Jesus Christ Is a Stone. • "Jesus saith unto them, Did ye never read in the scriptures, The *stone* which the builders rejected, the same is become the head of the corner: this is the Lord's doing, and it is marvellous in our eyes? . . . And whosoever shall fall on this *stone* shall be broken: but on whomsoever it shall fall, it will grind him to powder" (Matt. 21:42, 44; Mark 12:10–11; Luke 20:17–18). • "This is the *stone* which was set at nought of you builders, which is become the head of the corner" (Acts 4:11). • "ye are no more strangers and foreigners, but fellowcitizens with the saints, and of the household of God; And are built upon the foundation of the apostles and prophets, *Jesus Christ himself being the chief corner stone*" (Eph. 2:19–20). • "the Lord is gracious. *To whom coming, as unto a living stone,* disallowed indeed of men, but chosen of God, and precious" (1 Pet. 2:3–4). • "I lay in Sion *a chief corner stone, elect, precious*: and he that believeth on him shall not be confounded. Unto you therefore which believe he is precious: but unto them which be disobedient, the *stone* which the builders disallowed, the same is made the head of the corner, And *a stone of stumbling*" (1 Pet. 2:6–8). • "if the Gentiles shall hearken unto the Lamb of God in that day that he shall manifest himself unto them in word, and also in power, in very deed, unto the taking away of their *stumbling blocks*" (1 Ne. 14:1). • "O Lord, wilt thou encircle me around in the robe of thy righteousness! . . . Wilt thou not place a *stumbling block* in my way . . . hedge not up my way, but the ways of mine enemy" (2 Ne. 4:33). • "he shall be for a sanctuary; but for a *stone of stumbling*, and for a *rock of offense* to both the houses of Israel" (2 Ne. 18:14). • "by the stumbling of the Jews they will *reject the stone upon which they might build and have safe foundation.* But behold, according to the scriptures, *this stone shall become the great, and the last, and the only sure foundation*, upon which the Jews can build" (Jacob 4:15–16). • "the Father and I are one. . . . I am in your midst, and I am the good shepherd, and *the stone of Israel*" (D&C 50:43–44).

10. The Creator (See also Chapter 9)

The LORD *Jehovah Created the Heavens, Earth and Man.* • "These are the generations of the heavens and of the earth when they were created, in the day that the LORD *God made the earth and the heavens*" (Gen. 2:4). • "the LORD said, I will destroy *man whom I have created*" (Gen. 6:7). • "praise the name of the LORD: for *he commanded, and they were created*" (Ps. 148:5). • "the everlasting God, the LORD, *the Creator of the ends of the earth,* fainteth not" (Isa. 40:28). • "Thus saith God the LORD, *he that created the heavens,* and stretched them out; *he that spread forth the earth,* and that which cometh out of it; he that giveth breath unto the people upon it" (Isa. 42:5). • "thus saith the LORD *that created the heavens; God himself that formed the earth and made it*; he hath established it, he created it not in vain, he formed it to be inhabited" (Isa. 45:18). • "For, lo, *he that formeth the mountains, and createth the wind,* . . . The LORD, The God of hosts, is his name" (Amos 4:13).

Jesus Christ Created the Heavens, Earth and Man. • "we are his workmanship, *created in Christ Jesus unto good works*" (Eph. 2:10). • "he shall be called Jesus Christ, the Son of God, the Father of heaven and earth, *the Creator of all things from the beginning*" (Mosiah 3:8). • "we believe in Jesus Christ, the Son of God, *who created heaven and earth,* and all things" (Mosiah 4:2). • "the Lord their God, their Redeemer, . . . Behold, *the Lord hath created the earth* that it should be inhabited; and *he hath created his children* that they should possess it" (1 Ne. 17:30, 36). • "Know ye not that I, the Lord your God, *have created all men"* (2 Ne. 29:7). • "we believe in Jesus Christ, the Son of God, *who created heaven and earth,* and all things" (Mosiah 4:2). • "be steadfast and immovable, . . . that Christ, the Lord God Omnipotent, may seal you his, . . . may have everlasting salvation and eternal life, through the . . . *mercy of him who created all things, in heaven and in earth,* who is God above all" (Mosiah 5:15). • *"the Lord had created all men,* and had also redeemed all men; and, in the end, all men should have eternal life" (Alma 1:4). • "Jesus Christ, the Son of God, the Father of heaven and of earth, *the Creator of all things from the beginning"* (Hel. 14:12). • "Behold, I am Jesus Christ the Son of God. *I created the heavens and the earth, and all things that in them are"* (3 Ne. 9:15). • "I am Jesus Christ, the Son of the living God, *who created the heavens and the earth,* a light which cannot be hid in darkness" (D&C 14:9). • "that your fastings and your mourning might come up into the ears of the Lord of Sabaoth, which is by interpretation, *the creator of the first day,* the beginning and the end" (D&C 95:7).

II. The King

The Lord Jehovah Is King. • *"the Lord your God was your king"* (1 Sam. 12:12). • "The Lord is King for ever and ever: the heathen are perished out of his land" (Ps. 10:16). • *"Who is this King of glory?"* The Lord strong and mighty, the Lord mighty in battle" (Ps. 24:8). • *"The Lord of hosts, he is the King* of glory" (Ps. 24:10). • "For the Lord most high is terrible; *he is a great King over all the earth"* (Ps. 47:2). • "O Lord of hosts, *my King, and my God"* (Ps. 84:3). • "For the Lord is our defence; and *the Holy One of Israel is our king"* (Ps. 89:18). • "For the Lord is a great God, and *a great King above all gods"* (Ps. 95:3). • "make a joyful noise before *the Lord, the King"* (Ps. 98:6). • "mine eyes have seen *the King, the Lord* of hosts" (Isa. 6:5). • "the Lord is our judge, the Lord is our lawgiver, *the Lord is our king;* he will save us" (Isa. 33:22). • "I am the Lord, your Holy One, the creator of Israel, *your King"* (Isa. 43:15). • "But the Lord is the true God, he is the living God, and *an everlasting king"* (Jer. 10:10). • "As I live, saith *the King, whose name is the Lord of hosts"* (Jer. 46:18). • "his chosen young men are gone down to the slaughter, saith *the King, whose name is the Lord of hosts"* (Jer. 48:15). • "And the Lord *shall be king over all the earth:* in that day shall there be one Lord, and his name one" (Zech. 14:9). • "every one that is left of all the nations which came against Jerusalem shall even go up from year to year *to worship the King, the Lord of hosts,* and to keep the feast of tabernacles. And it shall be, that whoso will not come up of all the families of the earth unto Jerusalem *to worship the King, the Lord of hosts"* (Zech. 14:16–17). • *"for I am a great King,* saith the Lord of hosts, and my name is dreadful among the heathen" (Mal. 1:14).

Jesus Christ Is King. • "And Jesus stood before the governor: and the governor asked him, saying, Art thou *the King of the Jews?* And Jesus said unto him, Thou sayest" (Matt. 27:11). • "And set up over his head his accusation written, THIS IS JESUS THE KING OF THE JEWS" (Matt. 27:37). • "Let *Christ the King of Israel* descend now from the cross, that we may see and believe" (Mark 15:32). • "We found this fellow perverting the nation, and forbidding to give tribute to Cæsar, saying that *he himself is Christ a King"* (Luke 23:2). • "When Jesus therefore perceived that they would come and take him by force, *to make him a king,* he departed again into a mountain himself alone" (John 6:15). • "Then Pilate entered into the judgment hall again, and called Jesus, and said unto him, Art thou *the King of the Jews?"* (John 18:33). • "Pilate therefore said unto him, Art thou a king then? Jesus answered, *Thou sayest that I am a king.*

To this end was I born" (John 18:37). • "Pilate wrote a title, and put it on the cross. And the writing was, JESUS OF NAZARETH THE KING OF THE JEWS" (John 19:19). • "these all do contrary to the decrees of Cæsar, saying that *there is another king, one Jesus*" (Acts 17:7). • "our Lord Jesus Christ: . . , who is the blessed and only Potentate, *the King of kings,* and Lord of lords" (1 Tim. 6:14–15). • "These shall make war with the Lamb, and the Lamb shall overcome them: for he is Lord of lords, and *King of kings*" (Rev. 17:14). • "they sing . . . the song of the Lamb, saying, Great and marvellous are thy works, Lord God Almighty; just and true are thy ways, *thou King of saints*" (Rev. 15:3). • "These shall make war with the Lamb, and the Lamb shall overcome them: for he is Lord of lords, and *King of kings*" (Rev. 17:14). • "And he hath on his vesture and on his thigh a name written, KING OF KINGS AND LORD OF LORDS" (Rev. 19:16). • "Let the dead speak forth anthems of eternal praise *to the King Immanuel,* . . . and all ye seas and dry lands tell the wonders of *your Eternal King!*" (D&C 128:22–23). • *"I am Messiah, the King of Zion,* the Rock of Heaven, which is broad as eternity" (Moses 7:53).

12. Salvation

Salvation Is through the LORD Jehovah. • "I have waited for *thy salvation, O LORD"* (Gen. 49:18). • "The LORD is my strength and song, and *he is become my salvation*: he is my God" (Ex. 15:2). • "Sing unto the LORD, all the earth; *shew forth from day to day his salvation"* (1 Chr. 16:23). • "The God of my rock; in him will I trust: he is my shield, and *the horn of my salvation"* (2 Sam. 22:3). • "The LORD liveth; and blessed be my rock; and exalted be the God of *the rock of my salvation"* (2 Sam. 22:47). • *"Salvation belongeth unto the LORD"* (Ps. 3:8). • "The LORD is my rock, and my fortress, and my deliverer; my God, my strength, in whom I will trust; my buckler, and *the horn of my salvation"* (Ps. 18:2). • "Shew me thy ways, O LORD; teach me thy paths. Lead me in thy truth, and teach me: for *thou art the God of my salvation"* (Ps. 25:4–5). • "The LORD is my light and *my salvation;* whom shall I fear?" (Ps. 27:1). • "my soul shall be joyful in the LORD: *it shall rejoice in his salvation"* (Ps. 35:9). • "Shew us thy mercy, O LORD, and *grant us thy salvation"* (Ps. 85:7). • "The LORD is my strength and song, and *is become my salvation"* (Ps. 118:14). • "I will trust, and not be afraid: for the LORD JEHOVAH is my strength and my song; *he also is become my salvation"* (Isa. 12:2). • "truly in *the LORD our God is the salvation of Israel"* (Jer. 3:23). • "I will look unto the LORD; I will wait for *the God of my salvation"* (Mic. 7:7). • "I will rejoice in the LORD, I will joy in *the God of my salvation"* (Hab. 3:18).

Salvation Is through Jesus Christ. • "God hath not appointed us to wrath, but *to obtain salvation by our Lord Jesus Christ"* (1 Thess. 5:9). • "brethren beloved of the Lord, because God hath from the beginning *chosen you to salvation* . . . to the obtaining of the glory of our Lord Jesus Christ" (2 Thess. 2:13–14). • "we see Jesus, who was made a little lower than the angels for the suffering of death, crowned with glory and honour; that he by the grace of God should taste death for every man. For it became him, for whom are all things, and by whom are all things, in bringing many sons unto glory, to make *the captain of their salvation* perfect through sufferings" (Heb. 2:9–10). • "account that *the longsuffering of our Lord is salvation;* even as our beloved brother Paul also according to the wisdom given unto him hath written unto you . . . grow in grace, and in the knowledge of our Lord and Saviour Jesus Christ" (2 Pet. 3:15, 18). • "I heard a great voice of much people in heaven, saying, Alleluia; *Salvation,* and glory, and honour, and power, unto the Lord our God" (Rev. 19:1).

• *"all the earth shall see the salvation of the Lord,* saith the prophet; every nation, kindred, tongue and people shall be blessed. And I, Nephi, have written these things unto my people, that perhaps I might persuade them that they would remember the Lord their Redeemer" (1 Ne. 19:17–18). • "my beloved brethren, I would that ye should come unto Christ, who is the Holy One of Israel, and *partake of his salvation,* and the power of his redemption" (Om. 1:26). • "For salvation cometh to none such except it be through repentance and faith on the Lord Jesus Christ" (Mosiah 3:12). • "I say unto you, that there shall be no other name given nor any other way nor means *whereby salvation can come* unto the children of men, only in and through the name of Christ" (Mosiah 3:17). • "believe that *salvation was, and is, and is to come,* in and through the atoning blood of Christ, the Lord Omnipotent" (Mosiah 3:18). • "prepare ye the way of the Lord, for the time is at hand that all men shall reap a reward of their works, according to that which they have been—if they have been righteous they shall reap the *salvation of their souls,* according to the power and deliverance of Jesus Christ" (Alma 9:28). • "in the beginning of the seventh thousand years will the Lord God sanctify the earth, and complete *the salvation of man,* and judge all things, and shall redeem all things, except that which he hath not put into his power" (D&C 77:12). • "And then cometh the day when the arm of the Lord shall be revealed in power in convincing the nations, the heathen nations, the house of Joseph, of *the gospel of their salvation"* (D&C 90:10). • "now we ask thee, Holy Father, in the name of Jesus Christ, the Son of thy bosom, *in whose name alone salvation can be administered* to the children of men" (D&C 109:4).

13. The God of Abraham, Isaac, and Jacob

The Lord Jehovah Is the God of Abraham, Isaac and Jacob. • "Jacob said, O *God of my father Abraham, and God of my father Isaac,* the Lord" (Gen. 32:9). • "when the Lord saw that he turned aside to see, . . . I am the God of thy father, *the God of Abraham, the God of Isaac, and the God of Jacob"* (Ex. 3:4, 6). • "Thus shalt thou say unto the children of Israel, The Lord God of your fathers, *the God of Abraham, the God of Isaac, and the God of Jacob,* hath sent me unto you" (Ex. 3:15). • "say unto them, The Lord God of your fathers, *the God of Abraham, of Isaac, and of Jacob,* appeared unto me" (Ex. 3:16). • "That they may believe that the Lord God of their fathers, *the God of Abraham, the God of Isaac, and the God of Jacob,* hath appeared unto thee" (Ex. 4:5). • *"I appeared unto Abraham, unto Isaac, and unto Jacob,* by the name of God Almighty, but by my name JEHOVAH was I not known to them" (Ex. 6:3). • "I will bring you in unto the land, concerning the which *I did swear to give it to Abraham, to Isaac, and to Jacob;* and I will give it you for an heritage: I am the Lord" (Ex. 6:8). • "the Lord said unto Moses, Depart, and go up . . . unto *the land which I sware unto Abraham, to Isaac, and to Jacob,* saying, Unto thy seed will I give it" (Ex. 33:1). • "the Lord's anger was kindled . . . and he sware, saying, Surely none of the men . . . shall see *the land which I sware unto Abraham, unto Isaac, and unto Jacob"* (Num. 32:10–11). • "go in and possess *the land which the Lord* sware unto *your fathers, Abraham, Isaac, and Jacob"* (Deut. 1:8). • "that he may perform *the word which the Lord sware unto thy fathers, Abraham, Isaac, and Jacob"* (Deut. 9:5). • "the land which *the Lord sware unto thy fathers, to Abraham, to Isaac, and to Jacob,* to give them" (Deut. 30:20). • "the Lord said unto him, *This is the land which I sware unto Abraham, unto Isaac, and unto Jacob"* (Deut. 34:4).

Jesus Christ Is the God of Abraham, Isaac and Jacob. • "But as touching the resurrection of the dead, have ye not read that which was spoken unto you by God, saying, *I am the God of Abraham, and the God of Isaac, and the God of Jacob?* God is not the God of the dead, but of the living" (Matt. 22:31–32; Mark 12:26). • "I am the Lord your God, even *the God of your fathers, the God of Abraham and of Isaac and of Jacob"* (D&C 136:21). • "I, the Lord God, make you free, therefore ye are free indeed; and the law also maketh you free. . . . Behold, *this is the law I gave unto my servant Nephi, and thy fathers, Joseph, and Jacob, and Isaac, and Abraham,* and all mine ancient prophets and apostles" (D&C 98:8, 32). • "thus saith the Lord . . . *I, the Lord, justified my servants Abraham, Isaac, and Jacob"* (D&C 132:1). • "from Moses to Elijah, and from Elijah to John, who were with Christ in his resurrection, and the holy apostles, *with Abraham, Isaac, and Jacob, shall be in the presence of the Lamb.* And the graves of the saints shall be opened; and they shall come forth and stand on the right hand of the Lamb, when he shall stand upon Mount Zion" (D&C 133:55–56). • "Keep yourselves from evil to take the name of the Lord in vain, for *I am the Lord your God, even the God of your fathers, the God of Abraham and of Isaac and of Jacob"* (D&C 136:21).

14. Has Power, Is Omnipotent, Is Mighty

The Lord Jehovah Has Power, and Is Mighty • "For who is God, save the Lord? and who is a rock, save our God? *God is my strength and power:* and he maketh my way perfect" (2 Sam. 22:32–33). • "O Lord God of our fathers, . . . and in thine hand *is there not power and might,* so that none is able to withstand thee?" (2 Chr. 20:6). • "Praise ye the Lord. Praise God in his sanctuary: praise him *in the firmament of his power"* (Ps. 150:1). • "I prayed unto the Lord, saying, Ah Lord God! behold, thou hast made the heaven and the earth *by thy great power and stretched out arm,* and there is nothing too hard for thee" (Jer. 32:16–17). • "O Lord God, . . . what God is there in heaven or in earth, that can do according to thy works, and *according to thy might?"* (Deut. 3:24). • "the Lord thy God brought thee out thence through a *mighty hand and by a stretched out arm"* (Deut. 5:15). • "the Lord thy God is among you, *a mighty God and terrible"* (Deut. 7:21). "the Lord your God is God of gods, and Lord of lords, *a great God, a mighty, and a terrible"* (Deut. 10:17). • "Who is this King of glory? The Lord *strong and mighty,* the Lord mighty in battle" (Ps. 24:8). • *"The mighty God,* even the Lord, hath spoken" (Ps. 50:1). "Therefore saith the Lord, the Lord of hosts, *the mighty One of Israel"* (Isa. 1:24). • "come into the mountain of the Lord, *to the mighty One of Israel"* (Isa. 30:29). • "the Great, *the Mighty God,* the Lord of hosts, is his name" (Jer. 32:18).

Jesus Christ Has Power and Is Omnipotent. • "Jesus . . . spake unto them, saying, *All power is given unto me in heaven and in earth"* (Matt. 28:18). • "The Father loveth the Son, and *hath given all things into his hand"* (John 3:35). • "that ye may know that *the Son of man hath power* on earth . . . when the multitudes saw it, they marvelled, and glorified God, which had *given such power"* (Matt. 9:6, 8). • "there be some of them that stand here, which shall not taste of death, till they have seen the kingdom of God *come with power"* (Mark 9:1) • "Jesus rebuked the unclean spirit, and healed the child, and . . . they were all amazed at *the mighty power of God"* (Luke 9:42–43). • "God anointed Jesus of Nazareth with the Holy Ghost and *with power"* (Acts 10:38). • "his Son Jesus Christ our Lord, which was . . . declared to be the *Son of God with power"* (Rom. 1:3–4). • "To the only wise God our Saviour, be glory and majesty, *dominion and power,* both now and ever" (Jude 1:25). • "Now is come salvation, and strength, and the kingdom of our God, and *the power of his Christ"* (Rev. 12:10).

• "they sing . . . the song of the Lamb, saying, . . . just and true are thy ways, thou King of saints. . . . And the temple was filled with smoke from the glory of God, and from *his power*" (Rev. 15:3, 8). • "I heard a great voice of much people in heaven, saying, Alleluia; Salvation, and glory, and honour, *and power*, unto the Lord our God: . . . for the marriage of the Lamb is come, . . . worship God: for the testimony of Jesus is the spirit of prophecy" (Rev. 19:1, 7, 10). • "I heard as it were the voice of a great multitude, . . . saying, Alleluia: for *the Lord God omnipotent reigneth*. . . . give honour to him: for the marriage of the Lamb is come" (Rev. 19:6–7). • "I, Nephi, beheld *the power* of the Lamb of God" (1 Ne. 14:14). • "the time cometh . . . that *with power, the Lord Omnipotent* who reigneth, who was, and is from all eternity to all eternity, shall come down from heaven among the children of men" (Mosiah 3:5). • "there shall be no other name given . . . whereby salvation can come unto the children of men, only in and through the name of *Christ, the Lord Omnipotent*" (Mosiah 3:17). • "through the atoning blood of Christ, *the Lord Omnipotent*" (Mosiah 3:18). • "through repentance and faith on the name of *the Lord God Omnipotent*" (Mosiah 3:21). • "that *Christ, the Lord God Omnipotent*, may seal you his" (Mosiah 5:15).

15. Everlasting

The LORD *Jehovah Is Everlasting.* • "Abraham planted a grove in Beer-sheba, and called there on the name of the LORD, *the everlasting God*" (Gen. 21:33). • "Blessed be the LORD God of Israel *from everlasting, and to everlasting*" (Ps. 41:13). • "LORD, thou hast been our dwelling place in all generations. Before . . . thou hadst formed the earth and the world, even *from everlasting to everlasting, thou art God*" (Ps. 90:1–2). • "Blessed be the LORD God of Israel *from everlasting to everlasting*" (Ps. 106:48). • "*the everlasting God*, the LORD, the Creator of the ends of the earth, fainteth not" (Isa. 40:28). • "the LORD shall be unto thee *an everlasting light*, and thy God thy glory" (Isa. 60:19). • "the LORD is the true God, he is the living God, and an everlasting king" (Jer. 10:10). • "Art thou not *from everlasting*, O LORD my God, mine Holy One?" (Hab. 1:12).

Jesus Christ Is Everlasting. • "He that believeth on the Son *hath everlasting life*" (John 3:36). • "Labour . . . for that meat *which endureth unto everlasting life*, which the Son of man shall give unto you" (John 6:27). • "in me first Jesus Christ might shew forth all longsuffering, for a pattern to them which should hereafter believe on him *to life everlasting*" (1 Tim. 1:16). • "into *the everlasting kingdom of our Lord* and Saviour Jesus Christ" (2 Pet. 1:11). • "then shall the fulness of the gospel of the Messiah come unto the Gentiles, . . . And then at that day will they not rejoice and give praise unto *their everlasting God*, their rock and their salvation?" (1 Ne. 15:13, 15). • "that Christ, the Lord God Omnipotent, may seal you his, that you may be brought to heaven, *that ye may have everlasting salvation and eternal life*, through the wisdom, and power, and justice, and mercy of him who created all things, in heaven and in earth, who is God above all" (Mosiah 5:15). • "I am Alpha and Omega, Christ the Lord; yea, even I am he, the beginning and the end, the Redeemer of the world. . . . behold, *I am endless*, . . . *for Endless is my name*" (D&C 19:1, 10).

16. Light

The LORD *Jehovah Is the Light.* • "thou wilt light my candle: *the* LORD *my God will enlighten my darkness*" (Ps. 18:28). • "*The* LORD *is my light* and my salvation; whom shall I fear?" (Ps. 27:1). • "they shall walk, O LORD, *in the light of thy countenance*" (Ps.

89:15). • "God is the LORD, which *hath shewed us light"* (Ps. 118:27). • "come ye, and let us *walk in the light of the LORD"* (Isa. 2:5). • *"I form the light,* and create darkness: I make peace, and create evil: I the LORD do all these things" (Isa. 45:7). • "Arise, shine; for *thy light is come,* and the glory of the LORD is risen upon thee" (Isa. 60:1). • "the LORD shall be unto thee *an everlasting light,* and thy God thy glory. . . .the LORD shall be *thine everlasting light"* (Isa. 60:19–20). • "the LORD shall be *a light unto me"* (Mi. 7:8).

Jesus Christ Is the Light. • "In the beginning was the Word, and the Word was with God, and the Word was God. The same was in the beginning with God. All things were made by him; and without him was not any thing made that was made. In him was life; and the life was the light of men. And *the light shineth in darkness"* (John 1:1–5). • "He [John the Baptist] was not that Light, but was sent to bear witness of that Light. *That was the true Light, which lighteth every man that cometh into the world.* He was in the world, and the world was made by him" (John 1:8–10). • "That Christ should suffer, and that he should be the first that should rise from the dead, and should *shew light unto the people"* (Acts 26:23). • "they being led, the Lord their God, their Redeemer, going before them, leading them by day and *giving light unto them by night"* (1 Ne. 17:30). • "I, the Lord, the king of heaven, will be their king, and *I will be a light unto them forever"* (2 Ne. 10:14). • "and joy because of *the light of Christ* unto life" (Alma 28:14). • "remember the words of *him who is the life and light of the world,* your Redeemer, your Lord and your God" (D&C 10:70). • *"the word of the Lord is truth, and whatsoever is truth is light,* and *whatsoever is light is Spirit,* even the Spirit of Jesus Christ" (D&C 84:45). • *"to give the light* of the knowledge of the glory of God in the face of Jesus Christ" (2 Cor. 4:6). • "Christ shall *give thee light"* (Eph. 5:14). • "joy because of *the light of Christ"* (Alma 28:14). • "man can be saved, only in and through Christ. Behold, *he is the life and the light of the world"* (Alma 38:9). • "ye know the light by which ye may judge, *which light is the light of Christ,* . . . ye should search diligently in the light of Christ that ye may know good from evil" (Moro. 7:18–19). • "I am Jesus Christ, the Son of God. . . . *I am the light which shineth in darkness"* (D&C 6:21). • "I am Jesus Christ, the Son of God. *I am the life and the light of the world"* (D&C 11:28). • "I am Jesus Christ, the Son of the living God, who created the heavens and the earth, *a light which cannot be hid* in darkness" (D&C 14:9). • "He that ascended up on high, . . . *the light of truth;* Which truth shineth. *This is the light of Christ"* (D&C 88:6–7).

17. Truth

The LORD Jehovah Is, and Is Characterized by, Truth. • "The LORD God, merciful and gracious, longsuffering, and *abundant in goodness and truth"* (Ex. 34:6). • "now the LORD shew *kindness and truth"* (2 Sam. 2:6). • "All the paths of the LORD are mercy and truth" (Ps. 25:10). • "O LORD *God of truth"* (Ps. 31:5). • "the word of the LORD is right; and *all his works are done in truth"* (Ps. 33:4). • "O LORD: let thy lovingkindness and *thy truth* continually preserve me" (Ps. Ps. 40:11). • "O LORD; *I will walk in thy truth"* (Ps. 86:11). • "the LORD is good; his mercy is everlasting; and *his truth endureth* to all generations" (Ps. 100:5). • *"the truth of the LORD* endureth for ever" (Ps. 117:2). • "O LORD, thou art my God; . . . thy counsels of old are *faithfulness and truth"* (Isa. 25:1). • "The LORD liveth, *in truth,* in judgment, and in righteousness" (Jer. 4:2).

Jesus Christ Is, and Is Characterized by, Truth. • *"grace and truth came by Jesus Christ"* (John 1:17). • "I say the *truth in Christ"* (Rom. 9:1). • "the *truth of Christ* is in me" (2 Cor. 11:10). • *"in truth,* Christ is preached" (Phil. 1:18). • "I speak the *truth* *in Christ,* and lie not" (1 Tim. 2:7). • "Grace be with you, mercy, and peace, from God the Father, and from the Lord Jesus Christ, the Son of the Father, *in truth* and love" (2 Jn. 1:3). • "declare the word according to *the truth which is in Christ"* (Enos 1:26). • "Jesus Christ shall come, . . . full of grace, and mercy, and *truth"* (Alma 5:48). • "Christ. . . . is *the word of truth* and righteousness" (Alma 38:9). • *"the light of truth; Which* truth shineth. This is the light of Christ" (D&C 88:6–7). • "mine Only Begotten Son, who *is full of grace and truth,* which is Jesus Christ" (Moses 6:52).

18. Grace and Graciousness

The LORD *Jehovah Possesses, and Is Characterized by, Grace and Graciousness.* "The LORD God, *merciful and gracious,* longsuffering, and abundant in goodness and truth" (Ex. 34:6). • "the LORD *will give grace* and glory" (Ps. 84:11). • "The LORD make his face shine upon thee, and *be gracious unto thee"* (Num. 6:25). • *"the* LORD *was gracious* unto them, and had compassion on them, and had respect unto them" (2 Kgs. 13:23). • "the LORD your God is *gracious and merciful"* (2 Chr. 30:9). • "O Lord, art a God full of compassion, and *gracious"* (Ps. 86:15). • "The LORD is *merciful and gracious,* slow to anger, and plenteous in mercy" (Ps. 103:8). • *"the* LORD *is gracious* and full of compassion" (Ps. 111:4). • *"Gracious is the* LORD, and righteous" (Ps. 116:5). • "therefore will the LORD wait, that he may *be gracious unto you"* (Isa. 30:18). • "turn unto the LORD your God: for *he is gracious* and merciful, slow to anger, and of great kindness" (Joel 2:13). • "I pray thee, O LORD, . . . I knew that *thou art a gracious God,* and merciful, slow to anger, and of great kindness" (Jonah 4:2).

Jesus Christ Possesses, and Is Characterized by, Grace and Graciousness. • "through the *grace of the Lord Jesus Christ* we shall be saved" (Acts 15:11). • *"the gift by grace,* which is by one man, Jesus Christ" (Rom. 5:15). • "even so *might grace reign through righteousness* unto eternal life by Jesus Christ our Lord" (Rom. 5:21). • *"The grace of our Lord* Jesus Christ be with you" (Rom. 16:20; 1 Cor. 16:23; Gal. 6:18; Phil. 4:23; 1 Thess. 5:28; Philem. 1:25; Rev. 22:21). • *"The grace of our Lord Jesus Christ* be with you all" (Rom. 16:24). • *"the grace of God* which is given you by Jesus Christ" (1 Cor. 1:4). • "ye know *the grace of our Lord* Jesus Christ" (2 Cor. 8:9). • *"The grace of the Lord* Jesus Christ" (2 Cor. 13:14). • "unto every one of us is *given grace* according to the measure of *the gift of Christ"* (Eph. 4:7). • *"grace, which was given us in Christ Jesus* before the world began" (2 Tim. 1:9). • "be strong in *the grace that is in Christ Jesus"* (2 Tim. 2:1). • "the grace that is to be brought unto you at the revelation of Jesus Christ" (1 Pet. 1:13). • "Jesus Christ shall come, yea, the Son, the Only Begotten of the Father, *full of grace,* and mercy, and truth" (Alma 5:48). • "we know that justification *through the grace of our Lord* and Savior Jesus Christ is just and true" (D&C 20:30). • *"the grace of your Lord* Jesus Christ" (D&C 21:1).

19. Mercy

The LORD *Jehovah Is Merciful.* • "the LORD thy God, he is God, the faithful God, which *keepeth covenant and mercy* with them that love him" (Deut. 7:9). • "give thanks unto the LORD; for he is good; for *his mercy endureth for ever"* (1 Chr. 16:34). • "and praised the LORD, saying, For he is good; for *his mercy endureth for ever"* (2 Chr. 5:13; 7:3; Ezra 3:11). • "Praise the LORD of hosts: for the LORD is good; for *his mercy endureth for ever"* (Jer. 33:11). • "Remember, O LORD, *thy tender mercies and thy lovingkindnesses;* for they have been ever of old" (Ps. 25:6). • "All the paths of the LORD are *mercy and truth* unto such as keep his covenant and his testimonies" (Ps. 25:10).

• "the LORD is good; *his mercy is everlasting;* and his truth endureth to all generations" (Ps. 100:5). • *"the mercy of the* LORD is from everlasting to everlasting upon them that fear him" (Ps. 103:17). • "with everlasting kindness *will I have mercy* on thee, saith the LORD thy Redeemer" (Isa. 54:8). • "Praise the LORD of hosts: for the LORD is good; for *his mercy endureth for ever"* (Jer. 33:11).

Jesus Christ Is Merciful. • *"I obtained mercy,* that in me first Jesus Christ might shew forth all longsuffering" (1 Tim. 1:16). • *"looking for the mercy of our Lord Jesus Christ* unto eternal life" (Jude 1:21). • *"O have mercy,* and apply the atoning blood of Christ" (Mosiah 4:2). • "Jesus Christ shall come, . . . full of grace, and *mercy,* and truth" (Alma 5:48). • "I did cry out unto the Lord Jesus Christ *for mercy"* (Alma 38:8). • *"according to the mercy,* and the justice, and the holiness which is in Christ, who was before the world began" (3 Ne. 26:5). • "may Christ lift thee up, and may his . . . *mercy and long-suffering,* and the hope of his glory and of eternal life, rest in your mind forever" (Moro. 9:25). • "Listen to the voice of Jesus Christ, your Redeemer, the Great I AM, *whose arm of mercy* hath atoned for your sins" (D&C 29:1).

20. Makes and Fulfills Covenants

The LORD *Jehovah Makes/Fulfills Covenants.* • "In the same day *the LORD made a covenant with Abram"* (Gen. 15:18). • "Behold *the blood of the covenant,* which the LORD hath made with you concerning all these words" (Ex. 24:8). • "Behold, *I make a covenant:* . . . and all the people among which thou art shall see the work of the LORD" (Ex. 34:10). • "the LORD said unto Moses, Write thou these words: for after the tenor of these words *I have made a covenant with thee* and with Israel" (Ex. 34:27). • *"I will not . . . break my covenant* with them: for I am the LORD their God" (Lev. 26:44). • "I will for their sakes *remember the covenant* of their ancestors, whom I brought forth out of the land of Egypt in the sight of the heathen, that I might be their God: I am the LORD" (Lev. 26:45). • *"the ark of the covenant* of the LORD went before them" (Num. 10:33). • *"it is a covenant of salt* for ever before the LORD unto thee and to thy seed with thee" (Num. 18:19). • "Take heed unto yourselves, *lest ye forget the covenant* of the LORD your God, which he made with you" (Deut. 4:23). • "The LORD our God made *a covenant with us in Horeb"* (Deut. 5:2). • "the LORD thy God, he is God, the faithful God, *which keepeth covenant and mercy with them that love him* and keep his commandments to a thousand generations" (Deut. 7:9). • "remember the LORD thy God: for it is he that giveth thee power to get wealth, *that he may establish his covenant* which he sware unto thy fathers" (Deut. 8:18). • "the LORD gave me the two tables of stone, even *the tables of the covenant"* (Deut. 9:11). • "thou shouldest *enter into covenant* with the LORD thy God, and into his oath, which the LORD thy God maketh with thee" (Deut. 29:12). • "I the LORD have called thee . . . and will . . . give thee for *a covenant of the people,* for a light of the Gentiles" (Isa. 42:6). • "my kindness shall not depart from thee, neither shall *the covenant of my peace* be removed, saith the LORD" (Isa. 54:10). • *"this is my covenant* with them, saith the LORD; My spirit that is upon thee" (Isa. 59:20). • "I the LORD love judgment, . . . and I will *make an everlasting covenant* with them" (Isa. 61:8). • "the days come, saith the LORD, that I will *make a new covenant* with the house of Israel, . . . I will put my law in their inward parts, and write it in their hearts; and will be their God, and they shall be my people" (Jer. 31:31, 33; see Heb. 9:1–13). • "I will send my messenger, . . . *even the messenger of the covenant,* . . . saith the LORD of hosts" (Mal. 3:1).

Jesus Christ Makes/Fulfills Covenants. • "That the blessing of Abraham might come on the Gentiles through Jesus Christ; . . . Now to Abraham and his seed were the promises made. He saith not, And to seeds, as of many; but as of one, And to thy seed, which is Christ. . . . *the covenant, that was confirmed before of God in Christ,* the law, which was four hundred and thirty years after, cannot disannul, that it should make the promise of none effect" (Gal. 3:14–17). • "we are his workmanship, created in Christ Jesus unto good works, . . . remember, that ye being in time past Gentiles in the flesh, who are called Uncircumcision . . . at that time ye were without Christ, being aliens from the commonwealth of Israel, and strangers from *the covenants of promise,* having no hope, and without God in the world: But now in Christ Jesus ye who sometimes were far off *are made nigh by the blood of Christ"* (Eph. 2:10–13). • "When the day cometh that they shall believe in me, that I am Christ, then have *I covenanted with their fathers* that they shall be restored in the flesh, upon the earth, unto the lands of their inheritance" (2 Ne. 10:7). • "take upon you the name of Christ, all *you that have entered into the covenant with God* that ye should be obedient unto the end of your lives" (Mosiah 5:8). • "there was not one soul, except it were little children, but who *had entered into the covenant* and had taken upon them the name of Christ" (Mosiah 6:2). • "Behold, I [Jesus Christ] say unto you that the law is fulfilled that was given unto Moses. Behold, I am he that gave the law, and *I am he who covenanted with my people Israel;* therefore, the law in me is fulfilled, for I have come to fulfil the law; therefore it hath an end" (3 Ne. 15:4–5; see Matt. 5:17; 3 Ne. 9:17–18). "that ye may believe the gospel of Jesus Christ, which ye shall have among you; and also that the Jews, *the covenant people of the Lord,* shall have other witness besides him whom they saw and heard, that *Jesus, whom they slew, was the very Christ and the very God"* (Morm. 3:21). • "And again, every person who belongeth to this church of Christ, shall observe to keep all the commandments and *covenants of the church"* (D&C 42:78).

21. Shepherd

The Lord Jehovah Is a Shepherd, His Followers Are His Sheep. • "*The Lord is my shepherd;* I shall not want" (Ps. 23:1). • "Know ye that the Lord he is God: . . . we are his people, and *the sheep of his pasture"* (Ps. 100:3). • *"All we like sheep have gone astray;* . . . and the Lord hath laid on him the iniquity of us all" (Isa. 53:6). • "Woe be unto the pastors that destroy and scatter *the sheep of my pasture!* saith the Lord" (Jer. 23:1). • "thus saith the Lord God; Behold, I, even *I, will both search my sheep, and seek them out"* (Ezek. 34:11).

Jesus Christ Is a Shepherd, His Followers Are His Sheep. • "Simon, son of Jonas, lovest thou me? . . . *Feed my sheep"* (John 21:16, 17). • "our Lord Jesus, *that great shepherd of the sheep"* (Heb. 13:20). • "When the Son of man shall come in his glory, . . . before him shall be gathered all nations: and he shall separate them one from another, *as a shepherd divideth his sheep from the goats"* (Matt. 25:31–32). • *"I am the good shepherd:* the good shepherd giveth his life for the sheep" (John 10:11). • *"other sheep I have,* which are not of this fold: them also I must bring, and they shall hear my voice; and *there shall be one fold, and one shepherd"* (John 10:16; see 3 Ne. 15:21). • "Christ also suffered for us, leaving us an example, that ye should follow his steps . . . *For ye were as sheep going astray; but are now returned unto the Shepherd* and Bishop of your souls" (1 Pet. 2:21, 25). • "he gathereth his children from the four quarters of the earth; and *he numbereth his sheep,* and they know him; and there shall be *one fold and one shepherd;* and he shall feed his sheep, and in him they shall find pasture" (1 Ne. 22:25). • *"the good shepherd doth call you;* yea, and in his own name he doth call you, which is the name of Christ" (Alma 5:38; see Alma 5:60). • "they shall again be brought to the true knowledge, which is the knowledge of their Redeemer, and *their great and true shepherd,* and be numbered among his sheep" (Hel. 15:13).

22. The Unblemished Sacrificial Lamb/the Lamb of God

The LORD Jehovah Required from Israel the Sacrifice of an Unblemished Lamb, Prefiguring the Atonement of Christ. • "thou shalt make an atonement for the altar, and sanctify it; Now this is that which thou shalt offer upon the altar; two lambs of the first year day by day continually. . . .The one lamb thou shalt offer in the morning; and the other lamb thou shalt offer at even . . . according to the meat offering of the morning, and according to the drink offering thereof, for a sweet savour, *an offering made by fire unto the LORD"* (Ex. 29:37–41). • "And if his offering for a sacrifice of peace offering unto the LORD be of the flock; male or female, *he shall offer it without blemish.* If he offer a lamb for his offering, then shall he offer it before the LORD" (Lev. 3:6–7). • "the fat of the lamb is taken away from the sacrifice of the peace offerings; and the priest shall burn them upon the altar, according to the offerings made by fire unto the LORD: and *the priest shall make an atonement for his sin"* (Lev. 4:35). • "he shall bring his trespass offering unto the LORD for his sin which he hath sinned, a female from the flock, a lamb . . . for a sin offering; and *the priest shall make an atonement for him"* (Lev. 5:6). • "she shall bring a lamb of the first year for a burnt offering, . . . for a sin offering, . . . unto the priest: Who shall offer it before the LORD, and *make an atonement for her"* (Lev. 12:6–7). • "the priest shall make an atonement for him before the LORD. . . . he shall take one lamb for a trespass offering to be waved, to *make an atonement for him"* (Lev. 14:18, 21). • "ye shall offer that day . . . *an he lamb without blemish of the first year* for a burnt offering unto the LORD" (Lev. 23:12). • "This is the offering made by fire which ye shall offer unto the LORD; two lambs of the first year *without spot day by day,* for *a continual burnt offering"* (Num. 28:3).

Jesus Christ Is the Spotless Sacrificial Lamb of God. • "The next day John seeth Jesus coming unto him, and saith, Behold *the Lamb of God, which taketh away the sin of the world"* (John 1:29). • "the next day after John stood, and two of his disciples; And looking upon Jesus as he walked, he saith, *Behold the Lamb of God!"* (John 1:35–36). "For even *Christ our passover is sacrificed for us"* (1 Cor. 5:7). • "Christ also hath loved us, and *hath given himself for us an offering and a sacrifice to God for a sweetsmelling savour"* (Eph. 5:2). • "How much more shall *the blood of Christ,* who through the eternal Spirit *offered himself without spot to God,* purge your conscience from dead works to serve the living God?" (Heb. 9:14). • "ye were not redeemed with corruptible things, . . . But with the precious blood of Christ, *as of a lamb without blemish and without spot"* (1 Pet. 1:18–19). • "Ye also, as lively stones, are built up a spiritual house, an holy priesthood, *to offer up spiritual sacrifices,* acceptable to God by Jesus Christ" (1 Pet. 2:5). • "Blessed are they which are called unto the *marriage supper of the Lamb"* (Rev. 19:9). • "after he had baptized the Messiah with water, he should behold and bear record that *he had baptized the Lamb of God"* (1 Ne. 10:10). • "the angel said unto me: Behold *the Lamb of God,* yea, even the Son of the Eternal Father!" (1 Ne. 11:21). • "I saw the heavens open, and *the Lamb of God* descending out of heaven" (1 Ne. 12:6). • *"the Lamb of God* is the Son of the Eternal Father, and the Savior of the world" (1 Ne. 13:40).

Summary

1. The name Jehovah appears 14 times in the scriptures. However, the word "LORD," found thousands of times in the Bible, also represents that sacred name.

2. Latter-day Saints know for sure that Jesus Christ is the same being known before the creation of this earth, and during the Old Testament period, as Jehovah. They have this certainty, in part, because when the Lord Jesus Christ appeared to accept the Kirtland Temple, He told His prophet at that time that He was Jehovah (D&C 110:3).

3. D&C 110:1–10 was analyzed as an example of how one may determine which member of the Godhead is speaking in various passages. Examining the various clues found in "name" passages of Godhead members gives guidance. In this example, phrases such as *"the first and the last," "I am he who liveth, I am he who was slain," "I am your advocate with the Father,"* and the "my" words often used by the Savior in the Doctrine and Covenants (in this case *"my people," "my servants," "my commandments,"* and *"my name"*) all provided valuable clues that identified the appearing individual as the Lord Jesus Christ.

4. The way to show that Jehovah is Jesus Christ is to compare scriptural passages concerning Jehovah with other scriptural passages concerning Jesus. There are numerous areas where each of them assert that Jehovah and Jesus have the same qualities—enough that there really is no other rational alternative but to conclude that they are the same person: Jehovah is Jesus Christ; Jesus Christ is Jehovah!

5. A long-needed task of assembling scriptural passages on numerous topics concerning the two of them has been accomplished in this chapter. Significant correlations on 22 different topics, with numerous scriptures conveying parallel meanings on each of these topics, have been made.

CHAPTER 11

JESUS CHRIST AS THE FATHER

A significant landmark in the development of Latter-day Saint theology is a clarifying doctrinal exposition issued by the First Presidency and the Council of the Twelve in 1916. It was published to the Church in the *Improvement Era* (Vol. XIX, No. 10; August, 1916, pp. 934–42). The *Era* masthead defined it as the "Organ of the Priesthood Quorums, the Young Men's Mutual Improvement Associations and the Schools of the Church of Jesus Christ of Latter-day Saints."

At this time the President of the Church was Joseph F. Smith. He was ordained an Apostle by Brigham Young in 1866, at the age of 28, and was immediately called as a Counselor in the First Presidency. He served as a Counselor in the First Presidency under Presidents John Taylor, Wilford Woodruff, and Lorenzo Snow prior to becoming the sixth President of the Church in 1901. He served as the Prophet and President of the Church for 17 years, from 1901 until his death in 1918 at age 80.

This exposition clarifies four distinct uses of the term "Father" by the Church when referring to members of the Godhead: (1) as a *literal parent of the spirits of mankind;* (2) as a *creator;* (3) as *the father of those who accept the gospel;* and (4) as *a father by divine investiture of authority.* It is quoted here verbatim, in its entirety.

The Father and the Son

A Doctrinal Exposition by the First Presidency and the Twelve

The scriptures plainly and repeatedly affirm that God is the Creator of the earth and the heavens and all things that in them are. In the sense so expressed, the Creator is an Organizer. God created the earth as an organized sphere; but He certainly did not create, in the sense of bringing into primal existence, the ultimate elements of the materials of which the earth consists, for "the elements are eternal" (D&C 93:33).

So also life is eternal, and not created; but life, or the vital force, may be infused into organized matter, though the details of the process have not been revealed unto man. For illustrative instances see Genesis 2:7; Moses 3:7; and Abraham 5:7. Each of these scriptures states that God breathed into the body of man the breath of life. See further Moses 3:19, for the statement that God breathed the breath of life into the bodies of the beasts and birds. God showed unto Abraham "the intelligences that were organized before the world was"; and by "intelligences" we are to understand personal "spirits" (Abr. 3:22–23); nevertheless, we are expressly told that "Intelligence," that is, "the light of truth, was not created or made, neither indeed can be" (D&C 93:29).

The term "Father" as applied to Deity occurs in sacred writ with plainly different meanings. Each of the four significations specified in the following treatment should be carefully segregated.

1. "Father" as Literal Parent

Scriptures embodying the ordinary signification—literally that of Parent—are too numerous and specific to require citation. The purport of these scriptures is to the effect that God the Eternal Father, whom we designate by the exalted name-title "Elohim," is the literal Parent of our Lord and Savior Jesus Christ, and of the spirits of the human race. Elohim is the Father in every sense in which Jesus Christ is so designated, and distinctively He is the Father of spirits. Thus we read in the Epistle to the Hebrews: "Furthermore we have had fathers of our flesh which corrected us, and we gave them reverence: shall we not much rather be in subjection unto the Father of spirits, and live?" (Heb. 12:9). In view of this fact we are taught by Jesus Christ to pray: "Our Father which art in heaven, Hallowed be thy name."

Jesus Christ applies to Himself both titles, "Son" and "Father." Indeed, He specifically said to the brother of Jared: "Behold, I am Jesus Christ. I am the Father and the Son" (Ether 3:14). Jesus Christ is the Son of Elohim both as spiritual and bodily offspring; that is to say, Elohim is literally the Father of the spirit of Jesus Christ and also of the body in which Jesus Christ performed His mission in the flesh, and which body died on the cross and was afterward taken up by the process of resurrection, and is now the immortalized tabernacle of the eternal spirit of our Lord and Savior. No extended explanation of the title "Son of God" as applied to Jesus Christ appears necessary.

2. "Father" as Creator

A second scriptural meaning of "Father" is that of Creator, e.g. in passages referring to anyone of the Godhead as "The Father of the heavens and of the earth, and all things that in them are" (Ether 4:7; see also Mosiah 15:4 and Alma 11:38–39).

God is not the Father of the earth as one of the worlds in space, nor of the heavenly bodies in whole or in part, nor of the inanimate objects and the plants and the animals upon the earth, in the literal sense in which He is the Father of the spirits of mankind. Therefore, scriptures that refer to God in any way as the Father of the heavens and the earth are to be understood as signifying that God is the Maker, the Organizer, the Creator of the heavens and the earth.

With this meaning, as the context shows in every case, Jehovah, who is Jesus Christ the Son of Elohim, is called "the Father," and even "the very eternal Father of heaven and of earth." (See passages before cited, and also Mosiah 16:15.) With analogous meaning Jesus Christ is called "The Everlasting Father" (Isa. 9:6; compare 2 Ne. 19:6). The descriptive titles "Everlasting" and "Eternal" in the foregoing texts are synonymous.

That Jesus Christ, whom we also know as Jehovah, was the executive of the Father, Elohim, in the work of creation is set forth in the book *Jesus the Christ,* chapter 4. Jesus Christ, being the Creator, is consistently called the Father of heaven and earth in the sense explained above; and since His creations are of eternal quality He is very properly called the Eternal Father of heaven and earth.

3. Jesus Christ the "Father" of Those Who Abide in His Gospel

A third sense in which Jesus Christ is regarded as the "Father" has reference to the relationship between Him and those who accept His Gospel and thereby become heirs of eternal life. Following are a few of the scriptures illustrating this meaning.

In the fervent prayer offered just prior to His entrance into Gethsemane, Jesus Christ supplicated His Father in behalf of those whom the Father had given unto Him, specifically the Apostles, and, more generally, all who would accept and abide in the Gospel through the ministry of the Apostles. Read in our Lord's own words the solemn affirmation that those for whom He particularly prayed were His own, and that His Father had given them unto Him:

"I have manifested thy name unto the men which thou gavest me out of the world: thine they were, and thou gavest them me; and they have kept thy word. Now they are of thee. For I have given unto them the words which thou gavest me; and they have received them, and have known surely that I came out from thee, and they have believed that thou didst send me. I pray for them: I pray not for the world, but for them which thou hast given me; for they are thine. And all mine are thine, and thine are mine; and I am glorified in them. And now I am no more in the world, but these are in the world, and I come to thee. Holy Father, keep through thine own name those whom thou hast given me, that they may be one, as we are. While I was with them in the world, I kept them in thy name: those that thou gavest me I have kept, and none of them is lost, but the son of perdition; that the scripture might be fulfilled (John 17:6–12)."

And further:

"Neither pray I for these alone, but for them also which shall believe on me through their word; That they all may be one; as thou, Father, art in me, and I in thee, that they also may be one in us: that the world may believe that thou hast sent me. And the glory which thou gavest me I have given them; that they may be one, even as we are one: I in them, and thou in me, that they may be made perfect in one; and that the world may know that thou hast sent me, and hast loved them, as thou hast loved me. Father, I will that they also, whom thou hast given me, be with me where I am; that they may behold my glory, which thou hast given me: for thou lovedst me before the foundation of the world (John 17:20–24)."

To His faithful servants in the present dispensation the Lord has said: "Fear not, little children, for you are mine, and I have overcome the world, and you are of them that my Father hath given me" (D&C 50:41).

Salvation is attainable only through compliance with the laws and ordinances of the Gospel; and all who are thus saved become sons and daughters unto God in a distinctive sense. In a revelation given through Joseph the Prophet to Emma Smith the Lord Jesus addressed the woman as "My daughter," and said: "for verily I say unto you, all those who receive my gospel are sons and daughters in my kingdom" (D&C 25:1). In many instances the Lord has addressed men as His sons (e.g. D&C 9:1; 34:3; 121:7).

That by obedience to the Gospel men may become sons of God, both as sons of Jesus Christ, and, through Him, as sons of His Father, is set forth in many revelations given in the current dispensation. Thus we read in an utterance of the Lord Jesus Christ to Hyrum Smith in 1829: "Behold, I am Jesus Christ, the Son of God. I am the life and the light of the world. I am the same who came unto mine own and mine own received me not; But verily, verily, I say unto you, that as many as receive me, to them will I give power to become the sons of God, even to them that believe on my name. Amen" (D&C 11:28–30). To Orson Pratt the Lord spoke through Joseph the Seer, in 1830: "My son Orson, hearken and hear and behold what I, the Lord God, shall say unto you, even Jesus Christ your Redeemer; The light and the life of the world, a light which shineth in the darkness and the darkness comprehendeth it not; Who so loved the world that he gave his own life, that as many as would believe might become the sons of God. Wherefore you are my son." (D&C 34:1–3.) In 1830 the Lord thus addressed Joseph Smith and Sidney Rigdon: "Listen to the voice of the Lord your God, even Alpha and Omega, the beginning and the end, whose course is one eternal round, the same today as yesterday, and forever. I am Jesus Christ, the Son of God, who was crucified for the sins of the world, even as many as will believe on my name, that they may become the sons of God, even one in me as I am one in the Father, as the Father is one in me, that we may be one." (D&C 35:1–2.) Consider also the following given in 1831: "Hearken and listen to the voice of him who is from all eternity to all eternity, the Great I Am, even Jesus Christ—The light and the life of the world; a light which shineth in darkness and the darkness comprehendeth it not; The same which came in the meridian of time unto mine own, and mine own received me not; But to as many as received me, gave I power to become my sons; and even so will I give unto as many as will receive me, power to become my sons." (D&C 39:1–4.) In a revelation given through Joseph Smith in March, 1831, we read: "For verily I say unto you that I am Alpha and Omega, the beginning and the end, the light and the life of the world—a light that shineth in darkness and the darkness comprehendeth it not. I came unto mine own, and mine own received me not; but unto as many as received me gave I power to do many miracles, and to become the sons of God; and even unto them that believed on my name gave I power to obtain eternal life." (D&C 45:7–8.)

A forceful exposition of this relationship between Jesus Christ as the Father and those who comply with the requirements of the Gospel as His children was given by Abinadi, centuries before our Lord's birth in the flesh:

"And now I say unto you, who shall declare his generation? Behold, I say unto you, that when his soul has been made an offering for sin he shall see his seed. And now what say ye? And who shall be his seed? Behold I say unto you, that whosoever has heard the words of the prophets, yea, all the holy prophets who have prophesied concerning the coming of the Lord—I say unto you, that all those who have hearkened unto their words, and believed that the Lord would redeem his people, and have looked forward to that day for a remission of their sins, I say unto you, that these are his seed, or they are the heirs of the kingdom of God. For these are they whose sins he has borne; these are they for whom he has died, to redeem them from their transgressions. And now, are they not his seed? Yea, and are not the prophets, every one that has opened his mouth to prophesy, that has not fallen into transgression, I mean all the holy prophets ever since the world began? I say unto you that they are his seed. (Mosiah 15:10–13)"

In tragic contrast with the blessed state of those who become children of God through obedience to the Gospel of Jesus Christ is that of the unregenerate, who are specifically called the children of the devil. Note the words of Christ, while in the flesh, to certain wicked Jews who boasted of their Abrahamic lineage: "If ye were Abraham's children, ye would do the works of Abraham. . . . Ye do the deeds of your father. . . . If God were your Father, ye would love me. . . . Ye are of your father the devil, and the lusts of your father ye will do." (John 8:39, 41–42, 44.) Thus Satan is designated as the father of the wicked, though we cannot assume any personal relationship of parent and children as existing between him and them. A combined illustration showing that the righteous are the children of God and the wicked the children of the devil appears in the parable of the tares: "The good seed are the children of the kingdom; but the tares are the children of the wicked one." (Matt. 13:38.)

Men may become children of Jesus Christ by being born anew—born of God, as the inspired word states: "He that committeth sin is of the devil; for the devil sinneth from the beginning. For this purpose the Son of God was manifested, that he might destroy the works of the devil. Whosoever is born of God doth not commit sin; for his seed remaineth in him: and he cannot sin, because he is born of God. In this the children of God are manifest, and the children of the devil: whosoever doeth not righteousness is not of God, neither he that loveth not his brother." (1 Jn. 3:8–10.)

Those who have been born unto God through obedience to the Gospel may by valiant devotion to righteousness obtain exaltation and even reach the status of Godhood. Of such we read: "Wherefore, as it is written, they are gods, even the sons of God." (D&C 76:58; compare 132:20, and contrast paragraph 17 in same section; see also paragraph 37.) Yet, though they be Gods they are still subject to Jesus Christ as their Father in this exalted relationship; and so we read in the paragraph following the above quotation: "and they are Christ's, and Christ is God's." (76:59.)

By the new birth—that of water and the Spirit—mankind may become children of Jesus Christ, being through the means by Him provided "begotten sons and daughters unto God" (D&C 76:24.) This solemn truth is further emphasized in the words of the Lord Jesus Christ given through Joseph Smith in 1833: "And now, verily I say unto you, I was in the beginning with the Father, and am the Firstborn; And all those who are begotten through me are partakers of the glory of the same, and are the church of the Firstborn." (D&C 93:21–22.) For such figurative use of the term "begotten" in application to those who are born unto God see Paul's explanation: "for in Christ Jesus I have begotten you through the gospel." (1 Cor. 4:15.) An analogous instance of sonship attained by righteous service is found in the revelation relating to the order and functions of Priesthood, given in 1832: "For whoso is faithful unto the obtaining these two priesthoods of which I have spoken, and the magnifying their calling, are sanctified by the Spirit unto the renewing of their bodies. They become the sons of Moses and of Aaron and the seed of Abraham, and the church and kingdom, and the elect of God." (D&C 84:33–34.)

If it be proper to speak of those who accept and abide in the Gospel as Christ's sons and daughters—and upon this matter the scriptures are explicit and cannot be gainsaid nor denied—it is consistently proper to speak of Jesus Christ as the Father of the righteous, they having become His children and He having been made their Father through the second birth—the baptismal regeneration.

4. Jesus Christ the "Father" by Divine Investiture of Authority

A fourth reason for applying the title "Father" to Jesus Christ is found in the fact that in all His dealings with the human family Jesus the Son has represented and yet represents Elohim His Father in power and authority. This is true of Christ in His preexistent, antemortal, or unembodied state, in the which He was known as Jehovah; also during His embodiment in the flesh; and during His labors as a disembodied spirit in the realm of the dead; and since that period in His resurrected state. To the Jews He said: "I and my Father are one" (John 10:30; see also 17:11, 22); yet He declared "My Father is greater than I" (John 14:28); and further, "I am come in my Father's name" (John 5:43; see also 10:25). The same truth was declared by Christ Himself to the Nephites (see 3 Ne. 20:35 and 28:10), and has been reaffirmed by revelation in the present dispensation (D&C 50:43). Thus the Father placed His name upon the Son; and Jesus Christ spoke and ministered in and through the Father's name; and so far as power, authority and Godship are concerned His words and acts were and are those of the Father.

We read, by way of analogy, that God placed His name upon or in the Angel who was assigned to special ministry unto the people of Israel during the exodus. Of that Angel the Lord said: "Beware of him, and obey his voice, provoke him not; for he will not pardon your transgressions: for my name is in him." (Ex. 23:21.)

The ancient Apostle, John, was visited by an angel who ministered and spoke in the name of Jesus Christ. As we read: "The Revelation of Jesus Christ, which God gave unto him, to shew unto his servants things which must shortly come to pass; and he sent and signified it by his angel unto his servant John." (Rev. 1:1.) John was about to worship the angelic being who spoke in the name of the Lord Jesus Christ, but was forbidden: "And I John saw these things, and heard them. And when I had heard and seen, I fell down to worship before the feet of the angel which showed me these things. Then saith he unto me, See thou do it not: for I am thy fellowservant, and of thy brethren the prophets, and of them which keep the sayings of this book: worship God." (Rev. 22:8–9.) And then the angel continued to speak as though he were the Lord Himself: "And, behold, I come quickly; and my reward is with me, to give every man according as his work shall be. I am Alpha and Omega, the beginning and the end, the first and the last." (Verses 12–13.) The resurrected Lord, Jesus Christ, who had been exalted to the right hand of God His Father, had placed His name upon the angel sent to John, and the angel spoke in the first person, saying "I come quickly," "I am Alpha and Omega," though he meant that Jesus Christ would come, and that Jesus Christ was Alpha and Omega.

———

None of these considerations, however, can change in the least degree the solemn fact of the literal relationship of Father and Son between Elohim and Jesus Christ. Among the spirit children of Elohim the firstborn was and is Jehovah or Jesus Christ to whom all others are juniors. Following are affirmative scriptures bearing upon this great truth. Paul, writing to the Colossians, says of Jesus Christ: "Who is the image of the invisible God, the firstborn of every creature: For by him were all things created, that are in heaven, and that are in earth, visible and invisible, whether they be thrones, or dominions, or principalities, or powers: all things were created by him, and for him: And he is before all things, and by him all things consist. And he is the head of the body, the church: who is the beginning, the firstborn from the dead; that in all things he might have the preeminence. For it pleased the Father that in him should all fulness dwell." (Col. 1:15–19.) From this scripture we learn that Jesus Christ was the "firstborn of every creature" and it is evident that the seniority here expressed must be with respect to antemortal existence, for Christ was not the senior of all mortals in the flesh. He is further designated as "the firstborn from the dead," this having reference to Him as the first to be resurrected from the dead, or as elsewhere written "the firstfruits of them that slept" (1 Cor. 15:20, see also verse 23); and "the first begotten of the dead" (Rev. 1:5; compare Acts 26:23). The writer of the Epistle to the Hebrews affirms the status of Jesus Christ as the firstborn of the spirit children of His Father, and extols the preeminence of the Christ when tabernacled in flesh: "And again, when he bringeth in the firstbegotten into the world, he saith, And let all the angels of God worship him." (Heb. 1:6; read the preceding verses.) That the spirits who were juniors to Christ were predestined to be born in the image of their Elder Brother is thus attested by Paul: "And we know that all things work together for good to them that love God, to them who are the called according to his purpose. For whom he did foreknow, he also did predestinate to be conformed to the image of his Son, that he might be the firstborn among many brethren." (Rom. 8:28–29.) John the Revelator was commanded to write to the head of the Laodicean church, as the words of the Lord Jesus Christ: "These things saith the Amen, the faithful and true witness, the beginning of the creation of God." (Rev. 3:14.) In the course of a revelation given through Joseph Smith in May, 1833, the Lord Jesus

Christ said as before cited: "And now, verily I say unto you, I was in the beginning with the Father, and am the Firstborn." (D&C 93:21.) A later verse makes plain the fact that human beings generally were similarly existent in spirit state prior to their embodiment in the flesh: "Ye were also in the beginning with the Father; that which is Spirit, even the Spirit of truth." (Verse 23.)

There is no impropriety, therefore, in speaking of Jesus Christ as the Elder Brother of the rest of human kind. That he is by spiritual birth Brother to the rest of us is indicated in Hebrews: "Wherefore in all things it behoved him to be made like unto his brethren, that he might be a merciful and faithful high priest in things pertaining to God, to make reconciliation for the sins of the people." (Heb. 2:17.) Let it not be forgotten, however, that He is essentially greater than any and all others, by reason (1) of His seniority as the oldest or firstborn; (2) of His unique status in the flesh as the offspring of a mortal mother and of an immortal, or resurrected and glorified, Father; (3) of His selection and foreordination as the one and only Redeemer and Savior of the race; and (4) of His transcendent sinlessness.

Jesus Christ is not the Father of the spirits who have taken or yet shall take bodies upon this earth, for He is one of them. He is The Son, as they are sons or daughters of Elohim. So far as the stages of eternal progression and attainment have been made known through divine revelation, we are to understand that only resurrected and glorified beings can become parents of spirit offspring. Only such exalted souls have reached maturity in the appointed course of eternal life; and the spirits born to them in the eternal worlds will pass in due sequence through the several stages or estates by which the glorified parents have attained exaltation.

THE FIRST PRESIDENCY AND
THE COUNCIL OF THE TWELVE APOSTLES OF
THE CHURCH OF JESUS CHRIST OF LATTER-DAY SAINTS

SALT LAKE CITY, UTAH, JUNE 30, 1916

Examples of Jesus Speaking as God the Father

The above marks the end of the 1916 doctrinal exposition. What follows are observations made by this author.

Example #1: D&C 29. Doctrine and Covenants section 29 is an interesting example in which Jesus Christ gives a revelation, but somewhere in the middle He ceases speaking in first person for himself and begins speaking in first person as if He is God the Father, presumably using the power of "divine investiture of authority," referenced above, to do so.

He begins the revelation saying, *"Listen to the voice of Jesus Christ, your Redeemer, the Great I AM,* whose arm of mercy hath atoned for your sins" (D&C 29:1). He again makes reference to Himself in verse 5: *"I am in your midst, and am your advocate with the Father;* and it is his good will to give you the kingdom" (D&C 29:5), and also identifies Himself in verse 11 as He makes a clear reference to His Second Coming in glory: • *"I will reveal myself from heaven with power and great glory, with all the hosts thereof, and dwell in righteousness with men on earth a thousand years."* In verse 27 Jesus is still speaking in first person for Himself: • *"the righteous shall be gathered on my right hand unto eternal life; and the wicked on my left hand will I be ashamed to own before the Father"* (D&C 29:27).

But somewhere between verse 28 and verse 41 Jesus ceases speaking for Himself and begins speaking in first person as if He were God the Father, while twice referring to Himself as "mine Only Begotten Son." The "bridge" seems to be the usage of the title "I the Lord God," a descriptive name which is used both in reference to Himself, and in other passages to God the Father. In verse 18 it still appears to be a reference to Christ (because of His verse 27 allusion to "the Father," but by verse 41, "I, the Lord God" seems to be referring to God the Father. Several verses seem to identify the Father (as being spoken of, by Jesus, but in first person as if God the Father is speaking for Himself), beginning with verse 41:

> And it came to pass that Adam, being tempted of the devil—for, behold, the devil was before Adam, *for he rebelled against me, saying, Give me thine honor, which is my power; and also a third part of the hosts of heaven turned he away from me because of their agency;* . . .
>
> Wherefore, *I, the Lord God, caused that he should be cast out from the Garden of Eden, from my presence,* . . .
>
> But, behold, I say unto you that *I, the Lord God, gave unto Adam and unto his seed, that they should not die as to the temporal death, until I, the Lord God, should send forth angels to declare unto them repentance and redemption, through faith on the name* of **mine Only Begotten Son.**
>
> And *thus did I, the Lord God, appoint unto man the days of his probation* . . .
>
> But behold, I say unto you, that *little children are redeemed from the foundation of the world* through **mine Only Begotten** . . . (D&C 29:36, 41, 42, 43, 46).

This transition makes it very difficult to ascertain with certainty which of the two divine beings is giving voice, in verses 29 through 35 particularly. Presumably Jesus remains speaking, but He begins speaking for God the Father in first person, perhaps through "divine investiture of authority."

Example #2: *D&C 49.* Section 49 poses the same interpretive challenges. It ends with the Savior's identifying words • "Behold, I am Jesus Christ, and I come quickly. Even so. Amen." (D&C 49:28). But again, using the bridge title "I, the Lord God" (v. 7), much of the revelation is given in first person as if God the Father is speaking, particularly the following verses:

> Thus saith the Lord; for *I am God, and have sent* **mine Only Begotten Son** *into the world for the redemption of the world, and have decreed that he that receiveth him shall be saved, and he that receiveth him not shall be damned*—
>
> And *they have done unto the Son of Man even as they listed;* and *he has taken his power on the right hand of his glory,* and now reigneth in the heavens, and will reign *till he descends on the earth* to put all enemies under his feet, which time is nigh at hand—
>
> *I, the Lord God,* have spoken it; but the hour and the day no man knoweth, neither the angels in heaven, nor shall they know until he comes. . . .
>
> *Believe on the name of the Lord Jesus,* who was on the earth, and is to come, the beginning and the end;
>
> Repent and *be baptized in the name of Jesus Christ* . . .
>
> *the Son of Man cometh not in the form of a woman,* neither of a man traveling on the earth. . . .
>
> Behold, *I will go before you and be your rearward; and I will be in your midst* . . . (D&C 49:5–7, 12–13, 22, 27)

So the question again must be posed, is Jesus speaking in first person for God the

Father, fulfilling his revelatory responsibility through "divine investiture of authority," or is he repeatedly referring to Himself in third person for the sake of modesty, usually with the words "mine only begotten" as the signal that he is doing so? It appears that the second possibility, above, may be a likely interpretation.

Example #3: D&C 124. This section is of interest in like manner, because it apparently is Jesus Christ speaking, but referring to Himself as if it were God the Father speaking. Like many of the revelations, Jesus repeatedly identifies Himself by saying • "thus saith the Lord" (v. 1) • "saith the Lord" (v. 15, 34, 47, 50, 52, 53, 59, 69, 75, 76, 101, 119, 120, 122, 145), • "I, the Lord" (v. 20, 78, 83), • "I am the Lord your God" (v. 54), and • "I, the Lord, am God" (v. 71). The revelation is filled with things which Jesus did, does, or will do, expressed in first person (my servants, mine house, my people, my holy name, mine holy ordinances, my commandments, etc.). But suddenly, he refers to Himself in third person, as if he were speaking again for God the Father: • "Verily I say unto you, I now give unto you the officers belonging to my Priesthood, that ye may hold the keys thereof, even the Priesthood which is after the order of Melchizedek, which *is after the order of **mine Only Begotten Son***" (D&C 124:123).

The phrase "mine Only Begotten Son" again seems to be the Lord's modest indicator that He is going to speak of Himself in third person, typically as if it were God the Father speaking.

Example #4: the book of Moses. The deity speaking in the book of Moses, upon first reading, appears to be God the Father, because of its several references to Jesus Christ in the third person. Listed here are 16 passages where that seems to be the case. They will be followed by a series of interpretational clues, some of which are referenced in square brackets (for instance: [See clue #5, below.])

1. "I have a work for thee, Moses, my son; and thou art in ***the similitude of mine Only Begotten***; and ***mine Only Begotten*** is and shall be the Savior, for he is full of grace and truth; but there is no God beside me, and all things are present with me, for I know them all" (Moses 1:6). [See clue #5, below.]
2. "Get thee hence, Satan; deceive me not; for God said unto me: Thou art after ***the similitude of mine Only Begotten***" (Moses 1:16).
3. "And he also gave me commandments when he called unto me out of the burning bush, saying: Call upon God in the name of ***mine Only Begotten***, and worship me" (Moses 1:17). [See clue #1, below.]
4. "Moses stood in the presence of God, and talked with him face to face. And the Lord God said unto Moses: For mine own purpose have I made these things. Here is wisdom and it remaineth in me. And by the word of my power, have I created them, which is ***mine Only Begotten Son***, who is full of grace and truth" (Moses 1:31–32). [See clue #4, below.]
5. "worlds without number have I created; and I also created them for mine own purpose; and by the Son I created them, which is ***mine Only Begotten***" (Moses 1:33). [See clue #6, below.]
6. "I am the Beginning and the End, the Almighty God; ***by mine Only Begotten*** I created these things" (Moses 2:1). [See clues #2, 3, below.]
7. "I, God, ***said unto mine Only Begotten***, which was with me from the beginning: Let us make man in our image, after our likeness; and it was so" (Moses 2:26).

8. "I, God, created man in mine own image, *in the image of mine Only Begotten* created I him; male and female created I them" (Moses 2:27).

9. "I, the Lord God, *said unto mine Only Begotten,* that it was not good that the man should be alone; wherefore, I will make an help meet for him" (Moses 3:18).

10. "I, the Lord God, spake unto Moses, saying: That Satan, whom thou hast commanded *in the name of mine Only Begotten,* is the same which was from the beginning, and he came before me, saying—Behold, here am I, send me, I will be thy son, and I will redeem all mankind, that one soul shall not be lost, and surely I will do it; wherefore give me thine honor. But, behold, *my Beloved Son, which was my Beloved and Chosen from the beginning, said unto me—Father, thy will be done, and the glory be thine forever"* (Moses 4:1–2).

11. "because that Satan rebelled against me, and sought to destroy the agency of man, which I, the Lord God, had given him, and also, that I should give unto him mine own power; *by the power of mine Only Begotten,* I caused that he should be cast down" (Moses 4:3). [See clue #7, below.]

12. "I, the Lord God, *said unto mine Only Begotten:* Behold, the man is become as one of us to know good and evil" (Moses 4:28).

13. "God hath made known unto our fathers that all men must repent. *And he called upon our father Adam by his own voice, saying: I am God; I made the world, and men before they were in the flesh.* And he also said unto him: If thou wilt turn unto me, and hearken unto my voice, and believe, and repent of all thy transgressions, and be baptized, even in water, *in the name of mine Only Begotten Son,* who is full of grace and truth, which is *Jesus Christ, the only name which shall be given under heaven, whereby salvation shall come unto the children of men,* ye shall receive the gift of the Holy Ghost" (Moses 6:50–52).

14. "ye must be born again into the kingdom of heaven, of water, and of the Spirit, and be cleansed by blood, *even the blood of mine Only Begotten;* that ye might be sanctified from all sin" (Moses 6:59).

15. "This is the plan of salvation unto all men, through *the blood of mine Only Begotten,* who shall come in the meridian of time" (Moses 6:62).

16. "righteousness will I send down out of heaven; and truth will I send forth out of the earth, *to bear testimony of mine Only Begotten;* his resurrection from the dead" (Moses 7:62).

Interpretational clues concerning who is speaking in the book of Moses. Notice that every one of these 16 passages makes reference to *"mine Only Begotten."* This phrase appears to be an indication that Jesus is the speaker, though using the "mine only begotten" phrase as a means of describing Himself and His roles as though seen through the eyes of His Father, man's Heavenly Father.

Notice these other clues in the book of Moses that *the God who is speaking is Jehovah,* who later became known as Jesus Christ:

Clue 1. The God Moses was speaking to was the God who called to him out of the burning bush (Moses 1:17). Ex. 3:2–15, with Ex. 6:2–3, indicates that God was Jehovah.

Clue 2. The God who appeared to Moses was "The Beginning and the End." (Moses 2:1). That is a title of Jehovah/Jesus Christ. (See chapter 10.)

Clue 3. The God who appeared to Moses was the "Almighty God" (Moses 2:1). That is a title which is applicable to both Jehovah/Jesus Christ and God the Father. (See chapter 11.)

Clue 4. Moses talked to God face to face (Moses 1:31–32). The God Moses talked with face to face on all other occasions was Jehovah (see chapter 4).

Clue 5. The God who talked to Moses said that "There is no God beside me" (Moses 1:6). The God who asserted that repeatedly in the Old Testament was Jehovah. (See chapter 5.)

Clue 6. The God Moses talked to created "worlds without number," a project in which the Father and the Son labored together. (Moses 1:33; see chapter 7.)

Clue 7. Satan's rebellion, in mortality, apparently was against both the Father and the Son, but the responsibility of casting him out of heaven fell to Jehovah (Moses 4:3). (See chapter 9.)

Clue 8. The God Moses talked to is Endless. One of Christ's names is Endless (D&C 19:4–10).

Clue 9. The God Moses talked to created this earth. Almost all passages defining who created this earth state that it was Jehovah/Jesus Christ who did so. (See chapter 9.)

Clue 10. The God who interacted with Moses was called the "Lord God" (Moses 4:28, 5:1). This is a title which is attributed to both God the Father and Jehovah. However, it was Jehovah who continually interacted with Moses, gave him the ten commandments, and led him out of Egypt and up to the promised land (Ex. 20:2–3).

Clue 11. The book of Moses indicates that when Adam began to receive revelations, it was Jehovah who first came to him and instructed him (Moses 5:9) and who continued to function as the God of this earth.

These are some of the major clues which have led most students of the book of Moses to believe that the God who spoke with Moses was Jehovah, rather than God the Father. Jehovah, in His modesty, apparently elects to describe many of His accomplishments in the third person, rather than in the first person.

Summary

1. "The Father and the Son, A Doctrinal Exposition by the First Presidency and the Twelve" is cited verbatim, in its entirety. It clarifies four distinct uses of the term "Father" by the Church when referring to members of the Godhead: (1) as a *literal parent of the spirits of mankind;* (2) as a *creator;* (3) as *the father of those who accept the gospel;* and (4) as *a father by divine investiture of authority.*

2. Four examples are cited of how Jesus Christ may have spoken in behalf of God the Father, utilizing the "divine investiture of authority" from God the Father which granted Him permission to speak in the Father's name. The examples are D&C sections 29, 49, and 124, and the book of Moses from the Pearl of Great Price.

3. The phrase "I, the Lord God," may be an indicator of situations where Jehovah/Jesus Christ is speaking as God the Father.

4. The phrase "mine only begotten" may be another indicator of situations in which Jehovah/Jesus Christ is speaking as God the Father. Sixteen instances where this phrase is used are identified in the book of Moses.

5. Eleven clues were listed which appear to indicate that it was Jehovah/Jesus Christ who was speaking to Moses in the book of Moses.

PART FIVE

INDIVIDUAL INSIGHTS ON
GOD THE SON, GOD THE HOLY GHOST,
AND GOD THE FATHER

CHAPTER 12

GOD THE SON:
JEHOVAH—JESUS CHRIST

What a challenge! To write an informative chapter on Jesus Christ, after all the thousands of books that have been written about Him. An objective of this chapter is to add new insights concerning His premortal, mortal, and postmortal life and missions.

Much has already been covered in this book concerning Jehovah, who is also Jesus Christ. This chapter will briefly comment on a smorgasbord of other items: some things which are not known or understood by non-Latter-day Saints, plus a few things which are sometimes misunderstood by Latter-day Saint members. It will present several items that I have never seen in print elsewhere. The latter portion will deal with His mission here on this earth during the meridian of time.

Hopefully, the final result will lead to increased love, reverent awe and worshipful adoration. It is hoped, also, that it will inspire some with a yearning to mend their life to be more fully in harmony with the teachings and commandments of He who is the Creator, Example, Teacher, Father by adoption, Redeemer, and Eternal God of this earth and its inhabitants: Jesus the Christ.

Jehovah/Jesus Christ Is the God of This Earth and All Its Inhabitants

Undoubtedly, *the most significant message of this chapter, and this book, is that the Lord—Jehovah—Jesus Christ, is* the *God of this earth!* It is He who was commissioned to create it. It is He who chose Israel and covenanted with Abraham, Isaac and Jacob. It is He who walked this earth and here atoned for the sins of all mankind. It is He who controls earth's events today. It is He who shall return and cleanse the earth. It is He who shall rule as King during the millennium, and it is He who will be granted eternal supervision and Kingship of this earth as part of His forever-increasing glory.

God the Father and God the Holy Ghost also have important roles to play, but by premortal assignment and agreement, Jehovah—the Lord—Jesus Christ is *in charge* of this earth and all its inhabitants. He runs the show. He shoulders the responsibility. He carries the administrative load. He is *the main God* of this earth. Mankind, by scriptural commandment, is to place no other god, nor God, before Him!

That isn't a difficult principle for Latter-day Saints to grasp, for informative comparisons can easily be made. For instance, in their stake, their stake president is the man in charge. Yes, they recognize there are higher ecclesiastical authorities, but in almost all situations, communications to higher authorities are rerouted so that they flow through the stake president. Requests to hold intra-stake activities are to be directed through the stake president. Doctrinal questions are to be addressed to and through the stake president. Mission calls and releases flow through the stake president.

The stake president has selected two counselors by inspiration. They too are highly qualified, truly capable, often charismatic leaders. They are men who are entitled to seek and receive inspiration pertaining to the well-being of the stake's members, particularly for the stake organizations for which they have direct stake president-assigned responsibility and authority. One of the counselors may be more visible and beloved to the youth than the rest of the stake presidency. Another may be held in highest regard by the sisters of the Relief Society or the Primary. But regardless of personal closeness and affinities, all the stake members recognize that it is the stake president, not the counselors, who is *the* president, the leader, the final decision-maker concerning the affairs of that stake. It is he who bears ultimate responsibility for the progress and well-being of the entire stake membership, and by extension, for all the people who live within the stake's geographical area.

That stake-presidency channel mirrors, in significant but comparatively minuscule form, the organization on the whole-earth level. Jehovah/Jesus Christ is *the* God, the ruler, the great high priest, the king of this planet earth!

It is not unusual, when stakes are divided or when stake presidents are released after fulfilling their assigned terms, for one of the president's counselors to be chosen as the new stake president. His previous service has qualified him to be *the* leader in the new stake. That may well be the situation with Jehovah/Jesus Christ. He assisted His Father in creating worlds without number. Now, for this earth (and perhaps millions of other earths), He is *the* God who presides over this earth and all its inhabitants. His Father may have been in the "creation" business longer, but it is Jesus Christ who is appointed and functioning as *the* God of *this earth*, and He is entitled to the full respect, honor, and glory which that position entails. That is the message of this chapter!

Scriptural Witnesses That Jehovah/Jesus Christ Is the God of This Earth

The Old Testament bears repeated witness that Jehovah is the God of this earth. The **Psalmist** joyously proclaimed it: • *"The earth is the* LORD'S, *and the fulness thereof; the world, and they that dwell therein"* (Ps. 24:1). • Another Psalmist wrote, "LORD, thou hast been our dwelling place in all generations. Before the mountains were brought forth, *or ever thou hadst formed the earth and the world, even from everlasting to everlasting, thou art God"* (Ps. 90:1–2). • And yet another Psalmist wrote: *"For thou,* LORD, *art high above all the earth: thou art exalted far above all gods.* Ye that love the LORD, hate evil: *he preserveth the souls of his saints; he delivereth them out of the hand of the wicked.* Light is sown for the righteous, and gladness for the upright in heart" (Ps. 97:9–11).

Examples from the Pentateuch ("the law," the first five books of the Bible). As early as the *days of Abraham*, about 1900 BC, Jehovah asserted his place of pre-eminence as the Almighty God of this earth, and He established the Abrahamic covenant which still shapes the events of both the Church and the world: • "when Abram was ninety years old and nine, the LORD appeared to Abram, and said unto him, *I am the Almighty God;* walk before me, and be thou perfect. *And I will make my covenant between me and thee,* and will multiply thee exceedingly" (Gen. 17:1–2).

Five hundred years later, the Prophet *Moses* warned the Pharoah of Egypt, • "I will spread abroad my hands unto the LORD; and the thunder shall cease, neither shall there be any more hail; *that thou mayest know how that the earth is the LORD's*" (Ex. 9:29).

Next, while they wandered in the wilderness, Jehovah taught His chosen people the necessity of their loving Him, and their regarding Him as the one and only God who was guiding and directing them: • "Hear therefore, O Israel, and observe to do it; that it may be well with thee, and that ye may increase mightily, as the LORD God of thy fathers hath promised thee, in the land that floweth with milk and honey. Hear, O Israel: *The LORD our God is one LORD: And thou shalt love the LORD thy God with all thine heart, and with all thy soul, and with all thy might*" (Deut. 6:3–5).

Not many years thereafter, Jehovah clearly asserted that He, and none other, is the God mankind is to worship here on earth. He proclaimed it as the first of His Ten Commandments: • *"I am the LORD thy God,* which have brought thee out of the land of Egypt, out of the house of bondage. *Thou shalt have no other gods before me"* (Ex. 20:2–3). This commandment, as the keystone of the Ten Commandments, was repeated in Deuteronomy 5:6–7 ("none other gods") and Mosiah 12:34–35.

The book of Deuteronomy records many of Moses' teachings concerning how they should worship and interact with the LORD, their God of all the earth and its inhabitants. He instructed them, for instance, to • *"Know therefore that the LORD thy God, he is God, the faithful God,* which keepeth covenant and mercy with them that love him and keep his commandments to a thousand generations" (Deut. 7:9). And then he explained to them what their God would require of them: • "And now, Israel, what doth the LORD thy God require of thee, but to *fear the LORD* thy God, to *walk in all his ways,* and to *love him,* and to *serve the LORD thy God with all thy heart and with all thy soul,* To *keep the commandments of the LORD,* and his statutes, which I command thee this day for thy good? *Behold, the heaven and the heaven of heavens is the LORD's thy God, the earth also, with all that therein is"* (Deut. 10:12–14).

Moses gave them God's word that He could, and would, control the elements and plant life to their benefit if they would faithfully serve Him: • "if ye shall *hearken diligently unto my commandments* which I command you this day, to *love the LORD your God,* and to *serve him* with all your heart and with all your soul, That I will give you the *rain of your land in his due season,* the first rain and the latter rain, that thou mayest gather in thy corn, and thy wine, and thine oil. And *I will send grass* in thy fields for thy cattle, that thou mayest eat and be full" (Deut. 11:13–15).

Moses gave them their God's promise of military success, conditioned upon their obedience to his commandments, and promised them the lands of present-day Lebanon, Iraq, and even to the "uttermost sea": • *"if ye shall diligently keep all these commandments which I command you, to do them, to love the LORD your God, to walk in all his ways, and to cleave unto him*; Then will the LORD drive out all these nations from before you, and ye shall possess greater nations and mightier than yourselves. Every place whereon the soles of your feet shall tread shall be yours: *from the wilderness and Lebanon, from the river, the river Euphrates, even unto the uttermost sea shall your coast be.* There shall no man be able to stand before you: for the LORD your God shall lay the fear of you and the dread of you upon all the land that ye shall tread upon, as he hath said unto you" (Deut. 11:22–25).

Later, at the end of his life, Moses summarized many of his teachings to the

Israelites, focusing them on the continued need to love, serve and follow their God, Jehovah, and promising them rich blessings if they would do so: • *"the LORD thy God will circumcise thine heart, and the heart of thy seed, to love the LORD thy God with all thine heart, and with all thy soul, that thou mayest live*. . . . And the LORD thy God will make thee plenteous in every work of thine hand, in the *fruit of thy body*, and in the fruit of *thy cattle*, and in the fruit of *thy land*, for good: for the LORD will again rejoice over thee for good, as he rejoiced over thy fathers: If thou shalt hearken unto the voice of the LORD thy God, to keep his commandments and his statutes which are written in this book of the law, and *if thou turn unto the LORD thy God with all thine heart, and with all thy soul"* (Deut. 30:6, 9–10).

And then Moses admonished them to choose obedience to Jehovah so they would reap the blessings of long and fruitful lives: • "I have set before thee this day *life and good*, and *death and evil*; In that I command thee this day to love the LORD thy God, to walk in his ways, and to keep his commandments and his statutes and his judgments, that thou mayest live and multiply: and the LORD thy God shall bless thee in the land whither thou goest to possess it. . . . I call heaven and earth to record this day against you, that *I have set before you life and death, blessing and cursing*: therefore *choose life, that both thou and thy seed may live*: That thou mayest *love* the LORD thy God, and that thou mayest *obey* his voice, and that thou mayest *cleave* unto him: for he is thy life, and the length of thy days: *that thou mayest dwell in the land which the LORD sware unto thy fathers, to Abraham, to Isaac, and to Jacob, to give them"* (Deut. 30:15–16, 19–20).

Examples from "the prophets," the Old Testament prophetic books. Another seven hundred years (and more) later, Israel's prophets taught repeatedly concerning Israel's need to fear, worship, and serve Jehovah, the God of all the earth. But many of them prophesied in eras when Israel had strayed far from their true God and had gone whoring after other, false gods which had led them into abject wickedness. Not only did they warn of dire consequences in the near future, they prophesied of the scattering of Israel (an event which transpired long ago) and of a last-days gathering of Israel's remnants (a process in its early stages now, but with much more to transpire before all their prophecies are fulfilled).

Perhaps an often-overlooked aspect of their prophetic messages is that Jehovah's rule over all the earth wasn't just confined to ancient times. His rule continues, and will become increasingly visible as last-days events unfold.

The Prophet *Isaiah* spoke of how the people of ancient Israel had turned away from their true God, Jehovah, but prophesied that the day would come when Jehovah would again assert Himself to all the world, saying: • "thus saith the LORD, Ye have sold yourselves for nought; and ye shall be redeemed without money. For thus saith the Lord GOD, My people went down aforetime into Egypt to sojourn there; and the Assyrian oppressed them without cause. Now therefore, what have I here, saith the LORD, that my people is taken away for nought? they that rule over them make them to howl, saith the LORD; and *my name continually every day is blasphemed. Therefore my people shall know my name: therefore they shall know in that day that I am he that doth speak: behold, it is I"* (Isa. 52:3–6).

Isaiah made many prophecies concerning the Lord's mighty acts in the last days. His prophecy that the influence of the Lord will again be felt in the last days contains these descriptive phrases concerning Jehovah, the God of all the earth. In his prophecy, he compares Jehovah's future deeds with His past creative acts: • *Behold, the Lord GOD will come with strong hand*, and his arm shall rule for him: behold, his reward is with him, and his work before him. He shall feed his flock like a shepherd: he shall gather the lambs with his arm, and carry them in his bosom, and shall gently lead those that are with young. *Who hath measured the waters in the hollow of his hand, and meted out heaven with the span, and comprehended the dust of the earth in a measure, and weighed the mountains in scales, and the hills in a balance? Who hath directed the Spirit of the Lord, or being his counsellor hath taught him?"* (Isa. 40:10–13).

The Prophet *Ezekiel* also foretold how Jehovah will gather scattered Israel in the last days: *"As I live, saith the Lord God, surely with a mighty hand, and with a stretched out arm, and with fury poured out, will I rule over you:* And I will bring you out from the people, and will *gather you out of the countries wherein ye are scattered, with a mighty hand, and with a stretched out arm, and with fury poured out.* And I will bring you into the wilderness of the people, and *there will I plead with you face to face.* Like as I pleaded with your fathers in the wilderness of the land of Egypt, so will I plead with you, saith the Lord God" (Ezek. 20:33–36).

Joel, a prophet of the ancient nation of Judah, foretold Jehovah's future saving of latter-day Israel:

> Blow the trumpet in Zion, sanctify a fast, call a solemn assembly:
>
> Gather the people, sanctify the congregation, assemble the elders, gather the children, and those that suck the breasts: let the bridegroom go forth of his chamber, and the bride out of her closet.
>
> Let the priests, the ministers of the Lord, weep between the porch and the altar, and let them say, *Spare thy people, O Lord,* and give not thine heritage to reproach, that the heathen should rule over them: wherefore should they say among the people, Where is their God?
>
> *Then will the Lord be jealous for his land, and pity his people.*
>
> Yea, the Lord will answer and say unto his people, Behold, I will send you corn, and wine, and oil, and ye shall be satisfied therewith: and I will no more make you a reproach among the heathen:
>
> *But I will remove far off from you the northern army, and will drive him into a land barren and desolate, with his face toward the east sea, and his hinder part toward the utmost sea, and his stink shall come up, and his ill savour shall come up, because he hath done great things.* (Joel 2:15–20)

Another Prophet to ancient Israel, *Zephaniah,* described Jehovah's power as He will cast out Israel's enemies in the last days:

> Sing, O daughter of Zion; shout, O Israel; be glad and rejoice with all the heart, O daughter of Jerusalem.
>
> *The Lord hath taken away thy judgments, he hath cast out thine enemy: the king of Israel, even the Lord, is in the midst of thee: thou shalt not see evil any more.*
>
> In that day it shall be said to Jerusalem, Fear thou not: and to Zion, Let not thine hands be slack.
>
> *The Lord thy God in the midst of thee is mighty; he will save,* he will rejoice over thee with joy; he will rest in his love, he will joy over thee with singing.
>
> I will gather them that are sorrowful for the solemn assembly, who are of thee, to whom the reproach of it was a burden.
>
> Behold, at that time *I will undo all that afflict thee:* and I will save her that halteth, and gather her that was driven out; and I will get them praise and fame in every land where they have been put to shame.
>
> *At that time will I bring you again, even in the time that I gather you: for I will*

make you a name and a praise among all people of the earth, when I turn back your captivity before your eyes, saith the LORD. (Zephaniah 3:14–20)

Examples from the Book of Mormon. The Prophet **Lehi,** in the first chapter of the Book of Mormon, records a glorious vision which he saw while still in Jerusalem, which caused him to rejoice in the greatness and goodness of Jehovah. He exclaimed, • "Great and marvelous are thy works, *O Lord God Almighty! Thy throne is high in the heavens, and thy power, and goodness, and mercy are over all the inhabitants of the earth*; and, because thou art merciful, thou wilt not suffer those who come unto thee that they shall perish!" (1 Ne. 1:14).

The Prophet **Nephi** cited clues that the "Lord your God" of the Book of Mormon is the same being as the Jehovah of the Old Testament, saying, • "Know ye not that *I, the Lord your God, have created all men*, and that I remember those who are upon the isles of the sea; and that *I rule in the heavens above and in the earth beneath; and I bring forth my word unto the children of men*, yea, even upon all the nations of the earth?" (2 Ne. 29:7).

The newly converted **Alma,** when he began to preach at the Waters of Mormon (about 148 BC), taught about Jehovah, the Almighty God, as he baptized: • "And when he had said these words, the Spirit of the Lord was upon him, and he said: Helam, I baptize thee, *having authority from the Almighty God*, as a testimony that ye have entered into a covenant to serve him until you are dead as to the mortal body; and may the Spirit of the Lord be poured out upon you; and may he grant unto you eternal life, *through the redemption of Christ*" (Mosiah 18:13).

Ammon, the great missionary who ministered about 121 BC, taught the Lamanite King Limhi that Christ (who is Jehovah) is the God who would come to bless men here on this earth: • "he said unto them that *Christ was the God, the Father of all things*, and said that he should take upon him the image of man, and it should be the image after which man was created in the beginning; or in other words, *he said that man was created after the image of God*, and that *God should come down among the children of men, and take upon him flesh and blood, and go forth upon the face of the earth*" (Mosiah 7:27).

Helaman, another Book of Mormon prophet, wrote of the tremendous powers over the elements and geography of the earth which the "Lord their God" is able to exert:

> Behold, they do not desire that *the Lord their God, who hath created them,* should rule and reign over them; notwithstanding his great goodness and his mercy towards them, they do set at naught his counsels, and they will not that he should be their guide.
>
> O how great is the nothingness of the children of men; yea, even they are less than the dust of the earth.
>
> For behold, *the dust of the earth moveth hither and thither, to the dividing asunder,* at the command of our great and everlasting God.
>
> Yea, behold at his voice do the *hills and the mountains tremble* and quake.
>
> And by the power of his voice *they are broken up, and become smooth*, yea, even like unto a valley.
>
> Yea, by the power of his voice doth *the whole earth shake*;
>
> Yea, by the power of his voice, do *the foundations rock, even to the very center.*
>
> Yea, and if he say unto the *earth—Move—it is moved.*
>
> Yea, *if he say unto the earth—Thou shalt go back, that it lengthen out the day for*

many hours—it is done;

And thus, according to his word the *earth goeth back,* and it appeareth unto man that the sun standeth still; yea, and behold, this is so; for surely it is the earth that moveth and not the sun.

And behold, also, if he say unto *the waters of the great deep—Be thou dried up—it is done.*

Behold, if he say unto *this mountain—Be thou raised up, and come over and fall upon that city, that it be buried up—behold it is done.* (Hel. 12:6–17)

An interesting *song of rejoicing* sung by the Nephites who had just been liberated from the depredations of strong bands of secret-combination robbers about AD 21 contains interesting insights: • "they did rejoice and cry again with one voice, saying: *May the God of Abraham, and the God of Isaac, and the God of Jacob, protect this people in righteousness, so long as they shall call on the name of their God for protection.* And it came to pass that they did break forth, all as one, in singing, and praising their God for the great thing which he had done for them, in preserving them from falling into the hands of their enemies. Yea, they did cry: *Hosanna to the Most High God. And they did cry: Blessed be the name of the Lord God Almighty, the Most High God"* (3 Ne. 4:30–32).

Examples from the New Testament. When confronted by Satan on the mount of temptation, ***Jesus*** rebuffed him with the command, • *"Thou shalt not tempt the Lord thy God"* (Matt. 4:7; Luke 4:4). And as Satan tried to entice Jesus to worship him, Jesus rigorously asserted his own authority, stating that he was the only one to be worshiped here on earth during mankind's mortal probation: • "Get thee hence, Satan: for it is written, *Thou shalt worship the Lord thy God, and him only shalt thou serve"* (Matt. 4:10; Luke 4:8). Jesus knew full well the intended meaning of these passages, for it was He in His premortal role as Jehovah, who first revealed them.

Near the end of his ministry, Jesus took advantage of another opportunity to assert His role as God over all this earth. When he was asked, • "Master, which is the great commandment in the law? Jesus said unto him, *Thou shalt love the Lord thy God with all thy heart, and with all thy soul, and with all thy mind. This is the first and great commandment. And the second is like unto it, Thou shalt love thy neighbour as thyself"* (Matt. 22:36–39). He was harking back to the commandment He first revealed to Moses in his premortal role as Jehovah (see Deut. 6:5).

The Apostle ***John*** was shown in vision events beyond the veil. He beheld heavenly beings worshiping the Lord Jesus Christ, saying • *"Holy, holy, holy, Lord God Almighty, which was, and is, and is to come. . . .* The four and twenty elders fall down before him that sat on the throne, and *worship him that liveth for ever and ever,* and cast their crowns before the throne, saying, *Thou art worthy, O Lord, to receive glory and honour and power: for thou hast created all things, and for thy pleasure they are and were created"* (Rev. 4:8, 10–11).

In a later vision recorded in the book of Revelation, the Apostle John describes seeing angels in heaven, and reported that • "they sing the song of Moses the servant of God, and *the song of the Lamb,* saying, *Great and marvellous are thy works, Lord God Almighty; just and true are thy ways, thou King of saints.* Who shall not fear thee, O Lord, and glorify thy name? for *thou only art holy:* for *all nations shall come and worship before thee; for thy judgments are made manifest"* (Rev. 15:3–4. See also Rev. 11:17; 15:3–4; 16:5–7).

Examples from the Doctrine and Covenants. A revelation which was directly obtained from Jesus Christ (preface to D&C 20), in connection with the first formal meeting of the restored Church, asserts that: • "there is a God in heaven, who is infinite and eternal, from everlasting to everlasting the same unchangeable God, *the framer of heaven and earth, and all things which are in them; And that he created man, male and female, after his own image* and in his own likeness, created he them; And gave unto them commandments that *they should love and serve him, the only living and true God, and that he should be the only being whom they should worship*" (D&C 20:17–19).

Another revelation given by the Lord Jesus Christ (see D&C 59:2, 24), records that • "I give unto them a commandment, saying thus: *Thou shalt love the Lord thy God with all thy heart, with all thy might, mind, and strength;* and in the name of Jesus Christ thou shalt serve him" (D&C 59:5). [Note how the Savior switches from first to third person in the last phrase; a communication technique which he frequently employs when he describes Himself or gives instructions or commandments concerning other people's required interactions with Him. See other examples in chapter 11.]

In "the Vision," the glorious instruction on the nature of life after death which Jesus Christ, the Lord and Savior revealed, He described numerous eternal aspects of His role as the God of those who dwell on this earth: • "Hear, O ye heavens, and give ear, O earth, and rejoice ye inhabitants thereof, *for the Lord is God, and beside him there is no Savior.* Great is *his wisdom*, marvelous are *his ways*, and the extent of *his doings* none can find out. *His purposes* fail not, neither are there any who can stay *his hand.* From eternity to eternity *he is the same*, and his years never fail. For thus saith the Lord—*I, the Lord, am merciful and gracious unto those who fear me, and delight to honor those who serve me in righteousness and in truth unto the end.* Great shall be their reward and eternal shall be their glory" (D&C 76:1–6).

In another Doctrine and Covenants revelation, the Lord Jesus Christ speaks of the wide range of his powers, extending from His giving talents unto men to controlling the armies of the earth and ruling in the heavens above:

> Behold, *thus saith the Lord* unto the elders of his church, who are to return speedily to the land from whence they came: Behold, it pleaseth me, that you have come up hither;
> But with some I am not well pleased, for they will not open their mouths, but they hide *the talent which I have given unto them,* because of the fear of man. Wo unto such, for mine anger is kindled against them.
> And it shall come to pass, if they are not more faithful unto me, it shall be taken away, even that which they have.
> For *I, the Lord, rule in the heavens above, and among the armies of the earth; and in the day when I shall make up my jewels, all men shall know what it is that bespeaketh the power of God.* (D&C 60:1–4)

Joseph Smith's poignant prayer, offered while he endured the sordid conditions of Liberty Jail, was addressed to the Lord: "*O Lord God Almighty, maker of heaven, earth, and seas, and of all things that in them are, and who controllest and subjectest the devil,* and the dark and benighted dominion of Sheol—stretch forth thy hand; let thine eye pierce; let thy pavilion be taken up; let thy hiding place no longer be covered; let thine ear be inclined; let thine heart be softened, and thy bowels moved with compassion toward us" (D&C 121:4).

These passages, from the various standard works of the Church, make it clear that Jehovah, who is the LORD of the Old Testament and Jesus Christ of the New

Testament, (1) is the God of this earth, (2) is the principle creator of this earth and its heaven, (3) is He who exercises His powers to control the elements, and (4) is He who directs and controls many of the events and activities of men which transpire upon this earth.

While His followers are commanded by Jehovah/Jesus Christ to have no other Gods, in priority, *before* Him, that does not preclude their also worshiping the divine being who is the father of their spirits: *God the Father*. Nor does it prohibit them from worshiping the divine Comforter who frequently teaches, directs, protects, consoles and inspires them: *God the Holy Ghost*. The continually repeated assertions that Jehovah/Jesus Christ is *the* God of this earth in no way diminishes the stature and glory of God the Father and God the Holy Ghost, nor the importance of the many significant roles which They fulfill in the administration, blessing, and exalting of this earth and its inhabitants!

Jehovah/Jesus Christ "Owns" All Things

At least pertaining to this earth, Jesus Christ owns all things. Consider again the full import of what the Psalmist said: • *"The earth is the LORD's, and the fulness thereof; the world, and they that dwell therein"* (Ps. 24:1). The identification of Jehovah's ownership of the many items listed below becomes significant because it provides an identifying characteristic in numerous scriptural passages in which the identity of the Godhead member who is speaking is deemed uncertain at first glance.

In his profound discourse, **King Benjamin** conveyed this perspective concerning Jehovah's ownership of all things:

> *O how you ought to thank your heavenly King!*
>
> I say unto you, my brethren, that if you should render all the thanks and praise which your whole soul has power to possess, *to that God who has created you*, and has kept and preserved you, and has caused that ye should rejoice, and has granted that ye should live in peace one with another—
>
> I say unto you that *if ye should serve him who has created you from the beginning, and is preserving you from day to day, by lending you breath, that ye may live and move and do according to your own will, and even supporting you from one moment to another*—I say, if ye should serve him with all your whole souls yet ye would be unprofitable servants.
>
> And behold, all that he requires of you is to keep his commandments; and *he has promised you that if ye would keep his commandments ye should prosper in the land*; and he never doth vary from that which he hath said; therefore, if ye do keep his commandments he doth bless you and prosper you.
>
> And now, in the first place, *he hath created you, and granted unto you your lives, for which ye are indebted unto him.*
>
> And secondly, he doth require that ye should do as he hath commanded you; for which if ye do, *he doth immediately bless you; and therefore he hath paid you.* And *ye are still indebted unto him, and are, and will be, forever and ever;* therefore, of what have ye to boast?
>
> And now I ask, can ye say aught of yourselves? I answer you, Nay. Ye cannot say that ye are even as much as the dust of the earth; yet ye were created of the dust of the earth; but behold, *it belongeth to him who created you.* (Mosiah 2:19–25)

It is instructive to list the things the Lord specifically claims as being personally *His* in the scriptures. The list below is incomplete, since it is only based on a D&C

computer search of the word "my" which the Savior used hundreds of times in His modern revelations, but it puts the point being made in clear perspective. Searching the other standard works undoubtedly would add more items to the list.

Group One: The Church: Observe some of the many church-related things that Jesus Christ created and brought to pass and for which He claims full ownership. [A few of the most significant are highlighted in bold type. All citations are from the Doctrine and Covenants.] He speaks of [1] "my **church** (1:1), [2] my holy **priesthood** (119:4), [3] my holy **prophets** (10:46), [4] my **ministry** (6:29), [5] my everlasting **gospel** (27:5), [6] my **doctrine** (10:62), [7] my **covenant** (38:20), [8] my new and everlasting covenant (132:27), [9] my **testimony** (124:8), [10] my **kingdom** (100:11) and [11] my **glory** (78:8). He speaks of all these, and the many other things which will be listed, as [12] "my **works** (29:33), [13] my **purpose** (5:4), [14] my **cause** (30:11), [15] my **will** (25:2), [16] my **act** (101:95), [17] my strange act (95:4), and [18] my strange work (101:95)."

Group Two: The People: Jesus refers to His faithful followers as [19] "my **disciples** (6:32), [20] my **stewards** (104:86), [21] my **saints** (61:17), [22] my **Zion** (14:6), [23] my **servants** (1:6), [24] my counselor(s) (90:21), [25] my high council (120:1), [26] my jewels (60:4), [27] my **people** (39:11), [28] my creatures (104:13), [29] my **sheep** (112:14), [30] my young men (101:55), [31] my **warriors** (101:55), [32] my **army** (105:31), [33] my **vineyard** (21:9), [34] my **friends** (84:63), [35] my **son(s)** (31:1), [36] my **daughter(s)** (25:1), [37] my handmaid(s) (90:28), [38] my **little ones** (121:19), [39] my **church in Zion** (115:3), [40] my **redeemed** (133:52), and [41] my **beloved** (7:1)."

Group Three: The Revelations: The Savior speaks of His instructions and revelations which He gives to His followers as [42] "my **commandments** (1:6), [43] my command(s) (29:6), [44] my **statutes** (119:6), [45] my **laws** (38:22), [46] my holy laws (124:50), [47] my **words** (5:6), [48] my holy words (124:46), [49] my righteous purposes (17:9), [50] my sayings (72:23), [51] my **scriptures** (6:27), [52] my preface (1:6), [53] my strong reasoning (45:10), [54] my **knowledge** (101:25), [55] my **wisdom** (10:40), [56] my **judgments** (29:30), [57] my **blessings** (82:23), and [58] my **reward(s)** (54:10)."

Group Four: Property and Activities: The Lord also stresses His ownership of property, edifices, and activities with terms like: [59] "my **holy land** (84:59), [60] my footstool (38:17), [61] my **land** (101:57), [62] my **temple** (36:8), [63] my holy house (124:39), [64] my **tabernacle** (93:4), [65] my **houses** (104:34), [66] my boarding house (124:56), [67] my storehouse (42:34), and [68] my **general conference** (124:88)."

Other personal traits and rewards: Jesus also describes some of His personal emotions, traits and abilities (which others, obviously, also might possess) as [69] "my **love** (6:20), [70] my **goodness** (86:11), [71] my **grace** (17:8), [72] my **holy day** (59:9), [73] my pleasure (136:30), [74] my **work** (101:95), [75] my **rock** (11:16), [76] my **glory** (7:3), [77] my **name** (11:30), [78] my name's glory (19:7), [79] my sake (93:46), [80] my providence (78:14), [81] my **rebuke** (133:68), [82] my **anger** (19:15), [83] my **wrath** (19:15), [84] my **vengeance** (98:28), [85] my **judgments** (29:30), [86] my **power** (11:10), [87] my almighty power (19:14), [88] my **preparations** (19:19), [89] my rest (19:9), [90] my **salvation** (18:17), [91] my **reward** (112:34), and [92] my **seal** (101:61)."

Physical characteristics: Most definitely, the resurrected Christ still has a tangible, physical, glorified body. He refers to His various body parts frequently in the Doctrine and Covenants, making specific mention of [93] "my presence (29:41), [94] my body (27:2), [95] my bones (85:6), [96] my soul (25:12), [97] my face (39:20), [98] my countenance (88:52), [99] my ears (90:1), [100] my sight (66:3), [101] my mouth (19:15), [102] my voice (18:35), [103] my arm (133:67), [104] my hands (103:40), [105] my right hand (29:12), [106] my left hand (19:5), [107] my heart (104:5), [108] my [mortal] blood (27:2), [109] my side (6:37), [110] my bowels (101:9), and [111] my feet (103:7)." He also makes reference to His apparel and possessions: [112] "my covering (124:8), [113] my garments (133:51), [114] my raiment (133:51), [115] my whole armor (27:15), and [116] my scepter (106:6)." He alludes to His physical movements with references such as [117] "my coming (5:19), [118] my coming in a pillar of fire (29:12), and [119] my visitation (124:10)."

Relationships with other Godhead members: Jesus Christ also refers to His relationships to the other members of the Godhead in possessive form, speaking of [120] "my God (88:75), [121] my Father (50:41), [122] my Father's kingdom (84:38), [123] my Father's house (98:18), [124] my Spirit (8:1), and [125] my Holy Spirit (99:2)."

Above, then, are 125 scriptural clues which help to discern of whom various passages are speaking. It is a valuable list!

Three "Births" with Major "Nature of God" Implications

The scriptures speak of Jehovah/Jesus Christ having three "births." They are:

1. His *premortal* birth as the firstborn spirit child of God the Father.
2. His *mortal* birth, in the manger at Bethlehem.
3. His "birth" as the *firstborn of this earth's resurrected beings*.

As will be seen, each one of these three "birth" events, which will be discussed below, present major doctrinal challenges for those whose beliefs are based in "trinitarian" concepts of the nature of God.

"Trinitarians" do not believe in the premortal life of all mankind. Prior to the *Council of Nicæa* in AD 325, varying beliefs existed concerning the status of Christ before His mortal birth. However, when the Arian controversy arose and they sought some way to reconcile their different beliefs concerning the premortal existence and status of Jesus Christ, they finally settled on the words: "I believe in one God the Father Almighty, Maker of heaven and earth, And of all things visible and invisible. And in one Lord Jesus Christ, the Son of God, begotten of the Father" (Philip Schaff, ed., *The Creeds of Christendom*, 1:27).

In the second Catholic "ecumenical council," which was convened by Theodosius in Constantinople in AD 381, changes were made in the wording of the Nicæan creed, as follow: "We believe in one God the Father Almighty, Maker of heaven and earth, And of all things visible and invisible. And in one Lord Jesus Christ, *the only-begotten Son of God, Begotten of the Father before all worlds*" (Philip Schaff, ed., *The Creeds of Christendom*, 1:27).

Thus, the AD 381 revisers of the Nicæan creed confused the first and second births (Christ's premortal birth and His mortal birth, listed above).

They also added more wording concerning the Holy Ghost. The AD 325 *Nicæan creed* had originally said, only: "And in the Holy Ghost." But in the "updating" of the *Nicæan creed* in AD 381, the Holy Ghost portion was enlarged to read: "And in the Holy Ghost, *The Lord, and Giver of life; Who proceedeth from the Father; Who with the*

Father and the Son together is worshiped and glorified; Who spake by the prophets" (Philip Schaff, ed., *The Creeds of Christendom*, 1:29).

The "proceedeth" portion is apparently based on John 15:26: • "But when the Comforter is come, whom I will send unto you from the Father, even the Spirit of truth, *which proceedeth from the Father*, he shall testify of me."

Jehovah/Jesus Christ's *Premortal* Birth: the Firstborn Child of God the Father

What scriptural evidence is there that Jehovah is God the Father's firstborn son and child? Several brief verses communicate that knowledge:

The Lord Jesus Christ testified of Himself that • "I was in the beginning with the Father, *and am the Firstborn*" (D&C 93:21). D&C section 109 speaks of • "Jesus Christ, *the Son of thy* [God the Father's] *bosom*" (D&C 109:4).

The Apostle Paul wrote that God the Father's "dear Son," Jesus Christ, was • "*the firstborn of every creature*" (Col. 1:15). Obviously, there are only two births of Jesus Christ which can be considered: (1) His premortal birth in which His "intelligence(s)" became the spirit son and child of God the Father, or (2) the mortal birth of Jesus Christ where His mortal mother, Mary of Nazareth, was "overshadowed" by "the Highest" and hence was called "the Son of the Highest" (see Luke 1:32, 35). It is known that there are many (billions!) of spirit children of God the Father (hence He is called the "*Father of spirits*," see Heb. 12:9); all of which are similar and subsequent to Jehovah's premortal birth. The "firstborn" phrase cannot pertain to Jesus' mortal birth, for there were millions of humans born prior to His entry into mortality.

The author of Hebrews speaks of Jesus Christ as already being the Father's first-begotten before Jesus' entry into mortality, saying, "*when he bringeth in the firstbegotten into the world*, he saith, . . . let all the angels of God worship him" (Heb. 1:6).

Added to these verses are a brief series of passages which speak of the heavenly Church which is to be presided over by Jesus Christ, which is named the "church of the firstborn." That ecclesiastical church name, of course, attests to Jehovah/Jesus Christ being God the Father's firstborn spirit child: • "ye are come unto mount Sion, and unto the city of the living God, the heavenly Jerusalem, and to an innumerable company of angels, *To the general assembly and church of the firstborn*" (Heb. 12:22–23).

That passage in Hebrews is the only biblical allusion to the Church of the First-born; all the other passages which make reference to it are found in the Doctrine and Covenants: • "They are *they who are the church of the Firstborn*" (D&C 76:54). • "These are they who have come to an innumerable company of angels, to the general assembly and *church of Enoch, and of the Firstborn*" (D&C 76:67). • "these are they who are of the terrestrial, whose glory differs from that of *the church of the Firstborn who have received the fulness of the Father*" (D&C 76:71). • "*They who dwell in his presence are the church of the Firstborn*" (D&C 76:94). • "these all are they who will not be gathered with the saints, *to be caught up unto the church of the Firstborn*, and received into the cloud" (D&C 76:102). • "to bring as many as will come *to the church of the Firstborn*" (D&C 77:11). • "*ye are the church of the Firstborn, and he will take you up in a cloud*, and appoint every man his portion" (D&C 78:21). • "Which glory is that of *the church of the Firstborn, even of God, the holiest of all, through Jesus Christ his Son*" (D&C 88:5). • "*all those who are begotten through me are partakers of the glory of the same, and are the church of the Firstborn*" (D&C 93:22). • "to have the heavens opened unto them, *to commune with the general assembly and church of the Firstborn, and to enjoy the communion and presence of God the Father, and Jesus the mediator of the new covenant"* (D&C 107:14, 19).

These passages combine together to attest that Jehovah/Jesus Christ was the firstborn son and child of God the Father, obviously born as God the Father began His family of spirit children. All the inhabitants of this planet earth are members of that family.

Jehovah/Jesus Christ's *Mortal* Birth: The Only Begotten Son of God the Father

Latter-day Saints believe that Jesus Christ was born on earth as the Son of an *immortal Father*, God the Father, and a *mortal mother*, Mary of Nazareth. He is not the son of the Holy Ghost.

The creed-makers of early Christianity didn't understand the words of the Angel Gabriel to the virgin Mary: *"The Holy Ghost shall come upon thee*, and *the power of the Highest shall overshadow thee*: therefore also that holy thing which shall be born of thee shall be called the Son of God"* (Luke 1:35). Nor did they understand the words spoken to Joseph by the angel who • "appeared unto him in a dream, saying, Joseph, thou son of David, fear not to take unto thee Mary thy wife: for *that which is conceived in her is of the Holy Ghost"* (Matt. 1:20). Their teaching on the subject is based *entirely* on these two passages plus Matthew 1:18, which says: "When as his mother Mary was espoused to Joseph, before they came together, she was found *with child of the Holy Ghost."*

To assume that these three passages are stating that Jesus would be conceived by the Holy Ghost, rather than God the Father, is a gross error contradicted by hundreds of passages in the Bible and the other Latter-day Saint standard works in which *Jesus addresses and regards God the Father as His Father,* **not** the Holy Ghost.

What do various Catholic and Protestant key creedal statements say about Jesus' parentage? The *Apostles' Creed* says: "I believe in God the Father Almighty, Maker of heaven and earth. And in Jesus Christ, His only Son, our Lord, *Who was conceived by the Holy Ghost,* Born of the Virgin Mary; . . ." The *Nicene Creed*, while acknowledging that Jesus was "Begotten of His Father before all worlds," still states that Jesus "came down from heaven, And *was incarnate by the Holy Ghost* of the Virgin Mary, And was made man." Though this statement was dropped in various later creeds, the teaching that Mary was impregnated by the Holy Ghost still showed up in the *Old Catholicism 1911 Statement of Union*, in these words: Jesus "for us men and for our salvation came down from heaven, and *was Incarnate by the Holy Ghost of the Virgin Mary*, and was made man." It's also found in the Lutheran *Smalcald Articles* (1537), of which Martin Luther wrote the preface. The Articles said, "That the Son became man thus: that *he was conceived*, without the co-operation of man, *by the Holy Ghost*, and was born of the pure, holy [and always] Virgin Mary."

In contrast, Latter-day Saints believe that, as was indicated in Gabriel's prophecy to Mary, it was *"the power of the Highest,"* God the Father, which would "overshadow" her (Luke 1:32, 35), not the Holy Ghost, who is never referred to as "the highest" in the scriptures. Nephi's vision of the virgin Mary should be recalled in this context, which aids in understanding the Holy Ghost's role as a transporting facilitator in connection with Mary's becoming with child: • "I beheld that *she was carried away in the Spirit;* and *after she had been carried away in the Spirit for the space of a time* the angel spake unto me, saying: Look! And I looked and beheld the virgin again, bearing a child in her arms" (1 Ne. 11:19–20).

As will be seen, the combining of the power to live forever, through the parenthood of His immortal Father, with the power to die, through the parenthood of His mortal mother Mary, is what gave Jesus Christ the unique ability to perform His infinite Atonement. He alone, of all mankind, had the power to either live forever or to give His life, of His own volition, which made it possible for Him to literally sacrifice His life for all mankind on the cross. And it was that unique combination of immortality and mortality which somehow enabled Him to take up His life once again in the resurrection and break the bands of death so all mankind also could be resurrected. He, alone had this power; He, alone could die and rise again as He atoned for the sins of all mankind.

God the Father, Himself, repeatedly asserted that it was He who fathered Jesus here on earth, doing so by calling Jesus His *"Only Begotten Son"*—a phrase to which Latter-day Saints typically add the words "in the flesh," for they know that God the Father is "the Father of spirits" (Heb. 12:9), and that His son, Jehovah/Jesus Christ was in that sense • *"the firstborn among many brethren"* (Rom. 8:29) in the premortal spirit world. So, if Jesus had "many brethren" prior to mortality, the only situation where He could possibly be God the Father's "only begotten Son" would have to be His birth into mortality—His birth "in the flesh."

The *Bible* records numerous times when Jesus Christ is spoken of as the "only begotten Son" of God the Father. Probably the best-known passages are • "For God so loved the world, that *he gave his only begotten Son,* that whosoever believeth in him should not perish, but have everlasting life" (John 3:16). Other passages from the New Testament include: • "And the Word was made flesh, and dwelt among us, (and we beheld his glory, *the glory as of the only begotten of the Father,)* full of grace and truth" (John 1:14). • "No man hath seen God at any time; *the only begotten Son,* which is in the bosom of the Father, he hath declared [him]" (John 1:18). • "he that believeth not is condemned already, because *he hath not believed in the name of the only begotten Son of God"* (John 3:18). • "For unto which of the angels said he at any time, *Thou art my Son, this day have I begotten thee?* And again, I will be to him a Father, and he shall be to me a Son?" (Heb. 1:5). • and "In this was manifested the love of God toward us, because that *God sent his only begotten Son into the world,* that we might live through him" (1 Jn. 4:9).

Book of Mormon passages on the subject include: • "it was accounted unto Abraham in the wilderness to be obedient unto the commands of God in offering up his son Isaac, which is a similitude of God and *his Only Begotten Son,"* (Jacob 4:5). • "be reconciled unto him through the atonement of Christ, *his Only Begotten Son,"* (Jacob 4:11). • "God did call on men, in the name of his Son, (this being the plan of redemption which was laid) saying: If ye will repent and harden not your hearts, then will *I have mercy upon you, through mine Only Begotten Son"* (Alma 12:33). • "thus this holy calling being prepared from the foundation of the world for such as would not harden their hearts, being in and through *the atonement of the Only Begotten Son,"* (Alma 13:5).

Other passages referring to Jesus Christ as God the Father's only begotten Son are found in the *Doctrine and Covenants* and the *Pearl of Great Price:* • "Those things which were from the beginning before the world was, which were ordained of the Father, *through his Only Begotten Son,* who was in the bosom of the Father, even from the beginning" (D&C 76:13). • "[Satan] rebelled against *the Only Begotten Son whom the Father loved* and who was in the bosom of the Father, was thrust down from the presence of God and the Son" (D&C 76:25). • "[sons of perdition] having denied the Holy Spirit after having received it, and *having denied the Only Begotten Son of the*

Father, having crucified him unto themselves and put him to an open shame" (D&C 76:35). • *John*: "I beheld his glory, as *the glory of the Only Begotten of the Father*, ... which came and dwelt in the flesh, and dwelt among us" (D&C 93:11). • "all these had departed the mortal life, firm in the hope of a glorious resurrection, through the grace of God the Father and *his Only Begotten Son, Jesus Christ*" (D&C 138:14).

From the *Pearl of Great Price*: • "the angel spake, saying: This thing is a similitude of *the sacrifice of the Only Begotten of the Father*, which is full of grace and truth" (Moses 5:7). • "the Holy 'Ghost fell upon Adam, which beareth record of the Father and the Son, saying: *I am the Only Begotten of the Father* from the beginning, henceforth and forever" (Moses 5:9). See also: Alma 12:34; D&C 20:21; 29:42; 49:5; 76:57; 124:123; 138:14; 138:57; Moses 1:32; 5:57; 6:52.

Translation errors lead to creedal errors: Various Bible translations reflect the lack of understanding of their translators and interpretive editors concerning the King James Version phrase "only begotten Son." Since they don't perceive its meaning, they render John 3:16 without the phrase, saying such things as: *New International Version Bible* [NIV]: "For God so loved the world that he gave *his one and only Son*" and the *New Revised Standard Version*: "For God so loved the world that he gave *his only Son*."

This essential omission results in the false but commonly expressed notion that God the Son Jesus Christ is the *only* Son of God the Father—an apostate doctrine which causes those who believe it to fail to comprehend that God the Father is the premortal Father of the spirits of all mankind, and that He literally loves all of them as His children. Again, as the Apostle Paul wrote, Jesus Christ is • *the firstborn of every creature*" (Col. 1:15), so Jesus most definitely is not God the Father's "only Son."

The error goes back to ancient times, and is expressed in the early Catholic creeds: *The Apostles' Creed* states: "I believe in God the Father Almighty, ... And *in Jesus Christ His only Son*, our Lord." *The Nicene Creed* keeps the phrase Only-begotten Son, but applies the "only son" interpretation to Christ's premortal birth, which Latter-day Saints understand is His birth as the firstborn spirit child of God the Father, prior to the subsequent births of "many brethren" (Rom. 8:29). *The Nicene Creed* (following the changes made in the AD 381 Council of Constantinople) states: "I Believe in one God, the Father Almighty, ... And in one Lord Jesus Christ, *the only-begotten Son of God, Begotten of His Father before all worlds*."

Jehovah/Jesus Christ as the First Begotten of the Dead: His Resurrection "Birth"

In the eternal plan of redemption, transitions are required as (1) one passes from the premortal world to mortality (when spirit beings acquire a mortal body), (2) one goes from mortality back to the spirit world (in which spirit beings are separated from their mortal bodies), and (3) when one changes from being only a spirit in the spirit world to becoming a resurrected being (when spirit beings acquire their glorified, resurrected body). In each instance, a simultaneous death and birth appears to occur. Thus, "death" signifies an ending to a current phase of eternal life, and "birth" signifies a beginning to a new phase of eternal existence. With this understanding, it is easy to see why some scriptural passages refer to Jesus Christ's resurrection as being a type of "birth." They don't mean that He began life again as a tiny baby, but rather that *he had begun a new phase of the eternal plan*: that of existing as a resurrected, eternal being (never to have His body separated from His spirit again).

Several *Bible* passages refer to Christ as the "first begotten" or the "first fruits" or simply "the first" of the dead to be resurrected, which is why this section classifies His resurrection as one of His "births." These passages are: • "And from Jesus Christ, who is the faithful witness, and *the first begotten of the dead*, and the prince of the kings of the earth" (Rev. 1:5). • "That Christ should suffer, and that *he should be the first that should rise from the dead*, and should shew light unto the people, and to the Gentiles" (Acts 26:23). • "But now is Christ risen from the dead, *and become the firstfruits of them that slept.* For since by man came death, by man came also the resurrection of the dead" (1 Cor. 15:20–21). But every man in his own order: *Christ the firstfruits*; afterward they that are Christ's at his coming" (1 Cor. 15:22–23).

A significant **Book of Mormon** passage continues this theme, saying that He is • "the Holy Messiah, who layeth down his life according to the flesh, and taketh it again by the power of the Spirit, that he may bring to pass the resurrection of the dead, *being the first that should rise.* Wherefore, *he is the firstfruits unto God*" (2 Ne. 2:8–9).

There is no doubt that the resurrected Christ had a tangible, touchable, physical body after He was resurrected: when He appeared to his Apostles in Jerusalem, He invited them to • "Behold my hands and my feet, that it is I myself: *handle me, and see; for a spirit hath not flesh and bones, as ye see me have*" (Luke 24:39). And after they had seen and felt His resurrected body, He sat and ate fish and honeycomb before them (Luke 24:41–43). He mingled with them for forty days, appearing to them on numerous occasions. And finally, when they were together on the Mount of Olives, • "while they beheld, he was taken up; and a cloud received him out of their sight" (Acts 1:9). And then two angelic beings appeared to the Apostles and told them: • *"this same Jesus, which is taken up from you into heaven, shall so come in like manner as ye have seen him go into heaven,"* (Acts 1:10–11). So, just as He ascended into heaven in His tangible, resurrected body, and is to return with it in like manner, and cannot die (so His body can't ever again be separated from His spirit), it is undisputable Bible doctrine that Christ has a tangible, resurrected body in the heavens today.

The Apostle John bore witness of Christ's return in glory that • "we know that, when he shall appear, *we shall be like him; for we shall see him as he is*" (1 Jn. 3:2).

By definition, resurrection means that Christ's renewed, glorified, perfected physical body now is inseparably surrounding His immortal spirit. And because He broke the bands of death for all mankind, all shall be resurrected, never to die again. See, in the **Bible**: • *"Christ being raised from the dead dieth no more; death hath no more dominion over him"* (Rom. 6:9). • "the wages of sin is death; but the gift of God is *eternal life* through Jesus Christ our Lord" (Rom. 6:23). • "So when this corruptible shall have put on incorruption, and this mortal shall *have put on immortality*, then shall be brought to pass the saying that is written, Death is swallowed up in victory" (1 Cor. 15:54). • "our Saviour *Jesus Christ, who hath abolished death*, and hath brought life and *immortality* to light," (2 Tim. 1:10). • "I am he that liveth, and was dead; and, behold, *I am alive for evermore*" (Rev. 1:18). • "God shall wipe away all tears from their eyes; and *there shall be no more death*" (Rev. 21:4).

Book of Mormon passages convey the same understandings: • *"the spirit and the body is restored to itself again, and all men become incorruptible, and immortal,* and they are living souls, having a perfect knowledge like unto us in the flesh, save it be that our knowledge shall be perfect" (2 Ne. 9:13). • *"the sting of death is swallowed up in Christ.* He is the light and the life of the world; yea, a light that is endless, that can never be darkened; yea, and also *a life which is endless, that there can be no more death"*

(Mosiah 16:8–9). • "there is a death which is called a temporal death; and *the death of Christ shall loose the bands of this temporal death,* that *all* shall be raised from this temporal death. *The spirit and the body shall be reunited again in its perfect form; both limb and joint shall be restored to its proper frame,* even as we now are at this time" (Alma 11:42–43). • "this mortal body is raised to an immortal body, that is from death, even from the first death unto life, that *they can die no more; their spirits uniting with their bodies, never to be divided*; thus the whole becoming spiritual and immortal, that they can no more see corruption" (Alma 11:45). • "*The Father having raised me up unto you first,* and sent me to bless you in turning away every one of you from his iniquities; and this because ye are the children of the covenant" (3 Ne. 20:26).

The "trinitarian" quandary caused by Christ's resurrection. As seen above, the Bible clearly teaches that (1) Jesus Christ is a resurrected being, (2) that in the resurrection, the body is reunited to the spirit, (3) Christ ascended into heaven in bodily form, (4) Christ cannot die again, so His body and spirit are inseparably united for all eternity, (5) Christ is to return to earth in the same resurrected body in which He ascended to heaven. Therefore, it is clear Bible doctrine that Christ has a tangible, resurrected body in the heavens today.

The "trinitarian" problem is that their definition of the "trinity" specifies that (1) God is only a spirit, without physical shape or form, (2) that God the Father, God the Son, and God the Holy Ghost are all beings of the same inseparable "substance," (3) and that the Father, Son and Holy Ghost are only one God, not three Gods.

So, (1) how can Jesus Christ have a tangible, resurrected body and still be the same *only one* God as the God the Father and God the Holy Ghost, who according to the creeds are beings without tangible shape or form? and (2) how can Jesus Christ be of the same "substance" as God the Father and the Holy Ghost, as according to the creeds, and yet have a tangible, resurrected body?

No credible answer for this dilemma has been supplied in the last 1800 years, and it appears that no credible answer is going to be forthcoming. "It's a mystery!" certainly isn't ringing true to many thoughtful seekers after truth.

The Gospel of Jesus Christ Defined by the Savior

What, exactly, is the gospel of Jesus Christ, and what are its central doctrines? There are many allusions to it. As he began his gospel, Mark labeled his writings • "*The beginning of the gospel of Jesus Christ, the Son of God*" (Mark 1:1). The Apostle Paul gave a one-phrase description of it as he bore his testimony: • "I am not ashamed of the gospel of Christ: for *it is the power of God unto salvation to every one that believeth* . . . For therein is the righteousness of God revealed" (Rom. 1:16–17). In the Book of Mormon Nephi wrote • "behold, my beloved brethren, *this is the way*; and *there is none other way nor name given under heaven whereby man can be saved in the kingdom of God.* And now, behold, *this is the doctrine of Christ,* and the only and true doctrine of the Father, and of the Son, and of the Holy Ghost" (2 Ne. 31:21).

In an effort to get down to specifics on the subject, two key passages (3 Ne. 27:13–22 and 3 Ne. 11:31–40) will be cited. Together they represent an excellent summation of the gospel and basic doctrines of Jesus Christ.

First, 3 Ne 27:13–22, which contains the resurrected Jesus' definition of His gospel which He gave to His disciples in a special appearance to them, is a doctrine-filled and definitive passage:

Behold I have given unto you my gospel, and *this is the gospel which I have given unto you—that I came into the world to do the will of my Father,* because *my Father sent me.*

And *my Father sent me that I might be lifted up upon the cross;* and after that I had been lifted up upon the cross, *that I might draw all men unto me,* that as I have been lifted up by men *even so should men be lifted up by the Father, to stand before me, to be judged of their works,* whether they be good or whether they be evil—

And for this cause have I been lifted up; therefore, *according to the power of the Father I will draw all men unto me, that they may be judged according to their works.*

And it shall come to pass, that whoso *repenteth* and *is baptized in my name* shall be filled; and *if he endureth to the end,* behold, *him will I hold guiltless before my Father at that day when I shall stand to judge the world.*

And *he that endureth not unto the end, the same is he that is also hewn down* and cast into the fire, from whence they can no more return, *because of the justice of the Father.*

And this is the word which he hath given unto the children of men. And for this cause *he fulfilleth the words which he hath given,* and he lieth not, but fulfilleth all his words.

And *no unclean thing can enter into his kingdom;* therefore *nothing entereth into his rest save it be those who have washed their garments in my blood, because of their faith, and the repentance of all their sins,* and their faithfulness unto the end.

Now this is the commandment: **Repent, all ye ends of the earth**, and **come unto me** and **be baptized in my name,** that ye may **be sanctified by the reception of the Holy Ghost,** that ye may **stand spotless before me at the last day.**

Verily, verily, I say unto you, *this is my gospel*; and ye know the things that ye must do in my church; for *the works which ye have seen me do that shall ye also do*; for that which ye have seen me do even that shall ye do;

Therefore, *if ye do these things blessed are ye, for ye shall be lifted up at the last day.* (3 Ne. 27:13–22)

The second passage, 3 Nephi 11:31–40, is also from the record of the resurrected Christ's appearances to the Nephites in the land of Bountiful. These words were spoken to the multitude midday in his first day's appearance to them:

I will declare unto you my doctrine.

And *this is my doctrine,* and *it is the doctrine which the Father hath given unto me*; and *I bear record of the Father, and the Father beareth record of me, and the Holy Ghost beareth record of the Father and me*; and I bear record that *the Father commandeth all men, everywhere, to repent and believe in me.*

And *whoso believeth in me, and is baptized, the same shall be saved*; and *they are they who shall inherit the kingdom of God.*

And *whoso believeth not in me, and is not baptized, shall be damned.*

Verily, verily, I say unto you, that *this is my doctrine,* and *I bear record of it from the Father*; and *whoso believeth in me believeth in the Father* also; and *unto him will the Father bear record of me,* for *he will visit him with fire and with the Holy Ghost.*

And *thus will the Father bear record of me, and the Holy Ghost will bear record unto him of the Father and me*; for *the Father, and I, and the Holy Ghost are one.*

And again I say unto you, **ye must repent,** and **become as a little child**, and **be baptized in my name,** or ye can in nowise receive these things.

And again I say unto you, *ye must repent, and be baptized in my name, and become as a little child, or ye can in nowise inherit the kingdom of God.*

Verily, verily, I say unto you, that *this is my doctrine,* and *whoso buildeth upon this buildeth upon my rock,* and *the gates of hell shall not prevail against them.*

And *whoso shall declare more or less than this, and establish it for my doctrine, the same cometh of evil, and is not built upon my rock;* but he buildeth upon a sandy foundation, and *the gates of hell stand open to receive such* when the floods come and the winds beat upon them. (3 Ne. 11:31–40)

The numerous themes interwoven in these two passages constitute the central core of the Gospel of Jesus Christ. The most basic, and personally actionable teachings, are summarized in the *Fourth Article of Faith:* • "We believe that the first principles and ordinances of the Gospel are: first, *Faith* in the Lord Jesus Christ; second, *Repentance;* third, *Baptism* by immersion for the remission of sins; fourth, *Laying on of hands for the gift of the Holy Ghost"* (Articles of Faith 1:4).

As italicized in the passages above, more than a dozen other profound themes are interwoven with these four basic "first" principles. The study and contemplation of all of those themes together present a curriculum for lifetime study and an actionable program for personal refinement and sanctification. The diligent pursuit of these eternal truths is a course of action commended to all who read this book!

Jesus Christ Is the Mediator between Man and God and the Only Name whereby Man Can Be Saved

Abinadi's discourse, in Mosiah chapter 15, is a remarkable presentation on numerous aspects of the Lord's ministry and atoning sacrifice. It is a prophecy, spoken about 148 BC, which outlines many of the events that would take place in the Savior's mortal life. Three verses have special meaning in the present context. He said:

He shall be led, crucified, and slain, the flesh becoming subject even unto death, the will of the Son being swallowed up in the will of the Father.

And thus God breaketh the bands of death, having gained the victory over death; *giving the Son power to make intercession for the children of men—*

Having ascended into heaven, having the bowels of mercy; being filled with compassion towards the children of men; **standing betwixt them and justice;** *having broken the bands of death,* **taken upon himself their iniquity and their transgressions, having redeemed them, and satisfied the demands of justice."** (Mosiah 15:7–9)

The Lord's atoning sacrifice was • "an infinite atonement" (2 Ne. 9:7). What does that mean? It means that He suffered for *all mankind,* paying the debt for all their sins: • "I, God, have suffered these things *for all,* that *they might not suffer* if they would repent" (D&C 19:16).

It also means that Christ "purchased" all mankind from the demands of justice, so He *owns* every one of God the Father's children who has ever come or will come to mortality: • *"ye are bought with a price*: therefore glorify God in your body, and in your spirit, which are God's" (1 Cor. 6:20).

Christ's atonement allows mankind to be counted free from sin at Judgment Day because he has paid for us, with his grace bridging the gap between man's status at the end of his mortal probation and the perfection level of being completely free from sin. But, His payment also requires mankind to be His servants: • "he that is *called in the Lord, being a servant,* is the Lord's freeman: likewise also he that is called, being free, is *Christ's servant. Ye are bought with a price"* (1 Cor. 7:22–23).

Is Christ a tough taskmaster? See the answer through His eyes. He says, • "Listen to the voice of Jesus Christ, your Redeemer, the Great I AM, *whose arm of mercy hath atoned for your sins"* (D&C 29:1). He wants to extend His godly quality of mercy to all who will believe in Him and heed His commandments. They have to accept Him and follow His plan. What, exactly, is that plan? He explained it Himself:

> *For this cause have I been lifted up*; therefore, according to the power of the Father *I will draw all men unto me, that they may be judged according to their works.*
>
> *And it shall come to pass, that whoso **repenteth** and is **baptized** in my name shall be filled; and if **he endureth to the end**, behold, **him will I hold guiltless before my Father** at that day when I shall stand to judge the world.* (3 Ne. 27:15–16)

That's the ***two-sided bargain:***

Man's responsibility: If an individual will come to Him, repent, and cleanse himself from sin through baptism, and keep striving to be righteous to the end of His mortal probation,

Christ's responsibility: Christ will hold that individual guiltless before His Father at Judgment Day, thereby allowing the individual to continue progressing and to eventually enter into Heavenly Father's celestial realm. That's the celestial route.

The wickedness alternative: Those who won't come unto Christ, repent, be baptized, and endure to the end will have to suffer for their own sins, paying the price in hell and then, following the resurrection, be limited to eternal life in only the telestial or terrestrial level of glory. That, definitely, is ***not*** the best choice!

More details: first, how Christ will serve as man's mediator and advocate at Judgment Day:

> Listen to him who is *the advocate with the Father, who is pleading your cause before him—*
>
> Saying: Father, *behold the sufferings and death of him who did no sin,* in whom thou wast well pleased; behold the blood of thy Son which was shed, the blood of him whom thou gavest that thyself might be glorified;
>
> Wherefore, *Father, spare these my brethren that believe on my name, that they may come unto me and have everlasting life.* (D&C 45:3–5)

Second, more of what Christ requires of those who will come unto Him:

> And ye shall offer for a sacrifice unto me *a broken heart* and *a contrite spirit.* And whoso cometh unto me with a broken heart and a contrite spirit, *him will I baptize with fire and with the Holy Ghost, even as the Lamanites,* because of their faith in me at the time of their conversion, were *baptized with fire and with the Holy Ghost, and they knew it not.*
>
> Behold, *I have come unto the world to bring redemption unto the world, to save the world from sin.*
>
> Therefore, whoso *repenteth* and *cometh unto me as a little child,* him will I receive, for of such is the kingdom of God. Behold, for such I have laid down my life, and have taken it up again; therefore *repent, and come unto me* ye ends of the earth, and be saved. (3 Ne. 9:20–22)

Third, Latter-day Saints seem to grasp the requirements for repentance and baptism, but some apparently don't fully grasp the implications of the Lord's statement that "*him will I baptize with fire and with the Holy Ghost.*"

What does that mean, exactly? The ***lifetime process of being baptized by fire*** *is being led by the Holy Ghost in purging out personal coarseness and sin, learning to reject and hate sin and love righteousness, growing in knowledge and understanding of the broad* *spectrum of eternal things, acquiring the skills to become priests and kings unto the most-high God, and continually becoming more Godlike in spirit, character and attitude.*

That's the process Moroni explained in the very last chapter of the Book of Mormon:

> Yea, *come unto Christ,* and *be perfected in him,* and *deny yourselves of all ungodliness;* and if ye shall deny yourselves of all ungodliness, and *love God with all your might, mind and strength,* then is *his grace sufficient for you,* that by his grace *ye may be perfect in Christ;* and if by the grace of God ye are perfect in Christ, ye can in nowise deny the power of God.
>
> And again, if ye by the grace of God are perfect in Christ, and deny not his power, *then are ye sanctified in Christ by the grace of God, through the shedding of the blood of Christ,* which is in the covenant of the Father unto the remission of your sins, that ye become holy, without spot. (Moro. 10:32–33)

Fourth, the rule for being eligible to enter into exaltation is that • *"no unclean thing can enter into His kingdom."* After making that statement, Jesus continued with the caution that • *"nothing entereth into his rest save it be those who have washed their garments in my blood,* because of their faith, and the repentance of all their sins, and their faithfulness unto the end" (3 Ne. 27:19). That concept had been amplified 600 years previously by the Prophet Nephi, who wrote that • "if ye have sought to do wickedly in the days of your probation, then ye are found unclean before the judgment-seat of God; and *no unclean thing can dwell with God;* wherefore, ye must be cast off forever" (1 Ne. 10:21).

Fifth, those comforting words of the Savior to the Saints in His restored Church:

> Behold, ye are little children and *ye cannot bear all things now; ye must grow in grace and in the knowledge of the truth.*
>
> Fear not, little children, for *you are mine, and I have overcome the world, and you are of them that my Father hath given me;*
>
> And none of them that my Father hath given me shall be lost. (D&C 50:40–42).

And finally, **sixth,** accepting Christ and following the path of faith, repentance, baptism, sanctification by the Holy Ghost, and remaining faithful, obedient, growing, loving, preparing servants to Jesus Christ throughout one's remaining days in mortality and into the eternities is the only way these goals can be achieved.

> Behold, *Jesus Christ is the name which is given of the Father, and there is none other name given whereby man can be saved;*
>
> Wherefore, *all men must take upon them the name which is given of the Father,* for in that name shall they be called at the last day;
>
> Wherefore, *if they know not the name by which they are called, they cannot have place in the kingdom of my Father.* (D&C 18:23–25)

Aids for Studying and Understanding Christ's Mortal Ministry

At this point, the direction of this chapter shifts to Christ's mortal ministry, as recorded in the New Testament books of Matthew, Mark, Luke, and John. Little space is available, but comments are made on some often unknown or overlooked aspects of His mortal ministry coupled with several insights intended to facilitate more effective study of His life and ministry.

Insights Concerning the Mortal Birth of Jesus Christ

Some of the popular assumptions made when the Christmas story is heard may not be correct. For instance, were Mary and Joseph alone? It's not improbable that Mary's worried mother, perhaps with some other competent midwife and perhaps others accompanied them on their journey to Bethlehem. If recent research showing that Nazareth was resettled by members of a clan who were all descendants of King David is correct, many from the village may have come to Bethlehem to pay their taxes, and they may have been joined in their journey by other clan members from the northern village of Kochaba. Did they travel together to Bethlehem in a caravan? And did Joseph and/or Mary have kinfolk in the town who extended them hospitality and help?

They didn't just arrive the night of the Savior's birth—they were there for an undetermined number of days before Christ's arrival. The scripture specifically states that "while they were there, the *days* were accomplished that she should be delivered" (Luke 2:6). They may even have lodged at first in the inn, but then were moved out to make way for paying customers when the actual tax days arrived. These are all unsubstantiated conjectures, but they are worthy of consideration as realistic scenarios.

The actual day of the Lord's birth is unknown. The traditional December 25th date was first observed in Constantine's time, AD 325, and was officially set by the Roman church in the fourth century. (The Greek Christians celebrate Christ's birth on January 6; the Armenian church celebrates on January 19.)

It is believed that the birth of Christ did not take place in the winter, since Palestinian shepherds usually kept their flocks under cover from the November rains until the Passover (March or April) and the milder "latter rains" of those months. April is lambing season, when shepherds are caring for newborn animals in the fields around the clock. Many scholars assert that Jesus, the "Lamb of God" (John 1:29), was born in March or April, at the season when other Passover lambs were born. The Passover occurs at the first full moon after the first day of spring (the vernal or spring equinox—about March 21).

If Christ was born in 5 BC (a leap year), the year accepted by most modern biblical scholars, it would have been in the year of the Romans 749. Then, when Christ had His first birthday a year later (Roman year 750), that birthday would have fallen in AD 1 in modern time calculations. There is no year "zero" in the Before Christ [BC], Year of Our Lord [*Anno Domini* = AD] time scheme.

Bethlehem and Its Inn at the Time of Christ's Birth

At the time of Christ's birth, Bethlehem was probably a tiny hamlet of a hundred families or so. The inn there was probably one of the few edifices in the area, actually a caravan campground, and probably had only a single room. Visitors would hang curtains for privacy, and their animals would sometimes be inside with them.

Bethlehem was too close to Jerusalem (about six miles away) to be a popular overnight stopping point. Building construction then, as now, would have been of stone, not wood. The stable was almost certainly a cave; the manger was most likely a stone watering trough. That the shepherds knew where the manger was located in the village is a significant indication of how small Bethlehem actually was at that time.

The Church of the Nativity, built over the 11- x 38-foot cave, where it is believed Jesus was born, is the oldest church in Christiandom. It was originally constructed by direction of the Roman Emperor, Constantine, about AD 330, after his mother, Helena, determined the site.

The Meridian-of-time Size and Previous History of Nazareth

Since approximately the first 30 years of the Savior's life were centered in Nazareth, it is appropriate to give a brief description of the area. Recent excavations in Nazareth have shown that the population of the town at the time of Jesus probably numbered between 120 and 150 people. It is likely that in the time of Jesus, the tiny hamlet belonged to the larger village of Japhia, just a mile away. Japhia, in that era, was a strongly fortified village which played an important role in the Jewish war with the Romans (AD 66–70).

The Israelites first occupied the Galilee region about 1225 BC, when the tribe of Zebulon settled in the mountainous area where Nazareth is located, and the tribe of Naphtali received the lowlands around Lake Chinnereth (the Sea of Galilee). But the Assyrian king Tiglath-Pileser III invaded Galilee in 733 BC and took most of the northern Israelites into exile in Assyria. Nazareth was apparently without inhabitants from 733 to about 100 BC The general area, though, was made part of the Assyrian province of Megiddo. People from other conquered territories were brought into Galilee and the area became a region of Gentiles. For this reason, Isaiah wrote that the Lord "afflicted the land of Zebulon and the land of Naphtali . . . in Galilee of the nations [gentiles]" (Isa. 9:1).

As the Maccabean era began (c. 166 BC), there were only a few isolated Jewish groups in all of Galilee. But when the Hasmonean John Hyrcanus conquered the area about 104 BC, a strong immigration of Diaspora Jews from Persia and Babylon settled in the Galilee area. At the same time, John and his successors gave the gentile inhabitants a choice: either accept Judaism and be circumcised or leave the country.

About 100 BC, a clan which was descended from King David came back from Babylonian exile and settled two small villages: Nazareth ("village of the shoot") and Kochaba ("village of the star"). Kochaba was about 35 miles east of Nazareth (beyond the Jordan, and inland about 11 miles east from the Sea of Galilee, in the province of Batanea (Bashan), near the pilgrim route from Babylon to Jerusalem. It appears that both settlements were clan settlements, with almost everyone in the villages related to one another. It also appears that people in the two settlements had become reacquainted with their relatives in Bethlehem and Jerusalem, by the time of Jesus' birth. (See *Crowther, Jesus of Nazareth, Savior and King,* 56–57).

Not Necessarily a Carpenter: Christ's Mortal Occupation Is Uncertain

Was Jesus a carpenter? The only scriptural passages in which Jesus' worldly profession is alluded to are Mark 6:3 and Matt. 13:55, in which others ask, "Is not this the carpenter . . . ?" The New Testament word translated "carpenter" in these passages actually carries the more general meaning of "craftsman," so there is no evidence or indication that Jesus was a carpenter nor that he worked primarily with wood. The main work opportunity in His day and locality was work at a huge stone quarry located close to Nazareth, so Jesus may have been a stone mason.

Since Nazareth, in His day, was only a tiny village (recent archaeological excavations show it probably only had 120–150 inhabitants in Christ's day), it is likely that Jesus ranged throughout the Galilee region performing His labors as a general craftsman; work which today would be performed by a "general contractor" or by a "handy-man" or a "jack of all trades." Then, as now, construction workers went wherever they could find work and performed whatever work was available and needed. Jesus very likely performed some of His labors in growing areas such as the villages around the Sea of Galilee and in the rapidly growing Roman cities of Scythopolis and Caesarea, all of which were within a day's journey from His home in Nazareth.

Or, maybe He functioned in other professions. It should be noted that Jesus several times was called "rabbi" (John 1:38, 49; 3:2; 6:25; 20:26), which meant "master" or "teacher." The term clearly had the implied meaning that He was one "schooled in the law." This was the training of a "scribe," or in today's terminology, a "lawyer."

Christ's "Mission Statements"

In this day of MBAs, business and marketing plans, and the development of complex corporate strategies, it has become fashionable to develop corporate mission statements. The concept has branched out in many directions, and personal and family mission statements now are common.

What is a mission statement? It is a concise, carefully worded statement of reasons for existing, directions for growth, limits, and long-range goals. Mission statements appear in many forms, but they all in some manner characterize the objectives of the individuals or organizations who crafted them.

Jesus never posted or published a mission statement, but He made short, pithy statements that characterized His personal objectives. I selected a few such statements which He made that are recorded in the scriptures, and briefly present them in this context. I found identifying them to be a meaningful experience and suggest that readers might wish to amplify the list. Here are a dozen for starters:

• "this is my work and my glory—to bring to pass the immortality and eternal life of man" (Moses 1:39).

• "I am the way, the truth, and the life: no man cometh unto the Father, but by me" (John 14:6).

• "the Son of man shall come in the glory of his Father with his angels; and then he shall reward every man according to his works" (Matt. 16:27).

• "I must be about my Father's business" (Luke 2:49).

• "This is the work of God, that ye believe on him whom he hath sent" (John 6:29).

• "I honour my Father, . . . And I seek not mine own glory" (John 8:49–50).

• "I am . . . your advocate with the Father; and it is his good will to give you the kingdom" (D&C 29:5).

• "I am come to send fire [the Holy Ghost?] on the earth" (Luke 12:49).

• "the Son of man is not come to destroy men's lives, but to save them" (Luke 9:56).

• "I came not to call the righteous, but sinners to repentance" (Mark 2:17).

• "the Son of man is come to seek and to save that which was lost" (Luke 19:10).

• "the Son of man came not to be ministered unto, but to minister, and to give his life a ransom for many" (Mark 10:45).

Testimonies with Sure Knowledge: Devils Acknowledge Jesus Is the Son of God

When spirits are born on earth and take up mortal bodies, their memories of pre-mortal events and acquaintances are blocked so they can experience life in mortality as their time of probation. However, spirit beings who elected to follow Satan and his plan in the premortal council were cast out and prohibited from experiencing mortality. As a result of the "war in heaven," • "Satan . . . was cast out into the earth, and his angels were cast out with him" (Rev. 12:9). The desire for mortal bodies of many of these followers of Satan is so intense that they seek to enter and take over the bodies of vulnerable individuals throughout the world, often with more than one evil spirit crowding into a single mortal body.

Unlike mortals whose memories of pre-earth events have been blocked, these evil spirits have full remembrance of their premortal experiences. Most certainly they know who Jesus was and is, and they know beyond doubt that He is the Christ, the firstborn Son of God the Father. Their testimonies of this great truth aren't just faith-based, they are knowledge-based, so their repeated acknowledgments of Jesus in Bible accounts are highly significant witnesses of His divinity.

Early in His ministry, when Jesus first taught in the synagogue at Capernaum, His listeners recognized that He taught with authority, and they were "astonished at his doctrine." But • "there was in their synagogue a man with an unclean spirit; and he cried out, Saying, *Let us alone; what have we to do with thee, thou Jesus of Nazareth? art thou come to destroy us? I know thee who thou art, the Holy One of God"* (Mark 1:21–24; see also Luke 4:33–36). When Jesus cast out the unclean spirit(s), the man was torn and cried out with a loud voice before the spirit(s) came out of him. Word of this incident immediately spread throughout the entire Galilee region, which caused Jesus to confront other evil spirits He encountered in a different manner: • "he healed many . . . and cast out many devils; and *suffered not the devils to speak, because they knew him"* (Mark 1:34; see also Luke 4:41).

Jesus continued preaching in the Galilee area, with large crowds gathering from more than a hundred-mile radius. Among them were • "unclean spirits," who "when they saw him, fell down before him, and cried, saying, *Thou art the Son of God.* And he straitly charged them that they should not make him known" (Mark 3:11–12).

When Jesus sailed east across the Sea of Galilee and came • "into the country of the Gergesenes, there met him two possessed with devils, coming out of the tombs, exceeding fierce, so that no man might pass by that way. And, behold, they cried out, saying, *What have we to do with thee, Jesus, thou Son of God? art thou come hither to torment us before the time?"* (Matt. 8:28–29; see also Mark 5:6–9). There must have been many devils within the two men, for when Jesus cast them out they went into a whole herd of swine, which immediately went berserk, ran or fell into the sea and drowned.

So these, and other testimonies from evil spirits which are recorded in the Bible, are valuable because they are knowledge-based; they represent first-person witnesses of Jesus' stature—not just as a man, but as a God!

And what of the evil spirit's query: *art thou come hither to torment us before the time?* What is "the time" of which he speaks? No scripture explicitly answers that question, but it seems to have reference to the Savior's Second Coming in glory and the millennial period which will follow as He rules here on earth as King. The Apostle John, in the book of Revelation, wrote that • "I saw an angel come down from heaven, having the key of the bottomless pit and a great chain in his hand. And he laid hold on the dragon, that old serpent, which is the Devil, and Satan, and *bound him a thousand years,* And *cast him into the bottomless pit, and shut him up, and set a seal upon him, that he should deceive the nations no more,* till the thousand years should be fulfilled: and after that he must be loosed a little season" (Rev. 20:1–3).

Passovers during Christ's Mortal Ministry

Since major events in Christ's ministry revolved around the Passover feasts, the following listing is included here as a study aid. The gospels record four Passovers during Christ's ministry:

1. *First Passover* (John 2:12–3:21). Jesus cleansed the temple, answered the sign-seeking Jews, performed many miracles, and taught Nicodemus.

2. *Second Passover* (John 5:1–47). Jesus healed an impotent man at the pool of Bethesda who was then persecuted by the Jews. Jesus then bore witness of His divine Sonship to the Jews. (A few scholars don't recognized this feast as a Passover; in their view, Christ's ministry was only two years *long and only encompassed three passovers, rather than four.)*

3. *Third Passover* (No reference; see John 6:4). Jesus did not attend the Jerusalem celebration.

4. *Fourth Passover* (John 13:1; Matt. 21:1–27:66; Mark 11:1–15:47; John 12:2–19:42). Jesus' triumphal entry into Jerusalem, events of the Passion Week; His trial, crucifixion and burial.

A Correlation of the Periods of the Life of Christ, as Found in the Four Gospels

Many read the Gospels of Matthew, Mark, Luke, and John but fail to grasp the historical aspects of the Savior's mortal ministry because they read each gospel separately, with no attempt to study them chronologically. The following listing of the 11 periods of His mortal ministry are drawn from *Jesus of Nazareth, Savior and King: 414 Events in the Life of Christ.* (The dates are calculated with the assumption that Christ's mortal birth occurred in the year of the Romans 749, in April of 5 BC The year is not certain, but 5 BC appears to be best aligned with the calculations of most modern scholars.)

*Period 1: **Christ's Nativity and Preparation** (from the birth of John the Baptist to the beginning of John's ministry: 7 BC to AD 26). Matt. 2; Luke 1–2; John 1:1–14.

*Period 2: **Christ's Preliminary Ministry** (from the beginning of John's ministry to the first Passover of Christ's ministry: Summer, AD 26 to March–April, AD 27). Matt. 3–4:11; Mark 1:1–13; Luke 3–4:13; John 1:15–2:12.

*Period 3: **Christ's Early Judean Ministry** (from the first Passover of Christ's ministry to His return to Galilee: April, AD 27 to December, AD 27). Matt. 4:12; Mark 1:14; Luke 4:14; John 2:13–4:45.

*Period 4: **Christ's Early Galilean Ministry** (from Christ's return to Cana through the calling of the Twelve, to the second Passover: December. AD 27 to April, AD 28). Matt. 4:13–8:5; 8:14–17; 9:2–17; 10:1–42; 12:1–21; Mark 1:15–3:19; Luke 4:14–6:49; John 4:46–5:47.

*Period 5: **Christ's Great Galilean Ministry** (from after the second Passover to the time of the third Passover: April AD 28 to April A. D. 29). Matt. 8:5–13; 8:18–9:1; 9:18–33, 35–38; 11:1–30; 12:22–13:52; 13:54–14:36; Mark 3:22–6:56; Luke 7:1–9:17; John 6:1–71.

*Period 6: **Christ's Ministry to Phœnicia, Northern Judea and the Decapolis** (from Christ's visit to Phœnicia to the Feast of Tabernacles in Jerusalem: April AD 29 to October, AD 29). Matt. 15:1–18:35; Mark 7:1–9:50; Luke 9:18–62; John 7:1–10.

Period 7: **Christ's Late Judean Ministry** (from the Feast of Tabernacles to the Feast of Dedication: October, AD 29 to December, AD 29). Luke 10:1–13:22; John 7:11–10:39.

Period 8: **Christ's Ministry in Batanea and Peræa** (from after the Feast of Dedication to Christ's arrival in Bethany before the Passover: January, AD 30 to April, AD 30). Matt. 19:1–20:30; Mark 10:1–52; Luke 13:23–19:28; John 10:39–12:1.

Period 9: **Christ's Preparation for His Atoning Sacrifice** (from His triumphal entry into Jerusalem to His arrest in the Garden of Gethsemane: Sunday, April 2, AD 30 to Thursday, April 6, AD 30). Matt. 21:1–26:56; Mark 11:1–14:52; Luke 19:29–22:53; John 12:2–18:13.

Period 10: **Christ's Trial, Crucifixion and Burial** (from Christ's appearance before Annas to His burial: early Friday morning, April 7, AD 30 to early Sunday morning, April 9, AD 30). Matt. 26:57–27:66; Mark 14:15–15:47; Luke 22:64–23:56; John 18:13–19:42.

Period 11: **Christ's Resurrection and Ascension** (from the opening of Jesus' tomb through His ascension into heaven: Sunday, April 9, AD 30 to Thursday, May 18, AD 30). Matt. 28:1–20; Mark 16:1–19; Luke 24:1–53; John 20:1–21:25; Acts 1:1–12; 1 Cor. 15:5–7. (Crowther, *Jesus of Nazareth–Savior and King: 414 Events in the Life of Christ*, 41, 63, 77, 87, 115, 147, 164, 184, 202, 232, 243.)

The Major Discourses of Jesus Christ

During His mortal ministry in the meridian of time, the Lord Jesus Christ gave 24 major discourses. They are listed here with their titles, biblical scripture reference, place and to whom, ministry period, and approximate dates.

1. **Being Born Again and Receiving Heavenly Light and Salvation** [*The Lord's Counsel to Nicodemus*] (John 3:1–21). Jerusalem, to Nicodemus. Period 3, April, AD 27.
2. **Christ's Living Water Leads to True Worship** [*Instructions to the Samaritan Woman at Jacob's Well*] (John 4:5–27). Jacob's Well, to a Samaritan woman. Period 3, December, AD 27.
3. **Prophets Not Accepted by Their Own** [*The Lord's Sermon in the synagogue at Nazareth*] (Luke 4:16–28). Nazareth, in the synagogue. Period 4, Winter, AD 28.
4. **Eternal Relationships with Heavenly Father and Jesus Christ** [*The Sermon on the Mount*] (Matt. 5:1–7:29). Eremos (Galilee Mountain) to His disciples. Period 4, Spring, AD 28.
5. **The Golden Rule, and Following the Master** [*The Sermon on the Plain*] (Luke 6:17–49). Tabgha area, to a multitude. Period 4, Spring, AD 28.
6. **The Relationship of God the Son to God the Father** [*Christ's rebuke to the Jews near the pool of Bethesda*] (John 5:17–47). Jerusalem temple, to the Pharisees. Period 4, April, AD 28.
7. **The Role of John the Baptist as a Prophet and an Elias** [*Christ's message to many of John's followers*] (Matt. 11:7–30). Galilee, to a multitude. Period 5, Summer AD 28.
8. **Men Will Account for Their Words at Judgment Day** [*A rebuttal to the false accusation of the Pharisees*] (Matt. 12:25–45). Galilee synagogue, to the Pharisees. Period 5, Fall, AD 28.
9. **Parables of Preaching and Accepting the Gospel, and of Final Judgment**

[*Christ's first great day of parables*] (Matt. 13:3–52). On a boat, Sea of Galilee, to a multitude. Period 5, Fall, AD 28.

10. **The Son of Man Is the Bread of Life Sent from Heaven** [*Christ's explanation to the multitude gathered at Capernaum*] (John 6:25–59). Capernaum, to a multitude. Period 5, April, AD 29.

11. **Be Converted and as Humble as Children** [*Christ's teachings on the righteousness and eternal status of little children*] (Matt. 18:1–35). Capernaum, to His disciples. Period 6, September, AD 29.

12. **Christ's Teachings Are the Doctrines of God the Father** [*Rebuttals to the false assertions of Jewish critics*] (John 7:16–39). Jerusalem temple, to a multitude. Period 7, October, AD 29.

13. **If You Don't Believe in Me, You'll Die in Your Sins** [*Christ's debate with the Scribes and Pharisees in the Temple*] (John 8:12–59). Jerusalem temple, to the Pharisees. Period 7, October, AD 29.

14. **Christ Is the Good Shepherd Who Gave His Life for His Sheep** [*Christ's rebuttal to "blind" Pharisees*] (John 10:1–18). Jerusalem, to the Pharisees. Period 7, October AD 29.

15. **Let Your Eyes Be Single to God; Condemnation Comes to Those Who Do Evil** [*A rebuke to the Pharisees and lawyers*] (Luke 11:17–52). Judea, to a multitude. Period 7, Late Fall, AD 29.

16. **Trust in God and Prepare for the Lord's Coming** [*Counsel to the disciples of Christ*] (Luke 12:1–59). Judea, to a multitude. Period 7, Late Fall, AD 29.

17. **Gaining Immediate Versus Eternal Rewards** [*Christ's discourse in the home of a chief Pharisee*] (Luke 14:3–24). Batanea, to Pharisees at a feast. Period 8, Winter, AD 30.

18. **Sacrifice Is Required of Those Who Are the Lord's Disciples** [*Christ's second great day of parables*] (Luke 14:25–17:10). Batanea, to a multitude. Period 8, Winter, AD 30.

19. **The Kingdom of God Is Within You; Requirements for Inheriting Eternal Life** [*The Savior's response to the Pharisees in Galilee*] (Luke 17:20–18:30). Galilee, to the Pharisees. Period 8, March, AD 30.

20. **Rebuke and Condemnation of the Leaders of Israel** [*Christ's third great day of parables*] (Matt. 21:23–23:39). Jerusalem temple, to the Pharisees. Period 9; Tuesday, April 4, AD 30.

21. **Christ Will Die to Draw All Men to Him** [*Christ's instructions to Greek visitors during the Passover*] (John 12:20–36). Jerusalem temple, to the Greeks. Period 9; Tuesday, April 4, AD 30.

22. **Signs and Preparation Instructions for the Lord's Coming in Glory** [*The Lord's great Mount of Olives discourse*] (Matt. 24:3–25:46). Mount of Olives, to His disciples. Period 9; Tuesday, April 4, AD 30.

23. **The Love of Christ and the Guidance of the Comforter** [*Christ's parting instructions to His disciples in the upper room*] (John 14:1–16:33). Jerusalem room, to His disciples. Period 9; Thursday, April 6, AD 30.

24. **Father, Glorify Your Son, and Unite All Your Followers in One, as We Are One** [*Christ's great intercessory prayer*] (John 17:1–26). Jerusalem room, prayer to the Father. Period 9; Thursday, April 6, AD 30.

(Crowther, *Jesus of Nazareth–Savior and King*, 285–87)

Summary

1. Jehovah, who is also known as Jesus Christ, is the God who revealed the Ten Commandments and proclaimed: • "I am the LORD thy God . . . Thou shalt have no other gods *before* me" (Ex. 20:2–3). By assignment from the Godhead, he is the principal God of this planet earth and all its inhabitants. He created it, controls it, atoned for its inhabitants, and has been granted eternal Kingship over it. This, perhaps, is the most important message of this book.

2. Numerous passages were cited, from all the Latter-day Saint scriptures, which assert that • "The earth is the LORD's, and the fulness thereof; the world, and they that dwell therein" (Ps. 24:1). However, to worship him as *the* God of this earth does not prohibit man from also worshiping God the Father and God the Holy Ghost, who also fulfill prominent responsibilities in the administration, blessing and exalting of this earth and its inhabitants.

3. Jehovah/Jesus Christ "owns" all things pertaining to this earth. A listing of 125 things which He has specified as being "my" things in the Doctrine and Covenants was provided. The list was segregated into groups: the Church, the people, the revelations, property and activities, other personal traits and rewards, and physical characteristics.

4. Three "births" of Jesus Christ with major "nature of God" implications are discussed in the scriptures: his premortal birth as the firstborn spirit child of God the Father, his mortal birth in Bethlehem, and his "birth" as the firstborn of this earth's resurrected beings.

5. Each of these births have been misunderstood by "trinitarians," and their creeds treat them erroneously. They assert that the Holy Ghost is the Father of Jesus Christ and that Jesus is God the Father's only son. Though they accept that Jesus Christ was resurrected, they fail to reconcile his having an eternal, tangible physical body with their teaching that the Father, Son, and Holy Ghost are all one god who is a formless spirit being.

6. Jesus carefully defined the doctrinal elements of his gospel. Two of the most explicit passages which contain his definitions were cited: 3 Ne. 27:13–22 and 3 Ne. 11:31–40. His gospel centers in the first principles: faith, repentance, baptism, and being sanctified through the operations of the Holy Ghost. It also embraces enduring to the end, His obedience to the Father, justice and mercy, the Atonement, obedience to His commandments, and other basic doctrines.

7. Jesus Christ is the Mediator between man and God and functions as man's advocate. Since He "purchased" all mankind from the demands of justice by atoning and suffering for all mankind's sins, all men are positioned as His servants. For Him to serve as their advocate before God the Father at Judgment Day, He requires that they believe on him, repent, strive to cleanse themselves from sin, and obey His commandments.

8. No unclean thing can enter into God's kingdom. The grace of the Godhead will fill the gap between man's status at the end of his mortal probation and the essential perfection level of being completely free from sin, if Christ will secure mercy for His followers from the Father at the final Judgment Day.

9. The second portion of the chapter focuses on several little-known aspects of the Savior's mortal birth and life and provides useful aids to studying His life in the four New Testament gospels.

10. Insights concerning Jesus' mortal birth include recent archaeological findings concerning Nazareth and Bethlehem, and information that descendants of the royal Davidic line apparently returned to settle in Palestine about 100 BC, settling in Nazareth and Kochaba. These settlers apparently had reestablished ties with others of the royal Davidic line in Bethlehem and Jerusalem by the time of Christ's birth.

11. The two passages which allude to Christ's being a "carpenter," Mark 6:3 and Matthew 13:55, are mistranslated in the King James Version. The term really means "craftsman," not "carpenter," and it carries the general sense of being a "handyman" or a "general contractor." Tiny Nazareth, with only from 120 to 150 inhabitants during Christ's lifetime, probably wouldn't have supported a carpenter's shop. It is more likely that Jesus worked primarily in stone, the common building material of his day, and that he labored throughout the general Galilean area.

12. Several passages have been suggested by the author as representative "mission statements" for the Christ and His ministry.

13. Evil spirits who were cast out of heaven for following Satan did not have their memories blocked by mortal birth. Their testimonies that Jesus is the Son of God are powerful witnesses of His divinity, even though they come from Satan-influenced spirits, because they are knowledge-based rather than faith-based.

14. Christ's three-year mortal ministry often is chronicled based on the four Passovers which occurred. References for those scriptural citations are furnished.

15. A chronological listing of 11 periods in Christ's life was provided, with pertinent references given for reading His life in chronological order.

16. Twenty-four major discourses which Christ gave during His mortal ministry were identified, with biblical references cited.

CHAPTER 13

GOD THE HOLY GHOST

The Holy Ghost: A Member of the Godhead

The scriptures repeatedly depict the Holy Ghost as a member of the Godhead, in passages such as • "Go ye therefore, and teach all nations, baptizing them in the name of the *Father*, and of the *Son*, and of the *Holy Ghost*" (Matt. 28:19); • "this is the doctrine of Christ, and the only and true doctrine of the *Father*, and of the *Son*, and of the *Holy Ghost*, which is one God, without end" (2 Ne. 31:21); • "Having authority given me of Jesus Christ, I baptize you in the name of the *Father*, and of the *Son*, and of the *Holy Ghost*" (3 Ne. 11:25); • "after this manner shall ye baptize in my name; for behold, verily I say unto you, that the *Father*, and the *Son*, and the *Holy Ghost* are one" (3 Ne. 11:27); • "to sing ceaseless praises with the choirs above, unto the *Father*, and unto the *Son*, and unto the *Holy Ghost*, which are one God" (Morm. 7:7); etc.

A Male Being

The Holy Ghost is a living entity, not "an emanation of life-energy from God" as some modernistic teachers have attempted to describe Him. He is a "being" rather than a "force."

The scriptures make it clear that the Holy Ghost is a *male* being and should be referred to as "He" rather than "it." For instance, chapter 16 of the gospel of John repeatedly refers to Him with the masculine pronouns "he" and "him." In John 16:13–15 there are 13 male pronouns used concerning the Holy Ghost: "I will send *him*" (v. 7); "when *he* is come, *he* will reprove" (v. 8); "when *he*, the Spirit of truth, is come, *he* will guide you" (v. 13); "*he* shall not speak of *himself*" (v. 13); "whatsoever *he* shall hear, that shall *he* speak" (v. 13); "*he* will shew you" (v. 13); "*He* shall glorify me" (v. 14); "*he* shall receive" (v. 14); and "*he* shall take of mine" (v. 15).

The scriptures repeatedly describe Him as performing actions that are only possible for actual persons to perform. He speaks, He searches, He cries, He prays, He testifies, He teaches, He leads, He commands, He inspires! Likewise, the scriptures depict actions against Him that He must endure: He can be ignored, tempted, grieved, despised, blasphemed, and lied against.

A Personage of Spirit

After conveying the sure knowledge that both God the Father and God the Son have bodies "of flesh and bones as tangible as man's," D&C section 130 states that "*the Holy Ghost has not a body of flesh and bones, but is a personage of Spirit.* Were it not so, the Holy Ghost could not dwell in us" (D&C 130:22).

As was explained in detail in chapter 4 (in the section titled "Latter-day Saint Scriptures Teach about 'Spirit' and 'Spirit Beings' "), a personage of spirit has the same type of bodily shape and form as human beings. It is known, also, that spirit is matter, though of a more refined nature than the matter of human bodies.

There are two passages that make reference to the Holy Ghost appearing in physical form: one in the Bible and one in the Book of Mormon. Both are subject to different lines of interpretation and hence neither are regarded as definitive in the manner in which they are presented here, where in each case two differing interpretations are presented.

(Bodily?) Appearance Number One: Christ's Baptism: Luke's account of the Savior's baptism reads as follows: • "Now when all the people were baptized, it came to pass, that Jesus also being baptized, and praying, the heaven was opened, *And the Holy Ghost descended in a bodily shape* like a dove upon him, and a voice came from heaven, which said, Thou art my beloved Son; in thee I am well pleased" (Luke 3:21–22).

There are some, not particularly Latter-day Saints, who understand this passage as saying that the Holy Ghost descended in a bodily shape, and that He came gently—as a dove. (Perhaps they take their cue about a dove being a gentle animal from Matt. 10:16: "be ye therefore wise as serpents, and *harmless as doves.*") With this interpretation, Matthew's account is taken more literally, that the Holy Ghost was actually seen descending by the Savior: • "Jesus, when He was baptized, went up straightway out of the water: and, lo, the heavens were opened unto him, and *he* [Jesus] *saw the Spirit of God descending* like a dove, and lighting upon him" (Matt. 3:16).

Nephi saw Christ's baptism in vision and recorded that • "the Lamb of God went forth and was baptized of him; and after he was baptized, I beheld the heavens open, and *the Holy Ghost come down out of heaven and abide upon him in the form of a dove*" (1 Ne. 11:27).

So, was it the Holy Ghost in bodily shape that was seen descending and lighting upon Jesus, or was it literally a dove that glided down and perched on the Master? I don't know—it's on my list of questions to ask when I get beyond the veil. (Perhaps it belongs on your list too!)

Appearance Number Two: to Nephi. 1 Nephi 11 tells of the remarkable experiences granted to Nephi when he pondered and struggled to understand his father Lehi's dream of the tree, the river, and the rod of iron (see 1 Ne. 8). He desired to know the things that his father had seen, and believed that the Lord was able to make them known unto him. He recorded: • "*as I sat pondering in mine heart I was caught away in the Spirit of the Lord,* yea, into an exceedingly high mountain, which I never had before seen, and upon which I never had before set my foot" (1 Ne. 11:1).

Nephi and the Spirit of the Lord conversed, and the Spirit of the Lord praised Nephi because of his belief in the Son of God. He showed Nephi "the tree which is precious above all" and then committed Nephi to bear record of the Son of God. At this point, a unique conversation occurred, as Nephi later recorded:

> I said unto the Spirit: I behold thou hast shown unto me the tree which is precious above all.

And he said unto me: What desirest thou?

And I said unto him: To know the interpretation thereof—for *I spake unto him as a man speaketh; for I beheld that he was in the form of a man; yet nevertheless, I knew that it was the Spirit of the Lord; and he spake unto me as a man speaketh with another.*

And it came to pass that he said unto me: Look! And I looked as if to look upon him, and *I saw him not; for he had gone from before my presence.* (1 Ne. 11:9–12)

It was almost as if the Spirit of the Lord was concerned that He had been observed in bodily shape, which caused Him to change Nephi's vision view to behold the city of Jerusalem instead of Himself and to disappear immediately. Nephi then was shown the mother of the Son of God, the Christ as a new-born baby, the Son of God going forth among men, His baptism, the twelve, the Savior's mortal ministry, His death on the cross, and multitudes fighting against the Apostles (1 Ne. 11:12–34).

The interpretational question this passage raises is: is the being who caught Nephi away in the spirit (1) the premortal Christ, who also was known as the Spirit of the Lord; or (2) was it the Holy Ghost, who is frequently referred to in the scriptures as the Spirit of the Lord? Readers are left to their own interpretive skills to make their own tentative determinations of the proper interpretation. It seems to be a major interpretive indicator that in this instance, Nephi was "caught away" and transported elsewhere to observe his visions—this "catching away" or transporting of individuals is a clearly documented trait and responsibility of the Holy Ghost. (See "The Spirit Transports Man," later in this chapter.)

A very significant insight on the matter is found in the book *Determining Doctrine: A Reference Guide for Evaluating Doctrinal Truth*, by Dennis B. Horne. He adds his comments as personal observations made as a biographer of the Apostle Bruce R. McConkie. They are made in his chapter eight: "Church Correlation," where he is citing various critiques written by reading committees of various church manuals. At the end of his sub-section *Doctrinal Evaluation: Samples from some Critiques by Elder Bruce R. McConkie*, he writes:

> It is worth noticing here the comment made by Elder McConkie regarding the identity of the "Spirit of the Lord" mentioned in 1 Nephi 11, and the question which has developed over this identification—whether it is the spirit of the premortal Christ, or whether it is the spirit body of the Holy Ghost, the third member of the Godhead. In his book *Mormon Doctrine*, which was published the same year the above critique was written [1958], Elder McConkie took the qualified position that it was the premortal spirit of Jesus Christ. *I personally have not been able to find any other General Authority author who has committed himself to a like identification with Elder McConkie. I have found a number of others, including Joseph F. Smith, his son Hyrum M. Smith, George Q. Cannon, James E. Talmage, LeGrand Richards, and Marion G. Romney, all of whom have taken the position that the "Spirit of the Lord" who talked with Nephi face to face was in fact the Holy Ghost, in an exceptionally rare personal appearance to a mortal man.*
>
> In the 1990s, I heard a rumor that Elder McConkie, in his last book *A New Witness for the Articles of Faith*, had changed his former position as given in *Mormon Doctrine*, and stated that *he now believed that it was the Holy Ghost*, but that the publisher had removed the statement subsequent to Elder McConkie's death, but previous to publication. Since I was working on a biography of Elder McConkie at the time, I found this to be an intriguing rumor and in need of verification. I therefore

called Elder McConkie's son, Joseph Fielding McConkie, and questioned him about the rumor. I told him what I had heard and asked if it was true that the publisher had removed this material. Joseph McConkie answered, "No, I did," and then explained that *such a statement had indeed been included in this final book* (presumably on page 255) by Elder McConkie, but that after his death Joseph had removed it so that no awkward reversal of position would be in print to confuse readers. Thus, it seems Elder McConkie had eventually harmonized with others of the Brethren on this interesting subject. Further notable evidence of this change of opinion can be found in my earlier work, *Bruce R. McConkie: Highlights from His Life and Teachings* (Roy, Utah: Eborn Books, 2000), 68–69. See also the longer discussion of this issue in chapter 5 under the section on "mysteries." *Elder McConkie himself seems to have had little concern about changing his mind occasionally on doctrinal issues, even in print.* See Joseph Fielding McConkie, *The Bruce R. McConkie Story: Reflections of a Son* (Salt Lake City: Deseret Book, 2003), 299–301. (Horne, *Determining Doctrine*, 254)

Some Questions Concerning the Holy Ghost without Present Answers

There are several questions pertaining to the Holy Ghost which are sometimes discussed, but which as yet remain unanswered in the scriptures and, hence, in the doctrine of The Church of Jesus Christ of Latter-day Saints. So the proper answers to them, so far as I know at the present time, are "I don't know," "we don't know," and "the Church doesn't have any doctrine that answers these particular questions at the present time."

What are these questions that sometimes manage to pique a few curiosities?

1. Is the Holy Ghost a spirit child of God the Father?
2. Is the Holy Ghost a son, as Christ was, of God the Eternal Father?
3. Is the Holy Ghost a spirit brother of Jesus Christ?
4. Will the Holy Ghost, who presently is a spirit being, someday receive a physical body, as Christ did?

The answers to all these questions are "I don't know," "we don't know," and "the Church doesn't have any doctrine which answers these particular questions at the present time." So please don't ask my opinion on these matters because I don't have one.

The "Power" and the "Gift" of the Holy Ghost

There are two different levels of manifestations of the Holy Ghost among men. These are known as the *power* of the Holy Ghost and the *gift* of the Holy Ghost.

The *power of the Holy Ghost* can be experienced before one receives baptism. It serves as a witness to lead a person to Christ, to prompt him to investigate and learn for himself that the gospel is true, to convince him that Jesus is the Christ, the Son of God, and to help him perceive that The Church of Jesus Christ of Latter-day Saints is the Lord's organization through which he can grow and be led toward eternal blessings. The power of the Holy Ghost is a temporary blessing, bestowed and removed by the Holy Spirit as He sees fit, to whom He selects, and in the manner and situations which He selects. He has the overall goal of preparing individuals to come unto Christ and partake of His salvation.

The *gift of the Holy Ghost* is made available to those who have been baptized through the process of "confirmation," which is carried out by the laying on of hands by authorized priesthood holders. The *gift of the Holy Ghost* is the right to have and enjoy the companionship of the Holy Ghost on a more constant level, depending on one's worthiness and his desire to utilize the Spirit's promptings and guidance. Those who are being confirmed are typically instructed in the blessing to "receive" the Holy Ghost, an indication that they need to open their hearts through obedience to the commandments and thoughtful faith-based prayer seeking for the Spirit's guidance and companionship. The steady companionship of the Holy Ghost allows His ongoing purifying and sanctifying processes to cleanse the recipient and guide him toward conformity to God's will and eternal objectives. The purifying process of the Spirit is sometimes spoken of as "fire" (Matt. 3:11; Luke 3:16; 2 Ne. 31:17; 3 Ne. 9:20; 12:1–2; 19:13; Morm. 7:10; Eth. 12:14; D&C 20:41; 33:11; Moses 6:66).

The manifestation of the presence of the Holy Ghost by literal flames of spirit fire, on the day of Pentecost (Acts 2), was the gift of the Holy Ghost that was poured out upon the Savior's Apostles, which helped to prepare them for their ministries to the world. (See also Hel. 5.)

The Holy Ghost in Old Testament Times

The scriptures give solid indication that the Holy Ghost was functioning upon this earth, beginning right at the time of creation (see Gen. 1:2). After the spiritual and physical creations of this earth were accomplished, the book of Moses relates that
• "God . . . *called upon our father **Adam*** by his own voice, saying: I am God; I made the world, and men before they were in the flesh" (Moses 6:50–51). Then He taught Moses the doctrines of repentance, baptism, and receiving the gift of the Holy Ghost, with the promise that • *"ye shall receive the gift of the Holy Ghost,* asking all things in his name, and whatsoever ye shall ask, it shall be given you" (Moses 6:52).

The preaching process began to unfold. The scripture states that • "thus the Gospel began to be preached, from the beginning, being declared by holy angels sent forth from the presence of God, and by his own voice, and *by the gift of the Holy Ghost"* (Moses 5:58).

Adam "was caught away by the Spirit of the Lord" and "was baptized, and the Spirit of God descended upon him, and thus *he was born of the Spirit, and became quickened in the inner man.* And he heard a voice out of heaven, saying: *Thou art baptized with fire, and with the Holy Ghost"* (Moses 6:64–66).

Enoch recorded that the Lord gave him • "a commandment that I should baptize in the name of the Father, and of the Son, which is full of grace and truth, and *of the Holy Ghost,* which beareth record of the Father and the Son" (Moses 7:11).

In his day, ***Noah*** preached to the people, admonishing them to • "Believe and repent of your sins and be baptized in the name of Jesus Christ, the Son of God, even as our fathers, and *ye shall receive the Holy Ghost, that ye may have all things made manifest,"* and he warned them that "if ye do not this, the floods will come in upon you," but "they hearkened not" (Moses 8:24).

At this point, the record of the Holy Ghost's ministrations moves from the Pearl of Great Price to the Old Testament.

A considerable number of Old Testament scriptural passages speak of the Holy Ghost's functioning during those ancient times, though he is not mentioned prominently as compared to the thousands of mentions made of Jehovah during that same time span.

Rather than following the scriptures that speak of the Holy Ghost in the Old Testament chronologically, it seems just as productive to list representative passages about His ministrations while also considering the names of the Holy Ghost during the Old Testament period.

Old Testament Names of the Holy Ghost

Many of those Old Testament passages will be briefly cited here, in conjunction with a listing of the various names by which the Holy Ghost was known during that era. Those names are listed below in three groupings: (1) those names which express His relationship to the LORD, Jehovah; (2) those names which express His character, and (3) those names which describe His operations among men.

Old Testament names expressing the Holy Ghost's relation to "God" include:

Spirit • *"I will take of the spirit which is upon thee, and will put it upon them;* and they shall bear the burden of the people with thee" (Num. 11:17; see 11:25–29).

His Spirit • "By *his spirit* he hath garnished the heavens" (Job 26:13). • "The *Spirit of God* hath made me, and the breath of the Almighty hath given me life" (Job 33:4).

My Spirit • "the LORD said, *My spirit* shall not always strive with man" (Gen. 6:3).

Thy Spirit • "many years didst thou forbear them, and *testifiedst against them by thy spirit* in thy prophets" (Neh. 9:30).

Spirit of God • *"the Spirit of God* moved upon the face of the waters" (Gen. 1:2).

Spirit of the Lord • *"the spirit of the LORD shall rest upon him,* the spirit of wisdom and understanding, the spirit of counsel and might, the spirit of knowledge and of the fear of the LORD" (Isa. 11:2). • "Who hath directed *the Spirit of the LORD,* or being his counsellor hath taught him?" (Isa. 40:13).

Spirit of the Lord God • *"The Spirit of the Lord GOD* is upon me" (Isa. 61:1).

Old Testament names expressing aspects of the Holy Ghost's character include:

A New Spirit • "I will give them one heart, and *I will put a new spirit within you"* (Ezek. 11:19; see also 18:31; 36:26).

His Holy Spirit • "they rebelled, and vexed *his holy Spirit"* (Isa. 63:10, 11).

Thy Free Spirit • "uphold me with *thy free spirit"* (Ps. 51:12).

Thy Good Spirit • "Thou gavest also *thy good spirit* to instruct them" (Neh. 9:20).

Thy Holy Spirit • "take not *thy holy spirit* from me" (Ps. 51:11).

Old Testament names expressing various operations of the Holy Ghost upon **men** include:

The Breath of the Almighty • "The Spirit of God hath made me, and *the breath of the Almighty hath given me life"* (Job 33:4).

The Spirit of Burning • "When the Lord shall have . . . purged the blood of Jerusalem from the midst thereof by *the spirit of judgment,* and by *the spirit of burning"* (Isa. 4:4).

The Spirit of Grace and Supplications • "I will pour upon the house of David . . . *the spirit of grace and of supplications"* (Zech. 12:10).

The Spirit of Understanding, Counsel, Might, Knowledge, Fear of the Lord • "the spirit of the LORD shall rest upon him, *the spirit of wisdom and understanding, the spirit of counsel and might, the spirit of knowledge and of the fear of the LORD"* (Isa. 11:2).

The Spirit That Was Upon Moses • "the LORD came down in a cloud, and spake unto him, and *took of the spirit that was upon him,* and gave it unto the seventy elders" (Num. 11:25).

The Spirit of Wisdom • "thou shalt speak unto all that are wise hearted, whom I have filled with *the spirit of wisdom*" (Ex. 28:3).

Other scriptural allusions to the Holy Ghost in Old Testament times:

Several New Testament and Book of Mormon passages also indicate that the Holy Ghost was ministering here on earth during the Old Testament eras. They include:

• "Men and brethren, this scripture must needs have been fulfilled, *which the Holy Ghost by the mouth of David spake before concerning Judas*, which was guide to them that took Jesus" (Acts 1:16).

• "*Well spake the Holy Ghost by Esaias the prophet unto our fathers*, Saying, Go unto this people, and say, Hearing ye shall hear, and shall not understand; and seeing ye shall see, and not perceive" (Acts 28:25–26).

• "For the prophecy came not *in old time* by the will of man: but *holy men of God spake as they were moved by the Holy Ghost*" (2 Pet. 1:21).

• "Receiving the end of your faith, even the salvation of your souls. Of which salvation the prophets have enquired and searched diligently, who prophesied of the grace that should come unto you: *Searching what, or what manner of time the Spirit of Christ which was in them did signify*, when *it testified beforehand* the sufferings of Christ, and the glory that should follow" (1 Pet. 1:9–11).

• "Nephi, in 600 BC, already was familiar with the ministrations of the Holy Ghost. Concerning his quest for knowledge he wrote: • "I, Nephi, was desirous also that I might see, and hear, and know of these things, *by the power of the Holy Ghost*, which is the gift of God unto all those who diligently seek him, *as well in times of old* as in the time that he should manifest himself unto the children of men" (1 Ne. 10:17). And he prophesied, based on his faith, that • "he that diligently seeketh shall find; and *the mysteries of God shall be unfolded unto them, by the power of the Holy Ghost, as well in these times as in times of old*" (1 Ne. 10:19).

• "he that prophesieth, let him prophesy to the understanding of men; for *the Spirit speaketh the truth and lieth not*. Wherefore, it speaketh of things as they really are, and of things as they really will be; . . . But behold, we are not witnesses alone in these things; *for God also spake them unto prophets of old*" (Jacob 4:13).

New Testament Names for the Holy Ghost

Examples of names used for the Holy Ghost in the New Testament are listed below in four categories: (1) titles and names expressing the Holy Ghost's relationship to God the Son, Jesus Christ; (2) titles and names expressing His relationship to God the Father; (3) titles and names which express His own Godhood; and (4) titles and names expressing His character and personality.

Titles and names expressing the Holy Ghost's relationship to Jehovah/Jesus Christ include:

Comforter • "*I will pray the Father,* and he shall give you another *Comforter,* that he may abide with you for ever; Even *the Spirit of truth*" (John 14:16).

His Witness(es) • "The God of our fathers raised up Jesus, . . . Him hath God exalted with his right hand to be a Prince and a Saviour, . . . And *we are his witnesses* of these things; and *so is also the Holy Ghost*" (Acts 5:30–32).

My Spirit • "it shall come to pass in the last days, saith God, *I will pour out of my*

Spirit upon all flesh" (Acts 2:17; cf. Joel 2:27–28: this passage is quoting Jehovah).

The Spirit of Christ • "ye are not in the flesh, but *in the Spirit,* if so be that *the Spirit of God* dwell in you. Now if any man have not *the Spirit of Christ,* he is none of his" (Rom. 8:9). • "Searching what, or what manner of time *the Spirit of Christ which was in them* did signify" (1 Pet. 1:11).

The Spirit of His Son • "God hath sent forth *the Spirit of his Son* into your hearts" (Gal. 4:6).

The Spirit of Jesus Christ • "this shall turn to my salvation through your prayer, and the supply of *the Spirit of Jesus Christ"* (Phil. 1:19).

The Spirit of the Lord • "when they were come up out of the water, *the Spirit of the Lord caught away Philip,* that the eunuch saw him no more" (Acts 8:39).

Titles and names expressing the
Holy Ghost's relationship to God the Father include:

Gift of God • "Jesus answered and said unto her, If thou knewest *the gift of God,* . . . *whosoever drinketh of the water that I shall give him shall never thirst"* (John 4:10, 14). • "we should believe on the name of *his Son* Jesus Christ . . . hereby we know that he abideth in us, by *the Spirit which he hath given us"* (1 Jn. 3:23–24).

His Spirit • "he that raised up Christ from the dead shall also quicken your mortal bodies by *his Spirit* that dwelleth in you" (Rom. 8:11). • "God hath revealed them unto us by *his Spirit:* for the Spirit searcheth all things, yea, the deep things of God" (1 Cor. 2:10).

His Holy Spirit • "He therefore that despiseth, despiseth not man, but God, who hath also given unto us *his holy Spirit"* (1 Thess. 4:8).

Holy Spirit of God • "grieve not the *holy Spirit of God,* whereby ye are sealed unto the day of redemption" (Eph. 4:30).

Spirit of God • "I cast out devils by the *Spirit of God,* then the kingdom of God is come unto you" (Matt. 12:28).

Spirit of Him Who Raised Up Jesus • "*if the Spirit of him that raised up Jesus* from the dead dwell in you, he that raised up Christ from the dead shall also quicken your mortal bodies by *his Spirit* that dwelleth in you" (Rom. 8:11).

Titles and names expressing the
Holy Ghost's own Godhood include:

God • "Ananias, why hath Satan filled thine heart *to lie to the Holy Ghost,* . . . thou hast not lied unto men, but *unto God"* (Acts 5:3–4).

Eternal Spirit • "Christ, who through *the eternal Spirit* offered himself without spot to God" (Heb. 9:14).

Everywhere-present Spirit • "*Whither shall I go from thy spirit?* or whither shall I flee from thy presence? If I ascend up into heaven, *thou art there*: if I make my bed in hell, behold, *thou art there"* (Ps. 139:7–8).

Searching and Knowing Spirit • "*the Spirit searcheth all things,* yea, the deep things of God. . . . the things of God *knoweth* no man, but *the Spirit of God"* (1 Cor. 2:10–11).

Titles and names which express the
Holy Ghost's character and personality include:

Holy Ghost • "being sanctified by *the Holy Ghost"* (Rom. 15:16).

Holy One • "*ye have an unction* from the *Holy One,* and ye know all things" (1 Jn. 2:20).

Spirit of Adoption • "ye have received the *Spirit of adoption*, whereby we cry, Abba, Father" (Rom. 8:15).

Spirit of Faith • "We having the same *spirit of faith*, . . . we also believe, and therefore speak" (2 Cor. 4:13).

Spirit of Glory • "happy are ye; for the *spirit of glory* and of God resteth upon you" (1 Pet. 4:14).

Spirit of Holiness • "declared to be the Son of God with power, according to *the spirit of holiness"* (Rom. 1:4).

Spirit of Life • "the law of the *Spirit of life* in Christ Jesus hath made me free from the law of sin and death" (Rom. 8:2).

Spirit of Power, Love, Sound Mind • "For God hath not given us the spirit of fear; but *of power*, and *of love*, and *of a sound mind"* (2 Tim. 1:7).

Spirit of Promise • "ye were sealed with that holy *Spirit of promise*, Which is the earnest of our inheritance" (Eph. 1:13, 14).

Spirit of Truth • "Even the *Spirit of truth*; whom the world cannot receive, because it seeth him not, neither knoweth him: but ye know him; for he dwelleth with you, and shall be in you" (John 14:17; see also 15:26; 16:13; 1 Jn. 4:6).

Spirit of Wisdom and Revelation • "the God of our Lord Jesus Christ, the Father of glory, may give unto you *the spirit of wisdom and revelation* in the knowledge of him" (Eph. 1:17).

Did the Holy Ghost Function on Earth During Christ's Mortal Ministry?

Two passages in the gospel of John sometimes raise questions pertaining to whether the Holy Ghost was functioning on the earth during the mortal ministry of Jesus. The first is the account of a statement made by the Savior to the Pharisees in the temple in Jerusalem: • "If any man thirst, let him come unto me, and drink. He that believeth on me, as the scripture hath said, out of his belly shall flow rivers of living water. (*But this spake he of the Spirit, which they that believe on him should receive: for the Holy Ghost was not yet given; because that Jesus was not yet glorified.*)" (John 7:37–39).

The second question-causing statement is a remark Jesus made to His Apostles in His "last supper" discourse: • "It is expedient for you that I go away: for *if I go not away, the Comforter will not come unto you; but if I depart, I will send him unto you"* (John 16:7).

The many passages cited below make it abundantly clear that the *power* of the Holy Ghost was freely manifested during Christ's mortal ministry, as evidenced by the thousands who were drawn to Him while He walked among them. (Without that *power* being operational, no one would have received a testimony that He truly was and is the Christ and that His gospel was and is true.)

It appears that with Jesus present as a source of revelation and inspiration for His Apostles and other disciples, the *gift* of the Holy Ghost was withheld until the great outpouring of the Spirit upon the Apostles and other believers on the day of Pentecost (Acts 2:1–47). The then-present members of the church apparently received the *gift* of the Holy Ghost at that time (Acts 2:1–4). But on that same day, the *power* of the Holy Ghost also was manifested strongly; causing belief, building testimonies, and creating converts; so that "the same day there were added unto them about three thousand souls" (Acts 2:41).

An interesting exception to the *gift* of the Holy Ghost being conferred *after* baptism is John the Baptist, the Prophet who was forerunner of Jesus Christ. The scriptures relate that he was filled with the Holy Ghost *from his mother's womb* (Luke 1:15; D&C 84:27). He also was filled with *the spirit of Elias* (D&C 27:7), and *he was ordained by an angel when he was eight days old* (D&C 84:28). He, most definitely, was a very special case, and he ministered under the guidance of the Holy Ghost during the mortal ministry of Jesus Christ!

The Responsibilities and Blessings of the Holy Ghost

The scriptures bear witness of numerous specific actions that the Holy Ghost performs as He carries out His responsibilities as a member of the Godhead. The following is a representative listing of 63 of them; others probably could be added based on other passages of scripture:

1. **Aids in discerning truth:** • "they that are wise and have received the truth, and have *taken the Holy Spirit for their guide, and have not been deceived"* (D&C 45:57).

2. **Aids those who preach the gospel:** • "unto us they did minister the things, which are now reported unto you *by them that have preached the gospel unto you with the Holy Ghost"* (1 Pet. 1:12). • "if you shall ask the Father in my name, in faith believing, *you shall receive the Holy Ghost, which giveth utterance, that you may stand as a witness* of the things of which you shall both hear and see" (D&C 14:8).

3. **Baptizes by Fire** [purifies]: • "Thou art *baptized with fire, and with the Holy Ghost"* (Moses 6:66).

4. **Bears record in heaven:** • "For *there are three that bear record in heaven,* the Father, the Word, and *the Holy Ghost"* (1 Jn. 5:7).

5. **Bears record of the Father and Son:** • *"the Holy Ghost beareth record* of the *Father* and *me* [Jesus]" (3 Ne. 28:11). • "that the grace of God the Father, and also the Lord Jesus Christ, and *the Holy Ghost, which beareth record of them,* may be and abide in you forever" (Eth. 12:41).

6. **Bears witness of truth:** • "And it is *the Spirit that beareth witness,* because *the Spirit is truth"* (1 Jn. 5:6). • "And *by the power of the Holy Ghost ye may know the truth* of all things" (Moro. 10:5). • "he that receiveth the word by the Spirit of truth *receiveth it as it is preached by the Spirit of truth"* (D&C 50:21).

7. **Brings good fruits:** • *"the fruit of the Spirit is love, joy, peace,* longsuffering, gentleness, goodness, faith, Meekness, temperance" (Gal. 5:22–23). • "the remission of sins bringeth meekness, and lowliness of heart; and because of meekness and lowliness of heart cometh the visitation of the Holy Ghost, *which Comforter filleth with hope and perfect love"* (Moro. 8:26). • "I will impart unto you of *my Spirit,* which shall enlighten your mind, *which shall fill your soul with joy"* (D&C 11:13).

8. **Brings Christ's teachings to remembrance:** • "But the Comforter, which is the Holy Ghost, whom the Father will send in my name, he shall . . . *bring all things to your remembrance,* whatsoever I have said unto you" (John 14:26).

9. **Causes men to believe:** •"those who should come after, who should *believe in the gifts and callings of God by the Holy Ghost"* (D&C 20:27).

10. **Constant companion:** • "The Holy Ghost shall be *thy constant companion"* (D&C 121:46). • "the Holy Ghost has not a body of flesh and bones, but is a personage of Spirit. Were it not so, the Holy Ghost could not *dwell in us.* A man may receive the Holy Ghost, and it may descend upon him and not tarry with him" (D&C 130:22–23).

11. **Conveys Christ's commandments to Church leaders:** • "Jesus began both to do and teach, Until the day in which he was taken up, after that *he through the Holy Ghost had given commandments unto the apostles*" (Acts 1:1–2).

12. **Conveys the will of the Lord:** • "whatsoever they shall speak *when moved upon by the Holy Ghost* shall be scripture, shall be *the will of the Lord,* shall be the mind of the Lord, shall be the word of the Lord, shall be the voice of the Lord, and the power of God unto salvation" (D&C 68:4).

13. **Enabled Christ's sinlessness:** • "Christ, who *through the eternal Spirit offered himself without spot to God"* (Heb. 9:14).

14. **Enables priesthood ministrations:** • "a high priest, that is, after the order of Melchizedek, may be set apart unto the ministering of temporal things, *having a knowledge of them by the Spirit of truth"* (D&C 107:71).

15. **Enables prophesying:** • "when Paul had laid his hands upon them, *the Holy Ghost came on them;* and they spake with tongues, *and prophesied"* (Acts 19:6). • "For the *prophecy* came not in old time by the will of man: but *holy men of God spake as they were moved by the Holy Ghost"* (2 Pet. 1:21). • "the Spirit speaketh the truth and lieth not. Wherefore, it speaketh of things as they really are, and *of things as they really will be"* (Jacob 4:13). • "No sooner had I baptized Oliver Cowdery, than *the Holy Ghost fell upon him, and he stood up and prophesied* many things which should shortly come to pass. And again, so soon as I had been baptized by him, *I also had the spirit of prophecy, when, standing up, I prophesied concerning the rise of this Church,* and many other things connected with the Church, and this generation of the children of men" (JS—H 1:73).

16. **Enables sanctification:** • "Repent, all ye ends of the earth, and come unto me and be baptized in my name, that ye may *be sanctified by the reception of the Holy Ghost,* that ye may stand spotless before me at the last day" (3 Ne. 27:20).

17. **Enables the remission of sins:** • "For the gate by which ye should enter is repentance and baptism by water; and *then cometh a remission of your sins by fire and by the Holy Ghost"* (2 Ne. 31:17). • "the Spirit of the Lord came upon them, and they were filled with joy, *having received a remission of their sins,* and having peace of conscience" (Mosiah 4:3).

18. **Enables speaking in tongues:** • "they were all filled with the Holy Ghost, and *began to speak with other tongues, as the Spirit gave them utterance"* (Acts 2:4).

19. **Enables testimonies that Christ is the Lord:** • "no man speaking by the Spirit of God calleth Jesus accursed: and . . . *no man can say that Jesus is the Lord, but by the Holy Ghost"* (1 Cor. 12:3).

20. **Enables the spiritual gifts:** • "there are *diversities of gifts,* but the same Spirit" (1 Cor. 12:4). • "there are many gifts, and *to every man is given a gift by the Spirit of God"* (D&C 46:11).

21. **Enlightens minds:** • "thou knowest that thou hast inquired of me and *I did enlighten thy mind;* and now I tell thee these things that thou mayest know that *thou hast been enlightened by the Spirit of truth"* (D&C 6:15). • "I will impart unto you of *my Spirit, which shall enlighten your mind,* which shall fill your soul with joy" (D&C 11:13).

22. **Gives access to the Father:** • "through him we both have *access by one Spirit unto the Father"* (Eph. 2:18).

23. **Gives power to shake others:** • "my father did speak unto them in the valley of

Lemuel, with power, *being filled with the Spirit, until their frames did shake before him"* (1 Ne. 2:14). • "he hath spoken unto you in a still small voice, but ye were past feeling, that ye could not feel his words; wherefore, he has spoken unto you like unto the voice of thunder, *which did cause the earth to shake as if it were to divide asunder"* (1 Ne. 17:45). • "I, Nephi, said many things unto my brethren, insomuch that they were confounded and could not contend against me; neither durst they lay their hands upon me nor touch me with their fingers, even for the space of many days. Now *they durst not do this lest they should wither before me, so powerful was the Spirit of God"* (1 Ne. 17:52).

24. **Gives utterance:** • "they were all filled with the Holy Ghost, and began to speak with other tongues, *as the Spirit gave them utterance"* (Acts 2:4). • "it was *the Spirit of the Lord* which was in him, which *opened his mouth to utterance* that he could not shut it" (2 Ne. 1:27). • "now I, Nephi, cannot say more; *the Spirit stoppeth mine utterance"* (2 Ne. 32:7). • *"you shall receive the Holy Ghost, which giveth utterance,* that you may stand as a witness of the things of which you shall both hear and see" (D&C 14:8).

25. **Glorifies the Savior:** • "when he, the Spirit of truth, is come, . . . *He shall glorify me"* (John 16:13–14).

26. **Guide to discerning visions:** • "Moses cast his eyes and beheld the earth, yea, even all of it; and there was not a particle of it which he did not behold, *discerning it by the spirit of God"* (Moses 1:27).

27. **Guide to what should be said:** • "Yea, if it be according to the Spirit of the Lord, which is in me; for *I shall say nothing which is contrary to the Spirit of the Lord"* (Alma 11:22).

28. **Guides impromptu testimonies:** • "But when they shall lead you, and deliver you up, take no thought beforehand what ye shall speak, neither do ye premeditate: but *whatsoever shall be given you in that hour, that speak ye: for it is not ye that speak, but the Holy Ghost"* (Mark 13:11). • "But behold, *the Lord God poured in his Spirit into my soul,* insomuch that I did confound him [Sherem] in all his words" (Jacob 7:8).

29. **Guides in prayer requests:** • *"He that asketh in the Spirit asketh according to the will of God;* wherefore it is done even as he asketh" (D&C 46:30).

30. **Guides into truth:** • "when he, the Spirit of truth, is come, *he will guide you into all truth"* (John 16:13).

31. **Guides reproofs:** • *"Reproving* betimes with sharpness, *when moved upon by the Holy Ghost"* (D&C 121:43).

32. **Has grace:** • "that *the grace* of God the Father, and also the Lord Jesus Christ, and *the Holy Ghost,* which beareth record of them, may be and abide in you forever" (Eth. 12:41).

33. **Helps with infirmities:** • *"the Spirit also helpeth our infirmities:* for we know not what we should pray for as we ought" (Rom. 8:26).

34. **Inspires individuals to action:** • "I looked and beheld a man among the Gentiles, who was separated from the seed of my brethren by the many waters; and *I beheld the Spirit of God, that it came down and wrought upon the man;* and he went forth upon the many waters, even unto the seed of my brethren, who were in the promised land" (1 Ne. 13:12).

35. **Inspires the Savior:** • "That it might be fulfilled which was spoken by Esaias the prophet, saying, Behold my servant [Jesus Christ], whom I have chosen; my

beloved, in whom my soul is well pleased: *I will put my spirit upon him, and he shall shew judgment to the Gentiles"* (Matt. 12:17–18). • *"Jesus being full of the Holy Ghost* returned from Jordan, and *was led by the Spirit into the wilderness"* (Luke 4:1).

36. **Leads to do good:** • "put your trust in *that Spirit which leadeth to do good*—yea, to do justly, to walk humbly, to judge righteously; and this is my Spirit" (D&C 11:12).

37. **Makes intercession for the saints:** • *"the Spirit itself maketh intercession for us with groanings which cannot be uttered. . . . he maketh intercession for the saints* according to the will of God" (Rom. 8:26–27).

38. **Makes known thoughts of others:** • "thou [Zeezrom] hast lied unto God; for behold, he knows all thy thoughts, and thou seest that *thy thoughts are made known unto us by his Spirit"* (Alma 12:3).

39. **Manifests all things expedient:** • "you shall have the Holy Ghost, which *manifesteth all things which are expedient unto the children of men"* (D&C 18:18). • "Believe and repent of your sins and be baptized in the name of Jesus Christ, the Son of God, even as our fathers, and *ye shall receive the Holy Ghost, that ye may have all things made manifest"* (Moses 8:24).

40. **Manifests Christ to mankind:** • "it must needs be that the Gentiles be convinced also that Jesus is the Christ, the Eternal God; And that *he manifesteth himself unto all those who believe in him, by the power of the Holy Ghost;* yea, unto every nation, kindred, tongue, and people, working mighty miracles, signs, and wonders, among the children of men according to their faith" (2 Ne. 26:12–13). • "they understood me not that the Gentiles should not at any time hear my voice—that I [Christ] *should not manifest myself unto them save it were by the Holy Ghost"* (3 Ne. 15:23). • "then fulfilleth the Father the covenant which he made with Abraham, saying: In thy seed shall all the kindreds of the earth be blessed— unto *the pouring out of the Holy Ghost through me upon the Gentiles"* (3 Ne. 20:27). • "after he had been slain he should rise from the dead, and *should make himself manifest, by the Holy Ghost, unto the Gentiles"* (1 Ne. 10:11).

41. **Participates in spiritual rebirth:** • "Verily, verily, I say unto thee, Except a man be born of water and of the Spirit, he cannot enter into the kingdom of God. That which is born of the flesh is flesh; and *that which is born of the Spirit is spirit"* (John 3:5–6). • "thus he was baptized, and the Spirit of God descended upon him, and *thus he was born of the Spirit,* and became quickened in the inner man" (Moses 6:65).

42. **Pricks hearts of gospel investigators:** • "Now when they heard this, *they were pricked in their heart,* and said unto Peter and to the rest of the apostles, Men and brethren, what shall we do?" (Acts 2:37).

43. **Promises fulfillment of covenants:** • *"ye were sealed with that holy Spirit of promise, Which is the earnest of our inheritance* until the redemption" (Eph. 1:13–14). • "who overcome by faith, and *are sealed by the Holy Spirit of promise,* which the Father sheds forth upon all those who are just and true" (D&C 76:53). • "I give unto you Hyrum Smith to be a patriarch unto you, *to hold the sealing blessings of my church, even the Holy Spirit of promise, whereby ye are sealed up* unto the day of redemption" (D&C 124:124).

44. **Prompts writing:** • "And a book of remembrance was kept, in the which was recorded, in the language of Adam, for *it was given unto as many as called upon God*

to write by the spirit of inspiration; And by them their children were taught to read and write, having a language which was pure and undefiled" (Moses 6:5–6).

45. **Quickens mortal bodies:** • "he that raised up Christ from the dead shall also *quicken your mortal bodies by his Spirit* that dwelleth in you" (Rom. 8:11).

46. **Reproves the world of sin:** • "if I go not away, the Comforter will not come unto you; but . . . when he is come, *he will reprove the world of sin, and of righteousness, and of judgment*" (John 16:7–8).

47. **Sanctifies man:** • "ye are washed, but *ye are sanctified,* but ye are justified in the name of the Lord Jesus, and *by the Spirit of our God*" (1 Cor. 6:11). • "God hath from the beginning chosen you to salvation *through sanctification of the Spirit* and belief of the truth" (2 Thess. 2:13). • "through *sanctification of the Spirit,* unto obedience and sprinkling of the blood of Jesus Christ" (1 Pet. 1:2).

48. **Seals till redemption day:** "grieve not *the holy Spirit of God, whereby ye are sealed* unto the day of redemption" (Eph. 4:30).

49. **Searches all things:** • *"the Spirit searcheth all things,* yea, the deep things of God" (1 Cor. 2:10).

50. **Searches hearts:** • *"the Spirit . . . searcheth the hearts"* (Rom. 8:26–27).

51. **Shows things one should do:** • "if ye will enter in by the way, and *receive the Holy Ghost, it will show unto you all things what ye should do"* (2 Ne. 32:5).

52. **Shows things to come:** • "when he, *the Spirit of truth,* is come, . . . *he will shew you things to come"* (John 16:13).

53. **Speaks and conveys truth:** • *"the Spirit speaketh the truth* and lieth not. Wherefore, it speaketh of things as they really are, and of things as they really will be" (Jacob 4:13).

54. **Speaks through mortals:** • *"it is not ye that speak, but the Spirit* of your Father which speaketh in you" (Matt. 10:20).

55. **Spirit of revelation:** • "I have fasted and prayed many days that I might know these things of myself. And now I do know of myself that they are true; for *the Lord God hath made them manifest unto me by his Holy Spirit; and this is the spirit of revelation which is in me"* (Alma 5:46). • "I will tell you in your mind and in your heart, by *the Holy Ghost,* which shall come upon you and *which shall dwell in your heart.* Now, behold, *this is the spirit of revelation"* (D&C 8:2–3).

56. **Teaches all things:** • "But the Comforter, which is *the Holy Ghost, . . .* he shall *teach you all things"* (John 14:26).

57. **Teaches spiritual things:** • "the things of God knoweth no man, but the Spirit of God. . . . which things also we speak, not in the words which man's wisdom teacheth, but which *the Holy Ghost teacheth; comparing spiritual things with spiritual"* (1 Cor. 2:11, 13). • "you shall receive my Spirit, *the Holy Ghost,* even *the Comforter, which shall teach you the peaceable things* of the kingdom" (D&C 36:2). • "this is my gospel—repentance and baptism by water, and then cometh the baptism of fire and *the Holy Ghost,* even *the Comforter, which showeth all things, and teacheth the peaceable things of the kingdom"* (D&C 39:6).

58. **Teaches what to say:** • "when they bring you unto the synagogues, and unto magistrates, and powers, take ye no thought how or what thing ye shall answer, or what ye shall say: *For the Holy Ghost shall teach you in the same hour what ye ought to say"* (Luke 12:11–12).

59. **Testifies of Christ:** • "when the Comforter is come, *even the Spirit of truth, . . .*

he shall testify of me" (John 15:26). • "nothing that is good denieth the Christ, but acknowledgeth that he is. And *ye may know that he is, by the power of the Holy Ghost"* (Moro. 10:6–7).

60. **Transports individuals:** • "when the Lord had spoken with Adam, our father, that Adam cried unto the Lord, and *he was caught away by the Spirit of the Lord,* and was carried down into the water, and was laid under the water, and was brought forth out of the water" (Moses 6:64).

61. **Witnesses of gospel truths:** • *"we are his witnesses of these things; and so is also the Holy Ghost,* whom God hath given to them that obey him" (Acts 5:32).

62. **Witnesses of the Father and the Son:** • "ye have received *the Holy Ghost,* which *witnesses of the Father and the Son"* (2 Ne. 31:18).

63. **Witness of the Lord's covenants:** • *"the Holy Ghost also is a witness to us:* for . . . *This is the covenant that I will make with them* after those days, saith the Lord, I will put my laws into their hearts, and in their minds will I write them; And their sins and iniquities will I remember no more" (Heb. 10:15–17).

Symbolic Representations of the Presence or Manifestations of the Holy Ghost

A subject often overlooked by Latter-day Saint authors is symbolic representations of the presence or operations of the Holy Ghost. The scriptures, particularly the Bible, speak of many such representations, and examples of them are cited below. They are listed in two groups: (1) symbols of the Holy Ghost drawn from nature, and (2) symbols of the Holy Ghost drawn from animate life and the roles men fulfill.

Symbols from nature which sometimes represent the workings of the Holy Ghost include:

Breath [of God]. • "the LORD God formed man of the dust of the ground, and *breathed into his nostrils the breath of life;* and man became a living soul" (Gen. 2:7). • "But there is a spirit in man: and the inspiration of the Almighty giveth them understanding. . . .The Spirit of God hath made me, and *the breath of the Almighty hath given me life"* (Job 32:8, 33:4). • "Then said he unto me, Prophesy unto the wind, prophesy, son of man, and say to the wind, Thus saith the Lord GOD; Come from the four winds, *O breath, and breathe upon these slain, that they may live.* So I prophesied as he commanded me, and *the breath came into them,* and they lived, and stood up upon their feet" (Ezek. 37:9–10). • "Then said Jesus to them again, Peace be unto you: as my Father hath sent me, even so send I you. And when he had said this, *he breathed on them,* and saith unto them, *Receive ye the Holy Ghost"* (John 20:21–22).

Clothing [verb]. (The **verb** "clothing" is frequently used in a figurative sense.) For instance: • "the Spirit of the LORD *came upon* Gideon" (Jud. 6:34) literally means: "*The Spirit of Jehovah clothed himself with Gideon.*" • "Then the spirit *came upon* Amasai" (1 Chr. 12:18; 2 Chr. 12:18).

Dew. • *"I will be as the dew unto Israel:* he shall grow as the lily, and cast forth his roots as Lebanon" (Hos. 14:5).

Earnest. • "God; Who hath also *sealed us,* and given *the earnest of the Spirit in our hearts"* (2 Cor. 1:22). • "God, who also hath given unto us *the earnest of the Spirit.* Therefore we are always confident" (2 Cor. 5:5–6). • "we should be to the praise of his glory, who first trusted in Christ. In whom ye also trusted, after that ye heard the word of truth, the gospel of your salvation: in whom also after that ye believed, *ye were* *sealed with that holy Spirit of promise,* Which is *the earnest of our inheritance"* (Eph. 1:12–14).

Fire. • *"I will make my words in thy mouth fire,* and this people wood, and it shall devour them" (Jer. 5:14). • "But his word was in mine heart *as a burning fire* shut up in my bones, and I was weary with forbearing, and I could not stay" (Jer. 20:9). • *"Did not our heart burn within us,* while he talked with us by the way, and while he opened to us the scriptures?" (Luke 24:32). • "Every man's work shall be made manifest: for the day shall declare it, because *it shall be revealed by fire; and the fire shall try every man's work of what sort it is"* (1 Cor. 3:13). • "there appeared unto them *cloven tongues like as of fire,* and it sat upon each of them. And they were all filled with the Holy Ghost" (Acts 2:3–4). • "it came to pass that Nephi and Lehi were *encircled about as if by fire"* (Hel. 5:23). • "you must study it out in your mind; then you must ask me if it be right, and if it is right *I will cause that your bosom shall burn within you"* (D&C 9:8).

Floods. • "I will pour water upon him that is thirsty, and *floods upon the dry ground:* I will pour my spirit upon thy seed, and my blessing upon thine offspring" (Isa. 44:3).

Oil [anointing]. • "How *God anointed Jesus of Nazareth with the Holy Ghost* and with power" (Acts 10:38). • "God, even thy God, *hath anointed thee with the oil of gladness* above thy fellows" (Heb. 1:9).

Rain. • "He shall come down *like rain upon the mown grass:* as showers that water the earth. In his days shall the righteous flourish" (Ps. 72:6–7).

Rivers. • "He that believeth on me, as the scripture hath said, out of his belly shall flow *rivers of living water.* (But this spake he of the Spirit . . .)" (John 7:38–39).

Salt. • *"Ye are the salt of the earth:* but if the salt have lost his savour, wherewith shall it be salted? it is thenceforth good for nothing, but to be cast out, and to be trodden under foot of men" (Matt. 5:13). • *"every one shall be salted with fire,* and every sacrifice shall be salted with salt. *Salt is good: but if the salt have lost his saltness, wherewith will ye season it? Have salt in yourselves,* and have peace one with another" (Mark 9:49–50).

Seal [verb]. • "Labour not for the meat which perisheth, but for that meat which endureth unto everlasting life, which the Son of man shall give unto you: for *him hath God the Father sealed"* (John 6:27). • "Now he which stablisheth us with you in Christ, and hath anointed us, is God; Who hath also *sealed us,* and *given the earnest of the Spirit* in our hearts" (2 Cor. 1:21–22). • "In whom ye also trusted, after that ye heard the word of truth, the gospel of your salvation: in whom also after that ye believed, *ye were sealed with that holy Spirit of promise,* Which is *the earnest of our inheritance* until the redemption of the purchased possession" (Eph. 1:13–14). • "grieve not the holy Spirit of God, whereby *ye are sealed unto the day of redemption"* (Eph. 4:30).

Seed [verb; of the Spirit]. • "that which is *born of the Spirit* is spirit" (John 3:6). • "Whosoever is *born of God* doth not commit sin; for his seed remaineth in him: and he cannot sin, because he is *born of God"* (1 Jn. 3:9). • "Being *born again, not of corruptible seed, but of incorruptible,* by the word of God, which liveth and abideth for ever" (1 Pet. 1:23).

Seven. Representing "perfection," the numeral seven symbolizes the Holy Ghost in (1) the perfection of His Deity and (2) the perfection of His ministrations and mission. • "behold the stone that I have laid before Joshua; upon one stone shall be *seven eyes:* behold, I will engrave the graving thereof, saith the LORD of hosts, and I will remove the iniquity of that land in one day" (Zech. 3:9). • "they shall rejoice, and shall see the plummet in the hand of Zerubbabel with *those seven; they are the eyes of the* LORD, which run to and fro through the whole earth" (Zech. 4:10). • "in the midst of the elders, stood a Lamb as it had been slain, having seven horns and *seven eyes, which are the seven Spirits of God* sent forth into all the earth" (Rev. 5:6).

Springs. • "*whosoever drinketh of the water that I shall give him shall never thirst; but the water that I shall give him shall be in him a well of water springing up* into everlasting life" (John 4:14). • "all *my springs* are in thee" (Ps. 87:7).

Water. • "In the last day, that great day of the feast, Jesus stood and cried, saying, If any man thirst, *let him come unto me, and drink.* He that believeth on me, as the scripture hath said, out of his belly shall flow *rivers of living water.* (But this spake he of the Spirit, which they that believe on him should receive: for the Holy Ghost was not yet given; because that Jesus was not yet glorified.) (John 7:37–39). • "But whosoever drinketh of the water that I shall give him shall never thirst; but *the water that I shall give him shall be in him a well of water springing up into everlasting life*" (John 4:14).

Wind. • "*The wind bloweth where it listeth, and thou hearest the sound thereof, but canst not tell whence it cometh, and whither it goeth:* so is every one that is *born of the Spirit*" (John 3:8). • "And when the day of Pentecost was fully come, they were all with one accord in one place. And *suddenly there came a sound from heaven as of a rushing mighty wind,* and it filled all the house where they were sitting" (Acts 2:1–2).

Wine. • "Others mocking said, These men are full of *new wine.* But Peter, standing up with the eleven, lifted up his voice, and said unto them, . . . *this is that which was spoken by the prophet Joel;* And it shall come to pass in the last days, saith God, *I will pour out of my Spirit* upon all flesh: and your sons and your daughters shall prophesy (Acts 2:13–14. 16–17). • "be not drunk with wine, wherein is excess; but *be filled with the Spirit*" (Eph. 5:18).

Symbols of the Holy Ghost drawn from animate life and the roles men fulfill include:

Advocate. Not only is Christ man's advocate; the Holy Spirit also serves as an advocate for mankind: • "Likewise the Spirit also helpeth our infirmities: for we know not what we should pray for as we ought: but *the Spirit itself maketh intercession for us* with groanings which cannot be uttered. And he that searcheth the hearts knoweth what is the mind of the Spirit, because *he maketh intercession for the saints according to the will of God*" (Rom. 8:26–27).

Comforter. • "Then had the churches rest throughout all Judæa and Galilee and Samaria, and were edified; and walking in the fear of the Lord, and in *the comfort of the Holy Ghost,* were multiplied" (Acts 9:31).

Dove. • "the Holy Ghost descended in a bodily shape *like a dove* upon him" (Luke 3:22). See also: Gen. 8:8–12: six characteristics of doves—swift in flight: Ps. 55:6; beautiful plumage: Ps. 68:13; constant in love: S.S. 5:12; mournful: Isa. 59:11; gentle: Matt. 10:16; particular in food: Gen. 8:8–12.

Finger. The expression "the Finger of the Hand Divine" was utilized by the early church fathers. "The Finger of God" and "The Hand of God" carry the connotation of omnipotence. • "if *I with the finger of God cast out devils,* no doubt the kingdom of God is come upon you" (Luke 11:20; see Matt. 12:28 which shows that the finger of God is the Holy Spirit: • "*if I cast out devils by the Spirit of God,* then the kingdom of God is come unto you.")

Helper. • "the Spirit also *helpeth our infirmities"* (Rom. 8:26).

Paraclete. This word literally means *"counsel for the defense."* Characteristics of the Holy Ghost: (1) Christlike and abiding: • "I will pray the Father, and he shall give you another Comforter, that he may *abide with you for ever"* (John 14:16), (2) sent from the Father: • "the Holy Ghost, *whom the Father will send"* (John 14:26), (3) a gift from Christ: • "when the Comforter is come, *whom I will send unto you* from the Father" (John 15:26), (4) Christ's ascension gift: • "if I go not away, the Comforter will not come unto you; but *if I depart, I will send him unto you"* (John 16:7).

Porter. • Porter means *"door-keeper."* • "To him *the porter openeth;* and the sheep hear his voice" (John 10:3). • "For the Son of man is as a man taking a far journey, who left his house, and gave authority to his servants, and to every man his work, and *commanded the porter to watch"* (Mark 13:34). *The importance of porters:* • "I had rather be *a doorkeeper in the house of my God,* than to dwell in the tents of wickedness" (Ps. 84:10). • "Then saith *the damsel that kept the door* unto Peter" (John 18:17).

Witness. • "The *Spirit itself beareth witness* with our spirit, that we are the children of God" (Rom. 8:16). • "I say the truth in Christ, I lie not, *my conscience also bearing me witness* in the Holy Ghost" (Rom. 9:1).

Pardon. • "There is therefore now *no condemnation* to them which are in Christ Jesus, who walk not after the flesh, but *after the Spirit"* (Rom. 8:1).

Adoption: • "For as many as are led by the Spirit of God, *they are the sons of God"* (Rom. 8:14). • "because *ye are sons, God hath sent forth the Spirit* of his Son into your hearts, crying, Abba, Father" (Gal. 4:6).

Sanctification: • "Hereby know *we that we dwell in him, and he in us,* because *he hath given us of his Spirit.* . . . . Whosoever shall confess that Jesus is the Son of God, *God dwelleth in him, and he in God"* (1 Jn. 4:13, 15).

The Holy Spirit Transports Man

Entire books have been written about the Holy Ghost and His missions; it is impossible to cover so many aspects of His glorious ministry in a single chapter. The objective here has been to assemble information which might be new but useful insights to many Latter-day Saints. Before concluding the chapter, this one last subject is set forth for consideration.

A little-recognized, but very important role of the Holy Ghost is His transporting of individuals from one place to another, usually to accomplish or enable sacred events. Apparently this transportation, for the most part, is literal and physical. However, it apparently may, in some instances, be an opening of spiritual channels of communication. Listed here are scriptural instances of individuals who received Spirit-enabled transportation:

• ***Adam:*** "when the Lord had spoken with Adam, our father, that Adam cried unto the Lord, and *he was caught away by the Spirit of the Lord,* and was carried down into the water, and was laid under the water, and was brought forth out of the water" (Moses 6:64).

• ***Christ:*** "Then was Jesus *led up of the Spirit into the wilderness* to be tempted of the devil" (Matt. 4:1).

• ***Christ:*** "For Christ . . . being put to death in the flesh, but quickened by the Spirit: *By which also he went and preached unto the spirits in prison"* (1 Pet. 3:18–19).

• ***Elijah:*** "It shall come to pass, as soon as I am gone from thee, that *the Spirit of the LORD shall carry thee whither I know not;* and so when I come and tell Ahab and he cannot find thee, he shall slay me" (1 Kgs. 18:12).

• **Ezekiel:** "*the spirit lifted me up between the earth and the heaven,* and brought me in the visions of God to Jerusalem" (Ezek. 8:3).

• **Ezekiel:** "*the spirit lifted me up,* and *brought me unto the east gate of the* LORD's *house"* (Ezek. 11:1).

• **Lehi:** "being thus overcome with the Spirit, *he was carried away* in a vision" (1 Ne. 1:8).

• **Mary:** "I beheld that *she was carried away in the Spirit;* and *after she had been carried away in the Spirit for the space of a time* the angel spake unto me, saying: Look! And I looked and beheld the virgin again, bearing a child in her arms" (1 Ne. 11:19–20).

• **Nephi:** "as I sat pondering in mine heart *I was caught away in the Spirit of the Lord,* yea, *into an exceedingly high mountain"* (1 Ne. 11:1). • "now I make an end of speaking concerning *the things which I saw while I was carried away in the spirit"* (1 Ne. 14:30). • "it came to pass that *after I, Nephi, had been carried away in the spirit,* and seen all these things, I returned to the tent of my father" (1 Ne. 15:1).

• **Philip:** "he commanded the chariot to stand still: and they went down both into the water, both Philip and the eunuch; and he baptized him. And when they were come up out of the water, *the Spirit of the Lord caught away Philip,* that the eunuch saw him no more: and he went on his way rejoicing. But *Philip was found at Azotus"* (Acts 8:38–40).

• **Twelve Apostles:** "I also beheld twelve others following him. And it came to pass that *they were carried away in the Spirit from before my face,* and I saw them not" (1 Ne. 11:29).

• **Zion, People caught up to:** "the *Holy Ghost* fell on many, and *they were caught up by the powers of heaven into Zion"* (Moses 7:27).

There are other experiences recorded in the scriptures in which individuals were "caught up" to various locations. While these passages don't specifically indicate that the process was enacted by the Holy Ghost, the passages above present a broad-enough pattern to allow the tentative assumption that these other experiences also were accomplished through the Holy Spirit's actions:

• **Christ:** "a man child [Christ], who was to rule all nations with a rod of iron: and *her child was caught up unto God, and to his throne"* (Rev. 12:5).

• **Moses:** "The words of God, which he spake unto Moses at a time when *Moses was caught up into an exceedingly high mountain"* (Moses 1:1).

• **Paul:** "I knew a man in Christ above fourteen years ago, (whether in the body, I cannot tell; or whether out of the body, I cannot tell: God knoweth;) such an one *caught up to the third heaven"* (2 Cor. 12:2).

• **Paul:** "I knew such a man, (whether in the body, or out of the body, I cannot tell: God knoweth;) How that *he was caught up into paradise,* and heard unspeakable words" (2 Cor. 12:3–4).

• **Three Nephite Apostles:** "behold, the heavens were opened, and *they were caught up into heaven,* and saw and heard unspeakable things" (3 Ne. 28:13; see also 28:36).

In addition, prophecies of the future resurrection of the righteous repeatedly speak of the saints being "caught up" to heaven. It will be interesting to discover if this mass ascension will be under the sole administration of the Holy Ghost or will be delegated to others to accomplish.

• **Saints to be resurrected:** "Then we which are alive and remain *shall be caught up together with them in the clouds,* to meet the Lord in the air" (1 Thess. 4:17). • "be faithful until I come, and *ye shall be caught up,* that where I am ye shall be also" (D&C 27:18). • "the saints that are upon the earth, who are alive, shall be quickened and *be caught up to meet him"* (D&C 88:96).

Summary

1. The Holy Ghost is a member of the Godhead with eternal powers, perfection, and characteristics similar to and on a par with God the Father and God the Son.

2. The Holy Ghost is a male being, not a "force." He is a personage of Spirit, in the form of a human being, but does not have a physical body.

3. The scriptures contain two passages that *may* be records of the Holy Ghost appearing to man in a bodily shape: Luke 3:22 (at Christ's baptism) and 1 Ne. 11: 9–12 (when Nephi was caught up to a high mountain). Alternate interpretations for these two appearances also were presented.

4. Often-asked questions concerning the Holy Ghost were presented, with the observation that answers to the questions have not yet been revealed.

5. The difference between the *power* and the *gift* of the Holy Ghost was explained. The power is the before-baptism ministration of the Holy Ghost which helps people to encounter the gospel, gain a testimony, and to refine their lives to become worthy for baptism. The Holy Ghost gives and removes this power as He sees fit, with the overall goal of preparing individuals to come unto Christ and partake of His salvation.

6. The gift of the Holy Ghost is conferred by the laying on of hands as people are confirmed members of the Church. During confirmation they are instructed to "receive the Holy Ghost." Some make no effort to do so, and hence go without the constant companionship of the Holy Spirit until they learn to diligently seek and invite His guidance and companionship.

7. The Holy Ghost has been operative on this earth since the days of Adam. Numerous passages allude to His presence and guidance during Old Testament times, but they are relatively few in number compared to the thousands of allusions to Jehovah during the same period.

8. Names for the Holy Ghost used in Old Testament times were listed, in three categories: names expressing the Holy Ghost's relation to "God," names expressing aspects of the Holy Ghost's character, and names expressing various operations of the Holy Ghost upon men. Other passages from the New Testament and Book of Mormon alluding to the Holy Ghost's functions in Old Testament times were also cited.

9. New Testament names of the Holy Ghost were listed in four categories: titles and names expressing the Holy Ghost's relationship to God the Son, Jesus Christ; titles and names expressing His relationship to God the Father; titles and names that express His own Godhood; and titles and names expressing His character and personality.

10. It appears that the *power* of the Holy Ghost was abundantly manifested during the Christ's mortal ministry. However, as long as He was on earth and an available source of revelation and inspiration for His followers, the *gift* of the Holy Ghost apparently was withheld. It was bestowed upon His followers on the day of Pentecost, following His ascension into heaven (Acts 2).

11. Sixty-three responsibilities and blessings of the Holy Ghost were listed, all drawn from specific scriptural passages. Others probably could be listed from additional passages.

12. Symbolic representations of the Holy Ghost's presence or manifestations were listed in two categories: symbols of the Holy Ghost drawn from nature, and symbols of the Holy Ghost drawn from animate life and the roles men fulfill.

13. A final subsection dealt with a rarely discussed responsibility that the Holy Ghost fulfills: His transporting of various individuals for sacred purposes. Recipients of this blessing include Adam, Elijah, Ezekiel, Mary, Christ, Lehi, Nephi, Philip, and the people of Zion.

CHAPTER 14

GOD THE FATHER

God the Father Is *the* God of Jesus Christ and *a* God of All This Earth's Mankind

Although the scriptures assert, in numerous passages, that Jehovah/Jesus Christ is the Deity assigned as the God of this earth, Jesus still acknowledged that His Father, God the Father, stands as His personal God. Jesus also recognized God the Father as His own Parent, both as the Father in the birth of His spirit, and later as His Father in the birth of His mortal body.

Following His resurrection, the first person to whom Jesus identified Himself was Mary, who had come to visit his grave. • "Jesus saith unto her, Touch me not, for I am not yet ascended to my Father: but go to my brethren, and say unto them, *I ascend unto* **my Father**, *and* **your Father**; *and to* **my God**, *and* **your God**" (John 20:17).

Various passages in the New Testament book of Ephesians clearly assert (1) that God the Father stands as the God to the resurrected Christ and (2) that God the Father is to be recognized as a God by mankind and to be treated with worshipful and reverential awe: • "Blessed be *the God and Father of our Lord Jesus Christ*, who hath blessed us with all spiritual blessings in heavenly places in Christ" (Eph. 1:3). • "For this cause *I bow my knees unto the Father of our Lord Jesus Christ*" (Eph. 3:14). And • "That *the God of our Lord Jesus Christ, the Father of glory*, may give unto you the spirit of wisdom and revelation in the knowledge of him" (Eph. 1:17).

After the seventy He had sent out on short-term missions to Judea and Galilee returned and reported their success to Him, Jesus prayed to His Heavenly Father and addressed Him as "Lord of heaven and earth": • "In that hour Jesus rejoiced in spirit, and said, I thank thee, *O Father, Lord of heaven and earth*, that thou hast hid these things from the wise and prudent, and has revealed them unto babes: *even so, Father, for so it seemed good in thy sight*" (Luke 10:21–22). The term "Lord," as used in this sense, had the meaning of "Master," a term of respect in which Jesus seemingly acknowledged His respect as a Son for His Father. He also was acknowledging His realization that He was sent to earth by His Father and that He was implementing the many instructions that His Father had given Him. This sign of respect and reliance, however, should not be taken as a negation of Christ's assigned role as the God responsible for this earth.

Shortly thereafter, when Jesus taught His disciples about prayer, • "he said unto them, When ye pray, say, *Our Father* which art in heaven, Hallowed be thy name. *Thy kingdom come. Thy will be done, as in heaven, so in earth"* (Luke 11:2). This phrase "thy kingdom come" apparently has reference to the future time when this earth will be celestialized and be a "heaven" to its righteous inhabitants. By that time, Christ will have presented it to his Father and then had it restored to Him for His (Jesus Christ's) governance. (See D&C 76:106–108.)

In a latter-day revelation, Jesus indicated that: • "I may testify unto *your Father, and your God, and my God,* that you are clean from the blood of this wicked generation" (D&C 88:75). This statement acknowledges the Deity status of both God the Father and of Jesus Christ, and it seemingly speaks of the time of the final judgment when Jesus will stand as the Mediator between God the Father and mankind, advocating various individuals' eligibility to partake of their redeeming grace because of the individuals' righteousness.

Jesus, on several occasions, spoke with modest deference concerning His standing in relationship with His Father. He said, presumably speaking of God the Father, • *"with God all things are possible"* (Matt. 19:26; Mark 10:27; Luke 18:27), a phrase which could have equal import concerning Himself and also God the Holy Ghost, as well as God the Father. On another occasion He taught His followers, • *"Be ye therefore perfect, even as your Father which is in heaven is perfect"* (Matt. 5:48), modestly omitting Himself although knowing that He also qualified to be included as "perfect." (When He taught the same principle to the Nephites, He did include Himself as perfect (see 3 Ne. 12:48). On another occasion, when a questioner addressed Him as "good master," he responded, • "Why callest thou me good? *there is none good but one, that is, God:* but if thou wilt enter into life, keep the commandments" (Matt. 19:16–17; Mark 10:18; Luke 18:19). Again, this appears to be an expression of modesty, since Jesus knew that He, as well as His Father, was without sin and certainly eligible to be addressed both as "Good Master" and as "God."

On yet another occasion, in His "last supper" discourse, He told His Apostles that • *"my Father is greater than I"* (John 14:28). How? Apparently at this stage in their progression, both had all power, all knowledge, all wisdom—all the power and glory of Godhood. But God the Father is Jesus' Father. Plus, the Father has advanced further in His creations, in His posterity, in the glory which He has acquired. Later, in that same discourse, Jesus made another comparison between Himself and His Father. He said, • "I am the *true vine,* and my Father is *the husbandman"* (John 15:1). In this comparison, He reflected the mentoring which He was still receiving from His Father. He said, • *"Every branch in me that beareth not fruit he taketh away: and every branch that beareth fruit, he purgeth it, that it may bring forth more fruit"* (John 15:2), and He continued, • *"the branch cannot bear fruit of itself, except it abide in the vine"* (John 15:4), apparently signifying His ongoing dependence in His relationships with His Father.

In summation, the scriptures indicate that God the Father is **the God** of Jesus Christ and, as a member of the Godhead, **a God** of all mankind on this earth, though Jesus Christ stands as the Deity assigned as **the God of this earth** and its inhabitants. As members of the Godhead, God the Father, God the Son, and God the Holy Ghost are equal in their perfection and their powers, yet each has His own assignments as pertaining to the administration of this earth.

This is comparable, on a much-diminished scale, to a stake presidency: all three hold the same priesthood, all three have responsibility for the well-being of their stake, all three have specific governance assignments, but the stake president holds overall responsibility as *the* leader of their presidency and the one individual directly responsible to higher priesthood authorities in the priesthood hierarchal structure.

In the case of the Godhead, Jesus Christ holds the central responsibility for this earth, but the God to whom he reports in the hierarchal structure is His Father, God the Father, who has given considerable instruction to His Son and is assisting Him in his duties, but is intentionally standing back and having His Son be the appointed leader.

God the Father Made Covenants and Established Procedures Before This Earth Was Created

There is an interesting glimpse into premortality alluded to in section 76 of the Doctrine and Covenants, which reads as follows:

> By the power of the Spirit our eyes were opened and our understandings were enlightened, so as to see and understand the things of God—
>
> Even *those things which were from the beginning before the world was, which were ordained of the Father, through his Only Begotten Son,* who was in the bosom of the Father, even from the beginning. (D&C 76:12–13)

Most of the known details concerning these premortal events are covered in chapters 7, 8, and 9 of this book. However, there are some allusions to promises and commitments that were made by God the Father which were not covered there but which are being treated briefly here.

They pertain, in particular, to (1) the premortal introduction of the law concerning the eternity of the marriage covenant as discussed in Doctrine and Covenants section 132, (2) to premortal agreements made between God the Father and Abraham, and (3) to various premortal priesthood organizational items and how they have influenced last-days practices.

Though it isn't possible to ascertain exactly when various rules, commandments, and covenants were set into place by God the Father, the scriptures speak of their existence. A few examples follow:

1. *The Father's premortal covenant with Abraham pertaining to the law of the Holy Priesthood:* • "if ye enter not into my law ye cannot receive *the promise of my Father, which he made unto Abraham*" (D&C 132:33).

Another verse from section 132 helps defines this law, and indicates that it was established *prior to the creation of this earth*: • "I am the Lord thy God, and will give unto thee *the law of my Holy Priesthood, as was ordained by me and my Father before the world was*" (D&C 132:28). The subject of this D&C section is "the eternity of the marriage covenant" (D&C 132: Preface). Verse 11 also establishes the premortal occurrence of this event: • "And will I appoint unto you, saith the Lord, except it be by law, *even as I and my Father ordained unto you, before the world was?*" (D&C 132:11)

God the Father's premortal covenant with Abraham. What is of special interest in this context is what was Jehovah's role, and what was God the Father's role in this premortal covenanting situation. Jehovah is Jesus Christ, not God the Father. There are numerous passages detailing various acts of the God of Abraham, Isaac, and Jacob that easily and clearly fit in the scriptural pattern which indicates that *Jehovah* is the God of Abraham, Isaac, and Jacob who interacted with those ancient and revered prophets during their mortal lives and the lives of their descendants.

Two other passages, however, don't harmonize with that pattern; they seem to be speaking of *God the Father* rather than Jehovah in a relationship with Abraham. It is this premortal covenanting between God the Father and Abraham that appears to explain and rectify that interpretational problem.

First Nephi 22:9 says: • "it shall also be of worth unto the Gentiles; and not only unto the Gentiles but unto all the house of Israel, unto *the making known of the covenants of the Father of heaven unto Abraham, saying: In thy seed shall all the kindreds of the earth be blessed.*" (If "Father of heaven" refers to God the Father, it fits appropriately in this explanation as a premortal event. If, on the other hand, "Father of heaven" refers to He who created the heavens and the earth, then it would properly refer to Jehovah/Jesus Christ, and no conflict would exist with the "Jehovah is the God of Abraham, Isaac and Jacob" pattern.)

Assuming that 1 Nephi 22:9 is speaking of God the Father, then apparently it was in the premortal period, when the nature of eternal marriage was first laid out to future inhabitants of this earth, that this verse finds its fulfillment.

Facsimile 2, Figure 7 of the book of Abraham, reads: • "Represents *God sitting upon his throne, revealing through the heavens the grand Key-words of the Priesthood;* as, also, the sign of the Holy Ghost unto Abraham, in the form of a dove." That doesn't harmonize well with the Jesus is Jehovah passages, but it fits perfectly with the understanding that God the Father, prior to the creation of this earth, covenanted with Abraham, as alluded to in D&C 132:33.

2. *The Father's premortal promise to women that they may bear the souls of men and merit exaltation:* • "and *to fulfil the promise which was given by my Father before the foundation of the world,* and for their [women's] *exaltation in the eternal worlds, that they may bear the souls of men*; for herein is the work of my Father continued, that he may be glorified" (D&C 132:63). This promise, apparently, was made in the same general scenario as when the "eternity of the marriage covenant was being explained prior to this earth's creation. (See number 1, above.)

3. *The calling of Aaron by the Father and the Son:* The Lord Jesus Christ, who revealed D&C 132, alluded to His Father's calling of Moses' brother, Aaron, saying: • "*if a man be called of my Father, as was Aaron, by mine own voice, and by the voice of him that sent me,* and I have endowed him with the keys of the power of this priesthood, if he do anything in my name, and according to my law and by my word, he will not commit sin, and I will justify him" (D&C 132:59). It is very possible, if not probable, that this calling of Aaron was one of those premortal priesthood calls alluded to in Alma chapter 13.

4. *The oath and covenant of the Melchizedek Priesthood was established:* Another premortal event, which also harks back to Alma 13, is the establishing of the oath and covenant of the Melchizedek Priesthood. That oath and covenant is referred to in D&C section 84: • "he that receiveth my Father receiveth my Father's kingdom; therefore all that my Father hath shall be given unto him. And *this is according to the oath and covenant which belongeth to the priesthood.* Therefore, *all those who receive the priesthood, receive this oath and covenant of my Father, which he cannot break,* neither can it be moved" (D&C 84:38–40). [See Alma 13.]

5. *The privilege of faithful members to receive priesthood ordination:* At some

unidentified point in the eternal plan, God the Father apparently promised to the males of mankind that, if they were worthy, they would be entitled to receive and hold the priesthood—the authorization to speak and act for Him in their dealings with mankind. This promise is alluded to in D&C section 108: • "Wait patiently until the solemn assembly shall be called of my servants, then you shall be remembered with the first of mine elders, and *receive right by ordination* with the rest of mine elders whom I have chosen. Behold, *this is the promise of the Father unto you if you continue faithful.* (D&C 108:4–5). This is a December 26, 1835 revelation concerning a specific individual: Lyman Sherman.

6. *The privilege of faithful members to be Endowed in the temple:* That the Father also promised the privilege of receiving the holy endowment is mentioned in D&C section 95: • "I gave you a commandment that you should build a house, in the which house *I design to endow those whom I have chosen with power from on high; For this is the promise of the Father unto you*" (D&C 95:8–9). This is a June 1, 1833 revelation alluding to the as yet unbuilt Kirtland Ohio temple which was dedicated on March 27, 1836.

7. *Salvation is obtained through Jesus Christ only:* Presumably, this decision was made before or at the time Jehovah/Jesus Christ was named to be the Redeemer of this earth, prior to its creation: • "Jesus Christ is the name which is *given of the Father,* and *there is none other name given whereby man can be saved*" (D&C 18:23).

8. *The Father's commandment that children should walk in truth:* No scriptural record of the origin of this commandment has been found, but it is mentioned in the Second Epistle of the Apostle John: • "Grace be with you, mercy, and peace, from God the Father, and from the Lord Jesus Christ, the Son of the Father, in truth and love. I rejoiced greatly that *I found of thy children walking in truth, as we have received a commandment from the Father*" (2 Jn. 1:3–4). See also Matt. 18:14: • *"It is not the will of your Father which is in heaven, that one of these little ones should perish."*

God The Father Conferred the Fulness of His Power and Glory upon Jesus

Important tools and necessary capabilities for Jesus' fulfillment of His responsibilities upon this and other planets were conveyed to Him by God the Father, and perhaps by others, prior to the creation of this earth. Many such abilities probably required extensive periods of instruction and training. Other capabilities, apparently, were conveyed from God the Father to Christ during His (Christ's) mortal ministry. The scriptures don't provide those details. Many of these essential abilities were described in detail in chapters 7, 8, and 9. Other allusions to them are briefly mentioned in this context:

• *"All things are delivered to me of my Father"* (Luke 10:22).

• "and the Word was made flesh, and dwelt among us, (and *we beheld his glory, the glory as of the only begotten of the Father,) full of grace and truth*" (John 1:14).

• "Say ye *of him whom the Father hath sanctified, and sent into the world,* Thou blasphemest; because I said, I am the Son of God?" (John 10:36).

• *"All things that the Father hath are mine:* therefore said I, that he shall take of mine, and shall shew it unto you" (John 16:15).

• "Father, I will that they also, whom thou hast given me, be with me where I am; that they may behold *my glory, which thou has given me:* for thou lovedst me before the foundation of the world" (John 17:24).

• "For *it pleased the Father that in him should all fulness dwell*" (Col. 1:19).

• "For *he received from God the Father honour and glory,* when there came such a voice to him from the excellent glory, *This is my beloved Son, in whom I am well pleased*" (2 Pet. 1:17).

• "the Father and I are one—The Father because *he gave me of his fulness*" (D&C 93:3–4).

• "*I was in the world and received of my Father,* and the works of him were plainly manifest" (D&C 93:5).

• I, John, bear record that *he* [Jesus] *received a fulness of the glory* of the Father; And *he received all power, both in heaven and on earth,* and the glory of the Father was with him, for he dwelt in him" (D&C 93:16–17).

• "If you keep my commandments *you shall receive of his fulness, and be glorified in me as I am in the Father;* therefore, I say unto you, *you shall receive grace for grace*" (D&C 93:20).

God the Father Entrusted His Spirit Children to the Care of Jesus Christ

Sometime prior to this earth's creation, God the Father entrusted to the care of His Son Jehovah/Jesus Christ the responsibility for the care and well-being of all His spirit children who were to come to this earth for their mortal probation. The arrangement called for Jesus Christ to stand as the adopting Father of all those who would come to Him, follow Him, enter the waters of baptism and make themselves worthy to partake of the atoning sacrifice which He was to make in behalf of all mankind. Those who would come to Him in this way were to adopted as Christ's children, as was explained by the Apostle Paul:

> Blessed *be the God and Father of our Lord Jesus Christ,* who hath blessed us with all spiritual blessings in heavenly places in Christ:
>
> According as *he hath chosen us in him before the foundation of the world,* that we should be holy and without blame before him in love:
>
> Having predestinated us *unto the adoption of children by Jesus Christ to himself,* according to the good pleasure of his will,
>
> To the praise of the glory of *his grace, wherein he hath made us accepted in the beloved.* (Eph. 1:3–6)

Some representative passages in which the Savior alludes to the Father entrusting His spirit children into His (Christ's) care include:

• "And now I am no more in the world, but these are in the world, and I come to thee. Holy Father, *keep through thine own name those whom thou hast given me,* that they may be one, as we are" (John 17:11).

• "Father, *I will that they also, whom thou hast given me,* be with me where I am; that they may behold my glory, which thou has given me: for thou lovedst me before the foundation of the world" (John 17:24).

• "Giving thanks unto the Father, *which hath made us meet to be partakers of the inheritance of the saints* in light" (Col. 1:12).

• ". . . with *all those whom my Father hath given me* out of the world" (D&C 27:14).

• "Fear not, little children, for *you are mine, . . . and you are of them that my Father hath given me; and none of them that my Father hath given me shall be lost*" (D&C 50:41–42).

• "that through him all might be saved *whom the Father had put into his power* and *made by him"* (D&C 76:42).

• "You are mine apostles, . . . *ye are they whom my Father hath given me"* (D&C 84:63).

God the Father Sent Jesus Christ to This Earth

Jesus, during his mortal ministry, repeatedly stated that He was sent to this earth by His Father, God the Father. Oft-quoted biblical passages clearly set forth that doctrine:

• "God so loved the world, that *he gave his only begotten Son,* that whosoever believeth in him should not perish, but have everlasting life. For *God sent not his Son into the world to condemn the world; but that the world through him might be saved"* (John 3:16–17).

• ". . . that the world may believe that *thou hast sent me"* (John 17:21).

• "O righteous Father, . . . these have known that *thou hast sent me"* (John 17:25).

• "Peter, Put up thy sword into the sheath: *the cup which my Father hath given me, shall I not drink it?"* (John 18:11).

• "Then said Jesus to them again, Peace be unto you: as *my Father hath sent me, even so send I you"* (John 20:21).

• "We have seen and do testify that *the Father sent the Son to be the Saviour of the world"* (1 Jn. 4:14).

God the Father Implements His Will through Jesus Christ on This Earth

The Lord Jesus Christ, the Savior and Redeemer of all mankind on this earth, has forthrightly acknowledged that He came to this earth to accomplish various objectives which He and God the Father had specified in their premortal planning:

• "I am Jesus Christ; *I came by the will of the Father, and I do his will"* (D&C 19:24).

• In like manner, he indicated his objective was to accomplish His Father's will, by subduing all things unto Himself: *"I, having accomplished and finished the will of him whose I am, even the Father,* concerning me—having done this that I might subdue all things unto myself"* (D&C 19:2).

• In another passage He spoke of • "Those *things which were from the beginning before the world* was, *which were ordained of the Father, through his Only Begotten Son,* who was in the bosom of the Father, even from the beginning" (D&C 76:13).

God the Father Gives Commandments to His Children on This Earth through Christ

Though Jesus Christ has overall responsibility for this earth, the scriptures reveal that many decisions which he makes have previously been determined by His Father, God the Father. During his mortal ministry, the Savior made it abundantly clear that His Father was directing the words He was to speak: • "The Father which sent me, *he gave me a commandment, what I should say, and what I should speak.* And I know that his commandment is life everlasting: *whatsoever I speak therefore, even as the Father said unto me, so I speak"* (John 12:49–50).

Careful reading of the scriptures in which Jesus indicates the instructions He has received from God the Father is quite informative. The Father's instructions to Him are very specific. For example, the passages cited below are all from the book of 3 Nephi, though similar passages occur in other scriptures, primarily in the Book of

Mormon. In these 3 Nephi examples, the resurrected Jesus Christ is appearing to the Nephites gathered near their temple in the land of Bountiful:

• "this is my doctrine, and *it is the doctrine which the Father hath given unto me;* and I bear record of the Father, and the Father beareth record of me, and the Holy Ghost beareth record of the Father and me; and *I bear record that the Father commandeth all men, everywhere, to repent and believe in me"* (3 Ne. 11:32).

• "behold, this is the land of your inheritance; and *the Father hath given it unto you"* (3 Ne. 15:13).

• "And *not at any time hath the Father given me commandment that I should tell it unto your brethren at Jerusalem"* (3 Ne. 15:14).

• *"Neither at any time hath the Father given me commandment that I should tell unto them concerning the other tribes of the house of Israel, whom the Father hath led away out of the land"* (3 Ne. 15:15).

• *"This much did the Father command me, that I should tell unto them:* That other sheep I have which are not of this fold; them also I must bring, and they shall hear my voice; and there shall be one fold, and one shepherd" (3 Ne. 15:16–17).

• "And now, because of stiffneckedness and unbelief they understood not my word; therefore *I was commanded to say no more of the Father concerning this thing unto them"* (3 Ne. 15:18).

• "But, verily, I say unto you that *the Father hath commanded me, and I tell it unto you,* that ye were separated from among them because of their iniquity; therefore it is because of their iniquity that they know not of you" (3 Ne. 15:19).

• *"thus commandeth the Father that I should say unto you:* At that day when the Gentiles shall sin against my gospel, and shall reject the fulness of my gospel, and shall be lifted up in the pride of their hearts above all nations, . . . if they shall do all those things, and shall reject the fulness of my gospel, *behold, saith the Father, I will bring the fulness of my gospel from among them"* (3 Ne. 16:10).

• "Verily, verily, I say unto you, *thus hath the Father commanded me—that I should give unto this people this land* for their inheritance" (3 Ne. 16:16).

• "I perceive that ye are weak, that *ye cannot understand all my words which I am commanded of the Father to speak unto you at this time.* Therefore, go ye unto your homes, and ponder upon the things which I have said, and *ask of the Father, in my name, that ye may understand"* (3 Ne. 17:2–3).

• "Therefore blessed are ye if ye shall keep my commandments, *which the Father hath commanded me that I should give unto you"* (3 Ne. 18:14).

• "Therefore, keep these sayings which I have commanded you that ye come not under condemnation; for *wo unto him whom the Father condemneth"* (3 Ne. 18:33).

• "it came to pass that when they had all given glory unto Jesus, he said unto them: Behold *now I finish the commandment which the Father hath commanded me concerning this people,* who are a remnant of the house of Israel" (3 Ne. 20:10).

• "verily, I say unto you, *all these things shall surely come, even as the Father hath commanded me. Then shall this covenant which the Father hath covenanted with his people be fulfilled;* and then shall Jerusalem be inhabited again with my people, and it shall be the land of their inheritance" (3 Ne. 20:46).

• "Verily I say unto you, I commanded my servant Samuel, the Lamanite, that he should testify unto this people, that *at the day that the Father should glorify his name in me* that there were many saints who should arise from the dead" (3 Ne. 23:9).

• "it came to pass that *he commanded them that they should write the words which the Father had given unto Malachi,* which he should tell unto them. And it came to pass that after they were written he expounded them. And these are the words which he did tell unto them, saying: *Thus said the Father unto Malachi—Behold, I will send my messenger, and he shall prepare the way before me"* (3 Ne. 24:1).

• "These scriptures, which ye had not with you, *the Father commanded that I should give unto you;* for it was wisdom in him that they should be given unto future generations" (3 Ne. 26:2).

As can be seen from these passages, some of the items God the Father instructed Jesus to say probably were related to previously devised long-range plans. Other items, however, were dealing with more current matters where Jesus was instructed how to respond to either good or bad decisions which various peoples had made.

The Influence of God the Father Is Exerted and Felt in Church Activities

Various unrelated passages indicate the strong role God the Father has played in shaping The Church of Jesus Christ of Latter-day Saints. In the earliest days of the restored Church the Prophet Joseph Smith recorded the Savior's testimony that • "These words are not of man nor of men, but of me, even Jesus Christ, your Redeemer, *by the will of the Father"* (D&C 31:13). Examples of God the Father's shaping of both ancient and latter-day events are recorded in the scriptures in passages such as:

• *"Pure religion and undefiled before God and the Father* is this, To visit the fatherless and widows in their affliction, and to keep himself unspotted from the world" (James 1:27).

• In the church records Joseph Smith is to be called a seer, translator, prophet, and Apostle of Jesus Christ, and *"an elder of the church through the will of God the Father,* and the grace of your Lord Jesus Christ" (D&C 21:1).

• The early 1830 gathering of Church members took place because • *"The decree hath gone forth from the Father* that they shall be gathered in unto one place upon the face of this land" (D&C 29:8).

• The ancient propet Enoch *"received the priesthood by the commandments of God,* by the hand of his father Adam" (D&C 84:16).

• The Apostles of the Church are not only Christ's Apostles, they are also • *"God's high Priests"* (D&C 84:63).

Passages such as these indicate God the Father's active involvement in The Church of Jesus Christ of Latter-day Saints.

Man Is Commanded to Worship God the Father in the Name of Jesus Christ

The scriptures repeatedly instruct that man is to worship God the Father, and that he is to do so through Jesus Christ, by worshiping the Father in His (Christ's) name: • "For this cause *I bow my knees unto the Father* of our Lord Jesus Christ" (Eph. 3:14). • "You shall *fall down and worship the Father* in my name" (D&C 18:40). • "All men must repent and believe on the name of Jesus Christ, and *worship the Father in his name"* (D&C 20:29). • "I give unto you these sayings that you may *understand and know how to worship,* and *know what you worship, that you may come unto the Father in my name, and in due time receive of his fulness"* (D&C 93:19).

The final passage here cited shows the intent of this commandment: to prepare righteous followers to once again dwell in the eternal presence of their Heavenly Father and to receive the glorious blessings He is willing to bestow upon them.

How is worshiping God the Father in the Name of Jesus Christ accomplished? Latter-day Saint sacrament meetings furnish a good example:

1. The invocation and benediction are prayers to God the Father offered in the name of Jesus Christ.

2. Many of the hymns sung from the Latter-day Saint Hymnal are hymns that praise God the Father and speak of His relationship with His Son Jesus Christ, with the Holy Ghost, with the Church of Jesus Christ, and with the Saints who are members of that Church.

3. Both sacrament prayers are offered to God the Father in the name of Jesus Christ. In these prayers the partakers of the sacramental emblems specifically witness unto God the Father • "that they are willing to take upon them the name of [His] Son, and always remember him and keep his commandments which he has given them" (D&C 20:77, 79). • Jesus instructed Church members that when partaking of the sacrament they should be *"remembering unto the Father"* his body and blood (D&C 27:2).

4. Speakers in sacrament meetings often make reference to God the Father and His many works and blessings in their discourses.

5. An effort is made to feel and exhibit reverence for the members of the Godhead in sacrament meetings and other Church gatherings.

6. Latter-day Saints strive to worship and learn of God the Father in their teachings (Sunday School, Primary, Young Men and Young Women classes, priesthood and Relief Society classes); in general, area, stake, and mission conferences; in many publications prepared and distributed by the Church; in missionary lessons taught throughout the world; and in family home evenings, personal prayers, and other worship activities.

Mankind Is Commanded to Give Glory to God the Father

The next chapter is devoted to gaining a richer understanding of the principle of glory as it relates to each member of the Godhead and to every follower of Christ here upon the earth. In this context, it suffices to indicate that mankind is commanded to give glory to God the Father in word, in action, and in attitude and desire. Jesus set the example concerning giving glory to His Father and God; man is instructed to do likewise, as is shown in these representative passages:

Christ glorified and still glorifies the Father.

• *"Father, glorify thy name.* Then came there a voice from heaven, saying, I have both glorified it, and will glorify it again" (John 12:28).

• "These words spake Jesus, and lifted up his eyes to heaven, and said, Father the hour is come; *glorify thy Son, that thy Son also may glorify thee"* (John 17:1).

• *"O Father, glorify thou me with thine own self* with the glory which I had with thee before the world was" (John 17:5).

• "behold the blood of thy Son which was shed, *the blood of him whom thou gavest that thyself might be glorified"* (D&C 45:4).

•[Christ] *"glorifies the Father"* (D&C 76:43).

Mankind is to glorify God the Father through their praise.

• "That ye may *with one mind and one mouth glorify God,* even the Father of our Lord Jesus Christ" (Rom. 15:6).

• "And that *every tongue should confess that Jesus Christ is Lord, to the glory of God the Father*" (Philip. 2:11).

• "Now *unto God and our Father be glory* for ever and ever" (Philip. 4:20).

Mankind is to glorify God the Father through their obedience, Church service, good example, and good works.

• "*Let your light so shine before men, that they may see your good works,* and *glorify your Father* which is in heaven" (Matt. 5:16).

• "Herein is my *Father glorified, that ye bear much fruit;* so shall ye be my disciples" (John 15:8).

• "*to advance the cause . . .* to *the glory of your Father* who is in heaven" (D&C 78:4).

• "*by this law is the continuation of the works of my Father,* wherein *he glorifieth himself*" (D&C 132:31).

God the Father Has Infinite Love for His Children

As previously discussed (see chapters 4 and 7), God the Father dearly loves His Firstborn Son, Jehovah/Jesus Christ (see D&C 76:25). The love of God the Father is so powerful a bond that the Apostle John actually states that "God *is* love" (1 Jn. 4:8, 16).

The Father loves all His children. The scriptures repeatedly speak of the love of both Jesus Christ and God the Father being manifested and evident to those who follow Christ and keep his commandments. In His "last supper" discourse, Jesus declared to His Apostles: • "*He that hath my commandments, and keepeth them, he it is that loveth me:* and he that loveth me *shall be loved of my Father, and I will love him,* and will manifest myself to him" (John 14:21). When asked by one of the Twelve how He would manifest Himself, • "Jesus answered and said unto him, *If a man love me, he will keep my words: and my Father will love him,* and *we will come unto him, and make our abode with him*" (John 14:23). Later in His sermon, the Savior reiterated: • "*As the Father hath loved me, so have I loved you:* continue ye in my love" (John 15:9), and still later He said once again: • "*the Father himself loveth you, because ye have loved me,* and have believed that I came out from God" (John 16:27).

The Apostle Paul, in his second epistle to the Thessalonians, made reference to • "God, even our Father, *which hath loved us*" (2 Thess. 2:16), and the Apostle John pondered: • "*What manner of love the Father hath bestowed upon us,* that we should be called the *sons of God*" (1 Jn. 3:1). What a blessing it is that the followers of Jesus can rest secure in the knowledge that they are recipients of the abiding love of both the Father and the Son!

Warnings concerning losing the Father's love. However, the scriptures also warn that the love of God can and will be lost if one turns away from righteous obedience to the Lord's commandments. The Apostle John cautioned the Saints to • "Love not the world, neither the things that are in the world. *If any man love the world, the love of the Father in not in him*" (1 Jn. 2:15). A modern revelation from the Savior also admonished the Church, saying: "*If you keep not my commandments, the love of the Father shall not continue with you,* therefore you shall walk in darkness" (D&C 95:12).

God the Father Observes Men's Actions and Knows Their Needs

The Savior's "Sermon on the Mount" indicates that God the Father is well aware of every individual's daily activities and ongoing needs for divine assistance, and that His response to those needs can sometimes be dependent upon the recipient's actions and attitudes.

Performing charitable acts. For instance, the Savior said concerning the performing of charitable actions: • "Take heed that ye *do not your alms before men, to be seen of them: otherwise ye have no reward of your Father* which is in heaven" (Matt. 6:1). He continued by stressing the need for unpretentiousness, saying that if one's alms are given in secret • "*thy Father which seeth in secret himself shall reward thee openly"* (Matt. 6:4). He also spoke of the need to refrain from offering ostentatious public prayers, suggesting, rather, that • "When thou hast *shut thy door,* pray to thy Father which is *in secret;* and *thy Father which seeth in secret shall reward thee openly"* (Matt. 6:6).

Forgiveness and fasting. His teachings concerning forgiveness were of the same flavor: • "*If ye forgive* men their trespasses, *your heavenly Father will also forgive you:* But *if ye forgive not* men their trespasses, *neither will your Father forgive your trespasses"* (Matt. 6:14–15). Concerning fasting, the Master said not to make a public display of fasting, • "that thou *appear not unto men to fast,* but *unto thy Father which is in secret:* and *thy Father, which seeth in secret, shall reward thee openly"* (Matt. 6:18).

Food and other essential needs. Concerning the daily food one needs, Jesus taught: • "Behold the fowls of the air: for they sow not, neither do they reap, nor gather into barns; yet *your heavenly Father feedeth them. Are ye not much better than they?"* (Matt. 6:32). In a later sermon He told His newly ordained Apostles: • "Are not two sparrows sold for a farthing? and *one of them shall not fall on the ground without your Father [knowing]* . . . Fear ye not therefore, ye are of more value than many sparrows." (Matt. 10:29, 31).

But the central theme of this portion of the Savior's Sermon on the Mount was this: • "*your heavenly Father knoweth that ye have need of all these things"* (Matt. 6:32; Luke 12:30). Latter-day scripture conveys the same message: • "*Your Father, who is in heaven, knoweth that you have need of all these things"* (D&C 84:83). And it's not just Heavenly Father: *all three of the Godhead are aware of every individual's personal needs.* They, most certainly, are better qualified than the individuals themselves to separate "needs" from "wants," and they are more capable of discerning *if, when, how,* and *by whom* those needs should be answered. They also are able to evaluate factors such as *faith, belief, attitudes, intentions, worthiness, appropriateness,* and *other pertinent aspects.*

Concerning Heavenly Father's willingness to respond to proper prayer requests, Jesus taught: • "If ye then, being evil, know how to give good gifts unto your children, *how much more shall your Father which is in heaven give good things to them that ask him?"* (Matt. 7:11).

Again, that man approach Heavenly Father in prayer and that he humbly make his requests, asking specifically for the things he truly *needs,* for other things he *wants,* and for the needs and wants of *others* around him, is an essential element in the formula for having prayer petitions answered by the Heavenly Father.

Man Is to Pray to God the Father in the Name of Jesus Christ

Though Jesus had previously taught his disciples the rudiments of prayer (Matt. 6:9–13), it appears that they were accustomed to making their petitions to Him rather than to pray to their Heavenly Father. Near the end of His mortal ministry, He began to shift the mechanics of their prayer life, instructing them that their requests should be directed to God the Father, but that they should always address the Father in His name. He told His Apostles: • "Ye have not chosen me, but I have chosen you, and ordained you, that ye should go and bring forth fruit, and that your fruit should remain: that *whatsoever ye shall ask of the Father in my name, he may give it you"* (John 15:16).

A change: pray to the Father. In His "last supper" sermon, He spoke plainly about his impending death and the changes it would bring in the Apostles' lives and ministries. Concerning the new manner of prayer they were to follow, He said: • "in that day *ye shall ask me nothing. Verily, verily, I say unto you, Whatsoever ye shall ask the Father in my name, he will give it you.* . . . At that day ye shall ask in my name: and I say *not* unto you, that I will pray the Father for you" (John 16:23, 26).

In contrast, the Nephites had been praying to their Father in Heaven since their exodus from Jerusalem in 600 BC (see 2 Ne. 32:9; 33:12; Jacob 7:22; 3 Ne. 13:6, 9; 17:15, 17–18, 21; 18:19, 21, 23–24, 30; 19:6–8).

In these last times, the scriptural admonitions Jesus has revealed have consistently been instructions to pray to God the Father in the name of Jesus Christ (see D&C 14:8; 18:18; 20:77, 79; 42:3; 50:31; 88:64).

Ask, seek, knock. Since the time of the Sermon on the Mount, the instruction has been to • "*Ask, and it shall be given you; seek, and ye shall find; knock, and it shall be opened unto you*" with the accompanying promise, either expressed or implied, that "*For every one that asketh receiveth; and he that seeketh findeth; and to him that knocketh it shall be opened*" (Matt. 7:7–8; 3 Ne. 14:8; 27:29; D&C 4:7; 6:5; 11:5; 12:5; 14:5).

Prayer instructions. It is obvious that the Savior, who has revealed in detail how prayers should be offered to God the Father in order to be properly answered, fully intends that mankind be able to reap the joy that comes from having prayers answered: • "*ye shall receive, that your joy may be full*" (John 16:24). This is apparent because short, one-verse instructions have been revealed on numerous occasions which give specific guidance for how one should pray to God the Father. Some of them are:

• "Not every one that saith unto me, Lord, Lord, shall enter into the kingdom of heaven; but *he that doeth the will of my Father which is in heaven*" (Matt. 7:21).

• "And all things, whatsoever ye shall ask in prayer, *believing*, ye shall receive" (Matt. 21:22).

• "Ye ask, and *receive not, because ye ask amiss, that ye may consume it upon your lusts*" (James 4:3).

• "if our heart condemn us not, then have we confidence toward God. And *whatsoever we ask, we receive of him, because we keep his commandments, and do those things that are pleasing in his sight*" (1 Jn. 3:21–22).

• "If ye will *not harden your hearts*, and *ask me in faith, believing that ye shall receive*, with *diligence in keeping my commandments*, surely these things shall be made known unto you" (1 Ne. 15:11).

• "Whatsoever thing ye shall ask in faith, *believing that ye shall receive in the name of Christ*, ye shall receive it" (Enos 1:15).

• "if you shall *ask the Father in my name, in faith believing*, you shall receive the Holy Ghost, which giveth utterance" (D&C 14:8).

• "whatsoever ye *ask that is right*, in *faith, believing that ye shall receive* . . ." (Mosiah 4:21).

• "Alma *labored much in the spirit, wrestling with God* in mighty prayer" (Alma 8:10).

• "asking for whatsoever things ye stand in need, both spiritual and temporal; *always returning thanks unto God for whatsoever things ye do receive*" (Alma 7:23).

• "ye must always pray unto the Father in my name; And whatsoever ye shall ask the Father in my name, *which is right, believing that ye shall receive,* behold it shall be given unto you" (3 Ne. 18:19–20).

• "Whatsoever thing ye shall ask the Father in my name, *which is good,* in faith believing that ye shall receive, behold, it shall be done unto you" (Moro. 7:26).

• "I would exhort you that ye would ask God, the Eternal Father, in the name of Christ, if these things are not true; and if ye shall *ask with a sincere heart, with real intent, having faith in Christ,* he will manifest the truth of it unto you, by the power of the Holy Ghost" (Moro. 10:4).

• "surely shall you receive a knowledge of whatsoever things you shall ask in faith, *with an honest heart,* believing that you shall receive" (D&C 8:1).

• "Whatsoever ye ask the Father in my name it shall be given unto you, *that is expedient for you"* (D&C 88:64).

The Father desires that man initiate communications with Him. It is intriguing to ponder on the fact that • *"your Father knoweth what things ye have need of before ye ask him"* (Matt. 6:8), yet He requires man, in most cases, to **ask** for what he needs or desires, and if he fails to ask, man often does not receive the desired blessing. It seems that an essential element of prayer is that it requires one to humble himself and to approach his Father in Heaven properly and diligently. The Father desires, and requires, communication from His children, just like parents who send their children off to college, or into the mission field. The recipient of the requested blessings needs to do his part to initiate the communication and prayer request!

God limits one's temptations to one's personal capacity for resistance. One other thought, a promised assurance of protection, is linked to the prayer process: • "There hath no temptation taken you but such as is common to man: but *God is faithful, who will not suffer you to be tempted above that ye are able; but will with the temptation also make a way to escape,* that ye may be able to bear it" (1 Cor. 10:13). Protection, most assuredly, is available, whether it come from the Father, the Son, the Holy Ghost, or guardian angels or spirits or humans whom they have commissioned to protect the Saints. God knows man's needs, and seeks to bless, protect and guide those who will be receptive to communications from the Divine.

It should be recognized, also, that everything that happens does not necessarily represent God's will. One cannot assume, without proper prayerful communication, that various events which transpire are God-inspired. The Apostle John warned, • "For all that is in the world, the lust of the flesh, and the lust of the eyes, and the pride of life, *is not of the Father,* but is of the world" (1 Jn. 2:16).

Both God the Father and God the Son Send the Holy Ghost to Man

The Great Schism and the Filioque clause.

In AD 1054 contention caused the Catholic church to divide into Eastern and Western segments. Known as the "Great Schism," this contention, based on both ecclesiastical and political differences, had been moving toward eruption for centuries. The Western church, based in Rome and led by popes, became known as the Roman Catholic church. The Eastern church, based in Constantinople and led by Patriarchs, became known as the Greek or Eastern Orthodox church. Each maintained that *it* was the original church of Christ and that the other branch had separated from it.

The "straw that broke the camel's back" and caused the East and West to finally divide was three words which came to be known as the "filioque clause." The three words are: "and the Son." (*Filioque* is Latin for "and the Son.") The Roman Catholic church believed, and believes, that the Holy Spirit proceeds from God the Father and from God the Son. The Eastern Orthodox Church held, and holds, that the Holy Spirit proceeds only from God the Father.

The **Nicene Creed**, as revised in the council at Constantinople in AD 381, added several phrases concerning the Holy Ghost to the AD 325 Nicene creed, which originally stated concerning the Holy Spirit only: "*We believe in . . . And in the Holy Ghost.*" The AD 381 council changed the Holy Spirit phrase to read: "*We believe in . . . And in the Holy Ghost, The Lord, and Giver of life; Who proceedeth from the Father; Who with the Father and the Son together is worshiped and glorified; Who spake by the Prophets.*" The added words "and the Son" were pegged onto the phrase "*Who proceedeth from the Father **and the Son**"* following decisions made in the third council of Toledo in Spain in AD 589. By the eighth century the "and the Son" addition had gained acceptance in England and France, and in the ninth century the concept of "double procession" had spread throughout the western church and had become an established part of Roman Catholic belief. When the eastern church repudiated the clause and refused to accept it, it caused the long-impending rupture between the two Catholic bodies and the official formation of separate churches.

Latter-day Saints find scriptural evidence that the Holy Ghost can be sent to an individual either by God the Father or God the Son, or that He can come unto individuals of His own volition. As to the origin of the Holy Ghost, Latter-day Saints have not received scriptural information on the matter so they have no doctrine concerning His origin, only personal theories.

The Holy Ghost can be sent by God the Father.

• "If ye then, being evil, know how to give good gifts unto your children: how much more shall your *heavenly Father give the Holy Spirit to them that ask him?*" (Luke 11:13). • "But the Comforter, which is the Holy Ghost, *whom the Father will send in my name,* he shall teach you all things, and bring all things to your remembrance, whatsoever I have said unto you" (John 14:26). • "Therefore being by the right hand of God exalted, and *having received of the Father the promise of the Holy Ghost,* he hath shed forth this, which ye now see and hear" (Acts 2:33). • "Father, I [Christ] thank thee that *thou hast given the Holy Ghost* unto these whom I have chosen" (3 Ne. 19:20). • "and by the power of the Holy Ghost *which shall be given unto you of the Father*" (3 Ne. 21:2). • "who overcome by faith, and *are sealed by the Holy Spirit of promise, which the Father sheds forth upon all those who are just and true*" (D&C 76:53).

The Holy Ghost can be sent by God the Son.

• "ye are willing to take upon you the name of Christ, by baptism—yea, by following your Lord and your Savior down into the water, *according to his word, behold, then shall ye receive the Holy Ghost*" (2 Ne. 31:13). • "Angels speak *by the power of the Holy Ghost; wherefore, they speak the words of Christ*" (2 Ne. 32:3). • "I [John the Baptist] indeed have baptized you with water: but *he* [Christ] *shall baptize you with the Holy Ghost*" (Mark 1:8; Luke 3:16). • "Upon whom thou shalt see the Spirit descending, and remaining on him, *the same is he* [Christ] *which baptizeth with the Holy Ghost*" (John 1:33). • "But when the Comforter is come, *whom I* [Christ] *will send unto you from the Father, . .*" (John 15:26). • "whoso cometh unto me [Christ] with a broken heart and a contrite spirit, *him will I baptize with fire and with the Holy Ghost"* (3 Ne. 9:20). • "after that ye are baptized with water, behold, *I* [Christ] *will baptize you with fire and with the Holy Ghost"* (3 Ne. 12:1). • *"I will tell you in your mind and in your heart, by the Holy Ghost,* which shall come upon you and which shall dwell in your heart" (D&C 8:2). • *"I* [Christ] *will bestow the gift of the Holy Ghost upon them"* (D&C 33:15).

The Holy Ghost can come upon people by His own volition.

• "While Peter yet spake these words, *the Holy Ghost fell on all them* which heard the word" (Acts 10:44). • "And as I [Peter] began to speak, *the Holy Ghost fell on them,* as on us at the beginning" (Acts 11:15). • "I [Nephi] also saw and bear record that *the Holy Ghost fell upon twelve others"* (1 Ne. 12:7). • "but the disciples heard it; and on *as many as they laid their hands, fell the Holy Ghost"* (Moro. 2:3). • "in that day *the Holy Ghost fell upon Adam,* which beareth record of the Father and the Son" (Moses 5:9). • "and *the Holy Ghost fell on many,* and they were caught up by the powers of heaven into Zion" (Moses 7:27).

God the Father Actively Participates in Missionary Work

Numerous scriptures indicate that the Father has strong interest in the efforts of missionaries and that He works behind the scenes to aid them. Bringing people to Christ also means bringing people to God the Father, and bringing people to right-eousness results in bringing people into His kingdom and preparing them for eternal service and growth there. Jesus said, on one occasion: • "the hour cometh, and now is, when the *true worshippers shall worship the Father in spirit* and in truth: for *the Father seeketh such to worship him"* (John 4:23). Listed here are some ways in which God the Father participates in missionary work:

The Father draws men to Christ and instructs them.

• "No man can come to me [Christ], *except the Father which hath sent me draw him:* and I will raise him up at the last day" (John 6:44). • "It is written in the proph-ets, And *they shall be all taught of God.* Every man therefore that hath heard, and *hath learned of the Father,* cometh unto me" (John 6:45). • "No man can come unto me, *except it were given unto him of my Father"* (John 6:65). • "Every one that hearkeneth to the voice of the Spirit *cometh unto God, even the Father. And the Father teacheth him of the covenant* which he has renewed and confirmed" (D&C 84:47–48).

God the Father sanctifies man.

Like His Son Jesus, and God the Holy Ghost, God the Father also participates in the sanctification process: • "Say ye of him, *whom the Father hath sanctified,* and sent into the world, Thou blasphemest; because I said, I am the Son of God?" (John 10:36). • "Jude, the servant of Jesus Christ, and brother of James, to them that *are sanctified by God the Father,* and preserved in Jesus Christ, . . ." (Jude 1:1).

God the Father bears witness unto mortals.

• "Blessed art thou, Simon Barjona: for *flesh and blood hath not revealed it unto thee, but my Father which is in heaven"* (Matt. 16:17). • *"The Father himself,* which hath sent me, *hath borne witness of me."* (John 5:37). • "For *he received from God the Father* honour and glory, when there came such a voice to him from the excellent glory, *This is my beloved Son, in whom I am well pleased"* (2 Pet. 1:17). • "there are three that *bear record in heaven,* the Father, the Word, and the Holy Ghost" (1 Jn. 5:7). • "we heard the

voice *bearing record* that he [Christ] *is the Only Begotten of the Father"* (D&C 76:23).
• "I saw two Personages, whose brightness and glory defy all description, standing above me in the air. One of them spake unto me, calling me by name and said, pointing to the other—*This is My Beloved Son. Hear Him!"* (JS—H 1:17).

God the Father and Jesus Christ have promised to manifest themselves to believers.

• "He that hath my commandments, and keepeth them, he it is that loveth me: and he that loveth me *shall be loved of my Father*, and I will love him, and *will manifest myself to him"* (John 14:21). • "Jesus answered and said unto him, If a man love me, he will keep my words: and my Father will love him, and *we will come unto him, and make our abode with him"* (John 14:23).

Those who deny Jesus Christ will not have association with God the Father.

• "*Whosoever denieth the Son, the same hath not the Father:* but he that acknowledgeth the Son hath the Father also" (1 Jn. 2:23). • "*Whosoever transgresseth, and abideth not in the doctrine of Christ, hath not God.* He that abideth in the doctrine of Christ, he hath both the Father and the Son" (2 Jn. 1:9). • "they who believe not on your words, and are not baptized . . . *shall be damned, and shall not come into my Father's kingdom* where my Father and I am" (D&C 84:74). • "Whoso rejecteth you *shall be rejected of my Father and his house"* (D&C 99:4).

The Father and the Son as Missionary Companions

Second Nephi records an intriguing scenario found nowhere else in the scriptures. The aging prophet Nephi, writing to his people (the Nephites), apparently shortly before his death, chose to write about the doctrine of baptism. With the spirit of prophecy, he looked forward almost six hundred years and envisioned the baptism of the mortal Jesus Christ. He contemplated the efforts of the future prophet, John the Baptist, and then he told how he (Nephi) *repeatedly heard the voices of two different members of the Godhead: the Father and the Son.* They together taught him about repentance, baptism, receiving the Holy Ghost, and enduring to the end. They functioned just like modern missionaries, alternating in their teaching, with the Father bearing his testimony as to the truthfulness of his son's words, and with Nephi serving as the narrator. His account reads so much like today's missionaries teaching that it has been portrayed here as a script, all based on 2 Nephi chapter 31:

Nephi:

"Remember that I have spoken unto you concerning that prophet which the Lord showed unto me, that should baptize the Lamb of God, which should take away the sins of the world. [*John the Baptist:* see 1 Ne. 10:7–10; 11:27]

"And now, if the Lamb of God, he being holy, should have need to be baptized by water, to fulfil all righteousness, O then, how much more need have we, being unholy, to be baptized, yea, even by water!

"And now, I would ask of you, my beloved brethren, wherein the Lamb of God did fulfil all righteousness in being baptized by water?

"Know ye not that he was holy? But notwithstanding he being holy, he showeth unto the children of men that, according to the flesh he humbleth himself before the Father, and witnesseth unto the Father that he would be obedient unto him in keeping his commandments.

"Wherefore, after he was baptized with water the Holy Ghost descended upon him in the form of a dove.

"And again, it showeth unto the children of men the straitness of the path, and the narrowness of the gate, by which they should enter, he having set the example before them.

"And he said unto the children of men:" (v. 4–10).

Jesus:
"Follow thou me" (v. 10).

Nephi:
"Wherefore, my beloved brethren, can we follow Jesus save we shall be willing to keep the commandments of the Father? And the Father said:" (v. 10–11).

The Father:
"Repent ye, repent ye, and be baptized in the name of my Beloved Son." (v. 11).

Nephi:
"And also, the voice of the Son came unto me, saying: . . ." (v. 12).

Jesus:
"He that is baptized in my name, to him will the Father give the Holy Ghost, like unto me; wherefore, follow me, and do the things which ye have seen me do" (v. 12).

Nephi:
"My beloved brethren, I know that if ye shall follow the Son, with full purpose of heart, acting no hypocrisy and no deception before God, but with real intent, repenting of your sins, witnessing unto the Father that ye are willing to take upon you the name of Christ, by baptism—yea, by following your Lord and your Savior down into the water, according to his word, behold, then shall ye receive the Holy Ghost; yea, then cometh the baptism of fire and of the Holy Ghost; and then can ye speak with the tongue of angels, and shout praises unto the Holy One of Israel.

"But, behold, my beloved brethren, thus came the voice of the Son unto me, saying:" (v. 13–14).

Jesus:
"After ye have repented of your sins, and witnessed unto the Father that ye are willing to keep my commandments, by the baptism of water, and have received the baptism of fire and of the Holy Ghost, and can speak with a new tongue, yea, even with the tongue of angels, and after this should deny me, it would have been better for you that ye had not known me" (v. 14).

Nephi:
"And I heard a voice from the Father, saying:" (v. 15).

The Father:
"Yea, the words of my Beloved are true and faithful. He that endureth to the end, the same shall be saved" (v. 15).

Nephi:
"And now, my beloved brethren, I know by this that unless a man shall endure to the end, in following the example of the Son of the living God, he cannot be saved.

"Wherefore, do the things which I have told you I have seen that your Lord and your Redeemer should do; for, for this cause have they been shown unto me, that ye might know the gate by which ye should enter. For the gate by which ye should enter is repentance and baptism by water; and then cometh a remission of your sins by fire and by the Holy Ghost.

"And then are ye in this strait and narrow path which leads to eternal life; yea, ye have entered in by the gate; ye have done according to the commandments of the Father and the Son; and ye have received the Holy Ghost, which witnesses of the Father and the Son, unto the fulfilling of the promise which he hath made, that if ye entered in by the way ye should receive.

"And now, my beloved brethren, after ye have gotten into this strait and narrow path, I would ask if all is done? Behold, I say unto you, Nay; for ye have not come thus far save it were by the word of Christ with unshaken faith in him, relying wholly upon the merits of him who is mighty to save.

"Wherefore, ye must press forward with a steadfastness in Christ, having a perfect brightness of hope, and a love of God and of all men. Wherefore, if ye shall press forward, feasting upon the word of Christ, and endure to the end, behold, thus saith the Father: . . ." (v. 16–20)

The Father:
"Ye shall have eternal life" (v. 20).

Nephi:
"And now, behold, my beloved brethren, this is the way; and there is none other way nor name given under heaven whereby man can be saved in the kingdom of God. And now, behold, this is the doctrine of Christ, and the only and true doctrine of the Father, and of the Son, and of the Holy Ghost, which is one God, without end. Amen" (v. 21).

God the Father Controls Last-days Events

It appears that God the Father will exercise unique powers and will control the timing of such last-days events as the exact time of Christ's return to earth in His glorious Second Coming. Indeed, as Jesus spoke of His coming in glory, He stated that when He will come, He will descend from heaven not to do His own will, but to carry out the will of God the Father:

> All that the Father giveth me shall come to me; and him that cometh to me I will in no wise cast out.
>
> For *I came down from heaven, not to do mine own will, but the will of him that sent me.*
>
> And *this is the Father's will which hath sent me, that of all which he hath given me I should lose nothing, but should raise it up again at the last day.*
>
> And this is the will of him that sent me, that every one which seeth the Son, and believeth on him, may have everlasting life: and *I will raise him up at the last day.* (John 6:37–40)

Only God the Father knows the timing of Christ's Second Coming.

• "But of that day and hour knoweth no man, no, not the angels of heaven, *but my Father only*" (Matt. 24:36).

• "Of that day, and hour, no one knoweth; no, not the angels of God in heaven, *but my Father only*" (JS—M 1:40).

So far as been presently revealed to Church members at large, knowledge and decision-making of the exact time of the Lord's Second Advent has been reserved to God the Father only. That doesn't necessarily mean that as the event approaches, others won't be given that knowledge. Some, perhaps on both sides of the veil, may receive advance notice. After all, it will be a major worldwide project that will require considerable advance planning and coordination. But, by its very nature, the Lord's coming is intended to be a surprise event to all mankind:

> But *as the days of Noe were, so shall also the coming of the Son of man be.*
> For as in the days that were before the flood they were eating and drinking, marrying and giving in marriage, until the day that Noe entered into the ark,
> And knew not until the flood came, and took them all away; *so shall also the coming of the Son of man be.*
> Then shall two be in the field; the one shall be taken, and the other left.
> Two women shall be grinding at the mill; the one shall be taken, and the other left.
> *Watch therefore: for ye know not what hour your Lord doth come.*
> But know this, that if the goodman of the house had known in what watch the thief would come, he would have watched, and would not have suffered his house to be broken up.
> *Therefore be ye also ready: for in such an hour as ye think not the Son of man cometh.* (Matt. 24:37–44)

God the Father also has decreed the participation of Christ's Apostles in His Second Advent.

• "It hath gone forth *in a firm decree, by the will of the Father,* that mine apostles . . . *shall stand at my right hand* at the day of my coming in a pillar of fire" (D&C 29:12).

[In like manner, God the Father retains ultimate decision-making power over after-death relationships in His eternal realms: • "to sit on my right hand, and on my left, *is not mine* [Christ's] *to give,* but it shall be given to them *for whom it is prepared of my Father*" (Matt. 20:23).]

God the Father controls the times and seasons as that Second Advent draws near.

• "they asked of him, saying, Lord, wilt thou at this time restore again the kingdom to Israel? And he said unto them, It is not for you to know *the times or the seasons, which the Father hath put in his own power*" (Acts 1:6–7).

• "*God hath set his hand and seal to change the times and seasons,* and to blind their minds, *that they may not understand his marvelous workings; that he may prove them also and take them in their own craftiness*" (D&C 121:12; see also Matt. 5:45).

• "Every plant, *which my heavenly Father hath not planted,* shall be rooted up" (Matt. 15:13).

God the Father Will Preside and Judge at the Final Judgment Day

A preliminary announcement of the day of judgment.

In connection with the Second Coming of Christ, a series of seven angels will sound their trumpets, announcing end-of-the-earth events which will take place. The fifth angel will announce the final day of judgment, doing so in these words:

• "another trump shall sound, which is the *fifth trump,* which is the fifth angel who committeth the everlasting gospel—flying through the midst of heaven, unto all nations, kindreds, tongues, and people; And this shall be the sound of his trump, saying to all people, both in heaven and in earth, and that are under the earth—for *every ear shall hear it, and every knee shall bow, and every tongue shall confess, while they hear the sound of the trump, saying: Fear God, and give glory to him who sitteth upon the throne, forever and ever; for the hour of his judgment is come"* (D&C 88:103–104).

God the Father's "judgment personality" described.

• "Be ye therefore merciful, as *your Father also is merciful"* (Luke 6:36).

• "And if ye call on *the Father, who without respect of persons judgeth* according to every man's work, . . ." (1 Pet. 1:17).

Man's past actions will stand as a judgment norm.

• "and when ye stand praying, forgive, if ye have ought against any: *that your Father also which is in heaven may forgive you your trespasses.* But if ye do not forgive, *neither will your Father which is in heaven forgive your trespasses"* (Mark 11:25–26).

God the Father has given judgment responsibilities to Jesus Christ.

• "For *the Father judgeth no man, but hath committed all judgment unto the Son: that all men should honour the Son, even as they honour the Father.* He that honoureth not the Son honoureth not the Father which hath sent him" (John 5:22–23).

• "And *hath given him authority to execute judgment* also, because he is the Son of man" (John 5:27).

• "as I hear, I judge: and *my judgment is just; because I seek not mine own will, but the will of the Father* which hath sent me" (John 5:30).

Man to confess to the Father and to Jesus, and bow the knee to Christ.

• *"we shall all stand before the judgment seat of Christ.* For it is written, *As* I live, saith the Lord, *every knee shall bow to me,* and *every tongue shall confess to God.* So then *every one of us shall give account of himself to God"* (Rom. 14:10–12).

• "That at the name of Jesus *every knee should bow,* of things in heaven, and things in earth, and things under the earth; And that every tongue should confess that Jesus Christ is Lord, *to the glory of God the Father"* (Phil. 2:10–11).

• "The time shall come when all shall see the salvation of the Lord; when every nation, kindred, tongue, and people shall see eye to eye and *shall confess before God that his judgments are just. And then shall the wicked be cast out,* and they shall have cause to howl, and weep, and wail, and gnash their teeth; and this because they would not hearken unto the voice of the Lord; therefore the Lord redeemeth them not" (Mosiah 16:1–2).

• "I rejected my Redeemer, and denied that which had been spoken of by our fathers; but now that they may foresee that he will come, and that *he remembereth every creature of his creating,* he will make himself manifest unto all. *Yea, every knee shall bow, and every tongue confess before him. Yea, even at the last day, when all men shall stand to be judged of him, then shall they confess that he is God;* then shall they confess, who live without God in the world, that *the judgment of an everlasting punishment is just upon them;* and they shall quake, and tremble, and shrink beneath the glance of his all-searching eye" (Mosiah 27:30–31).

• "we saw the glory and the inhabitants of the telestial world, that they were as innumerable as the stars in the firmament of heaven, or as the sand upon the seashore; And heard the voice of the Lord saying: *These all shall bow the knee, and every tongue shall confess to him who sits upon the throne forever and ever; For they shall be judged according to their works"* (D&C 76:109–111).

God the Father passes final judgment upon all men after receiving the recommendations of Christ the mediator.

• "For there is *one God*, and *one mediator* between God and men, *the man Christ Jesus;* Who gave himself a ransom for all, to be testified in due time" (1 Tim. 2:5–6). • "if any man sin, *we have an advocate with the Father, Jesus Christ the righteous:* And he is the propitiation for our sins: and not for ours only, but also for the sins of the whole world" (1 Jn. 2:1–2). • "the Lord your God, even Jesus Christ, *your advocate, who knoweth the weakness of man and how to succor them"* (D&C 62:1). • *"Father, spare these my brethren that believe on my name,* that they may come unto me and have everlasting life" (D&C 45:5). • *"Fear not, little flock; for it is your Father's good pleasure to give you the kingdom. . . .* a treasure in the heavens that faileth not, where no thief approacheth, neither moth corrupteth. For where your treasure is, there will your heart be also" (Luke 12:32–34).

God the Father Grants Eternal Rewards

It appears that one of the many assignments that has fallen to God the Father, in connection with this earth and its inhabitants, is the providing of eternal rewards for those who are righteous followers of Christ and who have partaken of the Savior's redeeming grace. A passage in the Doctrine and Covenants promises that • *"If ye seek the riches which it is the will of the Father to give unto you, ye shall be the richest of all people, for ye shall have the riches of eternity"* (D&C 38:39). Another passage pricks the imagination with the message that • "ye have not as yet understood *how great blessings the Father hath in his own hands and prepared for you"* (D&C 78:17).

The scriptural verses cited below are but a representative sampling of the many passages which define with much specificity the many blessings which are promised to those who merit admittance to God the Father's heavenly kingdom. Those cited here are segregated into six categories: (1) *the fulness,* meaning all the powers and abilities of Godhood which will be granted to those who are • *"heirs; heirs of God, and joint-heirs with Christ"* (Rom. 8:17). • "They are *they into whose hands the Father has given all things*—They are they who are priests and kings, who have received of his fulness, and of his glory" (D&C 76:55–56); (2) *a crown,* or *a throne,* which symbolizes the kingship of those who have attained the highest degree of the celestial kingdom; (3) *kingdom admittance,* meaning that they are admitted into Heavenly Father's kingdom, though this phrase gives no indication of which of the levels of the celestial kingdom they are inheriting (see D&C 131:1); (4) *heavenly mansions,* though this phrase also gives no indication of which of the levels of the celestial kingdom they are inheriting; (5) *celestial companionship,* meaning fellowship with others who have partaken of Christ's salvation and have been found worthy to enter into the Father's celestial realms; (6) A *miscellaneous* category is also included.

These passages are representative scriptural citations:

The fulness—all that the Father hath:

• "Blessed be *the God and Father of our Lord Jesus Christ,* who hath blessed us with *all spiritual blessings in heavenly places* in Christ" (Eph. 1:3). • *"They are they into whose hands the Father has given all things"* (D&C 76:55). • [the terrestrial] "whose glory differs from that of *the church of the Firstborn who have received the fulness of the Father"* (D&C 76:71). • *"He that receiveth my Father receiveth my Father's kingdom; therefore all that my Father hath shall be given unto him"* (D&C 84:38). • "If you keep my commandments *you shall receive of his fulness,* and *be glorified in me* as I am in the Father; therefore, I say unto you, *you shall receive grace for grace"* (D&C 93:20).

A crown, a throne:

• "To him that overcometh *will I grant to sit with me in my throne, even as I also overcame,* and am set down with my Father in his throne" (Rev. 3:21). • *"They shall receive a crown in the mansions of my Father,* which I have prepared for them" (D&C 59:2). • *"you shall have a crown of eternal life* at the right hand of my Father" (D&C 66:12). • *"Thou shalt have a crown of immortality,* and eternal life *in the mansions which I have prepared* in the house of my Father" ((D&C 81:6). • *"I have prepared a crown for him* in the *mansions of my Father"* (D&C 106:8). • "I seal upon you *your exaltation,* and *prepare a throne for you in the kingdom of my Father,* with Abraham your father" (D&C 132:49).

Kingdom admittance:

• "Then shall the righteous *shine* forth as the sun *in the kingdom of their Father"* (Matt. 13:43). • "Come, ye blessed of my Father, *inherit the kingdom prepared for you* from the foundation of the world" (Matt. 25:34). • Lead men unto repentance, *"that they may come unto the kingdom of my Father"* (D&C 18:44). • "If you keep not my commandments *you cannot be saved in the kingdom of my Father"* (D&C 18:46). • Jesus said, "I am in your midst, and am your advocate with *the Father*; and *it is his good will to give you the kingdom"* (D&C 29:5). • *"The kingdom is given you of the Father,* and power to overcome all things which are not ordained of him" (D&C 50:35).

Mansions:

• "He who is faithful and wise in time is accounted worthy *to inherit the mansions prepared for him of my Father"* (D&C 72:4). • *"In my Father's house are many mansions,* and I have prepared a place for you; and *where my Father and I am, there ye shall be also"* (D&C 98:18; see also John 14:2). • "When I shall come in *the kingdom of my Father* to *reward every man according as his work shall be"* (D&C 101:65).

Celestial companionship:

• "Declare repentance unto this people, that you may bring souls unto me, *that you may rest with them in the kingdom of my Father"* (D&C 15:6). • "If you should . . . bring, save it be one soul unto me, *how great shall be your joy with him in the kingdom of my Father!"* (D&C 18:15–16).

Other blessings:

• "everyone that hath forsaken . . . shall *inherit everlasting life"* (Matt. 19:29). • "If any man serve me, *him will my Father honour"* (John 12:26). • "We . . . bear witness, . . . that *eternal life, which was with the Father,* . . . was manifested unto us" (1 Jn. 1:2). • "After it [this earth] hath filled the measure of its creation, *it shall be crowned with glory, even with the presence of God the Father"* (D&C 88:19). • "that ye also may have fellowship with us: and *truly our fellowship is with the Father, and with his Son Jesus Christ"* (1 Jn. 1:3). • "[Jesus Christ] Hath made us *kings and priests unto God and his Father"* (Rev. 1:6). • "The kingdom is given you of the Father, and *power to overcome all things which are not ordained of him"* (D&C 50:35). • *"Of as many as the Father shall bear record,* to you shall be given power to *seal them up unto eternal life"* (D&C 68:12). • "If you keep my commandments *you shall receive of his fulness,* and be glorified in me as I am in the Father; therefore, I say unto you, *you shall receive grace for grace"* (D&C 93:20).

"Exaltation," which is chapter 16 in **Life Everlasting**, provides a far more in-depth explanation of God's eternal rewards. The following extract from that chapter's summary may prove beneficial: "Exaltation consists of (A) Godhood; (B) Eternal association with the Father and Christ; (C) Membership in the Church of the Firstborn;

(D) Joint inheritance with Christ; (E) The fulness and glory of a celestial body; (F) Priesthood authority; (G) Eternal companionship of a beloved spouse; (H) Eternal powers of procreation; (I) Family relationship with progenitors and descendants; (J) Thrones, kingdoms, principalities, powers, and dominions; (K) Admittance to the city of the Living God; (L) Inheritance on the celestialized earth; (M) Association with celestial beings; (N) Perfect knowledge; (O) Governing and lawgiving jurisdiction; and (P) the powers of Godhood" (*Life Everlasting*, 481–82).

Summary

1. God the Father is *the* God of Jesus Christ. Since Jehovah/Jesus Christ is the appointed God of this earth, God the Father and God the Holy Ghost apparently stand in the role of counselors to Him as far as this earth is concerned, so God the Father is *a* God but not *the* God of this earth.

2. God the Father is to be recognized as a God by mankind and is to be treated with worshipful and reverential awe.

3. Jesus spoke with modest deference concerning His Father, God the Father, stating that "there is none good but one, that is, God," that "my Father is greater than I," and that "I am the true vine, and my Father is the husbandman."

4. As members of the Godhead, God the Father, God the Son, and God the Holy Ghost are equal in their perfection and their powers, yet God the Father has advanced further in His creations, in His posterity, and in His accumulated glory.

5. Each member of the Godhead has His own assignments as pertaining to the administration of this earth. This chapter serves to identify some of God the Father's assignments here.

6. God the Father made premortal covenants prior to the creation of this earth. He established the Law of the Holy Priesthood pertaining to the "eternity of the marriage covenant," developed the oath and covenant of the Melchizedek Priesthood, covenanted with Abraham and with women concerning their potentials for exaltation, and set various policies concerning the privileges of righteous individuals to receive the priesthood and to be endowed.

7. God the Father, and perhaps others, conferred "the fulness" of their powers and abilities upon Jesus prior to the creation of this earth. God the Father gave Him "all things that the Father hath."

8. God the Father entrusted His spirit children to the care of Jehovah/Jesus Christ during their mortal probation, with the instruction that none of them were to be lost.

9. God the Father sent Jesus Christ to this earth to minister and to perform His atoning sacrifice. The Father implements His will through Jesus on this earth. He gives commandments to His children here on earth through Christ. His influence is exerted upon the Church in its various activities.

10. Man is commanded to worship God the Father in the name of Jesus Christ, to give glory to God the Father, and to pray to God the Father in the name of Jesus Christ.

11. God the Father has and shows infinite love for all His children here on the earth. He is aware of their actions and needs, and is ready and willing to respond to their prayers addressed to Him. He wants His children to initiate contact with Him through prayer. They lose and forfeit blessings available to them if they don't pray

to the Father. Instructions on how to pray have been provided.

12. Both God the Father and God the Son send God the Holy Ghost to various individuals. However, since it is His responsibility to all mankind, the Holy Ghost often manifests his power to individuals of His own volition.

13. God the Father participates actively in missionary work, for He seeks true worshipers whom He can teach, sanctify and bless. The Father draws men to Christ, bears witness of Christ and His gospel, and has promised to visit with worthy believers as He sees fit.

14. God the Father controls some important last-day events. He controls and is changing the times and seasons, and only He knows when Christ is to come in His Second Advent. As the Second Coming draws nigh, others on both sides of the veil may receive revelation and assignments concerning its implementation, but the Second Coming is to come as a surprise to mankind as a whole.

15. God the Father will preside and be the final judge at Judgment Day, while Jesus will act as the Mediator and Advocate for His righteous followers. During the judgment, every knee will bow to Christ, and every tongue will confess to Christ and the Father, acknowledging their Godhood and also certifying that the judgments they receive are fair and appropriate for them.

16. God the Father grants eternal rewards to those who will be "heirs of God, and joint-heirs with Christ." A scriptural list of various rewards is provided.

PART SIX

THE ULTIMATE OBJECTIVES
OF DIVINITY

CHAPTER 15

MY WORK AND MY GLORY

A well-known verse in the Pearl of Great Price truly resonates with many Latter-day Saints. Why? Because it defines what God's ultimate work and objective is in His eternal plan. It also defines the glorious reward He seeks for Himself, for the other members of the Godhead, and for all those who inherit the highest degree of the celestial kingdom.

But it is a verse that needs to be understood in context. Just prior to making this memorable statement, the Lord God showed the Prophet Moses the worlds without number which had been created, and the Lord God told Moses:

> *The heavens, they are many,* and they cannot be numbered unto man; but they are numbered unto me, for *they are mine.*
>
> And as one earth shall pass away, and the heavens thereof even so shall another come, and *there is no end to my works, neither to my words.* (Moses 1:37–38)

And then, as God explained the process of eternal creations of new worlds, He made the profound explanation that summarizes His purposes in the eternal plan:
• *"This is my work and my glory—to bring to pass the immortality and eternal life of man"* (Moses 1:39).

His *work* is to create new earths, cause spirit beings to take on mortality as they inhabit them, guide them through the mortal testing process, and then summon them to move forward to more advanced training in the spirit world. There they are prepared to be resurrected so their spirits and bodies are reunited in a glorious eternal unison—they become "immortal beings" who have overcome the challenges of "physical death."

An essential element of this work is to provide examples, teachers, and opportunities for all His spirit children to hear and accept the gospel and the redemptive sacrifice of their Savior. To accomplish this goal they are to be cleansed, trained, refined, and motivated to reap the rich rewards of eternal righteousness known as "eternal life." A major task in this probationary process is that they must overcome the debilitating challenges of being separated from God known in gospel terms as "spiritual death."

All this vast program constitutes His "work." That's what He does.

But this chapter is not about His *"work."* Rather, it is about His *"glory."*

Definitions of Glory

The term "glory" involves many distinct definitions. These definitions shed light not only on what God does, but also on what all mankind is supposed to do as their part in the eternal plan of happiness. Fourteen different aspects of "glory" are defined and briefly described in this section. Numerous brief examples will be cited.

1. Glory as Reputation and Status. When used in this manner in the scriptures, the term refers to social status and frequently is used in a negative sense. For instance, the book of Esther tells of the bragging of the wicked Haman, who • "told them of *the glory of his riches,* and the multitude of his children, and all the things wherein the king had promoted him" (Esth. 5:11). In another example, as Job complained of losing the esteem of his neighbors, he said that • *"He hath stripped me of my glory,* and taken the crown from my head" (Job 19:9). Isaiah prophesied that the LORD would • "punish the . . . king of Assyria, and *the glory of his high looks"* (Isa. 10:12). Concerning Babylonia, Isaiah prophesied that • *"the glory of kingdoms,* the beauty of the Chaldees' excellency, shall be as when God overthrew Sodom and Gomorrah" (Isa. 13:19).

2. Glory as Praise and Adulation of God. The Psalmist wrote, concerning God: • *"Whoso offereth praise glorifieth me*: and to him that ordereth his conversation aright will I shew the salvation of God" (Ps. 50:23). The same psalm contains the LORD's instruction to • "Offer unto God thanksgiving; and pay thy vows unto the most High: And call upon me in the day of trouble: I will deliver thee, and *thou shalt glorify me"* (Ps. 50:14–15). Another psalm says, • *"I will praise thee, O Lord my God, with all my heart: and I will glorify thy name for evermore"* (Ps. 86:12). Isaiah wrote, • "O LORD, thou hast increased the nation: *thou art glorified"* (Isa. 26:15). When a crowd watched Jesus heal a man suffering with palsy, • *"they marvelled, and glorified God,* which had given such power unto men" (Matt. 9:8). When the Lord healed many individuals near the Sea of Galilee, • "the multitude wondered, when they saw the dumb to speak, the maimed to be whole, the lame to walk, and the blind to see: and *they glorified the God of Israel"* (Matt. 15:31).

3. Glory as Light, Truth and Knowledge. The scriptures frequently link the term "glory" with other words which, apparently, function as synonyms for it. For instance, they tell us that • *"The glory of God is intelligence, or, in other words, light and truth"* (D&C 93:36). The acquiring of light and truth, in turn, links with other principles such as obedience to God's laws and commandments. It is through this obedience that mortals partake of the cleansing powers of Christ's atoning sacrifice, which in turn allows them to attain light, together with the fulness of joy and eternal fellowship with God characteristic of exaltation in the celestial kingdom of God the Father. Thus the Apostle John wrote that • *"God is light,* and *in him is no darkness at all. . . . if we walk in the light, as he is in the light,* we have fellowship one with another, and the blood of Jesus Christ his Son cleanseth us from all sin" (1 Jn. 1:5–7 {1–10}).

A definitive revelation given by Jesus Christ in the Doctrine and Covenants speaks of those who become sons and daughters of Christ by accepting and obeying his gospel, thereby receiving glory, truth and light and knowledge of all things: • *"He that keepeth his commandments receiveth truth and light, until he is glorified in truth and knoweth all things"* (D&C 93:28–29 {21–32}).

4. Glory as the Light of Christ Given to All Mankind. While speaking of the light that emanates from God, a Doctrine and Covenants revelation indicates: • "Which *glory* is that of the church of the Firstborn, even of God, the holiest of all, through Jesus Christ his Son—He that ascended up on high, as also he descended below all things, in that *he comprehended all things, that he might be in all and through all things, the light of truth; Which truth shineth. This is the light of Christ*" (D&C 88:5–7). A revelation given less than five months later contains the Lord's explanation that • "every soul who forsaketh his sins and cometh unto me, and calleth on my name, and obeyeth my voice, and keepeth my commandments, shall see my face and know that I am; And that *I am the true light that lighteth every man that cometh into the world . . . The light* and the Redeemer of the world; the Spirit of truth, who came into the world, because the world was made by him, and in him was the life of men and *the light of men*" (D&C 93:1–2, 9).

5. Glory as the Light of the Sun, Moon, Stars, and the Immensity of Space. Doctrine and Covenants section 88 continues with this amazing revelation: • "*This is the light of Christ. As also he is in the sun, and the light of the sun,* and the power thereof by which it was made. As also *he is in the moon, and is the light of the moon,* and the power thereof by which it was made; As also *the light of the stars,* and the power thereof by which they were made; And the earth also, and the power thereof, even the earth upon which you stand. *And the light which shineth, which giveth you light, is through him who enlighteneth your eyes, which is the same light that quickeneth your understandings; Which light proceedeth forth from the presence of God to fill the immensity of space*" (D&C 88:7–12).

6. Glory as the Creative Power of God. The same power described above as "the light of the sun" is also • "*the power thereof by which it was made*" (D&C 88:7). It is also the power by which the moon was made (D&C 88:8), the power by which the stars were made (D&C 88:9), and the power by which this earth was created (D&C 88:10). Paul hinted of various aspects of this power when he wrote to the Colossians that he desired that they be • "increasing in the knowledge of God; . . . Giving thanks unto the Father, . . . Who hath delivered us from the power of darkness, and hath translated us into the kingdom of his dear Son . . . For by him were all things created, that are in heaven, and that are in earth, visible and invisible, whether they be thrones, or dominions, or principalities, *or powers: all things were created by him, and for him*: And he is before all things, and by him all things consist. (Col. 1:10, 12–13, 16–17).

Jacob, in the Book of Mormon, wrote that • "great and marvelous are the works of the Lord. . . . For behold, by the *power* of his word man came upon the face of the earth, which *earth was created by the power of his word*" (Jacob 4:8–9). And King Benjamin taught his followers to • "Believe in God; believe that he is, and that *he created all things, both in heaven and in earth*; believe that he has *all wisdom,* and *all power,* both in heaven and in earth; believe that man doth not comprehend all the things which the Lord can comprehend" (Mosiah 4:9).

7. Glory as the Source of Life for All Things. Doctrine and Covenants 88 also specifies that this glory is the light which • "*proceedeth forth from the presence of God* to fill the immensity of space—*The light which is in all things, which giveth life to all things*" (D&C 88:12–13). The resurrected Christ, when He appeared to the Nephites, taught them: • "Behold, I am Jesus Christ, . . . *I am the light and the life of the world*; and . . . have *glorified the Father*" (3 Ne. 11:10–11). While speaking in the Doctrine and Covenants, the Lord said: • *"Behold, I am the light and the life of the world,* that speak these words" (D&C 12:9).

8. *Glory as the Law by which All Things Are Governed.* That same revelation indicates that this glory • *"is the law by which all things are governed"* (D&C 88:13). While answering a question among the Nephites, Christ spoke of the law, saying: • *"Behold, I say unto you that the law is fulfilled that was given unto Moses. Behold, I am he that gave the law, and I am he who covenanted with my people Israel; therefore, the law in me is fulfilled, for I have come to fulfil the law; therefore it hath an end. . . . Behold, I am the law, and the light"* (3 Ne. 15:4–5, 9).

9. *Glory as the Power of God.* Thus, as the above passages indicate, the light by which the heavenly spheres were made, the light which fills the immensity of space, the light which gives life to all things, the light that is the law by which all things are governed—all these manifestations of light and glory combine as representations of • *"the power of God* who sitteth upon his throne" (D&C 88:13). The book of Revelation speaks of heaven where the exalted Saints will worship the Lord, and the power and light which is His: • "they sing . . . the song of the Lamb, saying, Great and marvellous are thy works, Lord God Almighty; just and true are thy ways, thou King of saints. Who shall not fear thee, O Lord, and *glorify thy name?* for thou only art holy . . . And *the temple was filled with smoke from the glory of God, and from his power"* (Rev. 15:3–4, 8). Later, in Revelation, John testifies that • "I heard a great voice of much people in heaven, saying, Alleluia; Salvation, and *glory,* and *honour,* and *power, unto the Lord our God"* (Rev. 19:1). Alma, in the Book of Mormon, prophesies that • *"the Son of God cometh in his glory, in his might, majesty, power, and dominion.* Yea, my beloved brethren, I say unto you, that *the Spirit saith: Behold the glory of the King of all the earth"* (Alma 5:50).

10. *Glory as a Definer of Heavenly Bodies and Kingdoms.* In the beloved revelation which became known as "The Vision" among the early members of the Church, the explanation is made that there are different levels of glory, and that those levels categorize the resurrected bodies of the inhabitants of the celestial, terrestrial and telestial kingdoms, and also the physical nature of those heavenly orbs:

> These are *they whose bodies are celestial, whose glory is that of the sun, even the glory of God, the highest of all,* whose glory *the sun of the firmament* is written of as being typical.
>
> And again, we saw the terrestrial world, and behold and lo, these are *they who are of the terrestrial, whose glory differs* from that of the church of the Firstborn who have received the fulness of the Father, even as that of the moon differs from the sun in the firmament. . . .
>
> These are they who receive of his glory, but not of his fulness.
>
> These are they who receive of the presence of the Son, but not of the fulness of the Father.
>
> Wherefore, *they are bodies terrestrial, and not bodies celestial,* and differ in glory as the moon differs from the sun. . . .
>
> And again, we saw *the glory of the telestial, which glory is that of the lesser,* even as the glory of the stars differs from that of the glory of the moon in the firmament. (D&C 76:70–71, 76–78, 81)

Paul, in his first epistle to the Corinthians, spoke of the resurrection, and of heavenly glories. He wrote: • "There are also celestial bodies, and bodies terrestrial: but the *glory of the celestial* is one, and the *glory of the terrestrial* is another. *There is one glory of the sun, and another glory of the moon, and another glory of the stars*: for one star differeth from another star in glory. So also is the resurrection of the dead. . . . *it is raised in glory*: it is sown in weakness; *it is raised in power*: It is sown a natural body; *it is raised a spiritual body*" (1 Cor. 15:40–44).

11. **_Glory as a Sanctifying Power._** The LORD, when teaching His Prophet Moses about the tabernacle the Israelites were to erect in the wilderness, revealed to him that • "there I will meet with the children of Israel, and *the tabernacle shall be sanctified by my glory. And I will sanctify the tabernacle of the congregation, and the altar*: I will sanctify also both Aaron and his sons, to minister to me in the priest's office. And I will dwell among the children of Israel, and will be their God" (Ex. 29:43–45). In the dedicatory prayer for the Kirtland temple, the Prophet Joseph beseeched God • "*That thy glory may rest down upon thy people, and upon this thy house*, which we now dedicate to thee, *that it may be sanctified* and consecrated to be holy" (D&C 109:12).

Even the earth must be sanctified: • "Therefore, it [the earth] must needs be *sanctified* from all unrighteousness, that it may be prepared for *the celestial glory*" (D&C 88:18).

12. **_Glory as a Power which Enables Mortals to Endure God's Presence._** Concerning Moses, in the Pearl of Great Price: • "he saw God face to face, and he talked with him, and *the glory of God was upon Moses; therefore Moses could endure his presence*" (Moses 1:2). Moses later testified, • "mine own eyes have beheld God; but not my natural, but my spiritual eyes, for my natural eyes could not have beheld; for I should have withered and died in his presence; but *his glory was upon me; and I beheld his face, for I was transfigured before him*" (Moses 1:11. See also Moses 1:5, 9, 14, 31; Ex. 33:18–23; Num. 14:21–22; Deut. 5:22–27).

13. **_Glory as a Cleansing Fire._** The Old Testament reports that in the days of Moses, • "the glory of the LORD abode upon mount Sinai, . . . *And the sight of the glory of the LORD was like devouring fire* on the top of the mount in the eyes of the children of Israel" (Ex. 24:16–17). The scriptures repeatedly indicate that at Christ's Second Coming, • "*the glory of the LORD shall be revealed*, and all flesh shall see it together" (Isa. 40:5). The Prophet Malachi taught that in that day which cometh, • "that *shall burn as an oven*; and all the proud, yea, and all that do wickedly, shall be stubble: and *the day that cometh shall burn them up*, saith the LORD of hosts, that it shall leave them neither root nor branch. . . . And ye shall tread down the wicked; for they shall be ashes under the soles of your feet in the day that I shall do this, saith the LORD of hosts" (Mal. 4: 1, 3). The Lord, in the Doctrine and Covenants, warns of • "the day . . . when the earth is ripe; and *all the proud and they that do wickedly shall be as stubble; and I will burn them up*, saith the Lord of Hosts, that wickedness shall not be upon the earth; . . . For *I will reveal myself from heaven with power and great glory*, . . . and the wicked shall not stand" (D&C 29:9, 11).

14. **_Glory as a Visible Light, Emanating from God's Body._** Isaiah foresaw the eternal future when the glorious light emanating from the Savior's body would furnish light for all mankind: • "The sun shall be no more thy light by day; neither for brightness shall the moon give light unto thee: but *the LORD shall be unto thee an everlasting light, and thy God thy glory. Thy sun shall no more go down; neither shall thy moon withdraw itself: for *the LORD shall be thine everlasting light*" (Isa. 60:19–20).

These passages indicate a variety of ways in which the term "glory" is defined and used in the scriptures. The few verses cited are but "the tip of the iceberg" of profound passages which reveal the amazing glory and nature of the members of the Godhead.

Now, the challenge is to convey, from the scriptures, the way which God the Father, His Son Jesus Christ, and the Holy Ghost, utilize their glory when directing mankind, and most importantly, how their use of their "glory" is related to their "work."

Godhead Members Increase Their Individual Glories

Central to understanding the nature of God is the need to recognize that the end results of their creating, populating, saving, and exalting worlds and populations "without number" and "without end" is to increase their own glory. Their individual and collective glory, which embodies all the definitions shown above, is cumulative, and it is continually crescendoing. (See Moses 1:4, 8, 27–40.)

How can this be envisioned in mortal terms? A weak but meaningful comparison of how they operate in expanding their glory is to compare it with today's practice of multi-level marketing (and please excuse my comparison if you happen to be among the few but vocal critics of this marketing practice and strategy). Indeed, this multiple-level approach may be a copy of the methodologies utilized by Deity in increasing their individual and collective glories, though the earthlings who devised their mortal multiple-level marketing approaches most likely had no realization of the methods they were emulating.

In this type of commercial venture, people learn of a product or service which they think is beneficial, and they purchase it from a sales person who is distributing it. As they purchase goods for their own use, they also sign up as sub-dealers under the sales person. Then they sell their product to others, as many as possible, whom they enlist as salesmen in their "down line." Their remuneration is an "override" on all the sales made by their downline people. They work to teach, motivate, and direct the activities of their down-line friends and acquaintances in order to increase the override from everything sold by anyone and everyone selling under their guidance. If their down-line people sell enough products, they personally receive both incremental overrides and also quantity discounts on the products they purchase.

They make rules that, if followed, will enhance the efficiency and productivity of their down-line personnel and which serve to protect the integrity and good name of their company and products. They also begin to receive increasingly widespread recognition for their efforts, skills and accomplishments within the company.

If these individuals generate enough sales through their downlines, they eventually develop so many multiple streams of income that they gain first local and then such company-wide prominence that they are designated as master salesmen, with broad powers and influence granted to them by the founding owners of the company.

This analogy, as weak as it is, still has meaningful correlations with how God the Father and the Son perform their work here upon this earth and in "worlds without number" elsewhere. The "products" they are distributing are "salvation" and "exaltation." The Savior strives to gather unto Him all those who will believe in Him, follow Him loyally, and keep His commandments. They become His "downline." They, in turn, enlist and convert others, all of whom are trusting in their Savior and relying on the merits and grace of His atoning sacrifice and His essential role as mediator with God the Father. And being the great "marketers" that they are, the Father, the Son, and the Holy Ghost are seeking and enhancing the righteous and diligent conduct of their "downline," and are ready and willing to lead them to the attaining of ultimate rewards of honor, glory, powers and dominions. When their "downlines" succeed to their highest goals and eternal aspirations, it glorifies the Father, the Son, and the Holy Ghost, as well as those who attain those lofty results. Hence, • *"this is my work and my glory—to bring to pass the immortality and eternal life of man"* (Moses 1:39).

The scriptures indicate that the Father and Son work harmoniously together to increase and enhance each other's glory. This is clearly shown in Christ's profound prayer that he offered following the last supper. John recorded that Jesus • "lifted up his eyes to heaven, and said, Father, the hour is come; *glorify thy Son, that thy Son also may glorify thee"* (John 17:1). Throughout His prayer, the Lord made repeated references to His Father's glory and to His own glory as well. He said, • *"I have glorified thee* on the earth: I have finished the work which thou gavest me to do. And now, O Father, *glorify thou me* with thine own self *with the glory which I had with thee* before the world was" (John 17:4–5). Concerning His disciples He prayed, • *"all mine are thine, and thine are mine; and I am glorified in them"* (John 17:10). He declared that • *"the glory which thou gavest me I have given them*; that they may be one, even as we are one" (John 17:22), and He prayed that those followers eventually would • "be with me where I am; *that they may behold my glory, which thou hast given me*: for thou lovedst me before the foundation of the world" (John 17:24).

On the preceding Sabbath, following His triumphal entry into Jerusalem, Jesus had told His disciples Philip and Andrew, • *"The hour is come, that the Son of man should be glorified"* as he anticipated His impending sufferings and death on the cross (John 12:23). Others were close by and heard Him as He spoke to His Father in Heaven, saying, • *"Father, glorify thy name."* Those standing nearby witnessed that then • "came there a voice from heaven, saying, *I have both glorified it, and will glorify it again"* (John 12:28). During the last supper the Master told His disciples, • *"Now is the Son of man glorified, and God is glorified in him. If God be glorified in him, God shall also glorify him in himself, and shall straightway glorify him"* (John 13:31–32). Also during the last supper, Jesus promised His Apostles that • "whatsoever ye shall ask in my name, that will I do, *that the Father may be glorified in the Son"* (John 14:13). And speaking of the Comforter, Jesus said, • *"He shall glorify me: for he shall receive of mine"* (John 16:14), apparently indicating that the Holy Ghost would also share Christ's glory. The Apostle Peter also wrote of the Holy Ghost's participation in the glorification process, saying that • "If ye be reproached for the name of Christ, happy are ye; for *the spirit of glory and of God* resteth upon you: on their part he is evil spoken of, but *on your part he is glorified"* (1 Pet. 4:14).

Numerous other passages speak of members of the Godhead acquiring glory through their interactions with one another or attributing it to one another. As Jesus taught His disciples "the Lord's Prayer," He instructed them to pray to God the Father, saying: • "After this manner therefore pray ye: Our Father which art in heaven, Hallowed be thy name. Thy kingdom come. Thy will be done in earth, as it is in heaven. . . . *For thine is the kingdom, and the power, and the glory,* for ever. Amen" (Matt. 6:9–10, 13).

The Apostle Peter, after healing a man who had been lame all his life, challenged the crowd of amazed onlookers, saying, • *"the God of our fathers, hath glorified his Son Jesus"* (Acts 3:13), signifying that the man had been healed through priesthood power rather than by his own words. Peter also wrote that • "if any man minister, *let him do it* as of the ability which God giveth: *that God in all things may be glorified through Jesus Christ,* to whom be praise and dominion for ever" (1 Pet. 4:11).

The Apostle Paul wrote to the Romans, instructing them to • "with one mind and one mouth *glorify God, even the Father of our Lord Jesus Christ.* Wherefore receive ye one another, as *Christ also received us to the glory of God"* (Rom. 15:6–7). The author of the epistle to the Hebrews taught that when Jesus Christ first received the priesthood, His ordination served to add to God the Father's glory: • "And no man taketh this honour unto himself, but he that is called of God, as was Aaron. So also *Christ glorified not himself* to be made an high priest; *but he that said unto him, Thou art my Son,* to day have I begotten thee" (Heb. 5:4–5).

The Book of Mormon account of the Savior's ministry among the Nephites following His resurrection contains the Master's testimony that • "I am Jesus Christ the Son of God. I created the heavens and the earth, and all things that in them are. I was with the Father from the beginning. I am in the Father, and the Father in me; and *in me hath the Father glorified his name"* (3 Ne. 9:15). He also told the Nephites that • "I am the light and the life of the world; and I have drunk out of that bitter cup which the Father hath given me, and *have glorified the Father in taking upon me the sins of the world"* (3 Ne. 11:11).

And the Doctrine and Covenants teaches that the shedding of Christ's blood ultimately accrued to God the Father's glory: • "Listen to him who is the advocate with the Father, who is pleading your cause before him—Saying: Father, behold the sufferings and death of him who did no sin, in whom thou wast well pleased; behold the blood of thy Son which was shed, *the blood of him whom thou gavest that thyself might be glorified"* (D&C 45:3–4).

Thus it is clearly seen that the Father, Son and Holy Spirit work together to mutually augment their glory as they enable mankind to obey and serve God, thus preparing man to also receive eternal glory.

Blessings that He Granted to Man Have Added to Christ's Glory

The scriptures identify numerous blessings which the Lord Jehovah, who is also the Lord Jesus Christ, has personally bestowed on mankind throughout the ages. Some passages make it clear that these acts also served to increase the Lord's glory. For instance, the Prophet Jacob, while teaching the people of Nephi, spoke of the creation of the world and asserted that • "all flesh is of the dust; and for the selfsame end hath he created them, that they should keep his commandments and *glorify him forever"* (Jacob 2:21).

While speaking of the creation of the house and tribes of Israel, the Prophet Isaiah conveyed a revelation of the LORD to them concerning the purpose of their origin: • "thus saith the LORD that created thee, O Jacob, and he that formed thee, O Israel, Fear not: for I have redeemed thee, I have called thee by thy name; thou art mine. . . . Even every one that is called by my name: for *I have created him* [combined Israel] *for my glory,* I have formed him; yea, I have made him" (Isa. 43:1, 7).

The LORD intervened in numerous battles during Old Testament times, using the defeat of enemy kings as a source of His glory. Ezekiel prophesied of one such situation, voicing the LORD's warning that • "Thus saith the Lord GOD; Behold, I am against thee, O Zidon; and *I will be glorified in the midst of thee: and they shall know that I am the LORD,* when I shall have executed judgments in her, and shall be sanctified in her" (Ezek. 28:22).

When Haggai sought to rebuild the temple of Solomon, the LORD commanded him to • "Go up to the mountain, and bring wood, and build the house; and I will take pleasure in it, and *I will be glorified, saith the LORD"* (Hag. 1:8).

Near the end of His mortal ministry, when Jesus heard of the sickness of Lazarus, • "he said, This sickness is not unto death, but *for the glory of God, that the Son of God might be glorified thereby*" (John 11:4). Several days later, when He traveled to Judea and found Lazarus had been dead for four days, He called him back from the grave and restored him to mortal life.

Many prophecies of the future restoration of Israel in the last days speak of that being an event which will bring great glory to the LORD. Thus, Isaiah prophesied that • "the LORD hath redeemed Jacob, and *glorified himself in Israel*" (Isa. 44:23). Prophesying of • "the city of the LORD, the Zion of the Holy One of Israel" (Isa. 60:14), the LORD proclaimed that • "*I will glorify the house of my glory*" (Isa. 60:7). He also prophesied that • "Thy people also shall be all righteous: they shall inherit the land for ever, the branch of my planting, the work of my hands, *that I may be glorified*" (Isa. 60:21). Again, he prophesied of the restoration of Zion when restored Israel will be called "the planting of the LORD," saying that • "To appoint unto them that mourn in Zion, to give unto them beauty for ashes, the oil of joy for mourning, the garment of praise for the spirit of heaviness; that they might be called trees of righteousness, *the planting of the LORD, that he might be glorified*" (Isa. 61:3). And he also said, • "I am God, . . . and I will place salvation in Zion *for Israel my glory*" (Isa. 46:9, 13).

In latter-day scripture, the Lord has spoken of the restoration of the new and everlasting covenant, specifying that • "*it was instituted for the fulness of my glory* . . . saith the Lord God" (D&C 132:6).

The pattern is clear: everything that the Lord does for the betterment of mankind not only blesses man but at the same time adds to His personal glory. That is a fundamental aspect of the eternal plan. Righteous mankind eventually will walk the same path, accruing personal glory as they obey God's commandments and render service both to God and to their fellow man.

Man Is to Function with His Eye Single to God's Glory

In His ministries here on the earth, Jesus repeatedly taught that man is to focus on adding to the glory of God rather than to labor for personal glory. In His "Sermon on the Mount," He told His followers to • "Let your light so shine before men, that they may see your good works, and *glorify your Father which is in heaven*" (Matt. 5:16). He taught the same principle when He repeated His discourse to the Nephites: • "let your light so shine before this people, that they may see your good works and *glorify your Father who is in heaven*" (3 Ne. 12:16). In His "last supper" discourse He told His Apostles that • "*Herein is my Father glorified*, that ye bear much fruit; so shall ye be my disciples" (John 15:8).

The Apostle Peter wrote concerning the same principle: • "If any man suffer as a Christian, let him not be ashamed; but *let him glorify God on this behalf*" (1 Pet. 4:16).

As he wrote concerning the coming forth of the Book of Mormon record in the last days, Moroni observed that • "none can have power to bring it to light save it be given him of God; for *God wills that it shall be done with an eye single to his glory*, or the welfare of the ancient and long dispersed covenant people of the Lord" (Morm. 8:15).

Numerous passages in the Doctrine and Covenants emphasize that the actions of Latter-day Saint members are to be performed with an eye single to the glory of God, no matter whether it be the glory of the Lord Jesus Christ or the glory of God the Father. For instance, concerning the nature of the sacramental emblems, the Lord instructed: • "it mattereth not what ye shall eat or what ye shall drink when ye partake of the sacrament, *if it so be that ye do it with an eye single to my glory*—remembering unto the Father my body which was laid down for you, and my blood which was shed for the remission of your sins" (D&C 27:2).

The proper attitude for those receiving baptism was revealed in a revelation given to William W. Phelps in 1831: • "thus saith the Lord unto you, my servant William, yea, even the Lord of the whole earth, thou art called and chosen; and after thou hast been baptized by water, which *if you do with an eye single to my glory,* you shall have a remission of your sins and a reception of the Holy Spirit by the laying on of hands" (D&C 55:1).

A revelation given on August 7, 1831 "in Zion, Jackson County, Missouri" (D&C 59: heading) promised that • "blessed, saith the Lord, are they who have come up unto this land *with an eye single to my glory,* according to my commandments" (D&C 59:1). But a revelation given in Kirtland, Ohio, later that month had a more critical tone: • "I, the Lord, am not pleased with those among you who have sought after signs and wonders for faith, and *not for the good of men unto my glory*" (D&C 63:12).

Concerning the need for forgiving others, the Master revealed that • "I, the Lord, will forgive whom I will forgive, but of you it is required to forgive all men. . . . And *this ye shall do that God may be glorified*" (D&C 64:10, 13).

In D&C 76, the great compilation of visions concerning life beyond the veil of death, the Lord admonished: • "*let no man glory in man*, but rather *let him glory in God,* who shall subdue all enemies under his feet" (D&C 76:61).

D&C 78, revealed in March, 1832, contains the Lord's organizational instructions for "the storehouse for the poor of my people" (D&C 78:3). The revelation stressed that • "thus saith the Lord, *it is expedient that all things be done unto my glory,* by you who are joined together in this order" (D&C 78:8).

In "the Olive Leaf," the great revelation which provided significant information concerning the light and glory of Christ, the saints received from the Savior the promise that • "*if your eye be single to my glory, your whole bodies shall be filled with light,* and there shall be no darkness in you; and that body which is filled with light comprehendeth all things" (D&C 88:67).

Thus, the pattern of receiving glory is completed. God the Father has shared His glory with His firstborn Son, Jesus Christ, and with the Holy Ghost. They, in turn, have labored to save and exalt all those upon this earth who have accepted Christ and faithfully obeyed His commandments, living and laboring with their eye single to His glory. If they endure in obedience unto the end, Jesus Christ will share His glory with them.

This was set forth previously in the prayer the Savior offered while ministering to the Nephites. Jesus asked that His listeners might be purified and united, which would add to His glory while also extending His glory to those who were hearing him that day: • "Father, I pray not for the world, but for those whom thou hast given me out of the world, because of their faith, that they may be purified in me, that I may be in them as thou, Father, art in me, that we may be one, *that I may be glorified in them*" (3 Ne. 19:29).

The Doctrine and Covenants, while speaking of why the Book of Mormon plates were preserved, says that it was so • "that the promises of the Lord might be fulfilled, which he made to his people; that the Lamanites might come to the knowledge of their fathers, and that they might know the promises of the Lord, and that they may believe the gospel and rely upon the merits of Jesus Christ, and *be glorified through faith in his name*, and that through their repentance they might be saved" (D&C 3:20). That pattern and promise extends to all who will be saved by Christ's grace and eventually exalted in the celestial kingdom.

The Lord Withholds His Glory from Evildoers

Glory—the power of God—is obviously a very precious commodity: a pearl of great price! Members of the Godhead protect it in all its aspects, ranging from their divine reputation to the visible radiance which emanates from their very beings when they allow mortals to see it. The scriptures make it abundantly clear that their glory is reserved for themselves and for the righteous; it will not be shared with those who do evil.

Concerning the pagan religions of old with their idols and images, Jehovah proclaimed: • "I am the LORD: that is my name: and *my glory will I not give to another,* neither *my praise* to graven images" (Isa. 42:8). When Nadab and Abihu, two of Aaron's sons, perverted the ordinances he had revealed and "offered strange fire before the LORD," Jehovah sent down fire which devoured them. • "Then Moses said unto Aaron, This is it that the LORD spake, saying, I will be sanctified in them that come nigh me, and before all the people *I will be glorified*" (Lev. 10:1–3).

A passage in the Doctrine and Covenants recalls the wickedness of the children of Israel whom Moses was attempting to instruct: • "Now this Moses plainly taught to the children of Israel in the wilderness, and sought diligently to sanctify his people that they might behold the face of God; But *they hardened their hearts and could not endure his presence*; therefore, the Lord in his wrath . . . swore that they should not enter into his rest while in the wilderness, *which rest is the fulness of his glory*" (D&C 84:23–24).

The Lord Jehovah will not allow His name to be polluted by evildoers. That's why in the second of His Ten Commandments He commanded that • "Thou shalt not take the name of the LORD thy God in vain" (Ex. 20:7; Deut. 5:11). Later, through His Prophet Isaiah, He revealed to the wayward Israelites this warning: • "for my name's sake will I defer mine anger, and *for my praise* will I refrain from thee, that I cut thee not off. For, behold, I have refined thee, I have chosen thee in the furnace of affliction. *For mine own sake, yea, for mine own sake will I do this*, for *I will not suffer my name to be polluted*, and *I will not give my glory unto another*" (Isa. 48:9–11; 1 Ne. 20:9–11).

Modern revelations also indicate that while the Lord is willing to manifest and share His glory with those who are righteous, He will withhold it from those who are wicked. For instance, concerning the building of the Kirtland, Ohio Temple, He said: • "*my glory shall be there*, and my presence shall be there. *But if there shall come into it any unclean thing, my glory shall not be there*; and my presence shall not come into it" (D&C 94:8–9).

Likewise, concerning the projected building of the Independence, Missouri Temple, He said: • "inasmuch as my people build a house unto me in the name of the Lord, and do not suffer any unclean thing to come into it, that it be not defiled, *my glory shall rest upon it; Yea, and my presence shall be there*, for I will come into it, and *all the pure in heart that shall come into it shall see God. But if it be defiled I will not come into it, and my glory shall not be there*; for I will not come into unholy temples" (D&C 97:15–17).

Concerning those in these last days who do not marry their spouse for eternity in one of God's holy temples, the Lord has warned: • "if a man marry a wife, and make a covenant with her for time and for all eternity, if that covenant is not by me or by my word, which is my law, . . . *they cannot, therefore, inherit my glory*; for my house is a house of order, saith the Lord God" (D&C 132:18).

Again, concerning murderers and concerning any Latter-day Saint who turns from the gospel and fights against it, thereby assenting to Christ's death, the warning is, • "The blasphemy against the Holy Ghost, which shall not be forgiven in the world nor out of the world, is in that ye commit murder wherein ye shed innocent blood, and assent unto my death, after ye have received my new and everlasting covenant, saith the Lord God; and *he that abideth not this law can in nowise enter into my glory*, but shall be damned, saith the Lord" (D&C 132:27; see verse 19; also D&C 76:28–38).

Christ's Glory Seen Prior to His Mortal Ministry

While it is only rarely that Christ has revealed the glorious light that emanates from His very being to mortals, the scriptures do record various instances in which the light of His glory has been seen. These unique manifestations range from the days of Moses to the meridian of time to the days of the Prophet Joseph Smith.

The ancient scriptures speak repeatedly of experiences in which the actual glory of the premortal Christ was seen, many years before His birth here on the earth. The book of Moses, in the Pearl of Great Price, tells of various manifestations granted unto the Prophet Moses:

> And he saw God face to face, and he talked with him, and *the glory of God was upon Moses; therefore Moses could endure his presence.*
>
> And God spake unto Moses, saying: Behold, I am the Lord God Almighty, and Endless is my name; for I am without beginning of days or end of years; and is not this endless?
>
> And, behold, thou art my son; wherefore look, and I will show thee the workmanship of mine hands; but not all, for my works are without end, and also my words, for they never cease.
>
> Wherefore, *no man can behold all my works, except he behold all my glory*; and *no man can behold all my glory, and afterwards remain in the flesh on the earth.* (Moses 1:2–5)

Later in the same chapter, it is recorded that • "Moses lifted up his eyes unto heaven, *being filled with the Holy Ghost*, which beareth record of the Father and the Son; And calling upon the name of God, *he beheld his glory again*, for it was upon him" (Moses 1:24–25).

Book of Mormon accounts also speak of prophets actually beholding the glory of the premortal Christ. Lehi testified that • "the Lord hath redeemed my soul from hell; *I have beheld his glory*, and I am encircled about eternally in the arms of his love" (2 Ne. 1:15). And, later in his life, the Prophet Lehi said to his son Jacob: • "I know that thou art redeemed, because of the righteousness of thy Redeemer; for thou hast beheld that in the fulness of time he cometh to bring salvation unto men. *And thou hast beheld in thy youth his glory*; wherefore, thou art blessed" (2 Ne. 2:3–4). Jacob later recorded that • "for this intent have we written these things, that they may know that we knew of Christ, and *we had a hope of his glory many hundred years before his coming*; and not only we ourselves had *a hope of his glory*, but also all the holy prophets which were before us" (Jacob 4:4).

Christ's Glory Seen in the Meridian of Time

During the short 33 years in which He experienced mortality in the era now known as the meridian of time, the glorious light of Christ's glory was also seen. About six months before His crucifixion, on what today is called the Mount of Transfiguration (most likely Mount Hermon, north of Caesarea Philippi), the following transpired:

> And it came to pass about an eight days after these sayings, he took Peter and John and James, and went up into a mountain to pray.
> And as he prayed, *the fashion of his countenance was altered, and his raiment was white and glistering.*
> And, behold, there talked with him two men, which were Moses and Elias:
> *Who appeared in glory,* and spake of his decease which he should accomplish at Jerusalem.
> But Peter and they that were with him were heavy with sleep: and when they were awake, *they saw his glory,* and the two men that stood with him. (Luke 9:28–32)

The Apostle John probably was referring to this experience when he later wrote his Gospel. He recorded that • "the Word was made flesh, and dwelt among us, (*and we beheld his glory, the glory as of the only begotten of the Father,*) full of grace and truth" (John 1:14).

A Doctrine and Covenants record also speaks of the glory of Jesus Christ being seen, though it does not make it clear whether what is described took place during Christ's mortal ministry or during his premortal labors. The revelation is speaking of the testimony of John the Baptist, the Prophet who was the forerunner to Christ's ministry in Judea:

> *John saw and bore record of the fulness of my glory,* and the fulness of John's record is hereafter to be revealed.
> And he bore record, saying: *I saw his glory,* that he was in the beginning, before the world was;
> Therefore, in the beginning the Word was, for he was the Word, even the messenger of salvation—
> The light and the Redeemer of the world; the Spirit of truth, who came into the world, because the world was made by him, and in him was the life of men and *the light of men.*
> The worlds were made by him; men were made by him; all things were made by him, and through him, and of him.
> And I, John, bear record that *I beheld his glory, as the glory of the Only Begotten of the Father,* full of grace and truth, even the Spirit of truth, which came and dwelt in the flesh, and dwelt among us.
> And I, John, saw that he received not of the fulness at the first, but received grace for grace;
> And he received not of the fulness at first, but continued from grace to grace, until he received a fulness;
> And thus he was called the Son of God, because he received not of the fulness at the first.
> And I, John, bear record, and lo, the heavens were opened, and the Holy Ghost descended upon him in the form of a dove, and sat upon him, and there came a voice out of heaven saying: This is my beloved Son.
> And *I, John, bear record that he received a fulness of the glory of the Father;*
> *And he received all power, both in heaven and on earth, and the glory of the Father was with him, for he dwelt in him.*

And it shall come to pass, that if you are faithful you shall receive the fulness of the record of John.

I give unto you these sayings that you may understand and know how to worship, and know what you worship, that you may come unto the Father in my name, and in due time receive of his fulness.

For if you keep my commandments you shall receive of his fulness, and *be glorified in me as I am in the Father*; therefore, I say unto you, you shall receive grace for grace.

And now, verily I say unto you, I was in the beginning with the Father, and am the Firstborn;

And all those who are begotten through me are partakers of the glory of the same, and are the church of the Firstborn. (D&C 93:6–22)

Christ's Glory Seen in These Last Days

In like manner, the glory of Jesus Christ has been seen various times in the dispensation of the fulness of times. The scriptures record several such experiences. Of special import is that the glory of God the Father was manifested with Christ's glory in two of these events. The first is Joseph Smith's vision received in the spring of 1820—his first vision. Of this experience Joseph later recorded: • "When *the light rested upon me* I saw two Personages, *whose brightness and glory defy all description*, standing above me in the air. One of them spake unto me, calling me by name and said, pointing to the other—*This is My Beloved Son. Hear Him!*" (JS—H 1:17).

The second appearance of both the Father and Son in their full glory occurred on February 16, 1832 at Hiram, Ohio. It was seen, together, by Joseph Smith and Sidney Rigdon as one of a series of visions: • "And while we meditated upon these things, *the Lord touched the eyes of our understandings* and they were opened, and the *glory of the Lord shone round about. And we beheld the glory of the Son, on the right hand of the Father*, and received of his fulness" (D&C 76:19–20).

The third experience occurred in Kirtland, Ohio, on April 3, 1836, in the newly completed Kirtland Temple. The manifestation was seen, together, by Joseph Smith and Oliver Cowdery: • "We saw the Lord standing upon the breastwork of the pulpit, before us; and under his feet was a paved work of pure gold, in color like amber. *His eyes were as a flame of fire; the hair of his head was white like the pure snow; his countenance shone above the brightness of the sun*; and his voice was as the sound of the rushing of great waters, even the voice of Jehovah, saying: I am the first and the last; I am he who liveth, I am he who was slain; I am your advocate with the Father" (D&C 110:2–4).

Private journals and the *History of the Church* record numerous other appearances of the Savior in these latter days, usually without making light and glory visible, but these three manifestations which describe both Jesus and the Father appearing in their glory suffice in this context.

Christ Will Return to the Earth in Glory

One of the most-prophesied events in all scripture is the near-future advent of the Lord Jesus Christ, commonly called His "Second Coming." Numerous books have been written on this long-expected event, and they elucidate many details that are related to His advent. That glorious return will be portrayed in this context by just three scriptural passages, one each from the New Testament, the Doctrine and Covenants, and the Book of Mormon.

Paul wrote, to the Saints of Thessalonika, the following warning and prophetic description of the Savior's coming:

the Lord Jesus shall be revealed from heaven with his mighty angels,
In flaming fire taking vengeance on them that know not God, and that obey not the gospel of our Lord Jesus Christ:
Who shall be punished with everlasting destruction from the presence of the Lord, and from the glory of his power;
When he shall come to be glorified in his saints, and *to be admired in all them* that believe (because our testimony among you was believed) in that day. . . . *That the name of our Lord Jesus Christ may be glorified in you, and ye in him.* (2 Thess. 1:7–10, 12)

Among numerous passages in the Doctrine and Covenants which speak of Christ's Second Advent is this succinct admonition to the Saints: • "be prepared for the days to come, in the which the Son of Man shall come down in heaven, *clothed in the brightness of his glory*, to meet the kingdom of God which is set up on the earth" (D&C 65:5).

In the Book of Mormon the words of the Savior to the three Nephite Apostles who were permitted to linger on earth and continue their ministry among mortals are recorded:

ye shall never taste of death; but ye shall live to behold all the doings of the Father unto the children of men, even until all things shall be fulfilled according to the will of the Father, *when I shall come in my glory with the powers of heaven.*

And ye shall never endure the pains of death; but *when I shall come in my glory* ye shall be changed in the twinkling of an eye from mortality to immortality. (3 Ne. 28:7–8)

The Eventual Glory and Reign of Jesus Christ

While describing what types of persons will inherit the heavenly kingdoms, the Lord reveals several of the final events pertaining to this earth and its inhabitants. He tells how He will deliver up this earthly kingdom (the results of His efforts pertaining to this earth) unto God the Father, and then will receive additional glory from His Father, and finally, this earth will be Christ's. Three passages combine to convey this highly significant transmittal of authority and glory: verses from D&C 76, D&C 130, and D&C 88. First, from Doctrine and Covenants section 76:

These are they who are cast down to hell and suffer the wrath of Almighty God, until the fulness of times, when Christ shall have subdued all enemies under his feet, and shall have perfected his work;
When *he shall deliver up the kingdom, and present it unto the Father, spotless*, saying: I have overcome and have trodden the wine-press alone, even the wine-press of the fierceness of the wrath of Almighty God.
Then shall he be crowned with the crown of his glory, to sit on the throne of his power to reign forever and ever. (D&C 76:106–108)

Then, from Doctrine and Covenants section 130:

The place where God resides is a great Urim and Thummim.
This earth, in its sanctified and immortal state, will be made like unto crystal and will be a Urim and Thummim to the inhabitants who dwell thereon, whereby all things pertaining to an inferior kingdom, or all kingdoms of a lower order, will be manifest to those who dwell on it; and *this earth will be Christ's*. (D&C 130:8–9)

And finally, from Doctrine and Covenants section 88:

> It is decreed that *the poor and the meek of the earth shall inherit it.*
>
> Therefore, it must needs be sanctified from all unrighteousness, *that it may be prepared for the celestial glory;*
>
> For after it hath filled the measure of its creation, *it shall be crowned with glory, even with the presence of God the Father;*
>
> *That bodies who are of the celestial kingdom may possess it forever and ever;* for, for this intent was it made and created, and for this intent are they sanctified. . . .
>
> *the earth abideth the law of a celestial kingdom,* for it filleth the measure of its creation, and transgresseth not the law—
>
> Wherefore, it shall be sanctified; yea, notwithstanding it shall die, it shall be quickened again, and shall abide the power by which it is quickened, and *the righteous shall inherit it.*
>
> For notwithstanding they die, they also shall rise again, *a spiritual body.*
>
> They who are of a celestial spirit shall receive the same body which was a natural body; even ye shall receive your bodies, and *your glory shall be that glory by which your bodies are quickened.*
>
> Ye who are *quickened by a portion of the celestial glory* shall then receive of the same, even a fulness. (D&C 88:17–20, 25–29)

So, in summary, God the Father previously has given His Son Jesus Christ authority, power and glory, and assigned Him to create and govern this earth. He has given Him great latitude in how He guides the affairs of humankind. He has caused that those who follow Christ, believe on Him and obey His commandments can be adopted as sons and daughters of Christ through the gospel plan. Finally, He has granted that this earth, the cumulative result of Christ's handiwork and careful tending and nourishing, will be returned back to Christ after the Savior first delivers it up to the Father, presenting it cleansed and spotless unto Him. Then the Father will convey additional glory to Jesus, and will give Him the eternal responsibility and ownership to rule over this earth forever. And Christ will, in turn, grant eternal power, glory and Godhood to all those earth-dwellers who have merited exaltation as the result of His labors, guidance and atoning sacrifice, as they dwell for eternity on this sanctified, celestialized earth.

So truly, the final result will be as Paul envisioned: • "For all things are yours; . . .Whether . . . the world, or life, or death, or things present, or things to come; *all are yours; And ye are Christ's; and Christ is God's*" (1 Cor. 3:21–23).

Righteous Sons and Daughters of Christ Will Receive Eternal Glory

The end result for those who will inherit the celestial kingdom is spelled out in greater detail in Doctrine and Covenants section 76:

> They are they who received the testimony of Jesus, and believed on his name and were baptized after the manner of his burial, being buried in the water in his name, and this according to the commandment which he has given—
>
> That by keeping the commandments they might be washed and cleansed from all their sins, and receive the Holy Spirit by the laying on of the hands of him who is ordained and sealed unto this power;
>
> And who overcome by faith, and are sealed by the Holy Spirit of promise, which the Father sheds forth upon all those who are just and true.

They are they who are the church of the Firstborn.

They are they into whose hands the Father has given all things—

They are they who are priests and kings, *who have received of his fulness, and of his glory;*

And are priests of the Most High, after the order of Melchizedek, which was after the order of Enoch, which was after the order of the Only Begotten Son.

Wherefore, as it is written, *they are gods, even the sons of God—*

Wherefore, *all things are theirs, whether life or death, or things present, or things to come, all are theirs and they are Christ's, and Christ is God's.*

And they shall overcome all things.

Wherefore, *let no man glory in man, but rather let him glory in God,* who shall subdue all enemies under his feet.

These shall dwell in the presence of God and his Christ forever and ever. (D&C 76:51–62)

Other passages convey the same message. For instance, as D&C 88 describes the events which will take place at the beginning of the millennium when Christ has just descended in glory, it records that

another angel shall sound his trump, which is the seventh angel, saying: It is finished; it is finished! The Lamb of God hath overcome and trodden the wine-press alone, even the wine-press of the fierceness of the wrath of Almighty God.

And *then shall the angels be crowned with the glory of his might, and the saints shall be filled with his glory, and receive their inheritance and be made equal with him.* (D&C 88:106–107)

In His prayer following the last supper, Jesus spoke of the righteous followers who will receive of His glory at that time and who will dwell with Him eternally:

Neither pray I for these alone, but for them also which shall believe on me through their word;

That they all may be one; as thou, Father, art in me, and I in thee, that they also may be one in us . . .

And *the glory which thou gavest me I have given them*; that they may be one, even as we are one:

Father, I will that they also, whom thou hast given me, be with me where I am; *that they may behold my glory, which thou hast given me*: for thou lovedst me before the foundation of the world. (John 17:20–22, 24)

In modern times, the Lord Jesus spoke of this relationship in His parable of a man sending his servants into the field and later visiting them, found in section 88 of the Doctrine and Covenants:

Behold, I will liken these kingdoms unto a man having a field, and he sent forth his servants into the field to dig in the field. . . .

Every man in his own order, until his hour was finished, even according as his lord had commanded him, *that his lord might be glorified in him, and he in his lord, that they all might be glorified.* (D&C 88:51, 60)

Consider the many blessings promised to those who will merit being glorified in Christ:

I, the Lord, am merciful and gracious unto those who fear me, and *delight to honor those who serve me in righteousness* and in truth unto the end.

Great shall be their reward and eternal shall be their glory.

And to them will *I reveal all mysteries*, yea, all the hidden mysteries of my kingdom from days of old, and for ages to come, will I make known unto them the good pleasure of my will concerning all things pertaining to my kingdom.

Yea, even *the wonders of eternity shall they know*, and *things to come will I show them*, even the things of many generations.

And *their wisdom shall be great, and their understanding reach to heaven*; and before them the wisdom of the wise shall perish, and the understanding of the prudent shall come to naught.

For *by my Spirit will I enlighten them*, and by my power will I make known unto them the secrets of my will—yea, *even those things which eye has not seen, nor ear heard, nor yet entered into the heart of man*. (D&C 76:5–10)

Another passage elucidates many of the glorious revelations which shall be granted to them:

A time to come in the which *nothing shall be withheld*, whether there be one God or many gods, they shall be manifest.

All thrones and dominions, principalities and powers, shall be revealed and set forth upon all who have endured valiantly for the gospel of Jesus Christ.

And also, *if there be bounds set to the heavens or to the seas, or to the dry land, or to the sun, moon, or stars—*

All the times of their revolutions, all the appointed days, months, and years, and all the days of their days, months, and years, and *all their glories, laws, and set times*, shall be revealed in the days of the dispensation of the fulness of times—

According to that which was ordained in the midst of *the Council of the Eternal God of all other gods before this world was*, that should be reserved unto the finishing and the end thereof, *when every man shall enter into his eternal presence and into his immortal rest*. (D&C 121:28–32)

Again, remember the key to understanding this eternal hierarchy of glory and power: • "Wherefore, *all things are theirs*, whether life or death, or things present, or things to come, *all are theirs and they are Christ's, and Christ is God's*" (D&C 76:59). The New Testament states the same message: • "let no man glory in men. *For all things are yours; . . . all are yours; And ye are Christ's; and Christ is God's*" (1 Cor. 3:21–23).

Summary

1. A favorite verse of many Latter-day Saints is Moses 1:39: • "For behold, this is my work and my glory—to bring to pass the immortality and eternal life of man." The rest of this book has focused primarily on the Godhead's *works* and how they are performed. This chapter, however, is focused on their *glory*.

2. Fourteen different definitions of "glory" were provided, ranging from reputation and status to the light which emanates from Godhead beings.

3. The end objective of the Godhead's creating, populating, saving, and exalting worlds and populations "without number" and "without end" is to increase their own glory and to provide avenues of glory for those who will follow them.

4. The individual and collective glory of the Godhead is cumulative, and it is continually crescendoing.

5. The system by which the Godhead functions in increasing their personal and collective glory has been copied on earth in numerous businesses. This has been done through

marketing systems organized on various levels, with rewards and overrides accruing to those on the intermediate levels as their downlines become more productive.

6. The scriptures indicate that the Father and Son work harmoniously together to increase and enhance each other's glory. Numerous passages speak of members of the Godhead acquiring glory through their interactions with one another or attributing it to one another.

7. Blessings which Jehovah/Jesus Christ has granted to man have served to increase His personal glory. Examples include helping His people to win battles, enabling them to prosper and grow economically to merit respect and acclaim, and the building of temples and other beautiful edifices which others admire.

8. Man is instructed to function on earth with an eye single to the increasing of God's glory. If one does so, a portion of that glory eventually will accrue to his own personal glory "stockpile."

9. The Lord withholds His glory from evildoers. Eternal glory is only attained and accrued through righteous actions and attitudes.

10. Examples of Christ's glory were cited from various periods: from prior to His mortal ministry, during his mortal ministry in the meridian of time, and during these last days.

11. Prophecies of Christ's future glory, as He returns to earth in His Second Coming, and also His eventual end-of-this-earth and afterwards' glory, were reviewed and analyzed.

12. At the end of this earth's mortal probation, when Christ will have finished His work, He will deliver this world and its inhabitants to God the Father. After the Father accepts it, He will convey additional glory to His Son, Jesus, and then return this earth to Jesus who will own and rule over it and its inhabitants forever. This earth will become a celestial kingdom for the exalted beings who will dwell upon it.

13. Righteous sons and daughters of Christ will receive their own eternal glory as they grow and progress in the eternal plan of happiness. The accruing of glory is a result of Heavenly beings' personal and collective progression.

CHAPTER 16

CHRIST RULES AMONG THE GODS, AND MANKIND CAN ATTAIN GODHOOD

Jehovah/Jesus Christ Is a God of Gods and Lord of Lords

The scriptures repeatedly assert that there are numerous Gods. In many cases, they do so in contexts that represent those Gods as righteous beings—exalted entities worthy to associate and serve with the members of the Godhead who govern the affairs of this particular earth: the Father, Son, and Holy Ghost.

The scriptures likewise assert that Jehovah/Jesus Christ stands pre-eminent among these many Gods. In authority he stands as Lord (Master) of these other righteous beings who also function as Lords—rulers of others who are participants in those rulers' kingdom and patriarchal hierarchies. Jehovah is repeatedly depicted as exceeding them in authority, glory, great deeds, and divine goodness.

Concerning the great Jehovah, the Psalmist wrote: • *"**God** standeth in the congregation of the mighty; he judgeth among the gods"* (Ps. 82:1). In the same psalm he refers to other beings—mortals who also have the potential to ascend to the pinnacles of personal perfection and exaltation: • "I have said, *Ye are gods; and all of you are children of the most High"* (Ps. 82:6).

Other psalms speak of many Gods, while asserting Jehovah's superlative status among them: • *"Among the gods there is none like unto thee, O Lord;* neither are there any works like unto thy works. All nations whom thou hast made *shall come and worship before thee, O Lord*; and shall glorify thy name. For thou art great, and doest wondrous things: thou art God alone" (Ps. 86:8–10). Yet another Psalm speaks of other righteous Gods in these words: • "O give thanks unto the Lord; for he is good . . . *O give thanks unto the God of gods . . . O give thanks to the Lord of lords"* (Ps. 136:1–3).

Guidelines for Discerning between "Good" and "Evil" Gods

Before proceeding further, several interpretational comments seem appropriate. *First,* discernment is needed, when reading the scriptures, to discern between references to (1) the many false gods of this earth's ancient times, as opposed to (2) the numerous righteous beings who, previous to the creation of this earth, have attained Godhood status—beings over whom Jehovah/Jesus Christ presides, in one capacity or another.

Second, the majority of Christian mankind is unaware of the second category—righteous beings who have attained Godhood or will someday attain their exaltation—though the Bible and other scriptures make significant allusions to them. Without the benefit of modern Latter-day Saint scriptures, they lack the knowledge of the vast numbers of other-world creations and of the numerous premortal events described in those sacred volumes. They also lack cognizance of the potential to achieve future exaltation and Godhood which has been revealed to mankind in these latter days.

Third, lacking the knowledge of these premortal events and promises of glorious rewards, they assume that all references to "gods" made in the Bible are allusions to the various false gods which proved to be stumbling blocks to mankind in ancient times.

How does one discern between the "good" Gods and the "false" or "evil" or "pagan" gods to which some scriptural allusions to "gods" refer? A little common sense and application of scriptural doctrines concerning the nature of Godhead beings provides guidance.

1. *The false gods of ancient scriptures were fictitious, nonexistent entities,* though their reputations sometimes reached mythological proportions. False priests created illusions of their existence, recruited widespread support for those illusions, and in some cases managed to beguile hundreds of thousands to worship the nonexistent beings which they proclaimed to be deities.

2. *Members of the Godhead are righteous: they abhor sin. They do not associate, nor allow themselves to be portrayed as associating with false, nonexistent gods.* However, they know of the existence of false priests, guided and motivated by Satan, who attempt to establish pagan worship entities, and they work to negate their evil effects on mankind.

3. *In contrast, Godhead members are portrayed in the scriptures as associating with, and ruling over "good" Gods.* Thus, when the Psalmist acknowledges that *"GOD standeth in the congregation of the mighty; he judgeth among the gods,"* one knows that the passage is speaking of righteous "mighty" beings and righteous "gods" rather that alluding to the presence of pagan deities.

4. *"Good" Gods worship and do obeisance to Godhead members.* Thus, they accept Jehovah and do homage to him.

5. *Since they are nonexistent, evil Gods neither worship nor obey Godhead members.* It is their false priests who fight against Jehovah as they seek to increase their powers through pagan rites.

6. *Jehovah is depicted in the scriptures as being more advanced than other "good" Gods* who, never-the-less, possess many of his virtues in varying degrees.

7. *In contrast, Jehovah is depicted in the scriptures as instructing his servants to fight against the priests of false gods, to destroy their idols and places of worship, and to thwart their advances and tactics.* In contrast, the scriptural commandment concerning righteous gods is to *be careful not to revile their names.*

8. *The scriptures repeatedly assert that members of the Godhead function according to the principles of divinely bestowed authority.* They grant their priesthood authority to others through proper ordination procedures. On the other hand, they chastise and condemn individuals who attempt to act in sacred things without proper authority. Usurpers and misusers of sacred priesthood authority are excommunicated and cast off from Gods' peoples, in modern as in ancient times. Thus, when the Psalmist refers to the LORD [Jehovah] as *"the God*

of gods" and *"the Lord of lords,"* it is properly assumed that the "gods" and "lords" over whom Jehovah presides are righteous participants in the true organizational plan established by the Godhead.

9. ***The scriptural admonitions to followers of Jehovah are to avoid and reject relationships with believers in false gods,*** *and to not participate in worship rites or partake of offerings made to pagan idols or gods.*

10. ***When scripture passages concerning Jehovah state that "thou art God alone," they are not asserting that only one being in all the vast universes and far-flung reaches of heaven is a God.*** Rather, *they are asserting that only one being holds the specific Godhood responsibility concerning **this earth**.* Thus, Jehovah, alone, is assigned as **the** God of **this** earth, even though God the Father and God the Holy Ghost frequently assist him in his administering of this earth's multiplicity of administrative affairs.

An analogy: in worldly terms, John Jones, and only John Jones, is the President of ABCDEFG Corporation. However, there are millions of other individuals who also are presidents of other corporate entities. While each of those other corporations have their own legal structures and their presidents may perform similar workplace functions as John Jones, their existence in no way precludes John Jones from being "President alone" of ABCDEFG Corporation.

Another analogy: many corporations have franchises or other related businesses functioning across the nation or worldwide, with each local unit also being governed by a president of that unit. There may be area divisions of those corporations which have area presidents. Each of those presidents are "presidents alone" for the units which are their responsibilities. This pattern also holds true for some religious organizations. Among the Latter-day Saints, for instance, there is a *First Presidency,* which presides over numerous areas; *Area Presidencies,* which preside over numerous stakes and missions; *stake presidents* and *mission presidents,* functioning within those Areas as presidents of stakes and missions, etc. Yet each of those presidents is a "president alone." In like manner, Jehovah/Jesus Christ is "a God alone," holding high authority in one or more higher administrative layers. *But the scriptures asserting that "thou art God alone" in no way indicates that there can be no other righteous, perfected, omnipotent God functioning on other worlds or in different administrative areas or layers of the vast divine organizational structure.*

Many Scriptural Passages Speak of Multiple Gods Who Are Not False Gods

Beginning with the accounts of this earth's creation in the first two chapters of Genesis, the scriptures repeatedly speak of a plurality of gods. The context of these scriptural references and allusions clearly indicate that these gods are righteous, exalted beings who are accepted in the authoritative framework in which the Godhead of this earth functions.

Genesis, chapter one, records that: • ***"God said, Let us make man in our image, after our likeness*** . . . So God created man in his own image, in the image of God created he him; male and female created he them" (Gen. 1:26–27; see Abr. 4:27).

Two chapters later, when it was observed that Adam and Eve had partaken of the fruit of the tree of knowledge of good and evil, it is recorded that • ***"the Lord God said, Behold, the man is become as one of us, to know good and evil"*** (Gen. 3:22; see also Gen. 3:1–5; and Moses 4:11).

Surely Moses, the recorder of the first five books of the Old Testament, knew of the revelations granted to his predecessor, Abraham. From the *spiritual creation* account in the Book of Abraham, one learns much concerning the plurality of Gods. Consider these brief extracts concerning "the Gods" and the many labors they performed in the creation process: • *"the Gods,* organized and formed the heavens and the earth"* (Abr. 4:1). • *"the Spirit of *the Gods* was brooding upon the face of the waters"* (Abr. 4:2). • *"they (the Gods)* said: Let there be light"* (Abr. 4:3). • *"they (the Gods)* comprehended the light"* (Abr. 4:4). • *"the Gods* also said: Let there be an expanse in the midst of the waters"* (Abr. 4:6). • *"the Gods* called the expanse, Heaven"* (Abr. 4:8). • *"the Gods* ordered, saying: Let the waters under the heaven be gathered together unto one place"* (Abr. 4:9). • *"the Gods* pronounced the dry land, Earth"* (Abr. 4:10).

• *"the Gods* saw that they were obeyed"* (Abr. 4:10). • *"the Gods* organized the earth to bring forth grass from its own seed, . . . yielding seed after his kind"* (Abr. 4:12). • *"the Gods* organized the lights in the expanse of the heaven"* (Abr. 4:14). • *"the Gods* watched those things which *they* had ordered until they obeyed"* (Abr. 4:18). • *"the Gods* said: Let *us* prepare the waters to bring forth abundantly the moving creatures that have life"* (Abr. 4:20). • *"the Gods* said: We* will bless them, and cause them to be fruitful and multiply"* (Abr. 4:22). • *"the Gods* organized the earth to bring forth the beasts after their kind"* (Abr. 4:25). • *"the Gods* took counsel among *themselves* and said: Let *us* go down and form man in *our* image, after *our* likeness"* (Abr. 4:26). • *"the Gods* said: We* will bless them. And *the Gods* said: We* will cause them to be fruitful and multiply"* (Abr. 4:28). • *"the Gods* said: We* will do everything that *we* have said, and organize them; and behold, they shall be very obedient"* (Abr. 4:31). • *"the Gods* concluded upon the seventh time, because that on the seventh time *they* would rest from all their works which *they (the Gods)* counseled among themselves to form; and sanctified it. And thus were *their* decisions at the time that *they counseled among themselves* to form the heavens and the earth"* (Abr. 5:3).

And concerning the actual *physical creation,* when the Gods' spirit-creation plans were finalized, some of the extracted phrases state: • *"the Gods* formed man from the dust of the ground, and took his spirit (that is, the man's spirit), and put it into him; and breathed into his nostrils the breath of life, and man became a living soul"* (Abr. 5:7). • *"out of the ground made *the Gods* to grow every tree that is pleasant to the sight and good for food"* (Abr. 5:9). • *"the Gods* took the man and put him in the Garden of Eden, to dress it and to keep it"* (Abr. 5:11).

• *"the Gods* said: Let *us* make an help meet for the man, for it is not good that the man should be alone, therefore *we* will form an help meet for him"* (Abr. 5:14). • *"Now I, Abraham, saw that it was after the Lord's time, which was after the time of Kolob; for as yet *the Gods* had not appointed unto Adam his reckoning"* (Abr. 5:13).

These representative extracts from Abraham's creation accounts clearly depict various beings, holding Godhood status and authority, planning and working together to bring to pass this earth's creation.

The knowledge possessed by Moses of these and other previously revealed statements concerning a multiplicity of righteous gods may have influenced Moses's understandings when he sang his jubilant song of praise unto Jehovah, proclaiming: • *"**Who is like unto thee, O Lord, among the gods? who is like thee, glorious in holiness, fearful in praises, doing wonders?**"* (Ex. 15:11). In other words, is the sense of Moses's praise: "who among the gods—who is similar to the Lord in glory, holiness, praise, and ability to do wonders—can do such things as well as the LORD"?

When one reads of Moses, in his reunion with Jethro, his father in law, he finds that • "Moses told his father in law all that the LORD had done unto Pharaoh and to the Egyptians for Israel's sake, and all the travail that had come upon them by the way, and how the LORD delivered them" (Ex. 18:8). His account undoubtedly included descriptions of the terrible plagues the LORD sent upon Egypt and the ineffectual efforts of the Egyptian priests to summon help from their false gods to counter Jehovah's miracles. His tale led Jethro to reply, • *"Now I know that the LORD is greater than all gods: for in the thing wherein they dealt proudly he was above them"* (Ex. 18:11). So the unanswered question is: Was Jethro only stating that Jehovah had power over the Egyptian Pharoah and his false Egyptian gods, or was he also asserting Jehovah's greatness over other, righteous gods as well? *Note that in Jethro's exclamation, he is attributing "greatness" to the other Gods which he is comparing with Jehovah. Presumably he would not attribute "greatness" to false gods.*

In Exodus 22:28, the LORD stipulated the divine commandment, • *"Thou shalt not revile the gods, nor curse the ruler of thy people."* This commandment seems to refer to the "good" Gods, since it links them with the Israelite rulers whom the Children of Israel were to follow and obey. *In contrast, presumably concerning the false, pagan gods, the LORD's instruction was:* • *"Make no mention of the name of other gods,* neither let it be heard out of thy mouth" (Ex. 23:13).

In other instructions given that same day the LORD revealed: • *"He that sacrificeth unto any god, save unto the LORD only, he shall be utterly destroyed"* (Ex. 22:20). *With the exception of the other members of the Godhead, "good" Gods, holding divine authority, are not called or authorized to function on this earth—it is not among their areas of jurisdiction.* Obviously, the Israelites were not to offer sacrifices to them, just as they were not to offer sacrifices to the false gods worshiped by their pagan neighbors.

In Deuteronomy, Jehovah speaks of himself, saying: • *"the LORD your God is God of gods, and Lord of lords, a great God,* a mighty, and a terrible, which regardeth not persons, nor taketh reward . . . Thou shalt fear the LORD thy God; him shalt thou serve, and to him shalt thou cleave, and swear by his name" (Deut. 10:17, 20). *The LORD, who abhors evil, obviously would not assert himself to be a God of false gods.* He might stress that he holds all power and can defeat or eradicate false gods, but *it would be completely foreign to his righteous nature to acknowledge that false gods have status among the righteous, or that he stands as their god and leader.*

The concept that Jehovah was the God and Lord of other righteous, not false pagan gods, played an important role in a conflict between various tribes of Israel, as reported in the book of Joshua. To define their allegiance to Jehovah, members of the tribes of Reuben, Gad and Manasseh proclaimed: • *"The LORD God of gods, the LORD God of gods, he knoweth,* and Israel he shall know; if it be [that we are] in rebellion, or if in transgression against the LORD (save us not this day)" (Josh. 22:22).

When King David had the Ark of the Covenant restored to its proper place in Israel, he wrote a psalm of praise to Jehovah in which he spoke of other gods who dwell in the LORD's presence.

He wrote: • "Give thanks unto the LORD, call upon his name, make known his deeds among the people. . . . *For great is the LORD, and greatly to be praised: he also is to be feared above all gods.* . . . Glory and honour are *in his presence; strength and gladness are in his place"* (1 Chr. 16:8, 25, 27). Obviously, King David was alluding to divine beings who dwell in the realms where the LORD dwells, for he stressed that they are *in his presence, . . . in his place.*" He expressly emphasized their location as being *in the heavens* by contrasting it with the earth-bound locale of false idols, saying, • "For all the gods of the people are idols: but *the LORD made the heavens"* (1 Chr. 16:26).

When King Solomon began his great temple-building project, he wrote: • "Behold, I build an house to the name of the LORD my God, to dedicate it to him, . . . And the house which I build is great: for *great is our God above all gods . . .* the heaven of heavens cannot contain him" (2 Chr. 2:4–5).

Other passages in Psalms, in addition to those cited above, make reference to other divine beings, while citing the LORD's preeminence among them by asserting that he is their king. Psalm 95:3 states that • *"the LORD is a great God, and a great King above all gods."*

Psalm 96:4 states: • *"the LORD is great, and greatly to be praised: he is to be feared above all gods."* (It should be remembered that to "fear" God meant to revere, to respect, to honor, and to obey when that term was used in Old Testament times.) So the Psalmist is actually saying, the LORD is to be revered even more than the other Gods who also deserve reverence and respect. In contrast, false gods are not to be respected nor reverenced; they are to be abhorred.

The same kind of understanding is required by Psalm 97:9: • *"thou, LORD, art high above all the earth: thou art exalted far above all gods."* Jehovah is to be exalted far above all other Gods, who also are to be exalted. And when Psalm 135:5 proclaims: • *"I know that the LORD is great, and that our Lord is above all gods,"* the implication is that all Gods are great, but Jehovah is even greater than they.

In another of the Psalms of David the King says: • I will praise thee with my whole heart: *before the gods will I sing praise unto thee . . .* for great is the glory of the LORD" (Ps. 138:1, 5).

David, it appears, was anticipating a place in the heavenly realms, where the LORD and other divine beings dwell; there he anticipated singing his praises to Jehovah—in the presence of the gods.

The book of Daniel contains several references which indicate that King Neb-uchadnezzar believed that there were multiple Gods and that Daniel's God, Jehovah, held preeminence among them. When Daniel, by revelation, interpreted his dream concerning future events, Nebuchadnezzar exclaimed, • *"Of a truth it is, that your God is a God of gods, and a Lord of kings,* and a revealer of secrets, seeing thou couldest reveal this secret" (Dan. 2:47; see also Dan. 5:14).

With the vast scriptural understanding which the Apostle Paul had obtained, and with these numerous Bible passages alluding to righteous divinities among whom Jehovah dwells and over whom he holds precedence, it is difficult to accept the typical "trinitarian" spin that his famous passage in 1 Corinthians 8:5–6 is *only* speaking of pagan gods and idols. This is the passage: • *"For though there be that are called gods, whether in heaven or in earth, (as there be gods many, and lords many,) But to us there is but one God, the Father, of whom are all things, and we in him; and one Lord Jesus Christ, by whom are all things, and we by him."*

Latter-day Saints believe that there literally are "gods many, and lords many," in numer-ous heavens and on earths "without number" (Moses 1:27–35). But they fully agree with Paul that *only the Godhead—consisting of God the Father, God the Son, and God the Holy Ghost—are ministering to this earth during its mortal probationary existence.*

Those Who Believe in Christ Can Attain Eternal Life

A basic precept of Christian doctrine is that those who gain a testimony that Jesus is the Christ may and can attain eternal life. Thousands of tracts, pamphlets, and books have been written on the multitude of ramifications of that profound sentence. They cannot be pursued in depth in this context. Cited are only a few of the numerous passages which assert the truthfulness of this basic premise: • "God so loved the world, that he gave his only begotten Son, that *whosoever believeth in him* should not perish, *but have everlasting life*" (John 3:16). • *"He that believeth on the Son hath everlasting life:* and he that believeth not the Son shall not see life; but the wrath of God abideth on him" (John 3:36). • *"Every one which seeth the Son, and believeth on him, may have everlasting life:* and I will raise him up at the last day" (John 6:40). • "He that *believeth on me hath everlasting life"* (John 6:47). • "Jesus saith unto him, I am the way, the truth, and the life: *no man cometh unto the Father, but by me"* (John 14:6). • "Thou hast given him power over all flesh, that *he should give eternal life to as many as thou hast given him.* And *this is life eternal, that they might know thee the only true God, and Jesus Christ, whom thou hast sent"* (John 17:2–3). • "And whoso *believeth* in me, and is *baptized,* the same shall be saved; and *they are they who shall inherit the kingdom of God"* (3 Ne. 11:33). • *"If ye receive me in the world, then shall ye know me, and shall receive your exaltation;* that where I am ye shall be also" (D&C 132:23).

The Riches of Eternity Are Christ's to Give to the Righteous

A key understanding of the process of man's attaining exaltation and eternal life is that, ultimately, *Jesus Christ is he who will oversee the decision-making process and will award man's eternal rewards.* He specifically asserts that • *"the heavens and the earth are in mine hands, and the riches of eternity are mine to give"* (D&C 67:2). Other passages convey this same principle: •*"Thou shalt guide me with thy counsel,* and *afterward receive me to glory. . . .* God is the strength of my heart, and *my portion for ever"* (Ps. 73:24, 26). • "Henceforth there is laid up for me *a crown of righteousness,* which *the Lord, the righteous judge, shall give me at that day: and not to me only, but unto all them also that love his appearing"* (2 Tim. 4:8). • "To him that overcometh *will I grant to sit with me in my throne,* even as I also overcame, and am set down with my Father in his throne" (Rev. 3:21). • *"Behold the Lord receiveth them up unto himself, in glory"* (Alma 14:11). • "Behold, *I, the Lord, . . . will crown the faithful with joy and with rejoicing. Behold, I am Jesus Christ, the Son of God, and I will lift them up at the last day"* (D&C 52:43–44). • "I must gather together my people, according to the parable of the wheat and the tares, that the wheat may be secured in the garners to possess eternal life, and be crowned with celestial glory, *when I shall come in the kingdom of my Father to reward every man according as his work shall be"* (D&C 101:66). • "do the things which I have commanded you, saith your Redeemer, even the Son Ahman, who prepareth all things before he taketh you; For ye are the church of the Firstborn, and *he will take you up in a cloud, and appoint every man his portion"* (D&C 78:20–21).

Eternal Life Is the Greatest of All Divine Gifts

Speaking in modern revelation, the Savior revealed a great truth as he stressed the necessity for man to keep his commandments: • "Keep my commandments in all things. And, if you keep my commandments and endure to the end *you shall have eternal life, which gift is the greatest of all the gifts of God"* (D&C 14:6–7). Other passages make reference to this eternal blessing, also labeling it as a gift.

The Apostle Paul, writing to the Romans, taught: • "But now being made free from sin, and become servants to God, ye have your fruit unto holiness, and *the end everlasting life*. For the wages of sin is death; but *the gift of God is eternal life through Jesus Christ* our Lord" (Rom. 6:22–23). The Book of Mormon prophet Helaman also described eternal life as a divine gift: • "lay up for yourselves a treasure in heaven, yea, which is eternal, and which fadeth not away; yea, that ye may have *that precious gift of eternal life*" (Hel. 5:8).

All Mortals Are Potential Gods, But Few Will Achieve Godhood

All mortal beings, since they are spirit children of God the Father, are possessed with the innate potential of becoming Gods. Several biblical passages allude to their divine potential. For instance: that same psalm which proclaims that • "GOD standeth in the congregation of the mighty; he judgeth among the gods" (Ps. 82:1) also contains the LORD's words concerning mortal beings: • "I have said, *Ye are gods; and all of you are children of the most High*" (Ps. 82:6). (Section 76 of the Doctrine and Covenants may be harkening back to the 82nd Psalm with the words • "Wherefore, *as it is written*, they are gods, even the sons of God" (D&C 76:58; see also Isa. 41:23.)

Jesus, on one occasion, was accused of blasphemy by a group of Pharisees. They sought to stone him because he asserted his Godhood unto them. In his defense, Jesus quoted the above verse from the 82nd Psalm, and provided an interpretation of its meaning, saying: • "Is it not written in your law, I said, *Ye are gods? If he called them gods, unto whom the word of God came,* and the scripture cannot be broken; Say ye of him, whom the Father hath sanctified, and sent into the world, Thou blasphemest; because I said, I am the Son of God?" (John 10:34–36).

But how many mortals will attain the exaltation and Godhood for which they have the potential? Jesus answered that query succinctly in his Sermon on the Mount, saying: • "strait is the gate, and narrow is the way, which leadeth unto life, and *few there be that find it*" (Matt. 7:14), and he continued: • *"Not every one that saith unto me, Lord, Lord, shall enter into the kingdom of heaven; but he that doeth the will of my Father which is in heaven.* Many will say to me in that day, Lord, Lord, have we not prophesied in thy name? and in thy name have cast out devils? and in thy name done many wonderful works? And then will I profess unto them, *I never knew you: depart from me, ye that work iniquity"* (Matt. 7:21–23).

Divine Sonship an Essential Aspect of Attaining Godhood

Since patriarchal orders and family relationships are integral parts of the eternal organizational plan, and since Jesus Christ ultimately is to rule over this earth in its final, celestialized state, the scriptures emphasize the sonship relationship (and, by extension, the daughtership relationship) whereby **beings from this earth who are to be exalted are adopted as sons of Jesus Christ.**

As pointed out in chapter 7, all human beings on this earth are spirit children of God the Father. Yet the Father has placed all mankind in the care of His Firstborn Son, Jesus Christ, and appointed Him the role of Father of all who will accept His gospel and partake of His atoning sacrifice. Thus, an integral part of the plan of progression is that when mortal beings believe in Christ and are baptized into his Church, they become his adopted children. Jesus becomes, and is, the adoptive father of all who truly come unto him and accept him as their Savior.

As part of the plan, those who become adopted children of Christ are accounted as

His heirs and also stand as joint-heirs with Christ with the same eternal entitlements and potentials as He has attained. Both the Apostles Paul and John write of this adoptive relationship in their New Testament works: • *"As many as are led by the Spirit of God, they are the sons of God. . . . ye have received the Spirit of adoption, whereby we cry, Abba, Father. The Spirit itself beareth witness with our spirit, that **we are the children of God: And if children, then heirs; heirs of God, and joint-heirs with Christ;** if so be that we suffer with him, that we may be also glorified together. For I reckon that the sufferings of this present time are not worthy to be compared with the glory which shall be revealed in us"* (Rom. 8:14–18). • *"God sent forth his Son, . . . To redeem them that were under the law, that we might receive the adoption of sons. And because ye are sons,* God hath sent forth the Spirit of his Son into your hearts, crying, Abba, Father. Wherefore **thou art no more a servant, but a son; and if a son, then an heir of God through Christ"** (Gal. 4:4–7). • "Beloved, *now are we the sons of God,* and it doth not yet appear what we shall be: but we know that, when he shall appear, *we shall be like him;* for we shall see him as he is. And *every man that hath this hope in him purifieth himself, even as he is pure"* (1 Jn. 3:2–3).

The Pearl of Great Price asserts the same message: • "And thou art after the order of him who was without beginning of days or end of years, from all eternity to all eternity. ***Behold, thou art one in me, a son of God; and thus may all become my sons"*** (Moses 6:67–68).

The Doctrine and Covenants also teaches that exalted mortals will be made equal with Jesus: • "And then shall the angels be crowned with the glory of his might, and ***the saints shall be filled with his glory, and receive their inheritance and be made equal with him"*** (D&C 88:107).

Christ Shall Rule Over the Exalted Righteous of This Earth as Both God and Father

Paul, when writing of the future role of the Savior, said: • *"Christ Jesus: Who, being in the form of God, thought it not robbery* **to be equal with God . . . Wherefore God also** *hath highly exalted him,* and given him a name which is above every name: That at the name of Jesus every knee should bow, of things in heaven, and things in earth, and things under the earth; And that every tongue should confess that **Jesus Christ is Lord, to the glory of God the Father. . . . That ye be blameless and harmless, the sons of God"** (Phil. 2:5–6, 9–11, 15).

The Lord, himself, spoke of the dual Father/God role he will play: • "I am Alpha and Omega, the beginning and the end. I will give unto him that is athirst of the fountain of the water of life freely. **He that overcometh shall inherit all things; and I will be his God, and he shall be my son"** (Rev. 21:6–7).

The Blessings of Exaltation and Eternal Life

Entire volumes have been written on this topic, and it can only be covered here with brevity.

Eight very informative scriptural passages concerning the many blessings of exaltation and eternal life will be cited here, and then a representative list will be extracted from those passages. That will have to suffice in this context.

Passage Number One: D&C 76:5–10

I, the Lord, am merciful and gracious unto those who fear me, and delight to honor those who serve me in righteousness and in truth unto the end.

Great shall be their reward and eternal shall be their glory.

And to them will I reveal all mysteries, yea, all the hidden mysteries of my kingdom from days of old, and for ages to come, will I make known unto them the good pleasure of my will concerning all things pertaining to my kingdom.

Yea, even the wonders of eternity shall they know, and things to come will I show them, even the things of many generations.

And their wisdom shall be great, and their understanding reach to heaven; and before them the wisdom of the wise shall perish, and the understanding of the prudent shall come to naught.

For by my Spirit will I enlighten them, and by my power will I make known unto them the secrets of my will—yea, even those things which eye has not seen, nor ear heard, nor yet entered into the heart of man. (D&C 76:5–10)

Passage Number Two: D&C 76:50–70

This is the testimony of the gospel of Christ concerning them who shall come forth in the resurrection of the just—

They are they who received the testimony of Jesus, and believed on his name and were baptized after the manner of his burial, being buried in the water in his name, and this according to the commandment which he has given—

That by keeping the commandments they might be washed and cleansed from all their sins, and receive the Holy Spirit by the laying on of the hands of him who is ordained and sealed unto this power;

And who overcome by faith, and are sealed by the Holy Spirit of promise, which the Father sheds forth upon all those who are just and true.

They are they who are the church of the Firstborn.

They are they into whose hands the Father has given all things—

They are they who are priests and kings, who have received of his fulness, and of his glory;

And are priests of the Most High, after the order of Melchizedek, which was after the order of Enoch, which was after the order of the Only Begotten Son.

Wherefore, as it is written, *they are gods, even the sons of God—*

Wherefore, *all things are theirs, whether life or death, or things present, or things to come, all are theirs and they are Christ's, and Christ is God's.*

And they shall overcome all things.

Wherefore, let no man glory in man, but rather let him glory in God, who shall subdue all enemies under his feet.

These shall dwell in the presence of God and his Christ forever and ever.

These are they whom he shall bring with him, when he shall come in the clouds of heaven to reign on the earth over his people.

These are they who shall have part in the first resurrection.

These are they who shall come forth in the resurrection of the just.

These are they who are come unto Mount Zion, and unto the city of the living God, the heavenly place, the holiest of all.

These are they who have come to an innumerable company of angels, to the general assembly and church of Enoch, and of the Firstborn.

These are they whose names are written in heaven, where God and Christ are the judge of all.

These are they who are just men made perfect through Jesus the mediator of the new covenant, who wrought out this perfect atonement through the shedding of his own blood.

These are they whose bodies are celestial, whose glory is that of the sun, even the glory of God, the highest of all, whose glory the sun of the firmament is written of as being typical. (D&C 76:50–70)

Passage Number Three: D&C 78:15–22

That you may come up unto the crown prepared for you, and be made rulers over many kingdoms, saith the Lord God, the Holy One of Zion, who hath established the foundations of Adam-ondi-Ahman;

Who hath appointed Michael your prince, and established his feet, and set him upon high, and given unto him the keys of salvation under the counsel and direction of the Holy One, who is without beginning of days or end of life.

Verily, verily, I say unto you, ye are little children, and ye have not as yet understood *how great blessings the Father hath in his own hands and prepared for you;*

And ye cannot bear all things now; nevertheless, be of good cheer, for I will lead you along. *The kingdom is yours and the blessings thereof are yours, and the riches of eternity are yours.*

And he who receiveth all things with thankfulness shall be made glorious; and the things of this earth shall be added unto him, even an hundred fold, yea, more.

Wherefore, do the things which I have commanded you, saith your Redeemer, even the Son Ahman, who prepareth all things before he taketh you;

For ye are the church of the Firstborn, and he will take you up in a cloud, and appoint every man his portion.

And he that is a faithful and wise steward *shall inherit all things.* (D&C 78:15–22)

Passage Number Four: D&C 84:35–40

All they who receive this priesthood receive me, saith the Lord;

For he that receiveth my servants receiveth me;

And he that receiveth me receiveth my Father;

And he that receiveth my Father receiveth my Father's kingdom; *therefore all that my Father hath shall be given unto him.*

And this is according to the oath and covenant which belongeth to the priesthood.

Therefore, all those who receive the priesthood, *receive this oath and covenant of my Father,* which he cannot break, neither can it be moved. (D&C 84:35–40)

Passage Number Five: D&C 109:76

• "That our garments may be pure, *that we may be clothed upon with robes of righteousness, with palms in our hands, and crowns of glory upon our heads, and reap eternal joy* for all our sufferings" (D&C 109:76).

Passage Number Six: D&C 130:1–2

• "When the Savior shall appear we shall see him as he is. We shall see that he is a man like ourselves. *And that same sociality which exists among us here will exist among us there, only it will be coupled with eternal glory,* which glory we do not now enjoy" (D&C 130:1–2).

Passage Number Seven: D&C 132:19–20

And again, verily I say unto you, if a man marry a wife by my word, which is my law, and by the new and everlasting covenant, and it is sealed unto them by the

Holy Spirit of promise, by him who is anointed, unto whom I have appointed this power and the keys of this priesthood; and it shall be said unto them—*Ye shall come forth in the first resurrection;* and if it be after the first resurrection, in the next resurrection; and *shall inherit thrones, kingdoms, principalities, and powers, dominions, all heights and depths*—then shall it be written in the Lamb's Book of Life, that he shall commit no murder whereby to shed innocent blood, and if ye abide in my covenant, and commit no murder whereby to shed innocent blood, *it shall be done unto them in all things whatsoever my servant hath put upon them, in time, and through all eternity;* and shall be of full force when they are out of the world; and *they shall pass by the angels, and the gods,* which are set there, *to their exaltation and glory in all things,* as hath been sealed upon their heads, *which glory shall be a fulness and a continuation of the seeds forever and ever.*

Then shall they be gods, because they have no end; therefore shall they be from everlasting to everlasting, because they continue; then shall they be above all, because *all things are subject unto them.* **Then shall they be gods,** because *they have all power,* and *the angels are subject unto them.* (D&C 132:19–20)

Passage Number Eight: D&C 132:37

• "Abraham received concubines, and they bore him children; and it was accounted unto him for righteousness, because they were given unto him, and he abode in my law; as Isaac also and Jacob did none other things than that which they were commanded; and because they did none other things than that which they were commanded, *they have entered into their exaltation, according to the promises, and sit upon thrones, and are not angels but are gods"* (D&C 132:37).

A Listing of Many of the Blessings of Exaltation and Godhood

This book is about the attributes, powers, and blessings of the three members of the Godhead.

However, if mortals who achieve exaltation are to become joint-heirs with Christ, and to be made equal to Him, and to receive all that the Father has, then this list appears to be valid descriptions of the nature of the Godhood possessed by this earth's Godhead members as well as the Godhood that is promised to mankind who reach the same exalted status.

Here are the lists extracted from the eight passages cited above:

Their previous accomplishments:
1. They received the testimony of Jesus
2. They believed on His name
3. They were baptized after the manner of His burial
4. They were washed and cleansed from all their sins
5. They received the Holy Spirit by the laying on of the hands from those ordained and sealed unto this power
6. They overcame by faith
7. They were sealed by the Holy Spirit of promise
8. They were just and true
9. They were faithful and wise stewards
10. They received the priesthood, the Lord, and the Father
11. They received the oath and covenant of the Priesthood
12. They married by the Lord's word and law

13. They married by the new and everlasting covenant
14. Their marriages were sealed unto them by the Holy Spirit of promise
15. Their names are written in the Lamb's Book of Life

Their eternal rewards:

1. Great shall be their reward
2. Eternal shall be their glory
3. To them the Lord will reveal all mysteries
   a. All the hidden mysteries of His kingdom from days of old, and for ages to come
   b. The good pleasure of His will concerning all things pertaining to His kingdom
   c. They shall know the wonders of eternity
   d. The Lord will show them things to come, even the things of many generations
4. Their wisdom shall be great
5. Their understanding shall reach to heaven
6. The wisdom of the wise shall perish before them
7. The understanding of the prudent shall come to naught before them
8. They will be enlightened by the Spirit of the Lord
9. The Lord will make known unto them the secrets of His will by His power
   a. those things which eye has not seen, nor ear heard
   b. those things nor yet entered into the heart of man
10. They shall come forth in the resurrection of the just
11. They shall have part in the first resurrection
12. They are members of the church of the Firstborn
13. The Father has given all things into their hands
14. They are priests and kings
15. They have received of the Father's fulness and of His glory
16. They are priests of the Most High, after the order of Melchizedek
17. They are gods
18. They are the sons of God
19. All things are theirs, whether in life or death
    a. things present
    b. things to come
20. They are Christ's, and Christ is God's
21. They shall overcome all things
22. They shall dwell in the presence of God and His Christ forever and ever
23. Christ shall bring them with Him when He comes to reign over His people on earth
24. They shall come unto Mount Zion
25. They shall come unto the city of the living God, the heavenly place, the holiest of all
26. They shall come to an innumerable company of angels
27. They shall come to the general assembly and church of Enoch, and of the Firstborn
28. Their names are written in heaven, where God and Christ are the judge of all
29. They are just men made perfect through Jesus the mediator of the new covenant
30. Their bodies are celestial
31. Their glory is that of the sun

32. Theirs is the glory of God, the highest of all
33. They will be made rulers over many kingdoms
34. The kingdom is theirs
35. The blessings of the kingdom are theirs
36. The riches of eternity are theirs
37. They shall inherit all things
38. They shall be made glorious
39. They will receive the Father's kingdom
40. They will receive all that the Father has
41. They will be clothed with robes of righteousness
42. They will receive palms in their hands
43. They will receive crowns of glory upon their heads
44. They will reap eternal joy for all their sufferings
45. They will see the Savior when He appears
36. They will receive sociality coupled with eternal glory
47. They shall inherit thrones
48. They shall inherit kingdoms
49. They shall inherit principalities
50. They shall inherit powers
51. They shall inherit dominions
52. They shall inherit all heights and depths
53. They shall pass by the angels and the gods to their exaltation and glory in all things
54. They shall have a fulness and a continuation of the seeds forever and ever
55. Then shall they be gods, because they have no end
56. They shall be from everlasting to everlasting, because they continue
57. All things shall be subject unto them
58. They shall be above all
59. They shall have all power
60. The angels shall be subject unto them
61. They sit upon thrones
62. They are not angels, but are gods
63. They have entered into their exaltation

Summary

1. The scriptures repeatedly assert that there are numerous Gods, doing so in contexts that represent those Gods as being righteous beings—exalted entities worthy to associate with members of the Godhead.
2. Various scriptures compare Jehovah with these other Gods, asserting His superlative status over and among them.
3. Jehovah/Jesus Christ is a God of Gods and Lord of Lords.
4. When reading the scriptures, one needs to discern between (1) various false gods of ancient times, and (2) righteous beings who have attained Godhood status.
5. Scriptural insights which aid in discerning between "good" Gods and "false" gods are presented:
   A. The false gods of ancient scriptures were fictitious entities, though they sometimes reached mythological proportions. False priests created illusions of their existence, recruited widespread support for those illusions, and in some

cases managed to beguile hundreds of thousands to worship the nonexistent beings which they proclaimed to be deities.

B. Members of the Godhead are righteous: they abhor sin. They do not associate with evil beings. In particular, they have no association with false, nonexistent gods.

C. In contrast, Godhead members are portrayed in the scriptures as associating with, and ruling over, or with "good" Gods.

D. "Good" Gods worship and do obeisance to Godhead members.

E. Since they are nonexistent, evil Gods neither worship nor obey Godhead members. However, the false priests who lead beguiled worshipers astray in this names fight against Godhead members.

F. Jehovah is depicted in the scriptures as being more advanced than other "good" Gods who apparently have His same virtues in lesser degrees.

G. Jehovah instructs His servants to vigorously oppose the priests of false gods, to destroy their idols and places of worship, and to thwart their advances and tactics.

H. The scriptures repeatedly assert that members of the Godhead function according to the principles of divinely bestowed authority. Good Gods are portrayed or alluded to as participating in or performing righteous acts. The priests of false, nonexistent gods are portrayed as opposing true priesthood authority.

I. The scriptural admonitions to followers of Jehovah are to avoid and reject relationships with believers in false gods, to not participate in their worship rites, and not to partake of offerings made to pagan idols or gods.

J. When scripture passages concerning Jehovah state that "thou art God alone," they are not asserting that only one being in all the vast universes and far-flung reaches of the heavens is a God. Rather, they are asserting that only one being holds the specific Godhood responsibility concerning this earth. Thus, Jehovah, alone, is *the* God of *this* earth, even though God the Father and God the Holy Ghost frequently assist Him in His administering of this earth's multiplicity of administrative affairs.

6. Numerous biblical passages allude to Gods who share righteous attributes, perform righteous actions, and who function with the approbation of Jehovah.

7. Latter-day Saints agree with Paul's teaching that "there be gods many, and lords many," but they fully agree with Paul that only the Godhead—consisting of God the Father, God the Son, and God the Holy Ghost—are ministering to this earth during its mortal probationary existence.

8. Numerous scriptures assert that those who believe in Christ can attain eternal life.

9. Jesus Christ is the Godhead member designated to pronounce the blessings of eternal life upon worthy candidates, and to assign them to responsibilities and locales in Heavenly Father's glorious realms.

10. As spirit children of God the Father, all mortals have the seeds of Godhood within them. However, Jesus taught that "strait is the gate, and narrow is the way, which leadeth unto life, and few there be that find it."

11. Divine sonship is an essential aspect of attaining Godhood. God the Father placed all His spirit children in the custodial responsibility of Jesus. When they

come unto Him and accept His gospel through true repentance and authorized baptism, they become adopted sons and daughters of Christ.

12. Adopted children of Christ become joint heirs with Him, and if righteous, will be entitled to inherit the same eternal blessings to which Jesus is entitled.

13. Jehovah/Jesus Christ will rule over the exalted righteous of this earth in the dual role as both their God and their Father.

14. The blessings of Godhood are glorious and numerous. Based on eight basic scriptural passages, 15 of them are listed under the heading "Their previous accomplishments." Sixty-three others are listed under the heading "Their eternal rewards." Combined, they present a useful summation of the eternal blessings, privileges, and capabilities of exaltation and Godhood.

THE SCRIPTURAL NAMES OF THE GODHEAD MEMBERS IN THE BIBLE

Gaining an in-depth understanding the names of Deity in the four standard works of the Church is a challenging task. The challenges presented by the names of God in the Old and New Testaments are very different from those pertaining to the names of Godhead members in the Book of Mormon, Doctrine and Covenants, and the Pearl of Great Price.

This chapter will be devoted to understanding the names of Deity in the Bible; the next chapter will deal with names of Deity in the other three Latter-day Saint scriptures.

The Primary Names of God in the Old Testament Explained

The four most-used names of Godhead members in the Old Testament are:

Elohim—God(s). (Gen. 1:1, 3, 4, 5, 6; appears thousands of times in the Bible).

Jehovah—LORD. (Gen. 2:4, 5, 7, 8, 9, 15; appears thousands of times in the Bible).

Adonai—Lord/Master. (Gen. 15:2, 8; Ex. 23:17; Deut. 3:24; 9:26; appears hundreds of times in the Bible).

El—The Strong One. (Gen. 14:18; Num. 23:22; appears hundreds of times in the Bible).

Each of these four names were used extensively in the Hebrew scriptures. What follows is a detailed explanation of each of them in outline form.

God(s) (*Hebrew: Elohim*) [*Pronounced: el-lo-HEEM*]

A. Elohim is a plural noun (the last two letters *im* represent a plural ending), and is sometimes translated in the plural: • "And *God* said, Let *us* make man in our image, after *our* likeness" (Gen. 1:26), • "And the LORD *God* said, Behold, the man is become as one of *us*, to know good and evil" (Gen. 3:22), • "let *us* go down, and there confound their language" (Gen. 11:7).

B. The term Elohim occurs about 3,000 times in the Bible. In over 2,300 of these references the term is applied to the being Christians identify as "God." (In about 700 places it is used in a secondary sense meaning idols, men, angels, judges, etc., where the ideas of might or authority are intended.)

C. Though a plural noun, Elohim is often used with a singular verb and/or adjective (as when the terms "the righteous" or "the living" are used). This has caused considerable interpretational conjecture, over the centuries, with meanings ascribed based on the personal beliefs of the various interpreters. Though these interpretations are sometimes quoted as fact, their "factual" nature should be regarded with considerable caution. The following, drawn primarily from "trinitarian" sources, are "interpretational theories" and should be perceived only as "theories," not "facts."

1. The use of the plural noun Elohim is an intimation of the three-in-one trinity.
2. The use of the plural noun Elohim is a plural of majesty, dignity or excellence such as that attributed to rulers and kings (but such use of the plural apparently was not employed in biblical times).
3. The use of the plural noun Elohim is a plural of intensity, to give the word stronger meaning (an interpretation doubted or rejected by many).
4. The use of the plural noun Elohim is an indication that God has combined in himself all the attributes which the heathens distributed over their numerous deities.
5. The use of the plural noun Elohim shows the enlargement of His vision and development of character over time.
6. The use of the plural noun Elohim is usually employed as an indication that God, or the Gods, is/are under the obligation of a premortal oath to perform certain conditions.

These "interpretational theories" appear in various theological treatises, sometimes even represented as "facts," but they remain "theories" and should be regarded only as such.

D. Though the word Elohim is always translated as the generic term "God" in the *King James Version*, it does not necessarily refer, consistently, to any single member of the Godhead. In most cases it has reference to Jehovah, the premortal name of Jesus Christ.

E. Though it is sometimes used as a "substitute proper name" for God the Father in Latter-day Saint literature, it is not a "given name" (like "Jehovah" or "Jesus"). Rather, it is a title of honor and respect (like "President" or "Governor").

F. *Allah* is an Arabian form of the Hebrew terms Elohim and Eloah. [*Pronounced: Ah-LAW*]

Jehovah (*English*: LORD). (See further discussion concerning this name throughout this appendix.)

A. This name has been distinguished in Jewish Rabbinical writings by euphemistic expressions such as "*The* Name," "The Distinguished Name," "The Great And Terrible Name," "The Holy Name," "The Incommunicate Name," "The Ineffable Name," "The Name of Four Letters," "The Peculiar Name," "The Separate Name," and "The Unutterable Name."

B. The exact pronunciation of the name is unsure, but mainline Hebrew translators have agreed that it probably is "Yahveh," "Yahweh," or "Yahve." They also agree that "Jehovah" may not be an altogether correct rendering of the name, but they have declined to substitute a different form because the name "Jehovah" has become familiar and has widespread usage.

C. It was called "The Name of Four Letters," or the "Tetragrammaton" ["four-letter name"] because the translation of the Hebrew letters is YHVH in English. The Jewish rabbis had so much reverence for this name that they refrained from pronouncing it, or even writing it, as much as possible. Why? See • "he that blasphemeth the name of the LORD, he shall surely be put to death, and all the congregation shall certainly stone him: as well the stranger, as he that is born in the land, when he blasphemeth the name of the LORD, shall be put to death" (Lev. 24:16).

D. The name occurs about 7,000 times in the Old Testament; about 700 times in the book of Psalms alone.

E. The name "Jehovah" is generally printed in small capitals (LORD) in the King James Version. The name remains as "Jehovah" in the American Standard Version (ASV).

F. The word "LORD" is distinguished from other Hebrew words translated as Lord (initial capital followed by *lower-case* letters). "LORD" is always applied to the word "Jehovah," but "Lord" is typically perceived as having other meanings; it sometimes also is applied to "Jehovah."

G. The words translated into English as "LORD," "Lord," and "lord" convey very different shades of meaning in both Hebrew and Greek.

H. The name is derived from the Hebrew verb "Havah," which means "to be," or "being."

I. When the words "Jehovah" and "Elohim" are combined, the entire God-head may sometimes be implied. It should be remembered, however, that in the Old Testament a concept of the other two Godhead members (God the Father and God the Holy Spirit) had not yet been revealed to the people at large.

J. Portions of the name "Jehovah" are combined into other personal names found in the Bible, like Jesus, Jehu, Jehiel, Jehoahaz, Jehoiada, etc., though the names "Jehovah" and "Jesus" are generally considered too sacred to be used as names for human beings in the English-speaking world. In some other languages, such as Spanish, however, the name "Jesus" is frequently used as a Christian name.

Master, Lord (*Hebrew: Adonai*) [*Pronounced: a-do-NAI*]

A. "Adonai" is an intensive plural of the Hebrew "Adon," meaning "master" or "lord."

B. The term appears about 300 times in the Old Testament as a name of Deity, and another 215 times in a more general sense where it is translated "Master," "Lord," or "Sir." The expression "Lord of lords" (Deut. 10:17) could appropriately be translated "Master of masters."

C. Because of their reluctance to write the name "Jehovah" as they made their copies, ancient Jewish scriptural copyists would substitute the "less awful" name of "Adonai," which to them meant "my ruler."

D. The word "Adonai" (or "Adonai-Jehovah") carries other related meanings when used in the scriptures, such as:

   1. *Authority*: identifying the word of God: • "Thus saith the LORD God of Israel" (Ex. 5:1).

2. **Power**: • "Trust ye in the LORD for ever: for in the LORD JEHOVAH is everlasting strength" (Isa. 26:4).
3. **Deity**: • "my God [*Elohim*] and my Lord [*Adonai*], (Ps. 35:23, see 38:15, John 20:28).
4. **Reverence**: • Daniel, as he confessed his nation's sin: "O Lord, hear; O Lord, forgive; O Lord, hearken and do; defer not, for thine own sake, O my God: for thy city and thy people are called by thy name" (Dan. 9:19).
5. **Relationship**: • "Thou art my Lord [*Adonai*]" (Ps. 16:2).
6. **Responsibility**: When Isaiah • "heard the voice of the Lord, saying, Whom shall I send, and who will go for us?" (Isa. 6:8), he responded, "Here am I; send me" (Isa. 6:8) and then asked "Lord [*Adonai*], how long?" (Isa. 6:11).

D. "Adonai" is sometimes compounded with "Jehovah" to mean "Lord Jehovah," which conveys the meaning that Jehovah is master and husband over His people Israel. (See Ezek. 16:8 and 16:30: "Lord GOD").

E. "Adonai" often appears in a compound with a portion of Jehovah when used as a proper given name, such as "Adoni-jah," meaning "Jehovah is LORD."

F. Heathen nations used this title in connection with their pagan gods (for instance, "Adonis" among the Phoenicians). It is similar to "Baal," which also implies "master" or "owner."

The Strong One (*Hebrew: EL*)

A. Some scholars believe that this is the root word from which Elohim is derived. It is the most primitive Semitic name. Its root meaning is probably "to be strong."

B. Though translated about 250 times as God in the KJV, the term is mainly poetical in its nature. It appears to have been used particularly in passages where indicating the great power of God is intended.

C. Examples of its use in the KJV: • "Melchizedek king of Salem . . . was the priest of the most high **God**" (Gen. 14:18). • "**God** brought them out of Egypt" (Num. 23:22). • "the LORD [*Jehovah*] your God [*Elohim*] is God of gods, and Lord of lords, a great **God** [*El*], a mighty, and a terrible" (Deut. 10:17). • "when Abram was ninety years old and nine, the LORD [*Jehovah*] appeared to Abram, and said unto him, I am the Almighty **God** [*El*]; walk before me, and be thou perfect" (Gen. 17:1). • "And God said unto him [Jacob], I am **God** Almighty: be fruitful and multiply" (Gen. 35:11). • "For unto us a child is born, . . . and his name shall be called Wonderful, Counsellor, The mighty **God** [El]" (Isa. 9:6).

D. When Christ, in His agony on the cross, cried Eloi, Eloi ("My God, My God"), He apparently was praying to El: "My Strength, My Strength." (Mark 15:34; see Ps. 22:1)

E. El is frequently combined with adjectives or nouns that express phrases or attributes which, by frequent usage, have become names or titles of God: Isra-*el*, *El*-elohe-Israel [House of Israel], Peni-*el*, Face of *El*, Prince of *El*, *El* Shaddai. (Jacob's blessing to his son, Joseph: • " Even by the **God** [El] of thy father, who shall help thee; and by the Almighty [*Shaddai*], who shall bless thee" Gen. 49:25.)

F. El is part of many biblical names: *Eli*akim, *Eli*hu, *Eli*melech, *Eli*sha, *Eli*za-beth, Michael.

G. El is often used for the word "God" when virtues are being described: Gen. 17:1 [Almighty *God*]; 21:33 [everlasting *God*]; Ex. 20:3–5 [jealous *God*]; Deut. 4:24 [*God* is a consuming fire]; 4:31 [merciful *God*]; 7:9 [faithful *God*]; Josh. 3:10 [living *God*]; Neh. 1:5 [terrible *God*]; Jonah 4:2 [gracious *God*].

Capitalization of the Names of God in the King James Version of the Bible

Old Testament Hebrew had no differences in type styles to allow for capitals, italics, etc. They were introduced by Sebastian Munster of Basel, Switzerland, in a Latin version published in 1534. The example was followed in several other translations, such as the *Geneva Bible* (1560), and the *Bishops Bible* (1568). The most extensive uses of special type styles appear in the *Authorized* or *King James Version* of 1611. There the translators used various combinations of capital letters to communicate the different meanings and interpretations of the names of God. Other English Bible translations followed the practice. Those who recognize this use of capitals can gain insight into the nature of God and how He relates to his people, even without knowing the original language. Following is a guide to the use of these capitals in the *King James Version:*

God (first letter capitalized)—Elohim or related words such as *El* and *Elohe*, the standard term for deity in many world religions.

God (first letter capitalized, last two letters in small capitals)—This is the word *Jehovah* (Lord), as it appears when preceded with Adonai (Lord). Apparently the translators thought it would be awkward to translate Adonai Jehovah "Lord Lord," so they kept *Adonai* as Lord and translated *Jehovah* (JHVH or YHWH) as "God"—hence, Lord God." When used in this combination, the term implies a headship relationship as that between a master and a slave, rather than emphasizing the self-revealing aspects of the name Jehovah.

GOD (all three letters capitals)—This is the Hebrew word *El*, which is a derivative of *Elohim*. This title shows God in all his strength and power. It could be rendered God the Omnipotent (see Ps. 63:1).

Lord (first letter capitalized, last three letters in small capitals)—This is *Jehovah* (or *Yahweh*), the Self-existent and Self-revealing Deity. He is the One who was, who is and who is to come. Because He reveals Himself to man, He thus forms a relationship with His people. Hence, Jehovah is known as the Covenant-keeping Deity.

JAH (all letters capitalized)—The word JAH (or YAH) appears 49 times in the Hebrew text, but is translated JAH only once in the King James Version (Ps. 68:4). *JAH* is a shortened form of the name Jehovah (or Yahweh), with emphasis on only one aspect of the name—salvation is to come. The full name, Jehovah, emphasizes past, present and future—"He who was, who is and who is to come." Most modern versions translate *JAH* Lord, since it is a derivative of Jehovah.

JEHOVAH (all letters capitalized)—God's name is printed in capitals (in Psalm. 83:18). Usually it is translated Lord. Perhaps it is emphasized here because it directly relates to what the name means: Whose name alone is JEHOVAH.

Lord (only the first letter capitalized)—This is *Adonai* (Lord/Master), a term carrying the meaning of headship, such as a master who is over a slave. God is the Lord who rules over His servants.

God Almighty (first letter of both words capitalized)—This is *El Shaddai*, God who is the source of strength and comfort. The emphasis is not on God's creative power so much as His power to supply man's needs.

Most High God (first letters capitalized)—This is *El Elyon*, God who possesses heaven and earth. This term is often used in relation to the Gentiles (see Deut. 32:8). It is used throughout the book of Daniel, which is set in a Gentile land. It is shortened to "most High" (first letter in "most" lower case, first letter in "High" capitalized) in Daniel 4:17, 24,25, 32, 34. It is printed lower case ("most high") in Daniel 3:26 and 5:18, 21. In Genesis 14:8–22, where the name is first introduced in Scripture, only "God" is capitalized ("most high God").

The Lord Most High (each word beginning with a capital, and the three last letters of Lord in small capitals)—though the most common title is Most High God (*El Elyon*), a few references are to Jehovah Most High (see Ps. 7:17). Jehovah is used here because His covenant people are exhorted to praise Him.

Lord God (only the first letter of Lord is capitalized, and God is printed with an initial capital followed by small capitals)—This is *Adonai Jehovah* (or *Yahweh*). While Jehovah is ordinarily printed "Lord," it would be awkward to translate the phrase "Lord, Lord" (see under God). "Abram said, Lord God (*Adonai Yahweh*), what wilt thou give me . . .?" (Gen. 15:2).

God the Lord (initial capital followed by small capitals for God; and only the first letter capitalized in Lord)—Again, the name God is *Jehovah* (or *Yahweh*) in the original followed by *Adonai*, but the translators wanted to avoid the repetition of "Lord the Lord." Here, however, the context seems to call for repetition for emphasis: "God the God (*El . . . El*) . . . Lord the Lord (*Yahweh Adonai*).

Random Capitalization

The following phrases were capitalized to show the importance the King James translators gave to the name of God. Many modern scholars find no basis for printing the titles in capitals, except to show respect for the names and qualities of the Deity.

I AM THAT I AM (Exod. 3:14).

I AM (Ex. 3:14).

JEHOVAH (Exod. 6:3, Ps. 83:18; Isa. 26:4).

HOLINESS TO THE LORD (Ex. 28:36).

THE LORD THY GOD (Deut. 28:58).

THE LORD OUR RIGHTEOUSNESS (Jer. 23:6).

BRANCH (Zech. 3:8; 6:12).

(This section was adapted from Towns, *My Father's Names*, Appendix B, 165–68.)

Explanations About the Name "Jehovah" and the Tetragrammaton

Interesting insights concerning this holy name can be gleaned from various Bible dictionaries.

One of the most easily understood explanations is found in the *Bible Dictionary* bound with the Latter-day Saint Bible. Under the heading "Jehovah" it states:

> *The covenant or proper name of the God of Israel.* It denotes the "Unchangeable One," "the eternal I AM" (Ex. 6:3; Ps. 83:18; Isa. 12:2; 26:4). The original pronunciation of this name has possibly been lost, as the Jews, in reading, never mentioned it, but substituted one of the other names of God, usually Adonai. Probably it was pronounced Jahveh, or Yahveh. In the KJV, the Jewish custom has been followed, and the name is generally denoted by Lord or God, printed in small capitals.

Jehovah is the premortal Jesus Christ and came to earth being born of Mary (see Mosiah 13:28; 15:1; 3 Ne. 15:1–5; D&C 110:1–10). Although Ex. 6:3 states that the God of Israel was not known by the name Jehovah before Moses' time, latter-day revelation tells us otherwise. (Abr. 1:16; 2:8; cf JST Ex. 6:3; see also Gen. 22:14)

The Evangelical Dictionary of Theology, in its article "**Tetragrammaton**," supplies more historical information:

> **Tetragrammaton.** The designation for the four (*tetra*) letters (*grammata*) in the Hebrew Bible for the name of the God of Israel, *yhwh*. The name was God's particular revelation to Moses and the Israelites (Exod. 6:2–3). It signifies that the God of Israel, unlike pagan deities, is present with his people to deliver them, to fulfill his promises to them, and to grant them his blessings. The pronunciation of the tetragrammaton *yhwh* was lost when the Jews avoided its usage for fear of desecrating the holy name (cf. Exod. 20:7). In OT times the name was pronounced and was at times used in theophoric names, which can be recognized in our Bibles by the prefixes Jo- or Jeho- (cf. *Jo*nathan and *Jeho*iada) and the suffix -jah (Adoni*jah*). The pronunciation fell into disuse after the Exile when the Jews began to pay careful attention to the practice of the law. (Ewell, *Evangelical Dictionary of Theology,* 1079–80)

Information was also given as to **how the name Jehovah has been handled in various English translations during the past century**: "The ASV of 1901 adopted the practice of using the name 'Jehovah' whereas most English versions continued the established practice of translating the tetragrammaton by LORD (capital letters) to distinguish it from 'Lord'" (*Adonai*) (Ewell, 1080).

Concerning **the meaning of the name Jehovah** as it is derived from the Tetragrammathon, the articles continues:

> Many scholars accept the widely held opinion that the tetragrammaton is a form of the root *hyh* ("be") and **should be pronounced as "Yahweh"** ("He who brings into being"; cf. Exod. 3:12, "I will be with you" and "I will be who I will be," vs. 14). Regardless of the editorial decision of substituting LORD for *yhwh* or of using the divine name "Yahweh," *the reader must keep in mind that LORD, Yahweh, or yhwh is the name of God that he revealed to his ancient people.* In reading the text of the OT, one should develop a feeling for the usage of the name itself over against such usages as "God" or "Lord" (Exod. 3:15; 6:3; Pss. 102:16, 22;113:1–3; 135:1–6; 148:5, 13). (Ewell, 1080)

Another useful dictionary, the *Expository Dictionary of Bible Words,* adds other valuable insights. Under the heading "LORD" it says, concerning the Hebrew derivations of the Tetragrammaton:

> *Two Hebrew words are translated "lord" in the OT. 'Ādôn* means "lord" in the sense of a superior, master, or owner. It is also used as a term of respect. *'Ādôn* is generally found in the OT in reference to human beings (e.g., Ge 18:12; 19:2; 24; 1 Sa. 16:16). But at times, especially in a series of names such as "the LORD, the God of Israel" it is used of God. A special intensified form, *ʰdōnāy,* is found over three hundred times in the OT, and this plural form refers only to God. Where *'ādôn* or *ʾdōnāy* refers to God, *the English versions show it by capitalizing the first letter,* Lord.
>
> The other Hebrew word translated "Lord" is *Yâhweh, God's revealed personal name.* **This name occurs 5,321 times in the OT in this form, and 50 more times in the poetic form Yâh.** *Yâhweh* is particularly significant, and when it occurs, most

English versions indicate this by the form LORD.

The pronunciation of *yhwh—the Tetragrammaton, the four letters without vowels that compose the divine name—is not certain*. But *the common pronunciation, Jehovah, was surely not used in ancient times*. The transcribers of the Hebrew OT in the *twelfth century* believed the divine name too holy to pronounce. They added the "o" and "a" from *ʾdōnāy* to the four Hebrew consonants, and when they read the hebrew aloud said *ʾdōnāy* in its place. It seems most likely that the original pronunciation is approximated in Yahweh. (Richards, *Expository Dictionary of Bible Words*, 416)

In this dictionary, the English translation of Yahweh differs from the translations cited above ("I will be with you" and "I will be who I will be"), and hence draws a different meaning: "Most scholars believe that the name is derived from an old form of the Hebrew verb meaning "to be" or "to become." The word stresses existence, with the meaning being that expressed in Exodus 3:14: "I am." This has been taken to emphasize the unchanging nature of God, particularly his changeless commitment to this people (Richards, 416).

More insights are presented in this dictionary concerning ***the Greek translation of Lord***, also:

The word translated "Lord" in the English versions is *kyrios*. In ordinary speech it may simply have been *a term of respect* or a form of address that *emphasized superior position, as that of the master of a slave*. When *kyrios* is so used, it is translated by an appropriate English equivalent, such as "master," "owner," or even "Sir."

When *kyrios* designates God or Jesus, *it is rendered "Lord."* In the Gospels, however, this should not be taken to mean that the speaker acknowledges Jesus as God (e.g., Matt. 8:2, 21; Luke 9:59). However, since the Septuagint uses *kyrios* for *Yâhweh*, it is clear that in many of its uses in the Gospels, *the title Lord is equivalent to the divine name. It seems certain that when Jesus spoke of himself—e.g., the time he called himself Lord of the Sabbath (Matt. 12:8)—he was ascribing deity to himself* (cf. Luke 20:42–44). Some uses of the title Lord by the disciples may also reflect the growing awareness that Jesus truly was divine, as Thomas finally confessed when he exclaimed, "My Lord and my God!" (John 20:28).

It is after the Resurrection, and in the Epistles, that we discover the significance of *kyrios* as applied to Jesus. (Richards, 416–17)

Explanations About the Name "Jesus"

The *Latter-day Saint Bible Dictionary* gives this information:

Jesus. The Greek form of the name Joshua or Jeshua, *God is help* or *Savior*. . . . The name given by Joseph to the Savior of the world at his circumcision (Matt. 1:25; Luke 2:21), in accordance with the direction of the angel Gabriel (Luke 1:31; cf. Matt. 1:21). *The name was not an uncommon one among the Jews.* ("Jesus," *Bible Dictionary*, 713)

Another Latter-day source adds these details:

The Name Jesus—The given name of Jesus is the Greek form of Joshua, which in Hebrew means "Yahweh is salvation." *The Aramaic form of Joshua is Jeshua* (Yeh-SHU-uh). By 700 BC Aramaic had become the common language of commerce and industry, and it was widely used throughout the Hellenistic period. *Aramaic was the common language of Palestine in the first century AD Jesus and His disciples spoke the Galilean dialect of Aramaic, so He was generally known as Jeshua throughout His mortal* *lifetime by those who spoke to him or about him.* (Crowther, *Jesus of Nazareth, Savior and King,* 49)

Baker's Dictionary of Theology provides other insights:

Jesus. The given name of God's incarnate Son—given before birth by divine intimation (Matt. 1:21; Luke 1:31) and then in due course by parental bestowment (Luke 2:21).

Jesus is the Greek form of Jeshua or Joshua (cf. the AV in Acts 7:45; Heb. 4:8) meaning "the Lord is salvation: or "the salvation of the Lord." . . .

Since Jesus was a common name, its application to our Lord necessitated mention of lineage and place of residence when full identification was needed—"Jesus, son of Joseph, the one from Nazareth" (John 1:45). During the public ministry "Jesus of Nazareth" was usually sufficient for public use, though it might have further adornment under special circumstances (Matt. 21:11; John 19:19). To his followers the name itself was enough. However, in speaking to him, they seem to have refrained from using it, *resorting to Teacher or Lord instead.* . . . (Harrison, *Baker's Dictionary of Theology,* 297)

Explanations About the Terms "Messiah" and "Christ"

Concerning the term "Messiah" the *Eerdman's Bible Dictionary* explains:

Messiah (Gk. *Messías*; from Heb. *māšîah* "anointed [one]"). God's anointed king; in the Old Testament specifically the expected Jewish Messiah, in the New Testament Jesus Christ.

In its basic sense the term "messiah" refers to a person who has been consecrated to a high office by ceremonial anointing with oil. In the ancient world priests and kings were so anointed, a practice reflected at 1 Kgs. 19:16; Ps. 133:2. *The anointing to an office gave a person high and sacred status and assured authority, reverence, and respect.* . . .

The history and memory of [King] David were revered for centuries during the development of the messianic ideal. *Many important prophetic constructs came into being that were applied in the expectation of the Coming One. He would be the son of David, the root of Jesse, a righteous branch, the servant of the Lord, and the anointed one on whom the spirit of the Lord would rest.* Such images of the Messiah represent themes of many Old Testament books, apocryphal writings, and Jewish apocalyptic texts. *The Psalms and the Prophets are filled with messianic vision.* The anointed would come with authority, glory, and sovereign power; all people everywhere would worship him—his kingdom would never end (Dan. 7:14). Isaiah specifically identified the coming Messiah as the Servant who would bring salvation to God's people through his vicarious suffering and death (Isa. 53:10). . . .

By the Roman times the focus of Jewish hope had become mainly political. Many Jews expected a Messiah who would deliver them from their Roman oppressors and reduce the burden of taxation.

Jesus of Nazareth, whom many would come to recognize as the Messiah, taught and performed miracles both publically and privately for the three years of his public ministry in Galilee and Judea. His primary claim was that he was the Messiah of the Old Testament prophecies. *Jesus persistently clarified the prophecies, answered criticisms, corrected false ideas about the messianic kingdom, and demonstrated in many indisputable ways that he was the promised Messiah.* . . .

The Hebrew term for Messiah (*māšîah*) occurs twice in transliterated form (John 1:41; 4:25). In both passages the Greek translation "Christ" also appears.

Jesus clearly claimed to be the promised Messiah or Christ (v. 26). He explained to his followers the full meaning of his coming as the Anointed (Mark 10:32–45), and he accomplished the promised salvation through his death on the cross. After the resurrection Jesus showed himself alive to the Apostles over a period of forty days, and taught them still more about the nature of the messianic kingdom of God before ascending into heaven (Acts 1:1–11). *The gospels were written to address what scholars call the christological question; the answer they provide is that Jesus is indeed the Messiah* (John 20:31). (Myers, *The Eerdman's Bible Dictionary*, 712–13)

Concerning the term "Christ" the above source says:

> **Christ** (Gk. *Christos*). "Christ is the New Testament designation of Old Testament "Messiah" (Heb. *māšîah* "anointed"). . . .
>
> The two names of Jesus Christ are not really interchangeable. "Jesus" was the name given to the child at his circumcision (Luke 2:21); *when the title, Christ, is used, that passage should be understood as a specific reference to the Savior's office as Mediator, the agent of reconciliation between God and mankind.* At times Paul inverts the usual order ("Christ Jesus," e.g., Rom. 3:24; 8:2, 39).
>
> *The appellation "anointed one" derives from the ancient Near Eastern custom of consecrating with oil persons who undertake the responsibilities of a high office.* Israel was familiar with this practice during Old Testament times, for prophets, priests, and kings were anointed (e.g., 1 Kgs. 19:16; Ps. 133:2) to confirm that they were officially installed in, and declared competent for, their respective offices. Because these Old Testament figures were anointed for only a short time and discharged their offices imperfectly, *Israel anticipated the arrival of the Anointed One, who would not be anointed by men and with oil prepared by human hands, but by God, with the Holy Spirit* (Matt. 3:16–17 par. Mark 1:10–11; Luke 3:21–22). For that reason Jesus could testify of himself: *"The Spirit of the Lord God is upon me, because the Lord has anointed me . . ."* (Luke 4:18 quoting Isa. 61:1; cfr. Acts 10:38). Thus, the name "Christ" connotes not only his sacred commission as Mediator and Redeemer of his people, but also the authority and power through which he was able to complete this mission. (Myers, 207)

One other insight concerning the title Christ should be considered:

> *After the resurrection it became common practice to link with the human name the titles Christ and Lord.* He could now be confidently proclaimed as the (promised) Christ (Messiah). *Before long Christ became so firmly yoked to Jesus, whether as Jesus Christ or Christ Jesus, as to be virtually a part of his name.* In this way personal faith approved the identification given long before by divine announcement (Luke 2:11). (Harrison, *Baker's Dictionary of Theology*, 297)

However, ***most Latter-day Saints are well aware that the term "Christ," or its equivalent in Book of Mormon language, was revealed to the Nephites and was frequently used long prior to the mortal advent of Jesus Christ.*** See 2 Nephi 10:3, 7; 11:4, 6–7; 25:16, 19–20, 23–29; 26:1, 8, 12; 27:11; 28:14; 30:5, 7; 31:2, 13, 19, 20, 21; 32:3, 6, 9; 33:9–12. ***Jacob*** 1:4, 6–8; 2:19; 4:4–5, 11–12; 6:8–9; 7:2–3, 6, 9, 11, 14, 17, 19. ***Enos*** 1:8, 15, 26. ***Omni*** 1:26. ***Words of Mormon*** 1:2, 4, 8, 15. ***Mosiah*** 3:8, 12–13, 16–19; 4:2–3; 5:7–10, 15; 15:21, 23–24; 16:6–8, 13, 15; 18:2, 13, 17; 25:23; 26:2. ***Alma*** 1:19; 4:13–14; 5:27, 38, 44, 48; 6:8; 9:28; 11:42, 44; 14:26, 28; 15:6, 8, 10; 18:39; 21:9; 22:13–16; 27:27–28; 28:14; 30:6, 12–13, 15, 22, 26, 39, 40; 31:16, 17, 29, 31–32, 34, 38; 34:2, 5, 6, 8, 37–38; 36:17; 37:9, 33, 44, 45; 38:8–9; 39:15; 40:2, 16, 18–20; 41:2; 44:3; 45:4, 10; 46:14–15, 18, 21, 27, 39, 41; 48:13. ***Helaman:*** 3:28–29, 35; 5:9, 12, 41; 8:22; 13:6; 14:12, 17; 15:9; 16:4, 18. ***3 Nephi*** 2:2, 7–8; 3:1; 5:2, 13, 20, 26; 6:20, 23; 7:15–16, 18, 21.

Less-used Names of God from the Old Testament

Seven other significant but less-used names of God used in the Old Testament are summarized below:

1. **The Everlasting God** (*Hebrew*: *Elah*) [*Pronounced*: *el-LAH*]
   Elah is a divine title identifying God with His people in captivity.
   A. The word Elah means an Oak tree, which symbolizes durability, and thus extols God as "the Everlasting God." Elah is the Chaldee form of *Eloah*.
   B. It occurs 43 times in Ezra, 46 times in Daniel, and once in Jeremiah (a total of 90 times in the Old Testament).
   C. Example of usage: • "no manner of hurt was found upon him [Daniel], because he believed in his **God**" (Dan. 6:23).

2. **The Adorable One** (*Hebrew*: *Eloah*) [*Pronounced*: *el-LO-ah*]
   Eloah is a "verbal noun." It is associated with the Hebrew verb *alah*, which means to fear, to worship, or to adore. Hence, it is translated as "The Adorable One," or "Worshipful One."
   A. Eloah is a singular form of Elohim. Both words are translated as "God" in the KJV without any distinguishing between the two terms.
   B. Eloah only occurs about 60 times in the Old Testament; 41 of them are in the book of Job, and is primarily considered a form of poetic expression.
   C. *Allah* is an Arabian form of the Hebrew terms Elohim and Eloah. [*Pronounced Ah-LAW*]
   D. Examples of usage: • "I know that my redeemer liveth, . . . And though after my skin worms destroy this body, yet in my flesh shall I see **God**" (Job. 19:25–26). • "For who is **God**, save the LORD?" (2 Sam. 22:32). • "Is there a **God** beside me?" (Isa. 44:8).

3. **God Most High** (*Hebrew*: *El Elyon*) [*Pronounced*: *el el-YOHN*]
   Elyon: "God Most High," "upper," "supreme," contains the added idea of "might."
   A. The term occurs four times in Genesis 14:18–22, in Numbers 24:16 and Deuteronomy 32:8, twice in Lamentations, 12 times in Daniel, and about 20 times in the Psalms (a total of 37 occurences).
   B. Examples of usage: • "Blessed be Abram of the **most high** God, possessor of heaven and earth: And blessed be the **most high** God" (Gen. 14:19–20). • "which heard the words of God, and knew the knowledge of the **most High**" (Num. 24:16). • "When the **most High** divided to the nations their inheritance" (Deut. 32:8).
   C. The related words *Heleyon*, or *Eleyon*, mean "Highest." They are translated "uppermost" in Genesis 40:17, "high" in Nehemiah 3:25, and as "higher" and highest in Ezekiel 9:2 and 41:7.
   D. When these words are associated with Jehovah, they are translated as "highest" in Psalms 18:13 and 87:5; "Most High" in Numbers 24:16, Deuteronomy 32:8; and 2 Samuel 22:14; "Most High God—El" in Genesis 14:18, 19, 20, and Psalm 78:56; "God Elohim **Most High**" in Psalm 57:2; and "Jehovah **most high**" in Psalms 7:17 and 47:2.

4. **God of [Israel]** (*Hebrew*: *El-Elohe-Israel*) [*Pronounced*: el e-LO-he YEE-srah-el]
   This term is used to identify God as being the God of a specific group or individual. • "he [Jacob, newly renamed Israel] erected there an altar, and called it El-elohe-Israel" (Gen. 33:20). The same usage is found for The God of Isaac, The God of Jacob, The God of Jeshurin, The God of Shem, The God of the Hebrews, The God of Daniel, and others.

5. **The Everlasting God, or God of the Universe** (*Hebrew*: *El Olam*) [*Pronounced*: el oh-LAHM*]
   El Olam is a term describing that which extends beyond one's furthest vision, whether forwards or backwards. The KJV translates it "The Everlasting God."
   A. Examples of usage: • "in the LORD JEHOVAH is *everlasting* strength" (Isa. 26:4). • "the *everlasting* God, the LORD, the Creator of the ends of the earth, fainteth not" (Isa. 40:28). • "thou, O LORD, art our father, our redeemer; thy name is from *everlasting*" (Isa. 63:16). • "the LORD is the true God, he is the living God, and an *everlasting* king" (Jer. 10:10). • "from *everlasting* to *everlasting*, thou art God" (Ps. 90:2).

6. **Almighty God** (*Hebrew*: *El Shaddai*) [*Pronounced*: el shad-DIE]
   The term El Shaddai occurs eight times in the Old Testament. The word Shaddai, which means "Almighty," is found 40 times in the Old Testament, 31 of them being in the book of Job.
   A. Examples of usage: • "the LORD appeared to Abram, and said unto him, I am the *Almighty God*" (Gen. 17:1). • "God said unto him [Jacob], I am *God Almighty* (Gen. 35:11). • "Jacob said unto Joseph, *God Almighty* appeared unto me at Luz" (Gen. 48:3). • "I appeared unto Abraham, unto Isaac, and unto Jacob, by the name of *God Almighty*, but by my name JEHOVAH was I not known to them" (Ex. 6:3). • "He that dwelleth in the secret place of the most High shall abide under the shadow of the *Almighty*" (Ps. 91:1).
   B. New Testament examples of usage: • "ye shall be my sons and daughters, saith the *Lord Almighty*" (2 Cor. 6:18). • "I am Alpha and Omega, . . . saith the Lord, which is, and which was, and which is to come, the *Almighty*. (Rev. 1:8). • "Lord God *Almighty*, which was, and is, and is to come" (Rev. 4:8). • "to gather them to the battle of that great day of God *Almighty*" (Rev. 16:14). • "Alleluia: for the Lord God *omnipotent* reigneth" (Rev. 19:6).

7. **The Independent One** (*Hebrew*: *JAH*) [*Pronounced*: YAH]
   A. This name signifies "He is," and corresponds to "I AM," just as Jehovah corresponds to the more complete expression "I AM THAT I AM" (Ex. 3:14). (*Literally, in Hebrew*: "I will be that [or who] I will be.") [See • "ye shall bear record of me, even Jesus Christ, that I am the Son of the living God, that *I was, that I am, and that I am to come*" (D&C 68:6).]
   B. The term JAH occurs more than 40 times in Isaiah, Psalms, and Exodus but is translated "the Lord" in the King James Version of the Bible.
   C. It appears that Jewish copyists sometimes wrote it when they were unwilling to write out the complete name Jehovah.
   D. This title appears untranslated in Psalm 68: • "Sing unto God, sing praises

to his name: extol him that rideth upon the heavens by his name JAH, and rejoice before him" (Ps. 68:4).

E. The term JAH is combined with "Jehovah" in Isaiah 12:2: • "for the Lord JEHOVAH is my strength and my song." It is repeated (JAH JAH) in Isaiah 38:11: • "I shall not see the Lord, *even* the Lord, in the land of the living."

(The above information is drawn primarily from Herbert Lockyer, *All the Divine Names And Titles in the Bible*.)

Compound Names of God (El, Elohim, and Elohe)

Cited below are examples from the Bible, primarily from the Old Testament. They are listed with the Hebrew terms first, followed by their King James Version English translations. It should be noted that many of these terms also appear in other Latter-day Saint scriptures, though they are not listed in this context.

Elohim—God (Gen. 1:1, 3, 4, 5, 6, thousands)
Elohim Bashamayim—God in Heaven (Deut. 4:39: Josh. 2:11; 2 Chr. 20:6; Dan. 2:28).
El Bethel—God of the House of God (Gen. 35:7).
Elohe Chaseddi—The God of My Mercy (Ps. 59:10, 17).
El Elohe Yisrael—God, the God of Israel (Gen. 33:20).
El Elyon—The Most High God (Gen. 14:18, 19, 20, 22; Ps. 57:2; 78:56).
El Emunah—The Faithful God (Deut. 7:9; 1 Cor. 1:9; 10:13).
El Gibbor—Mighty God (Gen. 49:24; Deut. 7:21; Ps. 50:1; 132:2, 5; Isa. 9:6; 10:21; Jer. 32:18).
El Hakabodh—The God of Glory (Ps. 29:3; Acts 7:2).
El Hay—The Living God (Deut. 5:26; Josh. 3:10; 1 Sam. 17:26, 36; 2 Kgs. 19:4, 16).
El Hayyay—God of My Life (Ps. 42:8).
Elohim Kedoshim—Holy God (Josh. 24:19).
El Kanna—Jealous God (Exod. 20:5; 34:14; Deut. 4:24; 5:9; 6:15).
El Kanno—Jealous God (Josh. 24:19).
Elohe Mauzi—God of My Strength (Ps. 43:2).
Elohim Machase Lanu—God Our Refuge (Ps. 46:1, 7, 11; 62:8).
Eli Malekhi—God My King (Ps. 5:2; 44:4; 68:24; 74:12; 84:3; 145:1).
El Marom—God Most High (Ps. 57:2; Mic. 6:6; Luke 8:28).
El Nekamoth—God that Avengeth (2 Sam. 22:48; Ps. 18:47).
El Nose—God that Forgave (Ps. 99:8)
Elohenu Olam—Our Everlasting God (Gen. 21:33; Ex. 3:15; Ps. 48:14).
Elohim Ozerli—God My Helper (Ps. 54:4).
El Rai—God Seest Me (Gen. 16:13).
El Sali—God, My Rock (2 Sam. 22:3, 47; Ps. 18:2, 46; 42:9; 62:7; 89:26).
El Shaddai—Almighty God (Gen. 17:1; 28:3; 35:11; 43:14; 48:3; Ex. 6:3).
Elohim Shophtim Ba-erets—God that Judgeth in the Earth (Ps. 58:11).
El Simchath Gili—God My Exceeding Joy (Ps. 43:4).
Elohim Tsebaoth—God of Hosts (Ps. 80:7, 14).
Elohe Tishuathi—God of My Salvation (Ps. 18:46; 51:14; 62:7).
Elohe Tsadeki—God of My Righteous (Ps. 4:1).
Elohe Yakob—God of Jacob (Gen. 49:24; Ex. 3:6, 15, 16; 4:5; 2 Sam. 23:1; Ps. 20:1; 46:7).
Elohe Yisrael—God of Israel (Ex. 5:1; 24:10; 32:27; 34:23; Num. 16:9; Ps. 59:5).

Compound Names of the Lord God (Jehovah El and Jehovah Elohim)

Jehovah El Elohim—The LORD God of Gods (Deut. 10:17; Josh. 22:22; Dan. 2:47).

Jehovah Elohim—The LORD God (Gen. 2:4; 3:9–13, 21; 9:26; 15:2; 24:7; thousands).

Jehovah Elosh Abothekem—The LORD God of Your Fathers (Ex. 3:15; Deut. 1:11; 4:1; Josh. 18:3; 2 Chr. 13:12).

Jehovah El Elyon—The LORD, the Most High God (Gen. 14:22).

Jehovah El Emet—The LORD God of Truth (Ps. 31:5; 86:15).

Jehovah El Gemuwal—The LORD God of Recompenses (Jer. 51:56).

Jehovah Elohim Tsebaoth—LORD God of Hosts (2 Sam. 5:10; 1 Kgs. 19:10, 14; Ps. 59:5; 69:6; 80:4, 19).

Jehovah Elohe Yeshuathi—LORD God of My Salvation (Ps. 88:1; Mic. 7:7; Hab. 3:18).

Jehovah Elohe Yisrael—The LORD God of Israel (Ex. 5:1; 32:7; Josh. 7:13, 19, 20; 8:30; 9:18, 19; Ps. 41:13).

BIBLIOGRAPHY

Abingdon. *The Interpreter's Bible: A Commentary in Twelve Volumes.* Nashville: Abingdon, 1980.

Achtemeier, Paul J., et al. *Harper's Bible Dictionary.* San Francisco: Harper SanFrancisco, 1985.

Allred, Gordon, comp. *God the Father.* Salt Lake City: Deseret Book, 1979.

Andrus, Hyrum L. *God, Man and the Universe.* Salt Lake City: Bookcraft, 1968.

Barker, James L. *The Protestors of Christendom.* Independence, MO: Zion's Printing & Publishing Company, 1946.

Barker, Margaret. *The Great Angel: A Study of Israel's Second God.* Louisville, KY: Westminster John Knox Press, 1992.

——. *The Great High Priest: The Temple Roots of Christian Clergy.* New York: T & T Clark, 2003.

Beisner, E. Calvin. *God in Three Persons.* Wheaton, IL: Tyndale House Publishers, 1984.

Bercot, David W., ed. *A Dictionary of Early Christian Beliefs: A Reference Guide to More Than 700 Topics Discussed by the Early Church Fathers.* Peabody, MA: Hendrickson Publishers, 1998.

Berkhof, Louis. *Principles of Biblical Interpretation: Sacred Hermeneutics.* Grand Rapids, MI: Baker Book House, 1992.

——. *The History of Christian Doctrines.* Grand Rapids, MI: Baker Book House, 1992.

The Bethany Parallel Commentary on the Old Testament: Three Classic Commentaries in One Volume. Minneapolis: Bethany House Publishers, 1985.

Bickersteth, Edward Henry. *The Trinity: Scriptural Testimony to the One Eternal Godhead of the Father, and of the Son, and of the Holy Spirit.* Grand Rapids, MI: Kregel Publications, 1980.

Boettner, Loraine. *Studies in Theology.* Phillipsburg, NJ: The Presbyterian and Reformed Publishing Company, 1989.

Bowman, Robert M. Jr. *Orthodoxy and Heresy: A Biblical Guide to Doctrinal Discernment.* Grand Rapids, MI: Baker Book House, 1992.

——. *Why You Should Believe in the Trinity: An Answer to Jehovah's Witnesses.* Grand Rapids, MI: Baker Book House, 1992.

Boyd, Gregory A. *Oneness Pentecostals & The Trinity: A Worldwide Movement Assessed by a Former Oneness Pentecostal.* Grand Rapids, MI: Baker Book House, 1992.

Bray, Gerald. *The Doctrine of God: Contours of Christian Theology.* Downers Grove, IL: InterVarsity Press, 1993.

Brewster, Hoyt W. Jr. *Doctrine & Covenants Encyclopedia.* Salt Lake City: Deseret Book, 2004.

Brown, Harold O. J. *Heresies: Heresy And Orthodoxy In The History Of The Church.* Peabody, MA: Hendrickson Publishers, 2003.

Burtler, Trent C., et al. *Holman Bible Dictionary.* Nashville: Holman Bible Publishers, 1991.

Carson, D. A. *Exegetical Fallacies.* Grand Rapids, MI: Baker Book House, 1984.

Chafer, Lewis Sperry and John F. Walvoord. *Major Bible Themes: 52 Vital Doctrines of the Scriptures Simplified and Explained.* Grand Rapids, MI: Zondervan Publishing House, 1974.

Charnock, Stephen. *Discourses upon the Existence and Attributes of God.* Grand Rapids, MI: Baker Book House, 1979, 2 volumes.

The Church of Jesus Christ of Latter-day Saints. *History of The Church of Jesus Christ of Latter-day Saints.* 2nd edition, revised. Salt Lake City: Deseret Book, 1959, 7 volumes.

Coleman, Richard J. *Issues of Theological Conflict: Evangelicals and Liberals.* Grand Rapids, MI: William B. Eerdmans Publishing Company, 1980.

Crowther, Duane S. *Doctrinal Dimensions: Major Missionary Messages of the Restored Gospel.* Bountiful, UT: Horizon Publishers, 1986.

————. *Jesus of Nazareth, Savior and King: 414 Events in the Life of Christ.* Bountiful, UT: Horizon Publishers, 2002.

————. *Life Everlasting: A Definitive Study of Life After Death.* 2nd revised edition. Springville, UT: Horizon Publishers, 2005.

Cruden, Alexander. *Cruden's Complete Concordance.* Philadelphia: The John C. Winston Company, 1949.

Dana, Bruce E. *The Eternal Father and His Son.* Springville, UT: Cedar Fort, 2004.

De Burgh, W. D. *The Legacy of the Ancient World,* Vol. 1 & 2. London: The Whitefriars Press, 1923. Reprinted: Baltimore, MD: Penguin Books, 1955.

Dockery, David S. *Biblical Interpretation Then and Now: Contemporary Hermeneutics in the Light of the Early Church.* Grand Rapids, MI: Baker Book House, 1992.

Douglas, J. D. *New Bible Dictionary.* 2nd edition. Wheaton, IL: Tyndale House Publishers, 1991.

Douglas, J. D. and Merrill C. Tenney et al. *The New International Dictionary of the Bible.* Grand Rapids, MI: Zondervan Publishing House, 1987.

Dowley, Tim et al. *A Lion Handbook: The History of Christianity.* Oxford: Lion Publishing, 1990.

————. *Eerdmans' Handbook to the History of Christianity.* Grand Rapids, MI: William B. Eerdmans Publishing, 1982.

Earle, Ralph. *Word Meanings in the New Testament: One-Volume Edition.* Grand Rapids, MI: Baker Book House, 1982.

Edersheim, Alfred. *The Life and Times of Jesus the Messiah.* Grand Rapids, MI: William B. Eerdmans Publishing, 1971.

Elwell, Walter A., ed. *Evangelical Commentary on the Bible.* Grand Rapids, MI: Baker Book House, 1989.

————. *Evangelical Dictionary of Theology.* Grand Rapids, MI: Baker Book House, 1984.

Enns, Paul. *The Moody Handbook of Theology.* Chicago: Moody Press, 1989.

Erickson, Millard J. *Christian Theology.* Grand Rapids, MI: Baker Book House, 1985.

————. *Evangelical Interpretation: Perspectives on Hermeneutical Issues.* Grand Rapids, MI: Baker Books, a Division of Baker Book House, 1993.

————. *Introducing Christian Doctrine.* Grand Rapids, MI: Baker Book House, 1992.

————. *Readings in Christian Theology: Volume 1: The Living God.* Grand Rapids, MI: Baker Book House, 1973.

Farrar, Frederic W. *History of Interpretation: Eight Lectures Preached Before the University of Oxford in the Year MDCCCLXXXV.* London: Macmillan and Co., 1886.

Ferguson, Sinclair B. et al., *New Dictionary of Theology.* Downers Grove, IL: 1988.

Frame, John M. *The Doctrine of the Knowledge of God.* Phillipsburg, NJ: Presbyterian and Reformed Publishing Company, 1987.

Frangopoulos, Athanasios S. *Our Orthodox Christian Faith: A Handbook of Popular Dogmatics.* Athens, Greece: The Brotherhood of Theologians, 1984.

Galbraith, Richard C. *Scriptural Teachings of the Prophet Joseph Smith.* Salt Lake City: Deseret Book, 1993.

Garrett, Duane A. et al. *Authority and Interpretation: A Baptist Perspective.* Grand Rapids, MI: Baker Book House, 1987.

Geisler, Norman. *False Gods of Our Time: A Defense of the Christian Faith.* Eugene, Oregon: Harvest House Publishers, 1985.

Gibson, Arvin S. *They Saw Beyond Death: New Insights on Near-Death Experiences.* Springville, UT: Horizon Publishers, 2006.

Gilbert, George Holley. *Interpretation of the Bible: A Short History.* New York: The Macmillan Company, 1908.

Grenz, Stanley J. and Roger E. Olson. *20th-Century Theology: God & the World in a Transitional Age.* Downers Grove, IL: InterVarsity Press, 1992.

Gruenler, Royce Gordon. *The Trinity in the Gospel of John: A Thematic Commentary on the Fourth Gospel.* Grand Rapids, MI: Baker Book House, 1986.

Guideposts. *Find It Fast in the Bible: The Ultimate A to Z Resource: Over 5,000 Common and Obscure Phrases.* Carmel, NY: Guideposts, 2000.

Guthrie, Donald. *New Testament Theology.* Downers Grove, IL: InterVarsity Press, 1981.

Harris, F. Donald, and Ronald A. Harris. *The Trinity: Is the Doctrine Biblical? Is It Important?* Neptune, NJ: Loizeaux Brothers, 1982.

Harris, James R. *The Names of God from Sinai to the American Southwest: An Alphabetic Script and Language Found in Ancient America and Israel.* Orem, UT: James R. Harris, 1998.

Harrison, Everett F. et al. *Baker's Dictionary of Theology.* Grand Rapids, MI: Baker Book House, 1988.

Harvey, Van A. *A Handbook of Theological Terms: Their Meaning and Background Exposed in Over 300 Articles.* New York: Collier Books, MacMillan Publishing Company, 1964.

Hayes, John H. and Carl R. Holladay. *Biblical Exegesis: A Beginner's Handbook.* Atlanta: John Knox Press, 1973.

Hicks, Robert and Richard Bewes. *God.* San Bernadino, CA: Here's Life Publishers, 1979.

Hopkins, Richard R. *How Greek Philosophy Corrupted the Christian Concept of God.* Springville, UT: Horizon Publishers, 2005.

Horne, Dennis B. *Determining Doctrine: A Reference Guide for Evaluating Doctrinal Truth.* Roy, UT: Eborn Books, 2005.

Horton, Stanley M. *Systematic Theology: A Pentecostal Perspective.* Springfield, MO: Logion Press, 1994.

Howells, Rulon S. *His Many Mansions: A Compilation of Christian Beliefs.* Hollywood: Murray & Gee Publishers, 1944.

Ironside, H. A. *The Holy Trinity.* Neptune, NJ: Loizeaux Brothers, 1941.

Jackson, Kent P. *Joseph Smith's Commentary on the Bible.* Salt Lake City: Deseret Book, 2006.

Jukes, Andrew. *The Names of God: Discovering God as He Desires to Be Known.* Grand Rapids, MI: Kregel Publications, 1980.

Kaiser, Christopher B. *The Doctrine of God: An Historical Survey.* Westchester, IL: Crossway Books, 1982.

Kaiser, Walter C. Jr. *Toward an Exegetical Theology: Biblical Exegesis for Preaching and Teaching.* Grand Rapids, MI: Baker Book House, 1981.

Kearley, F. Furman et al., ed. *Biblical Interpretation: Principles and Practice.* Grand Rapids, MI: Baker Book House, 1986.

La Due, William J. *The Trinity Guide to the Trinity.* Harrisburg, PA: Trinity Press International, 2003.

Lambert, Neal E. *Literature of Belief: Sacred Scripture and Religious Experience.* Provo, UT: Religious Studies Center: Brigham Young University, 1981.

Leith, John H., ed. *Creeds of the Churches: A Reader in Christian Doctrine from the Bible to the Present.* Garden City, NY: Anchor Books, Doubleday and Co., 1963.

Little, Paul E. *Know What You Believe: A Practical Discussion of the Fundamentals of the Christian Faith.* Wheaton, IL: Victor Books, 1984.

Lockyer, Herbert. *All the Divine Names and Titles in the Bible.* Grand Rapids, MI: Zondervan Publishing House, 1975.

Lockyer, Herbert Sr. et al. *Nelson's Illustrated Bible Dictionary.* Nashville: Thomas Nelson Publishers, 1986.

Loeks, Mary Foxwell. *The Glorious Names of God: Devotions for Church Groups.* Grand Rapids, MI: Baker Book House, 1986.

Ludlow, Daniel H. *A Companion to Your Study of The Doctrine and Covenants.* Salt Lake City: Deseret Book, 1978, 2 volumes combined.

Lyon, T. Edgar. *Apostasy to Restoration.* Salt Lake City: The Church of Jesus Christ of Latter-day Saints, 1960.

MacArthur, John, Jr. *God: Coming Face to Face with His Majesty.* Wheaton, IL: Victor Books, 1993.

MacDonald, William. *Believer's Bible Commentary: New Testament.* Nashville: Thomas Nelson Publishers, 1990.

Madsen, Truman G., *The Presidents of the Church: Insights into Their Lives and Teachings.* Salt Lake City: Deseret Book, 2004.

Marty, Martin E. *A Short History of Christianity.* Cleveland & New York: William Collins & World Publishing Co., 1974.

McConkie, Bruce R. *Mormon Doctrine: A Compendium of the Gospel.* Salt Lake City: Bookcraft, 1958.

McConkie, Clay. *In His Father's Image: The Father and Son Relationship Between God and Jehovah.* Springville, UT: Cedar Fort, 2004.

McGrath, Alister E. *Understanding the Trinity.* Grand Rapids, MI: Acadamie Books, Zondervan Publishing House, 1988.

Melton, J. Cordon, ed. *American Religious Creeds: An Essential Compendium of More than 450 Statements of Belief and Doctrine.* New York: Triumph Books, 1991, 3 volumes.

Miley, John. *Systematic Theology.* Peabody, MA: Hendrickson Publishers, 1989, 2 volumes.

Muller, Richard A. *Dictionary of Latin and Greek Terms: Drawn Principally from Protestant Scholastic Theology.* Grand Rapids, MI: Baker Book House, 1986.

Myers, Allen C. et al. *The Eerdmans Bible Dictionary.* Grand Rapids, MI: William B. Eerdmans Publishing Company, 1987.

Nibley, Hugh. *When the Lights Went Out: Three Studies on the Ancient Apostasy.* Salt Lake City: Deseret Book, 1970.

Pannenberg, Wolfhart. *Systematic Theology, Volume 1.* Grand Rapids, MI: William B. Eerdmans Publishing Company, 1991.

Petersen, Scott R. *Where Have All the Prophets Gone? Revelation and Rebellion in the Old Testament and the Christian World.* Springville, UT: Cedar Fort, 2005.

Plato. *The Dialogues of Plato; The Seventh Letter.* Chicago: Great Books of the Western World, Encyclopædia Britannica, 1952.

Pratney, W. A. *The Nature and Character of God: The Magnificent Doctrine of God in Understandable Language.* Minneapolis: Bethany House Publishers, 1988.

Priestley, Joseph. *An History of the Corruptions of Christianity, in Two Volumes.* Birmingham, England: Piercy and Jones, 1782. Reprinted: New York: Garland Publishing, 1974.

Qualben, Lars P. *A History of the Christian Church.* New York: Thomas Nelson and Sons, 1961.

Ramm, Bernard. *Protestant Biblical Interpretation: A Textbook of Hermaneutics.* Grand Rapids, MI: Baker Book House, 1993.

The Revell Bible Dictionary: Deluxe Color Edition. New York: Wynwood Press, 1990.

Richards, Lawrence O. *Zondervan Expository Dictionary of Bible Words.* Grand Rapids, MI: Zondervan Publishing House, 1991.

Richardson, Alan, ed. *A Theological Word Book of the Bible: 230 Articles Bringing the Resources of Modern Scholarship to Bear on the Meaning of the Key Words of the Bible.* New York: Collier Books Macmillan Publishing Company, 1950.

Richardson, Alan and John Bowden. *The Westminster Dictionary of Christian Theology.* Philadelphia: The Westminster Press, 1983.

Roberts, Brigham H. *Mormon Doctrine of Deity: The Roberts-Vander Donckt Discussion.* Bountiful, UT: Horizon Publishers, 1983.

———. *Outlines of Ecclesiastical History.* Salt Lake City: The Deseret News, 1902.

Ross, Bob L. *The Trinity and the Eternal Sonship of Christ: A Defense Against "Oneness" Pentecostal Attacks on Historic Christianity.* Pasadena, TX: Pilgrim Publications, 1993.

Rosten, Leo, ed. *Religions of America: Ferment and Faith in an Age of Crisis.* 33rd edition, New York: Simon & Schuster, 2005.

Ryrie, Charles C. *A Survey of Bible Doctrine.* Chicago: Moody Press, 1981.

Schaff, Philip. *The Creeds of Christendom: With a History and Critical Notes.* Grand Rapids, MI: Baker Book House, reprinted from the 1931 edition published by Harper and Row, 1990, 3 volumes.

Shaw, Mark. *Doing Theology with Huck & Jim: Parables for Understanding Doctrine.* Downers Grove, IL: InterVarsity Press, 1993.

Sheed, F. J. *Theology for Beginners.* Ann Arbor, MI: Servant Books, 1981.

Sire, James W. *Scripture Twisting: 20 Ways the Cults Misread the Bible.* Downers Grove, IL: InterVarsity Press, 1980.

Sizemore, Denver. *Thirteen Lessons In Christian Doctrine.* Joplin, MO: College Press, 1984.

Sjödahl, J. M. *The Reign of Antichrist: A Study in Ecclesiastical History.* Salt Lake City: The Deseret News, 1913.

Smullin, Ramon D. *The Father Is Not the Son: Godhead or Trinity?* Midvale, UT: Camden Court Publishers, 1998.

Stern, David H. *Jewish New Testament Commentary.* Clarksville, MD: Jewish New Testament Publications, 1992.

Stone, Nathan. *Names of God in the Old Testament.* Chicago: The Moody Bible Institute, 1944.

Swindoll, Charles R. *The Trinity: Discovering the Depth of the Nature of God.* Nashville, Tennessee: Broadman and Holman Publishers, 1997.

Talmage, James E. *A Study of the Articles of Faith: Being a Consideration of the Principal Doctrines of The Church of Jesus Christ of Latter-day Saints.* Salt Lake City: The Church of Jesus Christ of Latter-day Saints, 1952.

—————. *Jesus the Christ: A Study of the Messiah and His Mission according to Holy Scriptures both Ancient and Modern.* Salt Lake City: The Church of Jesus Christ of Latter-day Saints, 1962.

—————. *The Great Apostasy: Considered in the Light of Scriptural and Secular History.* Salt Lake City: Deseret Book, 1968.

Tate, W. Randolph. *Biblical Interpretation: An Integrated Approach.* Peabody, MA: Hendrickson Publishers, 1991.

Toon, Peter and James D. Spiceland. *One God in Trinity.* Westchester, IL: Cornerstone Books, 1980.

Torrey, R. A. *What the Bible Teaches: The classic reference on what Scripture teaches about God, Christ, the Holy Spirit, man, angels, and Satan.* 17th edition, Old Tappan, NJ: Fleming H. Revell Company, 1933.

Towns, Elmer L. *My Father's Names: The Old Testament Names of God and How They Can Help You Know Him More Intimately.* Ventura, CA: Regal Books, 1991.

—————. *The Names of Jesus: Over 700 names of Jesus to help you really know the Lord you love.* Denver: Accent Publications, 1987.

Turretin, Francis. *Institutes of Elenctic Theology.* Phillipsburg, NJ: P&R Publishing, 1992.

Unger, Merrill F. et al. *Nelson's Expository Dictionary of the Old Testament.* Nashville: Thomas Nelson Publishers, 1980.

—————. *The New Unger's Bible Dictionary.* Chicago: Moody Press, 1988.

Vos, Howard F. *An Introduction to Church History.* Chicago: Moody Press, 1984.

Wace, Henry and William C. Piercy. *A Dictionary of Early Christian Biography: A Reference Guide to Over 800 Christian Men and Women, Heretics, and Sects of the First Six Centuries.* Peabody, MA: Hendrickson Publishers, 1999.

Walker, Wilston et al. *A History of the Christian Church.* 4th edition, New York: Charles Schribner's Sons, 1946.

Warfield, Benjamin Breckinridge. *Biblical and Theological Studies*. Philadelphia: The Presbyterian and Reformed Publishing Company, 1968.

Watch Tower Bible and Tract Society. *Should You Believe in the Trinity? Is Jesus Christ the Almighty God?* Brooklyn, NY: Watch Tower Bible and Tract Society.

Watch Tower Bible and Tract Society of Pennsylvania, International Bible Students Association. *Insight on the Scriptures*. New York: Brooklyn, 1988, 2 volumes.

Worldwide Church of God. *God Is . . .*, 1992.

Zuck, Roy B. *Basic Bible Interpretation: A Practical Guide to Discovering Biblical Truth*. Wheaton, IL: Victor Books/Scripture Press Publications, 1973.

Electronic Sources

Bible Collection: Deluxe, The. Waconia, MN: ValuSoft, 2002.

Bible Library Deluxe. Waconia, MN: ValuSoft, 2001.

Britannica. Springfield, MA: Merriam-Webster, 2006.

Complete Bible Suite. Calabasas, CA: Ideasoft.

Complete Christian Collection, The. Packard Technologies, 1999.

Encarta Reference Library. Microsoft Corporation, 2006.

Quick Verse Starter Edition, Version 7. Omaha: Parsons Church Group.

Scriptures: Authorized Version Including the Official Study Aids, The; CD-ROM Edition 1.1. Salt Lake City: The Church of Jesus Christ of Latter-day Saints, 2005.

Talking Bible & Christian References. Rancho Dominguea, CA: Cosmi Corporation, 2002.

INDEX

(Chapter summaries are not included in this index.)

Council of the Eternal God of All Other Gods—170; passage contains important clues, 170–72; 212–13.

Councils, Early Christian—of *Nicaea* (AD 325)—helped formulate trinitarian doctrine, 14, 267–68; first ecumenical, 14; of *Constantinople* (AD 381)—second ecumenical, 14; 267–68; 323; anathemas of *2ⁿᵈ Council of Constantinople* (AD 553), 87; *3ʳᵈ Council of Toledo* (AD 589), 317; 323. *See: Creeds.*

Councils, Premortal and Early Mortal—*council 1*: Council of the Eternal God of all other gods, 170; 212; *council 2*: choosing of Christ and rebellion of Satan, 213–15; *council 3*: Gods who united to create this earth, 215; *council 4*: sons of God shouted for joy, 215.

Countenance, Head, and Face—of God, 146–48.

Covenants—Jehovah/Jesus Christ makes and fulfills, 239–40; God the Father made premortal c. , 311–13.

Creation, Creator—the LORD made man, 7; *Lutheran*: God the Father is creator: 16; man created in likeness of Christ's premortal spirit body, 36; 117–8; Father and Son and others combined efforts to create this earth, 71; creation of this earth a time marker, 160; Creator visits earth, 179–80; premortal instructions concerning this earth given to Jehovah by the Father, 301–4; spiritual and physical creation of this earth described, 204–5; this earth created nigh unto Kolob, 205–6; Jehovah/Jesus Christ is c., 231–2; "Father" as c. 244; glory is c. power of God, 339. *See: Jehovah; Jesus.*

Creation, Premortal Spirit—all things earthly first were created premortally, 71; spirit creation of earth described, 204–5.

Creeds—*Nicaean*: 14, 225, 267, 271, 323; *Nicaean C.* confused Christ's premortal and mortal births, 267–8; translation errors cause creedal errors, 271–72. *Apostles'*: 15, 225, 269–70, 271–72; *C. of Athanasius*: 97–98; *Congregational Churches* non–creedal, 18; *Disciples of Christ* reject creeds, 19.

Chrysostom, John—at school of Antioch, 129.

D

Death, Godhead's Attitude Toward Mortal—death a doorway to next phase of life, 63; death provides many with opportunity to learn and live the gospel, 63–64; death used to remove those obstructing God's plans, 65.

Deists—term defined, 23; of 17ᵗʰ and 18ᵗʰ centuries, 136.

Deuteronomists—worked to alter O. T. scriptures to establish monotheism, 88–91.

Disciple of Christ—beliefs concerning God, 19, 21.

Divine Investiture of Authority—Jesus spoke for the Father by d.i.o.a., 247–49.

Discrediting Labels Used by Theologians—terms used as d.l., 137–38. *See: Loaded Terminologies.*

Doctrine and Doctrinal Standards—*Methodists*: creeds not to be regarded as juridical norms for doctrine, 16; *Seventh–day Adventist*: not inventors of new d., 18: *United Church of Christ*: creeds as a testimony, not a test of faith, 18.

E

Earth—creation of e. is "beginning" marker, 169–70; Creator visits, 179–80; Jesus the God of this e., 257–65.

Ears—of God, 150–51.

Episcopalian—beliefs concerning God, 15; Methodists retain theology of the Anglican Church, 16, 21.

O

Oath and Covenant of Melchizedek Priesthood—established prior to the creation of this earth, 311–13.

Objects, Tangible—God owns, holds or wears, 162.

Omnipotent—members of Godhead are o., 43–44.

Omnipresence—fallacies in typical "trinitarian" understanding of o., 42–43.

Omniscient—Godhead members are o., 45–46.

One—means unity, not substance:, 103; Cruden's definitions, 101.

One Fold and Shepherd—Jesus the shepherd, church his fold, 106.

Oneness of Godhead—87–115; two statements of Jesus are basis for much of "trinitarian" three-in-one doctrine, 95–97; pivotal doctrinal choice: substance or purpose, 95–97; in LDS scriptures, 99–101; biblical passages where one means unity, not substance, 101–3; Cruden's Concordance definitions of "one," 101; oneness with God, 111–13.

Only Begotten Son—*LDS*: Jesus is the o.b.s. of the Father in the flesh, 17; future role of o.b.s. prefigured, 202–3; applies to Jesus's mortal birth, 451–55. *See: Jesus.*

Only One God Passages—91–95; all linked to rejecting of false gods and idols, 92.

Only Name Whereby Man Can Be Saved—275–78.

Oral Law—Jewish scribes exalted the o.l., 127.

Origen—"unum" meant "harmony of disposition, not "substance," 103; believed only allegorical interpretation contributed to real knowledge, 128; regarded as greatest theologian of his age, 128.

P

Pantheism—term defined, 23; p. emphasizes immanence, 136.

Patriarchal Order and Environment—Godhood members function in a p.e., 49–50.

Perfect—be p. like the Father and Son, 4–5; attain to p. knowledge of God, 7; p. knowledge attained through Spirit of Christ, 7; Godhood members are perfect beings, 38–39; man to strive for perfection, 39–40, 310; *commentary*: to seek to be as God is blasphemy, 40; man's eternal potential to attain perfection, 40–41; Jesus achieved p., 186–87.

Person—term redefined as "persona," signifying a character or a representation, 16.

Philo—early master of allegorical interpretation, 127–28; combined themes from Jewish scriptures with Stoic and Platonist philosophical ideas, 129–30.

Phrases Characterizing Godhead Members—*Greek Orthodox*, 14; *Episcopalian*, 15; *Lutheran*, 16; *Methodist*, 16; *Christian Scientist*, 18; *2ⁿᵈ Council of Constantinople*, 87.

Physical Attributes of God—117–65; twenty-four categories of g. described, 144–63.

Pictorial Language—language the early Church took over from Jewish background, 15.

Plainness of the Scriptures—plain and precious parts, 138–39.

Plan of Redemption—Godhood members follow premortal p.o.r. for mankind, 55–56; other names for, 55; thirteen elements of the plan listed, 55–56.

Plato, Platonic Philosophy—current in school of Alexandria, 128–29.

Pleasure in Righteousness—Godhood members take p.i.r., 59–60; different sources of God's p., 59–60; sources for God's displeasure, 60–61.

Power—Godhead members have all p., 43–45; extend their powers to men, 45; Jehovah/Jesus Christ has power, is omnipotent and mighty, 235–36; glory is p. which enables man to endure God's presence, 341.

ABOUT THE AUTHOR

Duane S. Crowther is a well-known author, theologian, teacher, and lecturer. He graduated with honors from Brigham Young University with a BA in music education and an MA in Old and New Testament. Brother Crowther also holds an MBA and completed course work for a PhD in music education at the University of Utah.

In his professional life he served as a Latter-day Saint Seminary instructor and principal, taught university classes, and still teaches music and writing classes in public schools. Brother Crowther was also President and Senior Editor of Horizon Publishers in Utah.

A creative and prolific author, Brother Crowther has written more than fifty books, including such well-known favorites as *Prophecy—Key to the Future, Life Everlasting, The Prophecies of Joseph Smith, Inspired Prophetic Warnings, Gifts of the Spirit, Prophets and Prophecies of the Old Testament, Jesus of Nazareth: Savior and King, How to Understand the Book of Mormon, How to Write Your Personal History, Key Choral Concepts,* and *You Can Read Music.* He is also the author of more than three dozen cassette talk tapes, numerous magazine articles and music compositions, and several national-award-winning patriotic pageants. He has lectured at numerous business and writers' seminars, BYU Education Weeks, youth conferences, and other Church events.

He has led a life of continued and varied service within the Church. He has served two full-time and three stake missions. A gifted and knowledgeable teacher, he has served as a Gospel Doctrine class instructor for more than twenty-five years. Other Church assignments have included callings as a temple worker in the Salt Lake Temple and as a guide on Temple Square. He and his wife currently serve as temple workers in the Bountiful Utah Temple.

Brother Crowther is married to Jean Decker, who is also an author, editor, teacher, and musician. The parents of eight children and grandparents of twenty-eight grandchildren, the Crowthers reside in Bountiful, Utah.